1986

# AN INTRODUCTION
## TO THE PSYCHOLOGY OF ADOLESCENCE

THE DORSEY SERIES IN PSYCHOLOGY

*Consulting Editor*  Wendell E. Jeffrey
*University of California,
Los Angeles*

# AN INTRODUCTION TO THE PSYCHOLOGY OF ADOLESCENCE

**BARBARA M. NEWMAN**
*The Ohio State University*

**PHILIP R. NEWMAN**

*1979*
THE DORSEY PRESS   Homewood, Illinois   60430
Irwin-Dorsey Limited   Georgetown, Ontario   L7G 4B3

*Cover photo:* Hiroji Kubota / Magnum

ISBN 0-256-02188-0
Library of Congress Catalog Card No. 78–70953
*Printed in the United States of America*

1 2 3 4 5 6 7 8 9 0 K 6 5 4 3 2 1 0 9

*To Sara and I. G.*

# Preface

In our treatment of adolescence, we will focus on three components of this period of life. First, we are concerned with the competences that adolescents acquire. These include the mastery of new motor skills, the acquisition of more abstract conceptual abilities, the formation of complex social relationships, and the formulation of a set of personal beliefs and values. Second, we are concerned with the social settings in which adolescents participate. The family, the peer group, the high school, college, work environments, and communities operate to structure the adolescent's experiences, and to provide the challenges of life for the adolescent. In our evaluation of these settings, we will look at how the demands and resources of the environment interact with the concerns and competences of adolescence. Third, we will look at the special life challenges that people face during adolescence and at the ways in which they cope with these challenges. As we examine these efforts to cope with challenges, we will explore deviant as well as creative adaptations.

Our primary orientation is to view adolescence as one of many periods in the life span. There are unique psychological developments in adolescence, just as there are in each period of life. There are unique social stresses and personal challenges during adolescence, just as there are during other periods of life. The events of adolescence are important both for the experiences of the period itself and for the pattern they set for future life choices. It is sometimes assumed that adolescence is the "stormiest" and most stressful period of life. For some people this is probably true. For the vast majority, however, it is not true. Each period of life can be difficult, stressful, and challenging. Although adolescence may be extremely stressful for some people, middle adulthood or early school age may be more stressful for others. For some people every period is extremely upsetting, and for others each period passes calmly. What we wish to communicate is that each period of life is qualitatively different from every other period. The adolescent years of your life are unique in your experience. The events that occur, the new learning, the emotional involvements, the growing sense of self, have never occurred before and will never happen again in quite the same way. The adolescent period is an original experience in the life of an individual. It is not necessarily better or worse than other periods, and it is not by definition easier or more difficult.

The book is divided into four parts. In Part I, we present the theoretical, cross-cultural, and empirical perspectives on the study of the psychology of the adolescent. The theoretical perspective in Chapter 1 considers the ways in which a variety of psychologists have conceptualized adolescence. We identify how each theory treats adolescence in relation to the rest of the life span. In Chapter 2, we explore the ways in which the life tasks of adolescence are dealt with in different cultures. We look for uniformities from one culture to another. We also look for the differences among societies in order to understand the ways in which culture acts to influence the psychological development of adolescents. Chapter 3 considers adolescence as a topic for research. We look at some of the techniques that have been employed to study adolescent development and at some of the problems that arise in doing research with adolescents.

In Part II, we discuss early adolescence. This period includes the time from the onset of puberty until roughly the end of high school, or about 18 years of age. Chapter 4 is a discussion of physical maturation. We are concerned both with the normal pattern of growth and with the environmental influences that might alter that pattern. Chapter 5 treats cognitive development, including changes in hypothetico-deductive reasoning. In this chapter, we begin to consider the ways in which differences in intellectual skills generate different life-styles. Chapter 6 focuses on social development, particularly the adolescent's relationships with parents, siblings, and peers. Chapter 7 looks in detail at the high school environment as a socialization setting for adolescents. We consider the impact of the high school on cognitive and social development. Architectural design, curriculum organization, and informal social interaction with adults and peers are examined in order to evaluate their impact. Chapter 8, the final chapter in Part II, treats a variety of maladaptive strategies for responding to the stresses of early adolescence. For each form of deviant behavior, we discuss the frequency and the meaning of the behavior, and the services and resources that have been developed to deal with it.

Part III presents the developmental changes of later adolescence—the years from 18 to the early 20s. Chapter 9 considers cognitive development, including morality, political orientation, and career selection. Chapter 10 discusses social development. Interpersonal skills, parent relations, sex role development, and the formation of loving relationships are each treated in depth. We also explore the ways in which cognitive and social skills contribute to the development of a sense of identity. In Chapter 11, the college environment is described in detail. We are concerned with who attends college, with the kinds of experiences that are encountered at different kinds of colleges, and with some of the ways in which college students change in the process of adapting to their college environments.

We recognize, of course, that many people between the age of 18 and the early 20s do not go to college. We treat the experiences of people who do not attend college in the chapter on cognitive development when we discuss career selection and training and the influences of the work setting on moral and political development. We also explore the differences among college and noncollege adolescents in the chapter on social development, particularly in the discussion of identity formation. Finally, in Chapter 11, we examine the effects of college on adaptation. Each chapter on later adolescence includes the experiences of noncollege adolescents. Because college has evolved as an institution that provides advanced training in a technological society, because there is an extensive literature on the psychological impact of the college environment, and because increasing numbers of people are attending colleges, we feel that it is important to explore the impact of the college environment on students. Chapter 12 treats some of the maladaptive strategies that have been observed during later adolescence. As in Chapter 8, we discuss the frequency and the meaning of each maladaptive strategy and the services or resources that have been developed to deal with it.

Part IV consists of a single chapter. In this chapter we present an integrated view of adolescence and its meaning for development across the life span. We trace patterns of continuity and change from childhood to adolescence and from adolescence to adulthood. We begin to evaluate how well the settings and resources designed for adolescents actually meet adolescents' changing needs for intellectual, emotional, and social growth.

One of the prominent features of adolescence is the emphasis on experimentation. During adolescence, young people acquire the intellectual capacity to imagine a variety of behaviors, roles, and relationships that they may not have actually experienced. They also have the freedom to try out some of these new behaviors apart from the supervision of parents or other adult authorities. Insofar as no other people are directly dependent on adolescents for their well-being or their livelihood, adolescents are freer to take risks in their behavior and to challenge existing social norms than they may be when they are older. The energy that adolescents can invest in experimentation and their opportunities to experiment without concern for risk sometimes lead adolescents to unfortunate consequences. Many of the topics that are described as examples of deviant behavior are best understood as the negative outcomes of a whole range of experimental efforts by adolescents. For the most part, experimentation during this life stage helps to clarify the content and the limits of the opportunities available in the culture for future growth.

We wish to thank our students for their reactions to earlier drafts of the manuscript. Andrea Anderman, Mary Aiello, and Susan Kugel provided technical assistance in various stages of preparation. Once again, we recognize the competence and encouragement of our typist Ethel Levin. We would also like to thank Kathleen M. White and Lawrence G. Shelton for their helpful comments.

*February 1979*                                    ***Barbara M. Newman***
                                                   ***Philip R. Newman***

# Contents

## PART II

actions. *Summary*. The Psychoses of Early Adolescence: *Schizophrenia. A Schizophrenic Reaction in an Adolescent Girl*. Behavior Disorders of Early Adolescence: *Juvenile Delinquency. Runaways. Drug Use.*

## PART III

## PART IV

# Part I

*We draw from many theories in order to appreciate the full range of behaviors that are observed during adolescence.*

1

# Theories of Adolescence

The purpose of this chapter is to present some of the major theories of psychological development in order to understand how they conceptualize the life stage of adolescence. One must ask certain questions of a theory in order to evaluate its usefulness. First, one must ask what phenomena the theory is trying to explain. If a theory is trying to explain intellectual development, it might hypothesize about the evolution of the brain, the growth of logical thinking, or the capacity for symbolism. We are less likely to expect insights about fears, motives, or friendship from such a theory. Understanding the frame of reference allows us to place a particular theory in perspective. We will expect cognitive theory to clarify the intellectual development of adolescents, but we will not expect it to tell us very much about social development. Social psychological theory may be expected to inform us about interpersonal relationships but not about logical reasoning. Since our goal is to understand the full range of behaviors that are observed during adolescence and to understand adolescents as psychologically integrated individuals, we will draw from the relevant aspects of many theories to accomplish this goal.

The second question one must ask of a theory is what specific predictions it makes about the phenomena under study. Some theories make very specific predictions about how individuals will be influenced by internal events or environmental pressures. Other theories make very general, vague, or circular predictions. The more clearly specified the predictions, the easier it is to test the theory in the laboratory or in the field.

The third question to ask of a theory involves the fundamental assumptions on which the theory is based. The assumptions of a theory are the guiding premises that provide the logic of the theory. Einstein assumed that the speed of light was a constant before he derived his famous equation. Darwin assumed that evolutionary progress from lower to higher life forms underlay the principle of the survival of the fittest. Freud assumed that all behavior was motivated, and this led him to derive the idea of unconscious mental processes and motives. The assumptions of a theory may be limited by the cultural context, by the sample of observations from which the theorist draws, by the current knowledge base of the field of study, and by the logical capacities of the theorist. The limitations of any theory can be attributed, in part, to the accuracy of the assumptions which generate the logic of the theory.

In this chapter, five groups of theories are discussed. The *evolutionary theories* include the works of Charles Darwin (1859) and G. Stanley Hall (1904). Darwin considers human development in relation to the development of other animal species. Hall, often considered the father of adolescent psychology, relates the life phases from childhood to adulthood to the cultural evolution of human societies.

The *normative theories* describe the average pattern of growth and change at each life stage. Arnold Gesell (Gesell and Ilg, 1949, 1956) and Robert Havighurst (1972) offer two different views of normative change. The former emphasizes a waxing and waning of inner- and outer-directed growth, whereas the latter considers the specific competences which are achieved at each stage.

*Psychodynamic theories* focus on changes in emotional and social functioning. The psychoanalytic theorists, including Sigmund Freud (1963a; Strachey, 1953–74), Anna Freud (1946, 1965), and Peter Blos (1962), emphasize the consequences associated with the expression or inhibition of sexual and aggressive motives at each life stage. Harry Stack Sullivan (1953) focuses on characteristics of interpersonal relationships during childhood and adolescene. Erik Erikson (1950, 1959, 1968, 1977) directs our attention to the interplay between individual competences and cultural expectations at every phase of development.

*Cognitive theories* offer explanations about the development of intellectual competences. Jean Piaget (1950, 1970, 1971, 1976) has developed a stage theory which describes qualitative changes in logical thinking from infancy through adolescence. Lawrence Kohlberg (1964, 1969) has elaborated this stage theory to explain patterns of moral reasoning based on a growing appreciation of abstract principles of justice, intentionality, and social contracts. Heinz Werner (1948, 1957) discusses changes in cognitive functioning as a result of a dynamic interplay between forces toward differentiation and specialization and forces toward integration and synthesis. George Kelly (1955) extends the cognitive approach to a theory of personality that focuses on the concepts individuals use to define themselves and others.

The *social psychological theories* include those of Kurt Lewin (1935, 1936, 1951), Orville Brim (1965, 1966, 1976), and Roger Barker (1963a, 1963b, 1968). Each of these theories describes the importance of interaction with the social and physical environment as a necessary component for growth. Lewin proposed the concept of psychological space as a primary determinant of a person's experiences. Brim considers the array of social roles which create the context for development. Barker has attempted to analyze specific settings in order to understand how individuals define their environments as well as how environments determine the behavior of individuals. Our discussion of each of these theories includes three sections: (1) a presentation of basic concepts; (2) an analysis of the predictions and assumptions of the theory; and (3) a statement of how the theory conceptualizes the life period of adolescence within its own framework.

## EVOLUTIONARY THEORIES

Evolutionary theories demonstrate that the natural laws which apply to plant and animal life also apply to humans. These theories are important for the study of psychological development because they integrate human beings into the vast array of all life forms. Evolutionary theories emphasize the power of natural forces to direct and modify growth.

### Biological Evolution: Charles Darwin

Charles Darwin was not the first person to speculate about a theory of evolution. In the century prior to Darwin's scientific work, a number of philosophers and naturalists, including Montesquieu, de Maupertuis, Diderot, Buffon, and Linnaeus, made observations which suggested that a species might change and evolve into a new species. Darwin's grandfather Erasmus Darwin argued that evolution was the result of the response of specific species to their own motives and needs. The pre-Darwinian theories of evolution tended to be intuitive, and none of them offered explanatory mechanisms to account for how species changed. The main resistance to theories of evolution was offered by religions that believed in the "creation." The theory of evolution directly contradicts the notion that a creator formed each species separately at a particular time (de Beer, 1974).

Charles Darwin was born in 1809 into a family that had an intellectual tradition of belief in the concept of evolution. In his childhood, he was not particularly good at his studies. During his adolescence he was sent to study medicine, but he found the lectures boring and the work disgusting. He left medical school to the serious disappointment of his father and was then sent to Cambridge to be trained for the clergy. He was no more interested in theology than he had been in medicine. Throughout his childhood and adolescence, he was mainly interested in collecting things and in being out in nature.

In 1831 an opportunity arose which provided the real training ground and sources of observation for Darwin's career as a naturalist. He became the ship's naturalist on the H.M.S. *Beagle* on a voyage that was undertaken to survey the coasts of South America and islands of the Pacific. The voyage lasted from 1831 to 1836. On this voyage, Darwin showed unending energy in the exploration of the natural phenomena that he encountered. Upon his return, he published several books based on his observations and developed a theory of evolution. He kept the theory to himself and finally published his ideas in 1859 in *On the Origin of Species* (Darwin, 1859) when he learned that someone else had developed a similar theory (de Beer, 1963).

Darwin believed that the same laws of nature apply uniformly throughout time. This assumption, called *uniformitarianism,* had been advanced by Charles Lyell (1830–33). The challenge that the assumption posed was to discover a basic mechanism that could account for species change when life first developed as well as in the modern day. The mechanism which Darwin discovered is called *natural selection.* Every species produces more offspring that can survive to reproduce because of (1) limitations of the food supply and (2) natural dangers. Darwin had observed that there was a considerable amount of *variability* among members of the same species within a particular location. Those individuals that were best suited to the characteristics of the immediate environment were more likely to survive, to mate, and to produce offspring that also had the desirable characteristics. Darwin referred to the development of environmentally suitable characteristics as *adaptation.* The principle of natural selection was used to explain changes within species as well as the evolution from one species to another. A corollary of this theory is that as the environment changes, for example, when climates change from hot to temperate or from cold to temperate, new variations within species and new species develop through the process of adaptation to new conditions. Forms of life which fail to adapt to environmental change may become extinct. It is important to recognize that it is the potential for variability within a species which ensures the continuation of the species, even though particular members with specific characteristics may not survive (Darwin, 1872).

The principle of natural selection was developed without a knowledge of genetics and the mechanisms of heredity. Modern genetics has provided evidence about the potential sources of species variability, the various patterns of genetic interaction, and the ability to predict the frequency of a specific trait in a population given the incidence of the genes in the gene pool.

One of the primary features of human adaptation has been the evolution of the large brain. The acquisition of thinking and reasoning skills has allowed humans to make significant alterations in their environment. Thus, adaptation in the human species has reduced the applicability of the principle of natural selection for humans. People can enhance their chances for survival by modifying the food supply, protecting themselves from changes in climate, and eliminating certain natural dangers. What we are now beginning to appreciate is that each human intervention in the alteration of the environment has ramifications for aspects of the total ecosystem, including the air, the water, plant and animal life, and of course humans themselves.

Sir Julian Huxley (1941, 1942) posited the notion of *psychosocial evolution.* The development of symbolic thought, speech, and reasoning has allowed humans to amass a body of knowledge about the world which is transmitted from generation to generation. Through child rearing, education, and a variety of communication forms, children of one generation can be taught information that has been acquired by all the generations that preceded them and add to it for the education of the next generation. Through this process, psychosocial evolution has proceeded at a rapid pace, bringing changes in technology, in social organization, and in techniques for making war. In comparison to the slow pace of biological evolution, psychosocial evolution is both rapid and constantly accelerating.

## Recapitulation: G. Stanley Hall

G. Stanley Hall, whose theory and research we will discuss in this section, studied with Wilhelm Wundt, who is regarded as the father of experimental psychology, and with the first American psychologist, William James. He was one of the first people to receive a Ph.D. in psychology in the United States, from Harvard University. He founded Clark University in Worcester, Massachusetts, and served as its president. He founded the American Psychological Association, which is the major professional affiliation of most present-day psychologists. He was the only American academician to persuade Sigmund Freud to lecture in the United States (Freud, 1963). He personally awarded Ph.D.'s to numerous people, including Arnold Gesell, who became leading scholars in psychology.

Hall also produced a tremendous quantity of psychological research (Pruette, 1926). One of his major contributions is a two-volume work entitled *Adolescence,* and his affection for the stage is apparent in the following quotation:

It is all a marvelous new birth, and those who believe that nothing is so worthy of love, reverence, and service as the body and soul of youth, and who hold that the best test of every human institution is how much it contributes to bring youth to the ever fullest possible development, may well review themselves and the civilization in which we live to see how far it satisfies the supreme test. (Hall, 1904, p. 6)

Hall was intellectually committed to an evolutionary theory when he thought about psychological development. He believed that early and later adolescence were two distinct periods of psychological development; and he believed that adolescence was the time of psychosocial development when the transition between the more primitive child and the truly human adult occurred. His particular version of evolutionary theory is called *recapitulation theory*. He believed that the human being went through all aspects of previous evolutionary development beginning with conception and concluding with the final days of life. He saw the infant as a primitive animal learning basic skills and emulating some early phase of the evolution of the human species. Adolescence was the time of life when the sexual and intellectual capacities of the adult human emerged, just as they had in the evolutionary order. Hall compared adolescence to a time when humans lived in tribes without technology. In this theory an individual's development is a reminder of the biological history of the human species. Hall believed that the individual acts as a contemporary mirror in which the history of the species is reflected.

Many of the observations which Hall made about adolescence remain relevant to our understanding of this life stage. In general, Hall saw adolescence as a vitally important period. During this time individuals were capable of changing the course of their lives. Adolescents, as a group, were capable of changing the course of their society. The capacity for personal and social change emerged as a result of a number of life events which occur simultaneously during adolescence. These include rapid physical growth, sexual maturation, increased emotional intensity and conflict, the achievement of hypothetico-deductive reasoning, and an awareness of complex moral, social, and political concerns.

Hall characterized adolescence as a period of "Storm and Stress." This phrase, taken from the works of Goethe and Schiller, captures the sense of conflict and confusion which accompanies a growing awareness of self and society. As adolescents acquire adult capacities for reasoning, they become sensitive to the contradictions, the hypocrisies, and the inhumanities of their society. As they seek to express their sexual impulses they experience both the thrill of love and the humiliation of rejection. Hall saw adolescence as a period of self-consciousness, impulsiveness, idealism, and intensity. He argued that because of the unique character of adolescence the methods of education should be carefully chosen to facilitate growth. Imagination was required to direct the energy and confusion of this period into productive channels. Hall criticized existing educational institutions because he felt that they did not respond to the emerging competences which adolescents demonstrated.

Of some interest is Hall's observation that male and female adolescents followed different patterns of development. Hall argued that females had an intense concern with the maternal role and were highly motivated to engage in maternal activities. He saw childbearing and child rearing as the female's central role. As an evolutionary theorist, he was concerned that women take their maternal role seriously. He advocated the fullest achievement of competences in females which would enhance child care and child education. He failed to see these competences as relevant to the development of males. Rather, he emphasized rationality and morality as the goals of male adolescent development.

## NORMATIVE THEORIES

The two theorists discussed below—Arnold Gesell and Robert J. Havighurst—have offered broad, descriptive analyses about the pattern of normal development. In its strictest sense, the idea of a statistical *norm* refers to the average of observations of a large number of people. In fact, few individuals may actually conform to the average observation, but an average can be established by pooling all the observations. The theorists who offer normative theories do not expect every individual to conform to their description of growth. Rather, they suggest for most people specific events tend to occur in a particular sequence or at a particular period of life. These theorists provide a description of normal growth which can be used as a guideline for the kinds of competences and conflicts that are likely to occur at a given age. In evaluating a normative theory, one must be careful to recognize the special qualities of the subject population that has been used to establish the norms. The responses of a sample may be influenced by variations in cultural expectations, in diet, or in comfort with the setting in which observations are made.

### The Developmental Spiral: Arnold Gesell

Arnold Gesell built his theory of development from the direct observation of children. As director of the Yale University Clinic of Child Development, Gesell had the opportunity to observe and test about 1,000 children each year. With the use of the motion-picture camera, Gesell was able to film about 12,000 children through a one-way screen. Observations, however, are never made in a vacuum. They depend for their selection and their interpretation on the theoretical assumptions which guide and organize them.

Gesell was heavily influenced by Hall's work and by the evolutionary approach to development. He believed that growth was a lawful, natural process which occurred as a result of the biological unfolding of the child's inherited potential.

Gesell saw adolescence as a prolonged period of patterned growth leading to maturity:

> Ten marks a turn in the spiral course of development. The behavioral beginnings of adolescence appear at about eleven. The adolescent cycle continues through the teens well into the twenties. The years from ten to sixteen therefore are significantly transitional in the long march to maturity.
>
> . . . Our studies of the first ten years of life predisposed us to think that a youth is a child achieving a larger growth; and that adolescence despite its apparent irregularities is a consistent ripening process. (Gesell and Ilg, 1956, p. 4)

In his description of the years from 10 to 16, Gesell focused on nine areas of development, including the total action system, or physical and motor growth; routines and self-care, including eating, sleeping, bathing, and personal habits; emotions; the self-concept; interpersonal relationships; activities and interests; school life; ethics; and philosophic outlook.

Gesell saw growth as a series of "rhythmic sequences," or cycles of development. He did not regard development as a continuous progression, but viewed some phases as more harmonious and other phases as more erratic. Individual rhythms of growth are influenced by the evolutionary plan for maturation of the species, the specific genetic inheritance of the person, and the environmental opportunities which stimulate growth. Gesell was especially sensitive to the reciprocity of the adult's growth cycle and the child's growth cycle.

> The guidance of psychological growth is a two-way transaction which requires a double awareness of the attitudes of the growing child in interaction with the attitudes of the growing adult. Two cycles of growth thus come into an interplay which changes profoundly with the advancing age of the child—and of the parent. (Gesell and Ilg, 1956, 17)

This point is particularly salient for our understanding of adolescent development. As adolescents acquire greater conceptual complexity and participate in more varied social relationships, they begin to be able to assume an adult perspective in problem solving and decision making. At the same time, adolescents are limited in their reasoning by their lack of experience with many life events. Adults, on the other hand, may fail to recognize the logic or accuracy of adolescents' perceptions. After many years of relating to children, who have a more limited cognitive scope, they may fail to adapt to the changes which have occurred.

### The Tasks of Development: Robert J. Havighurst

Robert J. Havighurst is a well-known educator who has observed the problems of human development for many years. He conducted a study in which he observed the process of growing up in a small city. His book describing this study is called *Growing Up in River City* (Havighurst, et al. 1962). His theory of human development is a relatively simple one, yet it has a great deal of intuitive appeal. It is an orderly and well-organized description of many experiences that we have all had. The central proposition of the theory is that much of human behavior is learning behavior. Havighurst believes that human development is a process in which each person attempts to learn the tasks that are required by the society into which the person is born. "Living in a modern society is a long series of tasks to learn" (Havighurst, 1972, p. 2). The person who learns well receives satisfaction and reward, and the person who doesn't learn well suffers unhappiness and social disapproval.

Learning does not proceed at an even, gradually uphill pace. There are not necessarily small units to learn each day in the gradual accomplishment of the tasks. Rather, there are times when learning is going on at an energetic pace, and there are times when little learning is going on.

The tasks that the person must learn are called *developmental tasks*. The tasks define what is healthy, normal development at different ages in a particular society. Individuals must learn to evaluate their own performance of the tasks of development. In this way they can gauge the progress of their own growth. Havighurst defined a developmental task as "a task which arises at or about a certain period in the life of an individual, successful achievement of which leads to his happiness and to success with later tasks, while failure leads to unhappiness in the individual, disapproval by the society and difficulty with later tasks" (Havighurst, 1972, p. 2).

He believed that there are sensitive periods for learning developmental tasks, and he called these periods *teachable moments*. Most people learn these tasks at the appropriate time and in the proper sequence. If a particular developmental task is not learned (or is not taught) during the correct time period, then the learning of that developmental task will be difficult if not impossible.

Havighurst identified the years from 12 to 18 as adolescence. During these years, he emphasized tasks associated with physical and emotional growth. This focus tends to overlook some of the significant cognitive changes which were of evolutionary importance to Hall and Gesell. Table 1–1 lists the eight developmental tasks of adolescence and their goals. Taken as a whole, they reflect challenges in the areas of sex role development, career choice, and morality. Havighurst suggests that the forces of biology, psychology, culture and social class all contribute to the person's ability to achieve success at each task. Some tasks, such as preparation for marriage, are trying for adolescents of every social class because of a combination of changing cultural attitudes and social class orientations. Other tasks, such as achieving emotional independence, are described as more stressful for middle-class adolescents than for upper- or lower-class adolescents. In other words, success in the business of development is dependent on the convergence of cultural norms, socioeconomic resources, and personal competences.

It must be clear from the description of development tasks that Havighurst does not consider such phenomena as conflict, rebellion, alienation, or deviance, as essential components of adolescent

**Table 1–1: Havighurst's Developmental Tasks of Adolescence**

| *Task* | *Goal* |
| --- | --- |
| 1. Achieving new and more mature relations with age-mates of both sexes. | To learn to look upon girls as women and boys as men; to become an adult among adults. |
| 2. Achieving a masculine or feminine social role. | To accept and to learn a socially approved adult masculine or feminine social role. |
| 3. Accepting one's physique and using one's body effectively. | To become proud, or at least tolerant, of one's body. |
| 4. Achieving emotional independence of parents and other adults. | To become free from childish dependence on one's parents; to develop affection for one's parents without remaining dependent upon them. |
| 5. Preparing for marriage and family life. | To develop a positive attitude toward family life and having children. |
| 6. Preparing for an economic career. | To organize one's plans and energies in such a way as to begin an orderly career; to feel able to make a living. |
| 7. Acquiring a set of values and an ethical system as a guide to behavior—developing an ideology. | To form a socio-politico-ethical ideology. |
| 8. Desiring and achieving socially responsible behavior. | To develop a social ideology; to participate as a responsible adult in the life of the community; to take account of the values of society in one's personal behavior. |

Source: Derived from R. J. Havighurst, *Developmental tasks and education,* 3d ed. (New York: David McKay, 1972).

growth. In this view, adolescence is a period in which individuals acquire the competences and the emotional commitment necessary to participate as adults in their society.

## PSYCHODYNAMIC THEORIES

The psychodynamic theorists focus upon the dynamic, changing qualities of the mental activity of individuals as they encounter the structure of their existence. For every person the structure of existence is an interweaving of culture, family, work, and other necessary life activities. The structure of one's existence may also be determined by personal characteristics, including (a) periods of biological growth and (b) physical and economic resources. Biologically, we unfold according to a pattern that has been established biochemically over a period of millions of years. One cannot influence whether one is growing as an infant, or as an adolescent, but the places one is allowed to enter change, depending on one's age (Barker and Wright, 1955). One's economic position will affect the places one has access to and what one may do in those settings.

Finally, the structure of an individual's life is determined by the man-made historical events and the natural conditions of the period in which he or she lives. A person who was 18–22 years old during the Vietnam War was psychologically stimulated in vastly different ways than a person who was 18–22 during the height of the British Empire. As you can see, the possible comparisons become quite vast.

The psychodynamic theorists have chosen to study and observe the lives of individuals and to try to develop explanations for what they have observed. In general the psychodynamic theorists believe that mental activity plays a very important role in determining the behaviors that an individual initiates during the activity record. The Freuds and Peter Blos focused on psychosexual development. Harry Stack Sullivan focused on interpersonal behavior. Erik Erikson focused on psychosocial development. We discuss the observations that each group made and the theories of psychodynamic functioning that were constructed from their observations.

### Psychosexual Theorists: Sigmund Freud, Anna Freud, and Peter Blos

The psychosexual theorists observed the impact of the sexual drives on the psychological functioning of the person. Sigmund Freud differentiated the impact of sexual drives on mental activity from their impact on reproductive functions (Freud, 1963a; Strachey, 1953–74). As an observer, he recognized the importance of sexuality in the mental activity of children. He argued that even though children were not capable of reproductive activity, sexual drives operated to direct aspects of their fantasies, their problem solving, and their social interactions (Freud, 1953, 1963a).

Sigmund Freud was trained as a neurologist in Vienna in the 1870s. His early research focused on the functions of the medulla, the conduction of nerve impulses in the brain and the spinal cord (Freud, 1884), and the anesthetic properties of cocaine (Freud, 1963b). In 1882 Freud turned his interest from physiology to psychology because of his association with Josef Breuer. Breuer and Freud developed a theory of hysteria in which they attributed certain forms of paralysis to psychological conflict rather than physiological damage (Breuer and Freud, 1955).

The historical period which provided the context for the structure of Freud's existence should be noted so that his theory can be properly evaluated and understood. Like Darwin, he lived during a time when the principles of human genetics were neither widely known nor fully understood. Freud had a greater awareness of the many scientific insights related to evolution and genetics than most physicians of his day. The time in which he lived was characterized by very rigorous restrictions on most forms of sexual expression. Freud was a middle-class Jew during a period in which there was considerable mobility in Austrian society. Jewish men of this period were expected to become lawyers, doctors, entrepreneurs, or industrialists. The various branches of the Rothschild family were engaged in many of the largest financial, industrial, and political transactions in all of Europe. Benjamin Disraeli, who was of Jewish descent served as the prime minister of England during Freud's adolescence and early adulthood.

The role of scientist was an emerging one. Wealthy gentlemen such as Newton or Darwin and talented entrepreneurs such as Benjamin Franklin could pursue the study of natural phenomena. Freud, a brilliant student, elected the study of medicine in order to gain a greater understanding of the nature of human psychological functioning. He was forced to pursue his scientific interests under the guise of a physician because the role of scientist was not accessible to him. He gathered his data by working with patients. Many of his writings include case presentations from which his theory of psychological functioning was derived. He was denied a professorial appointment at the University of Vienna because the public mention of childhood sexuality was not acceptable behavior. Needless to say, the concept of childhood sexuality was also unacceptable. For the rest of his life, Freud was criticized by physicians in Vienna because of this concept. His colleague and collaborator Josef Breuer found Freud's preoccupation with sexual motives distasteful and ceased his association with Freud. It should also be noted that throughout Europe and Russia there were periodic outbreaks of anti-Semitism. All through Freud's life, there were individuals and groups who harassed him simply because they did not like Jews. Toward the end of his life Freud was forced to leave his home in Austria, as Einstein had been forced to leave his home in Germany, in order to protect himself and his family from the threat of Nazi extermination (Jones, 1953, 1955, 1957). In the 1930s Freud and Einstein corresponded about their perceptions of anti-Semitism (Einstein and Freud, 1964). They shared their experiences as great thinkers who had been subjected to common experiences because of a common characteristic.

In response to his exclusion from the medical community, Freud helped to form the International Congress on Psychoanalysis. Freud became increasingly concerned that his theory would be dismissed because he was a Jew. In order to protect the field of psychoanalysis, he worked to have Carl Jung, a non-Jew, elected as the leader of the congress. When he felt that Jung was betraying him by deviating from the theory, he became less involved in the workings of the congress (Jones, 1953, 1955, 1957).

Freud battled cancer from 1923 until his death. He fled Vienna in 1938 and died in London in 1939. He devoted the last part of his life to extensive writing that would clarify his ideas so that they could be pursued by other analysts and scholars.

There are many excellent biographies on Freud. One of the best is by his disciple Ernest Jones (1953, 1955, 1957). Freud's complete works (1953–74) have been edited by James Strachey with the assistance of Alex Strachey, Alan Tyson, and Angela Richards in collaboration with Freud's daughter Anna Freud. Freud's theory is complex and provocative. It should be pointed out to the reader who is not familiar with the theory that its principles cannot be applied by amateurs and that it cannot be fully understood without serious study. Some of the major ideas will be presented here in order to convey a sense of how this influential theory conceptualizes the adolescent period of development.

Two assumptions guided Freud's thinking. First, he believed that all psychological events were tied to biochemical characteristics of the human body. He believed that eventually the mental functions he identified as id, ego, and superego would be tied to areas of the brain which governed impulse expression, reality assessment, and conscience, respectively.

The second assumption was that all behavior is motivated. Although Freud acknowledged the possibility that some behavior occurred as a result of fatigue, he was convinced that much of what people claimed to be a result of accident or chance was really the expression of a motive of which they were unaware. The two assumptions together resulted in the formulation of Freud's most powerful and troublesome concept, the unconscious. The unconscious is a reservoir of wishes, motives, and fears which are not readily accessible to conscious thought. The dynamic tension of psychological life is the conflict between the energy from unconscious wishes and the internalization of norms about the appropriate or permissible expression of those wishes.

Freud described the development of personality as a product of the changing focus of sexual impulses in various body zones. In his model, sexualized energy shifted according to a biological timetable from the mouth, to the anus, to the genitals. At each phase of development, new forms of sexual pleasure and new modes of social interaction emerge. The final stage of personality development occurs during adolescence, when sexual maturation results from the combination of hormonal changes which bring the capacity for reproduction and a social orientation toward heterosexual love. Freud believed that the psychological conflicts which adolescents and adults experienced were due to the failure to satisfy or express specific wishes during childhood. At any one of the childhood stages, sexualized impulses could be so frustrated that the person would continue to seek gratification of those wishes at later life stages. Given that no person can possibly satisfy all of his or her wishes at every life stage, normal development depends on the person's ability to channel the energy from those wishes into activities which either symbolize the wishes or express the wishes in a socially acceptable form, a process called sublimation. In summary, Freud saw adolescence as the final stage of personality development. During this stage, patterns of impulse expression and sublimation crystallize into a life orientation. From this point on, the content of the unconscious, balanced by the ability to evaluate reality and the regulating functions of the conscience, rework the struggles of childhood through repeated episodes of engagement, conflict, and impulse gratification or impulse frustration.

Anna Freud is Sigmund Freud's youngest daughter. She was born in 1895 in Vienna. Her major contribution to the field of psychoanalysis has been to extend its practice to the treatment and study of children. In one of her major works, *The Ego and the Mechanisms of Defense* (A. Freud, 1946), she outlines the aspects of psychosexual development from infancy through adolescence. In keeping with the theory of psychosexual development she views adolescence as a time of increased libidinal energy which is associated with biological maturation. She describes the period between latency and puberty in the following way:

There is more libido at the id's disposal and it cathects indiscriminately any id-impulses which are at hand. Aggressive impulses are intensified to the point of complete unruliness, hunger becomes voracity and the naughtiness of the latency-period turns into the criminal behavior of adolescence. Oral and anal interests, long submerged, come to the surface again. Habits of cleanliness, laboriously acquired during the latency-period, give place to pleasure in dirt and disorder, and instead of modesty and sympathy we find exhibitionistic tendencies, brutality and cruelty to animals. The reaction-formations, which seemed to be firmly established in the structure of the ego, threaten to fall to pieces. At the same time old tendencies which had disappeared come into consciousness. The Oedipus wishes are fulfilled in the form of phantasies and day-dreams, in which they have undergone but little distortion; in boys ideas of castration and in girls penis-envy once more become the centre of interest. There are very few new elements in the invading forces. Their onslaught merely brings once more to the surface the familiar content of the early infantile sexuality of little children. (A. Freud, 1946, p. 159)

At puberty, she observes, genital feelings, sexual objects, and sexual goals become the primary focus of libidinal energy. To some extent, this narrowing of focus gives adolescence a more controlled, predictable appearance than the period just before puberty. She warns, however, that two extreme consequences of the dynamic conflict of adolescence can have negative consequences for the person. First, the new surge of instinctual energy can make the id so strong that it dominates the ego. The result is an adult life characterized by impulsiveness, low tolerance for frustration, and continuous demands for self-gratification. The other negative consequence is the potential for a rigid, defensive response by the ego which rejects or denies the legitimacy of any aspect of the sexual instincts. The two ego defenses which Anna Freud described as adolescent responses to increased instinctual forces are asceticism and intellectuality. Asceticism refers to a mistrust of instincts and a refusal to engage in any form of pleasurable activity. Intellectuality refers to a preoccupation with the abstract concepts of friendship, love, marriage, or other conflict-laden themes. This preoccupation with abstractions is viewed as an attempt to gain ego control over threatening instincts. In spite of repeated discussions, ruminations, and reading about topics which are linked to sexuality, the adolescent's actions toward friends, family members, or potential sex objects may continue to be self-centered and impulsive. Thus, the threat of adolescence, as Anna Freud describes it, is that the ego may be overwhelmed by the quantity of instinctual forces which arise during puberty. The flow of contradictory behaviors, self-centered and passionately loving, submissive and rebellious, lighthearted and depressed, all reflect the struggle being waged to define and assert the ego as the dominant psychological force.

In *Normality and Pathology in Childhood,* a recent statement of her ideas, Anna Freud (1965) describes the differences between the child and the adult. The child is viewed as (1) egocentric, (2) sexually immature, (3) unable to accurately evaluate reality with the accompanying danger of being overwhelmed by impulses, and (4) lacking an adult appreciation of time. The implication of this view is that a child changes in each of these four dimensions as he or she attains adulthood. The time when most of the growth which results in the achievement of adult competences occurs is during the period of adolescence. Peter Blos (1962) has taken the psychoanalytic view of development and extended it to a full description of how the child is transformed into the adult during the adolescent years.

First, Blos (1962) makes clear that for the psychosexual theorists "adolescence" is the period of psychological adaptation to the biological maturation which is called "pubescence." Often, he notes, the psychological period extends for longer than the physical period. In addition, just as there is variation in the rate of physical growth for people, there is also variation in the rate of psychological growth. Blos also points out the great differences in experience that may exist between a sexually active 12-year-old and a sexually latent 12-year-old.

One important contribution of Blos's work is his focus on adaptation as well as defense. As Kroeber (1963) has pointed out, the adaptive system performs two important functions: coping and defending. Both Freuds elaborated the defending mode (A. Freud, 1946; S. Freud, 1963), but Blos added the importance of coping behaviors and outlined the evolution of a psychodynamic coping system for adolescents.

Coping refers to active efforts by the person to resolve stress and to create new solutions to personal problems. The need for coping is sometimes a result of intrapsychic conflict and sometimes a result of environmental pressures. There are three primary components to coping behavior: (1) the ability to gain and process new information, (2) the ability to maintain control over emotions, and (3) the ability to move freely in one's environment (White, 1974). While defending is a process of self-protection in the face of threat, coping involves the development of new responses that reduce or resolve conflict.

Remembering the theory of biological and psychosocial evolution, we know that the adaptive systems are vital in the biological realm. Why not, then, in the psychosocial? In fact, it is quite logical to assume psychosocial adaptive capacities (Kelly, 1966; Erikson, 1950; Newman and Newman, 1975, 1978). In sum, Sigmund Freud and Anna Freud have documented much of the psychological behavior that accompanies sexual motivation. Kroeber has identified the coping as well as the defensive functions of this type of mental activity. Blos has detailed these developments as well as the defensive function for the period of life that the psychosexual theorists term adolescence.

Blos describes three phases of the adolescent adaptation: (1) early adolescence, (2) adolescence proper, and (3) late adolescence. In early adolescence the person's psychological conflicts are primarily a result of biological motivation. Early adolescents are taken by surprise at their thoughts and impulses when they are unprepared for the onset of biological change.

In the phase of early adolescence, boys and girls who have been very deeply involved in relationships with members of their own sex become involved in relationships with members of the opposite sex. Impulse may lead a child of latency age who appears to be very orderly and competent to become rather inconsistent and perhaps slightly disordered in behavior. This is referred to as a developmental disturbance—a natural disturbance caused by a discrepancy between the biological events and psychological awareness (A. Freud, 1969; P. Blos, 1962). When biological events precede psychological awareness, the human tendency is toward defense. When psychological expectation precedes biological events, the outcome may be defensive or adaptive. The developmental disturbance tends to be a product of defensive behavior and is often encountered by psychotherapists. The developmental gain tends to be a function of a harmonious integration of psychological anticipation and biological growth. It tends to be observed by parents, teachers, friends, and other observers who are in positions to describe the creative accomplishments of a life period.

Adolescence proper is characterized by the removal of psychic investment from some people who were important in the oral, anal, phallic, and latency stages and by a reassessment of the fears, fantasies, conflicts, and aspirations that have crystallized around these people. Some of these psychic bonds must be dissolved so that the energy that was invested in them may be used to develop new involvements. Adolescent friendships are often particularly memorable. The free energy of dissolved bonds and the free energy which comes from biological growth can both be invested in adolescent relationships. The adolescent qualities of nostalgia and depression are interpreted as part of the process of saying good-bye to people whom one has thought about but perhaps not seen for a very long time. Adolescent experimentation and romanticism are interpreted as the qualities associated with a widening field of social interest.

Late adolescence is a period of consolidation. It is characterized by five major accomplishments: (1) judgment, interests, intellect and other ego functions emerge which are specific to the individual and very stable; (2) the conflict-free area of the ego expands, allowing new people and experiences to acquire psychological importance; (3) an irreversible sexual identity is formed; (4) the egocentrism of the child is replaced by a balance between thoughts about oneself and thoughts about others; and (5) a wall separating one's public and private selves is established. The late adolescent presents a relatively constant personal image.

Although the structure for one's personal identity is built during late adolescence, Blos believes that it is not until the adult years and considerable experience with the tasks of one's life that an integrated, comfortable sense of oneself is established.

At the close of adolescence, as I have remarked earlier, conflicts are by no means resolved, but they are rendered specific; and certain conflicts become integrated into the realm of the ego as life tasks. This was described as the achievement of late adolescence. It remains the task of postadolescence to create the specific avenues through which these tasks are implemented in the external world. (Blos, 1962, p. 150)

**Summary.**  Psychosexual theorists hypothesize about the psychological events that accompany the sexual drive as it develops in humans. They believe that there is a psychological energy that powers and directs the mental and behavioral apparatus. The mental apparatus includes many functions of the mind, including (1) fears, wishes, and impulses (the id); (2) reality-testing, defending, and coping mechanisms, including thinking, reasoning, judging, remembering, and planning (the ego); and (3) the moral restrictions, aspirations, and positive and negative emotions which reward "good" behavior and punish "bad" behavior (the superego). Psychosexual theorists recognize the independence of the behavioral system and the internal mental system. Although mental activity is sometimes the guiding force of behavior, there are times when impulses outside of consciousness guide behavior, with no cognitive awareness of their impact. Psychosexual theorists also recognize that impulses may lead to cognition but no action (fantasy). Sometimes an internal impulse leads to the construction of a fantasy that breaks down the reality-testing mechanisms and seems to be real (a delusion). Symptoms are viewed as the products of ineffective defenses. Defenses are replaced by symptoms that lead to some peace of mind but often also lead to restrictions in the individual's ability to function. Symptom patterns define conditions such as neurosis, psychosis, and character disorders when they become extremely noticeable and annoying (see Chapters 8 and 12).

In adolescence we find three phases of psychic development: (1) early adolescence, (2) adolescence proper, and (3) late adolescence. Psychosexual theory turns our attention to the events before, during, and after puberty. Physical and psychological events as well as the interrelationships among them are emphasized.

### Interpersonal Theory: Harry Stack Sullivan

Sullivan's theory focuses upon the development of communicative skills through the stages of infancy, childhood, the juvenile era, preadolescence, early adolescence, late adolescence, and adulthood. Sullivan was a psychiatrist who spent a good deal of time seeing adult patients with a wide variety of problems. He believed that the core of his patients' problems was a blockage of communication that was caused by anxiety or the threat of anxiety (Cohen, 1953).

Sullivan made two primary assumptions in his work: (1) that mental disorder was caused when communication was impaired by anxiety; and (2) that there was such a thing as an interpersonal field which affected all participants. He believed that from infancy through the rest of life the individual is communicatively part of a larger entity called an interpersonal field. Although the field may change during one's life, it has properties of its own and should, therefore, be measurable (Sullivan, 1953).

Sullivan hypothesized that three types of experience contribute to the structure of an individual's existence. The first type involves sensations, perceptions, and emotions which occur before the development of symbolic thinking. The second type involves symbols that are used privately, such as fantasies, daydreams, thinking, and private words, concepts, and images. The third type involves symbols whose meanings are agreed upon by two or more people, such as words (Sullivan, 1953).

According to Sullivan, dynamisms are the main mechanisms of individual stability. Dynamisms are patterns of interaction that are characteristic of a person at various stages of development. They usually develop in infancy and childhood and guide interactions as one grows older. Although dynamisms are relatively stable they do change over time. In fact, it is the de-investment of energy which has been expended in an older pattern that allows for the reinvestment of energy and the development of a new pattern.

The interactive network is, in part, an integration of the patterns of interaction of two or more people. Sullivan (1953) believed that anxiety resulted from characteristics of one's personal relationships. Fundamentally, he found that problems in interpersonal situations led to anxiety. Anxiety led to a communication blockage, and the communication blockage led to more anxiety. When the opportunities to communicate diminish, the resulting anxiety produces private symbolic responses (such as fantasy) or nonsymbolic responses (such as coping) instead of interpersonal responses. Persistent periods of high anxiety and infrequent interpersonal exchanges may lead to severe mental distress.

For most developing people, empathy allows problems in communication to be overcome. The ability to understand other individuals allows a person to understand the other persons' communication difficulty, to help them overcome it, and therefore to reduce the anxiety or tension level in the interpersonal field. The final important dimension of Sullivan's theory was his firm belief that individuals are very different from one another. Their specific personal experiences and, therefore, their dynamisms are quite unique. Interactive fields are even more unique because they result from the integration of the interaction patterns of two or more people. Empathy is a factor which separates growth-promoting from interpersonally pathological fields. *The basic principle of interaction* involves "helping each other overcome blocks in communication so that we may reduce the tension between us."

Sullivan agreed with the psychosexual theorists that there are three phases of adolescence. He called the phases preadolescence, early adolescence, and late adolescence. Preadolescence begins with the development of the need for a specific, close personal relationship with another person, usually of the same sex. These "best friend" relationships begin to teach the child about the characteristics of interpersonal intimacy. Although the predominant social unit of this phase is a "two-group," Sullivan observed that such pairs interlock with other pairs, forming the basis of preadolescent society. The society provides information to individuals about styles of dress, forms of slang, and expectations for other behaviors. Individuals come to evaluate themselves not only by personal and family standards but by the standards of the society. Differences in rates of physical maturation often mean extreme social consequences, particularly for late maturers. The final element in the interpersonal experience of the preadolescent period is the development of a sense of loneliness. Sullivan argued that the individual recognizes the need for intimate personal experience and fears its loss. Fantasies of being without a close friend lead the child to the experience of loneliness.

The interpersonal interest of the early adolescent shifts from members of the same sex to members of the opposite sex. How to have relationships with girls preoccupies boys, and vice versa.

In essence, children investigate the ways to have a meaningful personal relationship with members of the opposite sex. This concern also begins to preoccupy the two-person like-sex groups. The events of puberty initiate what Sullivan referred to as lust—an interpersonal derivative of the sexual drive. He believed that much of early adolescence involves working out the collisions and conflicts of the need for intimacy and lust. Both persist, and a lust dynamism develops, leading to very elaborate patterns of interaction based upon sexual needs and concerns. The fact that social events of the early adolescent years are structured to provide overt or covert expressions of sexuality is seen as an integration of biological and social life.

According to Sullivan:

Late adolescence extends from the patterning of preferred genital activity through unnumbered educative steps to the establishment of a fully human or mature repertory of interpersonal relations, as permitted by available opportunity, personal and cultural. In other words, a person begins late adolescence when he discovers what he likes in the way of genital behavior and how to fit it into the rest of his life. (Sullivan, 1953, p. 297)

Major intellectual events may occur in late adolescence. The enhancement of shared symbolic reasoning may occur in advanced education or through the challenge of a job. The expansion of this realm of experience varies a great deal from one person to another. Sullivan believed that increasing development of a sense of oneself and a sense of the other would determine the amount of intellectual growth during late adolescence. He saw major blocks to development growing out of an individual's tendency to escape the anxiety of adult maturity by engaging in daydreams and fantasy instead of more reality-oriented behavior. He felt, in fact, that late adolescence was the period when many people stopped growing psychologically. He believed that whether one continued to develop depended upon whether one developed a sense of self-respect. Self-respect could be the final product of the personal questioning that was stimulated during late adolescence. Self-respect would lead one to respect others, and if this were accomplished, maturity could result.

## Psychosocial Theory: Erik Homburger Erikson

Erik Erikson is probably the best-known student of human development among the current adolescent population. His name is associated with the concept of *personal identity,* which is the sense of oneself that Erikson believes develops during the adolescent period.

Erik Erikson was born in Frankfurt, Germany, in 1902. His Danish parents were divorced before his birth. His mother had only recently gone to Germany to visit friends when he was born (Coles, 1970). Erikson's mother married the boy's pediatrician, Dr. Homburger, before Erik was five. Erikson grew up in the home of a prosperous, Jewish physician and would in early adulthood serve as teacher, student, and patient in the household of another Jewish physician, Sigmund Freud.

Erikson attended elementary school from the ages of 6 to 10 and high school—the gymnasium—until he was 18. He then wandered around Europe for a year and spent several months on the shores of Lake Constance, reading, writing, and enjoying the views (Coles, 1970). He returned to his hometown, Karlsruhe, enrolled in art school, and studied there for a year. He then spent two years in Munich, attending art school and producing a large number of woodcuts. He traveled to Florence, gave up sketching completely, and just wandered about, along with the many other wanderers of that time. He was searching for himself, and he was trying to identify his personal resources. His friends were Peter Blos and a sculptor, Oscar Stonorov (Coles, 1970). Coles (1970) describes Erikson "as a wandering artist trying to come to grips with himself" (p. 15). How much he came to grips with himself remains unclear. It is known that at 25 he was home studying and preparing to teach art (Coles, 1970).

In his late teens, Erikson had decided to become an artist. He studied, traveled, worked, and had an exhibition with the now-famous Max Beckman. He decided that he was not good at his chosen field and befriended others like himself—Blos, who, as we know, was to become an analyst, and Stonorov, who was to become an architect. He returned home, having decided to become an art teacher, when a letter arrived from Blos that provided him with a unique opportunity to teach.

Erikson and Blos operated a private school that was sponsored by people who were living in Vienna to study psychoanalysis with Sigmund Freud. The school was for their children. Erikson studied the techniques of psychoanalysis at the analytic institute and underwent a training analysis with Anna Freud, who had also been a teacher. His decision to become an analyst was a choice encouraged by the proximity of a supportive and influential group of psychoanalysts who helped intelligent, interested people to enter the occupation that they had created.

After training and marriage, Erikson set off for America. He became a child analyst on the faculty of Harvard Medical School. Three years later he went to Yale, and two years after that he studied the Sioux Indians in South Dakota (Erikson, 1950). Next, he opened a clinical practice in San Francisco. At the same time, he conducted a study of the Yurok Indians (Erikson, 1943, 1950). In 1942, he was appointed a faculty member of the University of California at Berkeley. In 1950, his major theoretical work *Childhood and Society* was published. In the same year, he left his job at Berkeley and joined the staff of the Austen Riggs Center in Stockbridge, Massachusetts. In addition to other activities, including being a professor of human development at Harvard, Erikson has continued to write and to revise his theory. An excellent biography of Erikson, *Erik H. Erikson: The Growth of His Work*, has been written by Robert Coles (1970), a student of Erikson's and a well-known psychiatrist.

Erikson's psychosocial theory is a stage approach to the whole life span. Two assumptions about development dominate the theory. First, Erikson describes individuals at every life stage as having the capacity to contribute to their own growth. People are not merely shaped or governed by biological or environmental forces. Rather, they integrate, organize, and conceptualize their own experiences so that they can protect themselves and so that they can grow. Second, the social group makes active contributions in shaping the direction of personal growth. At every stage of life, cultural aspirations, expectations, and opportunities have an impact on individual development. Societies encourage patterns of parenting, opportunities for education, and attitudes toward sexuality, intimacy, and work that are designed to preserve and protect the culture.

Erikson describes development as occurring in eight life stages from infancy through later adulthood. At each stage, the person's changing competences emerge within a context of social expectations. Erikson sees growth as the product of a certain degree of conflict or tension at every life stage in which the person strives to adapt to cultural demands while trying to preserve a sense of individuality and personal meaning. Erikson describes the conflict of each life stage as a psychosocial crisis (see Table 1–2). The crises are characterized by growth around a central theme in which both positive and negative experiences are encountered.

Table 1–2: The Psychosocial Crises of Eight Life Stages

| *Life Stage* | *Psychosocial Crisis* |
| --- | --- |
| Infancy | Trust versus mistrust |
| Toddlerhood | Autonomy versus shame and doubt |
| Early school age | Initiative versus guilt |
| Middle school age | Industry versus inferiority |
| Adolescence | Identity versus role diffusion |
| Young adulthood | Intimacy versus isolation |
| Middle adulthood | Generativity versus stagnation |
| Later adulthood | Integrity versus despair |

*In Erikson's theory, adolescence is a period for experimentation and search for personal identity.*

In infancy, for example, the central theme is the development of mutuality with the caregiver. In the process of learning to count on the caregiver and learning to control one's own insistence on immediate gratification, infants learn both to trust and to mistrust others. Eventually, they also learn to trust and mistrust themselves. According to Erikson, every life stage brings its own sources of conflict and crisis as well as its sources of gratification and growth. In that sense, development is not viewed as a totally stagewise progress. At every life stage, one can anticipate developmental anxiety about the adequacy with which new challenges will be met. The child of 10 or 11 who has evolved a sense of industry may be more comfortable, more outgoing, or more creative than that same person at age 18, when he or she may be in the throes of conflict about personal identity.

In Erikson's theory, the life stage of adolescence plays a pivotal role. As one might guess from Erikson's own life experiences, he views this period as a time for search, experimentation, and introspection from which a personal identity evolves. For every person, identity is a creative integration of past identifications, personal competences, and future aspirations. The many life roles which the adolescent has come to play, including those of son or daughter, sibling, student, worker, citizen, religious believer, and lover, contribute many views of the person's meaning to self and to others. The personal identity is like the solution to the many-faceted puzzle of personal experience. As Erikson explains it, "The process of identity formation depends on the interplay of what young persons at the end of childhood have come to mean to themselves and what they now appear to mean to those who become significant to them" (Erikson, 1977, p. 106).

Work on identity formation can be disrupted by three rather different patterns of life events. First, Erikson explains that some adolescents resolve the question of their personal meaning without experiencing much search or experimentation. An identity that is achieved without crisis is called *identity foreclosure* (Erikson, 1959). This often occurs when a career choice is made early in adolescence that carries a person through an educational process, work activities, and socialization for professional values which are never challenged or evaluated in light of individual temperament or private hopes.

The second disruption to work on identity formation is described as *negative identity* (Erikson, 1959). When young people perceive themselves as devalued or rejected by the dominant culture, they may evolve a personal identity which is based on those negative characteristics. Although most people use their negative identity as a description of what they are trying to avoid becoming, some young people use it as a challenge to become the toughest, meanest, sliest, or crookedest member of the devalued group.

The third disruption to work on identity formation is described as *role diffusion* (Erikson, 1959). For some young people, it becomes impossible to integrate the many roles they play. When they are with their parents they fall into the subordinate child role. When they are with their peers, they feel autonomous and even rebellious. However, they never seem to mean the same thing to all of those who know them. They are afraid to relinquish their childhood roles and are unable to convince themselves of their authenticity in more contemporary roles.

In Erikson's scheme, adolescence is critical not only insofar as it serves to crystallize earlier components of development, but because it sets the course for later life choices. The decision to choose and care for a life partner, the manner in which one makes a personal contribution to one's children and to the society at large, and the degree of integrity with which one approaches aging and death are all influenced by the values and aspirations incorporated in the adolescent's identity (Erikson, 1968).

## COGNITIVE THEORIES

Probably the most significant consequence of human evolution has been the conceptual abilities made possible by the complexity of the human brain. Two cognitive competences are of particular importance to the direction of human development. First, there are those capacities which permit people to symbolize experiences so that they can leave exact records of events for future generations. Second, there are those skills which permit humans to hypothesize about conditions that do not exist currently but that could exist.

The psychologists whose theories are presented in this section have focused on aspects of cognition, that is knowing, conceptualizing, reasoning, thinking, and problem solving, as a key to understanding human behavior. In choosing this strategy, they have focused on the mental phenomena which one might categorize as conscious and rational rather than on phenomena which might be described as unconscious or emotional. Nevertheless, they consider many of the same life events that are of interest to the psychodynamic theorists. Characteristics of social relationships, the nature of dreams and play, the development of morality, and the content of the self-concept are all important themes that cognitive theorists attempt to explain. In addition, they emphasize the changing qualities of intelligence from childhood to adulthood. They offer varying descriptions of the characteristics of knowing and of the ways in which a particular kind of intelligence influences a person's orientation toward life events.

Piaget's theory is primarily a psychological approach to epistemology, or the acquisition of logical thought. He describes qualitatively unique stages in the growth of logical thinking, beginning in infancy and continuing through adolescence (Flavell, 1963; Piaget, 1970; Phillips, 1975). Kohlberg (1964, 1969) has used a stage approach to analyze the emergence of moral reasoning. He argues that a person's morality is directly influenced by the quality of the logical thought that governs decisions about right and wrong, personal responsibility, and justice.

Werner (1948, 1957; Wapner and Werner, 1957; Werner and Kaplan, 1963) is closest to being an evolutionary theorist. He describes stages of thought that reflect an evolutionary continuum from more global, primitive thought processes to highly abstract, conceptual networks. Kelly (1955) takes a cognitive approach to personality by emphasizing the mental constructs that operate in a person's definition of the self and of others. The openness or boundedness of mental constructs will determine how readily people can incorporate new information or how likely they are to change.

The importance of a cognitive analysis to adolescence cannot be underestimated. It has long been recognized that during adolescence something new, something potentially creative and even revolutionary, emerges in the conceptual sphere. Beginning with Plato, great philosophers have identified the adolescent years as the time in which people acquire the mental skills that make humans truly capable of shaping the future of their societies.

## Stages of Cognitive Development: Jean Piaget

Jean Piaget was born in Switzerland in 1896. Much like Darwin, he showed talent as a naturalist early in childhood. As a boy, he studied and observed birds, fossils, and seashells (Piaget, 1952a). At the age of ten he contributed a note on an albino sparrow to a scientific journal. While still an adolescent, he began to publish papers about the characteristics of mollusks. His work in this area was so impressive that he was invited to become the curator of the mollusk collection at the Geneva Museum while he was a high school student (Flavell, 1963). Continuing in this interest, Piaget earned his doctorate at the University of Neuchâtel in 1918. His dissertation topic was the mollusks of Valais.

And what, you may ask, has all this to do with cognitive psychology? Probably the most direct consequence of Piaget's training as a biologist was his sense that the principles of biology could be used to understand the evolution of knowledge. Further, through his training as a naturalist, Piaget developed skills of observation that were to serve him in developing his theory. He required a year or two of search after his doctoral studies had ended before he arrived at the definition of a set of problems and methods that would crystallize his program of study. Between 1918 and 1921, Piaget worked in the laboratory of Theodore Lipps, whose research focused on the study of empathy and aesthetics. He spent some time at Bleuler's clinic learning the techniques of the psychiatric interview. At the Sorbonne, Piaget had the opportunity to work at Binet's laboratory. There he began a project on children's responses to reasoning tests. He began to use the clinical interview method to discover how children arrived at their answers. He was as interested in children's incorrect responses as in their correct responses. His observations provided the basis for his first articles on the characteristics of children's thought. One of these articles brought him to the attention of the editor of *Psychological Archives,* who offered him the job of director of studies at the Institut Jean-Jacques Rousseau in Geneva. There he began a group of studies on children's moral judgments, children's "theories" about everyday events, and children's language. But it was not until the period from 1923–29, when Piaget conducted experiments and systematic observations with infants, that he began to unravel the basic problems about the growth of logical thought (Piaget, 1951, 1952b, 1954).

Piaget's theory of cognitive development emphasizes the importance of the continuous interaction between children and their environment (Piaget, 1950). Three concepts from his theory—scheme, adaptation, and stages of development—are introduced here. This introduction will provide a basis for more extensive discussions of cognitive competences in Chapters 5 and 9.

**Scheme.**   Piaget and Inhelder (1969) define scheme as "the structure or organization of actions as they are transferred or generalized by repetition in similar or analogous circumstances" (p. 4). Through repetition, infants begin to recognize a regular sequence of actions that eventually serves to guide behavior. In fact, two kinds of schemes emerge during infancy—those which guide a particular action, such as grasping a rattle or sucking a bottle, and those which link sequences of actions, such as climbing into the high chair in order to eat breakfast or crawling to the door in order to greet daddy when he comes home (Uzgiris, 1976). The word *scheme* is used instead of the word *concept* because it implies a greater action component than one usually attributes to concepts. It allows Piaget to talk about the counterpart of concepts and conceptual networks during the period of infancy before language and other symbolic forms are thought to develop.

**Adaptation.** Piaget (1952b) sees cognition as a continuously evolving activity in which the content and diversity of experience will serve to stimulate the formulation of new mental concepts. Knowledge is the result of adaptation, that is, a gradual modification of existing schemes which takes into account the novelty or uniqueness of each experience. Adaptation is a two-part process in which the continuity of existing schemes and the possibility of altering schemes interact. *Assimilation* contributes to the continuity of knowing. It refers to the tendency to interpret new experiences in terms of some existing scheme. Children begin to explore each new object by using the responses and behavior patterns that are already formed. In infancy, for example, children will use sucking and grasping as the primary modes for investigating new objects. Even if the object, for example, a balloon, is not really meant to be sucked, an infant will assimilate it to the sucking scheme. *Accommodation* refers to the ability to modify familiar schemes in order to respond to the new dimensions of the object. If sucking or grasping results in popping the balloon, or if the balloon is too big to fit into the baby's mouth, the infant will begin to modify those behaviors by blowing, licking, or nosing the balloon. With each new experience, successful adaptation involves responding to both the similarities and the differences between the familiar and the new.

**Stages of Development.** Piaget (1950, 1970, 1971) views intelligence as following lawful, predictable patterns of change from the infant's total reliance on sensation and motor activity to achieve knowledge to the adolescent's capacities to generate hypotheses, to anticipate consequences, and to formulate logical systems of experimentation. The brief description of the stages given here will be elaborated in Chapter 5. There we will also present evidence which supports and challenges Piaget's assumptions about the universality of these stages.

The earliest stage of *sensorimotor intelligence* begins at birth and lasts until approximately 18 months of age. Through the formation of increasingly complex sensory and motor schemes, infants begin to organize and control their environments.

The second stage, called *preoperational thought,* starts when the child begins to represent actions with symbols, that is, images, words, or drawings, and ends at about age five or six. During this transitional stage, children develop the tools for representing schemes internally through language, imitation, imagery, symbolic play, and symbolic drawing. Their knowledge is still very much tied to their own perceptions.

The third stage, *concrete operational thought,* begins at about age 5 to 6 and ends in early adolescence, at about age 11 or 12.

During this stage, children begin to appreciate the logical necessity of certain causal relationships. They can manipulate categories, classification systems, and hierarchies of groups. They are most successful at solving problems which have a clear tie to physical reality and less skilled at generating hypotheses about purely philosophic or abstract concepts.

The final stage of cognitive development, *formal operational thought*, begins in adolescence and continues through adulthood. This level of thinking permits the person to conceptualize about many simultaneously interacting variables. It allows for the creation of a system of laws or rules which can be used for problem solving. Formal operational thought is the quality of intelligence upon which science and philosophy are built.

As adolescents emerge from childhood they begin to be able to think about the world in new ways. Their thoughts become more abstract, and they are able to generate hypotheses about events that they have never perceived. These complex conceptual skills have been described by Piaget (Inhelder and Piaget, 1958; Piaget, 1970) as the stage of formal operations. Piaget means to suggest by this designation that the adolescent's thoughts are governed more by logical principles than by perceptions and experiences.

Several new conceptual skills are established during the stage of formal operations. First, adolescents are able to manipulate more than two categories or variables in their head at the same time. They can, for example, consider the relationship among speed, distance, and time in planning a trip. Second, adolescents are able to think about things changing in the future. They realize, for example, that their relationship to their parents will be much different in ten years. Third, adolescents are able to hypothesize about a logical sequence of events that might occur. For example, they are able to predict college and occupational options that might be open, depending on how well they do in school. Fourth, adolescents are able to anticipate the consequences of their actions. They realize, for example, that if they drop out of school certain career possibilities will be closed to them. The fact that adolescents can anticipate the consequences before acting allows them to decide whether or not they wish to do something given their prior knowledge of the possible outcomes. Fifth, adolescents have the capacity to detect the logical consistency or inconsistency in a set of statements (Kagan, 1972). They are puzzled by the apparent contradictions between a statement such as "All men are equal before the law" and the possibility of a presidential pardon for certain high-status lawbreakers. Finally, adolescents are able to think in a more relativistic way about themselves and the world in which they live. They know that they are expected to act in a particular way because of the norms of their own community and culture. They also know that in other communities or cultures different norms may govern the same behavior. Thus, their decisions to behave in a culturally accepted manner become a more conscious commitment to the culture of which they are a part. At the same time, adolescents are more easily able to accept persons of other cultures because they realize that these persons are the products of cultures with different sets of rules and norms.

In general, the changes in conceptual development that occur during early adolescence result in a more flexible, critical, and abstract view of the world. The abilities to hypothesize about logical sequences of action, to conceptualize about change, and to anticipate consequences of actions all serve to make a sense of the future a real part of the cognitive space of the individual.

## The Development of Moral Judgments: Lawrence Kohlberg

Kohlberg's theory concerns the understanding of how moral judgments are made. He believes that the evolution of moral reasoning is a process that coincides with the maturation of intellectual abilities. Piaget (1948) argued that a child's ability to evaluate a moral act was closely related to the child's relationship to adult authorities. In early childhood, from about four to eight, children are subject to the laws of adults. When children of this age group are asked about right and wrong conduct, they evaluate the situation in terms of the adult's sanctions. If an adult would punish such an act, it must be wrong. If an adult would approve of the act, it must be right. After age eight, coinciding with the acquisition of concrete operational skills, children become capable of a more autonomous moral reasoning. Children who participate with peers in active play discover that each peer brings his or her own experience, his or her own perspective, to the play. Peer interactions are the primary mechanisms that free a child's thinking from domination by adult sanctions and lead the way to an independent evaluation of right and wrong.

Kohlberg (1964, 1969, 1973) has expanded this cognitive orientation to moral judgment. He poses very complex stories to children and asks them to judge the rightness or wrongness of the actors. In Kohlberg's stories there is generally a conflict between personal interest and the larger good. Children have the opportunity to see ways in which a person might break a specific law in order to preserve a basic moral principle. These stories generate responses that Kohlberg categorizes in three levels of moral reasoning: preconventional, conventional, and postconventional morality. At the *preconventional stage,* from ages four to ten, Kohlberg finds that the child decides about right and wrong on the basis of whether an act is punished or rewarded. Acts that have good consequences are right. Acts that have bad consequences are wrong. During the *conventional stage*, which corresponds to adolescence, Kohlberg finds that young people express a concern with maintaining the social system. The influence of adult authorities continues to be felt quite strongly at this stage, as adolescents argue for the legitimate role of authorities in creating and upholding rules. In the *postconventional stage*, which begins to emerge during adulthood, Kohlberg finds that young adults begin to appreciate the relativity of their own cultural moral system. Morality is understood as a social agreement that requires mutual trust and reciprocity. During this final stage, individuals may formulate a personal moral code which takes priority over conventional principles under certain circumstances.

Kohlberg views adolescence as a vitally important period in the emergence of a personal morality. During this time of life, the awareness of one's subjective perspective of life events permits an appreciation of the relativistic nature of all moral principles. This relativistic thinking calls into question the adequacy or even the validity of the moral code which governs one's own social group. During adolescence, people first begin to evaluate the legitimacy of their society's morality. Once the prevailing code has been questioned, of course, there is always the possibility that a new, more compassionate, or more just ethic will emerge. Thus, adolescence becomes the period of life in which individuals can begin to contribute to the evolution of moral thought (Kohlberg and Gilligan, 1972).

## Comparative Organismic Theory: Heinz Werner

Heinz Werner was a displaced German scholar who left Nazi Germany in the early 1930s. For 2½ years he was a professor of psychology at the University of Michigan, where he studied perception and taught courses in comparative genetic psychology, characterology, and Gestalt psychology, among others (Senn, 1975). From 1936 to 1947, he made several moves before he was able to establish a permanent position on the faculty at Clark University. In Werner's work experiences, we begin to understand how the historical context can have direct impact on the ability of an individual to pursue a career. Displaced from his home during a time of persecution and preparation for war, Werner had to establish his academic credentials in an unfamiliar culture, wait out the tide of unfavorable political attitudes toward German scholars, and strive to transplant some of his ideas about psychology and development in a potentially hostile intellectual climate.

Werner's (1948) theory focuses on the development of thought in three stages: undifferentiated, differentiated, and integrated. His general developmental law was stated as follows: "The essence of organic development is the steadily increasing differentiation and centralization, or hierarchic integration, within the genetic totality" (1948, p. 53). Three assumptions provided a framework for Werner's thinking. First, in the tradition of the Gestalt psychologists, Werner assumed that any single behavior or thought had to be interpreted in the context of its function for the organism. This holistic assumption led Werner to be sensitive to the broad cultural context as well as to the individual meaning which might be associated with an image, a symbol, or an action.

The second assumption was that both biological and psychological activity are directed. This means that organisms strive to retain their existence and to undergo the changes that will bring them to their mature form. Werner did not believe that people were necessarily aware of the fact that their behavior had these goals. Nevertheless, he argued that an objective evaluation of behavior could identify the goals of survival and growth as central to the choices people make and the modes in which they express themselves.

The third assumption was a view of developmental change. Werner argued that there was a natural tendency to move through transformations from more global to more differentiated and integrated states. He viewed this change as both continuous and discontinuous. "On the one side, the orthogenetic principle in *overall terms,* that is, in terms of an increase in differentiation and hierarchic integration, necessarily implies continuity; on the other hand, in terms of the specific, concrete forms and operations, novel functions and structures 'emerge,' and in this respect changes are discontinuous" (Werner and Kaplan, 1963, p. 8). The goal of conceptual development was viewed as a hierarchical integration of both the content and the structure of thought. Categories of concepts would serve as organizing units that could be flexibly modified by interaction with unique aspects of the environment. Werner considered the unique aspect of humans' relationship to their environment to be the desire to know. As part of this desire, people are capable of altering their concepts and their responses in order to gather more information about the physical, social, and psychological elements in their environment.

Werner did not focus his studies on the adolescent years. He saw adolescence in technologically advanced cultures as "a slow, long-lasting, plastic transformation from one stage of life into the other" (1948, p. 27). He regarded the plasticity of adolescence in advanced culture as a result of more intense and varied interactions between older and younger people as well as less clearly defined definitions of both the child and the adult roles. The consequence of plasticity was more adequate preparation for a changing pattern of the future society. Werner's perspective on cognitive growth provides an important orientation for interpreting the phenomena of identity formation. The articulation of a personal identity is a complex symbolic creation that offers individuals a hierarchic organization with which to reconcile diverse roles and views of the self. Once the personal identity has been developed, one can approach settings and experiences with a new flexibility based on a well-integrated sense of self sameness.

## The Psychology of Personal Constructs: George Kelly

George Kelly was born in Kansas in 1905. He was an only child in a religious, rather restrictive family. Kelly received his undergraduate degree in physics and math in 1926 from Park College. He had expected to become an engineer, but while at college he became interested in social problems. In 1928 he received a master's degree in educational sociology from the University of Kansas. After two years of varied work experience, including teaching classes in public speech and classes in Americanization for students desiring citizenship, Kelly went abroad to study at the University of Edinburgh. He returned to complete a doctoral degree at the State University of Iowa in 1931. His dissertation focused on common factors in speech and reading disabilities.

Kelly's status as a psychologist was not really established until about 1946, when he was appointed director of the clinical psychology program at Ohio State University. Kelly's work with naval pilots during World War II and his development of traveling psychological clinics that consulted with Kansas school systems gave him diverse opportunities to observe the coping behaviors of people of various ages in varied settings. During his 20 years at Ohio State, Kelly worked to develop his theoretical framework, to train graduate students, and to develop a high-quality graduate program in clinical psychology. He also worked at a national level to develop standards for professional competence among clinical psychologists. Kelly died in 1966, one year after he had been appointed to the Riklis Chair of Behavioral Science at Brandeis University (Hjelle and Ziegler, 1976; Maher, 1969).

Kelly's psychology of personal constructs is described as a means of understanding human personality, particularly under conditions in which people are struggling to adapt to stress. He began with three ideas that directed his thinking about personality. First, he adopted the perspective that all people can be viewed as scientists, attempting to predict and to control events in their universe. Second, he suggested that people actively form constructs, or conceptual templates, through which they interpret both social and psychological events. Finally, Kelly saw the external universe as a continuous, real, and changing group of events that are bound together by time. The universe is always actively existing. It is the work of people to interpret and predict the relevance of events for their own actions.

The most important element of Kelly's theory was his assumption of *constructive alternativism.* "We assume that all of our present interpretations of the universe are subject to revision or replacement. . . . We take the stand that there are always some alternative constructions available to choose among in dealing with the world. No one needs to paint himself into a corner; no one needs to be completely hemmed in by circumstances; no one needs to be the victim of his biography" (Kelly, 1955, p. 15).

This position gives Kelly's theory a strong emphasis on the creative, growth potential in all human beings. Kelly argued that personal constructs can be modified, reorganized, or even disregarded if a person is willing to recognize that they do not adequately predict or explain the events of his or her universe. Change in the definition of constructs or their interrelation occurs most often when people encounter novel or unexpected events.

Of course, not all constructs are equally amenable to redefinition. Furthermore, people differ widely in the number and quality of the constructs that they create. Some people tend to view the universe through broad, abstract principles that can encompass a variety of situations. Others have narrowly defined constructs about specific events or specific relationships. Kelly suggested that people who use similar constructs to interpret experience actually have similar psychological realities.

Kelly did not take a stage approach to personality development. He regarded the process of construct formation and restructuring as one that occurs continuously through life. The content of constructs would, of course, be influenced by the person's cognitive capacities and role relationships. The merit of the theory in understanding adolescent development is the interpretive power it provides. During childhood, many of the child's constructs are built on experiences in the parent-child relationship. These authoritarian relationships are likely to generate constructs characterized by inequality in status, power, and skill. Childhood constructs are also integrated in a conceptual network which does not readily include abstract concepts, hypothetical thinking, or logical principles of evaluation. Thus, the child's constructs are likely to be organized and tested on rather different grounds than are the adult's. One of the central tasks of adolescence, then, would be a broad-ranging evaluation and recreation of the personal construct system, bringing it more into line with logical thinking and adult experiences.

We might also expect adolescents to encounter an array of new experiences for which they do not have adequate constructs. The expansion of social roles, including participation in heterosexual relations and responsibilities as a worker, a voter, or a teacher of younger children, confronts adolescents with an ocean of life events for which constructs need to be developed or redefined. Being "caught with one's constructs down" is probably more likely during adolescence than during earlier periods of life. If, as Kelly argued, anxiety is "the failure to produce a construction that appears wholly applicable to the events of which one is aware" (Kelly, 1955, p. 501), then we could expect adolescence to be a life stage in which anxiety is a normal result of the rapid expansion of one's relevant universe.

## SOCIAL PSYCHOLOGICAL THEORIES

Beginning with the evolutionary theories and the notion of psychosocial evolution, there have been repeated references to the importance of the social context in the process of development.

Dennis Stock/Magnum

*Social psychological theories offer strategies for understanding the impact of the social environment on development.*

We have discussed Havighurst's notion of developmental tasks as reflecting expectations from parents, peers, and the cultural group. Among the psychodynamic theorists, both Sullivan and Erikson consider the relevance of interpersonal relationships and the quality of social interactions in their descriptions of development. Among the cognitive theorists, Piaget, Kohlberg, and Kelly all acknowledge the importance of interpersonal events for stimulating cognitive growth and change. What the social psychological theorists add to the picture are strategies for systematically conceptualizing the nature of the social environment. Each theorist has an idea about which aspects of the social environment are relevant to development, how people perceive their social environment, and how the demands or expectations of people and social settings influence an individual's psychology.

In this section we will discuss the theories of three social psychologists, Kurt Lewin, Roger Barker, and Orville Brim. Lewin (1935, 1936, 1951) believed that behavior was a function of the interaction between a person and his or her environment. He provided a model for some of the ways in which people conceptualized their environments, arguing that the relevance of social settings was determined largely by the way in which a person perceived and experienced them. Barker (1963a, 1963b, 1968) has focused on conceptualizing the ways in which environments provide opportunities for participation. He has looked at the characteristics of physical settings in quite a bit more detail than most other psychologists. Brim (1966) has focused on roles and role relationships as the primary determinants of social behavior. His analysis of development emphasizes the content of specific roles and the effects of multiple roles in stimulating psychological development.

## Field Theory: Kurt Lewin

Kurt Lewin was born in 1890 in a village called Mogilno in a Prussian province which is now a part of Poland. His parents were economically comfortable, middle-class Jewish shopkeepers. As an elementary school student, Kurt was sent to the provincial capital to live in order to gain a better education than was available in his tiny village. He was a relatively undistinguished student until the final years of high school, when he discovered Greek philosophy and began to excel in his studies (Marrow, 1977).

After completing work at the gymnasium, he enrolled and left college several times before settling down at the University of Berlin to prepare himself for academic life. He enjoyed student life in Berlin and became interested in the study of psychology as well as philosophy. He completed his degree work in 1914 and served in the German army until the end of World War I. He entered the service as a private, rose to the rank of lieutenant, was decorated for bravery, and was wounded in action. He married while he was in the service.

While he was in the army, he wrote several papers that were to serve as forerunners for his basic theoretical work. In one paper (Lewin, 1917), he described the ways in which the soldier's psychological environment at the front changed from his "peace landscape" behind the lines. He showed how the situational demands of front-line conditions necessitated a very different set of perceptions of location in order to increase the probability of survival. In describing the importance of the psychological field and its characteristics, he was pointing the way toward a psychological internalization of environment which was to provide the key to his understanding of individual psychology.

After the war he worked at the Psychological Institute of the University of Berlin. During this period he developed the "topological" or field theory. He attracted many graduate students and worked closely with them as they conducted a group of studies testing various aspects of field theory. Many of these students and their studies have become very well known in psychology.

During the 1920s, Lewin became increasingly well known internationally as a result of a number of very well regarded papers. He traveled to the United States to deliver a series of lectures at Yale University. He and his wife were divorced, and he soon remarried. Even though his fame grew, he was only able to attain the rank of "associate professor without civil service status" at the University of Berlin because of his Jewish heritage.

As anti-Semitism grew with the rise of Nazism in Germany, Lewin accepted a visiting professorship at Stanford University. Upon his return to Germany, he was shocked at how quickly Nazi propaganda had affected intellectual life at the university. He appealed to American friends for help, and they were able to secure a temporary position for him at Cornell University.

After two years at Cornell, he was offered a position at the University of Iowa. Here he attracted many students. They conducted some extremely important studies which demonstrate the superiority of democratic leadership over authoritarian and laissez-faire leadership (Lewin, Lippitt, and White, 1960). As the Iowa years came to a close, Lewin became increasingly interested in "group dynamics" and in the application of the principles of group dynamics to industry.

He founded the Center for the Study of Group Dynamics and located it at MIT. Concepts of leadership, group cohesiveness, and sensitivity training were explored at the center as Lewin became increasingly convinced that groups, including families, classrooms, and informal peer alliances, had important influences on individuals. During this period, he also founded the Commission of Community Interrelations (CCI), which studied problems of prejudice and intergroup relations in real-world settings. Many of Lewin's former students worked at the Center for the Study of Group Dynamics and the CCI.

The Cambridge work was shaping up as among the most important of Lewin's career. Lewin was working extremely hard developing the theory of group dynamics and attempting to understand prejudice, intergroup hostility, and community action research when he died of a heart attack on February 11, 1947, at the age of 56.

Lewin's theory of behavior was influenced by two scientific principles. First, in harmony with field concepts in physics and the application of field theory to perception in Gestalt psychology, Lewin argued that all behavior must be understood in light of the field which provides a context for the behavior. Second, Lewin was striving for an analysis of behavior that could be expressed mathematically. This assumption that every psychological concept could be represented by a mathematical relationship led Lewin to build a theory in which characteristics of physical space, including distance, interconnectedness, boundaries, and enclosure in larger spaces, become the dimensions that dominate the theory (Lewin, 1935, 1936).

Field theory is based on a central law which is expressed as $B = f(L)$, or behavior is a function of the life space $(L)$. In Lewin's model of human behavior, the two elements of the life space were the person and all aspects of the environment of which the person is aware. The life space itself is bounded. In other words, objects, facts, and events which exist in the real world may not be known to the person. This part of the environment is not included in the life space, even though it may influence a person's behavior. In other words, Lewin was concerned primarily with those aspects of the environment that had meaning and relevance to the person's conscious thoughts.

Both the person and the environment are divided into regions. The person is divided into two kinds of elements—perceptual motor regions that have most immediate contact with the environment and inner-personal regions composed of thoughts and wishes that do not have direct contact with the environment. The environment is also divided into regions. These regions represent the areas of access, the settings, and the barriers that the person encounters.

Lewin identified three aspects of the psychological field that change during development (Lewin, 1951). First, both the inner-personal sphere and the environment become more differentiated. Adults are more aware than children of a variety of conceptual categories that can differentiate inner experience or social events. Second, the boundaries between regions grow firmer. There is less confusion about the difference between real and unreal, or me and other, for adults than for children. Third, development brings *organizational interdependence.* This refers to a hierarchical ordering of regions so that the person can use a variety of means to achieve a goal or release tension in one area while remaining controlled and effective in other areas. Lewin saw adults as more skillful than children at planning, organizing, and executing life tasks.

Lewin did not view behavior as a series of stages. He saw the process of developmental change as a continuous modification of regions, needs, and forces or valences which encourage or inhibit behavior. In a paper published in 1939, Lewin used the life stage of adolescence as an example of how field theory might be used to interpret complex life events. His primary analogy for adolescence was the image of the "marginal man" straddling the boundary between two regions, childhood and adulthood. This marginality includes being scornful of the group one desires to leave and uncertain about or even rejected by the group one wishes to join. Three events occur during adolescence that Lewin believed explain many of the phenomena which are characteristic of the life stage.

1. During a period of movement from one region to another, the total life space is enlarged, bringing the young person into contact with more information about the environment and, presumably, about oneself.
2. A widening life space results in greater uncertainty about the nature of each new region.
3. Biological changes associated with puberty alter the inner-personal regions and the perceptual-motor regions of the life space.

Lewin argued that the rapid expansion of regions and uncertainty about both the personal and environmental structure of the life space result in an emotional tension during the adolescent years. Characteristics of adolescent behavior, including emotional instability, value conflicts, hostility toward group members, and radical changes in ideology, are the result of the dramatic changes and persistent instability in the adolescent's life space.

## Ecological Theory: Roger Barker

Roger Barker first met Kurt Lewin while he was a student at Stanford and Lewin was a visiting professor. After completing his

Ph.D., Barker went to Iowa to work with Lewin at the Child Study Center. From 1938–39 he was an instructor at Harvard University. He worked at the University of Illinois, Stanford University, and Clark University before assuming the post of director of the Midwest Psychological Field Station at Oskaloosa, Kansas. It was during his years at the field station that he formulated his ideas about ecological psychology and tested them through field research.

While Lewin concerned himself primarily with the psychological representation of the environment, Barker is more concerned with the objective, measurable environment within which the person behaves (Barker, 1963a). He defines his interest in the following way: "Ecology is concerned with the naturally occurring environment of entities, i.e., with the environment as it occurs without the intervention of the investigator and with the distribution over the earth of the entity and its environmental variables" (Barker, 1960, p. 12).

He believes very strongly that behavior must be studied in a variety of naturally occurring settings in order to gain a sense of the phenomena of psychology (Barker, 1963b). He is interested in observing the "behavior stream" as it occurs naturally rather than the artificially induced behaviors that occur in laboratory settings. He believes that the "entity," or person, and the "environment" are separate from each other but are interrelated by ecological laws.

Barker uses the notion of "behavior setting" to characterize environments (Barker and Wright, 1955). Behavior setting is used to identify a specific location in which particular patterns of behavior are likely to occur. The patterns of behavior occur because of setting demands and expectations rather than because of individuals' characteristics. Behavior settings include a school dance, a basketball game, a party, a classroom, a school cafeteria, to name a few.

In their study of behavior settings in a small Kansas town— Midwest—Barker and Wright (1955) employ four useful categories for coding the behavior they observe:

1.  Occupancy time—the number of hours people spent in the behavior setting during the year.
2.  Penetration—the extent of involvement and responsibility of individuals in the setting.
3.  Action patterns—typical behavior patterns associated with a particular behavior setting.
4.  Behavior mechanisms—frequency of occurrence, tempo, or speed, and intensity of thinking, talking, manipulating, looking, listening, motor activity, and emotional behavior.

In order to accomplish the assessment of settings according to the above dimensions, Barker's researchers place trained observers in various places in the town. The observers keep field notes on the settings, the people in them, and the events that occur. Observations are made during a 30-minute period, and the "stream of behavior" is divided into distinct episodes that occur during that time (Barker, 1968). Over more than two decades of observation, Barker's group has been able to describe in detail the regular patterns of behavior that occur in the settings of an environment. The patterns of behavior are considered to be independent of specific individuals. The "expected" behaviors regulate the behavior of the specific individuals who enter a particular setting.

What have Barker and his colleagues learned about the ways in which adolescents utilize and are influenced by the settings they encounter? Initially, they have documented that, at least in Midwest, setting participation corresponds to one's age (Barker and Wright, 1955). Adolescents have considerably greater access to settings in their communities than do toddlers or children of middle-school age. This is a function of greater maturity and greater mobility.

In a very extensive study of high schools in Kansas, Barker and Gump (1964) compared schools which ranged in size from 35 students to 2,300 students. They discovered that although large and small schools differed greatly in number of students, they were much more alike in the number of behavior settings. The largest school contained 65 times as many students as the smallest, but only 8 times as many settings. Even more telling was the fact that the largest school contained only 1.5 times as many *varieties* of settings as the smallest. Students at smaller schools participated in more district events and extracurricular activities, and a much larger percentage of such students held positions of responsibility in a wide variety of activities. Small-school students reported feeling a greater pressure to participate in the life of the school than did large-school students. Barker and Gump concluded that there is a definite difference in adolescents' experiences, depending upon the size of the school attended. Small schools have relatively "undermanned settings." These schools need the participation of their students to function effectively. This need is transformed into a normative pressure for students to participate in school activities. Such participation leads to the development of a greater sense of responsibility among small-school students. Students in small schools tend to develop general, well-rounded competences, whereas students in large schools tend to become specialists in particular activities.

The final contribution of Barker's ecological orientation to the study of adolescent psychology involved a comparison of Midwest with the English community of Yoredale (Barker and Schoggen, 1973). Barker and Schoggen found that the two communities differ

quite markedly in adolescent setting participation, and they attributed the differences to underlying differences in the child-rearing
theories of the two cultures. In Midwest the adolescents tended
not to be segregated from the rest of the community, whereas in
Yoredale people in settings were segregated by age. The work on
behavior settings indicates that a person's behavior will be directly
influenced by the normative expectations and the opportunities
for participation of the environment in which he or she lives.

### Social Role Theory: Orville Brim

Orville Brim's theoretical orientation is more sociological than
the other theories presented thus far. He argues that "personality
can be viewed as a set of learned self-other relationships or systems" (Brim, 1965, p. 156). In this sense, factors associated with
maturation, temperament, or capacities to cognize the environment
are regarded as far less important than the nature of the roles
and role relationships that one encounters. Brim argues that the
social organization of every society brings individuals into contact
with expectations for behavior that are associated with specific
role relationships. It is essential to know how the individual views
those roles, that is, who the person identifies as "significant others,"
what expectations the person senses from those others, and how
the person feels about those expectations. Further, it is important
to evaluate the accuracy of these assumptions by identifying the
roles and role prescriptions which large groups of people recognize
as functioning in a given social context.

Although individuals bring their unique temperaments, skills,
personal philosophies, and value orientations to bear on the interpretation and enactment of the roles they play, nevertheless the
roles exist independently of the individuals who play them. In this
sense, social role theory focuses on the normative expectations
that a person is likely to encounter throughout development. For
example, we have expectations about the role of parent that guide
our decisions as we engage in parenting activities. Those expectations come from the mass media, from the law, from our families,
and from neighbors in the community. They also come from the
people with whom we share the parenting relationship, specifically
the spouse and the children. Knowledge of the functions and norms
associated with the parenting role, or any other role, will influence
the performance of the person who is playing the role and the
responses of a whole network of people who are associated with
that person (Goffman, 1959).

Development, according to social role theory, is the product of
participation in a greater number of roles which involve increas-

ingly complex skills (Parsons and Bales, 1955; Brim, 1966; Nye, 1976). As the number of simultaneous roles that people play increases, they must learn new skills of role playing, role differentiation, and role integration. With each new role, the individual's self-definition changes and his or her ability to influence the social environment increases (Brim, 1976). Of course, with each new role there are also new challenges to achieve the goals or conform to the expectations of the role prescription. New significant others emerge who hold expectations for one's behavior and contribute evaluative information about one's success or failure in the role. In this sense, personal change is viewed as a consequence of participation in role systems in which both the person and a variety of relevant others provide incentives for one's behavior.

In adolescence, the diversity of social roles increases. Brim (1965) has studied the perceptions that adolescents hold about the three primary roles of family member, peer group member, and student. In addition to performing these roles, adolescents are emerging into the new roles of worker, political participant, religious believer, and heterosexual partner (Gold and Douvan, 1969). However, although adolescents' sphere of influence is expanding, they are also coming under the scrutiny of new groups of significant others who may hold divergent expectations for their behavior. Finally, the expectations associated with the adolescent role itself have meaning for the growing person. Adolescents are faced with the challenge of adapting to the diverse and often incorrect assumptions held by adults about what adolescents are like.

## CHAPTER SUMMARY

Five theoretical orientations toward the study of development have been presented: evolutionary, normative, psychodynamic, cognitive, and social psychological. The work of 16 theorists has been discussed. Table 1–3 summarizes the general orientations and the specific contributions of each theorist. It states the assumptions, basic concepts, and view of adolescence of each theory. Taken as a whole, these theories represent the field of ideas about the relevance of the adolescent years for human development. We believe it important to remain open to the contributions of the varied perspectives, with the realization that as we narrow in on one topic, the others may tend to get slightly out of focus. In the remainder of the book, we pursue a view of adolescence that attempts to integrate the physical, cognitive, social, and emotional themes into a view of a total, functioning, proactive person.

A closer look at Table 1–3 helps to identify some of the major themes that will receive attention in later chapters. First, we notice

**Table 1–3: Summary of Theories of Adolescence**

| Theory | Theorist | Assumptions | Basic Concepts | View of Adolescence |
|---|---|---|---|---|
| Evolutionary | Charles Darwin | The laws of nature apply uniformly throughout time | Natural selection<br>Species variability<br>Adaptation | The pattern of sexual maturation is a product of evolutionary adaptation<br>Human sexual behavior is heavily influenced by learning |
| | G. Stanley Hall | Human development is a recapitulation of human evolution<br>Adolescence is a critical time in personal development and in human evolution—a period of transition from primitive to contemporary man | Simultaneous occurrence of sexual maturation; physical growth; emotional intensity; hypothetico-deductive reasoning; moral, social, and political awareness | Two distinct periods: early and later adolescence<br>A period of "Storm and Stress"<br>A period of potential personal and societal change |
| Normative | Arnold Gesell | Growth is a lawful, natural process which occurs as a result of biological unfolding | Rhythmic sequences or cycles of development<br>Reciprocity of adult's growth cycle and child's growth cycle | A transitional period toward maturity<br>Specific description of nine areas of development during the years from 10–16 |
| | Robert J. Havighurst | Much of human behavior is learned | Developmental tasks<br>Teachable moments—sensitive period for learning developmental tasks | The Years from 12–18<br>Tasks focus on sex role development, career choice, and moral development |
| Psychodynamic | Sigmund Freud | All psychological events are tied to biochemical characteristics of the human body<br>All behavior is motivated | The unconscious<br>Shifting sexual energy from the mouth, to the anus, to the genital area<br>Id, ego, and superego as the three basic mental functions<br>Defense mechanisms which protect ego from unacceptable wishes<br>Sublimation—channeling id impulses in socially acceptable directions | The final stage of personality development<br>Puberty results in reemergence of infantile themes, especially Oedipal or Electra conflicts<br>Patterns of impulse expression, defensive style, and sublimation crystallize into a life orientation<br>The genital stage, in which sexual intercourse is the primary mode for gratifying |

| | | | |
|---|---|---|---|
| | | | logical maturation<br>Ego is in danger of being overwhelmed by instinct<br>Emphasizes ascetuism and intellectuality as two powerful adolescent defenses |
| Peter Blos | Same as S. Freud | Adolescence is the psychological adaptation to biological maturation<br>The coping system | Three phases of adolescence: (1) early adolescence—the onset of puberty; (2) adolescence proper—autonomy from earlier objects of cathexis; (3) late adolescence—development of judgment, interests, and intellect; sexual identity established; consolidation of a personal identity |
| Harry Stack Sullivan | Mental disorder is caused when communication is blocked by anxiety<br>All persons exist in an interpersonal field which has properties of its own | Three kinds of experience: (1) sensations, perceptions, and emotions experienced before language; (2) private symbols, including fantasies and daydreams; (3) shared symbols<br>Dynamisms—patterns of interaction | Three phases of adolescence: (1) preadolescence—need for a close relationship with another person of the same sex; (2) early adolescence—interest in heterosexual relationships, conflict between needs for intimacy and needs for sexual gratification; (3) late adolescence—establishment of a mature repertoire of interpersonal relationships, emergence of self-respect |
| Erik H. Erikson | Individuals contribute to their own psychological development<br>The social group has expectations and resources that shape personal development | Eight life stages from infancy through later adulthood<br>Psychosocial crisis at each life stage | Adolescence the time when a personal identity is formulated; identity achieved through experimentation, search, and introspection; identity represents an integration of past identifications, competences, and aspirations |

**Table 1-3** *(continued)*

| Theory | Theorist | Assumptions | Basic Concepts | View of Adolescence |
|---|---|---|---|---|
| Cognitive | Jean Piaget | Knowledge is based on action. The structural properties of the human brain, sense receptors, and nervous system provide the universal bases for human cognition | Scheme. Adaptation, which consists of assimilation and accommodation. Stages of development: sensorimotor, preoperational, concrete operations, and formal operations | Adult reasoning achieved during adolescence. Thought governed by principles of logic. Hypothesis raising and testing. Simultaneous manipulation of more than two variables. Consequences of actions anticipated. Logical inconsistencies recognized. The future computeralized |
| | Lawrence Kohlberg | Moral reasoning reflects a child's level of cognitive maturity | Three levels of moral reasoning, each with two phases: (1) preconventional (4–10); (2) conventional (10–16); (3) postconventional (16–adulthood) | The period during which a personal morality emerges. Transition between conventional and postconventional levels may bring doubt, personal reflection, and confusion. The period when a new moral code or moral philosophy can emerge |
| | Heinz Werner | Any thought or behavior must be understood in the context of its function for the organism. All activity is directed to insure survival and growth. There is a natural tendency to move from global to more differentiated and integrated states | Differentiation. Hierarchic organization | Adolescence in technological societies viewed as a period of plasticity during which new conceptualization can prepare a person for a changing society |

| | | | | |
|---|---|---|---|---|
| | | tists who are trying to predict and control life events<br>The universe is actively existing<br>All present interpretations of events are subject to revision | | tion and recreation of the personal construct system<br>Need for new constructs to apply to the range of new experiences<br>Anxiety associated with construct inadequacies |
| Social psychological | Kurt Lewin | All behavior must be understood in the context of the field in which it occurs<br>Every psychological concept can be expressed by a mathematical relationship | Behavior is a function of the life space<br>The life space includes the person and all facts or events in the environment of which the person is aware<br>The person has a perceptual-motor region and an inner-personal region<br>The environment is divided into regions that represent settings, relationships, and barriers to access | Adolescent as "marginal man" straddling the boundary between childhood and adulthood<br>The life space enlarged and unstable<br>Greater uncertainty about the regions of the environment<br>Greater uncertainty about the inner-personal and perceptual-motor regions |
| | Roger Barker | Behavior must be studied in naturally occurring settings<br>The person and the setting are interrelated by ecological laws | Behavior setting<br>Behavior mechanisms<br>Behavior stream<br>Occupancy time<br>Penetration<br>Action patterns | A period of Greater access to settings<br>High school size influences the quality of student involvement and student responsibility<br>American communities appear to be more accessible to adolescents than British communities |
| | Orville Brim | Personality is a set of learned self-other relationships | Social roles<br>Significant others<br>Role prescriptions<br>Role enactment<br>Normative expectations for role behavior<br>Development a result of participation in more roles and more complex roles | Increased diversity of social roles<br>Sphere of influence expanding<br>Expectations from diverse role relationships—some may conflict<br>Adolescence a new age-related role with conflicting norms for behavior |

that both of the normative theories view adolescence as a predictable period of patterned changes in behavior. However, Gesell attributes these changes to maturation, whereas Havighurst attributes
them to learning. What is more important, both theories are correct
in their assumptions. Adolescence is a time of biological change
as well as a time of new learning. The key here is the question
of the harmony or discord that exists between socialization and
maturation. We must ask to what extent social experiences and
new learning during adolescence support or conflict with the natural unfolding of biological capacities.

Second, although some of the theories do not propose stages
of development, almost every theory recognizes some of the psychological changes that are associated with adolescence. Kelly and
Lewin both suggest a need for new concepts to deal with the expanded range of life events that confront the adolescent. Barker
has documented the adolescent's access to more varied settings,
and Brim has pointed out the adolescent's participation in more
diverse roles. Thus, even those theorists who are not primarily
concerned with biological maturation as the stimulus for growth
recognize adolescence as a time when life events are likely to
take a new turn.

Third, the themes of sexual maturation and cognitive maturation
dominate the discussion of developing competences. The theories
differ widely in how they handle these themes and their interrelationship. For example, three of the cognitive theorists, Piaget, Kohlberg, and Werner, have almost nothing to say about sexuality or
social intimacy as they contribute to the development of thought.
Similarly, Erikson's analysis of personal identity appears to be
dominated by cognitive competences, a creative reformulation of
personal history, skills, and aspirations.

In contrast, neither Sigmund Freud nor Anna Freud discusses
the contributions of sexuality to new levels of cognitive functioning.
Anna Freud appears to believe that the adolescent's intense efforts
at intellectuality are really defensive strategies to control sexual
energy. Lewin, who recognizes the relevance of sexuality for the
inner-personal sphere, views it, much as do the Freuds, as a source
of anxiety and uncertainty.

Peter Blos and Harry Stack Sullivan offer a perspective that begins to integrate these two important psychological changes. Adolescent sexuality begins as a means of motivating heterosexual
encounters. At first, these encounters are uncomfortable and anxiety provoking. At the same time, they stimulate increased self-
consciousness and the need to consider the needs, desires, and
pleasures of another person. In this way, sexual encounters can

help to foster perspective-taking and empathy which contribute to the development of a personal moral philosophy.

Fourth, the theories differ in the place they give to adolescence in the life span. Two of the most powerful theories, Freud's psychosexual theory and Piaget's cognitive theory, treat adolescence as the final period of qualitative change. Other theories, including the normative theories of Gesell and Havighurst, Erikson's psychosocial theory, Werner's organismic theory, Kelly's theory of personal constructs, and all the social psychological theories, recognize change as a continuous element of life. The forces of society, particularly the roles and responsibilities of work, marriage, parenthood, and community citizen, continue to exert pressures for the formulation of new concepts and new coping strategies. Biological change continues, but it is subordinated to aspects of the social context as a force toward psychological growth.

Finally, a number of theories reflect what we consider the secret magic of adolescence. Beginning with Darwin's principle of natural selection and including the work of Hall, Erikson, Piaget, Kohlberg, and Kelly, there is a clear message about the emergence in adolescence of a potential for changing the course of one's personal history and the course of social evolution. At many levels, including sexual activity, logical thinking, moral philosophy, and the definition of personal identity, adolescents have the possibility of making new choices and new solutions that will change the course of life events for themselves and for others. On the negative side, these choices may be destructive, ending the adolescents' own potential for growth or harming others. On the positive side, these choices may stimulate a new phase of human evolution. We do not suggest that adolescence is the time for most people to actually change large institutions or governments. Adolescents are not likely to have the power to implement social change. However, adolescence is the time to entertain new visions of the future, new goals for one's adulthood, and new values for the social community.

# REFERENCES

Barker, R. G.   Ecology and motivation. In M. R. Jones (Ed.), *Nebraska Symposium on Motivation*. Lincoln: University of Nebraska Press, 1960. Pp. 1–49.

Barker, R. G.   On the nature of the environment. *Journal of Social Issues,* 1963, *19,* 17–23. (a)

Barker, R. G.   *The stream of behavior.* New York: Appleton-Century-Crofts, 1963. (b)

Barker, R. G.   *Ecological psychology.* Stanford, Calif.: Stanford University Press, 1968.

Barker, R. G., and Gump, P. V. *Big school, small school.* Stanford, Calif.: Stanford University Press, 1964.

Barker, R. G., and Schoggen, P. *Qualities of community life.* San Francisco: Jossey-Bass, 1973.

Barker, R. G., and Wright, H. F. *Midwest and its children.* New York: Harper and Row, 1955.

Blos, P. *On adolescence: A Psychoanalytic interpretation.* New York: Free Press, 1962.

Breuer, J., and Freud, S. Studies on hysteria. In J. Strachey (Ed.), *The standard edition of the complete psychological works of Sigmund Freud.* London: Hogarth Press, 1955. (Originally published in German in 1895.)

Brim, O. G., Jr. Adolescent personality as self-other systems. *Journal of Marriage and the Family,* 1965, *27,* 156–162.

Brim, O. G., Jr. Socialization through the life cycle. In O. G. Brim, Jr., and S. Wheeler, *Socialization after childhood.* New York: Wiley, 1966.

Brim, O. G., Jr. Life-span development of the theory of oneself: Implications for child development. In H. W. Reese (Ed.), *Advances in child development and behavior,* vol. 11. New York: Academic Press, 1976. Pp. 241–251.

Cohen, M. B. Introduction. In H. S. Sullivan, *The interpersonal theory of psychiatry.* New York: Norton, 1953.

Coles, R. *Erik H. Erikson: The growth of his work.* Boston: Atlantic–Little, Brown, 1970.

Darwin, C. *On the origin of species by means of natural selection.* London: J. Murray, 1859.

Darwin, C. *The origin of species* (6th ed.). London: J. Murray, 1872.

deBeer, G. R. *Charles Darwin: Evolution by natural selection.* Garden City, N.Y.: Doubleday, 1963.

deBeer, G. R. Evolution. *Macropaedia,* vol. 7, *The New Encyclopaedia Britannica.* Chicago: Encyclopaedia Britannica, Inc., 1974. Pp. 7–23.

Deutsch, M. Field theory in social psychology. In G. Lindzey and E. Aronson (Eds.), *The handbook of social psychology,* vol. 1. Reading, Mass.: Addison-Wesley, 1968. Pp. 412–487.

Einstein, A. and Freud, S. Why war? In J. Strachey (Ed.), *The standard edition of the complete psychological works of Sigmund Freud,* vol. 22. London: Hogarth Press, 1964. Pp. 195–218. (Originally written in 1932 and 1933.)

Erikson, E. H. *Observations on the Yurok: Childhood and world image.* Monograph, University of California Publications in American Archaeology and Ethnology, 1943, *35,* 257–301.

Erikson, E. H. *Childhood and society.* New York: Norton, 1950.

Erikson, E. H. Identity and the life cycle. *Psychological Issues,* 1959, *1,* Monograph 1.

Erikson, E. H. *Identity: Youth and crisis.* New York: Norton, 1968.

Erikson, E. H. *Toys and reasons: Stages in the ritualization of experience.* New York: Norton, 1977.

Flavell, J. H.  *The developmental psychology of Jean Piaget.* Princeton, N.J.: Van Nostrand, 1963.

Freud, A.  *The ego and the mechanisms of defense.* New York: International Universities Press, 1946.

Freud, A.  *Normality and pathology in childhood: Assessments of development.* New York: International Universities Press, 1965.

Freud, A.  Adolescence as a developmental disturbance. In G. Kaplan and S. Lebovici (Eds.), *Adolescence: Psychosocial perspectives.* New York: Basic Books, 1969.

Freud, S.  A new histological method for the study of nerve tracts in the brain and spinal cord. *Brain,* 1884, *7,* 86.

Freud, S.  Three essays on the theory of sexuality. In J. Strachey (Ed.), *The standard edition of the complete psychological works of Sigmund Freud,* vol. 7. London: Hogarth Press, 1953. (Originally published in German in 1905.)

Freud, S.  Introductory lectures on psychoanalysis. In J. Strachey (Ed.), *The standard edition of the complete psychological works of Sigmund Freud,* vols. 15 and 16. London: Hogarth Press, 1963. (Originally published in German in 1917.) (a)

Freud, S.  *The cocaine papers.* Vienna and Zurich: 1963. (b)

Gesell, A., and Ilg, F. L.  *Child development: An introduction to the study of human growth,* vols. 1 and 2. New York: Harper and Brothers, 1949.

Gesell, A., Ilg, F. L., and Ames, L. B.  *Youth: The years from ten to sixteen.* New York: Harper and Brothers, 1956.

Goffman, E.  *The presentation of self in everyday life.* Garden City, N.Y.: Doubleday, 1959.

Gold, M., and Douvan, E.  *Adolescent development: Readings in research and theory.* Boston: Allyn and Bacon, 1969.

Grinstein, A.  *Sigmund Freud's writings: A comprehensive bibliography.* New York: International Universities Press, 1977.

Hall, G. S.  *Adolescence: Its psychology and its relations to physiology, anthropology, sociology, sex, crime, religion, and education,* vols. 1 and 2. New York: D. Appleton, 1904.

Havighurst, R. J.  *Developmental tasks and education* (3d ed.). New York: David McKay, 1972.

Havighurst, R. J., et al.  *Growing up in River City,* New York: Wiley, 1962.

Hjelle, L. A., and Ziegler, D. J.  *Personality: Theories, basic assumptions, research, and applications.* New York: McGraw-Hill, 1976.

Huxley, J.  *The uniqueness of man.* London: Chatto and Windus, 1941.

Huxley, J.  *Evolution: The magic synthesis.* New York: Harper and Brothers, 1942.

Jones, E.  *The life and work of Sigmund Freud,* 3 vols. New York: Basic Books, 1953–57.

Kelly, G. A.  *The psychology of personal constructs,* vols. 1 and 2. New York: Norton, 1955.

Kelly, J. G.  Social adaptation to varied environments. Paper presented at the

American Psychological Association meetings in New York, September 2, 1966.

Kohlberg, L.   Development of moral character and moral ideology. In M. L. Hoffman and L. W. Hoffman (Eds.), *Review of child development research,* vol. 1. New York: Russell Sage Foundation, 1964. Pp. 383–431.

Kohlberg, L.   *Stages in the development of moral thought and action.* New York: Holt, Rinehart and Winston, 1969.

Kohlberg, L.   Continuities in childhood and adult moral development revisited. In P. B. Baltes and K. W. Schaie (Eds.), *Life-span developmental psychology: Personality and socialization.* New York: Academic Press, 1973. Pp. 180–204.

Kohlberg, L., and Gilligan, C.   The adolescent as a philosopher: The discovery of the self in a post-conventional world. In J. Kagan and R. Coles (Eds.), *12 to 16: Early Adolescence.* New York: Norton, 1972. Pp. 144–179.

Kroeber, T. C.   The coping functions of the ego mechanisms. In R. W. White (Ed.), *The study of lives.* New York: Atherton, 1963.

Lewin, K.   Kreigslandschaft. *Zeitschrift für Angewandte Psychologie,* 1917, *12,* 440–447.

Lewin, K.   *A dynamic theory of personality.* New York: McGraw-Hill, 1935.

Lewin, K.   *Principles of topological psychology.* New York: McGraw-Hill, 1936.

Lewin, K.   Field theory and experiment in social psychology: Concepts and methods. *American Journal of Sociology,* 1939, *44,* 868–897.

Lewin, K.   Field theory in social science: Selected theoretical papers (D. Cartwright, Ed.). New York: Harper and Row, 1951.

Lewin, K., Lippitt, R., and White, R.   *Autocracy and democracy: An experimental inquiry.* New York: Harper and Row, 1960.

Lyell, C.   *Principles of geology,* 3 vols., 1830–33.

Maher, B. (Ed.).   *Clinical psychology and personality: The selected papers of George Kelly.* New York: Wiley, 1969.

Marrow, A. J.   *The practical theorist: The life and work of Kurt Lewin.* New York: Teachers College Press, 1977. (Originally published in 1969.)

Newman, B. M., and Newman, P. R.   *Development through life: A psychosocial approach.* Homewood, Ill.: Dorsey Press, 1975.

Newman, B. M., and Newman, P. R.   *Infancy and childhood: Development and its contexts.* New York: Wiley, 1978.

Nye, F. I.   *Role structure and analysis of the family.* Beverly Hills, Calif.: Sage Publications, 1976.

Parsons, T., and Bales, R. F. (Eds.).   *Family socialization and interaction process.* Glencoe, Ill.: Free Press, 1955.

Phillips, J. L.   *The origins of intellect: Piaget's theory* (2d ed.). San Francisco: W. H. Freeman, 1975.

Piaget, J.   *The moral judgement of the child.* Glencoe, Ill.: Free Press, 1948.

Piaget, J.   *The psychology of intelligence.* New York: Harcourt, Brace; London: Routledge and Kegan Paul, 1950.

Piaget, J.   *Play, dreams, and imitation in childhood.* New York: Norton, 1951.

Piaget, J.   Autobiography. In E. G. Boring et al., *History of psychology in autobiog-*

*raphy,* vol. 4. Worcester, Mass.: Clark University Press, 1952. Pp. 237–256. (a)

Piaget, J. *The origins of intelligence in children.* New York: International Universities Press, 1952. (b)

Piaget, J. *The construction of reality in the child.* New York: Basic Books, 1954.

Piaget, J. Piaget's theory. In P. H. Mussen (Ed.), *Carmichael's manual of child psychology,* vol. 1. New York: Wiley, 1970. Pp. 703–732.

Piaget, J. The theory of stages in cognitive development. In D. R. Green, H. P. Ford, and G. B. Flamer (Eds.), *Measurement and Piaget.* New York: McGraw-Hill, 1971.

Piaget, J. Intellectual evolution from adolescence to adulthood. *Human Development,* 1972, *15,* 1–12.

Piaget, J. *The grasp of consciousness: Action and concept in the young child.* Cambridge, Mass.: Harvard University Press, 1976.

Piaget, J., and Inhelder, B. *The psychology of the child.* New York: Basic Books, 1969.

Pruette, L. *G. Stanley Hall: A biography of a mind.* New York: D. Appleton, 1926.

Senn, M. J. E. Insights on the child development movement in the United States. *Monographs of the Society for Research in Child Development,* 1975, *40* (3–4, Serial No. 161).

Strachey, J. (Ed.). *The standard edition of the complete psychological works of Sigmund Freud.* London: Hogarth Press, 1953–74.

Sullivan, H. S. *The interpersonal theory of psychiatry.* New York: Norton, 1953.

Tanner, J. M. *Growth at adolescence* (2d ed.). Oxford: Blackwell, 1962.

Uzgiris, I. C. The organization of sensorimotor intelligence. In M. Lewis (Ed.), *Origins of intelligence: Infancy and early childhood.* New York: Plenum, 1976. Pp. 123–164.

Wapner, S., and Werner, H. *Perceptual development.* Worcester, Mass.: Clark University Press, 1957.

Werner, H. *Comparative psychology of mental development.* New York: International Universities Press, 1948. (Originally published in 1926.)

Werner, H. The concept of development from a comparative and organismic point of view. In D. B. Harris (Ed.), *The concept of development.* Minneapolis: University of Minnesota Press, 1957.

Werner, H., and Kaplan, B. *Symbol formation.* New York: Wiley, 1963.

White, R. W. Strategies of adaptation: An attempt at systematic description. In G. V. Coelho, D. A. Hamburg, and J. E. Adams (Eds.), *Coping and adaptation.* New York: Basic Books, 1974.

*A cross-cultural approach draws attention to the unique and the universal in adolescent socialization.*

2

# A Cross-Cultural View of Adolescence

What if there were no high schools or colleges? What if no special training were required to assume the work roles in the culture? What if there were no messages from the mass media trying to sell skin preparations, automobiles, or cigarettes to an adolescent population? If these and other cultural cues that define adolescence were absent, what would be the substance of the years from 10 to 25 in American society? The purpose of this chapter is to identify some of the ways in which culture shapes the pattern of adolescent development and to recognize some of the cultural differences in the ways adolescence is defined.

For the most part, the research, the settings, and the conflicts that are discussed in this book reflect adolescence in American culture. Before we become entwined in the complexity of concerns about adolescent development in our own society, we will take this opportunity to put some perspective on these experiences by discussing adolescence in a variety of cultures. The cross-cultural orientation raises two complementary questions. First, can we identify anything universal about the adolescent years in human cultures? Second, what is the range of experiences that adolescents encounter? The array of cultural patterns related to the rights and responsibilities of adolescents and the expectations for adolescent behavior alerts us to the enormous adaptive capacity of human beings.

We have selected six themes to guide our cross-cultural analysis: puberty rites, autonomy from parents, preparation for work, marriage, religious and political participation, and the characteristics of the adolescent peer culture. These themes reflect the ways in which social scientists have studied the process of change from childhood to adulthood. Each theme also offers a potential range of experiences that contribute to the adolescent's self-concept and to the expectations held by others for the adolescent's behavior.

The chapter samples material from a diverse array of cultures for which observations about the adolescent years are available. Differences in climate, differences in the development of technology, and differences in the degree of isolation from or integration with other cultures contribute to the patterning of life events in a specific culture. At another level, the kinds of resources, roles, and expectations that a society provides for adolescents tell us about the kinds of adults that the society hopes to produce. Since the topics of marriage, work, and religious or political commitment are central to the survival of a society, we can be certain that these themes will reflect important cultural goals.

## PUBERTY RITES

In all human societies, people have developed rituals and ceremonies to mark significant life events, such as birth, maturity, marriage, pregnancy, and death. Arnold van Gennep (1909; Eng. trans., 1960) was the first anthropologist to use the phrase "rites of passage" to describe ritual celebrations of new life roles. He argued that rites of passage are designed to smooth the transition from one status or role to another. Although the rites are frequently tied to biological events, Van Gennep viewed their function as primarily social and psychological. By means of ritualization, the individual could be helped through potentially painful transitions and the society could symbolize the enduring elements of its own character.

Puberty rites or initiation ceremonies are the rites of passage most closely associated with "coming of age" or with a cultural conception of maturity. The content and the timing of initiation rites vary widely from culture to culture (Muuss, 1970). There are also considerable differences in the patterns of initiation for males and females, in the severity of the rituals, and in the educational goals of the rituals. Among the Aranda of Central Australia, girls are initiated by rubbing their breasts with fat and ocher when they reach puberty. In contrast, Aranda boys must go through a series of difficult ceremonies that are designed to test their manhood, to teach obedience, and to impart the secrets of the tribe. The first of these rites includes separating the boy from women at about age 10 or 12, tossing him into the air several times, and beating him with a club as he falls to the ground. Later he is circumcised and taken to the bush to recover. While he is in the bush, men come and bite his scalp to help his hair grow. Five or six weeks later, a second surgical operation is performed on the boy's penis. Finally, there is a period of several months of celebration which ends when the boy goes through tests of fire, including kneeling down on hot coals. Sometime later, he is deemed capable of receiving the fetish object from the totem chief and is considered to be a man (Spencer and Gillen, 1966; Murdock, 1934)

Several explanations have been offered about the specific function of initiation rites. One view is to see the puberty rites as closely associated with the biological events of puberty. Mead (1949, 1955) argues that women's lives are marked by clear, well-defined events, including menarche, defloration, childbirth, and menopause. To enable males to achieve some comparable developmental sequence, society introduces rituals and social distinctions that identify the male's social status.

Puberty for the girl is dramatic and unmistakable, while for the boy the long series of events come slowly: uncertain and then deepening voice, growth of body hair, and finally ejaculations. There is no exact moment at which the boy can say, "Now I am a man," unless society steps in and gives a definition. One of the functions served by the variety of male initiation ceremonies that occur over the world . . . is that the rituals

serve to punctuate a growth-sequence that is inherently unpunctuated.
(Mead, 1949, 1955, p. 136)

Another explanation for the function of initiation ceremonies
is that they serve to emphasize the adult sex role expectations
held by the society for males and females (Brown, 1975; Munroe
and Munroe, 1975). In an analysis of cultures whose male initiation
ceremony involves circumcision, Burton and Whiting (1961) argue
that the purpose of the ceremony is to clarify the boy's identification
with the male sex role. They point out that in some societies which
give children exclusive sleeping privileges with their mother during
the first few years of life a strong mother-son bond develops, as
well as a father-son rivalry. Especially when fathers do not participate in the life events of young infants, there are few opportunities
for a strong male identification to develop. The society intervenes
at puberty to enforce the boy's commitment to the male group. In
societies where children sleep with both parents, or in the unusual
case in which the infant sleeps alone (as in the United States),
the initiation rites are generally not severe tests of manhood. The
transition to the adult male sex role is more gradual and continuous.

Few societies require painful initiation rites for females (Brown,
1963, 1969). When painful tests are part of the female initiation
ceremonies, they are also part of the male ceremonies. Brown (1975)
suggests that when there is conflict for either males or females
about the sex role group to which they wish to belong, the society
is likely to step in to emphasize the importance of a correct choice.

A third view about the meaning of initiation ceremonies is that
they reflect the continuity of discontinuity of the life events in
childhood and adulthood (Muuss, 1970). In cultures that are characterized by continuity, the information and experiences necessary
to participate in adult life are gradually integrated into the child's
daily life. In Samoa (Mead, 1928, 1949, 1955), for example, young
children are given increasing responsibilities for the care of their
siblings, for household chores, and for running errands. Cultural
taboos are explained and enforced. Children have the opportunity
to observe sexual behavior and to gradually participate in sexual
exploration. In all these ways, there is a comfortable accumulation
of skills and knowledge that prepare children for their adult status.

Some societies, in contrast, make very dramatic distinctions between the role of child and the role of adult. Children may be
prevented from participating in specific settings or from obtaining
certain information. In the example of the Aranda described above,
boys are grabbed away from their mothers and are eventually re-
born as males at the end of the initiation ceremonies (Benedict,
1938; Muuss, 1970). Because of all the secrecy in the adult religion

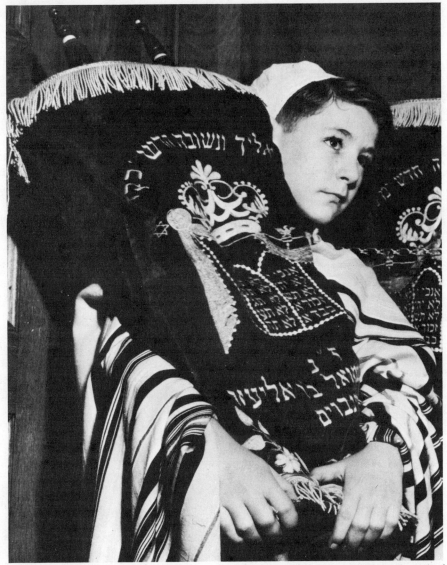

*The bar mitzvah is a ritual that marks attainment of a new status in the Jewish religion.*

and because of the intense hostility between males and females, male children have relatively few opportunities to learn the appropriate behaviors that are associated with the adult male role.

When there is cultural continuity between childhood and adulthood, there is less need for dramatic or elaborate initiation rituals.

The attainment of new status may be marked by celebrations and festivities that accompany the acquisition of a new role. Where there is cultural discontinuity, the initiation rituals may include specific education about sexual behavior, religious rites, cultural taboos, or adult skills. Children may be separated from their families in order to permit them to return after initiation in a new role and a new status (Munroe and Munroe, 1973). The society uses the initiation rituals as an opportunity to educate the child, the peer group, and the family about the child's new status.

The educational component is an important feature of many initiation ceremonies. In addition to the tests, trials, or festivities, initiation ceremonies may include the transmission of information about sexuality, training in some of the skills of adult work, and a passing on of the mythology and lore of the tribe. The Hopi ceremonies illustrate this educational emphasis. "At seven or eight years of age, all boys and some girls are initiated into the Kachina (or another) fraternity at the Powamu ceremony. After a flogging with yucca whips by the 'Kachinas,' masked dancers impersonating spirits, they receive new names and learn for the first time that the 'Kachinas' are not genuine divine beings but merely impersonations" (Murdock, 1934, pp. 342–343).

In American society, the change in status from child to adult occurs gradually during the years from 10 to 21. Specific subcultures retain their own initiation ceremonies, especially around the theme of religious commitment. Ceremonies of baptism, bar mitzvah, communion, and confirmation are conducted by religious groups to mark the beginning of adult status in the religious community. In addition to such subcultural celebrations, a variety of events mark the gradual recognition of the person's competences and the removal of the protections and restrictions that accompany childhood status (Muuss, 1970). The transitions from elementary school to junior high school, to high school, and to college involve ceremonies and festivities that celebrate increased intellectual competence. Adult privileges, including the right to a driver's license and the right to work without legal restriction at 16, the right to vote and the right to marry without parental consent at 18, and the full legal status associated with running for public office and participating in legal contracts at 21, all mark the passage from one status to another. The fact that these events are stretched out over a long period of time makes the change in status less clearly defined than it is for the Aranda or the Hopi child.

Given the explanations for initiation ceremonies discussed above, there are a number of ways to understand the American pattern. First, we might hypothesize that the absence of elaborate puberty rituals may reflect our desire to play down the importance of sex and sexuality in adult life. Instead of celebrating the arrival of adult reproductive capacities, we let them occur quietly, perhaps hoping that if adults take no notice, the children will ignore them as well (Davison and Davison, 1975). Second, we recognize that there are less clear sex role distinctions and status distinctions between males and females in our society than in cultures that practice severe initiation rituals. Males and females receive similar educations, participate in similar work roles, and have access to similar legal status.

There is another view that may be offered concerning the adolescent rites of passage in American society. First, let us point out that in addition to the transition to adulthood, a transition to adolescence occurs in the United States. The transition does not mark a movement into a new level of reproductive behavior. Rather, it confirms a movement into a stage of life when new intellectual skills may be attained. Graduation from junior high school, elementary school, or middle school (depending on the person's community) affirms the attainment of specific levels of intellectual accomplishment. The transition to high school, which is uniform and required in almost all American communities, states to child and family that the time has arrived when new levels of intellectual accomplishment are expected. As we explore the psychology of adolescence in the United States in greater detail, we will become aware that for some adolescents further levels of intellectual attainment are offered and expected (although college is offered to only a selected segment of the population).

We will speculate that rites of passage represent society's way of acknowledging necessary aspects of human development. Some societies identify mature reproductive behavior, others sensorimotor and problem-solving skills, as the passage to adulthood. American society identifies the psassage into a new stage of cognitive development which represents adolescence itself. Adolescence, though less observable in primitive cultures, is a clearly defined period in American society, offering the potential for at least two levels of intellectual attainment, in high school and in college. Although adolescence is the time for physical maturity of the reproductive system, it is, for most Americans, a time for learning about the psychological dimensions of heterosexual relations rather than a time for permanent mating. It is a time for developing a mature cognitive morality and becoming a member of a politicized society. Finally, it is a time for gaining the coping behavior of locomotion that is offered through the driving privilege. We do not whisk our adolescents into adulthood. We define a prolonged period of psychological development which involves cognitive, socioemotional, and physical accomplishments that we believe necessary for adult participation in the society.

## AUTONOMY FROM PARENTS

Modern psychologists working in industrialized societies have observed that the attainment of autonomy from parents is a task of considerable importance for the psychological development of the individual. The psychoanalytic theorists (A. Freud, 1965; Blos, 1962) have observed in clinical work with patients that many adolescents and adults who should be functioning autonomously are, in fact, operating from beliefs and feelings that are more characteristic of young children than adults. They have noted how strongly "infantile identifications" influence the adult behavior of some individuals. They have also observed that childlike ways of thinking and feeling often cause a great deal of psychic pain and limit the ability of persons to function effectively as adults. Blos (1962) has hypothesized that the dissolution of infantile dependencies and identifications is one of the fundamental tasks of adolescence. It is essential, from his point of view, for a person to dissolve these psychological bonds in order to become a free and autonomous individual. Freedom and autonomy are important for further personality development and for effective behavioral and psychological functioning.

Douvan and Adelson (1966) conducted a study of a large sample of youth of high school age. The subjects of their study were normal teenagers who were involved in rather typical school and community activities. The researchers discovered that the adolescents under study were extremely concerned with a large number of specific issues that were directly related to the attainment of autonomy from parents. They report that the students whom they studied spent a good deal of time debating with their parents about such issues as curfews and driving regulations. The authors conclude that in addition to the dissolution of infantile dependencies, the achievement of behavioral independence receives a good deal of attention and generates considerable conflict in the family.

Evolutionary theorists (Darwin, 1859; Huxley, 1941, 1942; deBeer, 1974) point out that humans spend a much longer period of time in physical and biological dependence than do members of other species. While some animals become independent within a few days or hours after birth, the human remains dependent upon caregivers for many years. We have noted in the previous section that in many human societies the transition from childhood to adulthood occurs in a relatively swift manner between the ages of 10 and

13. One might argue that in these societies puberty rites mark the transition from dependence upon others to personal independence. We have also noted that modern, technological society in the United States identifies a long period of development during which this autonomy occurs. Adolescence is a distinct period of life during which specific cognitive and emotional developments are expected to take place.

Margaret Mead (1928) pointed out that in the Samoan society of 1928 multiple caregivers were involved in the rearing of each child. She reported that strong psychological relationships with a few people (parents) were not characteristic of Samoan culture. She also noted that emotional disorders such as neuroses were not observed among adult Samoans. She implied that the neuroses observed in modern, Western culture did not exist in the Samoan culture of 1928 because of less intense psychological involvements and identifications with parents as primary caregivers. Her hypothesis was that less intense involvement with a larger number of caregivers made it easier for Samoan children to make the transition to adulthood. Modern observers (Feldman and Feldman, 1977) have noted that modernization and Westernization of the Samoan culture have produced conditions of child rearing which are similar to those that exist in American society.

From these observations we might speculate that social evolution toward increasing degrees of symbolization and abstraction in cognition and socioemotional development is accompanied by more intense involvement with and dependence upon one's parents (or a small number of caregivers). Part of the process of becoming an adult involves a relatively prolonged period of time during which, among other things, the psychological tie to one's primary caregivers must be modified in order to allow for the realization of the potential of individuals. If this individuation does not occur, then serious problems of personal functioning may develop. Before this premise is examined in relation to modern American society, the process by which autonomy from parents is attained in a variety of cultures will be described.

The meaning of autonomy from parents for an individual adolescent depends heavily on the nature of the family group during the childhood years. One cannot assume that all children experience the same family context during infancy and childhood. The notion of asserting one's own views, making independent decisions, or starting one's own family group may be accurate expressions of autonomy for one person, but not for another. In American society, the nuclear family consisting of two parents and their offspring is the predominant family form. The next most common family group in American society is the extended family, in which three or more generations of family members participate in child rearing.

If we look to other societies, we find an array of family patterns that are more diverse than the American forms. In studying a group of 554 societies, Murdock (1957) found that the dominant family pattern in 419 of them was polygamy. Among the societies that have a norm of polygamous marriage patterns, there are three varieties of marital arrangements: (1) polygyny, in which one male has more than one wife; (2) polyandry, in which one female has more than one husband; and (3) group marriage, in which two or more males marry two or more females (Adams, 1975). In all of these arrangements, children relate to more than two adults as parent figures. Further, the living arrangements of each marital pattern may differ. In 125 of the societies sampled by Murdock, men live separately from their wives and children. In some of those cultures, men travel for long periods and return only infrequently to their wives and children. In two African societies, the Hehe and the Thonga, children do not live with either their father or their mother. Once they are weaned, they live with their grandmother for a number of years. In the Israeli kibbutz, infants live in the children's quarters from the second week of life through adolescence. Although they have frequent interaction with their parents, kibbutz children come to see the metapalet, or caregiver, as the primary disciplinarian (Ben-Yaakov, 1972). In other words, the assumption one may tend to make that children emerge from a close, intimate daily association with mother and father into a more autonomous life-style in later adolescence or adulthood just does not hold for many children in many different societies.

Two cultural groups, the Israeli kibbutz and the Iroquois tribe of northern New York State, provide examples of some of the variability in child-rearing patterns that have implications for the emergency of autonomy. These examples illustrate that cultures vary in the physical autonomy and the socioemotional autonomy experienced during adolescence. One form of independence does not necessarily produce the other.

In the Israeli kibbutz, as mentioned above, children participate in communal child rearing, beginning in the second week of life. Collective children's houses are designed to care for infants and toddlers, school-age children, and adolescents. Beginning at the end of the first year of life, parents participate less frequently in their children's care and daily experience. They may drop in to the children's house for 10–15 minutes during the day, but the primary opportunity for interaction is in the evening hours from after dinner to bedtime. In contrast to family-reared Israeli children, the kibbutz children view their metapalet, their peers, and their teachers as highly involved in their life experiences. All of these figures serve as sources of support, discipline, and identification (Devereux et al., 1974).

Despite what might be viewed as limited opportunities for inter-action and a cultural emphasis away from the nuclear family, kib-butz adolescents continue to have a strong, somewhat idealized identification with their parents (Devereux et al., 1974; Long, Hen-derson, and Platt, 1973). Adolescents see their parents as supportive and concerned about their lives. They admire their parents' accom-plishments in the history of Israeli freedom and in the formation of their kibbutz (Bettelheim, 1969). The precariousness of the safety and freedom of the kibbutz settlements as well as the ideological commitment to individual responsibility for the success or failure of the settlements makes adolescent rebelliousness infrequent and inappropriate. The most obvious strategy for asserting autonomy during adolescence is to choose to leave the kibbutz and live in the city. Interestingly, Bettelheim suggests that the decision to leave the kibbutz seems to evoke more emotion about abandoning or being abandoned by the peer group than about a rejection of parents or kibbutz adults. In a sense, the struggle for an emerging identity and a set of personal life values is made easy by the great need that the kibbutz has for devoted, competent members. On the other hand, peer pressures rather than adult pressures appear to be the primary barriers to the emergence of autonomy for kibbutz-reared adolescents.

As they are described to Murdock (1934), the traditional Iroquois society households consisted of families in which the adult females shared common lineage with a female ancestor. A number of nu-clear families lived together in a "longhouse" of connected apart-ments and shared fireplaces. An older woman was the authority of the house, making major economic and political decisions for the group.

The pattern of child care in the Iroquois society reflected the importance of women in the nuclear unit. Mothers nursed their babies for two or three years. They had primary authority over their children's care and discipline. Fathers were minimally in-volved in their children's care. At puberty, both male and female children experienced temporary isolation. Girls were isolated dur-ing their first menstrual period. Boys were secluded for a year, being cared for in a hut in the forest. During these times of seclu-sion, the adolescents were tested for endurance, competence, and strength.

Soon after puberty, the female adolescents were married. Males married somewhat later, when they were able to show their profi-ciency as hunters. Marriages were arranged by the children's moth-ers. Females remained in the longhouse of their mothers, whereas males were expected to leave their family and live with their brides. After marriage, the male's main allegiance was shifted from his own chief matron to the chief matron of his wife's household. Not until the birth of his first child was the male fully accepted into his wife's family group (Murdock, 1934; Jacobs, 1964).

The pattern of socialization in the Iroquois tribe reflects the common expectation in many societies that there will never be full autonomy from one's parents or from parental authorities (Stephens, 1963). The cloaks of ancestry, religion, economic survival, and uniformity of values surround each new generation and draw it into the way of life of earlier generations. In the Iroquois society, males experience a harsher separation from their family group than do females. They must learn to shift their allegiance to a new household and a new chief matron. For neither the male nor the female is personal autonomy a highly valued or expected quality. Rather, the ceremonies, trials, and isolation at adolescence help males and females to recognize the importance of their membership in the complex political, economic, and religious units of their household, clan, and tribe.

## ASSUMING THE WORK ROLE

Among American psychologists, there is some consensus that the work role is a new and important aspect of intellectual and social experience during adolescence (Brim, 1966; Douvan and Gold, 1966; Douvan and Adelson, 1966; Gold and Douvan, 1969). For most American youth, adolescence marks the beginning of temporary paid work experiences such as baby-sitting, newspaper delivery, stock clerking, or waiting on tables, as well as educational training for more permanent work activities or careers. In a number of ways, work activities bring adolescents closer to an image of themselves as adults. First, the notion of being paid for one's efforts engages a person in the concrete reality of our economy. Labor → money → resources for purchasing goods → desire for more money, and so on. Second, the legitimacy of work as a positive, valued adult behavior extends to adolescent workers, providing them with a positive feeling of social worth. Third, work experiences help adolescents to identify their areas of competence and to acquire a sense of their importance to others and a notion of the consequences of particular work activities for future life-styles. Thus experimentation in the work role may contribute to a sense of personal identity.

Industrial and postindustrial societies differ from more traditional societies in the range of the work roles that they need and in their elaboration of training in skills that prepare children to assume those work roles. In industrial and postindustrial societies, the work roles are quite diverse. In American society, there is considerable freedom about the work activity for which one may prepare. Of course, family resources, community expectations, and personal competences may limit the variety of the work roles to which an adolescent aspires. However, the opportunities for training are vast and individuals are encouraged to pursue the work goals for which they feel best suited. In more authoritarian societies, individuals have less choice about their work. In China, for example, one's work depends as much on the social need to have a certain number of people employed in certain forms of work as on the individual's aspirations and competences. In both societies, however, the kinds of work roles that exist are varied, the amount of training necessary for each work activity is varied, and the kinds of life-styles that accompany different occupations are varied. A person who is trained to repair automobiles may complete training by the age of 18 and feel fully engaged in the work of auto repair. A person who is trained as a physician may not complete training until the age of 28 and may not be fully engaged in the work of health care until the age of 30 or 35. The contrast suggests that in our own society and in other industrial or postindustrial cultures, the various types of work-related experiences do not provide comparable transitions from adolescence to adulthood.

In comparison to other cultures, and other periods of history, contemporary American society appears to be rather protective in its attitude toward involving children in work activities. Gillis (1974) describes the pattern of child labor in peasant families of 16th-century England. At the age of six or seven, children were expected to perform major household chores. By the age of nine or ten, children were encouraged to leave home and work for wealthier families. This strategy helped peasant families to shed the burden of feeding and clothing their older children and may have enabled these families to increase their resources through their children's income.

Mead and Newton (1967) describe a variety of ways in which young children contribute to the economic survival of families in traditional societies. Children are frequently expected to gather food, catch small game, run errands, or help prepare food. Children as young as five or six are asked to look after younger brothers and sisters, carry infants on their backs, and feed younger children. In Samoa, for example, young children are expected to perform a variety of tasks at the bidding of their parents or older relatives. The chores demanded of children under the ages of nine or ten include "fetching water, gathering leaves, cleaning house, building fires, lighting lamps, serving drinks, running errands, and tending babies" (Murdock, 1934, p. 64). Especially for females, the rites associated with puberty bring greater freedom and fewer work responsibilities. From the time the female is inducted into the organization of young unmarried women until she is married, she has some years of leisure and pleasure.

The many examples of work done by young children suggest that the adolescent years do not mark the beginning of the capacity to contribute to the economic survival of the family group in all societies. We cannot even argue that young children do meaningful work in traditional societies but not in technological societies. In China, for example, part of the kindergarten curriculum includes planned experiences in "productive labor." Children at the Yu Yao Road kindergarten spend one period a week wrapping crayons and putting them in boxes or folding crayon boxes into their proper shape. The crayon factory pays for this work, and the kindergarten uses the money to purchase additional equipment (Sidel, 1972). This example suggests that the degree to which children and adolescents participate in meaningful work activities is closely linked to social attitudes or cultural values about the meaning of work and about the part work should play in the developmental experiences of children.

A final theme in the consideration of the work role is the practice of reserving adolescence as the occasion to teach important skills that will be relevant for adult survival. In American society, driver's education would be an example of such a practice. The society has chosen early adolescence as the time when students are taken aside to acquire the skills and knowledge necessary for driving a car. Among the Aranda of Australia, the long and severe initiation ceremonies provide a special opportunity to teach young men the lore, the customs, and the secrets of the tribe (Murdock, 1934; Benedict, 1938; Muuss, 1970). Puberty may provide the occasion to teach children about sexual intercourse and reproduction (Whiting, Kluckhohn, and Anthony, 1958). At puberty, some societies emphasize the importance of perfecting work-related competences such as weaving, grinding corn, or spinning cotton (Richards, 1956; Brown, 1975). Some cultures use puberty as the time to demand evidence of the child's fortitude and obedience to adult authorities. These tests are seen as necessary training to instill a commitment to the cultural pattern of work roles and family roles in adulthood (Muuss, 1970; Murdock, 1934).

## MARRIAGE

The marriage relationship is commonly viewed as a central element of adult life. Marriage generally involves a number of challenges that are associated with maturity. These include the ability to accumulate and share resources for survival, the ability to conceive and raise children, and the ability to experience physical and emotional mutuality with another person outside the nuclear family of origin. In the United States, marriage is clearly associated with adulthood. For just that reason, some adolescents who desire the independence and status they attribute to the adult role marry early, at the age of 16 or 17, in order to speed the transition out of adolescence. In contrast, some adolescents postpone marriage for much the same reasons. They view marriage as a relationship that brings more responsibility, more stability, or more commitment than they feel prepared to experience. The recognition that marriage brings adult status propels some adolescents toward it and others away from it.

## Mate Selection

In contrast to many Euro-American cultural groups, marriage in traditional societies usually does not permit the same degree of choice either in the selection of a mate or in the age at which marriage occurs. The selection of a mate is usually determined by two principles: (1) the range of eligible mates and (2) the involvement of other family members in mate selection (Freeman, 1958). Rules may limit the choice of eligible mates to members of a village, a religious group, a particular clan, or the extended family. For the Yaruros of Venezuela, for example, the ideal marriage partner for an adolescent male was a daughter of one of his uncles (Petrullo, 1938). Among the Hopi of Arizona, adolescents were quite free to choose their mates as long as they had the approval of their maternal relatives and as long as the prospective partner was not a member of the adolescent's clan (Murdock, 1934).

Marriage is frequently arranged by relatives and is not at all a reflection of the adolescent's preferences. Among the Iroquois, mothers of sons and daughters arranged a marriage for their children. Among the Aranda, two fathers arranged a special relationship between their son and daughter. The girl became the mother-in-law of the boy, and the boy had the right to marry any or all of her unborn daughters. By the time these daughters reached puberty they were already promised to men who would be quite a bit older than they (Murdock, 1934). Thus mate selection can range from free choice among partners to an agreement that is made even before birth.

## Age at Marriage

The age at which marriage takes place varies from one society to another. In the United States, the median age for first marriages was 23.5 for males and 21.1 for females in 1975 (U.S. Department of Commerce, 1975). This reflects an average delay of about one year for both males and females from 1960. Only 0.7 percent of males and 2.9 percent of females in the age range 14–17 were married in 1975. There has been a steady increase in the number of males and females who remain single during the ages 20–24 and 25–29, when the largest proportion of males and females tend to marry (U.S. Department of Commerce, 1975).

The pattern of females marrying at a younger age than males appears to be common in traditional as well as industrialized societies. Among the Aranda, as was mentioned above, girls were married at puberty to men who were quite a bit older than they were. The Todas of southern India arranged marriage for their children when the children were two or three years old. The bride lived at her own home until she was 15 or 16. Then she moved to her husband's home. If either the boy or the girl did not want to be married to this partner, they could annul the marriage at this point and return all gifts and buffalo that had been exchanged over the years since the marriage agreement was established (Murdock, 1934).

The Polar Eskimo permitted their children to exercise free choice in selecting a marriage partner. Girls married at about age 16 to boys who were about 20. Frequently, unmarried adolescents lived together in a young people's house where males and females formed temporary pairs. When a couple identified each other as well-suited and competent partners, a marriage was arranged (Murdock, 1934).

The traditional Crow of the Western plains of the United States offer another marriage pattern. Females were expected to marry before they reached puberty. If they were not married by this age, they were often objects for teasing and scorn. Males usually did not marry until the age of 25. Crow males had numerous lovers before they married. Crow warriors often married women whom they captured from other tribes. Usually, however, they purchased the bride and the right to marry all her younger sisters from her family (Murdock, 1934).

The differences in patterns of age at marriage suggest two conclusions that are relevant to our understanding of adolescence. First, the cross-cultural similarity of earlier marriage for females than males suggests that most societies perceive females as ready to participate in this adult role at an earlier age. This may be related to the biological readiness to conceive and the accompanying need for a partner to share in the responsibilities of economic survival and child care. It may also reflect a discrepancy in the length of time needed by males and females to acquire the skills and competences associated with their work roles. If the division of labor in a society requires males to have more physical strength, more information, or more complex skills to perform the tasks required for economic survival, males may have to wait longer than females before they enter into the obligations of a marriage relationship.

The second general conclusion is that as a result of the many variations in cultural orientations toward marriage the marriage relationship will have varied psychological meaning, depending on the way it is structured. If one has a significant role in selecting one's marriage partner, the sense of emotional commitment is likely to be quite different than if the marriage partner was selected by others. If the marriage occurs before puberty, the relationship is likely to have a different quality than if the marriage occurs after puberty. If a young girl moves into the household of her husband's family or if a young boy moves into the household of his wife's family, the marriage relationship is likely to be experienced differently from the way in which it is experienced by couples who live in their own home and are expected to generate their own resources. The cultural pattern of marriage will influence the quality of the bond between the partners, the resources available to the married couple, and the degree to which married brings adult status.

## RELIGIOUS AND POLITICAL PARTICIPATION

One way a society has of acknowledging the increased competences of its members is to open new avenues for participation in important religious or political activities. In general, increased rights and responsibilities in the religious or political sphere are a response to the obvious changes in intellectual functioning that occur during the adolescent years. Many cultures recognize that adolescents are capable of a new level of reasoning, problem solving, and decision making that makes them more valued members of the group. Many societies anticipate these cognitive changes, and use adolescence as a time to inform young people of the reality behind many of the political or religious myths that constitute the education of childhood. Rather than risk the disillusionment in cultural values that would result if adolescents were to discover for themselves that childhood stories or illusions were not accurate, the society makes a gift of the truth and thereby wins the adolescent's cooperation in continuing to maintain the underlying cultural values.

### Religious Participation

In the United States, the Christian ceremony of confirmation represents entry into a new status within the church. Occurring at around the age of 11 or 12, confirmation involves memorizing central beliefs of the faith; a religious ceremony in which family, friends, and peers recognize the change in status; and the acquisition of an additional name. Although many adolescents do not actually perceive the confirmation ceremony as bringing a meaningful change in their contribution to the church, the ceremony obviously symbolizes a traditional recognition of the emerging competences of the young adolescent.

In other Western religions, ceremonies such as bar mitzvah or baptism acknowledge a new commitment to the religious group and a new respect by the group for the individual. In the Orthodox Jewish religion, for example, a religious service can only take place if at least ten men who have been bar mitzvahed are present. These ten men are known as a minyan. Boys who have not been bar mitzvahed do not "count" toward a minyan even if they are present when the service is being conducted. Toward the end of the Middle Ages, bar mitzvah became a prerequisite for certain religious rights. Only those who had been bar mitzvahed were given the honor of reciting the blessing over the Torah during a service. The right to wear tefillin, a sacred prayer bound to the head and arm during morning prayers, was reserved for boys of bar mitzvah age (Schauss, 1950).

Many traditional societies use adolescent initiation ceremonies as a time to share sacred religious secrets or to instill religious beliefs. The custom cited earlier of the initiation of seven- or eight-year-old Hopi children into the Kachina fraternity is an example of such secret-sharing. Turner (1964, 1966, 1967) describes the initiation ceremonies of the Ndembu of Zambia. In these rituals males are taught the sacred mysteries of the culture. These mysteries include the symbolic meaning of specific masks and emblems and the mystical connection between the human body and the functions of the universe. Turner suggests that the sharing of these mysteries has several consequences. It teaches young males how to conceptualize their daily experience and gives them an organized value system to which they can refer. It changes their psychology, binding them more intimately to their fellow initiates and committing them more deeply to the legitimate authority of the elders in the society.

## Political Participation

Increased recognition and participation in the political system is evidenced in the United States by the attainment of voting age at 18. The right to vote, which is given at the beginning of later adolescence, is accompanied by other rights, including the right to marry without parental consent, and by other responsibilities, including the change in status from juvenile to adult in the eyes of the courts. A similar change in political status was part of adolescent development in ancient Greece. Young men of 16 or 17 were judged by a group of adults to verify their competence in athletic, muscial, and academic areas. After an adolescent had been adjudged competent, his name was entered into the registry of citizens.

Military service may be an expression of increased political involvement. In the United States, 16 is the minimum age for volunteering for the armed forces. In Israel, both males and females are expected to receive military training at the age of 17 or 18. Among the Dahomeans of West Africa, the king selected a special group from all unmarried females to be trained as the core force in his army. These Dahomean Amazons were all considered wives of the king. In addition to their contribution to battle, the Amazons protected all the women in the king's harem and their slaves (Murdock, 1934).

A final example of political participation is membership in a political organization. In Samoa, young men join an organization of all young men and older untitled men. Their roles include cooperative labor for fishing, cultivating, and cooking as well as entertaining and organizing community social life. Young females join a similar organization of women who entertain and serve as an honor court for the village princess (Murdock, 1934; Mead, 1939).

*Leonard Freed/Magnum*

*In Israel, both males and females are expected to receive military training at the age of 17 or 18.*

Politically oriented youth organizations emerge in technological societies as well. In the middle 1960s, a large group of Chinese high school and college students formed a powerful revolutionary youth movement called the Red Guards. Their goal was to carry forward the revolutionary spirit in culture, in education, and in government by destroying prerevolutionary artifacts and by disrupting "bourgeois" forces in government and business. In Russia, two youth organizations have operated to encourage education and discipline among youth. The Young Pioneers, a group for children aged 10–15, is viewed as a desirable and prestigious extracurricular activity for older elementary and secondary school children. The Komsomol (Leninist Young Communist League) organizes political and educational experiences for adolescents 14 through 25. Participation in both groups increases an adolescent's status in the community and raises his or her chances for admission to highly competitive universities.

Whether the political organizations are planned experiences that are sanctioned by the adult community or spontaneous groups that emerge from the sentiments of adolescents themselves, participation in them increases the adolescent's insight into the political and economic structure of his or her society. Political participation provides opportunities to learn about strategies for producing change. It highlights the value structure that is expressed by the dominant governing group. Finally, it alerts adolescents to the additional power and influence that can be achieved through group efforts.

## CHARACTERISTICS OF ADOLESCENT PEER CULTURES

During early adolescence, we expect young people to be involved in an increasingly differentiated, active, and complex peer group. The potential functions of peer group participation are varied. First, we expect the peer group to be a supportive setting that permits adolescents to establish increased autonomy from parents and older siblings. Second, the peer group offers avenues for experimentation with cultural values and for a restatement of one's own commitment or resistance to family or cultural ways. Third, peers are a nonfamily group that invites adolescents to feel a sense of bondedness or affection for a larger, more diverse segment of the society beyond the nuclear and extended family. Finally, peers operate to regulate and direct the behavior of individuals. In some cases, we view this control function as a press toward deviance and impulsiveness. In other cases, we view peer pressures toward conformity as socially desirable forces that reduce egocentrism and tendencies to act in self-centered, antisocial ways.

As one looks across cultures at the experiences adolescents share with their peers, it becomes clear that many societies make deliberate use of the adolescent peer group as an agent of socialization. In contrast to the sentiment often expressed in American society that adolescent peers challenge, deviate from, or ignore cultural values, many societies create peer cultures that actively support and encourage individual allegiance to the societal norms. Three functions of the peer group will be discussed below: (1) supporting and maintaining cultural values; (2) investing energy and affection in a large group that goes beyond family or kinship lines; and (3) providing an environment for realizing a new degree of autonomy and competence.

## Supporting and Maintaining Cultural Values

The pattern of Soviet character education and "upbringing" is an excellent example of how a culture can encourage peers to feel responsible for maintaining cultural values (Bronfenbrenner, 1970). Soviet society uses both the family and the school as socialization agents. The family emphasis includes open expression of affection and clear expectations for obedience and self-control. Parents have access to a variety of media which communicate the findings and views of child-rearing experts about how to function effectively in the parent role. Parents are told that obedience is to be encouraged through explanations of how to behave, praising when correcting faults, and punishing when disobedience occurs.

When children begin school at age seven, character education is continued through the school. A manual outlining specific goals for socialization guides the expectations, the activities, and the responsibilities that children encounter at each grade level. Within each classroom, children are organized into cells. At first, teachers identify the goals for the class and reward the cells that perform the best. Eventually student monitors take over this function, evaluating each cell's achievements.

The principle of *social criticism* is used to foster peer responsibility for group behavior. If a child is disobedient, the other children try to decide on a fitting plan to improve the child's behavior. Children compete with the class monitors, criticizing their performance. Within cells, children are encouraged to point out one another's errors and to figure out how to improve one another's performance so that they can compete more successfully with other cells. Even parents are asked to submit critical reports of the ways in which their children are achieving the goals of character education at home.

Research on moral behavior and on response to the peer group illustrates some of the consequences of this consistent and well-defined program of character education. A comparison of 12-year-old American and Soviet schoolchildren showed that the Soviet schoolchildren were less willing to participate in a wide variety of behaviors if these were disapproved by adults (Bronfenbrenner, 1966). A number of situations, including cheating on a quiz, neglecting homework, and taking fruit from someone's orchard, were presented to the children. They were asked to tell whether they would go along with friends or refuse to go along with friends in each situation. The children had to evaluate the situation under one of three conditions—(1) a condition in which they were told that no one except the experimenter would see their responses; (2) a condition in which they were told that parents and teachers would see their responses; or (3) a condition in which they were told that their classmates would see their responses. Among the Russian children, the knowledge that peers would see their responses increased the extent of their resistance to deviant pressures. Among the U.S. children, the knowledge that peers would see their responses increased their willingness to participate in deviant behavior.

In a comparison of Soviet and Swiss children, the same pattern was observed (Bronfenbrenner, 1970). Children were asked how they would handle 21 examples of peer misconduct. The children had four choices: telling a grown-up; telling the other children; handling it by themselves; or doing nothing. Of the Soviet children, 75 percent said that they would speak to the child themselves, whereas only 33 percent of the Swiss children chose that strategy. Twenty percent of the Swiss children, but less than 1 percent of the Soviet children, said that they would do nothing. Clearly, the Soviet strategy of gradually increasing the peer group's obligation for the maintenance of standards of excellence serves to create a sense that peers are responsible for one another's behavior.

## The Development of Bonds of Affection beyond Kinship Lines

The peer group represents a potential source of lifelong friendships and emotional commitments that range far beyond the kinship structure. Once adolescents direct the investment of positive emotion toward their peers, they become committed to a concern for a social organization that is larger than their family group. There are several examples of life patterns that appear to foster strong peer bonds.

In the Israeli kibbutz, strong peer bonds are created as a result of communal child rearing. Children in the same age group go through a number of transitions from one children's house to another, from one caregiver to another, and from one set of school and work expectations to another. By the time they reach adolescence, kibbutz adolescents have developed a sense of one another as members of a large family (Spiro, 1954; 1965; Barnouw, 1971). In Spiro's observations of kibbutz life, he noted, for example, that those adolescents who were born and raised in the kibbutz married individuals from outside the kibbutz. Although there were no rules to enforce this practice, it appeared to be a reflection of the sentiment that it would be inappropriate to marry someone who was so much like a sibling. The consequences of this intimate experience among peers are difficult to evaluate. On the one hand, kibbutz-reared children tend to see peers as exerting more of a controlling function in their lives than do urban, family-reared Israelis (Devereux et al., 1974). Bettelheim (1969) points out that there is strong pressure toward conformity among adolescent peers. A child who is rejected by the kibbutz peer group experiences intense alienation and isolation. On the other hand, one of the strongest motives for continuing one's commitment to the kibbutz community is a sense of obligation and love for one's peers. Peers coax one another into the decision to reject the diversity and potential luxury of noncommunal life for the security, warmth, and moral virtue of kibbutz existence (Spiro, 1965, 1968, 1970).

Samoan society offers another pattern of positive adolescent peer commitment (Mead, 1928). Boys and girls joined same-sex peer groups when they were about seven years old. The children played together often and developed some antagonism toward groups from other villages or neighborhoods. There was strong avoidance of opposite-sex peers. For girls, the intensity of these friendships was limited by the girls' responsibility to care for younger siblings during this time. As soon as a girl reached puberty, her family involved her in new and more difficult household tasks which left her few hours for peer play. As girls became interested in love affairs and seriously involved in courtship, the need for secrecy made any close friendship hazardous.

For Samoan boys, the pattern was somewhat different. They did not have the responsibility of caring for younger siblings, nor were they expected to assume heavy household tasks at puberty. Therefore, the male peer groups were freer to retain their camaraderie for a longer time. Peer cooperation was required in many of the tasks that adolescent and young adult males were expected to perform. These tasks included manning the canoes, fishing for eels, and laboring in the taro plantations. Finally, young men became members of the Aumaga, an organization of males who performed central work tasks and organized important social events for the village. Thus, while Samoan females were more likely to find friendship among the wives of one another's husbands, the peer group bonds of Samoan males were fostered and maintained throughout adult life.

## The Peer Group as an Environment for Building Autonomy and Competence

The third function of the adolescent peer group is to provide new opportunities for adolescents to rely on their own skills and problem-solving capacities rather than on the competences of adults. In order to achieve this goal, some societies create youth dormitories or age-graded communities where young people are expected to perform many of the tasks of daily survival. Among the Muria of eastern India, male and female children live in a dormitory from the time they are six until marriage (Elwin, 1947; Barnouw, 1971). The dormitory, or ghotul, is viewed as a religious sanctuary where members are dedicated to work and spiritual harmony. Children work for their parents and other villagers. They also perform ceremonial dances for the village. Marriage is arranged by a child's parents, and once children are married they must leave the ghotul.

The training for autonomy is even more pronounced among the Nyakyusa of East Africa (Wilson, 1951; Barnouw, 1971). Children leave their father's houses and begin a new village of reed huts when they are ten years old. As they get older, the boys build stronger huts to which they bring their wives when they marry. Before marriage, the boys continue to eat in their fathers' homes. After marriage, each young man and his wife and children begin to cultivate their own land and prepare their own fields. About ten years after most of the young men have been married and are functioning autonomously, their fathers transfer the responsibilities of government to the young men's village. Among the Muria and the Nyakyusa, adolescents have the opportunity to exercise their new skills and to experience many of the responsibilities of adult life before achieving adult status.

## CHAPTER SUMMARY

We have discussed six themes of adolescent experience: initiation ceremonies, autonomy from parents, the work role, marriage, religious and political involvement, and the adolescent peer culture. The life period of adolescence, though not of equal importance in all societies, rarely passes unmarked by some significant new social learning. Rather than view adolescence as a new stage that is the product of technological societies and their accompanying complexity, we begin to see adolescence as a common turning point in many societies, ancient and contemporary, traditional and industrial. Each society recognizes some newly emerging competences as particularly relevant for successful adaptation during adulthood. Clearly, adolescence is not a modern invention. It has existed as an important phase in human development, celebrated uniquely in various cultures, from the ancient Greeks to the Incas of Peru, from the ancient Chinese to the Polar Eskimo.

Initiation or puberty ceremonies are the rites of passage associated with the transition from childhood to adulthood or from adolescence to adulthood. Not every society has a specific initiation ceremony. Those initation ceremonies that have been observed vary in the degree of stress or pain involved, the degree of separation from the community, and the kind of new learning that occurs. Three theories have been offered to explain the purpose of initiation ceremonies. First, they may serve to mark an important biological transition. In this view, males may need more cultural emphasis to mark the events of puberty since the biological changes are more subtle in males than females. A second theory emphasizes the functions that initiation ceremonies serve in helping adolescents to accept adult sex role expectations. In this perspective, initiation ceremonies would be more marked and more severe if there were childhood experiences that led males or females to reject or resent their adult sex role. Finally, a general theory views initiation ceremonies as bridging the gap in experience and competence from childhood to adulthood. Cultures that isolate children from the knowledge or experiences of adulthood use elaborate initiation ceremonies to provide a clear transition experience from which the person emerges into a totally new status.

In Western, technological society, autonomy is viewed as a necessary element of adult functioning that occurs after a prolonged period of dependence. The difficulty in achieving emotional autonomy results from intense identification and involvement with a few caregivers for a long time. Since not all societies share this family pattern, not all adolescents experience this psychological process of differentiation and autonomy. Furthermore, not all societies expect or desire adults to experience a high degree of individuation and personal autonomy. The Israeli kibbutz provides an example of physical separation accompanied by enduring emotional commitment. Among the Iroquois, an adult continued to show allegiance to a household matron, even if the adult left his own household of origin.

In American society, work activities tend to be a new experience for adolescents. These activities provide new learning which brings adolescents closer to adult status and provides opportunities to participate in adult activities. In contrast to our culture, many traditional societies depend on children's work long before adolescence. Frequently, puberty is a time when young people are asked to demonstrate competence in work-related activities that will be required for adult survival.

Marriage is another social event that is associated with adult status in our society. Looking across cultures, we have seen that is is common for females to marry at a younger age than males. Beyond this regularity, the patterns of mate selection, the range of eligible partners, and the age at which marriage occurs differ widely across cultures. Often marriages are arranged before the partners reach puberty. Marriage does not always include a strong emotional commitment to the partner; marriage does not always remove the partners from their household of origin; and marriage does not always bring adult status in the eyes of the community.

Increased participation in religious or political organizations is a means of recognizing the new cognitive capacities of adolescence. In some cultures, adolescence marks the time for sharing religious secrets as well as for acquiring certain rights and responsibilities. Political participation may include new legal rights or legal status, participation in the military, or membership in political organizations. These activities help to educate youth about the structure of their government, about strategies for change, and about the group as a potential source of social influence.

Three functions of the adolescent peer culture were discussed. These were the support and maintenance of cultural values, the development of affectionate ties with age-mates outside the adolescent's kinship group, and opportunities to develop competence and autonomy in a context not dominated by adults. Many societies tend to structure specific peer experiences that will exercise these functions. In our own culture, the diversity of adolescent peer groups reflects the diversity of the ethnic and socioeconomic groupings that exist in adult life. Although our culture has less control over adolescent peer groups than is observed in the Russian or the Samoan examples, the peer group perform many of the same functions for the exercise of behavioral autonomy, the development of affectionate ties to age-mates, and the pressure toward value conformity.

# REFERENCES

Adams, B. N.   *The family: A sociological interpretation* (2d ed.). Chicago: Rand McNally, 1975.

Barnouw, V.   *An introduction to anthropology, vol. 2: Ethnology, rev. ed.* Homewood, Ill.: Dorsey Press, 1975.

Benedict, R.   Continuities and discontinuities in cultural conditioning. *Psychiatry,* 1938, *1,* 161–167.

Ben-Yaakov, Y.   Methods of kibbutz collective education during early childhood. In J. Marcus (Ed.), *Growing up in groups: Two manuals on early child care.* New York: Gordon and Breach, 1972. Pp. 197–295.

Bettelheim, B.   *The children of the dream.* New York: Macmillan, 1969.

Blos, P.   *On adolescence: A psychoanalytic interpretation.* New York: Free Press, 1962.

Brim, O. G., Jr.   Socialization through the life cycle. In O. G. Brim, Jr., and S. Wheeler, *Socialization after childhood.* New York: Wiley, 1966.

Bronfenbrenner, U.   Response to pressure from peers versus adults among Soviet and American school children. In U. Bronfenbrenner (Chariman), *Social factors in the development of personality.* Symposium 35 presented at the 18th International Congress of Psychology, Moscow, August 1966. Pp. 7–18.

Bronfenbrenner, U.   *Two worlds of childhood: U.S. and U.S.S.R.* New York: Russell Sage Foundation, 1970.

Brown, J. K.   A cross-cultural study of female initiation rites. *American Anthropologist,* 1963, *65,* 837–853.

Brown, J. K.   Female initiation rites: A review of the current literature. In D. Rogers (Ed.), *Issues in adolescent psychology.* New York: Appleton-Century-Crofts, 1969. Pp. 74–86.

Brown, J. K.   Adolescent initiation rites: Recent interpretations. In R. E. Grinder (Ed.), *Studies in adolescence* (3d ed.). New York: Macmillan, 1975. Pp. 40–51.

Burton, R. V., and Whiting, J. W. M.   The absent father and cross-sex identity. *Merrill-Palmer Quarterly,* 1961, *7,* 85–95.

Darwin, C.   *On the origin of species by means of natural selection.* London: J. Murray, 1859.

Davison, P., and Davison, J.   Coming of age in America. *New York Times Magazine,* March, 9, 1975.

deBeer, G.   Evolution. *Macropaedia,* vol. 7, *The New Encyclopaedia Britannica.* Chicago: Encyclopaedia Britannica, Inc., 1974. Pp. 7–23.

Devereux, E. C., Shouval, R., Bronfenbrenner, U., Rodgers, R. R., Kav-Venaki, S., Keely, E., and Karson, E.   Socialization practices of parents, teachers, and peers in Israel: the kibbutz versus the city. *Child Development,* 1974, *45,* 269–281.

Douvan, E., and Adelson, J.   *The adolescent experience.* New York: Wiley, 1966.

Douvan, E., and Gold, M.   Modal patterns in American adolescence. In M. L. Hoffman and L. W. Hoffman (Eds.), *Review of child development research,* vol. 2. New York: Russell Sage Foundation, 1966.

Elwin, V.   *The Muria and their Ghotul.* Bombay: Oxford University Press, 1947.

Feldman, H., and Feldman, M.   Personal communication, 1977.

Freeman, L. C.   Marriage without love: Mate selection in non-Western societies. In R. F. Winch (Ed.), *Mate selection.* New York: Harper and Row, 1958. Pp. 20–39.

Freud, A. *Normality and pathology in childhood: Assessments of development.* New York: International Universities Press, 1965.

Gillis, J. R. *Youth and history.* New York: Academic Press, 1974.

Gold, M., and Douvan, E. *Adolescent development: Readings in research and theory.* Boston: Allyn and Bacon, 1969.

Huxley, J. *The uniqueness of man.* London: Chatto and Windus, 1941.

Huxley, J. *Evolution: The magic synthesis.* New York: Harper and Brothers, 1942.

Jacobs, M. *Pattern in cultural anthropology.* Homewood, Ill.: Dorsey Press, 1964.

Long, B. H., Henderson, E. H., and Platt, L. Self-other orientations of Israeli adolescents reared in kibbutzim and moshavim. *Developmental Psychology,* 1973, *8,* 300–308.

Mead, M. *Coming of age in Samoa,* New York: William Morrow, 1928.

Mead, M. *From the South Seas: Studies of adolescence and sex in primitive societies.* New York: William Morrow, 1939.

Mead, M. *Male and female: A study of the sexes in a changing world.* New York: William Morrow; New York: Mentor Books, 1949, 1955.

Mead, M., and Newton, N. Cultural patterning of perinatal behavior. In S. A. Richardson and A. F. Guttmacher (Eds.), *Childbearing—Its social and psychological aspects.* Baltimore: Williams and Wilkin, 1967. Pp. 142–244.

Munroe, R. L., and Munroe, R. H. Psychological interpretation of male initiation rites: The case of male pregnancy symptoms. *Ethos,* 1973, *1,* 490–498.

Munroe, R. L., and Munroe, R. H. *Cross-cultural human development.* Monterey, Calif.: Brooks/Cole, 1975.

Murdock, G. P. *Our primitive contemporaries.* New York: Macmillan, 1934.

Murdock, G. P. World ethnographic sample. *American Anthropologist,* 1957, *59.*

Muuss, R. E. Puberty rites in primitive and modern societies. *Adolescence,* 1970, *5,* 109–128.

Petrullo, V. The Yaruros of the Canpanaparo River, Venezuela. Smithsonian Institution, Bureau of American Ethnology, *bulletin 123.* Anthropological Papers, no. 11, 1938, pp. 161–290.

Richards, A. I. *Chisungu: A girl's initiation ceremony among the Bemba of Northern Rhodesia.* New York: Grove Press, 1956.

Schauss, H. *The lifetime of a Jew: Throughout the ages of Jewish history.* New York: Union of American Hebrew Congregations, 1950.

Sidel, R. *Women and child care in China.* Baltimore: Penguin Books, 1972.

Spencer, B., and Gillen, F. J. *The Arunta: A study of a Stone Age people.* Atlantic Highlands, N.J.: Humanities Press, 1966. (Originally published in 1927.)

Spiro, M. E. Is the family universal? *American Anthropologist,* 1954, *56,* 840–846.

Spiro, M. E. *Children of the kibbutz.* New York: Schocken Books, 1965.

Spiro, M. E. Addendum, 1958, to Is the family universal?—The Israeli case. In N. Bell and E. Vogel (Eds.), *A modern introduction to the family.* New York: Free Press, 1968.

Spiro, M. E. *Kibbutz: Venture in Utopia.* New York: Schocken Books, 1970.

Stephens, W. N.   *The family in cross-cultural perspective.* New York: Holt, Rinehart and Winston, 1963.

Turner, V.   Betwixt and between: The liminal period in *Rites de passage.* In J. Helm (Ed.), *Symposium on New Approaches to the Study of Religion.* Proceedings of 1964 spring annual meeting of the American Ethnological Society. Seattle: University of Washington Press, 1964. Pp. 4–20.

Turner, V.   Colour classification in Ndemba ritual. In M. Banton (Ed.), *Anthropological approaches to the study of religion.* London: Tavistock Publications, 1966. Pp. 47–84.

Turner, V.   *Mulcanda:* The rite of circumcision. In V. Turner (Ed.), *The forest of symbols.* Ithaca, N.Y.: Cornell University Press, 1967. Pp. 151–279.

U.S. Department of Commerce, Bureau of the Census. Marital status and living arrangements, March 1975. *Current Population Reports,* series P–20, no. 287. Washington, D.C.: U.S. Government Printing Office, 1975.

van Gennep, A.   *Les rites de passage.* Paris: Libraire Critique Émile Nourry, 1909. (English translation by Monika B. Vizedon and Gabrielle Caffee. Chicago: University of Chicago Press, 1960.)

Whiting, J. W. M., Kluckhohn, R., and Anthony, A.   The function of male initiation ceremonies at puberty. In E. E. Maccoby, T. M. Newcomb, and E. L. Hartley (Eds.), *Readings in Social Psychology.* New York: Henry Holt, 1958. Pp. 359–370.

Wilson, M.   *Good company: A study of Nyakyusa age-villages.* London: Oxford University Press, 1951.

Charles Gatewood/Magnum

*Research provides the building blocks of new knowledge.*

**3**

# Research Methods for the Study of Adolescence

In the preceding chapters, we have raised many questions about development during the adolescent years. Each of the theoretical orientations toward adolescence suggests that certain experiences are characteristic of the adolescent period. Anna Freud (1965, 1969) believes that there is anxiety about heightened impulses during adolescence. Orville Brim (1966) has suggested that adolescence is a time when young people experience multiple and conflicting expectations about role performances. Kurt Lewin (1939) has likened the adolescent to a marginal man, straddling two important and well-defined role groups but feeling uncomfortable and unaccepted in both. How accurate are any of these views? Do these descriptions apply equally to males and females, to early and late adolescents, or to adolescents of all socioeconomic groups? A scientific understanding of adolescent development goes beyond theory. It goes beyond case observations and ethnographic description. As with all other areas of psychological investigation, we rely on a variety of carefully collected empirical observations in order to evaluate current theories and to generate better ones.

The purpose of this chapter is to discuss the research methods that have been used to study adolescent development. We are concerned with three general areas of questions. First, who is being studied? What are the strategies for sample selection? How can we know whether the sample involved in a study is an accurate representation of adolescents as a whole? Second, how are adolescents studied? What methods are available for collecting data, and what are the kinds of problems for which each method is best suited? Third, what are some of the unique issues associated with doing research with an adolescent population? What have we learned about the adolescent's willingness to participate in research? What are the advantages or disadvantages of the various methods for work with the adolescent age group? In this chapter, we will alert the reader to the importance of understanding research design and research methods in interpreting the results of studies about adolescents. Go cautiously; ask questions; be aware of the limitations of every study. This is not to say that research is unimportant because it is imperfect. Quite the contrary—every study should help us to formulate our concepts more precisely and to appreciate the complexity of our task. In psychological research, no single study is going to provide a definitive answer to a complex psychological question. We require validation in other studies with similar results and in replications of a particular study under similar conditions with a new sample. Researchers in the field of adolescent development have a broad range of interests. There are few lines of adolescent research that have been pursued in a systematic way. Replication and corroboration of existing findings will be the task of researchers in the second hundred years of the study of adolescence.

## SAMPLE SELECTION

It may seem obvious that in order to do research on adolescent development, one must make observations of people during their adolescent years. Just because a study uses adolescent-aged subjects, however, does not mean that the findings are applicable to all adolescents. The problem of sampling is as much with us in the study of adolescence as in all areas of psychological research. If we dip into the universe of people who are adolescents and pull out tenth graders from a high school in a suburb of Chicago, how well do they represent adolescents from other communities, from other age groups, from other cultural groups, or from other historical periods? If we expect adolescent experiences to be heavily influenced by cultural expectations, family resources, and community opportunities, then it would make sense that these and other variables will contribute to the pattern of responses that are observed in studies of adolescent subjects. Although it is possible to make an evaluation about how likely it is that the responses of a sample are characteristic of a larger population of similar subjects (see Winer, 1971; Hays, 1973), it is important to acknowledge that the unique properties of a sample might limits its generalizability.

### Cross-Sectional Samples

The study of stability and change during adolescence can be evaluated by using two different research strategies, the cross-sectional and the longitudinal. In cross-sectional studies, several groups of subjects are studied at the same time. These groups often differ in chronological age, and the question that is raised is whether a specific characteristic changes or remains stable with age.

In order to understand the cross-sectional strategy of sampling, let us think about a hypothetical study of identity formation. Erikson (1950, 1959, 1968) theorized that during adolescence young people work to establish a sense of values and aspirations that have personal meaning and that will guide future choices. Personal identity is an integration of past identifications with contemporary roles and competences. Marcia and his co-workers have tried to operationalize the notion of identity status through the design of an interview which reveals the person's psychological work on value themes of work, sexuality, politics, and religion (Marcia, 1966; Marcia and Freedman, 1970; Orlofsky, Marcia, and Lesser, 1973). Four possible resolutions of the effort to achieve identity have been described that reflect the degree to which the person has experienced *crisis* in the evaluation of goals and values, and the extent to which the person has made a personal *commitment* to specific goals and values. Identity foreclosure, in which the person decides about work goals and personal aspirations early in adolescence without much opportunity for experimentation or questioning, is an identity status that provides commitment without crisis. Moratorium refers to a period of withdrawal from pressures toward commitment during which the person can engage in wide-ranging questioning and experimentation. Identity achievement involves a commitment to values and goals that follows experimentation and questioning. Finally, identity confusion refers to an inability to integrate many roles and aspirations into a consistent set of personal goals. This results in a chronic state of crisis with no promise of impending commitment.

An important question about identity would reflect the progress that young people make on identity resolution from the beginning to the end of adolescence. A cross-sectional approach to this question might involve sampling groups of subjects, young people going through puberty (age 12), juniors in high school (age 16), juniors in college (age 20), and young adults who have been out of college for two years (age 24). This sample would provide information about the identity status of young people who are at different points in their lives. One would expect more of the youngest subjects to respond in ways that give evidence of foreclosure or confusion and more of the oldest subjects to respond in ways that give evidence of achievement. The middle age groups would be expected to contain the greatest number of subjects experiencing moratorium. One might be able to infer from data of this kind the period during which most people experience identity achievement.

### Longitudinal Samples

In longitudinal studies, repeated observations are made of the same group of subjects at several points in time. In the example described above, a longitudinal study of identity status might involve interviewing the same subjects four times: at puberty, during the junior year of high school, during the junior year of college, and two years after graduation from college. Longitudinal studies permit us to follow the progress of individual subjects. We can say something about how many subjects experience identity foreclosure or identity confusion at each phase of adolescence. We can also say something about the fate of individuals who begin work on identity at puberty in a foreclosed status. In other words, the longitudinal sample offers evidence about the pattern of transition and change during the adolescent years. Marcia has observed some of his original subjects after six–seven years (Marcia, 1975). The results of this work will be discussed in Part III.

Longitudinal studies frequently take a long time to complete. In contrast to the cross-sectional design, which could be completed during one calendar year, the longitudinal study would require about 12 years for subjects to move from puberty to the final data collection two years after graduation from college. On the other hand, certain questions really cannot be answered without the longitudinal data. In our example of the process of identity formation, we could not know how long lasting identity foreclosure at the high school level is from a cross-sectional sample. Questions about the disruptive effects of role confusion or the beneficial consequences of moratorium can only be clarified with the longitudinal design.

## A Design Which Combines Cross-Sectional and Longitudinal Samples

A further elaboration of the notion of longitudinal research is the model of sequential sampling that combines the cross-sectional and longitudinal designs (Schaie, 1965; Baltes, 1968; Baltes and Nesselroade, 1970; Nesselroade and Baltes, 1974). In this strategy, groups of subjects who compose a cross-sectional sample at time 1 are retested at regular intervals until the youngest subjects reach the age of the oldest subjects in the original sample. Table 3–1 illustrates the sequential longitudinal design for our hypothetical study of identity achievement.

The cohort refers to the age period during which the subjects were born. In the sequential design, the first data collection (1978)

Table 3–1: A Sequential Longitudinal Design for the Study of Identity Formation

| Cohort | Puberty (age 12) | High School Junior (age 16) | College Junior (age 20) | 2 years past college (age 24) |
|---|---|---|---|---|
| 1978 | 1990 | 1994 | 1998 | 2002 |
| 1974 | 1986 | 1990 | 1994 | 1998 |
| 1970 | 1982 | 1986 | 1990 | 1994 |
| 1966 | 1978 | 1982 | 1986 | 1990 |
| 1962 | | 1978 | 1982 | 1986 |
| 1958 | | | 1978 | 1982 |
| 1954 | | | | 1978 |

Note: The entries are the dates of data collection.
Source: Model adapted from M. R. Nesselroade and P. B. Baltes, "Adolescent Personality Development and Historical Change: 1900–1972," *Monographs of the Society for Research in Child Development*, 1974, *39* (1, Serial No. 154).

produces a standard cross-sectional study with subjects from four different cohorts. At every subsequent four-year period, both cross-sectional and longitudinal data are produced. Each column provides comparative data on the same age period from different cohorts. Each row provides longitudinal data from a single cohort. Each diagonal from top left to bottom right provides a new cross-sectional analysis.

In this design, one can evaluate the power of generational or cohort experiences as well as the contribution of changes due to maturation. Let us say that the scandal of the Nixon Administration during 1974 and 1975 had a special impact on the adolescents in the 1958 cohort, who were college juniors during 1978. We might expect more of the subjects in this cohort to show identity foreclosure in an effort to resist the anxiety of experimenting with or challenging cultural values. A cross-sectional study which includes those subjects might give us the impression that college juniors are characterized by foreclosure. A longitudinal study of this cohort alone would be likely to suggest that the college years offer little encouragement for experimentation and personal questioning. The sequential longitudinal design gives us an opportunity to test whether differences among groups are due to maturation or to unique generational characteristics in the experiences of a specific cohort. Although our example is a simplification of the kinds of findings that might emerge from a sequential longitudinal study, it begins to demonstrate the potential power of this approach for the study of development.

## Demographic Variables

Not all research with adolescent subjects focuses on the process of change during adolescence. Often, studies are conducted to describe or evaluate the attitudes or behaviors of adolescents. Studies of adolescent drug use, the characteristics of high school dropouts, and adolescent rebelliousness are all examples of empirical efforts to understand some particular aspect of adolescent behavior. Whether adolescent research has a developmental focus or emphasizes particular behaviors, it is important to ask about the characteristics of the adolescent population that has been sampled. Research with one adolescent sample may not be applicable to adolescents of other subcultures or socioeconomic groups. For example, Lippitt and Gold (1959) reported that students in a middle-class community liked peers who were friendly, supportive, and helpful. Pope (1953) found that students from a lower-class school district liked and admired peers who were aggressive and rebellious. The norms for peer acceptance and the models for peer identification were different in the two communities. This comparison serves to warn us that the applicability of research findings is limited by the nature of the sample included in the study. Among the characteristics of adolescent populations that are likely to make a difference in the response of subjects are the subjects' sex, physical maturation, race, religion, socioeconomic status, community (urban, suburban, or rural), years of schooling, and the historical context of the subjects' cohort. Any of these variables could reasonably influence the pattern of responses of a particular adolescent group in many areas, including intellectual performance, social behavior, values and aspirations, or self-concept. In reading research about adolescents, it is important to ask yourself, "Who are these subjects?" Subjects do not necessarily provide an accurate representation of the universe of adolescents just because they are a certain chronological age.

## Sample Size

The problem of determining the degree to which a sample of adolescents represents the universe of adolescents is closely related to decisions about sample size. Every kind of research project must set some limits on the number of subjects who will be included. It is certainly not the case that a large sample is needed in order to make meaningful observations about a particular phenomenon. One must weigh the advantages and disadvantages of working with a sample of a particular size in deciding how many subjects to include. Given some limit in time, energy, and financial resources, one can choose to study one or a few subjects in great depth or to work with larger groups at a less intense level.

Three studies of formal operational thought illustrate three researchers' orientations to the problem of sample size. Martorano (1977) selected 20 female subjects at grades 6, 8, 10, and 12 who were tested individually for two one-hour sessions. From this cross-sectional comparison, she suggested that the transition from concrete to formal thought occurs between the eighth and tenth grades. Neimark (1975) selected three cohorts from grades three–six and a control group from grades four–six. The sample included 44 males and 40 females in the longitudinal cohorts, and 28 males and 24 females in the control group. All of the testing was done individually in sessions that lasted about 50 minutes. Cohort 1 was tested nine times during a four-year period. Cohort 2 was tested six times in three years. Cohort 3 was tested seven times in three years. The control group was tested once. Neimark concluded from the longitudinal analysis that subjects move from the concrete operational to the formal operational problem-solving strategy "in a stepwise fashion through temporary transitional phases."

The third study of formal thought was conducted in British middle and secondary schools (Shayer, Kuchemann, and Wylam, 1976). Ten thousand subjects between the ages of 8 and 14 were tested on tasks of concrete and formal operational thought. Written tests were administered to groups. In this large survey of British youth, 20 percent of the sample were reported to have achieved formal operational thought. This finding is quite compatible with Martorano's smaller, cross-sectional study in that Martorano does not identify the transition to formal thought until after the eighth grade, or approximately age 13. Thus, according to her findings only the oldest subjects in the British sample would be expected to demonstrate formal thought. Neither the British study nor Martorano's study can discuss the changing strategies used by individual subjects as they move from one level of problem solving to another.

The question of sample selection and sample size is a complex matter. It is related to the nature of the problem under investigation, the talents of the researcher, and the limits of statistical inference associated with various sampling strategies (Kish, 1965). Erik Erikson (1958) provided a powerful example of the process of identity achievement through his psychohistorical case study *Young Man Luther.* The case study of individual lives continues to serve as an important strategy for understanding the complexity of psychological, social, and cultural forces in human growth (White, 1966, 1976; White, Riggs, and Gilbert, 1976; Goethals and Klos, 1976; Newman and Newman, 1976). On the other hand, surveys of large, representative samples also make important contributions to the study of adolescent development. Johnston's (1973) evaluation of adolescent drug use and Luchterhand and Weller's (1976) survey of patterns of aggression among lower-class youth are examples of studies in which large samples of adolescents can clarify for social scientists as well as concerned citizens just how adolescents might behave in a variety of situations.

## The Embeddedness of the Adolescent Sample in a Larger Community

One source of influence on all human subjects is the social context in which they behave. Research with adolescent subjects is particularly vulnerable to the power of the social context to modify young people's responses. Two social contexts that are often included but not controlled in adolescent research are the school and the community. Barker and Gump (1964) have demonstrated that students in small schools are more likely to be involved in a variety of school activities and settings, whereas students in large schools are more likely to be "specialists." They have also observed that students in small schools are more likely to feel a greater sense of responsibility for their own behavior and for the school, whereas students in large schools tend to feel more anonymous. These kinds of context differences are quite likely to influence the pattern of adolescents' responses on a number of psychological variables. Let us say that we decide to do a survey of adolescents' attitudes about vandalism in the community. We might expect the "big school–small school factor" to be an intervening variable that would influence an adolescent's sense of personal responsibility. If we do not control for this dimension, or as is likelier, if we do not have any data about school size for the respondents, we would not be able to evaluate the impact of the school context on patterns of responsibility.

Other context variables of school samples include academic tracks within schools, membership in specific peer groups, and attendance at senior high schools, junior high schools, middle schools, or elementary schools. Each of these variables may influence the status of adolescents, the kinds of expectations others hold for their behavior, and the aspirations adolescents have for their future. Rarely are these context variables included in a description of the sample, nor do we have much systematic evidence about how these variables influence responses.

The community itself offers an additional set of context effects. For example, communities differ in the extent to which they offer adolescents access to a variety of settings (Barker, 1968; Barker and Schoggen, 1973). Communities also differ in their dominant political attitudes, in the conservatism or liberalism of their views about sexuality, and in the orientation of adults toward the high schools or colleges that are within their boundaries. When we sample the attitudes of the adolescent members of a community we often do not know whether or not their views are different from those of the adult population. Thus, what we may wish to interpret as the opinions of adolescents may in fact be a reflection of the beliefs or attitudes of the larger social community.

## METHODS OF STUDY

A variety of methods have been used to study adolescent development. Each method has strengths and weaknesses insofar as it allows the investigator to focus on some set of behaviors at the expense of others. The choice of method is central to the success of any empirical study. Both the investigator and the subjects must be comfortable with the mode of data collection. The method must fit the problem, taking in a sufficiently wide range of observations to answer the questions under study and at the same time providing selectivity, so that not every thought and behavior is included.

The method must also fit the subjects. Tasks must be designed to maintain interest. Questions must be posed so that they fit the vocabulary and reading level of subjects. Designing questions and tasks for adolescent subjects requires some special attention and talent. The materials must be designed in such a way that they do not appear condescending or childish. On the other hand, they cannot be so complex or abstract that they are beyond the subject's comprehension. Four methods of research that have been used with adolescents are discussed in the following sections: survey research, laboratory experimentation, naturalistic observation, and field experiments.

## Survey Research

Survey methods are generally used to collect information about attitudes (How important is it to you to participate in family decision making?), about current practices (How many hours per week do you spend talking on the telephone?), about aspirations (What would you like to do when you graduate from high school?), and about perceptions (Who understands your problems best? [Check one] your mother, your father, your teacher, your friends). In successful surveys, the questions are asked clearly and the response choices do not overlap. The sample responding to the survey is carefully selected to be representative of the population under study (Nunnally, 1967). If the survey is only completed by volunteers or if a large number of respondents do not return the survey, the applicability of the findings is less certain. Surveys may be done by mail, in large classroom groups, over the telephone, or door to door. The questions must be asked in a standard form, and the responses are usually categorized according to a prearranged set of codes or choices (Chun, Cobb, and French, 1975; Robinson and Shaver, 1973).

The *Youth in Transition* study is an example of a six-year longitudinal study of adolescent boys in which the survey research methodology was used (Bachman et al., 1967; Davidson, 1972). The sample included approximately 2,200 tenth-grade boys from public schools in the United States. A single high school was selected from each of 88 geographic areas. Within each school, 30 tenth-grade boys were randomly selected for the study. This design produced clusters of boys within specific school environments, thus permitting an analysis of the effects of different school settings on boys of similar age. An additional group of ten "outstanding" schools was added to the sample in order to provide some contrast to the typical pattern. These schools were included as a way of illustrating the potential contributions of exceptional environments.

Four kinds of data were collected from this sample: (1) interviews, (2) group ability tests, (3) self-administered questionnaires, and (4) measurements of the school environments. Data were collected from the boys three times, during 1966, 1968, and 1969. Data about the school environments were collected only once, at the beginning of the project. This vast pool of data from a carefully selected group of subjects has been used to study a wide variety of topics. It has been the basis for analyses of such specific subjects as adolescent drug use (Johnston, 1973), adolescent attitudes and behavior relating to military service (Johnston and Bachman, 1972), and the characteristics of boys who drop out of high school as compared to those who remain until graduation (Bachman, Green, and Wirtanen, 1972). In addition, methodological studies about the study of change (Davidson, 1972) and theory building about the relationship of family variables to intelligence, personality, and personal aspirations during adolescence (Bachman, 1970) have been generated from this survey.

The advantages of the survey method include the ability to include large numbers of subjects, the wide variety of topics that can be studied, and the prearranged codification of the responses. There are also several disadvantages. Some subjects respond flippantly to the questions, making check marks on all the middle boxes or checking extreme responses to every third question. Surveys may create attitudes where they did not already exist. For example, if a survey asks about a student's views on the curriculum in the school, the student may check certain responses without having thought much about the problem before. In other words, the researcher often does not know how important or salient the questions being asked really are to the respondents. Finally, there is the problem of making inferences about behavior from survey responses (Thornburg, 1973; Albrecht, 1977). For example, a sample of adolescents was asked the following question: "If a family of a different race with about the same income and education as you moved next door to you, how would you feel about it?" Nine percent said that they would mind it a lot; 28 percent that they would mind a little; and 62 percent that they would not mind at all (Bachman and van Duinen, 1971). These data suggest a fairly high degree of openness toward racially mixed communities. However, what proportion of students would choose to live in a racially mixed neighborhood cannot be determined from the results of the survey.

## Laboratory Experimentation

Experimentation is the method of research which psychology has borrowed most directly from the physical sciences. It is a method intended to clarify the causal relationships among variables. In an experiment, some variable or group of variables is systematically manipulated while others are held constant. Any change in the subjects' responses or reactions are attributed to the manipulation (Rosenthal and Rosnow, 1975; Wuebben, Straits, and Schulman, 1974).

Control is the key to successful experimentation. Control must be exercised in selecting subjects to participate in a study. This means that the subjects must be able to bring equivalent competences to the situation. If this assumption is not met, then multiple groups of subjects must be used who vary systematically with regard to the competences required. Control must be used in presenting the task to the subjects so that such things as the instructions, the order of presentation, and the setting where the study is conducted do not interfere with the responses under study. Finally, control is required in comparing the behavior of the subjects after an experimental manipulation either to their own behavior prior to the manipulation or to the behavior of another group of subjects who did not experience the manipulation. (The latter are referred to as the control group.) The use of these controls permits the experimenter to draw conclusions about the impact of a specific manipulation on the behavior of the subjects. Without these controls, the effects of the manipulation are difficult to evaluate.

In one experimental study, the relationship of identity status to conformity behavior was evaluated for female college-age students (Toder and Marcia, 1973). Identity status was assessed by using Marcia's (1966) interview in areas of occupation, religion, politics, and sexual attitudes. Subjects were sampled at random from the junior and senior female students in the college directory of a large state university and from two large lecture classes containing freshmen and sophomores. Sixteen subjects at each of four identity status levels were selected for the study. The experimental procedure involved a situation in which subjects were asked to judge the length of a line in the presence of three other people who were confederates of the experimenter (Asch, 1951, 1956). These confederates were dressed in either "hippie" or "straight" clothing. Subjects were randomly assigned to the hippie or straight group. During the experimental procedure each "subject" was asked to judge which of three lines on a card at the right was identical in length to the standard line on a card on the left. Each of the confederates responded incorrectly on 12 of the 18 trials. Conformity was measured by the number of trials out of 12 in which the real subjects gave an incorrect answer about the length of the line. Of the 64 subjects, 36 gave either conforming responses or one conforming response. In a comparison of the four levels of identity status, identity achievement subjects conformed least often, foreclosure and moratorium subjects were intermediate, and identity diffusion subjects conformed most often. There was no difference in conformity among subjects who were in the hippie or straight conditions. In this experimental situation, women who had a stable identity were less likely to depend on peer judgments than were women who had persistent uncertainty or anxiety about their identity.

The experimental method has the advantage of providing conclusions about causal relationships. If we think that the subject's behavior will only change if one of the independent variables is varied or manipulated, then we can conclude that the variation or manipulation caused the change in behavior. In the experimental study of identity status and conformity behavior, the two independent variables were identity status and the presence of hippie or straight confederates during the experimental situation. The dependent variable was the number of conforming responses. The hypothesis that stable identity status will reduce peer conformity was confirmed. The hypothesis that subjects would conform more when in the presence of a similar (straight or hippie) reference group was not confirmed.

The experimental method also has some limitations. First, we cannot be certain that the laboratory situation is applicable to the "real world." In the study described above, for example, the conforming behavior consisted of a perceptual judgment about the length of a line. How similar is that kind of decision to real situations in which pressures toward peer conformity involve moral judgments about social behavior?

Second, in the study of development we are moving away from a search for unidirectional, causal relationships (personal identity → resistance to peer pressure) toward an appreciation of the continuous feedback among participants in an interaction (Riegel, 1976; Ainsworth, Bell, and Stayton, 1974; Lewis and Rosenblum, 1974; Bronfenbrenner, 1974a, 1974b). We need to understand the pressures toward conformity and toward individuality as elements that exist side by side in peer group interactions. One may be likely to conform because of uncertainty about one's own position or because of uncertainty about the acceptance or trustworthiness of other members of the group.

Finally, the experimental situation frequently takes away from the subject the meaningful cues that commonly guide behavior and replaces them with ambiguity or uncertainty. Under those conditions, adolescents may respond with more suspicion or with greater dependence on the experimenter's expectations than they might in a familiar situation (Orne, 1962).

### Naturalistic Observation

Perhaps the oldest form of studying children has been direct observation. Parents' diaries and observation logs have provided rich insights into the patterns of behavior during infancy and childhood (Kessen, 1965). Observational research may be highly structured or very open ended (Cohen and Stern, 1970). At the structured

*Jean-Claude Lejeune*

*Activities at a playground provide a basis for observational research.*

end of the continuum, we have studies that use carefully constructed coding systems and multiple forms of observation, including human coders, videotape, and teacher's observation logs, to characterize patterns of behavior. In an analysis of children's use of three kinds of playground settings, three measures were used. Observers recorded all the behaviors that took place in a specific location. They also observed specific children, the time they spent at each activity, and the kinds of activities that they participated in. As the children left the park, they were interviewed about their use of the playground, where they liked to play, and how often they came to the particular park at which they were observed (Hayward, Rothenberg, and Beasley, 1974). On the other hand, we have observational data from studies of language use in which all the verbal behavior of a subject is recorded and analyzed for patterns of grammar, phonetics, and meaning (Labov, 1972).

Careful observation remains a basic tool in the study of development. Ethological psychologists (Jones, 1972; Richards, 1974) argue that careful, objective observation of behavior without biasing assumptions about its meaning is the most accurate way to understand the function of activities and relationships. Controlled observation in natural settings is the key to documenting the reciprocal influence of persons and settings (Proshansky, 1976; Moos, 1974; Brandt, 1972). The need to describe behavior as it occurs in specific environments and to compare the quality of interactions among participants in various settings will most likely occupy the energies of many developmental psychologists for the next decade.

Systematic observation is somewhat more difficult than might be expected. Take a partner and go to a restaurant. Begin watching in a specific location for five minutes, and write down everything you see. Afterward, compare your notes. Most likely, you and your partner will not have noted exactly the same events, especially if you were watching more than two people. Furthermore, you will not always agree about the meaning of a behavior. A gesture that you may have described as a friendly pat, your partner may have described as hitting. Finially, if you were watching the events with a focus on one person whom you defined as the "main subject" and your partner was watching with an eye on another person as the "main subject," your records may be quite discrepant. The strength of observation is its ability to capture naturally occurring responses as they take place. The weaknesses include a difficulty in establishing agreement among observers (observer reliability) and the problem of being overwhelmed by the vast array of possible events to record. The latter problem can be resolved by means of a carefully defined coding scheme. Ideally, the coding scheme is based on a theory of what events are important and on frequent observations of events similar to those under study. Armed with a limited set of meaningful categories of behavior, observational research can succeed in preserving the authenticity of behavior and in clarifying many of the dynamics of interaction (Lindberg and Swedlow, 1976; Cartwright and Cartwright, 1974; Weick, 1968).

## Field Experiments

A fourth method that has been used in the study of adolescence is the field experiment. The field experiment differs from naturalistic observation in that the experimenter makes some specific manipulation or creates some unique circumstances that would not occur in the natural flow of events. The field experiment differs from the laboratory experiment in that it makes use of naturally occurring groups or settings as a context for observation (Swingle, 1973).

One of the most well known field experiments with adolescent subjects is the Sherifs' work on in-group and out-group relations (Sherif and Sherif, 1969). The research was carried out with 11- and 12-year-old boys who were attending a three-week summer camp. Three manipulations were planned to study the pattern of group formation, the emergence of intergroup conflict, and the resolution of that conflict. After the boys started camp and began to choose friends, they were split into two groups in such a way that most of the best friends were in different groups. For about a week, these two groups participated in camping activities and had little contact with each other. By the end of the week, the members of the new groups showed preference for one another and had abandoned their earlier friendship choices. The boys began to develop a unique identity for their group, giving it a name and establishing norms for group behavior.

The second manipulation was a tournament at the end of the first week in which intergroup competition was fostered. After the tournament, the camp leaders increased intergroup hostility by having a party at which one group arrived early and ate all the best snacks before the second group came. These competitive and frustrating experiences led to a week of pranks, name-calling, and stereotyping of the other group.

Finally, during the last week, the camp leaders devised a series of situations that required cooperation between the groups. These situations, such as pooling funds to go to the movies or looking for a problem in the water supply line, reduced group conflict and increased friendly interactions among the members of the two groups. Over the three weeks, experimental manipulations served to heighten in-group commitments, to generate intergroup hostilities, and eventually to modify those intergroup attitudes in the direction of greater intergroup friendliness and acceptance.

The advantage of the field experiment is the confidence it gives one about the authenticity of the behavior that is being observed. The shared meaning of the situation, the norms for behavior, and the presence of other participants all contribute to a sense that the subjects are acting much as they would in the absence of the observer. On the other hand, the field experiment is more difficult to control than the laboratory experiment, and field data collection requires more finesse than does data collection in the laboratory. The experimenter must be able to make observations or to collect data without interfering with the normal flow of events or detracting from the confidence of the subjects. The experimental manipulation must be powerful enough to evoke some response and yet appropri-

Bruce Davidson/Magnum

*A study of group behavior involved field experiments with boys who were attending summer camp.*

ate to the context in which it occurs. If the experimental manipulation radically changes the setting, then the purpose of a field experiment may be defeated.

The four general methods—survey research, laboratory experimentation, naturalistic observation, and the field experiment—are not mutually exclusive. Table 3–2 compares the strengths and limitations of each method. One can design studies that make use of

Table 3–2: A comparison of Four Methods for the Study of Adolescence

|  | Strengths | Limitations |
|---|---|---|
| Survey research | Ability to include a large sample | Subjects may not respond seriously |
|  | Wide variety of topics can be covered | Questions may create attitudes that did not exist |
|  | Prearranged codification | Hard to make inferences about behavior from survey responses |
| Laboratory experimentation | The control in this design permits conclusions about causal relationships | Cannot be sure about the applicability of laboratory situation to the "real world" |
|  |  | Does not incorporate the reciprocal quality of many interactions |
|  |  | Takes away meaningful cues that would normally guide behavior |
| Naturalistic observation | Allows observation of the natural stream of behavior | Difficult to achieve coder reliability |
|  |  | Observer may be overwhelmed by data |
|  |  | Observer's presence may disrupt the setting |
| Field experiment | Uses naturally occurring settings as a context for observation | Difficult to control |
|  |  | Data collection must be unobtrusive |
|  | Sense of authenticity about the observed behavior | Experimental manipulation may disrupt the setting |

several methods, or one can develop a series of studies that begin with observation, test out some specific hypotheses through experimentation, and then apply the findings to larger populations through a survey approach. The methods are not confined to any particular setting. Cross-cultural research can be done with any of the methods. Both experimentation and observation can occur in the laboratory or in the field. Studies of interventions such the Peace Corps or the Job Corps or of naturally occurring crises such as parental separation provide opportunities to create an experimental design from real-world events (Cook and Campbell, 1974). It is not the case that observation is real and experimentation artificial. Any of these methods can be authentic or clumsy, depending on how well they are executed.

## GENERAL RESEARCH ISSUES

The strategies of sample selection and the methods of research described above could well apply to the study of any age group or to any of a wide variety of psychological topics. We have emphasized some of the specific uses of these research techniques for the study of adolescent development as a way of heightening your appreciation of the empirical basis on which general statements about adolescent behavior are made. In this section we consider some of the unique properties of adolescents that might influence their performance as subjects in research. These qualities will be discussed in more detail in later chapters. However, they are not always taken into consideration in the planning or the execution of empirical work. At the end of the chapter, we will describe two studies that have made use of multiple strategies of sampling and multiple methods in order to characterize the diverse qualities of their adolescent subject populations.

## Some Unique Properties of Adolescents as Subjects in Research

If you go to an eighth-grade classroom and look at the boys in the class, you will recognize the first special quality of adolescent subjects. Chronological age and biological age diverge at adolescence. The pattern of growth during puberty (which will be discussed further in Chapter 4) leads to wide differences in physical maturity and sexual development among an age cohort. These differences are increased when one considers that most of the females in the eighth-grade group began to experience physical changes during the sixth and seventh grades. Chronological age groupings in the early years of adolescence include children who are at quite different points in their physical maturation.

A related point is that young adolescents are self-conscious and somewhat uncomfortable about heterosexual encounters. In a study of interpersonal skills, fictional stories were presented to subjects who were asked to answer a series of questions about each story. One of the stories involved a situation in which a girl, Nancy, asked a boy, Bob, to a party. Listening to this situation started a chain reaction of "oohs," "aahs," and giggles among members of an eighth-grade class as they turned to the "Nancy" and "Bob" in their own group to see whether they were blushing. The students' joking comments about why Nancy did not invite others to her party or about what Bob saw in Nancy anyway made it questionable whether the students were paying any attention to the task that the researcher had in mind. Although this behavior was unmistakable among 8th-grade subjects, it was not observed in the 6th or 12th grades (Newman, 1978).

A third characteristic of adolescent subjects is the variability in their competences. We do not design studies, for example, for kindergarten-age children that include material for the children to read because we do not assume that kind of competence among most five-year-olds. Many studies with adolescents ask the subjects to respond to written material. Yet the reading skills of high school students may vary from the third- or fourth-grade level to the college level. In a group situation, it is difficult to get students to indicate when they do not understand a question or problem in its written form. It may be more embarrassing for an adolescent to ask what a phrase means than to move quietly on to the next question or to check a box at random. Adolescents are characterized by a wide range of competence in many skill areas. Some individuals will demonstrate adult or near-adult competence, whereas an age-mate may demonstrate the ability of a child. The adolescent's need to mask areas of ability in which comparability with peers has not yet been attained and the need to avoid embarrassment in the eyes of peers or adults are special problems for researchers.

Adolescents tend to be more sensitive to the possibility of experimental manipulation than do infants or young children. They have grown wise to one-way mirrors, loudspeakers that are also listening devices, tape recorders, gimmicked lights on a control panel, and fake feedback. In one study of conformity and moral development, seventh-grade subjects were told that the lights on a console in front of them represented the judgments made by five other children in their group. In fact, the lights were manipulated by the experimenter in order to evoke conforming responses from the subjects. The experimenters make the following observation: "We will mention that some of our subjects, especially among boys, seemed suspicious of the experimental procedure and apparatus. The data of the three subjects (all boys) who were judged to have seriously doubted the genuineness of the group judgments were eliminated from the sample" (Saltzstein, Diamond, and Belenky, 1972).

College-age subjects also have some special characteristics that deserve consideration in planning or evaluating research. Many adolescents who participate in research during college are enrolled in psychology courses. This means that they are likely to be aware of some of the research methods that have been used in important and current areas of research. One could not expect a student who has had introductory psychology to be naive about the Asch-type conformity study described above. Reseach on achievement motivation, eating behavior, androgyny, sex role stereotyping and prejudice, to name just a few themes, is discussed in most introductory texts. In a study of these and many other familiar topics, one must evaluate whether or not one's subjects are providing authentic responses or responses that have been modified because of familiarity with the research method.

A closely related and even more pervasive question is the college context itself. Several issues are related to the study of a population of subjects who are enrolled in college. First, if one desires to study a representative sample of adolescents during the age period 18–22, it would be necessary to sample subjects who are not enrolled in college as well as subjects who are. We would expect certain differences among college and noncollege populations in intelligence, information, work experience, career aspirations, and previous school experiences, all of which might influence responses in a psychological study. We must remember that a college sample is not a random sample of all adolescents.

Furthermore, there is evidence that colleges differ in the impact they have on students (Thistlethwaite, 1959a, 1959b, 1960; Stern, 1962; Pace, 1963; Getzels, 1969; Astin, 1977; Newman and Newman, 1978). The characteristics of the college environment will be described in detail in Chapter 11. Here we will only point out that a random sample of subjects from one college cannot be assumed to be a representative group of college students. We must ask how much the results of studies in one college environment are a reflection of that specific community and how much they are a reflection of the developmental characteristics of the adolescents. Even in work with a noncollege population, the question of organizational context is relevant. Suppose that we did a study of value change among Vista volunteers or General Motors employees during the age period 18–22. We would need to identify the contribution that the work setting made to the subjects' value positions. We would expect that the reward structure, the kinds of skills necessary for the job, and the attitudes of employers, older workers, and the hiring personnel would all shape the value climate of a work setting. Once again, we must ask how much of what we observe is a reflection of the personal growth of an adolescent and how much is a reflection of the environmental context in which the adolescent is embedded.

The college experience itself makes an impact on students that is likely to alter their personal experience and to influence their behavior as research subjects. Freshmen, for example, are often deeply involved with the stresses and challenges of adapting to a new environment. They are experiencing interactions with a more varied group of peers in a new physical setting. They are working on more difficult academic tasks than they confronted in high school, and they may be experiencing more failure than they have experienced before. At the same time, freshmen are likely to be assuming certain responsibilities for their own life and personal care, making more day-to-day decisions, and feeling more uncertain about their competence than they did during the last years of high school. Although college freshmen might be an ideal group for studying adolescent coping skills and the impact of stress during adolescent development, they may be a less ideal group for documenting the achievements or developmental competences of 18- and 19-year-olds. In other words, the stress of the freshman year may temporarily interrupt the level of performance that freshman students are capable of achieving.

The college environment also tends to be a comparatively bounded system in which all participants are likely to be touched by the political, economic, or moral crises of a particular historical period. Since college-age students are a population that is likely to be experiencing value clarification and personal reevaluation, they may be particularly sensitive to the value issues that are raised during a specific era. We would expect each cohort of college students to be influenced by the issues or trends that are relevant during its college years. The college students of the 50s are perhaps more sensitive to the theme of communism among intellectuals, the violations of civil liberties involved in forcing employees to sign loyalty oaths, and the suspicious orientation of the cold war. The college students of the 60s may be more familiar with the issues of war, student rebellions, violent and nonviolent protests, racism, imperialism, and experimentation with hallucinogenic drugs. The college students of the 70s have been confronted with a growing interest in Eastern religions and in Eastern techniques of meditation, mind expansion, and mind control. The women's movement and its political, social, and personal implications have been a powerful force for change in all university settings. Finally, the decline in research funds and the threatened decline in college enrollments have forced a reorganization of colleges and a reallocation of resources that touches the student body. The students of the 70s probably viewed themselves as more valuable to the college and more actively engaged in college decision making than did the students of earlier cohorts. These generational differences warn us about the need for careful sample selection and cautious interpretation of research findings using college populations. The psychological impact of historical events on adolescents is a theme worthy of documentation in and of itself. However, it would be a mistake to use data that may be heavily influenced by the trends of their time as a guide to contemporary decisions or future planning without understanding their tie to a particular era (Lifton, 1974; Erikson, 1975).

The college population is likely to be highly transient. Most college students attend college elsewhere than in their hometown and plan to leave the college community after graduation. Studies that involve longitudinal sampling of the college sample are faced with a particularly difficult task. It is comparatively easy to keep track of a sample of young children many of whom remain in the same community during the years from birth through 15 or 16. However, if one begins with a college sample, one can be certain that after four years most of the subjects will disperse all across the country and that they may well move several more times before they settle into permanent residences. This means that longitudinal studies are more difficult. It also means that certain aspects of the college student's sense of community commitment or involvement are not yet fully developed. In this respect, the perspectives of college students about politics, ownership, education, or the functions of government may be quite different from those of adults.

Finally, we assume that all adolescents in the age range 18–22 are involved in private work on the formulation of a personal identity. (Erikson, 1950, 1959, 1968). Although the biological variation of early adolescence may have evened out during this later phase of adolescent development, the psychological variation has not. As we described above, there are at least four potential resolutions to the psychosocial crisis of personal identity versus role diffusion: achievement, foreclosure, confusion, and moratorium. Research on identity status tells us that these resolutions are associated with fundamental differences in ego strength, anxiety, moral outlook, and the capacity for intimacy. (Marcia, 1966, 1975; Marcia and Freedman, 1970; Orlofsky et al., 1973). Thus, a sample of chronologically similar adolescents will include subjects who vary on this powerful dimension of identity status. We need to understand this kind of variability as a meaningful dimension of growth during later adolescence rather than as another annoying source of error. In fact, if we selected to variables that we have identified as problems for the researcher, namely, the differences among colleges and the variations in the identity status of students, we could design a study to investigate the nature of person-environment interaction during the college years and to test whether college environments tend to have a greater impact on moratorium students than on identity-foreclosed or identity-achieved students (Newman and Newman, 1978).

## The Use of Multiple Methods in the Study of Adolescence

In this section we consider two studies, one with a focus on high school communities and the other with a focus on college classroom groups, that illustrate the use of varied research methods for the understanding of complex questions about adolescent behavior. The "Opinions of Youth" project was a longitudinal study of the adaptation of high school boys to their school environments. Preliminary work on this study began in 1966, and data analysis is still continuing. Over 30 researchers utilized tests, survey questionnaires, interviews, demographic data collection, naturalistic observation, and field experimentation to observe adolescents and their school environments (Kelly et al., 1971; Kelly, 1979).

Kelly (1969) began with a concern for coping preferences among adolescents in contrasting social environments. He identified social exploration, the desire to actively engage the social environment, as a personality variable that might guide the process of adaptation within a specific setting. The first phase of the research for Kelly and his co-workers involved designing a measure of social exploration that could be used to select subjects for the longitudinal sample and conducting preliminary demographic, experimental, and observational studies at the two schools which the subjects would eventually attend (Goldberg et al., 1967; Stillman, 1969; Kelly et al., 1971). During their eighth-grade year in junior high school, a sample of 20 high, 20 moderate, and 20 low explorers who would enter the same high school were selected in each of two communities. The study of adaptation to school involved the simultaneous use of diverse methods. Some efforts were directed at describing the perceptions of the school, the self-concepts, the attitudes, and the activities of the boys in the study. A self-report questionnaire was administered in the fall and in the spring of the school year during the students' three years of high school (Edwards, 1979). A subgroup of high, moderate, and low explorers were interviewed during their tenth-grade year. This interview was structured around the themes of exploration, identity, and personal competence (Gilmore, 1979). In an experimental study, the problem-solving strategies of high, moderate, and low explorers were evaluated in dyadic interactions between homogeneous pairs (two high explorers working together) or in mixed pairs (a low and a high explorer working together) (Jones, 1979). Finally, the interpersonal skills of high, moderate, and low explorers were described in an observational study of two discussion groups (B. Newman, 1979). Variables describing the boys' use of cognitive and affective interactive strategies as well as the nature of their interactions with the group leader have been evaluated (B. Newman, 1975).

Multiple methods were also used to assess the school environments. Initially, the two schools were selected because they differed in the dimension of stability versus change. School 1 was seen as a relatively changing environment, with a population exchange rate of 18.7 percent per year. School 2 was seen as a relatively stable environment with a population exchange rate of 8.0 percent per year (Goldberg et al., 1967; P. Newman, 1970, 1979; Rice and Marsh, 1979). Population exchange was determined by dividing the number of students who entered or left the school during the school year by the total student population. Other characteristics of the two schools were obtained from census data about the communities from which the schools drew their students; descriptive analyses of the school space; faculty reports about teaching experience, involvement in school events, expectations for student behavior, and perceptions of the influence structure at the schools; student ratings of school excellence; and student reports of school satisfaction, school involvement, and needs for school change (Rice and Marsh, 1979; P. Newman, 1979). In a survey of males and females at every grade level, P. Newman (1979) was able to characterize the patterns of interaction in various settings at each school, the students' perceptions of teacher involvement, and the characteristics of setting use. In an interview study of new students who arrived at the schools after tenth grade or in the middle of the school year, Fatke (1971) was able to identify the responsiveness of each school environment to newcomers. The variety of methods used to study adaptation permitted some converging views about the nature of the school environments as well as the characteristics of the coping strategies of adolescent boys. Both Edwards' self-report questionnaire and P. Newman's survey of the patterns of interaction across settings found more involvement and identification with the school in school 1 than in school 2. Fatke's study of new students found greater ambiguity about the process of acculturation at school 2. B. Newman's study of interpersonal behavior found greater use of the leader and more enthusiasm about the group situation at school 1 than at school 2. All of these findings combine to illustrate the qualitative difference in the social atmosphere of the two organizations. Similar converging data provided a sense of the boys' competences, their feelings of self-worth, the levels of social and problem-solving skills that they brought to the task of adaptation, and the ways in which they used their skills vis-à-vis the school setting. One particularly interesting pattern, for example, was that high explorers at school 1 found many opportunities to express their interest and initiative within the school. High explorers at school 2 were more reserved, less openly expressive, and more involved in deviant behavior than other groups or high explorers at school 1. There was some sense that the challenge of school 2 was to learn to redirect one's energy out of school events rather than to try to change the school. Because of their greater needs for interaction and activity, high explorers in school 2 may have experienced more repressive responses than they would have had they been students at school 1 (Kelly, 1979; Edwards and Kelly, 1977).

The second example of a research project which employed diverse methodology is a study of interpersonal behavior in the college classroom group (Mann et al., 1970). The subjects for the study were four introductory psychology teachers at a large midwestern university and the students enrolled in their sections during one semester. The study was designed to provide a detailed analysis of the affective life of the classroom group. The intent was to demonstrate the ways in which teachers' styles and students' orientations create an underlying set of meanings for and feelings toward the academic content of the classroom. The study also illustrates some of the ways in which this latent, affective content facilitates or inhibits work on meaningful intellectual themes in the classroom.

Six strategies were used to understand the classroom experiences of the students and teachers. Each class session was observed and tape-recorded. The tapes were later analyzed for the expression of emotional messages embedded in the interactions (Mann, Gifford, and Hartman, 1967). These data provided the core for an understanding of the patterns of affection, hostility, dependence, rebelliousness, guilt, and anxiety that were present during various phases of the groups' history. In order to validate the accuracy of the affective themes that were identified by scoring the tapes of class sessions, the teachers and students were interviewed during the semester. Questionnaire data were collected from the students four times, immediately before, during, immediately after, and two years after they had taken the course. The questionnaires included rating scales that described the students' evaluation of a variety of related subjects, including the teacher, the course, and other students in the class. The students were asked to describe their typical reaction to a variety of encounters between a younger and an older person. At the end of the term, they were asked to provide a detailed evaluation of the course and the instructor.

The classroom tapes were used in two other ways to understand the processes of interaction in the group. A new coding scheme was devised which emphasized the specific needs that students had for the teacher's behavior. These needs were characterized by six possible roles that teachers might serve: expert, formal authority, socialization agent, facilitator, ego ideal, and person. Every interaction was coded in order to understand the student presses for the teacher to increase some roles and to decrease others. This analysis also included messages sent by the teacher to the students showing his willingness or unwillingness to modify the emphasis of the roles he performed. The tapes also permitted a cluster analysis of student participation. Eight student styles were identified by grouping students who had similar styles of participation in the class. These style clusters have significantly different strategies for participation in the class; they enjoy different aspects of the course; they perceive their teachers as playing or needing to play different roles; and they respond differently to teachers' techniques for encouraging class participation or involvement.

In a final approach to the classroom group, a case study of one teacher integrated the observations, coded analysis, and student interviews into a descriptive picture of the affective climate of the classroom. The case approach provided a look at the teacher's efforts to respond to particular student needs. It also examined the teacher's conflicts about course goals, standards of excellence, and needs for student acceptance as they influence the classroom climate. Student reactions to the course and the teacher were understood in light of their own past experiences, current involvements, and competences.

The outcome of this study is a more realistic awareness of the variety of needs and styles that students bring to the classroom and the articulation of specific affective conflicts that prevent meaningful work from occurring during class sessions. The message to college teachers is to discover a balance of strategies that feels comfortable but also takes into account the real and diverse messages from students about the quality of classroom interactions. The class sessions where real communication and growth take place include a quality of responding to the variety of needs present in the group rather than denying, rejecting, scorning, or attacking them.

## CHAPTER SUMMARY

The chapter has emphasized the challenges of research about adolescent development. The first step in considering a research plan is to select the sample. The strategies for tracing developmental change include the cross-sectional, longitudinal, and sequential longitudinal sampling techniques. In the cross-sectional sample, normative patterns of change can be documented in a comparatively short period. In the longitudinal sample, patterns of stability or change among individuals can be traced. In the sequential longitudinal design, generational and maturational patterns can be compared. Only this last method offers a means of identifying the historic or generational effects that contribute to adolescent development.

Three other characteristics of the sample were discussed: demographic variables, sample size, and the embeddedness of the sample in a larger influential context. We do not yet have a clear sense of how specific environments, especially high schools, colleges, work organizations, and communities, contribute to the responses of adolescent subjects. This aspect of sample selection needs more careful attention in research design. A persistent question is how representative one adolescent sample is of adolescents in general.

Four methods of study that have been commonly used with adolescent subjects were described: survey research, laboratory experimentation, naturalistic observation, and field experimentation. The methods differ in the degree of control and intervention for which the experimenter is responsible. They also differ in the ease with which observations from research can be applied to other situations or samples. Each method requires unique strategies for collecting data. The methods can be used singly, or they can be interwoven in order to obtain comprehensive view of an area of behavior.

The adolescent subject population offers some unique challenges for any research method. Early adolescents are characterized by varied maturational levels, suspiciousness of manipulation, embarrassment about heterosexual encounters, and diverse intellectual and social skills. All of these qualities may influence their responses in psychological research. One of the major issues in research with later adolescents is whether or not the sample is in college. There are a number of reasons to expect basic differences in orientation and competence between college and noncollege groups. College provides a powerful context for adolescents. Differences among schools, stresses in adapting to school, experience with psychology courses, and historical trends may all have unique effects on the behavior and thought of college students.

The two studies described as examples of research with multiple methods illustrate the usefulness of employing converging methods to understand complex psychological phenomena. The methods were designed to be appropriate to the settings in which the research was conducted as well as to the populations under study. The exploratory nature of both studies is characteristic of much of the research in the area of adolescence. We have hunches, educated guesses about the processes of growth and the meaning of the adolescent experience. Researchers who seek to understand the adolescent experience find themselves mistrusting any single set of observations as an artifact of their methodology. The use of several methods, particularly methods that include observing adolescent behavior and asking adolescents about their behavior, help to inspire confidence in the genuineness of observations.

## REFERENCES

Ainsworth, M. D. S., Bell, S. M., and Stayton, D. J.  Infant-mother attachment and social development: Socialization as a product of reciprocal responsiveness to signals. In M. P. M. Richards (Ed.), *The integration of a child into a social world.* Cambridge: Cambridge University Press, 1974. Pp. 99–135.

Albrecht, S. L.    Adolescent attitude-behavior inconsistency: Some empirical evidence. *Adolescence,* 1977, *12,* 433–442.

Asch, S. E.    Effects of group pressure on the modification and distortion of judgments. In H. Guetzkow (Ed.), *Groups, leadership, and men.* Pittsburgh: Carnegie Press, 1951.

Asch, S. E.    Studies of independence and conformity: A minority of one against a unanimous majority. *Psychological Monographs,* 1956, *70* (9, Whole No. 416).

Astin, A. W.    *Four critical years: Effects of college on beliefs, attitudes, and knowledge.* San Francisco: Jossey-Bass, 1977.

Bachman, J. G.    *Youth in transition,* vol. 2: *The impact of family background and intelligence on tenth-grade boys.* Ann Arbor, Mich.: Institute for Social Research, 1970.

Bachman, J. G., Green, S., and Wirtanen, J. D.    *Youth in transition,* vol. 3: *Dropping out—Problem or symptom?* Ann Arbor, Mich.: Institute for Social Research, 1971.

Bachman, J. G., Kahn, R. L., Mednick, M. T., Davidson, T. N., and Johnston, L. D.    *Youth in transition,* vol. 1: *Blueprint for a longitudinal study of adolescent boys.* Ann Arbor, Mich.: Institute for Social Research, 1967.

Bachman, J. G., and van Duinen, E.    *Youth look at national problems: A special report.* Ann Arbor, Mich.: Institute for Social Research, 1971.

Baltes, P. B.    Longitudinal and cross-sectional sequences in the study of age and generation effects. *Human Development,* 1968, *11,* 145–171.

Baltes, P. B., and Nesselroade, J. R.    Multivariate longitudinal and cross-sectional sequences for analyzing ontogenetic and generational change: A methodological note. *Developmental Psychology,* 1970, *2,* 163–168.

Barker, R. G.    *Ecological psychology.* Stanford, Calif.: Stanford University Press, 1968.

Barker, R. G., and Gump, P. V.    *Big school, small school.* Stanford, Calif.: Stanford University Press, 1964.

Barker, R. G., and Schoggen, P.    *Qualities of community life: Methods of measuring environment and behavior applied to an American and an English town.* San Francisco: Jossey-Bass, 1973.

Brandt, R. M.    *Studying behavior in natural settings.* New York: Holt, Rinehart and Winston, 1972.

Brim, O. G., Jr.    Socialization through the life cycle. In O. G. Brim, Jr., and S. Wheeler, *Socialization after childhood.* New York: Wiley, 1966.

Bronfenbrenner, U.    Developmental research, public policy, and the ecology of childhood. *Child Development,* 1974, *45,* 1–5(a).

Bronfenbrenner, U.    Experimental human ecology: A reorientation to theory and research on socialization. Paper presented at 82d convention of the American Psychological Association, New Orleans, 1974(b).

Cartwright, C., and Cartwright, P.    *Developing observation skills.* New York: McGraw-Hill, 1974.

Chun, K. T., Cobb, S., and French, J. R. P.   *Measures for psychological assessment: A guide to 3,000 original sources and their applications.* Ann Arbor, Mich.: Institute for Social Research, 1975.

Cohen, D. H., and Stern, V.   *Observing and recording the behavior of young children.* New York: Teachers College Press, 1970.

Cook, T. D., and Campbell, D. T.   The design and conduct of quasi-experiments and true experiments in field settings. In M. D. Dunnette (Ed.), *Handbook of industrial and organizational psychology.* Chicago: Rand McNally, 1974.

Davidson, T. N.   *Youth in transition,* vol. 4: *Evolution of a strategy for longitudinal analysis of survey panel data.* Ann Arbor, Mich.: Institute for Social Research, 1972.

Edwards, D. W.   Coping preferences, adaptive roles, and varied high school environments. In J. G. Kelly (Ed.), *Adolescent boys in high school: A psychological study of coping and adaptation.* Hillsdale, N.J.: Lawrence Erlbaum, 1979.

Edwards, D. W., and Kelly, J. G.   A longitudinal field test of the person-environment transaction model: Coping and adaptation. Unpublished manuscript, 1977.

Erikson, E. H.   *Childhood and society.* New york: Norton, 1950.

Erikson, E. H.   *Young man Luther.* New York: Norton, 1958.

Erikson, E. H.   The problem of ego identity. *Psychological Issues,* 1959, *1* (1), 101–164.

Erikson, E. H.   *Identity: Youth and crisis.* New York: Norton, 1968.

Erikson, E. H.   *Life history and the historical moment.* New York: Norton, 1975.

Fatke, R.   The adaptation process of new students in two suburban high schools. In M. J. Feldman (Ed.), Studies in Psychotherapy and Behavioral Change, no. 2: *Theory and research in community mental health.* Buffalo: State University of New York at Buffalo, 1971. Pp. 134–172.

Freud, A.   *Normality and pathology in childhood: Assessments of development.* New York: International Universities Press, 1965.

Freud, A.   Adolescence as a developmental disturbance. In G. Kaplan and S. Lebovici (Eds.), *Adolescence: Psychosocial perspectives,* New York: Basic Books, 1969.

Getzels, J. W.   A social psychology of education. In G. Lindzey and E. Aronson (Eds.), *The handbook of social psychology,* vol. 5: *Applied social psychology* (2d ed.). Reading, Mass.: Addison-Wesley, 1969. Pp. 459–537.

Gilmore, G. E., Jr.   Exploration, identity development, and the sense of competency: A case study. In J. G. Kelly (Ed.), *Adolescent boys in high school: A psychological study of coping and adaptation.* Hillsdale, N.J.: Lawrence Erlbaum, 1979.

Goethals, G. W., and Klos, D. S.   *Experiencing youth: First person accounts.* Boston: Little, Brown.

Goldberg, R., Kaye, G., Groszko, M., Hichenberg, A., and Kelly, J. G.   A comparative analysis of the social characteristics of the four schools selected. Appendix F: Adaptive behavior in varied high schools environments. Research proposal (ROI-MH-15606-04) submitted as a privileged communication to the National Institute of Mental Health, 1967.

Hays, W. L. *Statistics for social scientists* (2d ed.). New York: Holt, Rinehart and Winston, 1973.

Hayward, D. G., Rothenberg, M., and Beasley, R. R. Children's play on urban playground environments: A comparison of traditional, contemporary, and adventure playground types. *Environment and Behavior,* 1974, *5*(2), 131–168.

Johnston, J., and Bachman, J. G. *Youth in transition,* vol. 5: *Young men and military service.* Ann Arbor, Mich.: Institute for Social Research, 1972.

Johnston, L. *Drugs and America youth.* Ann Arbor, Mich.: Institute for Social Research, 1973.

Jones, N. B. *Ethological studies of child behavior.* Cambridge: Cambridge University Press, 1972.

Jones, W. H. Exploratory behavior of adolescents in a dyadic problem solving situation. In J. G. Kelly (Ed.), *Adolescent boys in high school: A psychological study of coping and adaptation.* Hillsdale, N.J.: Lawrence Erlbaum, 1979.

Kelly J. G. Naturalistic observations in contrasting social environments. In E. P. Williams and H. L. Raush (Eds.), *Naturalistic viewpoints in psychological research.* New York: Holt, Rinehart and Winston, 1969. Pp. 183–199.

Kelly, J. G., in collaboration with Edwards, D. W., Fatke, R., Gordon, T. A., McClintock, S. K., McGee, D. P., Newman, B. M., Rice, R. R., Roistacher, R., and Todd, D. M. The coping process in varied high school environments. In M. J. Feldman (Ed.), Studies in Psychotherapy and Behavioral Change, no. 2: *Theory and research in community mental health.* Buffalo: State University of New York at Buffalo, 1971. Pp. 93–166.

Kelly, J. G. (Ed.) *Adolescent boys in high school: A psychological study of coping and adaptation.* Hillsdale, N.J.: Lawrence Erlbaum, 1979.

Kelly, J. G. Some closing comments. In J. G. Kelly (Ed.), *Adolescent boys in high school: A psychological study of coping and adaptation.* Hillsdale, N.J.: Lawrence Erlbaum, 1979.

Kessen, W. *The child.* New York: Wiley, 1965.

Kish, L. *Survey sampling.* New York: Wiley, 1965.

Labov, W. *Language in the inner city: Studies in the black English vernacular.* Philadelphia: University of Pennsylvania Press, 1972.

Lewin, K. Field theory and experiment in social psychology: Concepts and methods. *American Journal of Sociology,* 1939, *44,* 868–897.

Lewis, M., and Rosenblum, L. A. *The effect of the infant on its caregiver.* New York: Wiley, 1974.

Lifton, R. J. *Explorations in psychohistory: The Wellfleet papers.* New York: Simon and Schuster, 1974.

Lindberg, L., and Swedlow, R. *Early childhood education: A guide for observation and participation.* Boston: Allyn and Bacon, 1976.

Lippitt, R., and Gold, M. Classroom social structure as a mental health problem. *Journal of Social Issues,* 1959, *15,* 40–58.

Luchterhand, E., and Weller, L. Effects of class, race, sex, and educational status on patterns of aggression of lower-class youth. *Journal of Youth and Adolescence,* 1976, *5,* 59–71.

Mann, R. D., Arnold, S. M., Binder, J., Cytrynbaum, S., Newman, B. M., Ringwald, B., Ringwald, J., and Rosenwein, R.   *The college classroom: Conflict, change, and learning.* New York: Wiley, 1970.

Mann, R. D., Gibbard, G., and Hartman, J.   *Interpersonal styles and group development.* New York: Wiley, 1967.

Marcia, J. E.   Development and validation of ego identity status. *Journal of Personality and Social Psychology,* 1966, *3,* 551–558.

Marcia, J. E.   A six-year follow-up study of the identity statuses. Paper presented at the Eastern Psychological Association meetings in New York City, April 1975.

Marcia, J. E., and Friedman, M. L.   Ego identity status in college women. *Journal of Personality,* 1970, *2,* 249–263.

Martorano, S. C.   A developmental analysis of performance on Piaget's formal operations tasks. *Developmental Psychology,* 1977, *13,* 666–672.

Moos, R. H.   Systems for the assessment and classification of human environments: An overview. In R. H. Moos and P. Insel (Eds.), *Issues in social ecology: Human milieus.* Palo Alto, Calif.: National Press Books, 1974.

Neimark, E. D.   Longitudinal development of formal operations thought. *Genetic Psychology Monographs,* 1975, *91,* 171–225.

Nesselroade, J. R. and Baltes, P. B.   Adolescent personality development and historical change: 1970–1972. *Monographs of the Society for Research in Child Development,* 1974, *39* (1, Serial No. 154).

Newman, B. M.   Characteristics of interpersonal behavior among adolescent boys. *Journal of Youth and Adolescence,* 1975, *4* (2), 145–153.

Newman, B. M.   Interpersonal behavior and preferences for exploration in adolescent boys: A small group study. In J. G. Kelly (Ed.), *Adolescent boys in high school: A psychological study of coping and adaptation.* Hillsdale, N.J.: Lawrence Erlbaum, 1979.

Newman, B. M.   The development of interpersonal skills in early adolescence. Mimeographed, 1978.

Newman, B. M., and Newman, P. R.   *Development through life: A case study approach.* Homewood, Ill.: Dorsey Press, 1976.

Newman, P. R.   The effects of varied high school environments on student socialization. Appendix K: Adaptive behavior in varied high school environments. Research proposal (ROI-MH-15606-04) submitted to the National Institute of Mental Health, 1970.

Newman, P. R.   Persons and settings: A comparative analysis of the quality and range of social interaction in two suburban high schools. In J. G. Kelly (Ed.), *Adolescent boys in high school: A psychological study of coping and adaptation.* Hillsdale, N.J.: Lawrence Erlbaum, 1979.

Newman, P. R., and Newman, B. M.   Identity formation and the college experience. *Adolescence,* 1978, *13,* 311–326.

Nunnally, J. C.   *Psychometric theory.* New York: McGraw-Hill, 1967.

Orlofsky, J. L., Marcia, J. E., and Lesser, I. M.   Ego identity status and the intimacy vs. isolation crisis of young adulthood. *Journal of Personality and Social Psychology,* 1973, *27,* 211–219.

Orne, M. T.   On the social psychology of the psychological experiment: With particular reference to demand characteristics and their implications. *American Psychologist,* 1962, *17,* 776–783.

Pace, C. R.   Differences in campus atmospheres. In W. W. Chartes, Jr., and N. L. Gage (Eds.), *Readings in the social psychology of education.* Boston: Allyn and Bacon, 1963. Pp. 73–79.

Pope, B.   Socioeconomic contrasts in children's peer culture prestige values. *Genetic Psychology Monograph,* 1953, *48,* 157–220.

Proshansky, H. M.   Environmental psychology: A methodological orientation. In H. M. Proshansky, W. H. Ittelson, and L. G. Rivlin (Eds.), *Environmental psychology: People and their physical settings* (2d ed.). New York: Holt, Rinehart and Winston, 1976. Pp. 59–69.

Rice, R. R., and Marsh, M.   The social environments of the two high schools: Background data. In J. G. Kelly (Ed.), *The high school: Students and social contexts in two Midwestern communities.* Hillsdale, N.J.: Lawrence Erlbaum, 1978.

Richards, M. P. M.   First steps in becoming social. In M. P. M. Richards (Ed.), *The integration of a child into a social world.* London: Cambridge University Press, 1974. Pp. 83–98.

Riegel, K.   The dialectics of human development. *American Psychologist,* 1976, *31,* 689–700.

Robinson, J. P., and Shaver, P. R.   *Measures of social psychological attitudes.* Ann Arbor, Mich.: Institute for Social Research, 1975.

Rosenthal, R., and Rosnow, R. L.   *Primer of methods for the behavioral sciences.* New York: Wiley, 1975.

Saltzstein, H. D., Diamond, R. M., and Belenky, M.   Moral judgment level and conformity behavior. *Developmental Psychology,* 1972, *7,* 327–336.

Schaie, K. W.   A general model for the study of developmental problems. *Psychological Bulletin,* 1965, *64,* 92–107.

Shayer, M., Kuchemann, D. E., and Wylam, H.   The distribution of Piagetian stages of thinking in British middle and secondary school children. *British Journal of Educational Psychology,* 1976, *46,* 164–173.

Sherif, M., and Sherif, C. W.   *Social psychology.* New York: Harper and Row, 1969.

Stern, G. E.   Environments for learning. In N. Sanford (Ed.), *The American college.* New York: Wiley, 1962. Pp. 690–730.

Stillmans, H.   An exploratory study of two high school environments. Unpublished manuscript. Project archives of the Opinions of Youth Study, Institute for Social Research, University of Michigan, 1969.

Swingle, P. G.   *Social psychology in natural settings: A reader in field experimentation.* Chicago: Aldine, 1973.

Thistlethwaite, D. L.   College environments and the development of talent. *Science,* 1959(a), *130,* 71–76.

Thistlethwaite, D. L.   College press and student achievement. *Journal of Educational Psychology,* 1959(b), *50,* 183–191.

Thistlethwaite, D. L.   College press and changes in study plans of talented students. *Journal of Educational Psychology,* 1960, *51,* 222–239.

Thornburg, H. D.   Behavior and values: Consistency or inconsistency. *Adolescence,* 1973, *8,* 513–520.

Toder, N. L., and Marcia. J. E.   Ego identity status and response to conformity pressure in college women. *Journal of Personality and Social Psychology,* 1973, *26,* 287–294.

Weick, K. E.   Systematic observational methods. In G. Lindzey and E. Aronson (Eds.), *The handbook of social psychology* (2d ed.), vol. 1. Reading, Mass.: Addison-Wesley, 1968. Pp. 357–451.

White, R. W.   *Lives in progress.* New York: Holt, Rinehart and Winston, 1966.

White, R. W.   *The enterprise of living: A view of personal growth* (2d ed.). New York: Holt, Rinehart and Winston, 1976.

White, R. W., Riggs, M. M., and Gilbert, D. C.   *Case workbook in personality.* New York: Holt, Rinehart and Winston, 1976.

Winer, B. J.   *Statistical principles in experimental design.* New York: McGraw-Hill, 1971.

Wuebben, P. L., Straits, B. C., and Schulman, G. I.   *The experiment as a social occasion.* Berkeley, Calif.: Glendessary Press, 1974.

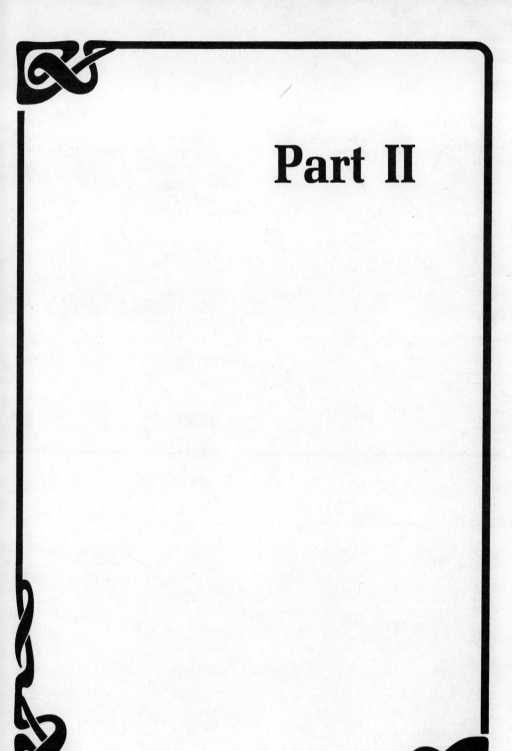

# Part II

*Adolescence brings rapid physical growth that propels the person out of childhood toward adulthood.*

# 4

# The Pattern of Growth at Puberty

From early childhood, the person becomes accustomed to a de-
celerating pattern of growth. Gains in height, for example, decrease
every year from age two to about age nine or ten. Then, at puberty,
there is a period of acceleration. The adolescent, his or her friends,
family members, and teachers recognize the emergence of a new
body shape, new physical competences, and a new capacity for
sexuality. After a long period of slow, gradual change, adolescence
brings relatively rapid and dramatic physical growth which propels
the person out of childhood and toward adulthood.

In this chapter the pattern of physical growth and sexual maturation is described. Individual differences and sex differences in physical growth are considered as contributors to individual variability.
Environmental influences on growth, especially the impact of nutrition, disease, and drugs, are discussed as they enhance or inhibit
growth. Considerable attention is given to the psychological consequences of physical changes. We are concerned about the changes
in personality, in social acceptance, and in anxiety or stress that
may occur as a result of biological growth during adolescence.
Finally, we recognize that adolescents and preadolescents are exposed to varied information about adolescent growth. We need
to understand what expectations and explanations adolescents
have about their physical growth. What kinds of information reach
adolescents, where does that information come from, and what
impact does it have?

## CHANGES IN SIZE AND STRENGTH

Five areas of physical growth have been used to mark the growth
spurt of early adolescence. These include changes in height, weight,
shoulder width, hip width, and muscle strength. An analysis of
these dimensions gives us a picture of the emergence of an adult
physique apart from its sexual characteristics. In describing the
events of physical growth, three kinds of variability must be kept
in mind. First, the age when growth begins may vary. Second, the
length of time from the beginning of growth until the tapering off
of growth may vary. Third, the increase in size or strength may
vary, resulting in the variability in adult heights, weights, body
shapes, and muscle strengths with which we are all familiar.

### Changes in Height

A normative picture of adolescent growth can be seen in Table
4–1's cross-sectional survey of U.S. adolescents between the ages
of 12 and 17. This table suggests that there is a nine-inch difference
between average 12-year-old males (60.0 inches) and average 17-

Table 4–1: Height in Inches of Youths Aged 12–17 Years by Sex and Age at Last Birthday (mean and selected percentiles, United States, 1966–1970)

| Sex and Age | X̄ | Percentile | | | | | | |
|---|---|---|---|---|---|---|---|---|
| | | 5th | 10th | 25th | 50th | 75th | 90th | 95th |
| Male | | | | | | | | |
| 12 years ........ | 60.0 | 54.6 | 55.7 | 57.8 | 60.0 | 61.9 | 64.0 | 65.2 |
| 13 years ........ | 62.9 | 57.2 | 58.3 | 60.4 | 62.8 | 65.4 | 68.0 | 68.7 |
| 14 years ........ | 65.6 | 59.9 | 60.9 | 63.2 | 66.1 | 68.1 | 69.8 | 70.7 |
| 15 years ........ | 67.5 | 62.4 | 63.7 | 65.7 | 67.8 | 69.3 | 71.0 | 72.1 |
| 16 years ........ | 68.6 | 64.1 | 65.2 | 67.0 | 68.7 | 70.4 | 72.1 | 73.1 |
| 17 years ........ | 69.1 | 64.1 | 65.7 | 67.2 | 69.2 | 70.9 | 72.6 | 73.7 |
| Female | | | | | | | | |
| 12 years ........ | 61.1 | 55.8 | 57.4 | 59.5 | 61.2 | 63.0 | 64.6 | 65.9 |
| 13 years ........ | 62.5 | 57.8 | 58.9 | 60.7 | 62.6 | 64.4 | 66.0 | 66.9 |
| 14 years ........ | 63.5 | 59.6 | 60.5 | 61.9 | 63.5 | 65.2 | 66.7 | 67.4 |
| 15 years ........ | 63.9 | 59.6 | 60.3 | 62.0 | 63.9 | 65.8 | 67.2 | 68.1 |
| 16 years ........ | 64.0 | 59.7 | 60.7 | 62.4 | 64.2 | 65.6 | 67.2 | 68.1 |
| 17 years ........ | 64.1 | 60.0 | 60.9 | 62.3 | 64.3 | 65.9 | 67.4 | 68.1 |

Source: U.S. Public Health Service, *Vital and Health Statistics*, series 11, no. 124, "Height and Weight of Youths, 12–17 Years, United States: January 1973." Reprinted by permission.

year-old males (69.1 inches). There is only a three-inch difference between average 12-year-old females (61.1 inches) and average 17-year-old females (64.1 inches). At 12 years of age, females are slightly taller than males. At every subsequent age, the mean height of males is greater than that of females. In the early years of adolescence the pattern of heights for males and females is quite close and overlaps. By age 17, however, the tallest females are not quite as tall as the average (50th percentile) males.

Longitudinal studies of growth provide information about the rate of growth, the age at which the growth spurt occurs, and the relationship, if any, between height before adolescence and adult height. Two analyses of physical growth during adolescence, one for boys (Stolz and Stolz, 1951) and one for girls (Faust, 1977), provide comparable data about patterns of physical development. The boys were subjects from the California Adolescent Growth Study (Jones, 1938, 1939). The data on them were collected from fifth grade through senior high school. The girls were subjects in the Guidance Study (Macfarlane, 1938) and the Berkeley Growth Study (Jones and Bayley, 1941). They were examined twice a year during the ages 6 through 18. For both the boys and the girls, the period of puberty was traced by establishing the rate of height growth between each examination. The height apex was the period in which the growth rate showed its greatest increase. The pubertal period was defined by those months when the rate of growth was above average during the five years before and after the apex in height. Thus, each subject's rate of growth rather than chronological age provided the basis for defining the boundaries of puberty.

Table 4–2 shows the chronological age and the height in centimeters of the male and female subjects. The table is divided into four developmental periods. The first is the age and height at the third semiannual examination before the pubertal period $(b-3)$.

**Table 4–2: Mean Chronological Age and Measurement of Height of Girls and Boys at Four Developmental Points**

| Sex | Prepubertal (b − 3) | | Pubertal Onset (b) | | Pubertal End (d) | | Postpubertal (d + 3) | |
|---|---|---|---|---|---|---|---|---|
| | M | SD | M | SD | M | SD | M | SD |
| Chronological age (years) | | | | | | | | |
| Girls . . . . . | 8.88 | 1.26 | 10.12 | 1.22 | 12.94 | 1.06 | 14.20 | 1.07 |
| Boys . . . . . | 11.51 | 0.92 | 12.76 | 0.92 | 15.57 | 0.87 | 16.77 | 0.87 |
| Height (cm) | | | | | | | | |
| Girls . . . . . | 133.1 | 7.07 | 140.1 | 7.15 | 159.7 | 6.19 | 163.3 | 5.88 |
| Boys . . . . . | 146.2 | 6.08 | 151.8 | 6.11 | 172.9 | 6.64 | 177.0 | 6.47 |

Note: N for girls is 94, and N for boys is 67. Boys' data taken from Stolz and Stolz (1951).

Source: Margaret S. Faust, "Somatic Development of Adolescent Girls," *Monographs of the Society for Research in Child Development,* 1977, *42*(1, Serial No. 169), Appendix B (adapted), p. 84. Reprinted by permission from the Society for Research in Child Development, Inc.

The second shows the age and height at the onset of the pubertal period *(b)*. The third marks the end of the pubertal period *(d)*, when the growth rate falls below the average for the five-year period around the height apex. The fourth period $(d+3)$ indicates the age and height at the third semiannual examination after the end of the pubertal period. As the table indicates, the pubertal period begins more than 2½ years later for males than for females. The pubertal period is equally long—about 2.8 years—for both males and females. However, there is more variability in chronological age for the female sample at each of the developmental periods. The youngest girl to begin pubertal growth was 7.52 years old, and the oldest was 13.32.

The pattern of height increase shows that girls gain fewer centimeters during the pubertal period than do boys. When growth is viewed in terms of developmental phases rather than chronological age, boys are taller than girls at every developmental period. One must keep in mind, however, that these comparable phases of development occur two years earlier for females than for males. Therefore, girls are likely to experience the greatest increases in height about two years before the growth rate for boys has begun to increase.

For both boys and girls, height at the beginning of puberty is positively correlated to height at the end of puberty ($r = .81$ for boys; $r = .76$ for girls). For most children, then, growth during puberty does not disrupt the sense of oneself as a tall, average, or short person. It should be noted that for a significantly large group, about 30 percent of the samples, height before puberty is not a good predictor of height after puberty. Some adolescents who were tall children do not grow much at puberty. Others who were short grow a great deal. Thus, one's body image and one's ranking in height may need considerable revision after puberty, particularly if one's height among peers is markedly different at the end of this developmental phase than it was before. For both boys and girls, the amount of height gain is related to the length of the pubertal growth phase. Early maturers grow somewhat more than late maturers. Those who have a long period of pubertal growth increase in height more than those who have a short period of pubertal growth.

## Changes in Weight

The U.S. Public Health Service data on weight during the adolescent years are summarized in Table 4–3. The average 12-year-old female is about eight pounds heavier than the average 12-year-old male. By age 17, however, males are over 15 pounds heavier than females in every percentile category. At the upper range, the heaviest boys are over 30 pounds heavier than the heaviest girls. Once again, the longitudinal data show that at the same develop-

Table 4–3: Weight in Pounds of Youths Aged 12–17 Years by Sex and Age at Last Birthday (mean and selected percentiles, United States, 1966–1970)

| Sex and Age | X̄ | Percentile | | | | | | |
| --- | --- | --- | --- | --- | --- | --- | --- | --- |
| | | 5th | 10th | 25th | 50th | 75th | 90th | 95th |
| Male | | | | | | | | |
| 12 years ...... | 94.8 | 67.5 | 72.1 | 80.6 | 91.7 | 105.8 | 124.0 | 132.4 |
| 13 years ...... | 110.2 | 76.9 | 81.2 | 91.2 | 106.5 | 124.5 | 142.6 | 156.1 |
| 14 years ...... | 124.9 | 86.4 | 92.2 | 107.0 | 122.0 | 139.4 | 158.0 | 172.1 |
| 15 years ...... | 135.8 | 102.1 | 107.4 | 119.2 | 113.2 | 147.9 | 165.3 | 184.6 |
| 16 years ...... | 142.9 | 107.6 | 114.2 | 127.4 | 139.7 | 154.7 | 173.5 | 187.2 |
| 17 years ...... | 150.0 | 115.9 | 122.1 | 133.6 | 145.9 | 162.2 | 180.5 | 200.4 |
| Female | | | | | | | | |
| 12 years ...... | 102.7 | 72.7 | 77.0 | 87.1 | 100.0 | 114.7 | 131.4 | 141.3 |
| 13 years ...... | 111.2 | 80.0 | 85.6 | 95.3 | 107.6 | 124.6 | 139.2 | 149.8 |
| 14 years ...... | 119.4 | 89.1 | 95.4 | 104.6 | 115.8 | 130.7 | 147.1 | 157.6 |
| 15 years ...... | 124.5 | 92.5 | 98.2 | 107.9 | 120.7 | 133.9 | 157.1 | 174.7 |
| 16 years ...... | 128.0 | 98.6 | 102.8 | 112.1 | 122.9 | 137.1 | 157.1 | 183.7 |
| 17 years ...... | 126.9 | 98.2 | 103.0 | 114.5 | 123.2 | 136.6 | 153.6 | 167.9 |

Source: U.S. Public Health Service, Vital and Health Statistics, series 11, no. 124, "Height and Weight of Youths 12–17 Years, United States: January 1973." Reprinted by permission.

mental level the average weight for boys is greater than the average weight for girls (Faust, 1977). During the examination periods from the prepubertal to the postpubertal period, many of the male and female subjects lost weight from one examination to another. Overall, the greatest weight gain for all subjects was during the pubertal period of height growth. The greatest increase in the rate of weight gain was most likely to occur after the increase in height for both boys and girls. For girls, however, weight gain was also positively associated with increases in subcutaneous tissue. The thickness of this tissue provides an estimate of body fat. For boys, weight gain and subcutaneous tissue were not significantly correlated. Further, for boys there was a general pattern of decreasing subcutaneous tissue during the pubertal period. The period of puberty, then, brings continued "plumping" for girls and thinning out for boys.

## Changes in Shoulder and Hip Width

The height spurt and weight gains of puberty are accompanied by changes in body proportions and body shape. For girls the apex in shoulder growth occurs before the height spurt, but for boys it often occurs after the height spurt. The increase in shoulder width during puberty is less for girls than for boys.

The pattern for hip width is just the opposite of the pattern for shoulder width. Boys have wider hips than girls at every developmental point, but the differences decrease. Boys' hips are wider than girls' hips during the prepubertal period. From that point, girls' hips increase in width more than do boys' hips, and they continue to increase in size at a greater rate than the hips of boys into the postpubertal period (Faust, 1977; Tanner, 1972).

Girls begin the pubertal growth phase with their shoulders slightly broader than their hips. For girls this shoulder width/hip width ratio decreases throughout puberty. Boys begin puberty with shoulders slightly broader than hips. For boys this ratio increases throughout puberty.

## Changes in Muscle Strength

There is a steady increase in muscle strength during puberty. At every developmental point, boys are stronger than girls. However, there is some overlap between the groups. By the end of the pubertal period, the strongest girls have muscle strength comparable to that of the weakest boys. The pattern of increasing rate of strength is different for males and females. For girls, the greatest rate of growth occurs simultaneously with the height spurt. Further, some girls show a decrease in strength between examinations

(Faust, 1977). For boys, the increased rate in strength is greater during the pubertal period than it is for girls. In the postpubertal period, boys show an even greater increase in strength (Stolz and Stolz, 1951; Carron and Bailey, 1974). The peak in strength increase occurs for boys approximately 12–14 months after the height spurt. This lag between height and strength may present the boy with some discrepancy between what he looks as if he should be able to accomplish physically and what he actually can accomplish. As Tanner (1972) describes it: "A short period may exist when the adolescent (male), having completed his skeletal and probably also muscular growth, still does not have the strength of a young adult of the same body size and shape. But this is a temporary phase; considered absolutely, power, atheletic skill, and physical endurance all increase progressively and rapidly throughout adolescence" (p. 7).

## The Pattern of Growth

There is a common pattern to the growth spurt for each aspect of growth. Generally, the feet, hands, and legs reach their apex first, then the height spurt, muscle strength, body breadth (shoulder and hip width), and body weight (Tanner, 1972). As has been noted, however, there are clear differences in the pattern for males and females. Shoulder width precedes the height spurt for females and follows it for males. The apex for hip width is later for females than for males. The strength apex is earlier for females than for males.

In addition to sex differences, there is considerable individual variability. In analyzing the sequential ordering in five skeletal apexes—height, stem length, leg length, shoulder width, and hip width—Faust (1977) found that 76 percent of the boys and 75 percent of the girls showed unique orderings. In other words, even though we can offer a normative picture of the pattern of physical growth, few adolescents actually follow the same pattern.

## SEXUAL MATURATION

Physical growth at adolescence is accompanied by a number of changes in the reproductive system and by the emergence of secondary sex characteristics. These changes accentuate the differences in physical appearance between boys and girls that were described above. They also mark the beginning of the reproductive capacity of males and females. Finally, sexual development at puberty clarifies the gender identity of most males and females by providing more pronounced physical characteristics associated with each sex. Although awareness of one's gender and the learning of sex-typed behaviors have been building since early childhood (Money and Ehrhardt, 1972; Gagnon and Simon, 1973), sexual maturation in adolescence forces each person to recognize the sexual implications of his or her gender.

The pattern of sexual development and the accompanying secondary sex characteristics are different for girls and boys. For girls, the secondary sex characteristics, including the growth of pubic hair, axillary (armpit) hair, and breast development, are all likely to be in the middle or toward the end of their growth before menarche begins (Tanner, 1966, 1972; Faust, 1977). All of these characteristics continue to develop well past the beginning of menarche. There is great variability in the length of time required for the full growth of breasts, pubic hair, and axillary hair. The breast development of some of the girls observed in Faust's sample had been completed by age 13, whereas other girls had not begun to show significant breast growth by that time. For almost all of Faust's subjects, the period of rapid height growth was also the period of rapid breast development.

Menarche itself tends to occur after the height apex. In fact, menarche tends to occur after most of the measures of skeletal growth have reached their peak velocity. In Faust's sample, the age at menarche varied from 10.5 to 15.8 years. The mean age was 12.79. This corresponds closely to other estimates of the mean age and the range of ages for menarche in British populations (Tanner, 1966; Marshall and Tanner, 1969). Menstruation and the menstrual cycle introduce a pattern of hormonal variations that are associated with ovulation, building up the lining of the uterus, and shedding the uterine lining. Three hormones, estrogen, progesterone, and androgen are responsible for the changes in the menstrual cycle. As the levels of each hormone increase or decrease, they signal a new phase of the menstrual cycle (Schwartz, 1968; Bardwick, 1971). These hormonal changes are also associated with changes in activity level and emotional state that will be discussed below.

Ovulation generally does not begin during the first menstrual cycles. Tanner (1962; Marshall and Tanner, 1969) estimates that females may be infertile for 12 to 18 months after the first menstrual period. However, individual variability in this aspect of physical development makes the matter of adolescent fertility somewhat unpredictable.

For boys, sexual maturation usually begins with the increased growth of the testes and the scrotum (Tanner, 1962; Marshall and Tanner, 1970). Pubic hair begins to grow around this time also. These changes occur about a year before the height spurt and the period of accelerated growth of the penis. For boys the growth of the testes and penis occurs during the period of accelerated height increase, whereas for girls menstruation usually comes about six months to a year after the height spurt.

The growth of axillary hair and facial hair usually begins about two years after the beginning of pubic hair growth. The first ejaculation of seminal fluid is likely to occur at about this time as well. Toward the end of the pubertal period, the larynx and the vocal cords grow, which results in a gradual change in the male's voice. During the transitional period of growth, the boy's voice may break or crack until his adult pitch is established.

Adolescent males also experience some changes in their breasts during the pubertal period. The size of the areola increases. For about 20–35 percent of boys, there is a temporary enlargement of the breasts that may last for about a year (Tanner, 1972).

Several changes in the skin occur for both males and females during puberty. These include the growth of sweat glands and the

Table 4–4: Normal Maturational Sequence in Girls

| Phase | Appearance of Sexual Characteristics | Average Ages | Age Range* |
|---|---|---|---|
| Childhood through preadolescence | No *pubic hair; breasts* flat; *growth* in height constant; no spurt | — | — |
| Early adolescence | Rounding of *hips; breasts* and nipples are elevated to form *"bud"* stage; no true *pubic hair,* may have down | 10–11 years | 9–14 years |
| Middle adolescence | *Pubic hair:* pigmented, coarse, straight primarily along labia but progressively curled and spreads over mons and becomes profuse with an inverse triangular pattern; *axillary hair* starts after pubic hair; marked *growth* spurt with maximum *height* increment 18 months before menarche; *menarche: labia* become enlarged, *vaginal secretion* becomes acid; *breast:* areola and nipple elevated to form "primary" breast | 11–14 years | 10–16 years |
| Late adolescence | *Axillary hair* in moderate quantity; *pubic hair* fully developed; *breasts* fill out forming adult-type configuration; *menstruation* well established; *growth* in height is decelerated, ceases at 16¼ ± 13 months | 14–16 years | 13–18 years |
| Postadolescence to adult | Further growth of *axillary hair; breasts* fully developed | Onset 16–18 years | Onset 15–19 years |

* The normal range was accepted as the first to the ninth decile (80 percent of cases).
Source: W. A. Schonfeld, "The Body and the Body-Image in Adolescents," Table 4–1 from *Adolescence: Psychosocial Perspectives,* edited by Gerald Caplan and Serge Lebovici, © 1969 by Basic Books, Inc. publishers, New York.

accompanying distinct odors of body areas; the enlargement of skin pores on the face and the increased likelihood of acne; and a roughening of the skin over the thighs and upper arms (Tanner, 1972).

Tables 4–4 and 4–5 show the patterns of sexual maturation for females and males. Once again, it is important to remember that the age at puberty and the sequence of growth are quite variable for both boys and girls. The importance of the chronological age

**Table 4–5: Normal Maturational Sequence in Boys**

| Phase | Appearance of Sexual Characteristics | Average Ages | Age Range* |
|---|---|---|---|
| Childhood through preadolescence | Testes and penis have not grown since infancy; no pubic hair; growth in height constant; no spurt | — | — |
| Early adolescence | Testes begin to increase in size; scrotum grows, skin reddens and becomes coarser; penis follows with growth in length and circumference; no true pubic hair, may have down. | 12–13 years | 10–15 years |
| Middle adolescence | Pubic hair—pigmented, coarse and straight at base of penis, becoming progressively more curled and profuse, forming at first an inverse triangle and subsequently extending up to umbilicus; axillary hair starts after pubic hair; penis and testes continue growing; scrotum becomes larger, pigmented, and sculptured; marked spurt of growth in height with maximum increment about time pubic hair first develops and decelerates by time fully established; prostate and seminal vesicles mature, spontaneous or induced emissions follow, but spermatozoa inadequate in number and motility (adolescent sterility); voice beginning to change as larynx enlarges | 13–16 years | 11–18 years |
| Late adolescence | Facial and body hair appear and spread; pubic and axillary hair become denser; voice deepens; testes and penis continue to grow; emission has adequate number of motile spermatozoa for fertility; growth in height gradually decelerates, 98 percent of mature stature by 17¾ years ± 10 months; indention of frontal hairline | 16–18 years | 14–20 years |
| Postadolescence to adult | Mature, full development of primary and secondary sex characteristics; muscles and hirsutism may continue increasing | Onset 18–20 years | Onset 16–21 years |

* The normal range was accepted as the first to the ninth decile (80 percent of cases).
Source: W. A. Schonfeld, "The Body and the Body-Image in Adolescents," Table 4–2 from *Adolescence: Psychosocial Perspectives,* edited by Gerald Caplan and Serge Lebovici, © 1969 by Basic Books, Inc. publishers, New York.

at which the person experiences sexual maturation will be discussed in detail below. Here, let us simply note that the age-graded organization of the school and of many community groups designed for preadolescent and adolescent participants brings together young people who are likely to be at vastly different points in their pubertal growth. To the extent that adolescents have come to see their chronological age-mates as a significant reference group, the events of puberty are likely to disrupt the sense of solidarity and comfort that children have grown accustomed to feeling among their peers.

## ENVIRONMENTAL INFLUENCES ON GROWTH DURING PUBERTY

The initiation and continuation of pubertal growth result from the increased production of a group of hormones, including pituitary growth hormones, thyroid hormone, the sex hormones testosterone and estrogen, and the pituitary hormones that stimulate the growth of the sex glands. The hypothalamus must mature to a certain size before the production of these hormones will begin. Thus the brain itself is the primary regulator of adolescent growth and sexual maturation.

We recognize that genetic information from both parents contributes to the growth potential of children. Some part of the pattern of growth and the eventual stature of an adolescent is a consequence of inheritance. If identical twins are raised in different homes, they reach almost identical heights (less than two centimeters' difference). In other words, given a basically normal nutritional environment, genetics appears to be the main regulator of height. On the other hand, identical twins reared apart showed an average difference of ten pounds in weight, whereas identical twins reared together showed an average difference of only four pounds. Both the environmental resources and the twins' tendencies for balancing eating and activity are more likely to influence weight than they are to influence height (Carson, 1963; Wilson, 1975, 1974).

Given a certain genetic potential for growth and for sexual maturation, the environment can play an important role in the eventual attainment of one's growth potential. The most global environmental influence has been the general tendency for children to mature earlier over the past 100 years. Since 1900, children aged 10–14 have increased in height on the average two–three centimeters every decade (Tanner, 1962, 1972). The age at menarche has also been occurring earlier as part of this "secular trend" toward more rapid maturation. In the United States, the average age at menarche was 14 in 1900 and about 12¾ in 1960. Data from Norway show the average age at menarche to have been about 17 in 1840 and about 13¼ in 1960 (Tanner, 1962). A combination of factors has been identified as responsible for this pattern. These factors include better nutrition, especially more protein and more calories in the diets of infants and young children; greater protection from childhood diseases; and increased mobility, which permits parents who are genetically more varied to mate and to produce taller children (Muuss, 1970).

The secular trend probably has a species-determined limit. A certain amount of brain growth is required before the onset of puberty can occur. There is some evidence from recent samples that the secular trend may have reached an end in the United States. In a sample of mothers and their daughters, the two generations reached menarche at about the same chronological age (*New York Times,* 1976). Nevertheless, the secular trend has already had two important consequences for adolescent development. First, the gap between the childhood years and the potential childbearing years is much shorter than it was 100 years ago. Second, the period of adolescence, which is marked by the years between physical maturation and total participation in adult roles, is much longer than it was 100 years ago.

## Nutrition

Within the general pattern of healthier, more robust generations of children who reach puberty at an earlier age than did the generations before them, there continue to be striking examples of malnutrition and its effects on development. The impact of malnutrition begins during fetal growth. The malnutrition of the pregnant woman can occur before, during, and after childbirth. The most severe consequences for the infant result when the mother has been malnourished during pregnancy and the baby continues to be malnourished after pregnancy (Brasel, 1974). Malnutrition during the prenatal period is associated with low birth weight, higher rates of infant mortality, more complications during the first days after delivery, and a high risk of mental and motor impairment (Sinclair, Saigol, and Yeung, 1974; Kaplan, 1972; Winick, 1970).

Because of the rapid growth that occurs during adolescence, the prepubertal years and the time just around the height spurt are another period of life when lack of nutritional resources can have particularly negative consequences. Adolescents have a need for greater calorie intake than do younger children or adults. For girls, the recommended calorie intake is 2,400 at ages 11–14 and 2,100 at ages 15–22. For boys, the recommended intake is 2,800 at ages 11–14, and 3,000 at ages 15–22. Most adolescents increase their calorie intake by responding to an increased appetite, during the period of accelerated growth. However, a national survey of health and nutrition in the United States reported that the average calorie intake of white adolescents and black adolescents in families above the poverty line was 2,423 and 2,164, respectively, whereas adolescent whites and blacks in families below the poverty line had diets of 2,076 calories and 1,877 calories, respectively (Abraham, Lowenstein, and Johnson, 1974). These data suggest that many adolescents do not consume as many calories during the adolescent growth phase as would be recommended.

The eating patterns of adolescents tend to be sporadic and vulnerable to fads (Gifft, Washborn, and Harrison, 1972). Adolescents are likely to skip breakfast or lunch, or both (Huenemann et al., 1968). Snacking replaces regular meals. The quality of the adolescent's diet then depends heavily on his or her selection of snacks from drugstore counters, vending machines, and neighborhood fast-food restaurants. Poverty adds to the likelihood of nutritional inadequacy by reducing the adolescent's resources for both regular meals and snacks.

Severe limitations in the availability of food have the consequence of slowing the growth rate and delaying the onset of menarche (Tanner, 1972). Wars and famines result in a decrease in height gains during puberty (Mitchell, 1964; Tanner, 1970). For example, children's heights in Stuttgart, Germany, increased steadily from 1911 through 1953 except for the last years of both world wars, during which there were drops in height for most age groups (Tanner, 1962; Howe and Schiller, 1952). The average age at menarche is greater in poor, undeveloped areas, such as those inhabited by the Bundi of New Guinea and the Bantu of South Africa, than it is in industrialized countries (Tanner, and 1970). Even within industrialized countries such as England and Scotland, the more children in the family, the later the onset of menarche (Tanner, 1970, 1972).

A special group of adolescents who are vulnerable to nutritional deficiencies during adolescence are the obese (Shenker and Schildkraut, 1975; Gifft et al., 1972). Adolescents tend to be very preoccupied about their weight. Girls, especially, worry about being fat and may respond to the normal changes in their body shape as evidence of the need to diet (Clifford, 1971; Dwyer and Mayer, 1968–69). Adolescents who have been overweight since childhood may reduce the amount of food they eat in order to achieve a more desirable profile. Since these obese adolescents are still in need of additional nutrition to support their body growth, they may suffer from malnutrition and still be overweight (Mayer, 1968; Stunkard, 1973).

## Disease

Most minor and short-term illnesses, such as measles, flu, and chicken pox, do not appear to interfere with growth or sexual maturation during adolescence (Tanner, 1970). Adolescents are less susceptible than younger children to many kinds of infectious diseases. In a health survey of adolescents between the ages of 12 and 17, slightly over 20 percent of the subjects showed some illness, deformity, or handicap (Roberts, 1973). However, when adolescents were asked to rate their own health from excellent to poor, only 0.4 percent rated themselves as being in poor health.

Venereal diseases are perhaps the most serious infectious diseases that threaten health during adolescence (Eberly, 1975). Gonorrhea is the most frequently reported communicable disease recorded by the U.S. Public Health Service. In 1972, there were an estimated 1,000 cases of gonorrhea reported for every 100,000 people in the age range 15–19. The incidence of syphilis is less frequent but also on the increase. In 1972, 20.4 adolescents per 100,000 in the age range 15–19 had syphilis. It is estimated that by 1983 between 3 and 4 million 15-year-olds will contract gonorrhea or syphilis if the rate of infection remains at its current level. Since many cases of venereal disease may not be reported, these estimates may be lower than the actual frequency.

The problem with the spread of venereal disease among young adolescents is the result of several converging factors. First, there are changing norms about the permissibility or even the desirability of sexual exploration for females as well as males. Second, many schools have reduced their commitment to sex education because of the conflict it has raised with parents. Third, programs that provide sex education often omit information or are vague about venereal diseases and their prevention. Fourth, medical facilities often require parental consent before they will prescribe medication for adolescents. Fifth, because adolescents do not recognize the symptoms of venereal diseases, they may not seek medical help. Particularly if the adolescent perceives his or her sexual activities as unacceptable to parents or adult authorities, problems with sex-related infections will be handled with secrecy (Gordon, 1972).

## Drugs

Growth and sexual maturation at puberty can be manipulated by programs of hormone injections (Money and Ehrhardt, 1972). When puberty is delayed, the adolescent is likely to be shorter than his or her peers as well as sexually immature. Depending on the cause of the delayed puberty, hormone injections can stimulate the growth of the genital organs, facial hair, and pubic hair. Often, however, the child with a chronic pituitary failure will remain infertile even with treatment. When puberty is delayed because of pituitary failure, adult height and full sexual functioning are difficult to achieve. If the cause of delay is the result of atrophied gonads, testosterone therapy can successfully maintain the development of male sexual characteristics.

## Chronic Stress

There are several examples of the influence of stressful environmental events on the pattern of growth. These examples suggest that under extreme conditions emotional strain can inhibit physical growth. Widdowson (1951) attempted to study the consequences of food supplements on the growth of children who had been receiving minimal diets. She worked with children living in two German orphanages at the end of World War II. After six months without any intervention, she gave dietary supplements to the children in orphanage B but not to the children in orphanage A. In contrast to her expectations, she found that even with 20 percent more calories, the children in orphanage B gained less weight and grew fewer inches than did the children in orphanage A. Widdowson learned that just at the time that the dietary intervention was made, a very harsh, critical caregiver was transferred from orphanage A to orphanage B. This caregiver often chose mealtime as the opportunity to scold and punish the children. The children at orphanage A thrived in her absence, and despite their additional nutritional resources the children at orphanage B suffered in her presence.

Another example of the effects of stress on growth was described as reversible hypopituitary dwarfism (Powell, Brasel, and Blizzard, 1967; Patton and Gardner, 1969; Wolff and Money, 1972). This condition involves a failure to grow while the child is living in his or her regular home. The absence of growth is accompanied by lack of sleep and the inability to produce growth hormone. Once the child is moved to a neutral setting, such as a hospital or a foster home, growth hormone levels increase rapidly and growth begins at a normal rate. In an extreme example, a boy of 16 who had been severely abused and frequently locked in a closet, had the size and physical maturity of an 8-year-old. Away from his home, growth began and the boy entered puberty (Money and Ehrhardt, 1972). Although these examples are extreme, they suggest that the same factors which contribute to hospitalism and the failure to thrive in young infants can disrupt growth at later points as well.

# PSYCHOLOGICAL CONSEQUENCES OF PHYSICAL GROWTH AT PUBERTY

After the growth spurt, the pant legs are too short, the sweaters and shirts are too tight and the styles are too babyish. The changing attire of the adolescent reflects the changing self-image of the person wearing the clothes. A sense of growth and change comes from within and is reflected in the reactions of others. Adolescents recognize and, for the most part, welcome the growth that brings them closer to their adult image. Growth brings increases in strength and endurance that contribute to the adolescent's physical competence. Physical changes also take on meaning because of the ways others react to them. Peer norms about physical appearance, adult expectations about behavior, and parental reactions to one's changing image all contribute to the ways an adolescent adapts to physical growth. We might expect that for all adolescents there would be some ambivalence about growth. On the one hand, adolescents may feel unwilling to give up the security and comfort of their childhood status. New growth forces them away from a view of themselves as young children. They are propelled toward a realization that they are getting older. There are not too many jumps from that realization to a fear of growing old and a dread about their own mortality (Goldburgh and Rotman, 1973). On the other hand, growth may be a signal to accelerate one's movement toward adult status. New height, new strength, and new sexual maturity may prompt adolescents to experiment with the variety of activities that are recognized as part of adult life. In every adolescent, we can hear the voice of Peter Pan struggling to retain childhood status and the voice of Lolita calling out prematurely for adult status.

## The Consequences of Early and Late Maturing

Given the range of ages at which physical maturation can begin, it makes sense to think about some adolescents as "early" maturers and about other adolescents as "late" maturers. A number of studies have evaluated the psychological consequences of these extreme patterns of maturation. The consequences associated with the timing of the onset of puberty appear to be different for males than for females.

Early-maturing males are taller and stronger than their agemates. These characteristics contribute to the development of greater athletic competence and greater physical endurance. In addition to these personal qualities which might contribute to personality development during adolescence, the physical stature of early-maturing boys generates admiration and positive responses from others (Clausen, 1975; Dwyer and Mayer, 1968–69). Tall, strong boys are more likely to be given responsibility, to be viewed as peer leaders, and to be treated as if they were more mature intellectually as well as physically.

Charles Harbutt/Magnum

*Early maturing boys tend to be viewed as peer leaders.*

When a group of 13–15-year-old boys were rated by trained observers, the physically more mature boys were seen as more self-assured and more attractive than the late-maturing boys. The late-maturing boys were described by peers as less attractive, more restless, and more likely to be show-offs than the early-maturing boys (Jones and Bayley, 1950). When these same subjects were studied at age 17, the late-maturing boys continued to express feelings of inadequacy and of rebelliousness toward their parents. (Mussen and Jones, 1957). By age 17, the boys did not differ in their participation or leadership in male groups. In mixed-sex groups, the late maturers seemed less poised and felt less adequate. An evaluation of the same sample in their 30s found some lasting differences between the early- and late-maturing groups (Jones, 1957). The physical differences in appearance were no longer present. However, the early maturers continued to make a better social impression than the late maturers. The late maturers were rated as "less settled" and more expressive than their early-maturing peers.

A similar pattern of advantages associated with early maturing was reported by Weatherley (1964). He surveyed college students, asking them to rate their own maturation along a scale from very early to very late. The late maturers were assessed as less dominant and more dependent than the early maturers. The late maturers were also more resistant to authority and more unconventional. These characteristics suggest that the late-maturing male is in a particular social conflict. On the one hand, he needs the reassurance and encouragement of friends, and on the other hand, he is fighting to be seen as responsible and mature by adults. The delay in puberty appears to blur the transition to adult status and to encourage a range of more childlike coping patterns.

From this picture, we might have a sense that the early-maturing male has all the benefits and none of the stress of his late-maturing peer. However, another kind of analysis tells us that the early-maturing male has his own challenges to meet. From the behavioral ratings of a longitudinal sample, Peskin (1967, 1973; Peskin and Livson, 1972) found early-maturing boys to be "more inhibited cognitively, socially, and athletically, and to be so from the onset of puberty through middle adolescence, but not before." Peskin argued that because early maturers have had a shorter time to develop the ego strengths which occur during the childhood years, they are more threatened by the rapid physical changes and sexual urges of puberty than are average- or later-maturing boys. In response to these early threats, early maturers try to master the rewards and responsibilities of the social environment. They find security and reassurance by succeeding in their social context. In contrast to late maturers, they may be more rigidly committed to specific goals and life choices at an earlier time in their life. Although this certainty has the immediate consequence of giving early-maturing males the appearance of being more settled and responsible, it may result in foreclosure on experimentation in the long run. In her assessment of early and later maturers during their adult years, Jones (1965) supported this argument. She described the early maturers as more conforming and more rigid in their adaptation to the challenges of adulthood. Late maturers, perhaps as a result of their earlier struggles, appeared to have more self-insight and greater flexibility.

The consequences of early and late maturing appear to be somewhat different for girls than for boys. Research has shown that both late- and early-maturing girls experience certain social and emotional stresses (Dwyer and Mayer, 1968–69). Early-maturing girls begin to develop physically long before any of their age-mates. For this reason, the early-maturing female may experience displeasure with her plumping figure and anxiety about her sexual interests. We must remember that early-maturing girls are only nine or ten years old. At that age, they are likely to be embarrassed by the height spurt and breast development that precede menstruation. They are certainly not able to share the reality of menstruation comfortably with their male peers, and they may have some reservations about talking these things over with their female friends. Early-maturing females may slouch, wear baggy sweat shirts, or become shy and withdrawn in order to avoid peer recognition of their changing body image (Jones and Mussen, 1958; Peskin and Livson, 1972).

In contrast to early-maturing girls, late-maturing girls may feel left out as most of their peers become involved in heterosexual dating. Late maturers, who are 14 or 15 when menstruation begins, may be anxious about the lack of breast development or of the accompanying curviness that characterizes the female figure. They would not, however, be at a social disadvantage because of their delayed height spurt or weight gain. In fact, late-maturing females would be maturing at about the same time as the average male. In this sense, their sexual development and sexual interests would be more appropriately timed to match their male cohort. In contrast to their early-maturing peers, late-maturing girls have less time to get used to their changing body image and sexual interests before the emphasis on heterosexual social activity actually dominates the peer group.

In general, the differences between late and early maturing are less marked for females than they are for males (Weatherley, 1964). Both early and late maturation pose challenges for females. Once physical development begins, early-maturing females may feel temporarily isolated and ill matched to their chronological peers. On the other hand, they are relieved of the prolonged uncertainty and naiveté that confront their late-maturing friends. Since the society does not especially value tall, robust females, early-maturing girls do not benefit from the social advantages that have been associated with early maturation for boys.

## Adolescent Reactions to Physique

Adolescents are critical observers of their own bodies and the bodies of their peers. Girl and boy watching are common pastimes that take place on street corners and in school halls, cafeterias, and shopping malls. The peer culture develops norms for physical attractiveness, and each adolescent works to achieve some approximation of those norms. Any family with adolescent children can verify the increased concern with physical appearance by observing the length of time that adolescents spend gazing at their reflection in the bathroom mirror.

The evaluation of one's physical attractiveness has consequences for peer relationships as well as for one's developing self-concept. These dimensions are likely to be interrelated because adolescents incorporate peer assessments about their attractiveness or popularity into their self-evaluation.

Three questions can be asked about the impact of physical appearance on psychological development. First, how much agreement is there among peers about the dimension of physical attractiveness? If there were no commonly held standards for physical attractiveness, then each person would stand an equally good chance of being perceived as attractive or unattractive by some other peers and adults. That does not appear to be the case. Physical attractiveness is a measurable dimension that is relatively consistent (Cavior and Dokecki, 1973). When 5th graders and 11th graders were asked to make judgments about the attractiveness of their classmates from black-and-white photographs, there was a high amount of agreement about how each person was rated. When these ratings were compared to ratings of the same people by students who did not know them, agreement was high for both 5th- and 11th-grade boys and for 11th-grade girls. Knowing the person had the most influence on judgments of fifth-grade girls. In this comparison, knowing the person led to higher ratings of attractiveness for people who were in the average range but did not affect judgments of people at the extreme attractive or unattractive ranges.

Given stable dimensions of physical attractiveness, a second question is, What is the social meaning of physical characteristics? One might ask whether boys have different criteria for judging attractiveness than girls or whether physical attractiveness and peer popularity are associated. The evidence suggests that boys and girls use similar criteria for judging physical attractiveness. Girls tend to be more dissatisfied about their appearance than boys, but both sexes emphasize the same level of satisfaction about their weight, their facial appearance, or their body build (Clifford, 1971).

When judging others, boys and girls tend to agree about which other boys and girls are attractive or unattractive (Cavior and Dokecki, 1973).

Physical characteristics are associated with social stereotypes. Sheldon (1940, 1942) hypothesized that there were important links between body type and personality type. He described three primary body types, each with its own closely associated personality characteristics. The endomorph, or the fat, rounded body type was associated with relaxation, affection, and love of physical comfort. The contrasting ectomorph, or the fragile, linear, delicate body type, was associated with restraint, love of privacy, and self-consciousness. The mesomorph, the third body type, had a muscular, rectangular physique and was associated with an adventurous, active, and assertive personality. In a recent assessment of the relationship between peer ratings and body build, Clausen (1975) confirmed the existence of social stereotypes associated with particular body shapes among a sample of junior high school students. In his analysis, however, he identified the importance of social class as an intervening factor that influenced the desirability of certain aspects of physical appearance. For boys, the mesomorphic build was positively associated with a variety of social traits, including aggressiveness, daring, leadership, and activity. Among the working-class sample, mesomorphic boys were seen as especially popular and happy. Clausen suggested that the characteristics of mesomorphy, including muscle strength and physical resilience, are especially relevant to the life activities of working-class boys.

The general pattern of peer reactions to boys with the ectomorphic body build was neutral to negative. In the working-class group, the tall, thin boys were seen as being fearful, lacking self-assurance, and more likely to be followers than leaders. The middle-class group of boys did not hold these same negative stereotypes for ectomorphs. No peer ratings were significantly associated with the endomorphic body build, although the middle-class boys saw their chubby peers less positively than did the working-class boys.

For the junior high school girls, Clausen found that social class also influenced the peer judgments that were related to body build. Among working-class girls, both mesomorphy and endomorphy were associated with positive ratings, but ectomorphy was seen more negatively. The middle-class girls were more neutral about ectomorphy and less positive about mesomorphy than were their working-class peers.

Here we begin to see the interweaving of cultural factors that may influence the evaluation of physical appearance. Ethnic ancestry and socioeconomic status may both influence the values placed on particular physical features. In the society as a whole, tall males receive higher salaries than shorter males and are more likely to be promoted to positions of responsibility than are shorter males. Within the adolescent peer group, however, the tall, thin boy may be viewed with some degree of scorn if the peer culture values muscular strength or athletic endurance.

The third question about the consequence of physical appearance concerns its contribution to the individual's self-image. Do judgments about one's attractiveness or one's physique influence one's self-concept? When adolescents in the age range 11–19 were asked to rate their body parts on a five-point scale from completely dissatisfied to completely satisfied, the average rating was 3.71 for males and 3.39 for females. Although this mean rating suggests that both boys and girls are generally satisfied about aspects of their body, females tended to express more dissatisfaction than males (Clifford, 1971).

In a study of the relationship between perceived attractiveness and self-concept, college students were asked to rate each of 24 body parts as attractive and then to rate those parts as effective or ineffective (Lerner, Orlos, and Knapp, 1976). For females, the attractiveness rating was more closely associated to the self-concept than the effectiveness rating ($r = .52$ and $r = .37$, respectively). For males, the two ratings were highly correlated with each other ($r = .77$) and effectiveness was more closely associated with the self-concept measure ($r = .58$) than was attractiveness ($r = .50$). These patterns suggest that the meaning of one's body image may differ for male and female adolescents. Females may be more concerned about the social appeal of their appearance. A positive self-concept is closely tied to a sense of social acceptance and heterosexual appeal. Males are more inclined to emphasize their physical competences as components of their self-worth. Their body is viewed as a resource for influencing the environment (Erikson, 1968; Schonfeld, 1969). Although physical attractiveness is an important component of the self-concept for both males and females, the socialization pattern leads to somewhat different emphases on the meaning of the body image for males and females.

To say that satisfaction about one's body is associated with satisfaction about oneself does not imply a causal connection from body image to self-image. It does not explain how physical appearance contributes to the self-image. It is important to realize that the body image is actually a mental concept, an idea about how one looks, how effective one's body is, and how much space one's body occupies (Schonfeld, 1969). Because adolescence is a period of rapid growth, there is new uncertainty about the dimensions of one's body and about the desirability of one's appearance. Intensified preoccupation with physical appearance seems to stimulate a kind of self-consciousness among early adolescents. When an adolescent girl enters a classroom or attends a dance, she may imagine that all eyes are on her, scrutinizing her appearance, her clothes, or her hair. This heightened self-consciousness makes adolescents overly concerned about how others may be reacting to them (Looft, 1971). They may not realize that their peers are equally concerned with their own appearance. The imagined audience becomes very real for an adolescent. Tapid physical changes and sexual maturation are quite likely the most powerful stimuli that provoke this new preoccupation with the social evaluation of peers.

## The Psychological Consequences of Sexual Maturation

Psychoanalytic theory emphasizes the sexual nature of human beings from their earliest moments in infancy throughout life. The concept of childhood sexuality alerts us to the fact that sexual interests and sexual fantasies do not begin in adolescence. Long before the person is sexually mature, wishes and fears about sexual intimacy are part of mental life (Freud, 1953, 1959a, 1959b, 1961, 1964). What is more, the genital area is sensitive to stimulation long before puberty. Kinsey (Kinsey et al., 1953) reported that 28 percent of males and 14 percent of females remembered participating in some form of sexual play by the age of nine. We do not have to begin the discovery of sexual satisfaction as complete novices during adolescence. Childhood masturbation; the pleasures of hugging, kissing, and being held closely by one's parents; and the sensual pleasures of a warm bath, an application of suntan lotion, or a vigorous bout of tickling are all examples of childhood behaviors that educate children about the potential pleasures of sexual encounters.

Freud (1953, 1955, 1959a, 1959b, 1961, 1964) warned us that in addition to these pleasures, there are also terrifying fears associated with the child's understanding of sexuality. He suggested that many children interpret the sexual act as a violent interaction in which the father injures the mother. The concept of castration anxiety suggests that boys may fantasy the loss of the penis during early childhood, as a punishment for either masturbation or for hostile feelings toward the father. According to the psychoanalytic view, these fears about sexual injury are repressed along with unacceptable Oedipal or Electra wishes at the end of the phallic stage of development.

What, then, are the special consequences of sexual maturation for the development of sexual behavior? The period of adolescence begins active experimentation with and conceptualization about adult sexuality. In Chapter 6, we will discuss adolescent sexual behavior and social dating in more detail. Here, let us consider two issues: (1) the process of learning how to translate sexual impulses and fantasies into an image of oneself as a mature sexual being and (2) the sexually mature adolescent in the family.

**Learning to Be a Sexual Adult.**  Three kinds of behaviors provide opportunities for developing a sense of one's sexual nature. These are masturbation, sexual encounters with others, and emotional commitment to another person. All of these behaviors take place in a cultural context, so that their meaning derives not only from the physical and emotional pleasures one derives but from the extent to which the behaviors fulfill or violate social expectations. The pattern of participation in these three forms of sexual activity are different for males and females.

Masturbation is much more frequent among high school–age males than females (Gagnon, 1972). In a sample of almost 600 males and 600 females of high school age, 77 percent of the males masturbated twice a week or more, whereas only 17 percent of the females masturbated that often and 60 percent of the females had never masturbated (Gagnon, Simon, and Berger, 1970). Masturbation for males provides an avenue for discovering about orgasm and for reinforcing the pleasure of sexual activity. A survey of adult sexual behavior conducted by the Playboy Foundation (Hunt, 1974) reported that 93 percent of males and 63 percent of females had masturbated to orgasm. About 60 percent of males but only 35 percent of females had experienced orgasm through masturbation by age 13. Given that sexual maturation begins earlier for females than for males, it appears that sexual activity of a nonsocial nature plays a more important role for males than for females. However, for both sexes, masturbation appears to be a primary mode of achieving sexual stimulation and of linking the physical act of orgasm with symbolic fantasies of social encounters.

The second kind of sexual learning occurs through sexual encounters. These experiences may be heterosexual or homosexual in nature. About 6 percent of females in the age range 13–19 have had at least one homosexual experience (Sorenson, 1973). About 15 percent of males have had at least one homosexual encounter during the age range 12–16, with no subsequent homosexual relationships (Simon and Gagnon, 1967). Often these experiences are the outcome of the strong, close commitment that develops among peers in the early adolescent years. Close physical contact, peer instruction about sexuality, or exploitation of a weaker or younger adolescent by an older adolescent can all be part of the context of early homosexual experiences. Most often, these experiences are interpreted as discrete events in the pursuit of a heterosexual direction (Gagnon, 1972).

Spanier (1975) has described four stages of heterosexual involvement. These include kissing, light petting, heavy petting, and intercourse. From a national sample of college students, he determined that most people begin with kissing and progress from one level to the next. The process of moving through these levels of involvement is closely related to when persons begin to date and how often they date.

Sexual practices in the United States suggest that this pattern of involvement is well under way during the high school years. A study in Illinois found that 50 percent of boys and 48 percent of girls had experienced light petting by their 15th birthday (Juhasz, 1976). Sorenson (1973) reported that 59 percent of boys and 45 percent of girls in the age range 13–19 had experienced sexual intercourse. Among this group of sexually experienced adolescents, 13 percent had had their first experience at the age of 12 or under. By the age of 15, 71 percent of males and 56 percent of females who were sexually experienced had had intercourse. These data indicate that a large group of adolescents make the transition to an adult form of sexual behavior through direct experience in sexual intimacy. Although this pattern continues to show females as less active than males in all stages of sexual activity, the pattern is toward increasingly large numbers of sexually active females at young ages (Micklin, Thomson, and Gardner, 1977; Gordon, 1973; Juhasz, 1976).

*Bruce Davidson/Magnum*

*The back seat of the car is a time-tested setting for sexual experimentation.*

The third element in the development of adult sexuality is the formation of an emotional commitment to a sexual partner. For the most part, adolescents are not promiscuous. They do not value nor do they participate in sexual activities with many different partners at the same period of time (Sorenson, 1973; Vener and Stewart, 1974; Dreyer, 1975). Nevertheless, there is a sense in which a double standard about the appropriateness of sex without commitment still exists. In a sample of over 1,000 students at 12 colleges, Carns (1973) found that males and females were just about opposite in the way they evaluated the nature of the relationship with their first sexual partner. Females were most likely to have intercourse with a person whom they planned to marry or with whom they had a strong emotional involvement. Males were most likely to have intercourse with someone described as a "pickup." When males are involved with casual sexuality, they tend to brag about ir or to share it with their male peers. Thus, an important part of early male sexual activity is the achievement of recognition among same-sex peers for one's virility. In contrast, females are more likely to focus on the romantic elements of the relationship. They are more likely than males to keep their sexual experiences to themselves rather than to share them, and they are more likely than males to get mixed reactions rather than approval for their sexual activities. In all of these ways, the picture emerges of females carrying on a private dialogue with an old standard of Victorian modesty. In fantasy and in reality, females see sexual intercourse as an element of a more elaborate emotional commitment to a partner. Males, on the other hand, begin their movement toward adult sexuality by exploring the satisfactions of sexuality per se. It is only later that they begin to merge sexual interests and social interests into an interpersonal commitment to a partner (Gagnon and Simon, 1973).

**The Sexual Adolescent in the Family.**   Much less thought has been given to the consequences of sexual maturation for the family group than for the emergence of mature heterosexuality. We might begin by recognizing that the prevalence of incest taboos must be a reaction to the very strong tendencies to begin one's sexual career with those who are nearest and most familiar. Rather than go through the embarrassment and uncertainty of learning about sex with a stranger, it would probably have been tempting to simply extend the family bonds to include sexual intimacy. Our revulsion at this notion suggests the powerful forces of socialization that have been at work through the generations of psychosocial evolution to prevent sexual bonds from developing in the family group.

In direct contrast to sexual attractiveness, what tends to happen as children move into puberty is a feeling of embarrassment about physical contact with parents. Opportunities for hugging, sitting on a parent's lap, crawling into bed on a Sunday morning, or snuggling close together in front of the fire diminish. In addition to the many ways that adolescents feel isolated or self-conscious, this new loss of nonverbal ways to show affection is a barrier to comfortable parent-child interactions.

The acceptance of one's sexuality depends to a large extent on the way sexuality is handled by one's parents. To the extent that parents are embarrassed, prudish, or anxious themselves, adolescents may feel the need to hide the physical changes they are experiencing. For example, of those college students who had experienced sexual intercourse, only 6 percent of males and 4 percent of females first told a family member about it. For those who did share this experience with a family member, the person told was usually a sibling, not a parent (Carns, 1973). In a sample of almost 1,000 university students, Thornburg (1975) found that 13 percent of the students received their initial information about sex from their mothers and that 2 percent received this information from their fathers. The kind of information parents share is also somewhat limited. For example, while mothers are likely to tell daughters about menstruation, they are less likely to tell them about sexual arousal or intercourse. Many boys have received no information about nocturnal emissions before they occur (Shipman, 1968). In fact, Shipman has found that during puberty parents became less willing to discuss sexual questions than they were during earlier periods of childhood. Clearly, then, puberty and the events of sexual maturation upset the equilibrium of the family group. Parents are, on the one hand, guarded and protective, and, on the other hand, proud, perhaps even envious, of their child's maturing physique. Adolescents are suddenly aware of their parents' sexuality at a new, concrete level. They may be disgusted, disappointed, delighted, or indifferent. In any case, they will probably find it hard to share their curiosity and their interest openly with their parents. At the same time, they are guarded about any action toward a parent that could possibly have a sexual implication. Finally, they are careful not to share any fantasies, sexual impulses, or sexual activities that would bring parental rejection. The events of puberty are likely to bring a period of emotional withdrawal and hostility which mark the beginning of prolonged work on individuation during the adolescent years.

## PREPARATION FOR PUBERTY: SOURCES OF INFORMATION

When parents are planning to move to a new city, they will most likely spend some time preparing their children for the move.

They will talk about their new home, explain the reasons for the move, perhaps take the children for a visit to the new city, and help share their children's fears about leaving a well-known, comfortable setting for something much less certain. The analogy to puberty is all too clear.

Before rapid physical growth and sexual maturation catch adolescents by surprise, it would make sense to begin to advise them about what to expect. Although most of the attention given to preparation for puberty has focused on sex education, we would suggest that all aspects of physical growth at puberty need explanation. Adolescents need an opportunity to ask questions and share their concerns about their total changing body image. The concepts that were presented earlier in this chapter about individual variation in the rate of maturing, the varied patterns of growth of each body part, the relationship between prepubertal and postpubertal height and weight, and the normative patterns of sexual maturation might all help adolescents put the experiences of physical growth into perspective. The discussion of physical growth might include an emphasis on diet, drugs, physical health, and activity as factors which influence growth. Armed with this information, adolescents might begin to understand how their contemporary life-style contributes to their current and future growth.

Information about sex comes from a number of sources, including parents, friends, the school, and literature. Early studies about the sources of sex information found that peers provided most of the information and that parents played a minimal role (Bell, 1938; Angelino and Mech, 1954, 1955; Shipman, 1968). In a recent survey of university students, Thornburg (1975) found that peers were still the most likely source of sex information. Parents, especially fathers, continue to play a small role, and literature and the school are increasing their contributions to sex information. This pattern does not necessarily match the preferences adolescents express for learning about sexuality. Gagnon (1965) found that an overwhelming majority of adolescents would prefer to learn about sex from their mother and father. Nevertheless, many adolescents find that parents are unwilling to talk about sex or that the discussions are very uncomfortable (Schofield, 1968; Gordon, 1973).

Information about sex is of varied quality and comes from varied sources. As we mentioned earlier, parents are most likely to tell about menstruation and childbirth. They usually do not talk about petting, intercourse, or venereal disease. Adolescents get most of their information about venereal disease from school and most of their information about abortion from literature. In other words, they seek out the information they need from the most accurate sources available. When asked to evaluate the accuracy of their information, adolescents rated their knowledge about homosexuality, masturbation, and intercourse as least accurate. We might speculate that these areas are also the sources of the most anxiety and uncertainty. They reflect areas of moral as well as biological doubt.

In general, the more information adolescents have at their disposal, the less likely they are to experience difficulties in their sexual encounters, especially venereal disease and unwanted pregnancy. In a survey of sexually active 15–19-year-olds, it was found that 53 percent did not use any form of contraception (Zelnick and Kantner, 1973). The reasons they gave for not using a contraceptive included the following: (1) they were too young to get pregnant; (2) they had sex too infrequently to get pregnant; (3) they could not get pregnant because it was the wrong time of the month. Most of the adolescent females who did not use contraceptives did not want to become pregnant. They simply did not realize that there was a serious risk of pregnancy, or they did not know where to obtain a contraceptive. When a group of unmarried pregnant adolescents were given a brief course in reproduction and birth control through the hospital where they delivered, only 7 percent had a second pregnancy before they married. In a matched group who did not receive the course, 57 percent of the young women were pregnant again within a year (Guttmacher, 1969; Rubin, 1968).

The goals of sharing information about sex are more complicated than the communication of biological information. Adolescents may already have most of the information about concepts related to foreplay, intercourse, birth, and menstruation by the age of 12. They need to learn how to weave sexuality into a nonexploitative, intimate relationship. They need to understand the nature of the various expressions of sexuality, including masturbation, homosexuality, and bisexuality, as these contribute to the total picture of human sexual behavior. Further, they need to understand the consequences of specific sexual activities and begin to see their own role in making decisions about sexual behavior (Gordon, 1973; Juhasz, 1976; McCary, 1978). In this sense, information about sex is intimately interwoven with the whole range of developmental issues that confront adolescents. Selfhood, one's sex role, the need for closeness and comfortable companionship with peers, the emergence from a family circle into a larger social community, and the anticipation of adulthood are significant life themes that need to be incorporated into education about physical growth at puberty.

## CHAPTER SUMMARY

Physical growth at puberty provides concrete evidence that one phase of life is coming to a close and a new phase is beginning. As Lewin has pointed out, changes about the inner personal region, including body boundaries, physical strength, and sexual impulses, lead to uncertainty and anxiety. On the other hand, physical growth may be greeted with enthusiasm and delight as a sign of movement toward a new adult status. This emotional ambivalence, nostalgia for childhood and desire for growth, is at the crux of the challenge of early adolescence. The very changes that move adolescents toward new modes of intimacy with peers may force them out of the comfortable stability of the family group. Preoccupation with one's appearance and physical growth may result in competition, jealousy, and feelings of inferiority with peers. The differences in timing of sexual maturation between males and females creates a new source of conflict and misunderstanding among age-mates. In a highly age-graded society such as ours, the early maturers have the advantage of greater competence and self-assurance. On the other hand, the extremely early maturers are in a position of having to cope with new information and new sexual impulses at a very early age. There is some evidence that the timing of maturity has personal and social meanings that continue to influence personality into adulthood.

An important theme in this chapter has been the differences in growth and adaptation to growth for males and females. Females mature earlier than males. There is not such a clear leadership advantage to early maturing for girls as there is for boys. On the other hand, there is not such a clear disadvantage for late-maturing girls as there is for late-maturing boys. Late-maturing girls are developing at about the same time as most of their male peers. The process of sexual learning appears to be different for males and females. Females are less likely to engage in masturbation than males. They are more likely to think of sexuality within a romantic context. Males are more likely to experience sexuality in an erotic context. Only later is the intimate relationship connected to this physical experience. Finally, females appear to be more dissatisfied about their appearance than males. They are less likely to be concerned about the effectiveness of their body and more likely to be concerned about the attractiveness of their body.

Adolescents begin to gather information about sexual maturation during childhood. By age 10–12, most adolescents have information about childbirth, intercourse, and menstruation. Although parents would be the most desirable sources of information, peers tend to be the largest source of information. The areas that are least well presented and in which the need for information is greatest are homosexuality, intercourse, and masturbation. In general, information about physical growth is not adequately presented. The importance of nutrition and physical activity for growth, the pattern of normal development, and the extent of individual variability are all areas in which information could reduce uncertainty and improve patterns of healthy development.


# REFERENCES

Abraham, S., Lowenstein, F. W., and Johnson, C. L.   *Preliminary findings of the first health and nutrition examination survey, United States, 1971–1972.* DHEW Publication no. (HRA) 74-1219-1. Washington, D.C.: U.S. Government Printing Office, 1974.

Angelino, H., and Mech, E. V.   Some "first" sources of sex information as reported by ninety college students. *Proceedings of the Oklahoma Academy of Science,* 1954, *35,* 117.

Angelino, H., and Mech, E. V.   Some "first" sources of sex information as reported by sixty-seven college women. *Journal of Psychology,* 1955, 321–324.

Bardwick, J.   *The psychology of women: A study of biocultural conflict.* New York: Harper and Row, 1971.

Bell, H. M.   *Youth tell their story,* Washington, D.C.: American Council on Education, 1938.

Brasel, J.   Cellular changes in intrauterine malnutrition. In M. Winick (Ed.), *Nutrition and fetal development.* New York: Wiley, 1974. Pp. 13–27.

Carns, D. E.   Talking about sex: Notes on first coitus and the double sexual standard. *Journal of Marriage and the Family,* 1973, *35,* 677–688.

Carron, A. V., and Bailey, D. A.   Strength development in boys from 10 through 16 years. *Monographs of the Society for Research in Child Development,* 1974, *39* (4).

Carson, H. L.   *Heredity and human life.* New York: Columbia University Press, 1963.

Cavior, N., and Dokecki, P. R.   Physical attractiveness, perceived attitude similarity, and academic achievement as contributors to interpersonal attraction among adolescents. *Developmental Psychology,* 1973, *9,* 44–54.

Clausen, J. A.   The social meaning of differential physical and sexual maturation. In S. E. Dragastin and G. H. Elder, Jr. (Eds.), *Adolescence in the life cycle: Psychological change and social context.* New York: Wiley, 1975. Pp. 25–47.

Clifford, E.   Body satisfaction in adolescence. *Perceptual and Motor Skills,* 1971, *33,* 119–125.

Dreyer, P. H.   Sex, sex roles, and marriage among youth in the 1970's. In R. J. Havighurst and P. H. Dreyer (Eds.), *Youth.* Chicago: University of Chicago Press, 1975.

Dwyer, J., and Mayer, J.   Psychological effects of variations in physical appearance during adolescence. *Adolescence,* 1968–69, *3,* 353–368.

Eberly, F. W.   Venereal disease in the adolescent. In A. J. Kalafatich (Ed.), *Approaches to the care of adolescents.* New York: Appleton-Century-Crofts/Prentice-Hall, 1975.

Erikson, E. H.   *Identity: Youth and crisis.* New York: Norton, 1968.

Faust, M. S.   Somatic development of adolescent girls. *Monographs of the Society for Research in Child Development,* 1977, *42* (1, Serial No. 169).

Freud, S.   Three essays on the theory of sexuality. In J. Strachey (Ed.), *The standard edition of the complete psychological works of Sigmund Freud,* vol. 7. London: Hogarth Press, 1953. (Originally published in German in 1905.)

Freud, S.   Analysis of a phobia in a five-year-old boy. In J. Strachey (Ed.), *The standard edition of the complete psychological works of Sigmund Freud,* vol. 10. London: Hogarth Press, 1955. (Originally published in German in 1909.)

Freud, S.   The sexual enlightenment of children. In J. Strachey (Ed.), *The standard edition of the complete psychological works of Sigmund Freud,* vol. 9. London: Hogarth Press, 1959. (Originally published in German in 1907.)(a)

Freud, S.   On the sexual theories of children. In J. Strachey (Ed.), *The standard edition of the complete psychological works of Sigmund Freud,* vol. 9. London: Hogarth Press, 1959. (Originally published in German in 1908.)(b)

Freud, S.   The dissolution of the Oedipus-complex. In J. Strachey (Ed.), *The standard edition of the complete psychological works of Sigmund Freud,* vol. 19. London: Hogarth Press, 1961. (Originally published in 1924.)

Freud, S.   New introductory lectures on psychoanalysis. In J. Strachey (Ed.), *The standard edition of the complete psychological works of Sigmund Freud,* vol. 22. London: Hogarth Press, 1964. (Originally published in German in 1933.)

Gagnon, J. H.   Sexuality and sexual learning in the child. *Psychiatry,* 1965, *28,* 212–228.

Gagnon, J. H.   The creation of the sexual in early adolescence. In J. Kagan and R. Coles (Eds.), *Twelve to sixteen: Early Adolescence.* New York: Norton, 1972. Pp. 231–258.

Gagnon, J. H., and Simon, W.   *Sexual conduct: The social sources of human sexuality.* Chicago: Aldine, 1973.

Gagnon, J. H., Simon, W., and Berger, A. J.   Some aspects of sexual adjustment in early and late adolescence. In J. Zubin and A. N. Freedman (Eds.), *Psychopathology of adolescence.* New York: Grune and Stratton, 1970.

Gifft, H. H., Washborn, M. B., and Harrison, G. G.   *Nutrition, behavior, and change.* Englewood Cliffs, N.J.: Prentice-Hall, 1972.

Goldburgh, S. J., and Rotman, C. B.   The terror of life—A latent adolescent nightmare. *Adolescence,* Winter 1973.

Gordon, S.   *The sexual adolescent: Communicating with teenagers about sex.* North Scituate, Mass.: Duxbury Press, 1973.

Guttmacher, A. F.   How can we best combat illegitimacy? *Medical Aspects of Human Sexuality,* March 1969, pp. 48–61.

Howe, P. E., and Schiller, M.   Growth responses of the school child to changes in diet and environmental factors. *Journal of Applied Physiology,* 1952, *5* 51–61.

Huenemann, R. S., et al.   Food and eating practices of teenagers. *Journal of the American Dietetic Association,* 1968, *53,* 17.

Hunt, M.   *Sexual behavior in the seventies.* Chicago: Playboy Press, 1974.

Jones, H. E.   The California Adolescent Growth Study. *Journal of Educational Research,* 1938, *31,* 561–567.

Jones, H. E.   The Adolescent Growth Study: principles and methods. Journal of Consulting Psychology, 1939, 3, 157–159.

Jones, H. E., and Bayley, N.   The Berkeley Growth Study. Child Development, 1941, 12, 167–173.

Jones, M. C.   The later careers of boys who were early or late maturing. Child Development, 1957, 28, 113–128.

Jones, M. C.   Psychological correlates of somatic development. Child Development, 1965, 36, 899–911.

Jones, M. C., and Bayley, N.   Physical maturing among boys as related to behavior. Journal of Educational Psychology, 1950, 41, 129–148.

Jones, M. C., and Mussen, P. H.   Self conceptions, motivations, and interpersonal attitudes of early and late maturing girls. Child Development, 1958, 29, 491–501.

Juhasz, A. M.   A cognitive approach to sex education. In J. F. Adams (Ed.), Understanding adolescence: Current developments in adolescent psychology (3d ed.). Boston: Allyn and Bacon, 1976. Pp. 441–463.

Kaplan, B. J.   Malnutrition and mental deficiency. Psychological Bulletin, 1972, 78, 321–334.

Kinsey, A. C., Pomeroy, W. B., Martin, C. E., and Gebhard, P. H.   Sexual behavior in the human female. Philadelphia: Saunders, 1953.

Lerner, R. M., Orlos, J. B., and Knapp, J. R.   Physical attractiveness, physical effectiveness, and self-concept in late adolescents. Adolescence, 1976, 11, 313–326.

Looft, W. R.   Egocentrism and social interaction in adolescence, Adolescence, 1971, 6, 487–494.

Macfarlane, J. W.   Studies in child guidance: Methodology of data collection and organization. Monographs of the Society for Research in Child Development, 1938, 3 (6, Serial No. 19).

Marshall, W. A., and Tanner, J. M.   Variables in pattern of pubertal changes in girls. Archives of the Diseases of Childhood, 1969, 44, 291–303.

Marshall, W. A., and Tanner, J. M.   Variations in the pattern of pubertal changes in boys. Archives of the Diseases of Childhood, 1970, 45, 13a.

Mayer, J.   Overweight: Causes, cost, and control. Englewood Cliffs, N.J.: Prentice-Hall, 1968.

McCary, J. L.   McCary's human sexuality (3d ed.). New York: Van Nostrand, 1978.

Micklin, M., Thomson, E., and Gardner, J. S.   Adolescent socialization and heterosexual behavior. Seattle: Battelle Human Affairs Research Center, 1977.

Money, J., and Ehrhardt, A. A.   Man and woman, boy and girl: The differentiation and dimorphism of gender identity from conception to maturity. Baltimore: Johns Hopkins Press, 1972.

Mussen, P. H., and Jones, M. C.   Self-conceptions, motivations, and interpersonal attitudes of late and early maturing boys. Child Development, 1957, 28, 243–256.

Muuss, R. E.   Adolescent development and the secular trend. Adolescence, 1970, 5, 267–286.

*New York Times.* When women mature. April 4, 1976.

Patton, R. G., and Gardner, L. I. Short stature associated with maternal deprivation syndrome: Disordered family environment as a cause of so-called idiopathic hypopituitarism. In L. I. Gardner (Ed.), *Endocrine and genetic diseases
of childhood.* Philadelphia: Saunders, 1969.

Peskin, H. Pubertal onset and ego functioning. *Journal of Abnormal Psychology,*
1967, *72,* 1–15.

Peskin, H. Influence of the developmental schedule of puberty on learning and
ego functioning. *Journal of Youth and Adolescence,* 1973, *2,* 273–290.

Peskin, H., and Livson, N. Pre and postpubertal personality and adult psychologic
functioning. *Seminars in Psychiatry,* 1972, *4,* 343–353.

Powell, G. F., Brasel, J. A., and Blizzard, R. M. Emotional deprivation and growth
retardation simulating idiopathic hypopituitarism. I. Clinical evaluation of
the syndrome. *New England Journal of Medicine,* 1967, *276,* 1271–1278.

Roberts, J. *Examination and health history findings among children and youths,
6–17 years, United States.* Data from the National Health Survey, series 11,
no. 129, DHEW Publications no. (HRA) 74-1611. Washington, D.C.: U.S. Government Printing Office, 1973.

Rubin, J. Changing college sex: New Kinsey report. *Sexology,* June 1968, pp.
780–782.

Schofield, M. *The sexual behavior of young people.* Gretna, La: Pelican Books,
1968.

Schonfeld, W. A. The body and the body-image in adolescents. In G. Caplan
and S. Lebovici (eds.), *Adolescence: Psychosocial perspectives.* New York:
Basic Books, 1969.

Schwartz, N. B. New concepts of gonadotropin and steroid feedback control
mechanisms. In J. J. Gold (Ed.), *Textbook of gynecologic endocrinology.* New
York: Harper and Row, 1968. Pp. 33–50.

Sheldon, W. H. *The varieties of the human physique.* New York: Harper and
Brothers, 1940.

Sheldon, W. H. *The varieties of temperament: A psychology of constitutional
differences.* New York: Harper and Brothers, 1942.

Shenker, I. R., and Schildkraut, M. Physical and emotional health of youth. In
R. J. Havighurst and P. H. Dreyer (Eds.), *Youth.* Chicago: University of Chicago
Press, 1975.

Shipman, G. The psychodynamics of sex education. *Family Coordinator,* 1968,
*17,* 3–12.

Simon, W., and Gagon, J. H. The pedagogy of sex. *Saturday Review,* 1967, *50,*
74–91.

Sinclair, J. C., Saigol, S., and Yeung, C. Y. Early postnatal consequences of fetal
malnutrition. In M. Winick (Ed.), *Nutrition and fetal development.* New York:
Wiley, 1974. Pp. 147–172.

Sorenson, R. C. *Adolescent sexuality in contemporary America.* New York:
World, 1973.

Spanier, G. B. Sexualization and premarital sexual behavior. *Family Coordinator,*
1975, *24* (1), 33–41.

Stolz, H. R., and Stolz, L. M.  *The somatic development of adolescent boys.* New York: Macmillan, 1951.

Stunkard, A. J.  The obese: Background and programs. In J. Mayer (Ed.), *U.S. nutrition policies in the seventies.* San Francisco: W. H. Freeman, 1973. Pp. 29–37.

Tanner, J. M.  *Growth at adolescence* (2d ed.). Oxford: Blackwell, 1962.

Tanner, J. M.  Galtonia eugenics and the study of growth. *Eugenics Review,* 1966, *58,* 122–135.

Tanner, J. M.  Physical growth. In P. H. Mussen (Ed.), *Carmichael's manual of child psychology* (3d ed.), vol. 1. New York: Wiley, 1970. Pp. 77–156.

Tanner, J. M.  Sequence, tempo, and individual variation in growth and development of boys and girls aged twelve to sixteen. In J. Kagan and R. Coles (Eds.), *12 to 16: Early adolescence,* New York: Norton, 1972. Pp. 1–24.

Thornburg, H. D.  Sources in adolescence of initial sex information. In H. D. Thornburg (Ed.), *Contemporary adolescence: Readings* (2d ed.). Monterey, Calif.: Brooks/Cole, 1975.

Vener, A. M., and Stewart, C. S.  Adolescent sexual behavior in middle America revisited, 1970–1973. *Journal of Marriage and the Family,* 1974, *36,* 728–735.

Weatherley, D.  Self-perceived rate of physical maturation and personality in late adolescence. *Child Development,* 1964, *35,* 1197–1210.

Widdowson, E. M.  Mental contentment and physical growth. *Lancet,* 1951, *1.* 1316–1318.

Wilson, R. S.  Twins: Mental development in the preschool years. *Developmental Psychology,* 1974, *10,* 580–588.

Wilson, R. S.  Twins: Patterns of cognitive development as measured on the Wechsler Preschool and Primary Scale of Intelligence. *Developmental Psychology,* 1975, *11,* 126–134.

Winick, M.  Nutrition and nerve cell growth. *Federation proceedings,* 1970, *29,* 1510–1515.

Wolff, G., and Money, J.  Relationship between sleep and growth in patients with reversible somatotropin deficiency (psychosocial dwarfism). *Psychological medicine,* 1972.

Zelnick, M., and Kantner, J. F.  Sex and contraception among unmarried teenagers. In C. F. Westoff (Ed.), *Toward the end of growth.* Englewood Cliffs, N.J.: Prentice-Hall, 1973. Pp. 7–18.

*New cognitive skills increase adolescents' awareness of the future and their appreciation for the consequences of events.*

# 5

# Cognitive Development in Early Adolescence

The focus of this chapter is on the emergence of new conceptual abilities that are associated with the life stage of early adolescence. In Chapter 1, we pointed out that many theories of development recognize adolescence as a time when new cognitive competences are established. The ability to think logically and abstractly, the ability to raise hypotheses about the consequen⟨...⟩ one event, and the ability to appreciate and to integrate sym⟨...⟩nships are all important components of intellectual ⟨...⟩ the adolescent years.

The emergence of more sophisticated th⟨...⟩ has become an increasingly prized human ⟨...⟩ ment to science, to complex social and politic⟨...⟩ to international systems of economics, resource ⟨...⟩ ernment increases, we become all the more dependent ⟨...⟩ tive abilities for survival. Elaborate educational syste⟨...⟩ emerged, including junior high schools, high schools, colleges, g⟨...⟩ uate schools, postgraduate training, and continuing education to nurture and sustain the growth of intellectual competence.

In this chapter, we will consider the new directions that emerge in this highly valued human competence—thought. In Chapter 1, we traced briefly the qualities of thinking that Piaget describes as characteristic of infancy, childhood, and adolescence. Here we will look in detail at the transition from concrete operational to formal operational thought. What new skills emerge? What accounts for this change? What are some consequences of this new level of thinking for adolescents? The characteristics of formal operation will be described, including the capacity for hypothesis generating and hypothesis testing, the concept of probability, and the conceptualization of the future. In addition, we will discuss some of the intellectual skills that foster problem solving, comprehension, and reasoning in early adolescence. In cognitive functioning, as in physical growth, there are important individual differences that influence life choices and day-to-day behavior. The last part of the chapter will focus on the measurement of intelligence and creativity in early adolescence, and on the implications of differences in these abilities for emerging life patterns.

We often find that a discussion of cognition and the emergence of new capacities for thinking strikes students as rather remote and even boring. Students who think back to their early adolescent years, from 11 or 12 to 18, do not retain very vivid memories of their thinking. Thinking is primarily important to us because of the content of our thoughts. The argument we have with a boyfriend, the plan we make to earn money during the summer, or the strategies we use to get dad to lend us the car are the experiences that hold a place in our thoughts. The way we figured out our plans, the chain of cause-effect links we made, or the logic in our arguments are not readily available to memory.

An appreciation of the excitement and energy associated with cognitive growth is also often dimmed by our recollections of the school as a setting for learning. Let us point out here that cognitive growth and going to school are two separate and perhaps only moderately related aspects of intellectual experience. The fact that you may remember school as tedious, boring, too easy, or too difficult does not mean that your mind was not expanding or that your thinking was not altered. In a brief autobiography written for his children, Charles Darwin assures us that attending school is in no way to be equated with intellectual growth.

Nothing could have been worse for the development of my mind that Dr. Butler's school,* as it was strictly classical, nothing else being taught, except a little ancient geography and history. The school as a means of education to me was simply a blank. During my whole life I have been singularly incapable of mastering any language. Especial attention was paid to verse-making, and this I could never do well. I had many friends, and got together a good collection of old verses, which by patching together, sometimes aided by other boys, I could work into any subject. (Darwin, 1929, p. 7)

Our goal in this chapter is to describe some of the important dimensions of logical thought that are part of an adolescent's mental resources and to point to some consequences of these new mental skills. In later chapters on social development, the high school environment, and cognitive growth in later adolescence, the implications of these early gains will become even more apparent.

In Chapter 1, we presented some of the basic concepts of Piaget's theory of cognitive development. We discussed the process of intellectual growth as a product of continuous interaction between the person and the environment. Through the reciprocal processes of assimilation and accommodation, familiar schemes are revised and elaborated into new schemes. We discussed four stages of intellectual growth: sensorimotor intelligence, preoperational or representational thought, concrete operational thought, and formal operational thought. Each of these modes of thinking is present in adult functioning. For example, we continue to use sensorimotor intelligence when we drive a car or type a letter. We use preoperational thought in designing the scenery for a school play or in daydreaming about a romantic encounter. We use concrete operational thought when we follow the rules of a new game or figure out our grocery bill. The fact that adults have the capacity for abstract thought

---

* A boarding school that Darwin attended from age 9 to age 16.

and logical reasoning does not mean that they only use those competences to the exclusion of all others.

During the period of early adolescence, young people are making the transition from one mode of thinking to another. From the age of 5 or 6 to about 11, children acquire the skills of concrete operational thinking. By about age 12, most young people are beginning to use formal operational strategies for solving some complex problems (Neimark, 1975b). We will look at the skills that are involved in concrete operational thought and at the process of transition to a more abstract, symbolic level of thought. Then we will examine the nature of formal operational thought and some of the ways in which it influences the adolescent's life orientation.

## CONCRETE OPERATIONAL THOUGHT

At around the age of 5 to 6, the child begins to apply certain principles of logic to explain experience. During the period of concrete operational thought (5–11 years), these principles of logic are still closely bound to concrete, observable events (Piaget and Inhelder, 1969). The kind of logical thinking that is characteristic of this stage requires the capacity for symbolic representation that was attained during the preoperational stage. In order to think about reversing an operation, for example, the child must be able to hold a mental image of the object before the operation, trace the transformation, and then mentally undo the transformation so that the object returns to its original form. Without representational skills this would be impossible.

Let us consider three kinds of logical skills that develop during the stage of concrete operational thought: *classification, conservation,* and *combinatorial skills.* Each of these kinds of skills requires the capacity to systematically interrelate separate mental actions. For each kind we will consider the types of problems involved and the nature of the child's approach to those problems in the concrete operational stage.

### Classification

In order to classify a group of objects, a child must be able to coordinate two dimensions which make the concept "class." First, the child must single out the criteria that define the class; second, the child must select all of the objects that fit the criteria, including all correct members of the class and omitting none.

For example, a group of objects might be sorted by four separate criteria: roundness, squareness, blackness, or whiteness. If the class were *blackness,* all black objects would be included, regardless of shape. If the class were *squareness,* all square objects would be included, regardless of color. The strategy of sorting objects into groups is the same, no matter what the specific array of objects, but the content of the sort depends on the specific objects which are sorted.

In the concrete operational stage, the mental operations that guide the sorting task are more stable than the arrangement of the objects themselves. During this stage, the child begins to identify the principles of class inclusion and class extension, correctly applying the criteria for each class to all available objects. Once children can manipulate the operations involved in classification, they still need information about which criteria apply to which objects. For example, the difference between first cousins and second cousins as distinct classes of relatives must be explained before the child can sort cousins into separate groups.

## Conservation

Conservation refers to the recognition that certain properties of matter, such as weight, amount, or volume, are not altered by changing the container or the shape of the matter itself.

Conservation tasks generally involve some manipulation of the shape of matter which does not alter the mass, the weight, or the volume of that matter (Piaget, 1954; Piaget and Inhelder, 1969). A typical conservation problem is the comparison of two balls of clay (see Figure 5–1). First, the child is asked to confirm that A and B are the same size. Then $B_1$ is changed to $B_2$, $B_3$, and $B_4$.

**Figure 5–1: Conservation of Substance**

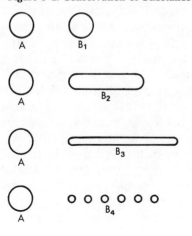

The child is asked to make comparisons between A and $B_2$, $B_3$, and $B_4$, each time stating whether A and B are still the same. Children who are in the preoperational stage are guided by their perception of the transformed shape. They tend to see $B_2$, $B_3$, and $B_4$ as greater than A. Children who are in the concrete operational stage preserve a sense of the equality between A and B that survives these physical transformations.

There are three operations which are eventually coordinated into a systematic conceptualization of conservation. They are: identity, reversibility, and reciprocity (Piaget, 1963). *Identity* refers to the appreciation that $B_2$ or $B_3$ or $B_4$ are still the "same B." The child who uses identity as an explanation in a conservation task might say: "It's still the same clay—you haven't taken any away or added any."

*Reversibility* is the operation of undoing an action. A child who uses reversibility as an explanation might say: "You could squeeze the sausage back into a ball," or "You could put all those little pieces back into one big one." The child does not have to see the transformation in order to imagine it.

*Reciprocity* is the interdependence of related dimensions. In the conservation of substance task, a child who understands reciprocity might say: "The sausage is longer, but it's thinner than the ball."

At the beginning of the stage of concrete operations, children may be able to apply one operation to the problem but not all three. By the end of the stage, identity, reversibility, and reciprocity operate in a synchronized grouping of operations that can be applied to any similar task. One very important consequence of the acquisition of these operations is the flexibility that this provides in problem solving. If conservation can be assumed as a constant property of matter, then identity, reversibility, and reciprocity can be manipulated to chart a variety of courses toward the same goal. Let us say that a 12-year-old child is planning a paper route. The child has to pick up the papers at a specific corner, deliver them to certain houses, and return home. The absolute distance from pickup point to home is constant, but the child must be able to conceptualize time, distance, and effort as interdependent variables in planning an efficient delivery route. During the course of the year, the route may change because of weather conditions, new customers, or customers who go on vacation. Each of these changes requires a remapping of the route, tracing through the transformations mentally before setting out with the papers. Through the use of mental operations, the child should be able to figure out many possible routes and then select the one which meets his or her criteria for efficiency and ease.

## Combinatorial Skills

A third group of operations which are acquired during this developmental stage are expressed in the following mathematical symbols (Phillips, 1975, p. 84):

$+$  combining
$-$  separating
$\times$  repeating
$\div$  dividing
$>$  placing in order
$=$  possible substitution

Basic to these numerical operations is an appreciation of numbers as symbols for quantities (Piaget, 1952). Each element in a group is *one* unit, and all the units together are symbolized by the number $N$. Children in the preoperational stage may be able to count, but they do not use numbers to symbolize quantities. Thus, five chips spread apart will be viewed as *more* chips than five chips close together. However, the skills involved in classification and conservation are reflected once again in the concrete operational child's use of numbers and combinatorial operations. Principally, the recognition of numbers as units, counting as a system of ordering units, and the associative relationships among units combine to form a logical system of numerical skills.

# THE TRANSITION FROM CONCRETE TO FORMAL OPERATIONAL THOUGHT

The transition to formal operational thought involves the recognition that a set of combinations or relationships can apply to a wide range of specific objects. As Piaget (1969) describes it:

The great novelty that results consists in the possibility of manipulating ideas in themselves and no longer in merely manipulating objects. In a word, the adolescent is an individual who is capable (and this is where he reaches the level of the adult) of building or understanding ideal or abstract theories and concepts. (p. 23)

In order to demonstrate the change in thinking from concrete to formal thought, Inhelder and Piaget (1958) developed a series of problems that require systematic strategies for their eventual solution. One of those problems, the combination of chemical substances, was designed to study the way a young person could generate a combinatorial system. In this experiment, the subject is shown five bottles of colorless liquid labeled 1, 2, 3, 4, and G. The experimenter shows the subject two glasses of clear fluid, one containing $1 + 3$ and one containing 2. The experimenter then adds some drops of G to each and shows the subject that by combining some of the fluids a yellow color will appear. The experimenter then asks the subject to try to create a similar colored fluid. What is more important, the subject is asked to explain how the task should be approached. The task itself requires a systematic approach to all the combinations of the five bottles. The bottles actually contain (1) plain water, (2) dilute sulfuric acid, (3) sodium thiosulfate solution, (4) hydrogen peroxide, and (G) potassium iodide. Only the combinations $1 + 2 + 4 + G$ or $2 + 4 + G$ will produce the yellow color. In these combinations iodine is released and colors the solution. The presence of liquid from bottle 3 bleaches the solution and removes the color. Of all the possible combinations of five bottles, only two will provide the desired effect. In order to achieve a solution, the subject must devise a systematic strategy for producing each possible combination of five bottles. The child who uses concrete operations is likely to begin by adding one liquid to each other liquid. If that does not work, the child may add all the liquids together or begin a random combination of groups of liquids. The systematic approach seems to deteriorate as the child faces a problem that requires the combination of more than two variables for the solution. The child who uses formal operational thought to find the solution recognizes right away that there is a need for a strategy that will generate all the possible combinations. Further, the capacity for formal operational thought allows the child to explore some of the properties of each fluid and to raise some hypotheses about their contribution to the experiment.

The transition from concrete to formal operational thinking occurs gradually as children apply the general systematic approach to a broader and broader range of specific tasks (Flavell, 1963; Neimark, 1975a). In a longitudinal study of children in grades four–six, Neimark (1975b) followed the changes in problem-solving strategies and successful problem solution over a 3½-year period. She found that among her subjects, the capacity to manipulate combinations was the first area to be submitted to a formal operational approach. Skills in handling permutations (generating all $n$-digit license plate numbers that can be made using $n$ digits) and correlations (the relationship of green germs to the presence or absence of disease) were achieved more slowly. If one holds a strict criterion for formal operational thought, requiring the ability to formulate a solution or a strategy to a variety of complex, multivariate tasks, then one would conclude that even the oldest of Neimark's subjects (15-year-olds) had not completely achieved formal thought.

One of the qualities of formal thought appears to be the realization that some kind of system or strategy is required for solving a problem. In other words, the person must anticipate that a number of dimensions or variables are involved in the solution to complex problems. Recognizing this, the person must then devise a system for keeping track of the contribution of each variable before any actual operations are performed. In this sense, the system for deriving the solution is more important than the actual solution itself. The system or the general problem-solving approach can be applied to a variety of problems with different content.

Siegler and Liebert (1975) demonstrated the importance of the planning function in formal thought by comparing the problem-solving strategies of 10-year-olds and 13-year-olds. The task involved an electric train set with four knife switches. When each of the switches was set in the proper position, the train would run. Otherwise it would not. The children were all advised to keep a record of which choices they tried so that they would not repeat their choices.

Before they approached the actual problem-solving situation, the children were divided into three groups. Group 1 was given conceptual training about how factors can effect something, how each factor can be at a particular level (on–off, high, medium, or low), and how factors are interrelated in the final solution to a problem. Group 2 was given this conceptual framework plus two tasks in which a diagram showing all possible solutions had to be drawn. Group 3, the control group, was given no training. The performance of the three groups of 10- and 13-year-olds is presented in Table 5–1.

In the train problem, 70 percent of the 10-year-olds and 100 percent of the 13-year-olds who had been given both the conceptual framework and the chance to solve similar tasks (group 2) generated all 16 possible positions for the switches. In contrast, none of the other ten-year-olds were able to find all the combinations. Only 20 percent of the ten-year-old control group kept a record of their problem-solving strategies. Among the 13-year-olds, 50 percent of those who had been given the conceptual training were able to

Table 5–1: Percentage of Children Producing All Possible Combinations and Percentage Keeping Written Records

| Treatment | 10-Year-Olds | | 13-Year-Olds | |
|---|---|---|---|---|
| | Combinations | Records | Combinations | Records |
| Conceptual framework with analogue ........... | 70 | 90 | 100 | 100 |
| Conceptual framework alone .................. | 0 | 10 | 50 | 90 |
| Control .................. | 0 | 20 | 10 | 40 |

Source: From R. Siegler and R. M. Liebert, "Acquisition of Formal Scientific Reasoning by 10 and 13 Year Olds: Designing a Factorial Experiment," *Developmental Psychology,* 1975, *11,* 402.

identify all the combinations, but only 10 percent of the control group succeeded at the task. The 13-year-olds seemed to be able to make use of the conceptual training alone to achieve a solution, whereas the 10-year-olds still needed actual practice in solving similar tasks. Many more of the 13-year-olds recognized that they would have to keep a record of their solutions in order to solve the problem. The ten-year-olds did not appear to anticipate the large number of possible solutions, even after they had been given a conceptual explanation of similar problems.

There are two interrelated aspects of the adolescent's experience that Piaget (Inhelder and Piaget, 1958) offers as an explanation for the gradual emergence of this systematic, abstract mode of thought. First, adolescents participate in an increasingly wide range of social roles. These experiences alert adolescents to the interaction of multiple variables at a behavioral level. They become used to perceiving themselves in a variety of relationships, governed by diverse norms and expectations for behavior. Second, adolescents are more likely than young children to anticipate the nature of their own adulthood. This future-oriented thinking fosters the generation of hypotheses about future possibilities and desired goals. Approaching adult status stimulates a kind of abstract conceptualization because of the need to make certain life decisions and because of the lure of desired freedoms and responsibilities.

In spite of these forces toward cognitive growth and increasingly abstract, logical thought, change does not occur quickly or uniformly. Dulit (1972) compared the formal reasoning of four groups: average young adolescents age 14, average older adolescents ages 16 and 17, gifted older adolescents ages 16 and 17, and average adults ages 20–55. Of these groups the subgroup with the greatest percentage of subjects functioning at a fully formal level of thought were the gifted older adolescent boys. Within this subgroup about 75 percent of the subjects approached problems from an abstract problem-solving strategy and showed an appreciation of the interaction of the variables involved in the solution. The average older adolescents and the average adults showed similar proportions of formal thinkers. Approximately 50 percent of males and 15 percent of females approached the problems from a fully formal operational level.

The majority of older adolescents and adults who were not using formal thought approached the problems from one of two strategies. Either they tried to solve the problems by applying a standard method that they had used in other situations, or they tried to intuit the solution, letting the facts of the situation lead them to an "inspired" best guess about the right answer. Dulit suggests that these two strategies may reflect two of the modes of thinking in addition to formal thought that are crystallized during adolescence. It is quite possible that adults use several problem-solving strategies, depending on the problem, their familiarity with the issues, and their level of emotional involvement or objectivity about the content (Piaget, 1972). For example, a young woman may use formal thought to design a research project for a college course and intuitive reasoning to choose a career (Berzonsky, Weiner, and Raphael, 1975). During adolescence, the potential for developing a logical, propositional conceptual system emerges. Whether it is used in day-to-day problem solving depends on the kinds of problems that call for solutions, the environmental supports for formal thought, and the person's expertise and confidence about the particular area in question.

## CHARACTERISTICS OF FORMAL OPERATIONAL THOUGHT

Formal thought suggests an expanding consciousness. Adolescents are able to hold in mind many more of the variables that may contribute to the solution of a problem. They are able to antici-

*Burk Uzzle/Magnum*

*Formal thought involves the expansion of consciousness.*

pate the need for a more elaborate system for arriving at the solution to a problem, a system that may involve more than one person, more than one procedure, even more than one data collection session. Adolescents can begin to approach the fantasies and playful wishes of their toddlerhood with logical plans for the achievement of "farfetched" goals. These cognitive achievements are closely tied to the adolescents' commitment to the future. Indeed, we have suggested that it is the appreciation of an approaching future that motivates adolescents to take on this more abstract, speculative, or hypothetical approach to problem solving. As Piaget (Inhelder and Piaget, 1958) describes it, an orientation toward a vision of oneself in the future requires a new level of thinking and planning.

The adolescent not only builds new theories or rehabilitates old ones; he also feels he has to work out a conception of life which gives him an opportunity to assert himself and to create something new (thus the close relationship between his system and his life program). Secondly, he wants a guarantee that he will be more successful than his predecessors (thus the need for change in which altruistic concern and youthful ambitions are inseparably blended). (Inhelder and Piaget, 1958, chap. 18)

Four characteristics of formal operational thought are considered below: the ability to generate and test hypotheses, the understanding of probability, a new conceptualization of future time, and egocentrism. These characteristics of formal thought have obvious implications for adolescents' problem-solving abilities and for their potential performance in academic areas. They also have implications for the quality of social relationships that emerge during adolescence and for the changing nature of the adolescent's self-concept.

## Hypothesis Raising and Hypothesis Testing

An important feature of formal thought is the ability to raise hypotheses to explain an event and then to follow along with the logic that a particular hypothesis implies. "Hypothetical reasoning implies the subordination of the real to the realm of the possible, and consequently the linking of all possibilities to one another by necessary implications that encompass the real, but at the same time go beyond it" (Piaget, 1972 p. 3).

One of the experiments that Inhelder and Piaget designed to demonstrate the importance of hypothetico-deductive reasoning was the explanation of the swing of a pendulum. The task is to find out what variable or combination of variables control the speed of the swing. Four factors can be varied: (1) the weight of the object, (2) the height from which the pendulum is pushed, (3) the strength with which it is pushed, and (4) the length of the string. In order to explain this phenomenon it is necessary to vary only one factor at a time while keeping the others constant. In this particular problem, only the length of the string actually influences the speed of the swing. The challenge is to demonstrate that the length of the string accounts for the speed and that the other factors do not. When the child who uses concrete operational thought tends to combine factors, the child who uses formal operational thought is able to test out each factor separately and evaluate its contribution (Inhelder and Piaget, 1958; Flavell, 1963).

Several skills are involved in problem solving of this kind. First, one must be able to identify the separate factors and the possible levels of each factor. Second, one must be able to recognize the possible interactions among the factors, for example short string and heavy weight or long string and light weight. Third, one must be able to develop a systematic method for testing out each factor in combination with each other factor. The conceptual system of possible solutions is the guide for problem solving (Neimark, 1975a; Siegler, Liebert, and Liebert, 1973).

## Probability

The concept of probability reflects the ability to integrate mathematical concepts of combinations and proportions (Piaget and Inhelder, 1951; Flavell, 1963). This complex notion begins with an appreciation that some events are random, such as the side of a coin that comes up on any single flip, and that some events are not random. The preoperational child does not really differentiate chance and nonchance events. In fact, preoperational children are likely to attribute more form and regularity to chance events than they really deserve. For example, in one experiment red and white beads were lined up at one end of a tray, the red ones on one side of a divider and the white ones on the other side. Then the tray was tipped and the children were asked to tell where the beads would end up after one, several, and many tippings. The youngest children guessed that all the beads would eventually end up on their original side or that all the reds would end up on the white side, and vice versa. They did not appreciate the random mixing that would result from this process.

The next component in understanding probability is to recognize that the observed event will reflect the proportion of each kind of element in the larger pool of elements. For example, if one draws a bead from a bag that has 20 black and 10 red beads, the bead is more likely to be black than red. As each bead is removed, the probability of drawing a red bead changes, depending on what color beads have already been removed. The probability of any event has to be viewed as a ratio of the kind of event in question to the total pool of possible events (Neimark, 1975b). It is not difficult for children to identify the similarity in the proportions of objects in two separate groups if they can inspect the elements of both groups (Hoemann and Ross, 1971). It is much more difficult for them to use the concept of proportions to base predictions about the probability of an event. The "gambler's fallacy" that if the last flip landed on heads the next flip is more likely to land on tails continues to be a source of confusion for adults (Ross and Levy, 1958).

Of course, not all events are random. In order to make accurate predictions it is necessary to be able to identify the nonchance factors that operate in a given situation. It is also necessary to be able to estimate the distribution of each element in the larger pool of events. If a girl is waiting to see whether someone will ask her to the junior prom, she can estimate the probability by knowing how many boys usually attend the prom and how many girls in the community might be considered appropriate dates. However, in the matter of dating, other factors, including attractiveness, status, age, and grade, may all enter into the selection of a partner.

A computer might be able to make a prediction about which girls will be asked to the junior prom, given the information about each of these factors and the ways they influence dating behavior. A single girl waiting by the phone is less likely to be able to take this kind of rational, probabilistic problem-solving approach.

## Conceptualizing the Future

In contrast to the child at the level of concrete operational thinking, who is preoccupied with the specific details of the present, the person at the stage of formal operational thought is capable of generating a more realistic or perhaps probabilistic view of future time (Inhelder and Piaget, 1958). The two skills described above, hypothesis raising and an understanding of probability, permit adolescents to develop a plan or even alternative plans about future events. In fact, Piaget has argued that this capacity to conceptualize the future is made necessary by the abstract and complex nature of impending adult roles. Thoughts about a career or about a marriage partner require the ability to create various scenarios and to imagine the consequences of each hypothetical choice. This kind of active conceptualization anticipates by five or ten years the time when a decision will have to be made. In this sense, the future events of one's life begin to take shape at an abstract, hypothetical level long before they occur. In adolescence, one begins to build the future by thinking about it. This is not to say that nothing will intervene to change one's plan. In fact, many of the specific details of the future plan are missing and await additional experience or information. However, beginning in adolescence the realm of future choices begins to emerge more clearly. What is more, adolescents begin to recognize their own aspirations. They begin to link positive emotional investments with some life goals and negative investments with others. Looking back from adulthood, the bridges from these adolescent life plans to contemporary life events are easy to trace. We can see where we have traveled by recalling the hopes and aspirations of those adolescent plans. Since we are likely to be involved in some form of work and some form of intimate relationship as adults, it is not difficult to retrieve the way those general adult roles were defined during the adolescent years. The bond between adolescence and adulthood is built by the future orientation of the adolescent and the capacity for reminiscence of the adult.

Studies of the development of future time perspective make a distinction between a cognitive understanding of the course of future events and a motivational investment in future events (Lessing, 1972; Davids and Parenti, 1958). In two studies with quite different samples, similar patterns of thinking about the future were described. Lessing (1972) studied girls in the age range 9–15 who attended a summer girl scout camp. Klineberg (1967) studied boys in the age range 10–16 years 11 months who attended private schools near Paris, France. Two kinds of measures were used to evaluate the ways in which future time was incorporated into the person's thought. One type tapped the organization of life events by asking subjects when they thought each of 20 life events would happen to them. Another type evoked a more fantasy-oriented use of the future. In Klineberg's study, the subjects were asked to tell a story about a picture. The story was scored for references to future time events. The subjects were also asked to tell about ten things that they had talked about during the past week. These conversations were evaluated for their reference to past, present, or future time. The two studies converge in their description of the quality of future orientation from childhood to adolescence. As children grow older, they have a clearer, more realistic orientation about the course of life events. Important life events are, in fact, closer to adolescents than they are to younger children. Adolescents do not tend to project farther into the future than young children. Rather, they tend to have a more coherent picture of the order and meaning of future events. The use of fantasy about the future appears to change from childhood to adolescence. The young, preadolescent subjects who were described as maladjusted or dissatisfied made a greater use of the distant future in projective-type material. The older, adolescent subjects who were described as maladjusted or dissatisfied made less use of the distant future in their fantasy projections. As young people move into adolescence, the expectations that they will be able to cope with approaching future challenges may remove these future fantasies as a source of sublimation or escape from contemporary life stresses. We might even suggest that it is just these impending challenges that generate anxiety. It would be interesting to see whether adolescents who are experiencing significant stress and little life satisfaction shift to reminiscing about the past instead of daydreaming about the future.

## EGOCENTRISM

Piaget (1926; Inhelder and Piaget, 1958) has used the term *egocentrism* to refer to the limited perspective of the child at the beginning of each new phase of cognitive development. In the sensorimotor phase, egocentrism refers to an inability to separate one's own actions from the consequences they have on specific objects or people. As the scheme for causality is developed, the first process of decentering occurs. Infants recognize that certain actions have predictable consequences. They also recognize that new situations call for new, relevant behaviors. One cannot turn the light on by turning the knob on the radio.

In the phase of preoperational thought, egocentrism refers to an inability to separate one's own perspective from the point of view of the listener. When a four-year-old girl tells you about something that happened to her at the zoo, she may not take into account the fact that you were not present. She will explain events as if you had seen them. When a three-year-old boy is explaining something to his grandmother over the phone, he may point to objects in the room, unaware that his grandmother cannot see through the phone.

The third phase of heightened egocentrism occurs when the young person begins to make use of formal operational thought. As adolescents develop the capacity to formulate hypothetical systems, they begin to generate assumptions about their own behavior and the behavior of others that will fit into these abstract formulations. An adolescent may assert that cooperation is a more highly desired mode of interaction than competition. In theory, cooperation ought to enhance each participant and to provide more resources for the group as a whole. This adolescent may become angry or disillusioned to discover that teachers, parents, and even peers seek competitive experiences and appear to find pleasure in them. "If the cooperative system is so superior, why do people persist in their illogical joy in triumphing over an opponent?" Egocentrism of this kind reflects an inability to recognize that one's own hypothetical system is not shared by others. Decentering in adolescence requires an ability to realize that one's ideals are not shared by all. We live in a pluralistic society in which each person is likely to hold different goals, different aspirations. Adolescents gradually discover that their neat, logical plans for life must constantly be adapted to the expectations and needs of relevant others.

Adolescent egocentrism has two characteristics that have relevance for social interaction as well as for adaptive problem solving. First, adolescents are preoccupied with their own thoughts. They may tend to become somewhat withdrawn and isolated as the domain of their consciousness expands. Thoughts about the possible and the probable, the near and distant future, and the logical extension of contemporary events to future consequences all flood the mind. This tendency to withdraw into one's own speculations may cut off access to new information or new ideas. Second, adolescents may assume that others share their preoccupations. Instead of assuming that each person is equally wrapped up in his or her own concerns and plans, adolescents envision their own thoughts as the focus of the attention of others (Elkind, 1967). This kind of subjectivity generates a kind of embarrassed self-consciousness that makes interaction uncomfortable. In an observational study of group interaction, Newman (1975) described the young male adolescents as uncomfortable and unresponsive to one another. Each boy enjoyed talking and joking about his own experiences. However, few of the boys were able to respond with support or encouragement to another boy in the group.

We begin to see a picture of early adolescence as a time when the young person's version of reality takes on convincing intensity. Young adolescents are likely to believe that their interpretation of an interaction is correct, and therefore they are less flexible about casting around for alternative interpretations.

Two experiences help to reduce adolescent egocentrism (Looft, 1971). These are social interaction with peers and participation in the work setting (Piaget, 1967; Inhelder and Piaget, 1958). Through interactions in which adolescents are motivated to understand the other person's world view, especially in early loving relationships, egocentrism may give way to a more empathic perspective. The world of work with its structured requirements for participation helps adolescents to trade an abstract system for a real system. Adolescents can experience the work setting as a complex set of interrelated systems in which real needs and goals have real implications for workers and supervisors. The perfection of the hypothetical system is modified by the functional imperfection of real work commitments.

Needless to say, egocentrism is not fully conquered in the adolescent years. At every phase of expanding awareness, there is a tendency to rely heavily on one's own experiences and perceptions in order to minimize the anxiety associated with uncertainty. Part of the progress of formal thought implies a reliance on the logic of reason over the power of experience. We have more confidence in what we know than in what we can see or hear, and this can trap us into an egocentric perspective. We may interpret new experiences as examples of a familiar concept rather than as novel events. We may reject evidence for an argument because it does not support an already carefully derived explanation. The business of casting around for new evidence and new explanations is a lifelong challenge. It is so much easier to rely on earlier assumptions and to take them as a guide than to continuously call one's subjectivity into question.

## INTELLECTUAL SKILLS

The concept of intelligence refers to a wide array of mental abilities that contribute to the person's effective coping with life challenges (Wechsler, 1975; Bayley, 1970). The characteristics of formal operational thought that have been described in the previous section depend on the continued growth and integration of a variety of mental abilities, including memory, concept formation, logical reasoning, and problem-solving strategies. In addition, the growth of intelligence is fostered by the accumulation of new information, exposure to new methods of experimentation, and opportunities for seeking out answers to unanswered questions. Much of the research that addresses intellectual growth during adolescence focuses on one or more of these aspects of mental functioning rather than on evaluating formal operational thought as a total cognitive orientation (Neimark, 1975a).

When repeated measures of intelligence are taken on the same people over a period of years, the picture is one of rapid growth through adolescence and a leveling off of ability during adulthood and into old age (Horn, 1970; Bayley, 1970). In one view of mental abilities, two kinds of intelligence were identified, fluid intelligence and crystallized intelligence (Cattell, 1963, 1967; Horn and Cattell, 1966). Fluid intelligence depends most heavily on neurological functioning and the healthy maintenance of the brain, the sense receptors, and the motor responses that are necessary for intellectual functioning. Crystallized intelligence is characterized by the accumulation of information and problem-solving strategies, through experience and education. Crystallized intelligence continues to increase steadily throughout adolescence and well into adulthood. On the other hand, fluid intelligence, which is related to memory span, speed in thinking, and the ability to keep separate elements available for recall, tends to decline toward the end of adolescence or the beginning of young adulthood (Horn, 1970). Figure 5–2 compares the patterns of scores on vocabulary, an ability that reflects crystallized intelligence, and on digit span, an ability that reflects fluid intelligence. The data are taken from longitudinal studies using the Wechsler scales for five ages from 16 to age 36. This figure

**Figure 5–2: Patterns of Scores on Vocabulary and Digit Span in the Wechsler Intelligence Tests**

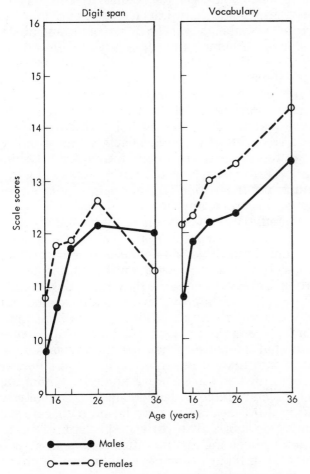

Source: N. Bayley, "Development of Mental Abilities, in P. H. Mussen (Ed.), *Carmichael's Manual of Child Psychology*, 3d ed., vol. 1 (New York: Wiley, 1970), pp. 1184 and 1185. Reprinted by permission.

suggests that the period of early adolescence is a time of continued growth in both fluid and crystallized intelligence.

Important abilities that increase measurably during adolescence are memory span (Mishima and Inone, 1966) and memory skills (Neimark, Slotnick, and Ulrich, 1971). Adolescents are more skilled than younger children in imposing memory strategies, or mnemonic devices, to help them organize and retrieve larger amounts of information (Lehman and Goodnow, 1972; Neimark, 1975a).

In a nationwide study of cognitive growth during the high school years, one of the impressive, if obvious, areas of achievement was the increase in information (Shaycroft, 1967). Between grades 9 and 12, students showed an increase in information about law, accounting, business, electronics, and mechanics. In tests of general ability, boys made greater gains than girls on measures of creativity, mechanical reasoning, visualizing in three dimensions, and abstract reasoning. Girls showed greater gains than boys in literature information, memory for words, and spelling. This kind of assessment suggests that encounters with the school environment, especially the academic curriculum, contribute to the content of the adolescent's intellectual competence. It also suggests that the pattern of abilities that are fostered by going to high school will differ, depending on one's sex. This statement reflects a theme that will be raised later on in this chapter and again in Chapter 7. Developmental growth that occurs in early adolescence is a result of individual competences and predispositions in interaction with environmental expectations, resources, and barriers.

A third area of increased competence is problem-solving ability. The general term *problem solving* is really an umbrella for the integration of a variety of cognitive competences. The specific competences involved will depend, of course, on the kind of problem that requires solution. Three related skills that make for more effective problem solving tend to improve during adolescence. First, adolescents are more flexible than children in generating concepts from pictures, words, or concrete objects (Elkind, 1975). This kind of flexibility means that adolescents can search across modes to find a needed bit of information or experience in the solution to a problem. A concept from knowledge about animal behavior might help in solving a problem related to leadership in a school group. Principles learned in auto mechanics may be used to help solve problems in geometry or sports. The varied aspects of life experience are interrelated through the abstract dimensions along which they may be similar, even though they have quite diverse physical properties or uses.

The second problem-solving skill that improves during adolescence is the internalization of stable, accurate mental representations of external objects or environments. Children as young as six can draw a picture of their bedroom or their house. With their eyes closed, they can tell you where objects are in a room. In other words, they have the ability to represent physical space in mental images. However, it is not until adolescence that these mental representations can themselves be manipulated (Piaget and Inhelder, 1967; Smothergill, 1973).

In a study of the manipulation of cognitive maps, subjects were asked to "sight" four objects in a room through a cardboard tube attached to a compass. In one condition, the subjects were asked to sight the objects from behind a screen so that they had to approximate the location of the objects. In a comparison of first graders, fifth graders, and college students, the accuracy of the sighting increased with age. In another condition, each subject was asked to make sightings for the objects as if he or she had moved to another location in the room. Finally, each subject was asked to imagine that the room had been rotated so that a target previously in front was now located in back of where the subject was standing. Sightings were made after this instruction for mental rotation was given. Only the oldest subjects were able to maintain an accurate image of the objects through these latter manipulations (Hardwick, McIntyre, and Pick, 1976). This kind of competence has relevance for adaptive problem solving in real-world situations. It reflects the ability to read maps, to give directions to others, and to plan paths or routes from one location to another.

The third skill in problem solving that improves during adolescence is the ability to develop efficient strategies for gaining information. A familiar example is the game of 20 questions. In this game, each question is designed to get as much information as possible by eliminating some categories or classes of objects. Young children tend to ask questions that test a specific hypothesis—"Is it a blue sneaker?" Older children ask series of questions that limit the possible categories of correct answers. They only ask the specific hypothesis-testing question toward the end as they narrow in on the solution (Mosher and Hornsby, 1966; Berlyne, 1970). In a nonverbal variation of this kind of problem-solving task, Neimark (Neimark and Lewis, 1967, 1968; Neimark, 1975b) found that with increasing mental age subjects shifted from a very specific trial and error strategy to a more general problem-solving strategy. This shift inevitably resulted in needing fewer bits of information to disclose the underlying concept.

In summary, the intellectual competences that improve during adolescence include memory span and memorization skills; the acquisition of information; concept production across verbal, perceptual and experiential modes; mental representations of physical space; and problem-solving strategies. None of these competences is totally new in adolescence (Fitzgerald, Nesselroade, and Baltes, 1973). Rather, the competences reflect the higher levels of integration, abstraction, and generalization that bring the realm of the possible into convenient range.

## THE SELF-CONCEPT

The self-concept is a general term for the attributes and expectations we have about ourselves. Usually, we think of the self-concept evaluatively. A person may be described as having a positive or a negative self-concept, an accepting or a critical orientation toward the self. Here we would like to consider the more literal meaning of the term, that is, the conceptual categories one uses to describe or understand the self. We would argue that the self-concept, like any other concept, undergoes revision and reorganization as the person's cognitive capacities mature. The cognitive growth that takes place during adolescence ought to bring observable changes in the person's understanding of the self just as it brings changes in the understanding of other complex systems (Inhelder and Piaget, 1958; Okun and Sasfy, 1977).

Perhaps the clearest way to understand the contribution of cognition to the self-concept is to follow Epstein's analysis of the self-concept as a self theory. The self theory is an organized set of ideas about the self that are accumulated through daily interactions. Epstein (1973) has argued that the self theory has three purposes:

1. To optimize the pleasure/pain balance of the individual over the course of a lifetime.
2. To facilitate the maintenance of self-esteem.
3. To organizate the data of experience in a manner that can be coped with effectively (p. 407)

The self theory is a set of hypotheses about the self and subjective reality. It is, in Kelly's (1955) terms, a system of personal constructs about where one stands on such variables as worthiness, competence, morality, and lovableness. If the self-concept shares the properties of a theory, then we would expect theorizing about the self to take on new levels of abstractness, complexity, and integration during adolescence.

A variety of methods have been used to evaluate developmental changes in the self-concept during adolescence. The interpretation of research on the self-concept is made somewhat difficult because of the variety of definitions of the self that are implied in the methods of measuring the self-concept. Few studies have taken a totally cognitive approach to the study of the self-concept (Flavell,

1977; Elkind, 1975). The studies that we will review here suggest some of the dimensions along which the self-concept is being revised during early adolescence.

In a very straightforward approach to the question of developmental changes in self-concept, Montemayor and Eisen (1975) asked subjects in grades 4, 6, 8, 10, and 12 to give 20 responses to the question "Who am I?" The answers were coded into 30 categories that reflected roles, personality, activities, membership in groups, and physical characteristics. From childhood to adolescence there was significant increase in the use of five categories: Existential (I am myself), Abstract (a person, a human), Self determination (ambitious, a hard worker), Interpersonal (friendly, nice), and Psychic style (happy, calm). The biggest change came between the fourth and sixth grades. Sixth graders responded more like 12th graders than they did like 4th graders.

Three subjects' responses provide a feeling for the characteristic changes in self-perceptions at ages 9, 11½, and 17.

These first responses are from a nine-year-old boy in the fourth grade. Notice the concrete flavor of his self-descriptions, and the almost exclusive use of terms referring to his Sex, Age, Name, Territory, Likes, and Physical Self.

My name is Bruce C. I have brown eyes. I have brown hair. I have brown eyebrows. I'm nine years old. I *love!* Sports. I have seven people in my family. I have great! eye site. I have lots! of friends. I love on 1923 P. Dr. I'am going on 10 in September. I'am a boy. I have a uncle that is almost 7 feet tall. My school is P. My teacher is Mrs. V. I play Hockey! I'am almost the smartest boy in the class. I *love!* food. I love fresh air. I *love* School.

The next protocol is from a girl aged 11½, in the sixth grade. Although she frequently refers to her likes, she also emphasizes her interpersonal and personality characteristics.

My name is A. I'm a human being. I'm a girl. I'm a truthful person. I'm not pretty. I do so-so in my studies. I'm a very good cellist. I'm a very good pianist. I'm a little bit tall for my age. I like several boys. I like several girls. I'm old-fashioned. I play tennis. I am a *very* good swimmer. I try to be helpful. I'm always ready to be friends with anybody. Mostly I'm good, but I lose my temper. I'm not well-liked by some girls and boys. I love sports and music. I don't know if I'm liked by boys or not.

The final response is from a 17-year-old girl in the 12th grade. Note the strong emphasis on interpersonal description, characteristic mood states, and the large number of ideological and belief references.

I am a human being. I am a girl. I am an individual. I don't know who I am. I am a Pisces. I am a moody person. I am an indecisive person. I am an ambitious person. I am a very curious person. I am a confused person. I am not an individual. I am a loner. I am an American (God help me). I am a Democrat. I am a liberal person. I am a radical. I am a conservative. I am a pseudo-liberal. I am an atheist. I am not a classifiable person (i.e.—I don't want to be).(Montemayor and Eisen, 1977, 317-318)

Long, Ziller, and Henderson (1968) considered the self as a social system with seven components: esteem, dependency, power, centrality, complexity, individuation, and identification. Their measures relied more on perceptual gestalts than on verbal responses. Their subjects were 420 students from grades 6 through 12. They found that self-esteem increased with age. They also found that dependency (seeing oneself as part of a group rather than as a separate entity) increased until ninth grade and then declined. Power scores in relation to teachers remained stable across grades, but power in relation to one's father *decreased* with age.

Carlson (1965) reported that the changes in the adolescent's self-image were highly related to a personal versus social orientation. Her studies with preadolescents (150 sixth graders) showed that both males and females were personally oriented, that is, their self-concepts were independent of concerns with social experience. They were based on inner feelings of competence and worth. In adolescence, she found that girls were significantly more socially oriented (their self-concepts were dependent on social appraisals and interpersonal experiences) and that boys were more personally oriented. Further, she found that changes in self-esteem from preadolescence to adolescence were not related to sex. She concluded that self-esteem and social versus personal orientation are two separate components of the self-image that develop independently.

A related study (Tome, 1972) identified three components of the adolescent's self-concept: (1) egotism, or the tendency to feel superior; (2) self-control, or the ability to solve problems autonomously; and (3) sociability, or interpersonal confidence. These three components were part of the way in which adolescents saw themselves as well as part of the way in which others saw them. Throughout adolescence, young people tend to recognize these elements as meaningful dimensions of the self-concept.

Katz and Zigler (1967) considered the discrepancy reported in perceptions of the real, the ideal, and the social self by 5th-, 8th-, and 11th-grade middle-class children. They used two instruments, a 20-statement questionnaire and a 20-item adjective checklist. Their main findings were that the 8th and 11th graders reported larger self-ideal discrepancies than did the 5th graders. With age, the real-self scores were more negative and the ideal scores more positive. They concluded that the increased discrepancy scores reflected a more mature level of self-differentiation and evaluation. They also suggested that the anxiety which has been found to relate to real-ideal discrepancy scores (Coopersmith, 1967; Horowitz, 1962) may be reevaluated as a necessary part of the process of cognitive differentiation.

The notion that the discrepancy between the real and the ideal self increases during adolescence is supported by Sinha's (1972) study of adolescent girls living in India. These Indian girls became increasingly unwilling to reveal aspects of their personality at older ages. The implication is that these subjects were expressing greater awareness of what was socially acceptable and greater anxiety about how adequately they measured up to a social standard of desirability.

The extent of this self-image discrepancy is put into perspective by looking at some cross-cultural comparisons of adolescent self-image. The Offer self-image questionnaire has been used to evaluate adolescent functioning in the following 11 areas:

1. Impulse control.
2. Emotional tone.
3. Body and self-image.
4. Social relationships.
5. Morals.
6. Family relationships.
7. Mastery of the external world.
8. Vocational-educational goals.
9. Psychopathology.
10. Superior adjustment.
11. Sexual attitudes and behavior.

The questionnaire has been used with subjects in the United States, Australia, Ireland, and Israel (Offer, Ostrov, and Howard, 1977). American adolescents in the age range 13–19 appear to be happier, more hopeful, and experiencing more life satisfaction than adolescents in the other three cultures. Even though the adolescent years are described as a period of reevaluation and redefinition, the real context of opportunities and resources can make a difference in the degree of optimism or alienation that is likely to be incorporated into the self-concept during this phase.

## INDIVIDUAL DIFFERENCES IN INTELLECTUAL DEVELOPMENT

Just as there are wide variations in the rate and pattern of physical development, so there are wide variations in the rate and pattern of intellectual growth. These differences are important contributors to the process of adaptation during adolescence. They not only influence academic performance during the high school years, but they influence adolescents' career aspirations and their decisions about continuing education. The rate and pattern of intellectual growth may also influence adolescents' abilities to make effective adaptations to social and personal challenges. One's capacity for reason and problem solving will contribute to the kinds of personal solutions that one is likely to generate about personal values, friendship commitments, and peer group participation.

Individuality in intellectual functioning can result from three factors. First, there are differences in the rate of development. Second, there are differences in cognitive style or cognitive organization. Third, there are differences in talent or unique areas of intellectual competence. Each of these factors contributes to a personal profile of intellectual functioning that can influence successful adaptation during early adolescence.

## Rate of Development

In Piaget's stage theory, the order of the stages is fixed, but the rate of development is not. Piaget (1972) estimates that formal operational skills will emerge during the age range 12–15. Although we might not expect even the brightest six-year-olds to be able to make use of the hypothetical reasoning of formal thought, there is evidence that some children make use of formal strategies earlier than others.

Keating (1975) compared four groups of boys who had been tested for general intelligence with the Iowa Tests of Basic Skills. There were bright (98th and 99th percentile) and average (54th and 55th percentile) boys from the fifth and seventh grades in the sample. Each boy was evaluated for his response to an advanced concrete operational task (conservation of volume) and three formal operational tasks.

Figure 5–3 shows the percentage of each group that passed all three formal operational tasks. Three observations can be made from this figure. First, even among the bright seventh graders (average age 13.1), not all subjects were using formal strategies consistently. Second, within age groupings, the brighter students were more likely to use formal strategies than were the average students. Third, the bright fifth graders (average age 11.3) were twice as likely to use formal operational strategies as were the average seventh graders, who were two years older. In other words, in Keating's sample some 11-year-olds were consistently using abstract, systematic strategies for solving complex problems, and some 13-year-olds were not.

Figure 5–3: Percentage Demonstrating Formal Operations on Three Tasks

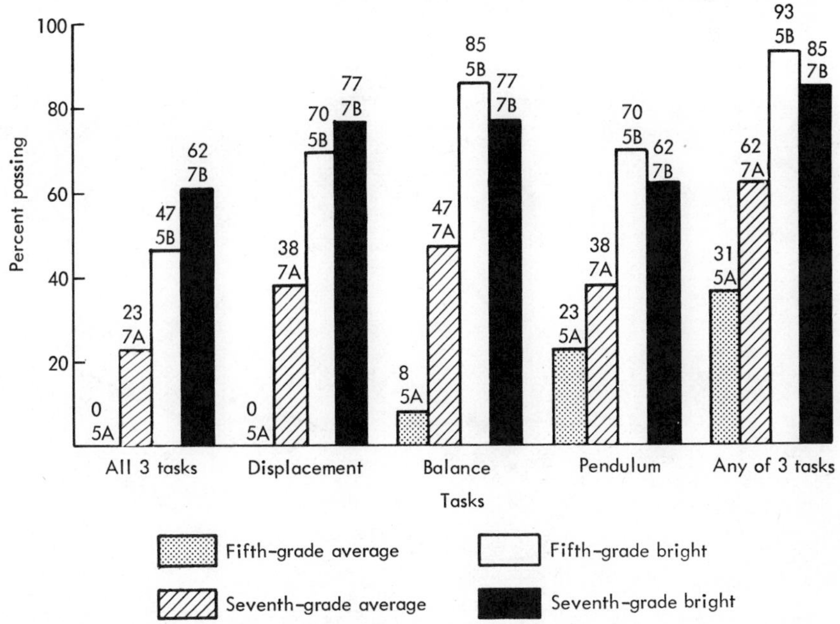

Source: D. P. Keating, "Precocious Cognitive Development at the level of Formal Operations," *Child Development*, 1975, *46*, p. 278. Reprinted by permission.

The notion of individuality in the rate of development is extended if we consider longitudinal data on the patterns of IQ change. McCall, Appelbaum, and Hogarty (1973) evaluated IQ patterns. They analyzed the scores of 80 subjects who had been tested an average of 14 times between the ages of 2½ and 17. These subjects were all part of the Fels longitudinal study. They were born between 1930 and 1938 in small- to medium-sized towns in Ohio. From the longitudinal data, five clusters or patterns of change were identified (see Figure 5–4). Cluster 1 included 36 of the 80 subjects. This pattern was one of slightly rising scores throughout childhood. Cluster 2 included nine subjects who had comparatively high initial scores, a preschool decline, some recovery during the elementary school years, and another decline during adolescence. Cluster 3 included ten subjects who showed a preschool decline and then steady recovery and an increase during adolescence. Cluster 4 included seven subjects whose scores increased through age ten and then declined. Even with this decline, cluster 4 remained highest in tested intelligence through age 17. Cluster 5 included five subjects who showed a pattern similar to that of cluster 4 but with less dramatic rises and declines. We see, then, that some adolescents experience

Figure 5–4: Mean IQ over Age for Five IQ Clusters (adjusted for differences between Binet revision)

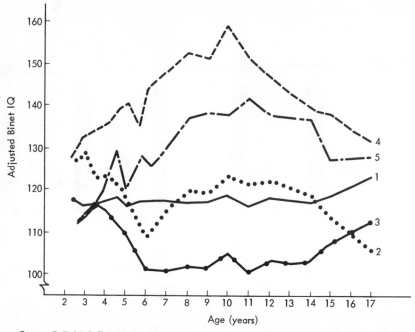

Source: R. B. McCall, M. I. Appelbaum, and P. S. Hogarty, "Developmental changes in mental performance," *Monographs of the Society for Research in Child Development*, 1973, *38* (ser. no. 150) Figure 5, p. 48. Reprinted by permission.

slow, steady increments in competence, that others are declining in competence after an earlier burst in ability, and that still others begin to recover earlier losses as adolescence gets under way.

We begin to get a more differentiated picture of intellectual growth from such data. Rather than considering intellectual development as a stable, stepwise increment in competences, we can appreciate the possibility of gains and losses in functioning that may be related to opportunities, motivation, and psychosocial expectations as well as to personal competence.

## Cognitive Styles

A second factor that contributes to individual differences in intellectual functioning is the dimension of cognitive style. Cognitive style refers to a consistent strategy for selecting and integrating information (Messick, 1976). It refers to the manner in which intellectual tasks are approached rather than to the content of what is known. It is not a description of a person's abilities or talents, but of the typical orientation that a person takes across a variety of tasks.

One of the most carefully investigated dimensions of cognitive style is the variable of field independence versus field dependence. This dimension refers to "the extent to which a person is able to deal with a part of a field separately from the field as a whole" (Witkin, 1976, p. 41). Three tests have been devised to evaluate a person's stylistic preference for field dependence or independence. One measure requires adjusting a rod to the upright position inside a frame. Both the rod and the frame can be tilted separately. Field independence is measured by whether the subject can adjust the rod to the true upright position without being influenced by the tilt of the frame. The second measure is the adjustment of the person's own body to an upright position in a tilted chair and a tilted room. Once again, people differ in how much they judge their own upright position by how much the surrounding room is tilted. The third measure is the embedded figures test. Subjects are shown a figure. Then they are shown a complex design and asked to find the figure hidden in the design.

It is important to point out that field dependence and independence represents a continuous dimension. People can be characterized as relatively more field independent or more field dependent. This characteristic of relying on or resisting environmental cues for interpreting information appears to be a stable aspect of functioning (Witkin, Goodenough, and Karp, 1967). It extends to problem solving, social interaction, and the self-concept. For example, field-dependent people are more likely to look at the faces of others in a social interaction. They appear to be better at remembering faces and better at remembering the content of social interactions than are field-independent people (Nevill, 1971; Ruble and Nakamura, 1972; Fitzgibbons and Goldberger, 1971; Goldberger and Bendich, 1972).

The dimension of field dependence and field independence is relevant for guiding interests and career decisions. Field dependence is associated with interest in interpersonal relations and involvement with people. This includes careers in the social sciences, advertising and promotion, elementary school teaching, and real estate. Field independence is associated with preference for analytic skills and for careers that make use of those skills, especially mathematics, engineering, and the physical and biological sciences (Clar, 1971; DeRussy and Futch, 1971; Krienke, 1969). As early as ten years of age, the dimension of field dependence influences career aspirations by making field-dependent boys more likely to show an interest in the careers preferred by their peers (Witkin, 1976). Field-independent students are more likely than field-dependent students to take optional advanced courses in math and science during high school (Witkin, 1976).

Field dependence and independence is only one dimension of cognitive style. In a glossary of dimensions of cognitive style, Messick (1976) has noted 19 factors that have been identified and studied as characteristics of perceptual and cognitive strategies. Table 5–2 describes five of these dimensions. The existence of individual

Table 5–2: Five Dimensions of Cognitive Style

| | |
|---|---|
| 1.  Breadth of categorization | Preferences for inclusiveness or exclusiveness in establishing the acceptable range for a specific category. |
| 2.  Leveling versus sharpening | Patterns of memory. Leveling is the tendency to blur or merge similar memories. Sharpening is the tendency to exaggerate small differences so that memories of past and present are quite distinct. |
| 3.  Reflection versus impulsivity | The speed and accuracy with which information is processed and hypotheses are formed. |
| 4.  Risk taking versus cautiousness | The willingness to take chances or to seek certainty in trying to solve a problem. |
| 5.  Sensory modality preferences | The reliance on kinesthetic, visual, or auditory information. |

differences in cognitive style suggests differences in adaptation to the learning environment (Messick, 1976; Snow, 1976; Witkin, 1976). Those differences will be reflected in the kinds of learning experiences that students seek out, in the academic areas in which they are most likely to succeed, and in the kinds of future aspirations that are built on contemporary experiences of success or failure.

## Abilities and Talents

The third component of individual variability in intellectual functioning is ability or talent. Terman's longitudinal study of exceptionally bright children has demonstrated that intellectual talent can be identified early in childhood and that it has long-enduring properties, including good physical health, mental stability, and academic achievement (Terman and Oden, 1947; Terman and Oden, 1959). The talented children in Terman's sample have been periodically assessed over the past 50 years. They appear to have resources that continue to foster successful adaptation throughout life (Kagan, 1964; Seagoe, 1975).

The kinds of talents that have captured the interest and energy of the scientific community tend to be those related to intellectual and scientific abilities (Nauman, 1974). At Johns Hopkins, Julian Stanley has developed a program to study mathematically precocious children in the 12–14-year age range (Stanley, Keating, and Fox, 1974). The project involves identifying mathematically gifted children and developing their talents. Some special program has been developed to nurture the skills of each student. Some students have attended accelerated courses, some have enrolled in junior college night classes, some have attended university summer sessions, and some have enrolled early in universities. One of the students involved in the program is Eric Jablow. He entered Brooklyn College after sixth grade and graduated summa cum laude. He won a National Science Foundation graduate fellowship to help support his graduate work at Princeton. At the age of 15, Eric was Princeton's youngest doctoral candidate (Nevin, 1977).

It is important to note that intellectual ability is not limited to mathematical and scientific areas. Intellectual achievement can be expressed through involvement in art, dramatics, debating, creative writing, music, or political leadership, to name a few. These areas of ability are not necessarily related to outstanding classroom achievement or to test scores on standard achievement tests (Wallach, 1976; Wing and Wallach, 1971). On the other hand, areas of productivity and achievement during high school are good predictors of later accomplishments. (Albert, 1975; Wallach, 1971; Richards, Holland, and Lutz, 1966). The skill and pleasure that are experienced while one exercises areas of special talent can be considered sources of motivation. In line with White's (1960) notion of competence motivation, personal talents guide individual youths toward areas of interest and aspiration that are intrinsically satisfying.

## THE MEASUREMENT OF INTELLIGENCE

The early work on the measurement of intelligence began in the last part of the 19th century (Brody and Brody, 1976). In England, Sir Frances Galton (1883) developed tests to measure individual variation in physical strength and sensory competences. Influenced by Galton's work, James Cattell in America developed a battery of mental tests that included the assessment of sensory acuity, reaction time, sensitivity to pain, color preference, memory, and imagery (Cattell, 1890).

In France, at about the same time, Alfred Binet was working on a mental test that was designed to evaluate "higher" mental abilities, including comprehension, aesthetic appreciation, judgment of visual space, and suggestibility. In an effort to help the French minister of public instruction to identify children who were "mentally defective," Binet and Simon (1905) developed standardized tests that would provide a quantitative score or measure of intelligence. In these early tests, items were age-graded. The tests were designed so that normal intelligence would permit performance to increase with age.

Beginning in 1916, Lewis Terman in California revised and standardized Binet's scale. The Stanford-Binet continues to be a valuable diagnostic tool for the assessment of intelligence (Terman and Merrill, 1960). It is an individually administered test that can be taken by a wide range of people from slow learners at the preschool level to gifted adults. Terman then began work with Arthur S. Otis to develop multiple-choice items that could be used as a quick way of assessing intelligence in groups of people. The Stanford Achievement Test Battery was developed during World War I, and it continues to be a useful group method for assessing ability (Seagoe, 1975).

Throughout the years of research on intelligence and its measurement there has been controversy about the definition of intelligence. In early work, Spearman (1904) identified two factors in all intelligence tests, $g$ and $s$. The $g$ factor referred to general ability as it would be measured in any specific test. The $s$ factor referred to the specific ability that was tapped by any particular test. Spearman defined $g$ as the "education of relations and correlates" (Spearman, 1927). It referred to a general capacity to comprehend the logical implications of relationships. Raymond Cattell (1971) has provided a contemporary analysis of this view. He has described a list of 17 primary mental abilities, from which five general factors of intelligence can be derived. The two most frequently discussed of these factors are $gf$, or fluid abilities and $gc$, or crystallized abilities. As we discussed earlier, fluid abilities are closely linked to perception, memory, and general capacities to understand relationships. Crystallized abilities are closely linked to verbal skills and information that is associated with formal education.

In contrast to theorists who suggest a general intellectual capacity as the basic underlying content being measured by intelligence tests, Guilford has devised a model of 120 different abilities that he considers to be separate elements of intelligence (Guilford, 1967; Guilford and Hoepfner, 1971). He has rejected the concept of general intelligence and has developed specific tests to assess each area of ability. Given this wide range of separate abilities, one would expect to find individual variability, such that a person could be in the top 10 percent on some tests and in the bottom 10 percent on others. Rather than a summary score of intelligence, Guilford's model would suggest a profile of mental abilities.

To these two views of the meaning of intelligence Wechsler (1975) has added another perspective. "To be rated intelligent, behavior must not only be rational and purposeful; it must not only have meaning but it must also have value, it must be esteemed" (Wechsler, 1975, p. 136). This third perspective suggests an emphasis on the adaptive, coping skills that are expressed in intelligent behavior. In this respect, Wechsler differentiates mental abilities from intelligence. The former refer to mechanisms for perceiving, interpreting, and organizing information. The latter refers to meaningful, purposeful, worthwhile mental activity.

Despite these diverse interpretations of the general concept of intelligence, intelligence tests have been widely used in the military, in elementary and secondary schools, in colleges, and in industry (Cronbach, 1975). Since the 1920s there have been repeated controversies over the use of intelligence tests, and, probably more important, over the decisions that are made on the basis of these tests. The tests are designed to identify individual variation. Whether this variation is the result of inherited capacities or environmental opportunities has plagued psychologists and educators. To date, there is strong evidence that a variety of factors contribute to performance on intelligence tests, including genetics, neurological impairment during the prenatal period, low birth weight, prenatal and postnatal nutrition, parenting practices, preschool enrichment experiences, and schooling (Brody and Brody, 1976; Resnick, 1976; Loehlin, Lindzey, and Spuhler, 1975; Scarr-Salapatek, 1975). Since most intelligence tests were designed to identify variation among subjects, the fact that such variation has been found should not be a source of surprise. Nonetheless, the very fact of individual variation has probably been the most troublesome aspect of intelligence testing. It is troublesome precisely because performance on intelligence tests has been used to make decisions about children and adolescents that alter the educational settings and resources that provide the context for further learning.

## CREATIVITY

Another argument about the heavy reliance on tests of intelligence is that most of these tests appear to tap crystallized rather than fluid intelligence. In other words, the content of most intelligence tests, especially those administered to large groups of students in the school setting, draw on information and ideas that are acquired in school. They test how well an individual knows what is already known in the society as a whole. The notion of creativity has been studied from many perspectives (Dellas and Gaier, 1970). One approach is to identify creativity with the quality of the productions that a person has created. For example, Albert (1975) has offered the following definition of genius: "A person of genius is anyone who, regardless of other characteristics he may possess or have attributed to him, produces, over a long period of time, a large body of work that has a significant influence on many persons for many years" (p. 144).

In this line of thinking, Wallach (1976) has argued that real-life accomplishments during high school and college are more predictive of later attainments than are grades or test scores. What is more, the range of attainment tends to be quite specific. A person who excels in theater is not necessarily going to create unusual science experiments or new mathematical models. Thus, to nurture creativity during adolescence it is necessary to link individual talents to experiences or programs that especially value those talents.

A second view identifies creativity with the quality of thought that is involved in a creative response (Kogan and Pankove, 1972). Here we see an effort to differentiate between convergent thinking, or finding the single, best answer, and divergent thinking, or finding many, varied, and unusual answers (Guilford, 1967; Wallach, 1971; Kogan, 1973). Of course, both kinds of thinking are part of normal cognitive functioning. Sometimes we search for the one best answer or solution to a problem. Often, however, we try to generate a list of the many possible explanations or options before selecting one.

In an attempt to differentiate between the adaptive capacities of highly intelligent and highly creative adolescents, Getzels and Jackson (1962) selected two groups of subjects from the total population of a private midwestern secondary school. The highly creative group scored in the top 20 percent on the creativity measures but below the top 20 percent on tests of intelligence. The highly intelligent group scored in the top 20 percent on tests of intelligence and below the top 20 percent on measures of creativity. Three comparisons between the two groups are of interest. First, both the highly intelligent and the highly creative groups earned higher grades in school than the average student population. Second, when teachers were asked to rate how much they would enjoy having students in their class, the highly intelligent group received higher ratings than the highly creative group. Third, when the two groups were asked to report what kinds of occupations they would like to have, the highly creative group named more possible occupations and more "unconventional" occupations than did the highly intelligent group. Several implications can be drawn from these findings. First, creativity appears to be a personal, inner resource that permits students with average intelligence to make highly effective responses in the academic setting (Walberg, 1971). Taylor (1975) has elaborated this component in an analysis of creative actions. He describes creative actions as those that bring aspects of the environment into line with the person's talents, motives, and inner experiences. In his model, creativity permits the person to modify or select elements of the environment, rather than be shaped by it.

Second, findings suggest that creative adolescents are not particularly highly valued in the student role. We can understand that creative students may resist coming to a final conclusion, that they may offer more suggestions than the teacher has time to pursue, or that they may ask questions that embarrass or perplex teachers (Torrance, 1970; Walberg, 1971). Torrance has described several aspects of the academic environment that inhibit the emergence of creative responses. These include the resistance that both teachers and students offer to divergent or unusual responses, the orientation toward success and external evaluation rather than toward achievement for its own sake, the conforming emphasis of peer pressure, and the cultural assumption that work is serious and productive but play is not. Within the pattern of developmental changes in creativity, Torrance finds that the seventh grade is one period in the decline of creativity. At this entry point into adolescent development, the temporary increase in anxiety, academic expectations, peer pressures, and social roles all serve to decrease the nonevaluative approach that is conducive to divergent thinking (Torrance, 1962, 1965, 1975; Torrance and Myers, 1970).

## THE IMPLICATIONS OF INDIVIDUAL DIFFERENCES IN INTELLIGENCE FOR THE EMERGENCE OF LIFE-STYLE PATTERNS

The idea that individual differences in intelligence have consequences for future life choices has already been implied in our discussions of genius, creativity, special intellectual abilities, and the pattern and tempo of intellectual growth. During adolescence choices are made and paths are followed that have implications for a total life course. Of course, these decisions are not irreversible. One may find at age 20 or age 30 or even much later that an opportunity that was rejected or ignored during adolescence can be retrieved. On the other hand, for many adolescents the decision to pursue a college preparatory curriculum or a vocational curriculum, to attend a liberal arts college or a professional school, or to drop out of high school or remain enrolled are all major choice points that can influence subsequent opportunities, work roles, and personal resources. These and other decisions that direct the future life course are closely tied to an individual's assessments of his or her intellectual abilities. This assessment is built on feedback from school authorities, performance in academic tasks, and an inner appraisal of areas of competence or ability. In the following discussion, three possible consequences of differences in ability are considered: academic tracking, peer group identification, and career choice. The decision to drop out of school will be discussed in Chapter 7 as an example of one pattern of adaptation to the total high school environment.

### Academic Tracking

Because of the compulsory attendance laws, a large and diverse population of adolescents attend secondary schools. Some communities have established specialized high schools to respond to this diversity. Vocational schools and schools for the gifted, such as the Bronx High School of Science, are examples of total school

*Burk Uzzle/Magnum*

*Academic tracking is one strategy for responding to the diversity of student abilities.*

settings that are designed to meet the individual needs of high school students. Most comprehensive schools use a variety of strategies to adapt to the diversity of student abilities. Thomas and Thomas (1965) list ten of the most frequent administrative techniques that are designed to respond to the many levels of competence among students.

1. Ability groupings.
2. Special classes for slow learners.
3. Special classes for the gifted.
4. Other special classes.
5. Ungraded classes.
6. Retention and acceleration.
7. Frequent promotion plans.
8. Contract and unit plans.
9. Team teaching.
10. Parallel track plan.

In the parallel track plan, a student is assigned to a curriculum that is presumed to match his or her ability and interests. The tracks may be differently defined in different high schools. One model offers four tracks: Basic or Special Academic, for slow learners; General, a vocational program for students who do not plan to attend college; Regular, for college-bound students; and Honors, for intellectually gifted students (Hansen, 1964; Hobson, 1967). Other track models are more finely differentiated, providing fine arts, business education, vocational education, practical arts, general, and college-bound tracks (Tanner, 1965). In most track systems, some general education courses are required in every track. This means that all students will take courses in Freshman English, U.S. History, or Biology. Usually these courses are taught at different levels in the college-bound, general, and vocational tracks.

Assignment to a track is based on six factors: aptitude, achievement, teachers' opinions, elementary and junior high school performance, social maturity, and the student's interests (Tanner, 1965). This assignment usually occurs during junior high school or upon entrance to high school. Several criticisms of the procedures for track assignment have been raised. First, the assignment to tracks often discriminates against low-income and minority-group children. In contrast to middle-class white students these children tend not to be assigned to the college-bound track. Thus, despite what is known about the culture-bound nature of intelligence tests, and despite the high aspirations and life goals of many low-income and minority adolescents (Kurlesky and Thomas, 1971), many low-income, black, and Spanish-speaking adolescents are guided away from a college education and prepared for a career in areas that are associated with less skill, less training, and less income.

A second criticism of the tracking system is that it is based on past performance. Given the variability in maturational rate that has been documented thus far, it makes sense to assume that the school record and test performance of many children reflect a slower tempo of intellectual development. There is some evidence to suggest that early maturers perform better on verbal tasks than do late maturers. In contrast, late maturers perform better on spatial tasks than do early maturers (Waber, 1976). Since decisions about high school tracking are usually made during the seventh- and eighth-grade years, young adolescents are directed toward an educational pattern before their mental abilities are fully developed.

In an assessment of the tracking system, Schafer and Olexa (1971) compared the effects of tracking in two comprehensive high schools. One, Industrial City High School, was near the center of the business district of a midwestern city. The other, Academic Heights High School, was on the outskirts of a university town. Industrial City had two tracks, college prep and general. Academic Heights had four tracks: Special Room; General, Business, and Industrial; College and University; and Advanced Placement.

Several findings of this study reflect the impact of the tracking experience at the two schools. First, even when IQ and previous school records were held constant, students whose fathers held blue-collar jobs were more likely to be in the non–college prep tracks than were students whose fathers held white-collar jobs. Black students were more likely than white students to be in the non–college prep tracks. These track assignments were relatively permanent. About 7 percent of the college prep students moved into the noncollege programs, and about 7 percent of the noncollege students moved into the college-bound programs.

Of course, these patterns might not be very important if students in all the tracks were experiencing intellectually stimulating, positive academic experiences. However, Schafer and Olexa did not find this to be the case. In a controlled comparison of grade point averages, 73 percent of the noncollege group showed grades in the low or low-average categories and only 39 percent of the college group had grades in this range. Looking at grade change over the 10th, 11th, and 12th grades, students whose grades were in the 2.5–1.5 range were more likely to show drops in grades if they were in the noncollege track and were more likely to show improvements in grades if they were in the college track. These findings suggest a general depressing effect on the academic record for those who are in the noncollege track, and an enhancing effect for those who are in the college track. Within this pattern, low-income and minority students are "disproportionately subject to whatever negative effects are associated with the non–college prep track" (Schafer and Olexa, 1971, p. 36).

In areas of social adaptation, the track system also manifested undesirable characteristics. As illustrated in Table 5–3, students in the noncollege tracks showed less participation in extracurricular activities, higher rates of delinquency, and a greater tendency

Table 5–3: Differences between Tracks in Extracurricular Participation, Dropout Rates, and Delinquency Rates, Standardized for Father's Occupation, IQ, and Previous Achievement

| | Activities | | | | |
| --- | --- | --- | --- | --- | --- |
| | 3 or More | 1–2 | None | Total | N |
| College prep . . . . . . . . . . . . . | 41% | 35% | 24% | 100% | 512 |
| Non–college prep . . . . . . . . | 15 | 35 | 50 | 100 | 199 |

| | Dropout Rate | | | | |
| --- | --- | --- | --- | --- | --- |
| | Graduated | Transferred | Dropped Out | Total | N |
| College prep . . . . . . . . . | 88% | 8% | 4% | 100% | 681 |
| Non–college prep . . . . . | 74 | 7 | 19 | 100 | 326 |

| | Delinquency Rate | | | |
| --- | --- | --- | --- | --- |
| | Nondelinquent | Delinquent* | Total | N |
| College prep . . . . . . . . . . . | 94% | 5% | 100 | 708 |
| Non–college prep . . . . . . . . | 86 | 12 | 100 | 354 |

* Determined by juvenile court records
Source: Adapted from W. E. Schafer and C. Olexa, *Tracking and opportunity: The locking-out process and beyond.* Scranton, Pa.: Chandler, 1971; Pps. 42, 46, 48.

to drop out of school. To the extent that the school values the college-bound students and prides itself on their future accomplishments, the non-college-bound students experience less reinforcement and less encouragement to work hard. Involvement in the school itself and getting good grades have decreasing payoff for a student who is planning to leave the world of schools, courses, and teachers for the world of work. Add to this a variety of teacher expectations about the lower ability of the non-college-bound students, and it is not difficult to see a pattern of low incentives, few reinforcements, and negative assessments about one's ability, leading to a gradual disengagement from school.

## Peer Group Cohorts

Friendship patterns are usually influenced first by proximity and later by similarity of interests and values (Newcomb, 1961). In moving to a new community, starting at a new school, or going off to college, the first friendships we are likely to form are among those who are nearby. Thus, the homeroom group that meets together every day or the people who ride the bus to school in the morning are the most likely initial source of peer friendships in the high school. After a while, however, people begin to seek out friends who share their interests, hold similar aspirations, and participate in similar activities. In this way, the diversity of ability groupings present in the comprehensive high school frequently serves as a force toward peer group formation. Students who are following the same academic curriculum are more likely to have repeated interactions with one another; similar course schedules; similar concerns about homework, papers, tests, or projects; and similar aspirations about the direction of their life after high school. This is not to say that vocational and college-bound students cannot be friends, but that such friendships are unlikely in schools which separate students into highly differentiated groupings or academic tracks.

Several studies of peer group identification suggest that ability groupings not only make cross-group friendships difficult, but that they serve to foster cross-group antagonisms (Hargreaves, 1967; Stinchcombe, 1964; Frease, 1969; and Kelly, 1970). These antagonisms result from differences in the aspirations of the groups, differences in involvement in school activities, and differences in the responsiveness and punishment experienced from adults in the school setting. In Hargreaves' (1967) analysis of a secondary school in England, the conflict between the high stream and the low stream was so great that negative stereotypes of the members of the opposite stream began to emerge. These negative stereotypes themselves prevented students in the low stream from aspiring to an improved academic status. In fact, Hargreaves suggests that some boys in the low stream actually performed less well than they might have, for fear of being promoted to the high stream.

Extreme consequences of individual differences in intellectual ability for peer group functioning are experienced by students in the genius and slow learner groups. At both ends of the intellectual ability continuum, adolescents are likely to experience peer rejection or alienation. At the genius end of, unusually gifted adolescents find few peers who can share their interests or follow their thinking. As they move through their elementary and high school years at an accelerated pace, they may have little time or desire to interact with peers.

In his study of gifted children, Terman found that these particularly bright youngsters tended to become absorbed in reading, experimentation, or projects. He urged parents to encourage such children to play outdoors and to engage with other children at a young age in order to prevent them from becoming socially withdrawn

(Terman, 1947, in Seagoe, 1975). Exceptionally bright children may not begin to find academic age-mates (not chronological age-mates) who are intellectual companions until they reach college or even graduate school (Nevin, 1977; Stanley et al., 1974).

## Career Choice

The challenge of selecting an appropriate, satisfying work role can be viewed as one of the most concrete consequences of intellectual development during early adolescence. We view work as a basic focus of life activity that has implications for social relationships, the development of special competences, the accumulation of material resources, and the formulation of a sense of worth in the larger social community. A picture of the development of a work role is presented here. We suggest a view of the working person that begins in childhood and continues through later adulthood (Borow, 1976). At every phase, the components of the work role include personal aspirations and motives for work, personal abilities and talents that may direct the choice of the work activity, training opportunities and experiences, and the economic reality of the job market.

Two developmental models have been offered that emphasize the gradual evolution of the work role. Ginzberg (1972; Ginzberg et al., 1951) describes three kinds of thinking about work. In the *fantasy* period, until about 11, children do not differentiate between what they would like to be and what they really can be. One would expect the range of career aspirations at this stage to be broad, reflecting the child's awareness of diverse work roles and influenced by the status or "glamour" associated with specific work roles. During the second, *tentative* period, at about 12–17, adolescents begin to understand more about the aptitudes and training that a specific career requires. They also become aware of their own relevant talents, values, and goals that make some occupations more attractive than others. The third phase of career development is termed the *realistic* period. During this phase, the person seeks to optimize personal talents and goals through the selection of an appropriate career. This may involve experimentation and the rejection of certain work activities, processes that can continue well into adulthood. It may also involve an assessment of the contemporary demand for some work roles and the anticipation of future job roles as economic, historic, and technological realities change.

Superimposed on this view of an evolving appreciation of work activity is another developmental picture of changing conceptualizations of the self as a worker. In his description of developmental tasks, Havighurst (1964) has identified three psychological stages in the emergence of the concept of self as worker. In the first stage, children identify with workers, especially parents, relatives, and older siblings. During this process, children come to idealize some work roles. Working becomes an essential component of the ego ideal. In the second stage, children acquire a sense of industry. The strategies of being an effective worker, including planning a task, organizing one's time, enjoying feelings of accomplishment, and beginning to evaluate one's progress, are all being learned. The third stage is acquiring an identity as a worker in an occupational role. This may include technical training, on-the-job experience, and experimentation with a variety of work roles. In Table 5–4 the two views of career development are combined, showing the kinds of thinking and the kinds of psychological experiences that contribute to the formation of a worker role.

It is clear from both of these views that many factors contribute to an eventual commitment to work activity. What is more, neither system anticipates that a clear, consolidated decision will be reached during early adolescence. This is the stage for becoming aware of the requirements and rewards of various occupations. It is also the time for evolving an effective work strategy, enjoying the positive aspects of a whole range of productive activities. During the age range 14–16 almost all adolescents are still in school. About 25 percent are working in unskilled occupations, including delivering papers, baby-sitting, doing farm chores, and waiting on tables (U.S. Bureau of Labor Statistics, 1966, 1970). Young adolescents are not only beginning to accumulate work experiences, but they are developing a sense of the meaning of work and what they hope for in a job. In a poll of high school adolescents, characteristics of a work setting that were described as desirable included active work versus inactive work, work with others rather than

Table 5–4: The Emergence of The Work Role during Childhood and Adolescence

| Evolution of the Work Role | Developmental Tasks That Provide the Competences for Work |
| --- | --- |
| *Fantasy:* No differentiation between what one wishes to be and what one can be | Identification with workers |
| *Tentative:* Understanding about the skills and training that specific work roles require | The development of a sense of industry |
| *Realistic:* Trying to otpimize one's talents and aspirations through the selection of an appropriate career | Experimentation with work roles leading to the formation of an identity as a worker in a specific occupation |

*Sepp Seitz/Magnum*

*Early adolescents have greatest access to unskilled jobs.*

work alone, and self-guided work versus work guided by others (Erlick and Starry, 1972).

In a retrospective study of career plans among college women, Harmon (1971) asked students to respond to a list of 135 occupations. For each occupation, the subject was asked whether she had ever considered it as a career, the age at which she first thought of it, and the age at which she rejected it. The pattern of responses showed that the most popular and earliest occupational choices were housewife and actress. These were first considered in the age range six–nine, and thereafter many of the subjects continued to look forward to becoming housewives. Later choices tended to be more specific and reflected more understanding of actual professions. For example, careers such as nurse and veterinarian were chosen during the 10–12-year range, whereas biologist, nurse's aid, and physical therapist were chosen at around 15. The subjects also tended to express interest in a narrow range of career choices. Less than 3 percent of the sample had ever thought of such careers as accountant, governor, dentist, weather forecaster, museum director, children's clothes designer, or hotel manager, to name just a few. As Shafer (1975) argues, a major obstacle to expanding women's career aspirations is the absence of female role models in visible career positions. Thus, even though almost half of the women between the ages of 18 and 65 are in the labor force, many women do not begin an active period of career investigation or conceptualization that ranges broadly over possible work activities and goals.

Another factor that limits the conceptual work on career development is the learning environment. We will talk more about the nature of the high school experience in Chapter 7. Here, let us refer to our earlier discussion of ability tracking and the creation of discrete educational opportunities for students of various abilities. High school adolescents are likely to find themselves in one of three very general educational programs—the college-bound program, the general curriculum, or the vocational curriculum. The college-bound program makes no pretense of training students in specific work skills, but is intended to enhance the general sense of industry by increasing students' abilities to pose problems, plan solutions, and gather information. All of these skills are supposed to be preparation for further education that will eventually lead to a career. The general curriculum does not prepare graduates for college, nor does it teach specific skills (Rogers, 1973). As the tracking literature suggests, students in the non-college-bound, general curriculum are likely to find the learning experience irrelevant to their future goals, and they may even experience declines in their sense of industry. The vocational curriculum is of quite varied quality across the United States. In some states, there is a close working relationship between large industry and vocational training programs. In these states, the selection procedures for the vocational training programs are quite rigorous. No students who might require prolonged training or remedial education are admitted. The schools really provide training programs for industry and are successful in placing students in work settings after graduation. In other states, the instruction, the equipment, and the curriculum are so outmoded that graduates are not really prepared to function in the work role for which they have been trained (Rogers, 1973). In the short run, a close collaboration between industry and vocational training programs seems essential to insure employability after this experience. In the long run, vocational training seems to cut short the phase of career experimentation or investigation that one expects during the early adolescent years.

Havighurst and Gottlieb (1975) point to a very powerful dilemma that youth face with respect to the formation of an identification with work and work activities. First, many young people look forward to work that will be personally meaningful, that will provide satisfying social interactions, and that will not be manipulative or exploitative. Their aspirations about finding satisfying careers are high. Even among low-income and minority groups, adolescents aspire to jobs that require a high level of education, involve skill and prestige, and provide substantial incomes (Kurlesky and Thomas, 1971). However, several barriers stand in the way of these positive expectations. First, there has been a substantial increase in unemployed youth among nonwhite males and females since 1960 (Havighurst, 1975). Thus, many young people who want to work are turned away. Second, the kinds of jobs that adolescents can get do not provide them with the experiences of responsibility, the range of contact with others, or the sense of contributing to larger, meaningful goals that would feed into a positive sense of the self as worker. As expectations about work rise, as more and more women are socialized to anticipate an active career phase, and as the influences of school and home press all adolescents to view work as an avenue for self-enhancement, the challenge is posed to create work activities that match adolescent expectations. This challenge involves expanding the adolescent's knowledge of the careers that are possible and of the avenues that lead to these careers. It also involves modifying work settings so that jobs are designed to provide the personal satisfactions that adolescents seek. In the transition phase, there is a great need to create work roles that can provide opportunities for temporary commitments as adolescents evolve a fuller sense of their own competence as workers.

## CHAPTER SUMMARY

During early adolescence, there is a gradual transition from concrete operational thought to formal operational thought. The concrete skills, including classification, conservation, and combinatorial operations remain central to later functioning. In this phase of development, however, adolescents begin to integrate these skills, to apply the skills to more abstract problems, and to approach complex problems more systematically. Formal thought, including hypothesis raising and testing, probabilistic thinking, and a more coherent view of the future, is fostered by expanded experiences in a variety of roles, increased self-awareness, and an awareness of the importance of future events. Nevertheless, not all young adolescents make use of formal thought, and those who do may not apply formal strategies to the whole range of problems that they encounter. One consequence of the transition from concrete to formal operational functioning is a heightened egocentrism. There is a preoccupation with one's own thoughts and an expectation that others are also focused on one's inner concerns. This egocentrism is thought to be reduced through peer interaction and participation in the work setting. Some degree of egocentrism remains a characteristic of adult thought. In addition to the skills described as elements of formal operational thought, other intellectual abilities continue to improve during early adolescence. Measures of both fluid and crystallized intelligence show continued growth. Memory span, the acquisition of information, and problem-solving abilities improve.

A view of the self-concept as a theory about oneself was offered. This orientation suggests that the conceptual gains of adolescence should contribute to a changing self-concept. The changes that have been documented include a greater real-ideal discrepancy, the inclusion of more abstract qualities as relevant definitions of the self, and a clearer differentiation of the private and public characteristics of the self.

Within the picture of normal patterns of development, the theme of individual differences emerged. It is clear that there is quite a bit of variability in the rate and pattern of intellectual growth. There are also differences in cognitive style, abilities, talents, and creativity that have implications for the kinds of intellectual experiences that one will pursue and for the ways in which one is likely to adapt to the challenges of the school setting.

Three implications of intellectual growth during early adolescence for later life-style patterns were discussed. Academic tracking separates students of different abilities and aspirations into different school curricula. The system itself tends to overselect blue-collar and minority students into the noncollege tracks. Once the tracks are established, the students in the lower tracks appear to receive lower grades, to show less grade improvement, to participate in fewer school activities, to drop out more frequently, and to participate in more delinquent acts than do the college-bound students. Intellectual growth also contributes to the emergence of peer cohorts of similar competence. In some situations, tracking can create strong peer reference groups that develop antagonisms toward one another. Precocious or delayed intellectual development can result in peer isolation.

The final theme of the chapter, career choice, suggests the integration of a variety of factors related to intellectual growth. Career choice is in a formative phase during early adolescence, when young people are trying out the work role in jobs that are usually not very complicated or that do not require elaborate training. The conceptualization of oneself as a worker during this phase includes recognition of one's talents, abilities, motives, and aspirations. It also includes knowledge of the training or experience that is required for a particular career and of the access to that training or experience. Finally, it involves an assessment of economic realities that might make some career choices more desirable, more lucrative, or more secure than others.


# REFERENCES

Albert, R. S.   Toward a behavioral definition of genius. *American Psychologist,* 1975, *30,* 140–151.

Bayley, N.   Development of mental abilities. In P. H. Mussen (Ed.), *Carmichael's manual of child psychology* (3d ed.), vol. 1. New York: Wiley, 1970. Pp. 1163–1209.

Berlyne, D. E.   Children's reasoning and thinking. In P. H. Mussen (Ed.), *Carmichael's manual of child psychology* (3d ed.), vol. 1. New York: Wiley, 1970. Pp. 939–981.

Berzonsky, M. D., Weiner, A. S., and Raphael, D.   Interdependence of formal reasoning. *Developmental Psychology,* 1975, *11,* 258.

Binet, A. and Simon, T.   Applications des methodes nouvelles au diagnostic du niveau intellectual chez des enfants normaux et anormaux d'hospice et d'école primaire. *Année Psychologie,* 1905, *11,* 245–336.

Borow, H.   Career development. In J. F. Adams (Ed.), *Understanding adolescence: Current developments in adolescent psychology* (3d ed.). Boston: Allyn and Bacon, 1976. Pp. 489–523.

Brody, E. B., and Brody, N.   *Intelligence: Nature, determinants, and consequences.* New York: Academic Press, 1976.

Carlson, R.   Stability and change in adolescents' self-image. *Child Development,* 1965 *36,* 659–666.

Cattell, J. McK.   Mental test and measurements. *Mind,* 1890, *15,* 373–381.

Cattell, R. B.   Theory of fluid and crystallized intelligence: A critical experiment. *Journal of Educational Psychology,* 1963, *54,* 1–22.

Cattell, R. B.   The theory of fluid and crystallized intelligence checked at the 5–6 year old level. *British Journal of Educational Psychology,* 1967, *37,* 209–224.

Cattell, R. B.   *Abilities: Their structure, growth, and action.* Boston: Houghton Mifflin, 1971.

Clar, P. N.   The relationship of psychological differentiation to client behavior in vocational choice counseling. Doctoral dissertation, University of Michigan, 1971. Ann Arbor, Mich.: University Microfilms, no. 71-23, 723.

Coopersmith, S.   *The antecedents of self-esteem.* San Francisco: W. H. Freeman, 1967.

Cronbach, L. J.   Five decades of public controversy over mental teting. *American Psychologist,* 1975, *30,* 1–14.

Darwin, Sir Francis.   *Autobiography of Charles Darwin.* London: Watts, 1929.

Davids, A., and Parenti, A. N.   Time orientation and interpersonal relations of emotionally disturbed and normal children. *Journal of Abnormal and Social Psychology,* 1958, *3,* 299–305.

Dellas, M., and Gaier, E. L. Identification of creativity: The individual. *Psychological Bulletin*, 1970, *73*, 55–73.

DeRussy, E. A., and Futch, E. Field dependence-independence as related to college curricula. *Perceptual and Motor Skills*, 1971, *33*, 1235–1237.

Dulit, E. Adolescent thinking à la Piaget: The formal stage. *Journal of Youth and Adolescence*, 1972, *1*, 281–301.

Elkind, D. Egocentrism in adolescence. *Child Development*, 1967, *38*, 1025–1034.

Elkind, D. Recent research on cognitive development in adolescence. In S. E. Dragastin and G. H. Elder, Jr. (Eds.), *Adolescence in the life cycle: Psychological change and social context*. New York: Wiley, 1975. Pp. 49–61.

Epstein, S. The self-concept revisited: Or a theory of a theory. *American Psychologist*, 1973, *28*, 404–416.

Erlick, A. C., and Starry, A. R. *Vocational plans and preferences of adolescents, Poll 94*. West Lafayette, Ind.: Purdue University, 1972.

Fitzgerald, J. M., Nesselroade, J. R., and Baltes, P. B. Emergence of adult intellectual structure: Prior to or during adolescence? *Developmental Psychology*, 1973, *9*, 114–119.

Fitzgibbons, D., and Goldberger, L. Task and social orientation: A study of field dependence, arousal, and memory for incidental material. *Perceptual and Motor Skills*, 1971, *32*, 167–174.

Flavell, J. *The developmental psychology of Jean Piaget*. Princeton, N.J.: Van Nostrand, 1963.

Flavell, J. H. *Cognitive development*. Englewood Cliffs, N.J.: Prentice-Hall, 1977.

Frease, D. *The schools, self-concept, and delinquency*. Unpublished doctoral dissertation, University of Oregon, 1969.

Galton, F. *Inquiries into human faculty and its development*. London: Macmillan, 1883.

Getzels, J. W., and Jackson, P. W. *Creativity and intelligence: Explorations with gifted students*. New York: Wiley, 1962.

Ginzberg, E. Toward a theory of occupational choice: A restatement. *Vocational Guidance Quarterly*, 1972, *20*, 169–176.

Ginzberg, E., et al. *Occupational choice*. New York: Columbia University Press, 1951.

Goldberger, L., and Bendich, S. Field dependence and social responsiveness as determinants of spontaneously produced words. *Perceptual and Motor Skills*, 1972, *34*, 883–886.

Guilford, J. P. *The nature of human intelligence*. New York: McGraw-Hill, 1967.

Guilford, J. P., and Hoepfner, R. *The analysis of intelligence*. New York: McGraw-Hill, 1971.

Hansen, C. F. *The four track curriculum*. Englewood Cliffs, N.J.: Prentice-Hall, 1964.

Hardwick, D. A., McIntyre, C. W., and Pick, H. L., Jr. The content and manipulation of cognitive maps in children and adults. *Monographs of the Society for Research in Child Development*, 1976, *41* (3).

Hargreaves, D. H. *Social relations in a secondary school*. New York: Humanities Press, 1967.

Harmon, L. W. The childhood and adolescent career plans of college women. *Journal of Vocational Behavior*, 1971, *1*, 45–56.

Havighurst, R. J. Youth in exploration and man emergent. In H. Borow (Ed.), *Man in a world at work.* Boston: Houghton Mifflin, 1964.

Havighurst, R. J. Youth in social institutions. In R. J. Havighurst and P. H. Dreyer (Eds.), *Youth: The seventy-fourth yearbook of the National Society for the Study of Education.* Chicago: University of Chicago Press, 1975. Pp. 115–144.

Havighurst, R. J., and Gottlieb, D. Youth and the meaning of work. In R. J. Havighurst and P. H. Dreyer (Eds.), *Youth: The seventy-fourth yearbook of the National Society for the Study of Education.* Chicago: University of Chicago Press, 1975. Pp. 145–160.

Hobson versus Hansen. 269 F. Supp. 401. Washington, D.C.: U.S. Government Printing Office, 1967.

Hoemann, N. W., and Ross, B. M. Children's understanding of probability concepts. *Child Development*, 1971, *42*, 221–236.

Horn, J. L. Organization of data on life-span development of human abilities. In L. R. Goulet and P. B. Baltes (Eds.), *Life-span developmental psychology: Research and theory.* New York: Academic Press, 1970. Pp. 424–466.

Horn, J. L., and Cattell, R. B. Refinement and test of the theory of fluid and crystallized intelligence. *Journal of Educational Psychology*, 1966, *57*, 253–270.

Horowitz, J. D. The relationship of anxiety, self-concept, and sociometric status among fourth, fifth, and sixth grade children. *Journal of Abnormal and Social Psychology*, 1962, *65*, 212–214.

Inhelder, B., and Piaget, J. *The growth of logical thinking.* New York: Basic Books, 1958.

Kagan, J. American longitudinal research on psychological development. *Child Development*, 1964, *35*, 1–32.

Katz, P., and Zigler, E. Self-image disparity: A developmental approach. *Journal of Personality and Social Psychology*, 1967, *5*, 186–195.

Keating, D. P. Precocious cognitive development at the level of formal operations. *Child Development*, 1975, *46*, 276–280.

Kelly, D. H. Social class, school status, and self-evaluation as related to adolescent values, success, and deviance, Unpublished doctoral dissertation, University of Oregon, 1970.

Kelly, G. A. *The psychology of personal constructs*, 2 vols. New York: Norton, 1955.

Klineberg, S. L. Changes in outlook on the future between childhood and adolescence. *Journal of Personality and Social Psychology*, 1967, *7*, 185–193.

Kogan, N. Creativity and cognitive style: A life-span perspective. In P. B. Baltes and K. W. Schaie (Eds.), *Life-span developmental psychology: Personality and socialization.* New York: Academic Press, 1973.

Kogan, N., and Pankove, E. Creative ability over a five year span. *Child Development*, 1972, *43*, 427–442.

Krienke, J. W. Cognitive differentiation and occupational-profile differentiation on the Strong Vocational Interest blank. Doctoral dissertation, University of Florida, 1969. Ann Arbor, Mich.: University Microfilms, no. 70-20, 599.

Kurlesky, W. P., and Thomas, K. A.   Social ambitions of Negro boys and girls from a metropolitan ghetto. *Journal of Vocational Behavior,* 1971, *1,* 177–187.

Lehman, E. B., and Goodnow, J.   Memory of rhythmic series: Age changes in accuracy and number coding. *Developmental Psychology,* 1972, *6,* 363.

Lessing, E. E.   Extension of personal future time perspective, age, and life satisfaction of children and adolescents. *Developmental Psychology,* 1972, *6,* 457–468.

Loehlin, J. C., Lindzey, G., and Spuhler, J. N.   *Race differences in intelligence.* San Francisco: W. H. Freeman, 1975.

Long, B. H., Ziller, R. C., and Henderson, E. H.   Developmental changes in the self-concept during adolescence. *School Review,* 1968, *76,* 210–230.

Looft, W. R.   Egocentrism and social interaction in adolescence. *Adolescence,* 1971, *6,* 485–494.

McCall, R. B., Appelbaum, M. I., and Hogarty, P. S.   Developmental changes in mental performance. *Monographs of the Society for Research in Child Development,* 1973, *38.*

Messick, S.   Personality consistencies in cognition and creativity. In S. Messick and associates (Eds.), *Individuality in Learning.* San Francisco: Jossey-Bass, 1976. Pp. 4–22.

Mishima, J., and Inone, K.   A study on the development of visual memory. *Experimental Psychology and Research,* 1966, *8,* 62–71.

Montemayor, R., and Eisen, M.   The development of self-perceptions from childhood to adolescence. *Developmental Psychology,* 1977, *13* (4), 314–319.

Mosher, F. A., and Hornsby, J. G.   On asking questions. In J. S. Bruner et al., *Studies in cognitive growth.* New York: Wiley, 1966.

Nauman, T. F.   A first report on a longitudinal study of gifted preschool children. *Gifted Child Quarterly,* 1974, *18,* 171–172.

Neimark, E. D.   Intellectual development during adolescence. In F. D. Horowitz (Ed.), *Review of child development research,* vol. 4. Chicago: University of Chicago Press, 1975a. Pp. 541–594.

Neimark, E. D.   Longitudinal development of formal operations thought. *Genetic Psychology Monographs,* 1975b, *91,* 171–225.

Neimark, E. D., and Lewis, N.   The development of logical problem-solving strategies. *Child Development,* 1967, *38,* 107–117.

Neimark, E. D., and Lewis, N.   Development of logical problem-solving: A one year retest. *Child Development,* 1968, *39,* 527–536.

Neimark, E. D., Slotnick, N. S., and Ulrich, T.   Development of memorization strategies. *Developmental Psychology,* 1971, *5,* 427–432.

Nevill, D. D.   Expected manipulation of dependency motivation and its effect on eye contact and measures of field dependency. Doctoral dissertation, University of Florida, 1971. Ann Arbor, Mich.: University Microfilms, no. 72-16, 639.

Nevil, D.   Young prodigies take off under special program. *Smithsonian,* 1977, *8,* 76–81.

Newcomb, T. M. *The acquaintance process.* New York: Holt, Rinehart and Winston, 1961.

Newman, B. Characteristics of interpersonal behavior among adolescent boys. *Journal of Youth and Adolescence,* 1975, *4,* 145–153.

Offer, D., Ostrov, E., and Howard, K. I. The self-image of adolescents: A study of four cultures. *Journal of Youth and Adolescence,* 1977, *6,* 265–280.

Okun, Morris A., and Sasfy, Joseph H. Adolescence, the self-concept, and formal operations. *Adolescence,* 1977, *12,* 373–381.

Phillips, J. L. *The origins of intellect: Piaget's theory* (2d ed.). San Francisco: W. H. Freeman, 1975.

Piaget, J. *The language and thought of the child.* New York: Harcourt, Brace, 1926.

Piaget, J. *The child's conception of number.* New York: Humanities Press, 1952.

Piaget, J. *The construction of reality in the child.* New York: Basic Books, 1954. (Original French edition, 1937.)

Piaget, J. *The psychology of intelligence.* Paterson, N.J.: Littlefield, Adams, 1963.

Piaget, J. *Six psychological studies.* New York: Random House, 1967.

Piaget, J. The intellectual development of the adolescent. In G. Caplan and S. Lebovici (Eds.), *Adolescence: Psychological perspectives.* New York: Basic Books, 1969. Pp. 22–26.

Piaget, J. Intellectual evolution from adolescence to adulthood. *Human Development,* 1972, *15,* 1–12.

Piaget, J., and Inhelder, B. La genèse de l'idée de hasard chez l'enfant. Paris: Presses Univer, 1951.

Piaget, J., and Inhelder, B. *The child's conception of space.* New York: Norton, 1967.

Piaget, J., and Inhelder, B. *The psychology of the child.* New York: Basic Books, 1969.

Resnick, L. B. The nature of intelligence. New York: Lawrence Erlbaum, 1976.

Richards, J. M., Jr., Holland, J. L., and Lutz, S. W. The assessment of student accomplishments in college. ACT Research Report, no. 11. Iowa City, Iowa: American College Testing Program, 1966.

Rogers, D. Vocational and career education: A critique and some new directions. *Teachers College Board,* 1973, 471–511.

Ross, B. M., and Levy, N. Patterned predictions of chance by children and adults. *Psychological Reports,* 1958, *4* (monograph supplement 1), 87–124.

Ruble, D. V., and Nakamura, C. Y. Task orientation versus social orientation in young children and their attention to relevant social cues. *Child Development,* 1972, *43,* 471–480.

Scarr-Salapatek, S. Genetics and the development of intelligence. In F. D. Horowitz (Ed.), *Review of child development research,* vol. 4. Chicago: University of Chicago Press, 1975. Pp. 1–57.

Schafer, W. E., and Olexa, C. *Tracking and opportunity: The locking-out process and beyond.* Scranton, Pa.: Chandler, 1971.

Seagoe, M. V. *Terman and the gifted,* Los Altos, Calif.: William Kaufmann, 1975.

Shafer, S. M.   Adolescent girls and future career mobility. In R. E. Grinder (Ed.), *Studies in adolescence* (3d ed.). New York: Macmillan, 1975. Pp. 114–125.

Shaycroft, M. F.   Cognitive growth during high school. *Project Talent,* bulletin no. 6, April 1967.

Siegler, R. S., Liebert, D. E., and Liebert, R. M.   Inhelder and Piaget's pendulum problem: Teaching preadolescents to act as scientists. *Developmental Psychology,* 1973, *9,* 97–101.

Siegler, R. S., and Liebert, R. M.   Acquisition of formal scientific reasoning by 10 and 13-year-olds: Designing a factorial experiment. *Developmental Psychology,* 1975, *11,* 401–402.

Sinha, V.   Age differences in self-disclosure. *Developmental Psychology,* 1972, *7,* 257–258.

Smothergill, D. W.   Accuracy and variability in the localization of spatial targets at three age levels. *Developmental Psychology,* 1973, *8,* 62–66.

Snow, R. E.   Aptitude-treatment interactions and individualized alternatives in higher education. In S. Messick and associates (Eds.), *Individuality in learning.* San Francisco: Jossey-Bass, 1976. Pp. 268–293.

Spearman, C.   General intelligence, objectively determined and measured. *American Journal of Psychology,* 1904, *15,* 201–293.

Spearman, C.   *The abilities of man.* New York: Macmillan, 1927.

Stanley, J. C., Keating, D. P., and Fox, L. H. (Eds.).   *Mathematical talent: Discovery, description, and development.* Baltimore: Johns Hopkins Press, 1974.

Stinchcombe, A.   *Rebellion in a high school.* Chicago: Quadrangle, 1964.

Tanner, D.   *Schools for youth: Change and challenge in secondary education.* New York: Macmillan, 1965.

Taylor, I. A.   An emerging view of creative actions. In I. A. Taylor and J. W. Getzels (Eds.), *Perspectives in creativity.* Chicago: Aldine, 1975. Pp. 297–325.

Terman, L. M.   Educating and training the gifted child. Unpublished manuscript, 1947. In M. V. Seagoe, *Terman and the gifted.* Los Altos, Calif.: William Kaufmann, 1975. Pp. 230–234.

Terman, L. M., and Merrill, M. A.   *Stanford-Binet intelligence scale: Manual for 3rd revision.* Boston: Houghton Mifflin, 1960.

Terman, L. M., and Oden, M. H.   *Genetic studies of genius,* vol. 4: *The gifted child grows up: Twenty five years follow-up of a superior group.* Stanford, Calif.: Stanford University Press, 1947.

Terman, L. M., and Oden, M. H.   *Genetic studies of genius,* vol. 5: *The gifted group at mid-life: Thirty five years follow-up of the superior child.* Stanford, Calif.: Stanford University Press, 1959.

Thomas, R. M., and Thomas, S. M.   *Individual differences in the classroom.* New York: David McKay, 1965.

Tome, H. R.   *Le moi et l'autre dans la conscience de l'adolescent.* Paris: Delachaux et Niestle, 1972.

Torrance, E. P.   *Guiding creative talent,* Englewood Cliffs, N.J.: Prentice-Hall, 1962.

Torrance, E. P.  *Rewarding creative behavior,* Englewood Cliffs, N.J.: Prentice-Hall, 1965.

Torrance, E. P.  Achieving socialization without sacrificing creativity. *Journal of Creative Behavior,* 1970, *4,* 183–189.

Torrance, E. P.  Creativity research in education: Still alive. In I. A. Taylor and J. W. Getzels (Eds.), *Perspectives in creativity.* Chicago: Aldine, 1975. Pp. 278–296.

Torrance, E. P., and Myers, R. E.  *Creative learning and teaching.* New York: Dodd, Mead, 1970.

U.S. Bureau of Labor Statistics.  Employment of school age youth: 1966, 1970. Special Labor Force Report, no. 87, 1967; Special Labor Force Report, no. 135, 1971.

Waber, D. P.  Sex differences in cognition: A function of maturation rate? *Science,* 1976, *192,* 572–573.

Walberg, H. J.  Varieties of adolescent creativity and the high school environment. *Exceptional Children,* 1971, 111–116.

Wallach, M. A.  Intelligence tests, academic achievement, and creativity. *Impact of Science on Society,* 1971a, *21,* 333–345.

Wallach, M. A.  *The intelligence/creativity distinction.* Morristown, N.J.: General Learning Press, 1971b.

Wallach, M. A.  Psychology of talent and graduate education. In S. Messick and associates (Eds.), *Individuality in learning.* San Francisco: Jossey-Bass, 1976. Pp. 178–210.

Wechsler, D.  Intelligence defined and undefined: A relativistic appraisal. *American Psychologist,* 1975, *30,* 135–139.

White, R. W.  Competence and the psychosexual stages of development. In M. R. Jones (Ed.), *Nebraska Symposium on Motivation.* Lincoln: University of Nebraska Press, 1960. Pp. 97–141.

Wing, C. W., Jr., and Wallach, M. A.  *College admissions and the psychology of talent.* New York: Holt, Rinehart and Winston, 1971.

Witkin, H. A.  Cognitive styles in learning and teaching. In S. Messick and associates (Eds.), *Individuality in learning.* San Francisco: Jossey-Bass, 1976. Pp. 38–72.

Witkin, H. A., Goodenough, D. R., and Karp, S. A.  Stability of cognitive style from childhood to young adulthood. *Journal of Personality and Social Psychology,* 1967, *7,* 291–300.

The photography of H. Armstrong Roberts

*Spontaneous group activity is part of the exploding social experience of early adolescence.*

**6**

# Social Development in Early Adolescence

It is all well and good to present a picture of the young adolescent as a planner, as a strategist, as one who deals in abstractions and hypothetical realities, but what about the rest? What about the friends that are made, the feelings of elation and self-doubt, the struggles with parents for a later curfew or beer at parties, the nostalgia about a past childhood, or the daydreams about a special girl or boy. Just as adolescents are experiencing expanded mental competences, they are also experiencing new and diverse social interactions. The focus of this chapter is on the range of social relationships that are likely to be encountered during early adolescence. We view these social encounters as essential contributors to emotional and intellectual growth. They pose challenges to every aspect of socialization that has taken place in the first ten years of life. During early adolescence, the person's ability to trust, to function independently and cooperatively, to handle competition, to defend moral principles, and to express deep feelings of commitment and love will all be tested.

The interpersonal relationships of early adolescence are a patchwork of contradiction and paradox. Young adolescents will insist on independence from the restrictions of parents, only to bind themselves intimately to a boyfriend or a girlfriend. They will reject peers who appear different from themselves and then wail about being accepted for who they are. They will boss younger brothers and sisters and then criticize teachers for being condescending. They will try desperately hard to be accepted into a group or club and then lose interest once they are.

The point is that in thinking about social development in early adolescence, we must remember that we are thinking about an unfinished product. This is not the end but only the beginning of the formation of a life pattern of social interactions. During these years, we are looking at peer group interaction in its formative phase. We are looking at heterosexual intimacy as it just begins to be expressed. We are focusing on the earliest, most tentative steps toward autonomy from parents, many years before a true camaraderie can even hope to be formed.

Wherever possible, we will try to draw links between the cognitive achievements that were described in Chapter 5 and the social development that is the focus of this chapter. The concept of egocentrism will be expanded to consider its implications for social relations. The self-concept will be elaborated here by considering the dimension of self-esteem, or self-worth, especially as it is reflected in the evaluations of others. Themes of peer conformity, peer group affiliations, and the experiences of adolescent parenthood must be understood in light of the cognitive skills that such choices reflect as well as the emotional commitments that are required. Nevertheless, the picture of social development does not reflect the image of the adolescent as one solely guided by reason. Of equal importance are the strong motives that demand satisfaction, the social roles that provide expectations, the social incentives for certain commitments over others, and, above all, the fact that young adolescents are comparative novices in the complicated array of social groupings and encounters that they experience.

## INTERPERSONAL BEHAVIOR

In order to appreciate the social development that takes place during early adolescence, it is necessary to begin by describing some of the characteristics of adolescent interpersonal behavior. The modes of interaction, the social style of the adolescent, and the settings or opportunities for interaction all contribute to a unique pattern of interpersonal behavior that unfolds during adolescence. Three developing competences underlie the person's interpersonal abilities at every life stage (Newman, 1976a). These are (1) the ability to establish feelings of intimacy, closeness, and involvement with others; (2) the ability to use language effectively; and (3) cognitive maturation. Several theories of adolescent development bear directly on one or more of these three components of interpersonal behavior.

The psychoanalytic tradition suggests that a resurgence of Oedipal or Electra fantasies accompanies the onset of puberty (Blos, 1968). Although the aggressive and sexual fantasies may have been anxiety provoking for the child at age five or six, they are even more intolerable to the entire family unit when the child reaches puberty. Adolescents tend to defend against their sexualized and dependent wishes by finding fault with their parents and by avoiding intimate contact with them. At the same time, adolescents find opposite-sex peers toward whom they direct the expression of their heightened sexual impulses. Changes in adolescents' relationship with parents often bring about periods of moodiness when adolescents are withdrawn, secretive, and sullen. One outcome of the distancing process that occurs between adolescents and their parents may well be a new quality of interpersonal behavior that is more guarded or censured than it had been. On the other hand, the heightened interest in heterosexual relationships ought to motivate adolescents to be more aware of their impact on others and more carefully tuned in to messages about their desirability than are younger children.

Cognitive theory, as expressed both in Piaget's notions of formal operations (Piaget and Inhelder, 1969) and in Kohlberg's stages of moral development (Kohlberg and Gilligan, 1971), has implications for changes in the adolescent's interpersonal behavior. New conceptual skills emerge in adolescence, including the ability to manipulate more than two groups of variables at one time; to think about future changes; to hypothesize about a logical sequence of events, even if these events have never happened; to detect logical inconsistencies; and to think in a relativistic way about the norms and values which govern one's behavior. The cognitive changes that take place during adolescence result, eventually, in a more flexible, critical, and abstract view of the self and of the social environment.

The conceptual gains described by cognitive theorists suggest that it should be easy for adolescents to separate their own point of view from the point of view of the other. They should be able to predict their impact on another person, and perhaps to manipulate that impact toward a specific end. They should be able to detect discrepancies in the verbal messages that others send. They may also begin to create an ideal for the kinds of interpersonal interactions that they wish to achieve.

These gains may, however, be temporarily overshadowed by a quality of egocentrism that Elkind (1967) describes as the adolescent's failure "to differentiate between what others are thinking about and his own mental preoccupations." Anxiety about personal inadequacies and desires for peer acceptance, coupled with a new-found fascination for the mental constructions that occupy the adolescent's thoughts, may prevent adolescents from being as socially effective as they might wish to be or as we might expect them to be, given their level of conceptual maturation. Consequently, we might expect to find a period in early adolescence when young people are particularly susceptible to feelings of alienation as they distance themselves from their parents and struggle through their own self-consciousness to attain a sense of closeness with their peers.

Finally, the social psychological orientation highlights changes in social roles and role relationships that facilitate new interpersonal skills and pose new interpersonal challenges. Sullivan (1949) stressed the shift from capacities for intimacy in same-sex peer relationships to the conflict between desires for lust and intimacy in early adolescence.

Thus, one of the ways of attempting to solve this collision between the intimacy need and lust is by something which is about the opposite of diffidence—namely, the development of a very bold approach in the pursuit of the genital objective. But the approach is so poorly addressed to the sensitivities and insecurities of the object that the object is in turn embarrassed and made diffident; and so it overreaches and has the effect of making the integration of real intimacy quite improbable. (Sullivan, 1953, p. 269)

Role theorists emphasize the diverse roles that adolescents play. As young adolescents become aware of the variety of expectations that exist for their behavior, the concept of a "performance" in Goffman's (1959) sense becomes more clearly articulated. Interpersonal behaviors can be planned to meet expectations, thereby strengthening one's legitimacy in a particular role.

All of these theoretical orientations suggest that there are reasons to expect adolescents to be more conscious of the impact that their interpersonal behavior has on others and to be more skillful at altering that impact than younger children. The theories also suggest that adolescent interpersonal behavior may be characterized by unique inadequacies or limitations, specifically withdrawal or suspiciousness in interactions with adult authorities, preoccupation with the self, and a tendency toward stilted performances in roles that do not yet feel authentic. The quality of adolescent interpersonal behavior may vary quite dramatically, depending on the degree of familiarity of the situation, the presence or absence of authority figures, and the level of anxiety that the situation arouses with respect to emotionally sensitive areas such as sexual intimacy, physical appearance, or family bonds.

## The Range of Interpersonal Interactions

Two studies using quite different methods provide a picture of the usual array of interpersonal encounters that adolescents experience. Newman (1971) surveyed a stratified random sample of 10th-, 11th-, and 12th-grade males and females in two large suburban high schools in the Midwest. The sample consisted of 248 females and 249 males. The students were asked to tell how many times they talked to a variety of people during the time that they were not in school. They reported that their most frequent out-of-school interactions had been with parents (13.35) and close friends (13.7). They had about the same number of interactions with these two groups of people. The next most frequent interactions were with siblings (10.2). Girlfriends, boyfriends, and other adults were each involved in about six daily interactions. Other relatives and clergy were encountered less frequently. Within the school setting, the principal, assistant principals, counselors, coaches, and all other school workers were each encountered an average of less than one time during a normal school day. The students reported about six daily interactions with teachers. The most frequent interactions were with other students. The average number of student-student interactions was 35.3, almost six times as great as the frequency of interactions with teachers.

Another very intriguing strategy for mapping the pattern of student activities was described by Czikszentmihalyi, Larson, and Prescott (1977). Twenty-five students were given electronic paging devices. During the hours from 8:00 A.M. to 11:00 P.M., the subjects were "beeped" on a random schedule five–seven times a day for one week. When signaled, the subjects had to fill out a questionnaire describing the activities they were involved in, why they were doing these things, and how they were feeling. Once again, talking with peers was the most frequent single activity recorded. Of 542 observations, 111, or about 20 percent, involved talking with peers. (In contrast, only 31 observations, or about 6 percent, involved interactions with adults. What is more, ten of the subjects never mentioned talking with adults in any observation.) Another frequently mentioned activity was watching TV. Close to 15 percent of the observations reported watching television as either a primary or secondary activity. Activities involving work or skill, including sports, reading, studying, or attending class, each accounted for about 5 percent of the total number of times that the subjects were signaled.

The subjects said that they felt happy, friendly, sociable, and free in talking with peers. On the other hand, they were likely to feel somewhat weaker and more passive in peer interactions than in sports or work. They described their interactions with adults as somewhat more exciting than their interactions with peers, but as more constrained, more passive, and weaker.

These two studies suggest that the adolescent's predominant social encounters occur with peers, both in and out of school. Interactions with adults are less frequent, and those adults are more likely to be parents than any other role group, including teachers. This pattern suggests that even though we expect adolescent participation in adult roles to be increasing, parents continue to be the predominant adult socialization agents in the young adolescent's life. For some adolescents, however, interactions with parents are infrequent and are perceived as constraining.

A third study of interpersonal behavior begins to take a glimpse at the quality of the interactions that characterize social encounters within the school setting (Newman, 1976b; Newman and Newman, 1974). Eighteen male high school juniors from two midwestern high schools were observed during two normal school days. The boys were accompanied by a male undergraduate who had been trained to code social interactions. Table 6–1 describes the characteristics of the interactions that were observed. It must be remembered that the observer's presence tied the observations to the public

**Table 6–1: Characteristics of Interaction in the Naturalistic Observation Study**

| | |
|---|---|
| *Mean Number of Interactions* | *93* |
| Interactions with adults | 21% |
| Interactions with students | 79 |
| Interactions with females | 23% |
| Interactions with males | 77 |
| Socioemotional content | 40% |
| Task content | 60 |
| Joking | 15% |
| Serious | 85 |
| Formal | 6% |
| Casual | 94 |
| Discouragement | 2% |
| Dramatization | 11 |
| Sarcasm/teasing | 15 |
| Negative affect | 3% |
| Neutral affect | 18 |
| Positive affect | 79 |

Source: B. M. Newman, "The Study of Interpersonal Behavior in Adolescence," *Adolescence*, 1976, *11*, p. 137.

domain of encounters. Nevertheless, the subjects appeared to be comfortable in continuing their normal range of daily interactions with minimal interruptions. If they had intended to skip class, to get high between classes, or to tease friends, the observer's presence did not seem to interfere. Only those subjects with girlfriends reported some feelings of embarrassment or intrusiveness at the observer's presence.

Once again, there were far fewer interactions with adults than with peers. Somewhat surprisingly, there were also few interactions with females. The total number of male-female interactions was accounted for largely by two or three boys who had girlfriends at school. Thus, even in a heterosexual school setting the social context of these boys tended to be primarily male.

Several themes in the content of the interactions are of interest. First, within the school setting, the boys' interactions seemed to be mostly task related, serious, and casual. Thus many interactions were about homework assignments, a game or sports practice, or how they did on a test or paper. Yet the boys also had a rather high frequency of socioemotional interactions in the serious and casual modes. They discussed things that they were excited about, hoping for, worried about, or pleased about.

The categories of discouragement, dramatization, and sarcasm/ teasing deserve some description. Discouragement refers to expressions of disappointment and depression. It was an infrequently used mode for these boys. As will be discussed in Chapter 8, depression is not a commonly observed overt mode in early adolescence. However, adolescents use other behavioral strategies to express their feelings of self-doubt or worthlessness. The two that were commonly seen here were dramatization and sarcasm or teasing. Dramatization refers to telling "tall tales," blowing things up, or describing situations in a way tht enhances one's own importance. Dramatization was a relatively common technique used by these boys to impress others. Sarcasm and teasing are the other side of the coin. Rather than inflate one's own image, this mode minimizes the importance or worth of the other person. The put-down is a favorite interpersonal strategy. Adolescent males tend to use this mode to keep some distance from their close friends as well as to demolish their rivals and to dominate those peers who are not "cool."

The most impressive form of the put-down is the competitive language game of *sounding,* or *playing the dozens* (Labov, 1972a). This is a ritualized exchange of insults that had its origin in black communities across the country. The traditional sounds were rhymed couplets. Others follow the form:

Your mother is like . . .

Your mother got . . .

Your mother so _____ , she _____ .

Your mother eat _____ .

Your mother raised you on _____ .

If I went to your house, _____ .

A sample of sounds from a group session with an adolescent group in south-central Harlem gives an idea of the range of images that contribute to ritual sounding.

Bell grandmother so-so-so ugly, her rag is showin'.

Bell mother was so small, she bust her lip on the curve.

Your mother so white, she hafta use Mighty White.

Your mother so skinny, she ice-skate on a razor blade.

. . . so skinny, she can reach under the doorknob.

. . . so low, she play Chinese handball on a curve.

. . . so low, got to look down to look up.

. . . so ugly, she got stinkin' with a glass of water.

. . . so black, she sweat chocolate.

. . . so black that she had to steal to get her clothes.

(Labov, 1972b, p. 133)

Sounds are ritual insults, not personal insults. They make use of exaggeration, rhymes, puns, or unexpected images and comparisons that usually deride a target that is very near to the person, usually one's father, one's mother, or oneself. Yet these insults are not taken as personal affronts, but as moves in a challenging verbal competition.

## Individual Differences

Within the overall pattern of interpersonal behavior that has been described thus far, important individual differences have been observed. Of the 25 adolescents who were asked to report what was happening while they were signaled at random times during the day, 10 were never talking to parents or other adults, 14 were never participating in sports, and 15 were never doing something that they described as work. The activities that provide stimulation, a feeling of sociability, or friendship are not experienced with equal frequency in each adolescent's life.

The observations of boys in the school setting disclosed three quite different patterns of interaction (Newman and Newman, 1974). One group of boys had very few interactions with anyone. One of these boys attended school infrequently and for very brief periods of time. After homeroom, this boy would often leave school and go home. In contrast, three boys were extremely high participators. They used a lot of sarcasm and teasing in their interactions and seemed almost unable to restrain themselves from engaging in verbal interactions. A third group was described as having many more interactions with peers than with adults. These boys seemed uncomfortable and restrained in their interactions with adults, but expressive and joking in their interactions with peers. These three interaction patterns all differ from the normative picture that is based on data taken from the group as a whole. The patterns suggest the use of different strategies for adapting to the school setting. Some boys used their interpersonal skills to form bonds of friendship, to defend against threat, or to exert dominance. Those who judged themselves to be interpersonally less competent may have withdrawn from certain kinds of interactions or they may have withdrawn from the school setting altogether. Peers can evaluate one another's interpersonal competences. If they think that they will be outdone in a verbal confrontation, they may not "play."

## THE RELATIONSHIPS BETWEEN EARLY ADOLESCENTS AND THEIR PARENTS

In the psychoanalytic view of adolescent development, early adolescence brings a gradual loosening of emotional ties with earlier love objects, especially parents (Blos, 1962; Freud, 1958). On the other hand, the cognitive and social psychological views emphasize the growing importance of adult roles and adult responsibilities in the life plans of early adolescents (Piaget, 1972; Kohlberg and Gilligan, 1972; Lewin, 1939; Brim, 1965). These different theoretical views of the process of adolescent development suggest different possible characteristics of adolescent-parent relationships. On the one hand, we might expect adolescents to become more secretive, more withdrawn, and more sensitive to parental dominance or intrusiveness. On the other hand, we might expect adolescents to desire information and guidance from adults about work roles and career choice, about loving and intimacy, and about the development of personal competences. Because of their experience, their resources, and their status in the community, adults hold the key to the opportunities to which adolescents aspire. Nevertheless, the push toward individuation makes adolescents cautious of being manipulated or exploited by adults. Particularly in the case of adolescents and their parents, the need to feel reassured about one's autonomy may make it difficult for adolescents to make use of the expertise that their parents have to offer. Thus, it might be expected that the ability to enjoy and profit from interactions with parents during adolescence is related to the sense of freedom or independence that exists within the parent-child relationship.

Three themes are treated in our discussion of adolescents and their parents. First, we are concerned with the dimension of independence and dependence. How are these two terms expressed in adolescent behavior? To what extent are adolescent-parent relationships characterized by conflict over dependence and independence? The second theme concerns the similarities and differences in attitudes and values that are held by young adolescents and their parents. How much of a "generation gap" exists between parents and children? Are some areas of values more likely to show similarity to parent values than others? The third theme concerns the impact of different family constellations on adolescent-parent relationships. How do patterns of authority, parent absence, or parental resources influence adolescent identification with, attitudes toward, and participation in the family group?

## Independence and Dependence

An analysis of independence and dependence in adolescent-parent relationships requires an appreciation of the context of the family group as children emerge into adolescence. Before puberty, parents have been growing accustomed to a gradual changing, increasingly competent child. Prepubertal children are capable of performing tasks that require increased strength, coordination, and planning. They can follow instructions, and they see difficult tasks—cleaning the attic or building a boxcar—through to the end. Then, at puberty, the previous picture of stability and competence changes. Young adolescents are experiencing rapid physical changes, expanding intellectual competences, and new challenges in peer relationships. They are physically larger and thus less readily intimidated by their parents' physical power. They are curious, excited, and perhaps somewhat embarrassed by the sexual impulses that accompany puberty. These new impulses lead to new conflicts in heterosexual interactions as well as some amount of competition or jealousy among same-sex peers. Discussions of "sex" with parents are often experienced as a source of tension and caution. Parents do not want to disclose their ignorance, and neither do adolescents. What is more, such discussions often contain some implication that the parent suspects the child of inappropriate experimentation. Parents may assume the role of the "grand inquisitor" in an effort to make sure that their child will be safe as well as careful. Questions about who will be at a particular party, how the child will get home, whether alcohol will be served, or whether adults will be present are all legitimate parental concerns that make adolescents feel small and unprepared. The answer "I don't know" seems weak. Yet more often than not, that is the truth. In order not to appear incompetent or "immature," adolescents may fabricate a story that will appease parents even though it is inaccurate. Here begins a voyage of estrangement, with the parents pushing and the adolescents backing and filling.

The fact is that in early adolescence young people are likely to have a temporary setback in independence and self-assurance. All of the physical, cognitive, and social changes of this phase open up new areas of uncertainty. Just as parents were beginning to anticipate a stable, predictable relationship, they are confronted with mood swings, withdrawal, secrecy, anger, and helplessness. Adolescents may be so preoccupied with their thoughts that they do not listen to instructions or give the kind of help that they gave in the past. They may daydream, talk on the phone, spend long periods in the bathroom, set out for long walks, or become devotedly religious. They may be more easily frustrated, disappointed, or hurt. What is more, they may feel resentful that parents do not understand them better. Egocentrism works to distort adolescents' perceptions of the preoccupations of others. Adolescents may feel that their problems are not only terribly serious, but that they should be of great concern to parents, siblings, and peers. It comes as quite a blow that mother and father have not even thought about what you are going to tell Joe when he calls or whether you should lend Betty the money she asked for.

One of the powerful experiences of early adolescence is the

realization that parents are imperfect. This realization begins with the recognition that they, like you, are sexual beings who experience lust. It includes a recognition that parental advice may not always be helpful or accurate. It also includes a powerful insight that parents do not understand you perfectly. In other words, the introspection and egocentrism of early adolescence heighten young persons' awareness of the dynamics of their inner life. These thoughts about love, about work, about sex, or about religion are rich, vivid, energized events. They have a brilliant existence within your own head, but seem to dwindle to shallow platitudes when they are communicated. Of course, parents cannot know this inner life intimately. Some parents try to tune in; others do not. Some parents seem impatient with adolescent speculations, whereas others are deeply moved by them. In some families, the child's explosive growth is a signal for celebration and delight. In other families, it is viewed as a threat to parental power and authority. The degree to which growth on all levels is met with enthusiasm or resentment will set the tone for the process of individuation, the evaluation of values, and the emergence of a personal identity in later adolescence.

In 1955 and 1956 a national sample of boys aged 14 through 16 and girls aged 11 through 17 were interviewed. Douvan and Adelson (1966) have summarized many of the central life themes that emerged from those interviews. Both the boys and the girls showed a pattern of increased independence during early adolescence. For the girls, independence was expressed by increased responsibility for jobs and for work around the house and by more time away from home with friends. At an emotional level, there was no dramatic change but a gradual expression of independence. They continued to express a tendency to be tied to their parents. As they grew older, however, they tended to be less likely to think of their mothers as their confidantes and they less frequently selected their mother as the person whom they most wanted to be like in adulthood.

The pattern of conflict between girls and their parents showed a progression of independence around three different themes. Early daughter-parent conflicts were about dress, makeup, and appearance. These conflicts were most frequent before the age of 14. From 14–16 the disagreements were about dating, friends, or driving the car. Conflicts about ideas, especially religion or politics, were low at the earlier ages and peaked in the later ages. In general, these conflicts took place within an atmosphere that the girls perceived as fair rather than extremely restrictive or arbitrary.

One of the projective questions the interviewers asked was the following: "Jane sometimes wishes her parents were different. What does she have in mind?" The most frequent response made reference to fewer restrictions or limitations. However, another answer suggested that some girls wished for a closer relationship with their parents. This kind of answer was given by 17 percent of the girls under 14 and by 32 percent of the girls who were 17–18. In other words, whatever gains in independence were being made were balanced by feelings of nostalgia for or regret about the absence of feelings of intimacy.

The picture of emerging independence is somewhat different for the boys than for the girls. The boys started to date and to earn money later than the girls. However, the boys spent less time at home with parents and shared fewer leisure activities with parents. They were less likely to see their fathers as their ideal for adulthood. Only 31 percent of the 14-year-olds and 18 percent of the 16-year-olds said that they wanted to be like their fathers when they were adults. The boys were more likely than the girls to resist a parental restriction or to tell a parent that they had disobeyed. In response to the question "Have you ever broken a rule?" 26 percent of the girls and only 10 percent of the boys answered no.

Douvan and Adelson drew the following conclusion about the importance of independence for males and females: "We know that independence is a more salient issue for boys—they more often speak of it in discussing their conscious concerns, ideals, hopes and aspirations. They are more actively 'on the move' toward independence during the adolescent period" (1966, p. 168).

The emergence of independence takes place within the context of the family organization. Different patterns of decision making, different patterns of discipline, and different patterns of resource allocation will all have an effect on the adolescent's opportunities to experience responsibility and to exercise autonomy.

Douvan and Adelson approached this issue of the family context for independence by looking at three different matters. First, autonomy could be inferred from the answers to the question "What are the most important things your parents expect of you?" Answers that reflected an expectation for independence or autonomy in the girls' sample increased from 8 percent at age 14 to 25 percent at ages 17–18. No similar data were available for boys. Parents who expected their daughters to function independently were viewed as more lenient, more likely to involve girls in making rules, and more likely to use psychological discipline than physical punishment or deprivation. Nonetheless, it is striking to learn that only 25 percent of the oldest female subjects saw autonomy as a clear parental expectation.

The second matter that highlighted the context for autonomy was the use of discipline. Three forms of discipline were described:

physical punishment, deprivation (grounding, no use of the car), and psychological punishments. Table 6–2 compares the frequency of these three kinds of punishment for males and females. The patterns are quite similar, although females were slightly more likely to experience physical punishment and slightly less likely to experience psychological punishment. The use of physical punishment techniques declined with age.

The kind of punishment that parents use has clear implications for the emergence of autonomy. The girls who experienced physical

Table 6–2: The Use of Punishment for Males and Females

|  | Types of Punishment | | |
|  | Physical | Deprivation | Psychological |
| Girls .............. | 261 (15%) | 1197 (67%) | 318 (18%) |
| Boys .............. | 79 (12%) | 420 (64%) | 161 (24%) |

Source: Adapted from Douvan and Adelson, 1966, pp. 399 and 400.

punishment appeared to be submissive, docile, and unlikely to resist parental ideas or to question parental restrictions. In projective stories they were more likely to deceive their parents, but in real life they were very compliant. The physically punished boys were submissive to parents as well as other authority figures. They were more likely to follow parental advice, to choose a family member as an ideal adult, and to insist on obedience to parents and other formal authorities. The boys, however, gave evidence that in fantasy they would rebel against physical punishment even though they did not in real situations. The consequences of physical punishment reached into the boys' social development. Boys who experienced physical punishment did not date much and had less self-confidence and fewer interests than other boys.

The picture that Douvan and Adelson provide of the consequences of physical punishment for adolescents is, however, incomplete. As will be discussed in Chapter 8, physical punishment may also provoke delinquent behavior or running away. The modeling of aggression in physical punishment contributes to adolescents' use of aggression in peer interactions. Especially for girls, extreme restrictiveness is associated with leaving home.

The third index of the family context for autonomy is the question "Do you have any part in making the rules at home?" Data on this question were only available for females. Participation in rule making increased from 45 percent of the girls under age 14 to 62 percent of the girls aged 17–18. Still, at ages 17–18, 34 percent of the girls had no part in rule making. The girls who participated in rule making saw their parents as encouraging autonomy. They experienced little physical punishment. They appeared to be able to resist adult authorities or to break rules when necessary. Their participation in rule making served to increase their internalization of moral standards and to enable them to regulate their impulses effectively.

The relationship between emerging independence and parental power has been assessed in other samples as well. Elder (1963) reported the results of a study of adolescents in grades 7–12 who were sampled from a population of 19,200 white subjects from unbroken homes in North Carolina and Ohio. Two parental variables were described: (1) the level of parental power and (2) the frequency of parental explanations. Three levels of parental power were described: autocratic, democratic, and permissive. In autocratic families, parents tell their children what to do. In democratic families, children are encouraged to make their own decisions, but parents "have the last word." In permissive families, there is a range from asking children to include parents' opinions when reaching a decision to expressing indifference about children's decisions. Democratic and permissive parents are quite a bit more likely than autocratic parents to use frequent explanations for their rules. Four aspects of adolescent independence were related to parental power and the frequency of parental interactions:

1.  The greater the amount of parental interaction, the more likely adolescents are to want to be like their parents.
2.  Parents who use frequent explanations have children who are more likely to comply with parental wishes in response to a conflict about a friend.
3.  The group of subjects who are most likely to feel self-confident and independent in decision making have permissive or democratic parents who provide frequent explanations.
4.  Dependence and lack of confidence are greatest in children from autocratic families with low amounts of interaction.

Across all levels of parental power, girls were more compliant than boys in going along with parental objections to a friend.

The adolescent's perception of parental power is associated with the desire to be like the parents as well as the internalization of parental values. Most adolescents see their parents as having equal power in family decisions (Bowerman and Bahr, 1973). This pattern seems to be most highly associated with high identification with both parents. Families in which the father or the mother is viewed as most powerful are associated with lower identification with *both* parents. Identification with fathers is significantly lowered when adolescents perceive their mothers to have primary power in the family. The interpretation is offered that uneven power in families generates tension and conflict that make both parents less desirable models for identification.

The pattern of family relationships and its contribution to independence is further illustrated by Kandel and Lesser's (1972; Lesser and Kandel, 1969b) analysis of families in the United States and Denmark. Several differences between Danish and American families have been documented. First, there are more democratic families in Denmark and more authoritarian families in the United States. American parents have more rules for their adolescent children than do Danish parents. Danish parents talk more with their children and give more frequent explanations than do American parents. Danish adolescents are less likely than American adolescents to turn to their mothers for advice, less close to their mothers, and less likely to see their mothers as models for adult life. They are more likely than American children to feel close to their fathers and to want to be like their fathers.

Observations about American and Danish adolescents suggest that Danish adolescents are more likely to internalize parental values in the absence of specific rules for behavior. In other words, Danish adolescents are more likely than American adolescents to spend two hours or more doing homework when there are no rules about how many hours they should spend. Danish adolescents are also more likely to feel independent and more comfortable exercising their own judgment in cases of conflict with parents. In both countries, a greater feeling of independence is associated with fewer rules. American dissatisfaction about freedom is accurately associated with greater parental restrictions.

The achievement of independence is clearly linked to the parents' ability to involve adolescents in decision making, to provide explanations for rules, and to emphasize independence of judgment rather than conformity with rules. We are faced with an intriguing paradox as we consider these studies. On the one hand, feelings of confidence, freedom, and autonomy are associated with democratic, egalitarian families. On the other hand, adolescents in such families are most apt to be fond of their parents, to want to be like them, and to consider their rules and judgments fair and reasonable. In other words, the same conditions that foster a sense of independence also build a bond of closeness and affection between parents and children. The image of adolescence as a period of angry conflict and dramatic differentiation is missing from these studies. Rather, identification, in which parental values are internalized, continues to preserve the adolescent-parent bond and yet to permit effective, reasoned decision making.

## Attitudes and Values

The "generation gap" has become a popular phrase which is used to explain feelings of adolescent-parent antagonism, alienation from school, disillusionment with political and economic systems, and a whole manner of intergenerational disgruntlements. Basic to the concept of the generation gap is an assumption that parents and children or adults and adolescents do not share a common value system. A number of questions must be raised in order to assess the relationship between the value orientations of adolescents and the value orientations of their parents. First, what are the values of adolescents and their parents? Second, do these values differ, and if so, how? Third, and this is least often assessed, are the differences among parents and children today any more extreme than the differences in past generations? In other words, is the discrepancy we document a result of our particular sociohistorical context or a result of the psychosocial stage of adolescent development? The studies that are presented in this section focus on the values and atittudes of younger adolescents in the junior high school and high school ages. The theme of attitude formation will be raised again in Chapter 10 in our discussion of social development in later adolescence. One might expect the articulation of a unique value position to emerge more clearly during this later phase, particularly as adolescents leave home and have more experience in making their own decisions about life choices.

In an important analysis of social class differences in parental values, Kohn (1959, 1963) has offered a description of the characteristics that parents consider especially important for their children. Table 6–3 details the proportion of middle-class and working-class mothers who have selected each of 17 characteristics as important for fifth-grade children. There is general agreement among both middle-class and working-class mothers about the importance of honesty, happiness, and consideration for others as highly desirable qualities.

Few mothers in either group picked acting serious, playing alone, or being liked by adults as very important characteristics. Differences between middle-class and working-class mothers emerge in relation to the clusters of variables that tend to go together, in the characteristics they consider desirable for male and female children, and in the importance they attach to some intermediate characteristics such as self-control, neatness, and curiosity. For middle-class mothers, honesty, consideration, manners, and dependability form a cluster. These qualities form a description of a "standard of conduct" that is viewed as desirable. For working-class mothers, honesty is associated with being happy, popular,

Table 6–3: Proportion of Mothers Who Select Each Characteristic as One of Three "Most Desirable" in a 10- or 11-Year-Old Child

| | For Boys | | For Girls | | Combined | |
|---|---|---|---|---|---|---|
| Characteristics | Middle Class | Working Class | Middle Class | Working Class | Middle Class | Working Class |
| 1. That he is honest ..................... | 0.44 | 0.57 | 0.44 | 0.48 | 0.44 | 0.53 |
| 2. That he is happy...................... | 0.44* | 0.27 | 0.48 | 0.45 | 0.46* | 0.36 |
| 3. That he is considerate of others ........ | 0.40 | 0.30 | 0.38* | 0.24 | 0.39* | 0.27 |
| 4. That he obeys his parents well ........ | 0.18* | 0.37 | 0.23 | 0.30 | 0.20* | 0.33 |
| 5. That he is dependable................. | 0.27 | 0.27 | 0.20 | 0.14 | 0.24 | 0.21 |
| 6. That he has good manners ............. | 0.16 | 0.17 | 0.23 | 0.32 | 0.19 | 0.24 |
| 7. That he has self-control .............. | 0.24 | 0.14 | 0.20 | 0.13 | 0.22* | 0.13 |
| 8. That he is popular with other children .. | 0.13 | 0.15 | 0.17 | 0.20 | 0.15 | 0.18 |
| 9. That he is a good student ............. | 0.17 | 0.23 | 0.13 | 0.11 | 0.15 | 0.17 |
| 10. That he is neat and clean ............. | 0.07 | 0.13 | 0.15* | 0.28 | 0.11* | 0.20 |
| 11. That he is curious about things ........ | 0.20* | 0.06 | 0.15 | 0.07 | 0.18* | 0.06 |
| 12. That he is ambitious .................. | 0.09 | 0.18 | 0.06 | 0.08 | 0.07 | 0.13 |
| 13. That he is able to defend himself ...... | 0.13 | 0.05 | 0.06 | 0.08 | 0.10 | 0.06 |
| 14. That he is affectionate ............... | 0.03 | 0.05 | 0.07 | 0.04 | 0.05 | 0.04 |
| 15. That he is liked by adults ............. | 0.03 | 0.05 | 0.07 | 0.04 | 0.05 | 0.04 |
| 16. That he is able to play by himself...... | 0.01 | 0.02 | 0.00 | 0.03 | 0.01 | 0.02 |
| 17. That he acts in a serious way.......... | 0.00 | 0.01 | 0.00 | 0.00 | 0.00 | 0.01 |
| N | 90 | 85 | 84 | 80 | 174 | 165 |

* The social class differences are statistically significant at the 0.05 level or better, using the chi-square test.
Source: M. L. Kohn, "Social Class and Parental Values," *American Journal of Sociology*, 1959, *64*, p. 340.

and able to defend oneself. Honesty, then, is not viewed by working-class mothers as a quality of social interaction but as an element of personal integrity that contributes to overall life satisfaction. Honesty and popularity are seen as convergent characteristics by working-class mothers but as in conflict by middle-class mothers. The former think of honesty as a quality that is valued and respected by peers, whereas the latter sense that honesty may be offensive to peers.

Surprisingly, studies that attempt to evaluate the existence of the generation gap do not tend to ask about such basic values. With both early and later adolescents, the focus tends to be on discrepancies about specific behaviors (your choice of clothing) or about contemporary issues ("Birth control devices and information should be made available to all who desire them"). It is not really possible to assess the convergence of the generations on values for honesty, obedience, or curiosity from such assessments of attitudes.

The available evidence suggests that early adolescents are in basic agreement with their parents on many social issues. LoSciuto and Karlin (1972) evaluated student-parent agreement among 2,362 high school students in the state of Pennsylvania. Table 6–4 shows

Table 6–4: "Do You and Your Parents Feel Exactly the Same, Much the Same, Somewhat the Same, or Not at All the Same About Each of the Following Subjects?"

| Social Issues | Exactly the Same | Much the Same | Somewhat the Same | Not at All the Same | No Answer |
|---|---|---|---|---|---|
| Religion | 16.2% | 38.6% | 30.4% | 11.6% | 0.7% |
| Your homework | 16.3 | 32.1 | 31.6 | 17.0 | 0.6 |
| Your choice of friends | 18.9 | 42.4 | 25.2 | 10.7 | 0.5 |
| How you spend your money | 13.9 | 35.8 | 31.5 | 16.0 | 0.4 |
| Your choice of clothing | 18.5 | 42.3 | 25.7 | 10.7 | 0.4 |
| The way you wear your hair | 18.8 | 33.1 | 25.2 | 20.1 | 0.4 |
| A college education | 47.4 | 23.6 | 15.5 | 10.6 | 0.4 |
| Living in your neighborhood | 46.9 | 30.6 | 13.5 | 6.0 | 0.5 |
| The war in Vietnam | 25.9 | 32.6 | 26.3 | 11.9 | 0.9 |
| Smoking cigarettes | 49.0 | 15.8 | 11.8 | 20.6 | 0.3 |
| Smoking marijuana | 69.2 | 7.9 | 5.2 | 14.8 | 0.4 |
| Drinking alcohol | 49.9 | 17.4 | 31.1 | 16.8 | 0.3 |
| Driving cars | 34.2 | 36.4 | 18.3 | 8.3 | 0.3 |
| Sex before marriage | 41.3 | 18.9 | 17.8 | 18.7 | 0.8 |
| Discipline | 22.0 | 35.5 | 26.9 | 12.8 | 0.4 |

The totals across the table are not equal to 100 percent, since some of the respondents (2.4 percent) were not living with their parents.

Source: L. A. LoSciuto and R. M. Karlin, "Correlates of the Generation Gap," *Journal of Psychology,* 1972, *81,* p. 255.

that in only three categories—homework, how money is spent, and hairstyle—were the total disagreements greater than the total agreements. Two family variables were associated with the amount of discrepancy that adolescents saw between their views and the views of their parents: (1) adolescents who were more likely to share experiences with their parents were also more likely to share their parents' values; and (2) adolescents who were more likely to share their personal problems with their parents were also more likely to agree with their parents' attitudes. When adolescents said that they got their best advice about personal problems from a friend or from no one at all, they were more likely to express attitudes that were discrepant from the attitudes of their family.

Another analysis of adolescent-parent values focused on educational goals (Lesser and Kandel, 1969b). A comparison of educational plans from adolescents, their mothers, and their best friends suggested that mothers had a major role in influencing the aspirations of their adolescent children. The agreement between mothers and children was higher for daughter-mother pairs than for son-mother pairs. The most obvious way in which mothers influenced the child's choice was by having interactions in which she actually recommended or discouraged college attendance. Of the adolescents whose mothers strongly encouraged attending college, 85 percent planned to attend. Only 14 percent of the adolescents whose mothers discouraged college attendance planned to attend. The best friend's college aspirations were positively associated with the subject's own plans, but the association was not as strong as it was with the aspirations of the subject's mother. Best friends who had the strongest, most clearly positive, and mutual friendships had the most similar aspirations. Yet these best friends did not appear to have as much similarity in their views as did mother-child pairs.

There is a strong sense that during early adolescence young people continue to share many of their parents' attitudes and values. This does not mean that they always agree with their parents, that they do not resist some parental advice, or that they do not disobey parental rules when necessary (Douvan and Adelson, 1966). In fact, we would argue that the ability to question parental restrictions and to evaluate parental opinions is associated with a healthy independence and a growing personal value system. We do not want adolescents to emerge from this phase of life totally submissive to adult demands or totally convinced of parental attitudes. This is a time when the adolescent's ability to evaluate, to see logical implications, and to hypothesize about the future should permit the formulation of some new value positions that are more appropriately suited to his or her historical period than are the attitudes of previous generations. On the other hand, it would be surprising if there were to be dramatic gaps in the value systems of parents and children. After all, adolescents are just emerging from the intense socialization experiences of early and middle childhood. It is more than likely that during these earlier years children have internalized the interpersonal and social values of their family group. Lacking the benefit of an abstract analysis of values or a long-range perspective on changing social conditions, young children are likely to believe that what their parents say is good is good and that what they say is bad is bad. It may take a long time, maybe even a lifetime, to disentangle the value orientations that one learned as a child from the more carefully reasoned value system that one adopts throughout adolescence and young adulthood. To the extent that some essential moral values are embedded in the unconscious material that is repressed at the end of the phallic stage of development, there will always be an essential continuity between the values of childhood and the values of adulthood.

## The Family Constellation and Adolescent Development

A number of questions have been raised about the impact of particular aspects of the family constellation on adolescent development. How do such factors as family size, family income, parent absence, and maternal employment contribute to the socialization experiences of adolescents? In this section we will briefly examine some of the findings on the impact of these diverse ecological characteristics of the family group. It is important to point out, however, that we would expect few direct, causal relationships to exist between family structure and psychological growth during adolescence. At this phase of life, adolescents are able to supplement their life experiences by finding relationships with peers and adults outside the home. They are able to conceptualize and reinterpret their life experiences so that the negative impact of some childhood experiences may be diluted by a new perspective. Finally, adolescents are more aware than young children of the diversity of life patterns that exists in our society. This awareness raises the possibility of choice and change so that the young person need not feel trapped by the circumstances of the past.

**Family Size.**  The impact of family size is most clearly documented in two areas: parental control and children's intellectual achievement. Parents of large families (four or more) are more authoritarian, more likely to use physical punishment, and less likely to explain their rules than are parents of smaller families (Elder and Bowerman, 1963; Clausen, 1966). Particularly in middle-class families, adolescents perceive greater parental control when they come from larger families (Peterson and Kunz, 1975).

Studies of intelligence find that children from small families score higher than children from larger families. A similar pattern of decreasing scores with increasing family size has been found in samples of British, American, and Dutch families (Douglas, 1964; Scott and Seifert, 1975; Belmont and Marolla, 1973). The issue of child spacing has also been introduced to explain this decline (Zajonc, 1976). When children are born in close succession, parental resources are continuously taxed, there may be increased use of authoritarian methods of control, and there are fewer opportunities to develop the verbal and conceptual skills of each child.

**Family Income.**  The impact of family income has far-reaching implications for the life pattern of young adolescents. Some children from low-income families are too poor to continue attending school (Children's Defense Fund, 1974). They may not be able to afford the books, the transportation fees, or the activity fees that school participation requires.

Health care and nutrition are likely to be severely neglected among poor adolescents. Children from poor families are also more likely to try to obtain employment and more likely to fail in their search for work (Havighurst and Gottlieb, 1975). In 1973, the unemployment rate for adolescents in the 16–19-year-old range was 13.5

percent. That was 3.2 times as great as the total unemployment rate. What is more, these figures do not include many younger adolescents aged 10–15 who are searching for work.

In general, adolescents from very poor families are more likely to have an early transition into adult roles, including work, marriage, childbearing, and living away from home. The fewer resources parents have, the more children are forced to seek their own means of survival.

Rosenberg (1975) has emphasized the particular consequences of the dissonant context on self-esteem. He compared groups of children and adolescents from upper-, middle-, working-, and lower-class families who were attending either upper- or lower-class schools. There were more children with low self-esteem scores in the upper- and middle-class group who attended lower-class schools and in the lower-class group who attended upper-class schools than in any of the other subgroups. In other words, Rosenberg suggests that it is less painful to have few resources if those around you also have few. However, in a context that confronts you daily with the visible abundance of your peers, the implication of your own lack of worth becomes much more powerful. It is interesting that the children with more resources experienced a comparable reduction of self-esteem in the context of a predominantly poor school environment. It is possible that these children and adolescents did not share in the peer culture of the school, that they were rejected because of their differences, or that they felt guilty for having more resources than their peers.

**Parent Absence.**   There can be no question that parent absence puts a tremendous strain on the family group. In 1975, 15.5 percent of American children under 18 were living with their mothers only and 1.5 percent were living with their fathers (U.S. Department of Commerce, 1975). Although the vast majority of children live in two-parent families, the rate of single-parent families is increasing rapidly. There are almost twice as many children in one-parent families now as there were in 1950 (Advisory Committee on Child Development, 1976). Among the sources of strain on these families are the following: (1) the family is likely to be living on minimal income; (2) the parent may feel isolated; (3) the dual role of caregiver and provider creates role strain; and (4) because of inadequate child care facilities, the single parent will be forced to leave young children unattended, to place them in the care of older siblings, or to remain at home, unable to work or to learn new skills (Schlesinger, 1977; George and Wilding, 1972).

Interestingly, the impact of parent absence on adolescent development is not as severe as one might expect. In a large sample of two-child families, there were no differences in the quality of the relationship with the mother or in self-concept in father-present and father-absent families (Feldman and Feldman, 1976). There was a small but significant difference in grade point average in father-present families. In general, the Feldmans argue that even in father-present families, fathers are viewed as far less salient, less involved in interactions, and therefore less a force in the socialization process than mothers. When children with high- and low-interacting fathers were compared, the children who had frequent interactions with their fathers had more positive attitudes toward school, their peers, and their siblings and were more favorable about their relationship with their parents.

The following perceptions of fathers by adolescent girls provide some sense of why an absent father may not be too much different than a father who is home.

"I'm not that close to him. I just know him as the father, and that's it." (16, Chicana, urban).

"I get along, but, I mean, we're really not that close. Like he's got his business and I've got my schoolwork. He just doesn't seem interested in what I do." (17, American Indian, small town).

"It don't seem like, he really don't understand, about my feelings. So I hardly talk to him." (15, white, small town) (Konopka, 1976, p. 69)

There is some suggestion that parent absence can influence socioemotional development. For example, Hetherington (1972) described adolescent girls whose fathers were absent as less comfortable and less skilled in interactions with males than were adolescent girls whose fathers were present. In her comparison, Hetherington differentiated the daughters of divorced mothers from the daughters of widowed mothers. The daughters of divorced mothers tended to be more eager to have interactions with males. They were more involved with boys, spent more time in the presence of boys, smiled and spoke more openly to a male interviewer, and reported earlier and more frequent dating and sexual activity than did girls whose fathers were present. In contrast, the daughters of widows were shier and more reserved around boys and less likely to talk or smile during an interview with a male. Both groups of father-absent girls expressed anxiety about their relationship with males and had fewer contacts with males than did other girls. The daughters of widowed mothers tended to idealize their fathers, whereas the daughters of divorced mothers tended to be critical and to recall conflict with their fathers. These observations suggest that father absence may have significant implications for heterosexual relations, an area of development that is articulated rather early. This influence may be as much related to the mother's feelings and communications about the absent father as to the father's absence itself.

A final point about parent absence is to recognize that contextual dissonance has a bearing on its impact. Approximately one child in seven is growing up today in a one-parent family (U.S. Department of Commerce, 1976). If children from one-parent families grow up in a community in which most of their peers live in intact, two-parent groups, the feelings of uncertainty, discomfort, and doubt are likely to be much greater than they will be if parent absence is a comparatively frequent occurrence.

**Maternal Employment.** In the past, there has been some concern that maternal employment might result in a form of neglect of caregiving that would have negative consequences for both the intellectual and the socioemotional development of children (Nye and Hoffman, 1963; Stolz, 1960; Wallston, 1973). In recent studies, the impact of a mother's employment has been shown to have mixed effects, depending on the mother's satisfaction with her work, the total picture of family resources, and the implications that the mother's achievement has for the image of the father in the family group (Hoffman, 1974). In general, the positive effects of maternal employment appear to include the greater independence of working mothers' daughters, a higher value placed on female achievement, and a less stereotyped view of the female sex role. The daughters of working mothers tend to have higher career aspirations, but no consistent pattern of achievement or IQ measures differentiates the children of working mothers from the children of nonworking mothers.

One of the primary questions about maternal employment is its effect on supervision of the children. Although it has been suggested that working mothers provide less adequate supervision than nonworking mothers, this has not been shown to be true (McCord, McCord, and Thurber, 1963; Hoffman, 1974). What is more, there is no direct link between lack of supervision and delinquent behavior or between maternal employment and delinquent behavior (Woods, 1972). In fact, the stability of full-time employment may give children a sense of predictability. When mothers work they are likely to give more responsibility as well as more independence to their children. The children of working mothers frequently have important household tasks to perform, which can give them a feeling of contributing to the overall survival of the family group.

Of course, all of these strategies for redefining the contributions of family members to the family's functioning can be abused. Mothers can communicate neglect by being too tired or too preoccupied to interact with their children. Children can have long, unsupervised periods before and after school. Parents can burden children with difficult and time-consuming household chores that severely limit the children's time for peer interaction or study. However, it would appear that none of these abuses are more likely to occur in families with working mothers than in families with nonemployed mothers.

## PEER RELATIONS

During early adolescence, the peer group tends to become a more structured and organized entity than it was previously. The individual's relationship to the peer group has more clearly defined implications than has been the case. Although friends are important to the preadolescent, it is less important to the preadolescent to be a member of a definable group. His or her friends are often found in the neighborhood, local clubs, community centers, or classrooms. Friendship groups are homogeneous. They are the product of informal associations, residential area, and convenience.

During early adolescence, this process begins to change somewhat. The adolescent enters the more heterogeneous environment of the high school. There is a reordering of students according to a variety of kinds of abilities at this point, and a corresponding reordering of friendships also occurs. When the "leading crowd" of a particular neighborhood elementary school goes off to a more centralized high school, its members find that they are, to some degree, in competition with the "leading crowds" of the other neighborhood schools from which the high school draws its students. After some contact at the high school, there is a reordering of the several "leading crowds" into a single "leading crowd." Some students find that their social positions have been maintained or enhanced, while others find that their social positions have deteriorated somewhat as a result of a reevaluation of their abilities, skills, or traits.

Popularity and acceptance into a peer group at the high school level may be based on one or more of the following characteristics: good looks, athletic ability, social class, academic performance, future goals, religious affiliation, ethnic group membership, and special talents. Although the criteria for membership may not be publicly articulated, the groups tend to include or exclude members according to consistent standards. Some of the well-known peer groups present in American high schools today are affectionately known as frats or preppies, greasers or hoods, freaks or hippies, and athletes or "jocks" (P. Newman, 1971).

In the following sections, we will consider the structure of adolescent peer groups, the patterns of peer pressure and conformity within adolescent peer groups, and the extent to which adolescent peer relations influence the development of values. Dating, sexual behavior, and adolescent parenthood are discussed as special characteristics of social development during early adolescence. At the end of the chapter, the processes of socioemotional growth and group identification that take place during early adolescence are tied to the life-style patterns that emerge during later adolescence and young adulthood.

## The Peer Group Structure

The characteristics of the adolescent peer group structure have been described in some detail by Dexter Dunphy (1963). He based his analysis on naturalistic observation of peer interactions in Sydney, Australia, in the period 1958–60. His observations "on streetcorners, in milkbars and homes, at parties and on Sydney beaches" were complemented by questionnaires, diaries, and interviews that provided a conceptual map of the evolving peer group structure. Two areas of group structure emerge from his work: group boundaries and group roles. The group boundaries outlined two types of groups: cliques and crowds. The cliques were small, with an average of six members in each. The crowds were associations of two–four cliques. The feeling of intimacy and closeness extends to the clique, but the crowd is needed for larger social events, especially parties and dances. Dunphy observed that clique membership seemed to be a prerequisite for crowd membership. Not every clique was included in a crowd, but no one claimed to be a member of a crowd and not a member of a clique.

The formation of the crowd appeared to take a developmental trend. Adolescents began their group experience in same-sex cliques. The next stage was the interaction of a girl's clique and a boy's clique in some kind of group activity, such as a bike trip or a volleyball game. The third stage involved individual meetings between leaders of the two cliques and the beginning of dating. After these early heterosexual interactions, the cliques themselves began to be heterosexual and to join with other cliques to form a heterosexual crowd. At this stage most peer contacts, including friendships, dates, and larger group activities, were confined to other members of the crowd. In the last stage, the crowd began to disintegrate as couples who were going steady began to limit their heterosexual experimentation and had less need for an elaborate peer group context.

Dunphy described two central group roles as those of the leader and the sociocenter. There were two kinds of leaders, the clique leader and the crowd leader. Cliques were often described by referring to the leader's name. Clique leaders were notable for participating in more advanced heterosexual activities, for being in touch with other cliques, and for serving as advisers or counselors in matters of dating and love.

The sociocenter is the crowd joker. That person is usually popular and outgoing. The task of the sociocenter is to maintain good feelings within the group and to provide the group with a playful affiliative atmosphere. The more dominant and assertive the goup leader is, the more clearly articulated is the role of the sociocenter.

Studies of American peer groups suggest that the pluralistic nature of American society is reflected in a diversity of adolescent crowds or groups. Petroni (1971) states that high school students in a desegregated Topeka, Kansas, high school reported the following 12 types of students: "middle-class whites, hippies, peaceniks, white trash, 'sedits' (upper-class blacks), elites, conservatives, racists, niggers, militants, athletes and hoods."

Poveda (1975) asked the seniors in a working-class community near San Francisco to rate the student types for girls in their school. The students described two social types, the "high society" girls and the "party" girls. The high society group were significantly more involved in school activities. The party girls viewed school as constraining, and were more involved with social life, adventure, and autonomy from parental control. In between these two groups, there were the "average" girls, who were less visible and less active in school activities. These girls said that they could be friends with anyone, but in fact they were not likely to be included in the social activities of the other types. Finally, there were the social outcasts, or "duds," of the female peer structure. The "duds," who included about 12 percent of the senior girls, either looked and dressed differently ("dorks"), did not like to party, or tended to be very critical of others ("weirdos"). Another type of outcast was the "tramp," who had a bad reputation and did not seem to care what others thought of her.

As in Dunphy's description, these peer groups have boundaries. Some students try to push their way into a certain high-status group, whereas others may fall out of a crowd. Dating someone of a higher status or getting involved in a high-status school activity (athletics or cheerleading) may be ways of moving into a new peer group. When the school population is relatively stable, however, it is very difficult to lose the group identity that has already been established (Jones, 1976). What is more likely is that through gossip, through refusal to adhere to group norms, or through failure in heterosexual relationships individuals can slip outside the boundaries of their clique and therefore lose access to the larger social crowd.

## Peer Pressure and Conformity

The process of affiliating with a peer group involves opening oneself up to the pressure and social influence of that group. Adolescents are at a point in their intellectual development at which they are able to conceptualize themselves as objects of expectations. These expectations may be perceived by adolescents as a force drawing them to be more than they think they are, that is, to be braver, more outgoing, more confident, and so forth. In these cases, peer pressure has a positive effect on the adolescent's self-image and serves as a motive for group identification.

As members of a peer group, adolescents have more influence than they would as single individuals. They begin to understand the value of collective enterprise. In offering membership, the peer group enhances adolescents' feelings of self-worth and protects them from loneliness. When conflicts develop in the family, the adolescent can seek comfort and intimacy among peers. In order to benefit in these ways from the peer group affiliation, adolescents must be willing to suppress some of their individuality and to find pleasure in focusing on those attributes that they share with peers. We would not suggest that total conformity is demanded within the peer group. In fact, most peer groups depend on the unique characteristics of their members to lend definition and vigor to the roles that emerge within the group. However, we do suggest

*Luis Medina*

*Peer group membership can enhance the adolescent's self-image.*

that the peer group places considerable importance on some maxi-
mally adaptive level of conformity in order to bolster the structure
of the group and to strengthen its effectiveness in satisfying members' needs. In fact, most adolescents find some security in peer
group demands to conform. The few well-defined characteristics
of the group lend stability and substance to the adolescent's self-
concept. In complying with group pressure, each adolescent has
an opportunity to state, unambiguously, that he or she is someone
and that he or she belongs somewhere.

Several studies have tried to provide evidence about the strength
of the tendency to conform to peer pressure during early adolescence. Costanzo (1970) asked male subjects in four age groups—
7–8, 12–13, 16–17, and 19–21—to make judgments of the length of
a line and to give their answers by lighting a button on a response
panel. Each subject saw his own answer as well as what he thought
were the answers of three other subjects. Figure 6–1 shows the
percentage of subjects in each age group who made errors in the
direction of the peer judgments. The pattern of peer conformity
appears to peak at the 12–13-year age range and to decrease slowly
during the high school years. Other comparisons of early and later
adolescents confirm the tendency for early adolescence to be a

**Figure 6–1: Percentage of Conformity as a Function of Age
Level ($n = 36$ per age level)**

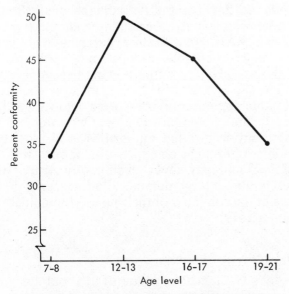

Source: P. R. Costanzo, "Conformity Development as a Function of Self-Blame," *Journal of Personality and Social Psychology,*
1970, *14,* p. 372. Copyright (1970) by the American Psychological
Association. Reprinted by permission.

peak period for peer conformity, especially when conformity is measured by the readiness to change one's judgment in the direction of peers' perceptions, even when those perceptions are in error (Brownston and Willis, 1971).

A somewhat disturbing fact is that pressures toward peer conformity appear to increase young adolescents' willingness to be involved in pranks or behavior of which adults would disapprove. Children at three grade levels (grades three, six, and eight) were asked whether they would go along with peers in certain hypothetical situations involving misbehavior. At each higher grade level, children saw the pranks as less serious and said that they would be more likely to get involved with their peers in the misbehavior (Bixenstine, DeCorte, and Bixenstine, 1976). Bronfenbrenner (1966; Rodgers, Bronfenbrenner, and Devereux, 1968) compared the willingness of American and Russian children to engage in misbehavior, including cheating on a test or denying responsibility for damage that one had done. The Russian children were equally unlikely to engage in such behavior if parents, peers, or school adults might learn of the act. The American children were *more likely* to participate in misbehavior if they thought that their peers might find out about it. In general, Soviet children are trained to use peer pressure and social criticism to enforce moral behavior. Soviet peers come through a consistent program of moral education in which they learn to correct one another, to help one another to succeed, and to feel shamed if they are the object of peer disapproval (Bronfenbrenner, 1970). In American society, there is no such clear picture of one correct way to behave. What is more, peers have not generally been taught to feel responsible for one another. More than likely, they have experienced peer competition in the school setting. Children come to learn that adults in the school are responsible for monitoring and punishing misconduct. Norms against "tattling" become very strong in the elementary grades. One way to begin to demonstrate autonomy from adult authorities is to participate in behavior of which adults might disapprove. Although this misconduct may be minimal and may never result in any form of discipline or police intervention, a large number of adolescents do perform delinquent acts in the company of their peers (Reynolds, 1976; Schimel, 1974; Weiner, 1970).

## The Impact of the Peer Group on Values

Two rather different questions have been raised about the impact of the peer group on values. First, do peer group values influence individual behavior? Second, do peer group values dominate or conflict with parental values?

Coleman (1961) has addressed the first question in his description of a system of cliques within the American high school. The cliques generate a value profile for the school that determines the status or importance of individual students. In most schools, the hierarchy of the peer group structure is determined by success in the primary areas that are valued by the cliques. These tend to include athletic skills, student activities, and social leadership, but not academic excellence. Thus, peer group values determine the acceptance of students, the boundaries around clique groupings, and the kinds of behaviors that are likely to be approved, rejected, or ignored among clique members.

The impact of friendship groups can be seen in the kinds of behaviors that friends engage in together and in their orientation toward school. Kandel (1978) found that high school friends tend to be in the same grade in school and of the same sex and race. Of all the many activities and attitudes that friends were asked about, the highest degrees of similarity were in drug use, educational expectations, and involvement with peer activities. In general, friends, even friends who had liked each other for more than three years, did not hold similar attitudes about such things as politics, materialism, career aspirations, closeness with parents, or evaluation of teachers. This picture of peer friendships suggests that peer groups tend to be structured around several rather obvious characteristics—age, race, and sex—and that they are probably fostered by frequent interactions or physical proximity within the school. Similarities in behavior may eventually produce similarity in attitudes, but attitudes do not tend to be the force that binds most adolescent peers together.

The second question about the impact of peer groups on values focuses on the extent to which parents' values and peers' values are in harmony or conflict, and if in conflict, on whether peers have more influence over adolescents than their parents. One approach to this question has been to survey the attitudes of adolescents and their parents on a range of issues, including sex, drugs, religion, war, law and law enforcement, racism, and politics. In surveys of this kind, attitudes of the two groups tend to be similar in most areas (Lerner and Weinstock, 1972; Weinstock and Lerner, 1972).

Another approach has been to pose hypothetical situations in which parents and peers offer opposing views of how to behave. The subjects are then asked whether they would follow the advice of parents or peers. Early studies of this type suggested that adolescents turned to peers when the situation involved a current question about popularity or membership in a club but that they turned to parents in deciding about future plans or moral decisions with consequences for the future (Brittain, 1963, 1967–68, 1969).

Later studies modified the method somewhat and came out with a rather different picture. In these studies (Larson, 1972a, 1972b), the subject was asked to tell what he or she would do in a given situation. The situation was described in two different ways, once so that the parents urged against some behavior that friends supported, and again so that friends urged against the behavior and the parents supported it. The majority of subjects (73.6 percent) were neither parent oriented nor peer oriented. They made their decision about the situation and did not modify it, regardless of who approved or disapproved. The next largest group (15.7 percent) were parent compliant. They went along with their parents' decisions in at least four of the six situations. In general, the group of adolescents tested in this situation were strongly parent oriented. In other words, they felt that their parents understood them, supported them, and generally had good advice. Nonetheless, when the decision about how to behave in a particular situation had to be made, the adolescents made their judgments independent of their parents' wishes.

A third approach to the question of the respective impact of parents and peers on the values of adolescents is to simply ask adolescents directly how highly they regard parental advice. Curtis (1975) described the responses of over 18,000 adolescents in grades 7–12 to questions about the degree to which they valued father's, mother's, and friends' opinions. At every age, parents were more valued sources of advice and opinions than friends. However, the number of students who gave a high rating to parents declined rather steadily from seventh through tenth grade. At grade 11, the middle-class and working-class boys seemed to show an increased valuation of fathers. The value of friends' opinions and advice remained much more stable across ages. About 28 percent of boys and 50 percent of girls placed high value on their friends' opinions at every age. Although friends do not become more important, parents become somewhat less important, suggesting a gradual process of individuation and a strengthing of the individual's own value system.

An interesting comparison is provided in a survey of friendship relations among Soviet students aged 14 to 17 (Kon and Losenkov, 1978). The students felt that their friends understood them better than either their mother or father. They also felt more comfortable sharing confidential problems with their friends rather than with their parents. On the other hand, in response to the question "With whom would you consult in a complicated life situation?" boys and girls both chose their mothers.

We see a picture of adolescent friendship as providing companionship in activities, emotional support, and understanding. However, adolescents appear to realize that on some matters parental opinions are likely to be sounder, perhaps more protective of their well-being, and more likely to result in a positive outcome than the opinion of peers. In addition, personal judgment is emerging to provide a more autonomous basis for value decisions. Individual adolescents become increasingly capable of evaluating situations and making their own choices without guidance from parents or peers.

## DATING AND SEXUAL BEHAVIOR

Dating is a delightful, troublesome, intense, compelling, mysterious experience that serves a variety of functions for the early adolescent. Winch (1971) offers seven functions of dating that provide

The photography of H. Armstrong Roberts

*The "prom" is a highlight of the dating season.*

a general conceptual framework for our understanding of the contribution of this experience to socioemotional development.

1.   Dating is a form of recreation.
2.   Dating is a means of achieving status.
3.   Dating provides opportunities to learn about the opposite sex.
4.   Dating provides opportunities to learn about one's own personality and needs.
5.   In a comparison of experiences, dating allows one to evaluate which relationships are satisfying and which are not. This leads to a better understanding of one's criteria for mate selection.
6.   In a dating relationship, values about marriage, child rearing, sexuality, and life-style can be clarified before a marriage partner is chosen.

To Winch's list, we would add that dating provides a context for experimentation with heterosexual behavior. For most adolescents, dating provides opportunities for physical intimacy with a member of the opposite sex on a continuum from holding hands to sexual intercourse. Within these relationships, young people learn how to handle their feelings of vulnerability and fear about physical contact, how to cope with difficulties that arise about sexual demands, and how to provide and receive physical pleasure without alarming each other (Estep, Burt, and Milligan, 1977).

Given this background of important functions of the dating relationship, what do we know about the dating behavior of young adolescents? Three themes are discussed in the following section: (1) learning to date; (2) who is a desirable date; and (3) emotional and sexual intimacy in dating.

## Learning to Date

Jackson (1975) asked 11- and 12-year-olds who were not yet dating two questions: (1) What does the word *dating* mean to you? (2) When you go out on a date, where do you usually go? Table 6–5 shows the categories of answers given by males and females to the question about what dating meant to them. Clearly, most of the children knew what dating was in the abstract sense, although 18 percent of the boys and 5 percent of the girls thought that the whole idea was rather stupid. When the children were asked what one does on a date, however, the concept of dating became much less clear. Forty-three percent of the females and 73 percent of the males did not know what a date involved. Activities that were mentioned included going to movies, eating, going to a party or a special place, and going to a school function. Clearly,

**Table 6–5: What Does Dating Mean to You?**

| Females | Frequency | Percent | Males | Frequency | Percent |
|---|---|---|---|---|---|
| To go out with opposite sex ...... | 101 | 58 | To go out with opposite sex ........ | 50 | 35 |
| To go out with a special person (friend) .......... | 32 | 18 | It's "dumb," don't know ......... | 27 | 18 |
| To go to a special place (party) ............ | 12 | 7 | It's "fun" (recreation)......... | 26 | 18 |
| To go out for a special time span .. | 11 | 6 | To go out without parents ............ | 14 | 10 |
| To get to know someone better .... | 11 | 6 | To go to a special place .............. | 13 | 9 |
| It's "dumb," "gross," etc., don't know ... | 9 | 5 | To get to know some-one better .......... | 13 | 9 |

Source: D. W. Jackson, "The Meaning of Dating from the Role Perspective of Non-dating Pre-adolescents," *Adolescence*, 1975, *10*, p. 124.

then, the role prescriptions associated with dating are learned. Where to go, what to do, and how to act are gradually established in the early dating experiences. If Dunphy's description of the peer group structure holds true, young adolescents tend to figure out the behaviors of dating by interacting in large groups at first and then moving into dyadic pairing. This allows some of the problems about the logistics of a date to be solved in a group before they are tried out in a one-to-one situation.

One of the special problems of dating involves obtaining parental permission to go out. In one study of high school sophomore girls, most parents had set 16 as the age when they though their daughters ought to begin dating (Place, 1975). All the girls in the sample tried to get permission to go on a date long before that. They report some of the strategies they used to convince or manipulate their parents into giving their approval.

My parents said I couldn't date until I was 16. Last year I started going steady with Ed. I wanted to go out and we [parents and she] had a fight. I just begged every weekend until she gave up.

Dad, can I go to the show? (Dad: I don't know, ask your mother.) Mom, Dad said it's OK to go to the show if you say yes. Then my Mom says yes, and then I say to my Dad, "Mom said yes."

As long as I name off a whole group of girls that are going, my Mom let me go, I told her [mother] all the kids were going and if I couldn't go to the city, I couldn't go to the dance. She said, "OK, but that's once and for all." But the next time I asked to go to the city, she said, "OK, go ahead."

I use older brothers and sisters to plead for me. I plead for my older sister when she wants to go somewhere. That way, when my times comes, I can go. (Place, 1975, pp. 158–161)

## Who Is a Desirable Date?

What characteristics do adolescents look for in a date? In early studies of dating, Waller (1937) proposed a prestige system of dating in which both males and females placed higher value on material, external variables such as money, dress, or owning a car than on internal values such as intelligence, consideration, or a good sense of humor. In a recent assessment of important characteristics of a date, Hansen (1977) asked black and white high school students to choose the 12 most important items on a list of 33 items. The students were asked to choose the items under three conditions: those that were important to their peers, those that were important in their own choice of a date, and those that were important in their choice of a mate. Table 6–6 shows the first 12 rankings for each category. The students thought that others regarded certain prestige characteristics as important but that they were more concerned with personal qualities. The students did, however, see neatness and dress as external qualities that make a person a desirable companion. In general, there is quite a bit of overlap among the lists. Only four qualities in the first list do not appear on the other lists:

1. Is popular with the opposite sex
2. Has a car or access to one

**Table 6–6: Rank Order Choices on the Dating-Rating Checklist**

| Characteristics Important to Respondents' Peers | Characteristics Important in a Date | Characteristics Important in a Mate |
|---|---|---|
| 1. Is pleasant and cheerful. | 1. Is pleasant and cheerful. | 1. Is pleasant and cheerful. |
| 2. Is neat in appearance. | 2. Is dependable. | 2. Is dependable. |
| 3. Has a sense of humor. | 3. Is considerate. | 3. Is considerate. |
| 5. Is dependable. | 4. Has a sense of humor. | 4. Is honest, straight-forward. |
| 5. Is popular with the opposite sex. | 5. Is neat in appearance. | 5. Is affectionate. |
| 6. Is natural. | 6. Is honest, straight-forward. | 6. Is natural. |
| 7. Is affectionate. | 7. Is natural. | 7. Is neat in appearance. |
| 8. Is considerate. | 8. Is affectionate. | 8. Has a sense of humor. |
| 9. Has a car or access to one. | 9. Has good sense, is intelligent. | 9. Has good sense, is intelligent. |
| 10. Knows how to dance. | 10. Thinks of things to do. | 10. Is a good listener. |
| 11. Is willing to neck on occasion. | 11. Is appropriately dressed. | 11. Is a good sport. |
| 12. Thinks of things to do. | 12. Is a good sport. | 12. Thinks of things to do. |
|  |  | 13. Is appropriately dressed. |

Source: S. L. Hansen, "Dating Choices of High School Students," *Family Coordinator*, 1977, *26*, p. 135. Copyright (1977) by the National Council on Family Relations. Reprinted by permission.

3.  Knows how to dance
4.  Is willing to neck on occasion

These choices suggest that some of the qualities that make a person a desirable date at a recreational level may not be so important for a more serious relationship. The other possibility is that the students were providing a socially desirable response in the second and third conditions, disclaiming their own interests in such "superficial" qualities but projecting them onto others.

It may be reassuring to some and disconcerting to others that physical appearance continues to be a primary basis for judging attractiveness. Good looks, a good build (shapely for girls, muscular for boys), and an attractive face are qualities that both boys and girls can rate consistently and that contribute to a person's desirability (Berg, 1975; Place, 1975; Cavior and Dokecki, 1973). However, there are several indications that personality characteristics, especially understanding, gentleness, and dependability or loyalty, are more important qualities than appearance in a girls' judgment of a boy. For boys, physical attractiveness appears to be the most salient quality in choosing a date (Hansen, 1977; Konopka, 1976; Berg, 1975).

## Emotional and Sexual Intimacy in Dating

We begin this discussion of adolescent intimacy with some of Hall's comments.

The development of the sex function is normally, perhaps, the greatest of all stimuli to mental growth. The new curiosity and interests bring the alert soul into rapport with very many facts and laws of life hitherto unseen. Each of its phenomena supplies the key to a new mystery. Sex is the most potent and magic open sesame to the deepest mysteries of life, death, religion, and love. It is, therefore, one of the cardinal sins against youth to repress healthy thoughts of sex at the proper age, because thus the mind itself is darkened and its wing clipped for many of the higher intuitions, which the supreme muse of common sense at this its psychologic moment ought to give. (Hall, 1904, vol. 2, pp. 108–109)

Intense romantic involvements appear to be a common characteristic of adolescent heterosexual relationships. In a national sample of high school seniors, only 35 percent of the white subjects and 23 percent of the black subjects had never gone steady during the previous three years (Larson, Spreitzer, and Snyder, 1976). White males were the largest group with no experience in a "steady" relationship (40 percent had never gone steady).

Sorenson (1973) described the primary expectations of young adolescents in an intimate relationship. Love is seen as mutual participation in a satisfying relationship. Love does not require a long-term commitment. The partners share a feeling of understanding and closeness that is expressed in part through sexual intimacy. In Sorenson's national sample, 44 percent of the boys and 30 percent of the girls had experienced sexual intercourse before age 16. By age 19, 72 percent of the boys and 57 percent of the girls had experienced sexual intercourse. This reflects a significant increase in sexual experience among girls, especially younger girls, when compared to Kinsey's data from the late 40s and early 50s (see Table 6–7).

**Table 6–7: Adolescent Sexual Activity as Reported by Sorenson (1973) and Kinsey (1948, 1953)**

|  | Percent Having Sexual Intercourse | |
| --- | --- | --- |
|  | *Before Age 13* | *By Age 19* |
| Males |  |  |
| 1948 .................... | 39 | 72 |
| 1973 .................... | 44 | 72 |
| Females |  |  |
| 1953 .................... | 3 | 20 |
| 1973 .................... | 30 | 57 |

Source: R. C. Sorenson, *Adolescent Sexuality in Contemporary America: Personal Values and Sexual Behavior, Ages 13–19* (New York: World, 1973); A. C. Kinsey, W. B. Pomeroy, and C. E. Martin, *Sexual Behavior in the Human Male* (Philadelphia: Saunders, 1948); and A. C. Kinsey, W. B. Pomeroy, C. E. Martin, and P. H. Gebhard, *Sexual Behavior in the Human Female* (Philadelphia: Saunders, 1953).

The meaning of sexuality in a relationship seems to differ for two subgroups in Sorenson's sample: the "serial monogamists" and the "sexual adventurers." The serial monogamists do not have sexual relations with other partners while they are involved in a relationship. However, they are likely to move from one close relationship to the next. The sexual adventurers do not make a commitment to the partner in a sexual encounter. They view sex as a pleasurable experience that does not require a context of love or emotional intimacy to be enjoyed. In Sorenson's sample, more of those who experienced intercourse described themselves as serial monogamists than as sexual adventurers. Although the latter had more sex partners, the former experienced intercourse more frequently.

Whether or not sexual intercourse is part of the relationship, there can be no doubt that sexual intimacy is an important, enjoyable, and common element in adolescent dating. Even adolescents who do not approve of intercourse before marriage will experiment with a range of sexual activities that may result in orgasm. In general, adolescents see sexual activity as a positive, natural part of a tender, caring relationship. Even the sexual adventurers among them do not intend to use sex to exploit or harm others. Rather, they see sexuality as a component of personal freedom, a part of having an open, natural relationship rather than a relationship that is bound by stereotypes and formality (Conger, 1975). On the other hand, especially in early adolescence, girls and boys can feel pressured into striving for a greater degree of sexual intimacy than they find genuinely comfortable. As with all other pressures toward peer conformity, adolescents confront peer expectations for sexual openness that may not match their own needs or that may increase their feelings of vulnerability. Learning to experience sexuality in a satisfying way that meets one's ideals about mutual respect, tenderness, and physical pleasure requires more psychological maturity than many junior high– and high school–age adolescents can bring to a relationship.

## PARENTHOOD IN EARLY ADOLESCENCE

Among the sexually active adolescent females, only one in five consistently uses contraceptives. The result of this inconsistent use or rejection of contraception is that 30 percent of sexually active adolescents become pregnant (Green and Lowe, 1976; Kantner and Zelnik, 1973). Despite the legalization of abortion, an increasing number of young adolescents are deciding to have their babies rather than abort. In 1974, almost 20 percent of all births were to teenage mothers. From 1972 to 1973, when the birthrate for all other age groups was declining, the birthrate for girls under 15 increased 8 percent (Green and Lowe, 1975). The phenomenon of teenage parenthood is a complex one that touches the lives of the adolescent mother and father, the child or children born to an adolescent mother, the parents of the adolescent parents, and the schools, counseling services, or planned parenthood services that are developed to help very young parents cope with parenthood (Furstenberg, 1977).

One of the great paradoxes of adolescent parenthood is the contrast between young girls' aspirations about mothering and the actual outcome of child rearing. Here are the comments of some young mothers.

**Ann** (14): When I got pregnant, my parents wanted me to have an abortion, but I'm an only child, and it's a lonely feeling when you're an only child. I just said, "Well, I'm going to keep the baby because now I'll have somebody I'll feel close to, instead of being lonely all the time." (Fosburgh, 1977, p. 34)

**Mary** (17): It was great, 'cause now I got him and nobody can take him away from me. He's mine, I made him, he's great. Something real who can give me happiness. He can make me laugh and he can make me cry and he can make me mad. (Konopka, 1976, p. 39)

In contrast to this romantic view of a close, loving relationship, the life experiences of the adolescent parent and child are filled with a number of hardships. Infants born to young mothers are at greater risk than infants born to women in their 20s and 30s. They have a higher risk of dying during the first year, a higher risk of being born prematurely or at a low birth weight, and a higher risk of neurological damage due to complications associated with delivery (Menken, 1972; Honig, 1978). Thus, young parents are more likely to have to cope with the special needs of a developmentally handicapped child.

The young mother is also likely to face the dissolution of the relationship with the father of the child. Of 180 unmarried young girls who received care at the Young Mother's Clinic of Yale–New Haven Hospital, 30 of the fathers were at the hospital during the delivery. By 26 months after the baby was born, 23 percent of the 180 girls had married the father. Of those who did not marry the father, 23 percent were still seeing the father at 26 months. For 54 percent of the 180 mothers, the father of the baby was pretty much out of the picture by 26 months after the baby was born (Lorenzi, Klerman, and Jekel, 1977).

In general, the adolescent mother who marries is not better off than the adolescent mother who can raise her child in her parent's home. About half of teenage marriages are likely to break up in five years. Those that involve pregnancy are three times as likely to end in divorce as other teenage marriages (Coombs et al., 1970). When a young girl with a baby marries, she is likely to drop out of school. She and her husband will be living on minimal resources. They may both be trying to work; they will have less time to establish the trust and reciprocity of their own relationship; and their poverty will impose health risks to their baby as well as to themselves. The failure of the marriage may add an additional negative experience that will influence the adolescent's self-image as well as her orientation toward her child.

Finally, there is some evidence that the pregnant adolescent begins her parenting career with low self-esteem and an inability to respond to the changing reality of her physical and social development (Lindeman, 1974; Schiller, 1974; Abernathy et al., 1975). In a comparison of pregnant school-age girls with age-mates who were not pregnant, the pregnant girls had lower self-esteem, greater feelings of worthlessness, more conflict with family members, and greater evidence of defensiveness (Zongker, 1977). Whether these characteristics were present before pregnancy or were a result of pregnancy cannot be determined from this study. In any case, these qualities do not provide a very hopeful context for a warm, supportive parenting relationship. In fact, these qualities combined with the stress of minimal resources, conflicts with parents, and a dissolving relationship with the father are likely to produce mothers who are critical, impatient, and likely to resort to abusive behaviors.

Very little has been written about the adolescent father. In the study of adolescent parents in New Haven cited above, 23 percent of the young mothers married the young fathers. Another 23 percent continued to have frequent contact with the fathers over a two-year period. Of the mothers who were not married, 49 percent were still receiving some financial support from the fathers after two years. These data suggest a continuing allegiance by many adolescent boys to the mother and the child, even if that allegiance is not expressed in marriage. Producing a child is bound to stimulate conflicting feelings of pride, guilt, and anxiety for the adolescent boy. He must struggle with the reality that his sexual adventures have resulted in a pregnancy that might bring conflict and pain to someone he cared for. He must confront the choices that he and his girlfriend have in coping with an unplanned pregnancy. Finally, he may experience the sense of being shut out from the birth of a child he has fathered.

## THE IMPLICATIONS OF GROUP IDENTITY AND ALIENATION FOR THE EMERGENCE OF LIFE PATTERNS

In psychosocial theory, a central concept for understanding the pattern of growth and change during life is the psychosocial crisis. The concept of crisis refers here to the predictable stresses and challenges that occur as individuals attempt to cope with the demands of their social environment at each period of development. We have theorized that in early adolescence the primary psychosocial crisis involves a striving for group identity and the threat of alienation (Newman and Newman, 1976).

Adolescents experience a search for membership, an internal questioning about the group of which they are most naturally a part. They ask themselves: "Who am I, and with whom do I belong?"

Although membership in a peer group may be the most pressing concern of adolescents, questions also arise about other group identifications. Adolescents may seek commitment to a religious organization; they may evaluate the nature of their ties to the members of the immediate or extended family; or they may begin to consider their place in their neighborhood or community. In the process of seeking a group identity, adolescents are confronted with the fit or lack of fit between their personal needs and values and the needs and values of relevant social groups in the environment. The process of self-evaluation takes place within the context of the meaningful groups that are available for identification. Individual needs for social approval or affiliation, for leadership or power, or for status or reputation are expressed in the kinds of group identifications that are made and rejected during early adolescence.

A positive resolution of the conflict of group identity versus alienation is one in which adolescents perceive an existing group which meets their social needs and provides them with a sense of group belonging. It is this sense of group belonging that facilitates the psychological growth of the individual and serves as an integrating force in efforts to cope with the challenge of physical, cognitive, and socioemotional growth that occur during early adolescence. By achieving a feeling of group identity, young adolescents will develop a preference for certain activities and they may develop a special mode of dress or a particular style of talk that links them to their group. Within the group, adolescents develop their skills in group participation, learning how to collaborate with peers in a group project, how to reach a group decision, how to use the group as a source of support in conflicts with adults, and how to express unique roles in the group's functioning, including the roles of "leader," "joker," "hero," or "parent." We have described how group membership in cliques links adolescents to a larger social crowd. As part of that smaller peer group, adolescents feel included in dances, athletic events, or parties that involve the larger group. The peer group is also an avenue for beginning to establish social contacts between boys and girls. Peer group membership offers a code for behavior, a sense of social status, a reputation, and a feeling of connectedness with the larger school or community population.

Peer group membership has a number of consequences for future life patterns. First, there is the positive feeling of having been a part of the group. This feeling of having been included provides a sense of optimism about engaging in more complex social groupings or about seeking peer associations in adulthood. Second, if one remains in the same community one begins life after high school with a group of friends who continue to function as companions, filling in the gap that dispersion to various work settings may create in the high school graduate's life. Third, participation in the peer group allows adolescents to develop the social skills of group functioning that will continue to be important in work and family settings as well as in later social contexts.

A negative resolution of the conflict leaves one with a pervasive sense of alienation from one's peers. One does not experience a sense of belonging to a group. Rather, one is continually uneasy in the presence of peers. One way in which the negative outcome may occur is for parents to press the adolescent to restrict his or her associations to a peer group that does not offer the adolescent membership. Another possibility is that the adolescent may look over the existing groups and not find one that would really meet his or her needs. In this case, the adolescent may never become a member of a peer group. A third possibility is that no peer group offers acceptance or friendship, so that the adolescent is gradually shut out of all the existing groups in the social environment.

During early adolescence, it is not uncommon for young people to become preoccupied with their own feelings and thoughts. They may withdraw from social interactions, feeling unwilling to share the areas of vulnerability and confusion that accompany rapid growth and changing expectations. In this sense, we would argue that most adolescents feel some of the loneliness and isolation that is implied in the term *alienation*. Even with peers, there is a need to exercise caution about sharing one's most troublesome concerns for fear that others will reject or ridicule you because of your weaknesses or fears. The maintenance of an interpersonal "cool," a desire to be perceived as someone who is together rather than confused, may stand in the way of building strong bonds of commitment to social groups. In other words, the crisis of group identity versus alienation is a tension between expectations for group affiliation and barriers to group commitment that are a product of the self-consciousness and egocentrism of this life stage as well as potential rejection from existing groups.

The consequences of alienation during early adolescence include lack of opportunities to develop group skills; a feeling of being shut off from an accepting, supportive social context; and a growing barrier to the formation of commitments to other people or groups. In analyzing the peer group structure, Dunphy suggested that without clique membership, adolescents had little involvement with the activities of the crowd. Adolescents can slip out of a peer group by rejecting group norms, by tarnishing their "reputation," or by becoming heavily involved with a "steady." We find, for example, that one of the major sources of stress among young pregnant adolescents is the feeling of being shut off from peers. Pregnant girls may want to stop attending school; they may become very inactive and unwilling to participate in activities with their peers (Adams et al., 1976). After childbirth, these girls have strong needs for peer involvement and companionship that simply cannot be met by a newborn.

We would emphasize that for most adolescents the negative

resolution of this conflict is far less likely than the positive. In this case, however, we begin to see the emergence of personal choice in the resolution of the psychosocial conflict. Adolescents may reject peer group identification because of conflicts with personal interests or values. Also, for the first time, a resolution of the psychosocial crisis does not depend on the relationship of an individual to an adult in the environment but depends heavily on the interaction between adolescents and their peers.

## CHAPTER SUMMARY

In our discussion of social development in early adolescence we have considered the range and quality of interactions, the characteristics of adolescent-parent relationships, and the characteristics of adolescent peer relationships. In school as well as out, adolescents have their primary social encounters with peers. There are far fewer interactions with adults, and often those feel uncomfortable and strained.

Three themes were considered in the analysis of parent-adolescent relationships: (1) How is independence from parents achieved? (2) How much discrepancy exists between parent and adolescent values? (3) What impact do specific family variables have on adolescent development? In general, independence is related to how much parents permit adolescents to be involved in decision making, how often parents give explanations for the rules they set, and whether or not parents value independent judgment in their children. Most adolescents do not see their parents as having very high expectations for them to function independently. Girls tend to express their independence by assuming more responsibility and by beginning to date and to earn money. Boys show their independence by spending more time away from home and by resisting parental restrictions. Interestingly, those adolescents who feel the most freedom and are the most comfortable about exerting their own judgment even in conflict with parents also feel the most affection and closeness with parents. In value areas as well, frequency of interaction and shared experiences tend to increase the similarity between the views of parents and adolescents. The evidence suggests that adolescents and their parents do not hold strikingly different views on most value issues.

Family characteristics influence the social experiences of adolescents. Children from large families tend to experience greater parental control. Low family income is associated with poor health care, a likelihood of dropping out of school, lack of success in finding or keeping work, and, particularly in a dissonant economic context, lowered feelings of self-worth. The absence of a parent does not appear to alter the child's relationship with the other parent or to contribute negatively to the child's self-concept. On the other hand, father absence does seem to influence adolescent girls' relationship to males. Maternal employment, the final family variable to be considered, is associated with increased independence among daughters, the placing of higher values on female achievement, and less stereotyped views of sex roles for both males and females. Supervising younger brothers and sisters can give adolescents a feeling of responsibility and competence, but it can also overburden adolescents. There is no evidence that the children of working mothers are more likely to be neglected, overworked, or ignored than the children of nonemployed mothers.

Adolescent peer groups have been described as small cliques that merge to form a larger crowd of friends. These friendship groups have a reputation, a leader, and a set of shared activities. Heterosexual involvement appears to be a major goal of peer interactions at the crowd level, and crowd leaders tend to be among the most active or precocious in their relationships with the opposite sex.

Peer group conformity tends to be at its strongest during early adolescence, especially the years from 12 to 14. Peers are especially likely to encourage or support one another in behavior that would be devalued by the adult community during these years. In general, however, peer relationships do not seem to be based as much on similarity of values or attitudes as on the sharing of daily experiences. Adolescents value their friends for the understanding and support they provide. When it comes to advice about important decisions, adolescents still see parents as a better source of opinions than peers. The overall pattern is to see an emergence of independent judgment as adolescents move through the high school years. By the age of 17 or 18, peer group conformity and reliance on parental opinion both decline. They give way to a greater reliance on one's own evaluation of each specific situation.

A special characteristic of peer group relations in early adolescence is the beginning of dating. Dating serves a number of functions for young people, including recreation, status, learning about one's own personality, learning about members of the opposite sex, beginning to identify the criteria for a permanent relationship, and experimenting with sex. Physical attractiveness is an important dimension in the choice of a date. However, adolescents tend to value such personal qualities as gentleness, understanding, and loyalty above prestige variables.

Adolescents tend to have more permissive views about sexual intimacy than do their parents or their grandparents. Sexual intercourse is viewed as an acceptable part of a loving relationship, even by adolescents who do not experience intercourse themselves. The trend seems to be toward earlier sexual experience for females and a relatively stable pattern of sexual experimentation for boys. For the most part, adolescents tend to see sexuality as an expression of love, not as a form of pleasure that is sought for its own sake.

The problem of adolescent pregnancy results from earlier involvement with sexual intercourse and inconsistent use of contraceptives. Many more adolescent girls are planning to keep their babies than used to be the case. Although abortion is more accessible today than it has been, many females think that it is wrong to destroy their babies. What is more, they look forward to the love and dependence that they expect from their babies. Often, young mothers are faced with a multitude of problems, including conflicts with parents or boyfriend, health problems, a lack of resources, and feelings of isolation. The mother's decision to marry because of pregnancy tends to create many more problems than does her decision to stay at home and raise the child with the help of her parents.

The psychosocial crisis of early adolescence is viewed as a conflict between group identity and alienation. The resolution of this crisis influences adolescents' opportunities to develop group skills, a sense of support from peers, and an ability to experience commitment to a social group. In searching for group identity, adolescents engage in value clarification and acquire an appreciation of their potential contribution to the group and a clearer sense of their needs for affiliation, status, or power. This conflict involves personal choice as well as acceptance or rejection from age-mates.

## REFERENCES

Abernathy, V., et al.   Identification of women at risk for unwanted pregnancy. *American Journal of Psychiatry,* 1975, *132,* 1027–1030.

Adams, B. N., Brownstein, C. A., Rennak, I. M., and Schmitt, M. H.   The pregnant adolescent—A group approach. *Adolescence,* 1976, *11,* 468–485.

Advisory Committee on Child Development.   *Toward a national policy for children and families.* Washington, D.C.: National Academy of Sciences, 1976.

Baumrind, D.   Early socialization and adolescent competence. In S. E. Dragestin and G. H. Elder (Eds.), *Adolescence in the life cycle: Psychological change and social context.* New York: Wiley, 1975. Pp. 117–143.

Belmont, L., and Marolla, F. A.   Birth order, family size, and intelligence. *Science,* 1973, *182,* 1096–1101.

Berg, D. H.   Sexual subcultures and contemporary heterosexual interaction patterns among adolescents. *Adolescence,* 1975, *10,* 543–548.

Bixenstine, V. E., DeCorte, M. S., and Bixenstine, B. A.   Conformity to peer-sponsored misconduct at four grade levels. *Developmental Psychology*, 1976, *12*, 226–236.

Blos, P.   *On adolescence: A psychoanalytic interpretation.* New York: Free Press, 1962.

Blos, P.   Character formation in adolescence. *Psychoanalytic Study of the Child*, 1968, *23*, 245–263.

Bowerman, C. E., and Bahr, S. J.   Conjugal power and adolescent identification with parents. *Sociometry*, 1973, *36*, 366–377.

Brim, O. G., Jr.   Adolescent personality as self-other systems. *Journal of Marriage and the Family*, 1965, *27*, 156–162.

Brittain, C. V.   Adolescent choices and parent-peer cross pressures. *American Sociological Review*, 1963, *28*, 385–391.

Brittain, C. V.   An exploration of the bases of peer-compliance and parent-compliance in adolescence. *Adolescence*, 1967–68, *2*, 445–458.

Brittain, C. V.   A comparison of rural and urban adolescents with respect to peer vs. parent compliance. *Adolescence*, 1969, *3*, 59–68.

Bronfenbrenner, U.   Response to pressure from peers versus adults among Soviet and American school children. In U. Bronfenbrenner (chairman), *Social factors in the development of personality.* Symposium 35 presented at the 18th International Congress of Psychology, Moscow, August 1966. Pp. 7–18.

Bronfenbrenner, U.   *Two worlds of childhood: U.S. and U.S.S.R.* New York: Russell Sage Foundation, 1970.

Brownston, J. E., and Willis, R. H.   Conformity in early and late adolescence. *Developmental Psychology*, 1971, *4*, 334–337.

Cavior, N., and Dokecki, P. R.   Physical attractiveness, perceived attitude similarity, and academic achievement as contributors to interpersonal attraction among adolescents. *Developmental Psychology*, 1973, *9*, 44–54.

Children's Defense Fund.   *Children out of school in America.* Cambridge, Mass.: Children's Defense Fund of the Washington Research Project, Inc., 1974.

Clausen, J. A.   Family structure, socialization, and personality. In L. W. Hoffman and M. L. Hoffman (Eds.), *Review of child development research*, vol. 2. New York: Russell Sage Foundation, 1966.

Coleman, J. S.   *The adolescent society*, New York: Free Press, 1961.

Conger, J. J.   Sexual attitudes and behavior of contemporary adolescents. In J. J. Conger (Ed.), *Contemporary issues in adolescent development.* New York: Harper and Row, 1975. Pp. 221–230.

Coombs, L. C., et al.   Premarital pregnancy and status before and after marriage. *American Journal of Sociology*, 1970, *75*, 800–820.

Costanzo, P. R.   Conformity development as a function of self-blame. *Journal of Personality and Social Psychology*, 1970, *14*, 366–374.

Curtis, R. L.   Adolescent orientations toward parents and peers: Variations by sex, age, and socioeconomic status. *Adolescence*, 1975, *10*, 483–494.

Czikszentmihalyi, M., Larson, R., and Prescott, S.   The ecology of adolescent activity and experience. *Journal of Youth and Adolescence*, 1977, *6*, 281–294.

Douglas, J. W. B.   *The home and the school: A study of ability and attainment in the primary school.* London: MacGibbon and Kee, 1964.

Douvan, E., and Adelson, J.  *The adolescent experience.* New York: Wiley, 1966.

Dunphy, D. C.  The social structure of urban adolescent peer groups. *Sociometry,* 1963, *26,* 230–246.

Elder, G. H.  Parental power legitimization and its effect on the adolescent. *Sociometry,* 1963, *26,* 50–65.

Elder, G. H., Jr., and Bowerman, C. E.  Family structure and child-rearing patterns: The effect of family size and sex composition. *American Sociological Review,* 1963, *30,* 81–96.

Elkind, D.  Egocentrism in adolescence. *Child Development,* 1967, *38,* 1025–1034.

Estep, R. E., Burt, M. R., and Milligan, H. J.  The socialization of sexual identity. *Journal of Marriage and the Family,* 1977, *39,* 99–112.

Feldman, H., and Feldman, M.  The effect of father absence on adolescents. Mimeographed, 1976.

Fosburgh, L.  The make-believe world of teen-age maternity. *New York Times Magazine,* August 7, 1977, pp. 29–34.

Freud, A.  Adolescence. In *Psychoanalytic Study of the Child,* vol. 13. New York: International Universities Press, 1958. Pp. 255–278.

Furstenberg, F. F.  *Unplanned parenthood: The social consequences of teenage childbearing.* Riverside, N.J.: Free Press, 1977.

George, V., and Wilding, P.  *Motherless families.* London: Routledge and Kegan Paul, 1972.

Goffman, E.  *The presentation of self in everyday life.* Garden City, N.Y.: Doubleday, 1959.

Green, C. P., and Lowe, S. J.  Teenage pregnancy: A major problem for minors. *Zero Population Growth National Reporter,* 1975, *7,* 4–5.

Hall, G. S.  *Adolescence: Its psychology and its relations to physiology, anthropology, sociology, sex, crime, religion, and education,* vols. 1 and 2. New York: D. Appleton, 1904.

Hansen, S. L.  Dating choices of high school students. *Family Coordinator,* 1977, *26,* 133–138.

Havighurst, R. J., and Gottlieb, D.  Youth and the meaning of work. In R. J. Havighurst and P. H. Dreyer (Eds.), *Youth: The seventy-fourth yearbook of the National Society for the Study of Education.* Chicago: University of Chicago Press, 1975. Pp. 145–160.

Hetherington, E. M.  Effects of father absence on personality development in adolescent daughters. *Developmental Psychology,* 1972, *7,* 313–326.

Hoffman, L. W.  Effects of maternal employment on the child: A review of research. *Developmental Psychology,* 1974, *10,* 204–228.

Honig, A. S.  What we need to know to help the teenage parent. *Family Coordinator,* 1978, *27,* 113–119.

Jackson, D. W.  The meaning of dating from the role perspective of non-dating pre-adolescents. *Adolescence,* 1975, *10,* 123–126.

Jones, S.  High school social status as a historical process. *Adolescence* 1976, *11,* 327–333.

Kandel, D. B.   Similarity in real-life adolescent friendship pairs. *Journal of Personality and Social Psychology*, 1978, *36*, 306–312.

Kandel, D. B., and Lesser, G. S.   *Youth in two worlds.* San Francisco: Jossey-Bass, 1972.

Kantner, J. F., and Zelnik, M.   Contraception and pregnancy: Experience of young unmarried women in the United States. *Perspectives*, 1973, *1*, 22.

Kohlberg, L., and Gilligan, C.   The adolescent as a philosopher: The discovery of the self in a post-conventional world. In J. Kagan and R. Coles (Eds.), *12 to 16: Early Adolescence.* New York: Norton, 1972. Pp. 144–179.

Kohn, M. L.   Social class and parental values. *American Journal of Sociology,* 1959, *64*, 337–351.

Kohn, M. L.   Social class and parent-child relationships: An interpretation. *American Journal of Sociology*, 1963, *68*, 471–480.

Kon, I. S., and Losenkov, V. A.   Friendship in adolescence: Values and behavior. *Journal of Marriage and the Family*, 1978, *40*, 143–156.

Konopka, G.   *Young girls: A portrait of adolescence.* Englewood Cliffs, N.J.: Prentice-Hall, 1976.

Labov, W.   *Language in the inner city: Studies in the black English vernacular.* Philadelphia: University of Pennsylvania Press, 1972. (a)

Labov, W.   Rules for ritual insults. In D. Sudnow (Ed.), *Studies in social interaction.* New York: Free Press, 1972. Pp. 120–169. (b)

Larson, D. L., Spreitzer, E. A., and Snyder, E. E.   Social factors in the frequency of romantic involvement among adolescents. *Adolescence*, 1976, *11*, 7–12.

Larson, L. E.   The influence of parents and peers during adolescence: The situation hypothesis revisited. *Journal of Marriage and the Family*, 1972, *34*, 67–74. (a)

Larson, L. E.   The relative influence of parent-adolescent affect in predicting the salience hierarchy among youth. *Pacific Sociological Review*, 1972, *15*, 83–102. (b)

Lerner, R. M., and Weinstock, A.   Note on the generation gap. *Psychological Reports*, 1972, *31*, 457–458.

Lesser, G. S., and Kandel, D.   Parent-adolescent relationships and adolescent independence in the United States and Denmark. *Journal of Marriage and the Family*, 1969, *31*, 348–358. (a)

Lesser, G. S., and Kandel, D. B.   Parental and peer influences on educational plans of adolescents. *American Sociological Review*, 1969, *34*, 213–223. (b)

Lewin, K.   Field theory and experiment in social psychology. *American Journal of Sociology*, 1939, *44*, 868–897.

Lindeman, C.   Birth control and unmarried young women. New York: Springer, 1974.

Lorenzi, M. E., Klerman, L. V., and Jekel, J. F.   School-age parents: How permanent a relationship? *Adolescence*, 1977, *12*, 13–22.

LoSciuto, L. A., and Karlin, R. M.   Correlates of the generation gap. *Journal of Psychology*, 1972, *81*, 253–262.

McCord, J., McCord, W., and Thurber, E.   Effects of maternal employment on lower-class boys. *Journal of Abnormal and Social Psychology*, 1963, *67*, 177–182.

Menken, J.   The health and social consequences of teenage childbearing. *Family Planning Perspectives*, 1972, *4*, 45–53.

Newman, B. M.   The development of social interaction from infancy through adolescence. *Journal of Small Group Behavior*, 1976, *7*, 19–32. (a)

Newman, B. M.   The study of interpersonal behavior in adolescence. *Adolescence*, 1976, *11*, 127–142. (b)

Newman, P. R.   Person and setting interactions: A comparative analysis of the quality and range of social interaction in two suburban high schools. Unpublished doctoral dissertation, University of Michigan, 1971.

Newman, P. R., and Newman, B. M.   Naturalistic observation of student interactions with adults and peers in the high school. Paper presented at the Eastern Psychological Association Convention, Philadelphia 1974.

Newman, P. R., and Newman, B. M.   Early adolescence and its conflict: Group identity versus alienation. *Adolescence*, 1976, *11*, 261–274.

Nye, F. I., and Hoffman, L. W.   *The employed mother in America*. Chicago: Rand McNally, 1963.

Peterson, E. T., and Kunz, P. R.   Parental control over adolescents according to family size. *Adolescence*, 1975, *10*, 419–426.

Petroni, F. A.   Teenage interracial dating. *Trans-action*, September 1971.

Piaget, J.   Intellectual evolution from adolescence to adulthood. *Human Development*, 1972, *15*, 1–12.

Piaget, J., and Inhelder, B.   *The psychology of the child*. New York: Basic Books, 1969.

Place, D. M.   The dating experience for adolescent girls. *Adolescence*, 1975, *10*, 157–174.

Poveda, T. G.   Reputation and the adolescent girl: An analysis. *Adolescence*, 1975, *10*, 127–136.

Reynolds, D. J.   Adjustment and maladjustment. In J. F. Adams (Ed.), *Understanding adolescence: Current developments in adolescent psychology* (3d ed.). Boston: Allyn and Bacon, 1976. Pp. 334–368.

Rodgers, R. R., Bronfenbrenner, U., and Devereux, E. C., Jr.   Standards of social behavior among children in four cultures. *International Journal of Psychology*, 1968, 3 (1), 31–41.

Rosenberg, M.   The dissonant context and the adolescent self-concept. In S. E. Dragastin and G. H. Elder (Eds.), *Adolescence in the life cycle: Psychological change and social context*. New York: Wiley, 1975. Pp. 97–116.

Schiller, P. A.   Sex attitude modification process for adolescents. *Journal of Clinical Child Psychology*, 1974, 50–51.

Schimel, J. L.   Problems of delinquency and their treatment. In G. Caplan (Ed.), *American handbook of psychiatry* (2d ed.), vol. 2: *Child and adolescent psychiatry, socio-cultural and community psychiatry*, New York: Basic Books, 1974. Pp. 264–274.

Schlesinger, B.   One parent families in Great Britain. *Family Coordinator*, 1977, *26*, 139–142.

Scott, R., and Seifert, K.   Family size and learning readiness profiles of socioeconomically disadvantaged preschool whites. *Journal of Psychology*, 1975, *89*, 3–7.

Sorensen, R. C.   *Adolescent sexuality in contemporary America*, New York: World, 1973.

Stolz, L. M.   Effects of maternal employment on children: Evidence from research. *Child Development*, 1960, *31*, 799–782.

Sullivan, H. S.   *The collected works of Harry Stack Sullivan*, vols. 1 and 2. New York: Norton, 1949.

Sullivan, H. S.   *The interpersonal theory of psychiatry*, New York: Norton, 1953.

U.S. Department of Commerce.   *Current population reports: Marital status and living arrangements*, series P-20, no. 287. Washington, D.C.: U.S. Government Printing Office, 1975.

U.S. Department of Commerce.   *Current population reports: Household and family characteristics*, series P-20. Washington, D.C.: U.S. Government Printing Office, 1976.

Waller, W.   The rating and dating complex. *American Sociological Review*, 1937, *2*, 727–734.

Wallston, B.   The effects of maternal employment on children. *Journal of Child Psychology and Psychiatry*, 1973, *14*, 81–95.

Weiner, I. B.   *Psychological disturbances in adolescence*. New York: Wiley-Interscience, 1970.

Weinstock, A., and Lerner, R. M.   Attitudes of late adolescents and their parents toward contemporary issues. *Psychological Reports*, 1972, *30*, 239–244.

Winch, R. F.   The functions of dating. From R. F. Winch, *The modern family* (rev. ed.). New York: Holt, Rinehart and Winston, 1971. Pp. 530–532.

Woods, M. B.   The unsupervised child of the working mother. *Developmental Psychology*, 1972, *6*, 14–25.

Zajonc, R.   Family configuration and intelligence, *Science*, 1976, *192*, 227–235.

Zongker, C. E.   The self concept of pregnant adolescent girls. *Adolescence*, 1977, *12*, 477–488.

*The most important settings of the high school may be ones the students define for themselves.*

**7**

# The High School

The high school is the main setting in which adolescents spend time away from home. Although it is a large, complex institution with a variety of educational and socialization goals, these are not the elements of the high school that seem to make the deepest impressions on young adolescents. Rather, it is the tempo, the climate, the relationships, and the activities that provide a rich set of images about the meaning of high school. We think of the high school setting as a lively convergence of adolescents and adults, functioning in some moderate degree of order or rhythm that is periodically interrupted by explosive outpourings of feelings, spontaneous laughter, ridiculous antics, and loudspeaker messages from the principal's office.

High school is a complex cognitive scheme that includes settings, people, activities, and a period of time. From the point of view of the student, the important high school settings may include the bus ride to school, the coffee shop across the street, the bathrooms, certain sections of hallway, or a particular set of back hall stairs, as well as such more obvious settings as the classrooms, the athletic fields, and the cafeteria. Being in high school is a characteristic of the person. Even when the student is away from school or on vacation, the phrase "I'm a high school student" serves to identify and locate the adolescent's relevant life framework. High school is perceived as a time of one's life. Adults often look back upon the high school years with nostalgia. The meaningfulness of this period, whether positive or negative, seems to persist well into adulthood. It is a time of all kinds of awakenings: physical awakening, cognitive awakening, social and emotional awakening. It is the arena in which the energy and confusion of adolescent growth and development are housed. Given all that we know about psychological development during early adolescence, what kinds of contributions can be attributed to the high school environment itself? In this chapter, our goal is to understand the high school on several levels: as a physical environment, as a context for socialization, and as a system of educational programs. The chapter attempts to evaluate the impact of the high school on cognitive and social development while keeping in sight the variety of adaptive responses that students make to their high schools.

## A TYPICAL HIGH SCHOOL DAY

Let us look at the daily experiences of a few students as they attend high school. As you read these brief sketches, you will undoubtedly be able to add other scenarios that are a product of your own recollections. From the sketches we begin to see the interaction between student needs and talents and the kinds of school environments that they encounter.

I.  *Brad* attends a large, urban high school. He has a vocational curriculum and is in a work-study program. He comes to school on a city bus which is usually crowded early in the morning. After a half-hour ride during which he stands most of the way, Brad goes to his locker, talks with a few friends, and is in his homeroom for roll call by 8:00 A.M. At 8:10 he reports to the machine shop. There is a car that needs a tune-up and a carburetor that needs repair. These projects are the focus of Brad's attention for that morning. He works in the shop for an hour and a half. Then he leaves for two periods for math and English classes. During the math class, one of the kids falls asleep and starts snoring loudly at the back of the room. The class breaks up, and there isn't much more work done that period. In English, a student teacher is in charge of the lesson. She asks Brad to read a poem out loud, and when he is done, she asks him to say what it meant. Brad is embarrassed and just shrugs his shoulders. He tells her that he is working on a big project in the shop and asks to be excused early to get back to it. Then he returns to the shop, where he completes his work on the tune-up by noon. He asks his teacher whether he can leave the carburetor for the next day, since he has to be to work by 1:00. The teacher agrees, but points out that Brad works too slowly and that he just has to learn to speed things up.

II.  *Mary* is a senior at a small, private school in a large, urban area. She also rides the city bus to school, and she meets a lot of her friends along the way. As they ride, they are talking about college applications, where they want to go, and who has already heard from some schools. At school, Mary goes to her locker, grabs the books and notebooks for her first two classes, and then goes to homeroom. There are annoucements, a brief discussion about the senior party, and the students are off.

In English class, they are reading the Book of Job. There is a lively argument about why Job suffered, and Mary offers an existential analysis that Job's suffering gave his life meaning. The class ends in an excited confrontation between a very religious student and an atheist about why humans believe in God.

In French class, the students rehearse a play they are working on. Then, in art class, they begin designing the sets for the senior class play. There is some discussion about the design, and Mary offers to draw up some quick sketches so that they can get an idea of how the different plans would look. While she is working, Clark, a boy in her class, sits down next to her and starts talking about how badly he is going to feel to leave the school. After art class, they go to the students' lounge together and talk for a while more. Mary suddenly feels very sad herself and is glad to be able to share her feelings with Clark. Then the conversation turns more personal. Clark tells Mary that he has been fond of her for a very long time but had always been too shy to say anything. Mary is surprised and confused. She is already dating another boy and has never really thought about Clark as anything other than a friend. Soon some other students come into the lounge and Mary goes off to her anthropology class. There are class reports, but Mary's mind wanders over the conversation with Clark and the troubled feelings she has about it. Her mind is miles away when the teacher asks if the class has any questions. Embarrassed at having tuned out so completely, Mary looks at the clock and is glad to be moving on. She makes sure to have lunch with lots of other kids that day, trying to avoid Clark's gaze. After lunch there is a long rehearsal for the senior play. While Mary is back stage, Clark comes to talk to her again. He is sobbing, telling her how deeply he cares for her. Mary tries to comfort him and to explain her feelings, but nothing seems to help. Mary leaves school feeling sad, angry, and a little bit flattered.

   **III.**   *Paul* is the fourth child in a family of six children. His mother and father both work, mother on the morning shift and father on the afternoon and evening shift. Paul usually leaves home without breakfast to ride the school bus to the suburban school he attends. On the way, he is quiet, not interested in joining in the gossip, the teasing, or the conversations about sports that fill the bus. He goes to his homeroom for attendance, and then to his first class, which is biology. Paul has about a sixth-grade reading level. He usually does not read the homework assignments, or if he does read some of them, he usually does not understand what he reads. The biology teacher is describing the parts of a plant, and Paul's stomach is rumbling. When it rumbles very loudly, a student in the next seat starts to giggle, and pretty soon the back of the class is giggling. Paul cuts his next class and goes over to the fast-food restaurant across from school. He has a sandwich, plays pinball, and talks with some of the boys who are there. Paul buys a few "joints" from one of them and goes into the bathroom to get high. When he is feeling good, he walks around the school neighborhood, wanders around some of the stores, and then drifts back to the school grounds in time to catch the bus back home.

   **IV.**   *Terry* always goes to bed late after finishing his homework. His parents must work hard to wake him up. Breakfast is ready by the time he struggles into the kitchen. He eats with the family, gathers his homework and books, and thinks about whom he will try to see during the day and what meetings he must go to after school. He is a junior in a large high school in a city of about 100,000 people. His father drives Terry to school. Along the way they pick up two friends. During the drive they talk about courses, the prom, and which parties they will go to after the basketball game on Friday night.

When they arrive at school, Terry proceeds to the main entrance to have a cigarette with some guys who are active in clubs and sports. They talk about activities, team records, and girls. At 8:25 Terry goes to his locker to leave his lunch and pick up his books for the first three classes of the day. He then walks to the counselors' office to see his friend the debate coach and Student Council adviser, Mr. Collins. They quickly talk over several matters, and then Terry heads to another locker room to meet his girlfriend. She has been waiting for five minutes, and she asks why he can't be there more promptly. They walk through the halls together, talking about a variety of things and casually saying hello to other students who pass by. They stop at the school office, where Terry picks up a batch of announcements for a Student Council dance on Saturday night which he will post around the school during the day.

At 9:00 A.M. a bell rings and the students all head for different classes. Terry drops his girlfriend at her English class and arrives at his biology class before the second bell rings. The teacher asks questions; Terry answers periodically to keep things moving and is somewhat bored as the teacher tries to prod the slower students to learn. In the ten minutes between classes Terry walks with a variety of friends to a college preparatory English class. The group speculate about basketball, Student Council, romances, and the English teacher.

The English teacher composes a panel of several of Terry's friends. Terry escapes the spotlight. He listens while his friends discuss the play and feels uneasy when the teacher systematically embarrasses one student after another. Only Mel Garber is able to provide reasonably satisfying answers to her probing questions. Terry is glad to be able to relax during this class.

After English, Terry rushes to meet his girlfriend and walk her to history. He is glad to see her and gets all the information about the first two classes. After he drops her off, he attends his American history class. The teacher talks about the U.S. Constitution, and Terry prepares his Debate Club agenda while listening. From history, Terry and several boys go to gym, where they play a game that the coaches devised, called "mass murder." Terry plays strongly enough not to be labeled a "sissy" but not so intensely as to risk injury. Terry is very hungry after gym, but he must endure French class before lunch. Luckily, the French teacher is a bit of a comedian. Terry is one of the best students in French, so the teacher rarely calls on him. He tries to keep up to date, but is glad to see the other students play a more active role. When no one else can conjugate an irregular verb, the teacher calls on Terry, and luckily he remembers. The teacher smiles when his hero comes through, and Terry is glad he stayed up late the night before memorizing his French.

After French, Terry goes to his locker to get his lunch and then stands in the "milk" line to get a drink. He then goes to the table which he and some friends always sit at. They talk about classes, sports, and girls until everyone is finished eating. Terry then heads toward the school entrance to have a cigarette. After lunch he attends typing class and study hall. During study hall he talks with the teacher about the Drama Club. When the final school bell rings, he meets his girlfriend and then goes to the Debate Club meeting. He is the president of the Debate Club and leads the meeting. He talks with his friend the counselor (who is the club adviser) after the meeting and then goes home. He has dinner with his family. They watch television together. Terry does his homework, talks to his girlfriend on the phone, and goes to bed.

## THE PHYSICAL SETTING OF THE HIGH SCHOOL

The physical plant of the high school has effects on the pattern of student-teacher interactions, the formation of student groups, opportunities for privacy, and resources for a variety of types of learning. We begin this section with a brief historical review of the program for the construction of high school facilities in the United States, in the realization that many of the schools that were built over the past 60 years continue to serve our adolescent population as learning environments.

During the 1920s, one of the signs of the country's prosperity was the building of lavish, massive high schools. These structures were a symbol of civic pride, much like government buildings or national monuments. They were ostentatious, cold, and impersonal institutions "that daily processed several thousand students with efficiency and dispatch" (Krug, 1972, p. 43).

There were two main problems with the building program that was carried on in the 20s. First, most of the high schools that were planned early in the 20s were already overcrowded by 1930. During this period high school enrollments doubled, so that buildings that were expected to serve the community for 25–50 years were strained within a decade. Second, the money that was used to build the expensive, architecturally powerful high schools left little for other necessary resources, including libraries and budgets for teachers' salaries. These schools began the phase of burgeoning enthusiasm for secondary education by being overcrowded and underresourced.

During the depression years and World War II, few new high schools were built. The next phase of active school construction occurred during the late 1950s and early 1960s (American Association of School Administrators, 1958). Once again, the plan was for buildings that would meet community needs for 50 years or more. Greater emphasis was placed on planning and incorporating the views of major groups, including the school staff, the school board, government groups, contractors and builders, and educational consultants. The plan for these schools included attention to the site of the campus, especially the location and the number of acres for the building and the grounds; the adequacy of teaching space for various kinds of classroom activities; and flexibility of design, so that space could be redefined as needs changed. These

*Alex Webb/Magnum*

*The campus plan provides the model for many contemporary high school buildings.*

guidelines have influenced the designs for high schools that have been built in the past 20 years.

Contemporary plans for school buildings have included five different approaches (American Association of School Administrators, 1958):

1. *The campus plan*—a single-story, decentralized building with arms, branches, or interconnected building groups on a 40–100-acre site with parking facilities, sports fields, and outdoor classroom space.

2. *Schools within a school.* Small groups of 300 to 600 students across all grades form one school, with its own teachers, classrooms, and building areas. A single school may include three or four smaller schools. Major facilities, including the physical education facilities, the library, and the lunchroom, may be shared by all students, but students spend most of the school day with the smaller groups in the more limited physical settings.

3. *Consolidated or central schools*—a K–12 school that serves several rural areas, villages, or small suburbs. This involves a very flexible design in which some spaces are used and designed especially for the smallest children and others can be used comfortably by all groups.

4. *Adding to existing facilities.* This may involve renovating old buildings, adding new classroom space, or converting space from one use to another. Problems with adding to an existing old building include limitations in the flexibility of the total structure, the site of the school, and the already inadequate space of the old structure. On the other hand, some old school buildings have such special meaning to the community that they evoke commitment for preservation.

5. *Schools without walls*—schools that emphasize learning in community settings and community use of school resources. The students meet in small learning groups at the school for part of the day and take classes, have job training, or participate in community settings for the other part. Adults and students generate ideas for new classes or courses, which emerge and dissolve as interests change.

### The Psychological Effects of the Physical Environment

School size is the physical dimension of the high school that has been most systematically studied for its contribution to the students' adaptation to school. In an analysis of behavior in Kansas high schools, Barker and Gump (1964) were able to trace differences in participation and involvement in schools with enrollments of different sizes. The schools ranged in size from very small (total enrollment = 40) to very large (total enrollment = 2105). Some of the results of observing student participation in a wide variety of behavior settings were the following:

1.  Larger schools offer a wider variety of instruction. However, in order to observe a 17 percent increase in instructional variety, the enrollment had to double. What is more, the average student was not involved in a more varied academic curriculum at the large schools.
2.  The students at large schools engage in a few more kinds of extracurricular activities, but the students at small schools engage in a wider range of activities.
3.  The students in small schools are "performers" more than twice as often as the students in large schools. This means that they are twice as likely to be essential participants in some activity or setting.
4.  The students at large schools are more likely to experience satisfaction vicariously through their enrollment at the schools. The students at small schools are more likely to experience satisfaction directly through their own actions and participation.

In other words, the supposed benefits of the larger schools in being able to provide more resources and a greater diversity of courses and extracurricular activities is not actually translated into greater feelings of involvement or competence for the students who attend such schools. Rather, it is at the small schools that students are more likely to be needed to participate in activities so that those activities can be carried out.

Other studies of the effects of school size have shown that even the marginal students at small schools feel a strong sense of obligation to the school, whereas in the large schools the marginal students feel almost no obligation (Willems, 1967). Because of their greater involvement across a variety of settings, the students at smaller schools have a more complex conception of their school, including a greater number of dimensions along which they evaluate school settings and a more highly differentiated view of the participants and functions associated with the school (Wicker, 1968, 1969).

The spatial arrangement of the school can also contribute to the patterns of interaction. Myrick and Marx (1968) have described school designs along the dimension of cohesive versus isolating. Cohesive schools allow students to congregate in large groups, so that there are more frequent opportunities for informal interactions and more interactions with teachers outside the classroom. In a comparison of two high schools with the older, vertical building design and one school with the campus design, the campus plan was viewed as more isolating. At the campus school, more time was spent in moving from one classroom to another, there were fewer student-teacher interactions in the classroom, and there were fewer settings in which large groups could congregate.

Windows are another characteristic of school design. There was a period when architects experimented with the concept of the windowless school. This design was intended to eliminate the expenses due to window breakage and to force students to focus their attention on school activities rather than to permit gazing, daydreaming, or responses to distractions from the outside. When students at windowless schools were compared with students at schools that had windows, they were more likely to design school buildings with windows. Because they lacked the opportunity to look outside and let their thoughts wander for a few moments, the students at the windowless schools found it more difficult to concentrate and perform at a high level (Karmel, 1965; Architectural Research Laboratory, 1965).

One big problem that high schools encounter is difficulty in providing security for the building. Concerns about vandalism, student and teacher safety, and the monitoring of persons who enter or leave the school are all related to the school design, especially the placement of doorways, street-level windows, and courtyard areas. Campus schools with many branching arms and corridors are vulnerable to intruders. A design that may have originally been intended to permit free access to the school building for students and teachers may be gradually modified by locking most of the entrances or by stationing student or adult guards in the hallways. The problem with creating security and surveillance measures to protect students is that the students themselves may feel that these measures are working to "lock" them into the school rather than to keep trouble out.

## THE PROGRAMMATIC EMPHASES OF THE HIGH SCHOOL: WHAT DO STUDENTS NEED TO KNOW?

The question of the content or orientation of the high school curriculum has been a focus of continuous debate since the early 1900s, when the decision to make high school attendance compulsory was being forged (Krug, 1972). In 1918 the U.S. Bureau of Education published the *Cardinal Principles of Secondary Education,* in which seven objectives were stated that became the object of curriculum revision and reform. These objectives were health, citizenship, vocation, the worthy use of leisure, worthy home membership, ethical character, and the command of fundamental processes. The press in these early years was to move away from a college preparatory function that mimicked the private academies and to offer a curriculum that would be relevant to the immediate and future occupational and family needs of the majority of high school students. Despite the involvement of many schools with curriculum reform and the dramatic increase in high school enrollment, at the end of the 1920s Latin, ancient history, medieval and modern history, English composition and English literature, and mathematics remained the mainstay of most high school programs.

In fact, the question about what the high school student really needs to know has not yet been satisfactorily resolved. As the diversity of students increases and the demands on the high school to perform a variety of training and socialization functions increase, the question of the content and structure of the high school curriculum becomes increasingly problematic. In his analysis of the American high school, Conant (1959) identified three main objectives of the comprehensive high school: "First, to provide a general education for all the future citizens; second, to provide good elective programs for those who wish to use their acquired skills immediately on graduation; third, to provide satisfactory programs for those whose vocations will depend on their subsequent education in a college or university" (p. 17). Clear as these objectives may appear to be, the diversity of the American student population makes them quite difficult to attain. Several questions should serve to clarify the problematic nature of devising a high school curriculum that would satisfy Conant's three objectives.

## General Education

Let us begin with the goal for general education. What is the relevant content that should be part of the education of all future citizens? Is there any course content that is essential for adult functioning or for participation as a citizen? Is this core of information best communicated through separate courses in such subjects as history, English literature, and mathematics, or would it be more appropriately communicated through a topical integration of subjects, as in the study of democracy or the problem of poverty in America? Perhaps the core experience is not the assimilation of knowledge but experience in learning methods of problem solving or strategies for gathering information. In other words, it could be argued that there are no content areas that should be learned by all students, that the development of conceptual approaches allowing students to ask their own questions and seek their own answers should be the focus of general education. Yet another point of view in that the general education of all students should focus on personal enhancement, that is, the appreciation of beauty; of poetry, art, and music; of authentic inspirational experiences. In this sense, the goal of a general education would be to humanize students, to give them a glimpse of what is noble and admirable about human accomplishments.

## Vocational Training

The objective of vocational training, "the use of acquired skills immediately on graduation," raises still other difficult questions. How should work experience be incorporated into the secondary school program? Should all students be prepared to use some acquired skills immediately on graduation? How can the school make its resources available to students who work?

The goal of vocational preparation has always been a major objective of the American public high school (Deal and Roper, 1978). It has also been subjected to considerable criticism. Students in vocational programs may not have access to other academic experiences. The training for many occupations is outmoded, so that students who graduate from high school do not have the skills they need to function on the job. The range of career directions offered in the vocational curriculum has been limited, so that adolescents are not free to explore the variety of career directions that may exist in the community. Recent recommendations on high school reform emphasize the need to collaborate with community industries, business leaders, and professionals in the development of the vocational curriculum. Industry might support the purchase of modern equipment so that high school students could receive more appropriate training. On-the-job training could be incorporated into the high school program. Students could have the opportunity for some vocational experimentation before selecting one area of training (Porter, 1975; Brown, 1973). Because of the high cost of a college education and the reduced vocational advantage of having a college degree, more and more communities are increasing the vocational emphasis of the high school. The notion that all students should leave school with a vocational skill, whether or not they plan to attend college, is gaining acceptance. Having a "marketable skill" increases the adolescent's sense of competence, reduces his or her dependence on parents for financial support, and makes college attendance an option rather than a necessity.

Some advance the view that the high school should offer not only vocational training but also a service experience for all students. This view emphasizes the need of students to feel responsible, to experience a commitment to their community. It also reflects the reality that high school students represent a virtually untapped

resource of human energy, ideas, and competences that could benefit the community (Havighurst, 1966). Rather than sequester high
school students from their communities, this goal would move more
adolescents into interaction with other age groups, other socioeconomic, religious, and cultural groups. It would give high school
students some experience in providing help, entertainment, service,
or companionship to those in the community who might benefit
from such efforts.

## College Preparation

The third objective in Conant's assessment involved college preparation. Once again, many questions arise. Who should have access
to college preparatory courses? As we mentioned in our discussion
of tracking (Chapter 5), for some students the decision to follow
a general or a vocational curriculum can eliminate the option of
college preparatory courses as early as the seventh or eighth grade.
Because many schools rank their students on the basis of the grades
earned in each course, students may avoid more difficult, advanced-
level courses in order to maintain their grade point average. In
smaller schools, it is difficult to offer high-level courses because
the demand for them is so low. Many students who plan to go
on to college complete their high school requirements in less than
four years. They might benefit by taking courses at junior colleges
or four-year colleges rather than continuing to take advanced-level
high school courses.

The challenge of the high school is to design a curriculum that
is truly responsive to the individual needs of students. This means
a curriculum that offers encouragement, stimulation, and support
to students who have a history of poor performance and alienation
from school as well as students who are highly motivated and
have continuing academic aspirations. The curriculum has to respond to students whose native language may not be English, who
come to high school with minimal reading skills, who are ridiculed
by parents or peers for spending time at school, or who have very
limited ideas about how to survive as adults in the community
(Ravitch, 1978). The curriculum has to be designed so that it offers
students a variety of ways to learn, a sense of personal accomplishment, and a growing respect for their own competences and talents.
Amid all of this, however, the recent call for a return to basics
reminds us of the essential need for a literate population. The high
school must develop competences in reading, spoken and written
communication, fundamental mathematics, and the principles of
health care. The high school must provide all of its students with
the tools for both survival and growth.

## Directions for Change

In 1973, the National Commission on the Reform of Secondary Education published its recommendations. This report must be seen in the light of certain historical realities. During the 1960s, increased funds were provided for innovation and experimentation in the public schools. The experiments focused heavily on new methods of instruction that could be flexible and responsive to individual differences in students' interests, background, and competences. Among the projects that received funding were team teaching, programmed instruction, computer-assisted instruction, learning centers, modular scheduling, and the formulation of behavioral objectives. During the same period, a series of troubles grew in the public schools, including a decline in achievement scores, especially in city schools; an increase of crime in schools, including assaults on teachers and students; and decrease in school attendance. As we look to the future, the diversity of students is likely to remain high, but the absolute number of students will decrease. The Census Bureau has projected a decrease of over 2 million in the population of secondary school age between 1973 and 1984. Declining enrollments will confront high schools with the task of meeting diverse needs with reduced resources. This makes changes in the high school curriculum essential. In particular, the changes must include making greater use of existing community resources; providing diverse routes to education, not all of which are offered by the high school itself; and reducing the high school's expenditure of energy on custodial or control functions for students who would rather not be in school. In this context, the 32 recommendations of the National Commission on the Reform of Secondary Education can be taken as guidelines for strengthening secondary education, not for abolishing it.

---

RECOMMENDATIONS FOR IMPROVING SECONDARY EDUCATION

The reform of secondary education cannot be accomplished by educators working alone. It requires the ingenuity and assistance of many peole in the community served by a particular school. The recommendations of the Commission must be considered in this framework.

Recommendation No. 1: Defining Secondary School Expectations

Every secondary school and its subordinate departments must formulate a statement of goals and develop performance criteria for students. Goals and objectives should be published in information bulletins for students and parents and be posted in a conspicuous place within the school building.

Recommendation No. 2: Community Participation in Determining Secondary School Expectations

Schools will not be able to achieve their purposes without increased help from the people in the communities they serve. Communities must participate in the formulation of goals and in continuing efforts to refine and adapt the statements of goals and objectives. The communities as a whole, not solely the subsection called schools, must achieve the goals.

### Recommendation No. 3: The Basis for Curricular Revision

The high schools should no longer be required to perform purely custodial functions. Attempts to keep in school adolescents who do not wish to be there damage the environment for learning. The content of traditional high school curricula should be revised to eliminate busy-work components designed merely to occupy the time of adolescents who are in school only because the law requires it. Revitalization of the curriculum will require attention to the earlier maturation of adolescents. Intelligent evaluation of curricular revision must grow from valid measurements of the degree to which students are achieving the stated goals and objectives of their school.

### Recommendation No. 4: Teacher Training

Teacher training institutions should revise their programs so that prospective teachers are exposed to the variety of teaching and learning options in secondary education. New teachers should be able to work in several instructional modes.

Extensive in-service programs should be instituted to retrain teachers presently employed to equip them with a greater variety of approaches and skills. This need will become increasingly acute as the decline in birth rate encumbers the schools with aging teaching staffs.

### Recommendation No. 5: Bias in Textbooks

State legislatures must ensure that procedures are established so that textbooks and materials used in the schools do not present inaccurate accounts of the contributions of various ethnic groups or inaccurate portrayals of the role of women.

### Recommendation No. 6: Bias in Counseling

Counselors should ensure that all students, regardless of sex or ethnic background, are afforded equal latitude and equally positive guidance in making educational choices.

### Recommendation No. 7: Affirmative Action

Every high school should establish an affirmative action committee composed of students, former students, faculty, and community representatives. The purpose of his committee is to examine and report to the administration on instances of inequality and discrimination involving students or groups of students at the school.

### Recommendation No. 8: Expanding Career Opportunities

Secondary schools must realign their curricula to provide students with a range of experiences and activities broad enough to permit them to take full advantage of career opportunities in their communities. To meet this objective, basic components of the school program will have to be offered in the late afternoon or in the evening for some students.

### Recommendation No. 9: Career Education

Career education advisory councils including representatives of labor, business, community, students, and former students should be established to assist in planning and implementing career education programs in comprehensive high schools.

Career awareness programs should be initiated as an integral part of the curriculum to assure an appreciation of the dignity of work.

Opportunities for exploration in a variety of career clusters should be available to students in grades 8 through 10.

In grades 11 and 12, students should have opportunities to acquire hard skills in a career area of their choice. This training should involve experience in the world outside school and should equip the student with job-entry skills.

Recommendation No. 10: Job Placement

Suitable job placement must be an integral part of the career education program for students planning to enter the labor force upon leaving school. Secondary schools should establish an employment office staffed by career counselors and clerical assistants. The office should work in close cooperation with the state employment services. Agencies certifying counselors for secondary schools should require such counselors to show experience in job placement as a condition for granting initial certification.

Recommendation No. 11: Global Education

The education of the nation's adolescents must be superior to that of their parents. Part of this superiority must be an enhanced sense of the globe as the human environment, and instruction to this end must reflect not only the ancient characteristics of the world, but emerging knowledge of biological and social unity. All secondary school students should receive a basic global education.

New instructional material for global education must be prepared if this recommendation is to be effective. State departments of education should require teacher training institutions to design programs which prepare teachers to present such programs.

Recommendation No. 12: Alternative Paths to High School Completion

A wide variety of paths leading to completion of requirements for graduation from high school should be made available to all students. Individual students must be encouraged to assume major responsibility for the determination of their educational goals, the development of the learning activities needed to achieve those goals, and the appraisal of their progress.

Recommendation No. 13: Local Board Responsibilities for Funding Alternatives

Whenever a student chooses an acceptable alternative to the comprehensive high school, local school boards should fund his education at the level of current expenditure computed for other students.

Recommendation No. 14: Credit for Experience

Secondary schools should establish extensive programs to award academic credit for accomplishment outside the building, and for learning that occurs on the job, whether the job be undertaken for pay, for love, or for its own sake. Community involvement will, of course, be required in such a program and should be as encompassing as possible.

Recommendation No. 15: Secondary Level Examination Program

The College Level Examination Board should expand its College Level Examination Program to include a comparable Secondary Level Examination Program. The tests should be routinely administered quarterly or monthly to help adolescents to obtain credit for work done outside the classroom.

### Recommendation No. 16: Broadcast Television

Major funding sources, including both foundations and the National Institute of Education, should initiate and support extensive research into the influence of television on students' attitudes, perceptions, and life styles. The purpose of this research should be to suggest changes in school curricula and instructional approach.

The broadcasting industry should establish media fellowships designed to afford secondary school teachers and instructional leaders the opportunity to study the use of broadcast commercial television for educational purposes.

### Recommendation No. 17: Classroom Use of Broadcast Material

Copyright laws and union contracts should be written to make sure that classroom use of broadcast materials copied off the air is not unnecessarily restricted. Television programs should never be asked to carry instructional burdens alone. Books and pamphlets must be specially and carefully prepared to accompany all instruction via television. Both the instructional television program and the printed materials should be available in public libraries as well as in schools.

### Recommendation No. 18: Cable Television

When cable franchises are awarded, the local school system should have exclusive use of three channels during the daytime, with possible use of more as needed. At least one—and preferably all three—of these cable channels should continue to be available for nighttime viewing by school students or for purposes of adult education.

### Recommendation No. 19: Flexibility of Alternative Programs

Differing time sequences—hourly, daily, weekly, yearly—must be made available so that educational programs can be adapted to the needs of individual students.

Schools are already moving away from the Carnegie Unit and are beginning to grant credit on the basis of competence, demonstrated experience, and a host of other assessments. It is recommended that this practice be expanded and that the Carnegie Unit become merely one of the alternative ways of granting credit.

### Recommendation No. 20: Rank in Class

Articulation between secondary schools and post-secondary schools must be improved, with each level seeking to support the educational efforts of the other. Personnel representing both levels must cooperatively develop alternatives to grade-point average and rank in class for assessing the scope and quality of the education received by students at the secondary level. High schools should stop calculating student rank in class for any purpose.

### Recommendation No. 21: Planning for School Security

All secondary school systems should develop security plans to safeguard students, faculty, equipment, and facilities. Specific procedures must be developed for faculty members to follow in case of disruption.

### Recommendation No. 22: Records of Violence

State legislation should be enacted to require principals to file a detailed report on all serious assaults within schools. The information contained should form a data base from which security personnel could identify potential trouble areas and move to alleviate future problems.

## Recommendation No. 23: Code of Student Rights and Obligations

Every secondary school should develop and adopt a code of student rights and obligations. This code should be published and distributed to every student. It should include all school rules, regulations, and procedures for suspension and expulsion with explanations of how students can defend themselves through established process.

## Recommendation No. 24: School Newspapers

A school newspaper is a house organ which is operated, financed, and therefore controlled by the school system, which may be legally liable for its contents. In cases where students and school administrators become deadlocked over censorship, a student-faculty-community committee should decide the issue. Some schools may find it necessary to withdraw financial support, allowing students complete freedom of expression in what would then be entirely their own publication, with a corresponding liability for what is printed.

## Recommendation No. 25: Right of Privacy

A student's school records must contain only factual information necessary to the educative process. The entire file must be available at all times for review by students and their parents but must not be accessible to "persons not in interest." Records should be forwarded to another school system, university, or prospective employer only at the written request of the student, his parents, or the receiving school.

That part of a student's records which pertains to his mental health should contain only entries made under the direction of the student's physician and must be kept separately from his academic records. The complete record or any of its contents should be released only to the student, his parents, or to his physician at the student's or parent's request.

## Recommendation No. 26: Corporal Punishment

Several states have outlawed corporal punishment with no resulting loss in control or authority. Corporal punishment should be abolished by statute in all states. In the modern world, corporal punishment is necessarily "cruel and unusual."

## Recommendation No. 27: Student Activities

Scholarship should not be a requisite for participation in sports, band, singing, cheerleading, or other student activities important to the social development of adolescents. Neither the local school nor state activities associations should establish scholarship standards. Any student in good standing in a school should have the right to participate in any of the school's activities with the exception of honor societies specifically established to reward scholarship.

## Recommendation No. 28: Compulsory Attendance

If the high school is not to be a custodial institution, the state must not force adolescents to attend. Earlier maturity—physical, sexual, and intellectual—requires an option of earlier departure from the restraints of formal schooling.

The formal school-leaving age should be dropped to age fourteen. Other programs should accommodate those who wish to leave school, and employment laws should be rewritten to assure on-the-job training in full-time service and work.

### Recommendation No. 29: Free K–14 Public Education

The Congress of the United States in conjunction with state legislatures should enact legislation that will entitle each citizen to fourteen years of tuition-free education beyond kindergarten, only eight of which would be compulsory. The remaining six years should be available for use by anyone at any stage of his life. Congressional involvement is essential to assure equal access in an age of interstate mobility.

### Recommendation No. 30: Youth Organizations

The National Association of Secondary School Principals, a professional organization for school administrators, currently operates two of the largest organizations affecting public high school youth: the National Student Council Association and the National Honor Society. The principals' group should dissociate itself from these organizations and help them become independent national youth organizations.

### Recommendation No. 31: Sexism

School administrators and school boards, at both the state and local levels, must set forth commitments to eliminate all vestiges of sexism in the schools.

Areas of immediate concern and equal employment and treatment of the sexes in instructional and administrative positions, equal opportunities for female students to participate in all curricular areas, including career education, and the elimination of all courses required of only one sex.

Individual teachers should make sure they are not focusing their teaching toward either sex.

All female students who become pregnant should be permitted to remain in school for the full term of pregnancy if they wish to do so and their physician considers it feasible. They should be permitted to return to school following childbirth as soon as released by their physician. There must be no denial of the right to participate in activities because of pregnancy or motherhood, whether the girl is wed or unwed.

### Recommendation No. 32: Females in Competitive Team Sports

School boards and administrators at the local level must provide opportunities for female students to participate in programs of competitive team sports that are comparable to the opportunities for males. The programs must be adequately funded through regular school budgets.

Outstanding female athletes must not be excluded from competition as members of male teams in noncontact sports. The fact that a school offers the same team sport for girls should not foreclose this option.

State activities associations should be required by statute to eliminate from their constitutions and bylaws all constraints to full participation in competitive team sports by females.

If state activities associations are to continue to have jurisdiction over female sports, they should be required by state statute to have equal sex representation on all boards supervising boys' and girls' athletics.

# THE IMPACT OF THE HIGH SCHOOL ON INTELLECTUAL DEVELOPMENT

What does going to high school do for the mind? This is, perhaps, an audacious question to ask. Obviously there must be some intellectual benefits to four years of secondary schooling, or why spend the time and money on such an enterprise? Yet it is surprising how little documentation there is about the intellectual growth that results from high school attendance. In this section, we consider three sources of influence on intellectual development during the high school years: the curriculum and participation in the school program, involvement with teachers, and peer influences on achievement. Taking these three factors together, we begin to get a picture of the ways in which the high school can contribute to the acquisition of knowledge, receptivity to new ideas, and the development of educational and occupational aspirations that will involve increasingly complex intellectual skills.

## The High School Curriculum

One part of attending high school is participation in a program of study. Although this may not be the most memorable or satisfying part of one's high school experience, it certainly deserves examination as a potential contributor to intellectual growth. Is there any evidence that intellectual competences are enhanced due to participation in the high school curriculum? As you might expect, the answer to this question is equivocal.

Shaycoft (1967) reported that the results of a three-year follow-up of students who had participated in Project Talent in 1960 as 9th graders and were tested again in 12th grade. The results suggested clear increases over the three years in information and ability in school-related subjects, including law, accounting, business, electronics, mechanics, and mathematics. Specific course work was correlated with gains in particular test scores. Some examples include improvement in the Mathematics Information and Introductory and Advanced High School Mathematics tests, which was associated with taking math courses, and on the Word Functions in Sentences test, which was associated with the study of foreign languages.

Of all the variables associated with gains in achievement during the high school years, the best predictor of increases in scores was the initial aptitude of the student at ninth grade. In other words, those students who gained the most at the 12th grade testing were those who had already shown a high level of intellectual competence and information when they entered high school. Those students who gained little or who scored lower in the 12th grade were already among the lowest ability group upon entrance to high school. In fact, some evidence suggests that 75 percent of students who will drop out of high school have had their first failure by the fourth grade. Early failures in English (especially reading) and math seem to spread to other subjects, so that by the time students who have had such failures reach high school they do not have the basic skills to perform at the high school level (Fitzsimmons et al., 1969). These patterns of achievement and failure suggest that the high school does not basically alter the ordering of students. It has not, in the past, effectively intervened to prevent school failures or to motivate the "middle-level student to greater intellectual involvement. Rather, the amount of intellectual growth that occurs during the high school years appears to reflect the individual's initial interests, competences, and investment in academic achievement.

What about the long-term effects of high school attendance? Are adults who have graduated from high school more knowledgeable than those who have not? Do students who drop out of school suffer intellectually, or occupationally? In an effort to evaluate the enduring effects of education, Hyman, Wright, and Reed (1975) compared responses to national surveys that were conducted at four time periods—in the early 50s, the late 50s, the early 60s, and the late 60s. At each time period, four age cohorts were analyzed; adults aged 25–36, 37–48, 49–60, and 61–72. Within each age cohort, the subjects were categorized by the amount of education they had received. Thus comparisons could be made for a single age cohort that had been educated during different periods of history as well as for changes in information or knowledge at various age levels. The general findings were that for all four periods studied, increments in education were associated with greater amounts of information in both academic and public affairs areas. Subjects who had attended school for more years were both more knowledgeable and more receptive to new information than subjects who had attended school for fewer years. In every area of information, subjects who had completed high school were more highly informed than those who had only completed elementary school, no matter how old the subjects were when they were tested or when they attended school. In thinking about the vast increase in the proportion of adolescents who have been enrolled in secondary schools since 1900, we cannot help but be optimistic about the increased pool of adults who, by virtue of school attendance, have gained access to a wide pool of information and ideas.

The counterarguments about the effectiveness of secondary schooling do not deny that adolescents learn something by attending school. Rather, they emphasize that schools do not correct disadvantages which result from socioeconomic status or ethnic prejudice, that schools do not intervene to correct the course of failing or alienated students, and that schools do not achieve the kind of intellectual impact on highly motivated students that they might (Jencks et al., 1972; Coleman et al., 1966).

## Involvement with Teachers

Teachers can have both positive and negative effects on their students' intellectual growth. On the positive side, we know that teachers can encourage independent thinking and questioning, that they can provide opportunities to develop areas of interest and expertise, that they can confront students with ideas that challenge the students' existing concepts and stimulate the formation of a

*The photography of H. Armstrong Roberts*

*Interaction with teachers can stimulate new interests and new ideas.*

new conceptual organization. Through informal interaction with teachers, students can begin to identify with the intellectual interests that teachers express and with the aspirations for academic achievement teachers hold for their students (P. Newman, 1978).

In some cases, teachers play an important role in encouraging students to attend college or in counseling them about areas of talent that they should pursue. Athletic coaches, for example, play a very important role in encouraging high school athletes to attend college. This role is especially strong for students from lower-class families and for athletes who are most heavily involved in the sport they play (Snyder, 1972, 1975).

On the negative side, teachers can be indifferent, unfair, biased, belittling, or even punitive in response to students' academic efforts. In a paper on student evaluation and victimization, Poole (1976) cites the following example:

During 1st marking period of my senior year of high school, a student was caught copying from my paper during an English exam. The teacher assumed I was letting the other student cheat so he gave us both a 0%." (p. 341)

In addition to the use of arbitrary or punitive evaluations, teachers' marks can also be inconsistent across types of students. For example, McCandless, Roberts, and Starnes (1972) found that teachers' grades were rather highly correlated with achievement test scores for disadvantaged students and black students, but only minimally correlated with achievement test scores for advantaged students and white students. For white boys, grades and achievement scores correlated $-.01$, an indication of almost complete independence. For disadvantaged girls, grades and achievement scores correlated $.64$, suggesting a rather high degree of interdependence. In other words, teachers' grades are more subjective and less closely related to tested competence for some groups than for others. This subjectivity may well interfere with the students' capacity to make a realistic assessment of his or her intellectual ability.

## Peer Influences on Intellectual Achievement

In an early analysis of the adolescent subculture within the high school, Coleman (1960, 1961) argued that the peer group does not really value academic achievement. This position was based on the fact that academic achievement does not provide peer group status, that it does not lead to membership in the "leading crowd," that it is not highly visible or dramatically rewarded by the school, and that it is not a characteristic for which either boys or girls are eager to be remembered in years to come. Behind this picture of an anti-intellectual or intellectually indifferent peer culture is the recognition that peer pressure and norms for popularity or acceptance can contribute to adolescent achievement and educational aspirations (McDill, Meyers, and Rigsby, 1967). The desirability or undesirability of intellectual competence among a group of friends can influence individuals to strive for good grades, to become involved in extracurricluuar projects, to participate actively in class discussions, or to reject any signs of academic involvement. Damico (1975) found that clique membership was a better predictor of high school grades than were aptitude scores, race, or sex. She argued that within the same high school class, some peer groups exert positive influences toward academic achievement and others reject intellectual goals in favor of athletics, social activities, or popularity. The important point is that the peer group exerts its own influence on its members' commitment to academic or intellectual goals. Depending on the stability of the peer group and on the extent of peer group identification, influences on achievement could be potentially more enduring and more predictive of future educational and occupational decisions than either the high school curriculum or the teachers.

## THE IMPACT OF THE HIGH SCHOOL ON SOCIAL DEVELOPMENT

The development of social competences that takes place within the context of the high school is a vital part of the total learning experience, even though it may be a less direct objective of the institution than cognitive growth. Through daily interactions with teachers and peers, through participation in a variety of school activities, and through various demands for decision making, students have the opportunity to elaborate their social skills. Although we are intuitively confident about the contribution of high school attendance to social development, the evidence on this issue is scattered and unsystematic (McClintock, 1979). In this section, we can only begin to point out a number of areas in which the potential for growth seems quite likely. Four themes are considered: learning that results from participation in a complex social institution, involvement with adults as role models and targets for identification, participation in the social status system of the peer culture, and political socialization.

### Participation in a Complex Institution

As we have already discussed, the high school is an elaborate institution with a variety of role groups striving to fill a diverse set of functions. As members of this organization, students acquire skills and concepts that have application to other organizational structures that they may encounter in adult life. This kind of learning includes participation in predefined roles as student, school leader, athlete, student government representative, or yearbook photographer. In addition to learning the specific roles one plays, one learns about the other roles, gains an appreciation of the interrelatedness of roles, and develops a sense of readiness to play any of a variety of roles that are required by the organization (Katz and Kahn, 1978).

Part of membership in the high school organization is learning to identify the norms for behavior. Probably the most agreed-upon norm that students perceive is the expectation to conform. This includes expectations to obey school rules, to do what teachers say, and to cooperate with classroom goals (Ringness, 1967; Martin, 1972; P. Newman, 1979). The norm derives from the school's need to work with large numbers of students and to maintain an orderly atmosphere. Students are expected to internalize school rules and procedures, functioning without much personal supervision or individual attention in accordance with a prescribed program of daily activities. To ensure conformity, the school uses such surveillance techniques as cameras in the hallways; loudspeakers in the classrooms; roving principals or assistant principals who patrol bathrooms, locker rooms, and study halls; and security guards. Disciplinary techniques, including corporal punishment, reprimand, detention, fines, conferences, suspension, and expulsion, are all part of the arsenal of strategies that are available for promoting rule conformity within the school structure (Findley and O'Reilly, 1971). Even students who do not experience these discipline techniques directly know of their existence. Students are well aware of the teacher's role as a disciplinarian, one who is responsible for maintaining rule compliance, as well as their own responsibility to abide by and enforce school rules.

Of course, schools differ in the intensity or severity with which they enforce rules. Some schools are literally under siege. Student riots, fights, or assaults on teachers and the presence of dope pushers, loan sharks, or organized gambling in the school push many schools into programs of heavy surveillance and strict rule enforcement. At other schools, however, the students may not even be certain what the school rules are or whether they have violated any of these rules. Nonetheless, even in very open, permissive school environments students are expected to attend class, to arrive on time, to abide by rules about leaving the school grounds, and to respect certain settings as "quiet" areas which are used for studying or conferences. Although students may differ in their willingness to conform or in their approval of existing regulations, they are all aware that the expectation for conformity is a central component of the norm structure.

Another aspect of the school as a complex social organization is the opportunity that the school provides to participate in a variety of school-sponsored extracurricular activities. Participation in these activities gives students visibility and some degree of status in the school (Jones, 1958; Coleman, 1961). Although in many schools only about one third of the students are actually involved in school activities, such involvement does provide opportunities to develop technical skills and to experience leadership during the high school years. In our discussion of school size, we noted that while larger schools offer a more diverse array of activities, students in smaller schools participate in a greater number of activities. This results in a greater sense of involvement in or commitment to the smaller school (Barker and Gump, 1964; Wicker, 1968; Willems, 1967).

In a sense, the high school offers a special opportunity for participation. This is a time when a student with minimal training or skill can take on an important function for the school community as a member of the yearbook or newspaper staff, as a participant in the drama club or the school orchestra, as a leader in student government, or as a member of an athletic team. For many students who do not attend college, this is the last opportunity for such activities. For others, the period of young adulthood is too full of commitments to work and family to permit this kind of "extracurricular" involvement. For still others, a skill that is discovered through a high school activity may become a lifelong career direction or a lifelong leisure-time activity.

## Involvement with Teachers

In general, high school students tend to have more role-bound and less personalized relationships with teachers than do elementary school students. This is probably because that high school teachers encounter many groups of students every day and have only brief opportunities for interaction with students outside the classroom. However, when teachers and students have more frequent opportunities for informal interactions across several school settings, students tend to feel more comfortable about their interactions with teachers and tend to perceive their teachers as being more interested in them as individuals (P. Newman, 1979). This ability to respond to students as individuals is a central component of successful teaching (Stern, 1963; Getzels, 1969; Alexander et al., 1971; Martin, 1972). A teacher's interest and supportiveness can increase both academic performance and friendly, cooperative behavior.

Fisher (1976) developed a four-week consultation program to work on the nature of the student-teacher relationship at the high school level. Groups of four students, three teachers, and an outside consultant met weekly to discuss perceptions, problems, and directions for change in student-teacher relations. From these discussions five areas of concern emerged:

1. The control of daily behavior. The students saw teachers as overly preoccupied with enforcing rules.
2. Outmoded and formal instruction. The students sought more flexibility and individuality in instruction.
3. Lack of respect. The students saw many teachers as sarcastic, unresponsive, and mistrustful of students.
4. Lack of social status. The students sought more collegial, less submissive relationships with teachers.
5. Lack of hope about change. The students felt that the teachers who should change the most would be the least interested in adolescents' needs.

These concerns do not mean that students have no positive interactions or relations with teachers. In fact, many students identify certain teachers as responsive, deeply involved, and intellectually inspiring. What these concerns do indicate is the importance of the socioemotional element of the student-teacher relationship. Students look to their teachers as potential role models, as targets for identification. They want to be treated as people with legitimate interests and needs. They also want to be able to use their teachers as sources of information about adult life.

## Participation in the Social Status System

There is considerable evidence that a dynamic peer structure operates within the high school environment (Coleman, 1961; Trickett, Kelly, and Todd, 1972; Jones, 1976). The precise impact of this peer status system on social development is not clear. Several kinds of learning are going on at the same time as one confronts an existing status structure. First, students learn to identify the existing groups and their defining features. They know what each group wears, where its members hang out, what their reputation is in the school, and what kinds of activities they are likely to engage in. One might call this the ability to read the status system. This kind of social skill is essential to the adaptive efforts of the student at the school and also contributes to later participation in the adult community.

Among the paths to status are physical appearance, including early maturation for boys; good looks and good grooming; athletic ability; leadership in school activities; and popularity (Jones, 1958; Coleman, 1961). In his analysis of ten midwestern high schools, Coleman (1961) was discouraged to find that the adolescent culture gave little emphasis to academic achievement as a prerequisite for status or popularity. Two more recent analyses of this problem suggest that adolescents may be developing their status system in response to patterns of reinforcement from the community and the school. Friesen (1968) analyzed the responses of Canadian students about characteristics that were descriptive of the leading crowd, characteristics that they perceived to be important for success in life, and characteristics that they perceived as important to their own future. Only 2.5 percent of the samples saw academic excellence as important for membership in the leading crowd, and only 15.6 percent viewed academic excellence as important to success in life. However, 80 percent saw academic excellence as important for their own future. Thus, although adolescents perceive the immediate and even the long-term rewards of academic excellence to be less important than friendliness, good looks, or personality, they recognize the importance of the sequential chain of life events that are tied to academic achievement in their culture.

Eitzen (1975) asked high school males the same question that Coleman used in his study from the 1950s:

If you could be remembered here at school for one of the three things below, which would you want it to be?

Athletic star
Brilliant student
Most popular

Table 7-1 compares the responses of Coleman's and Eitzen's samples to these choices. Athletic star continues to be viewed as a desirable characteristic for status in the high school and as an "unusual achievement." In the more recent sample, the importance of the brilliant student has dropped somewhat as a valued source of status.

Eitzen suggests that the importance of athletics for high school

Table 7-1: Percent of High School Boys Who Would Rather Be Remembered as . . . in 1950 and 1970

|  | Coleman | Eitzen |
|---|---|---|
| Athletic star | 44% | 47% |
| Brilliant student | 31 | 23 |
| Most popular | 25 | 30 |

boys varies, depending on characteristics of the school, the boy, and the community. The role of athletic star is less important to seniors than to sophomores. It is more important to students who are highly involved in school activities than to those who are uninvolved. Athletics is seen as a greater source of status in small than in large schools, and in highly structured, authoritarian schools than in permissive schools. Finally, athletics is less important in large communities with a high percentage of professionals and with comparatively few (less than 5 percent) very poor families. Although sports continues to be a highly visible area for success in high school, variations in student responses suggest that aspects of the school organization and the opportunity structure of the larger community clearly feed into the status characteristics of high school athletics.

In addition to learning to read the status system, adolescents eventually come to identify with some peer group. As we discussed in Chapter 6, involvement with the peer group and commitment to a particular group of friends provide the adolescent with a sense of peer understanding and support. They also carry pressures for peer conformity. We have argued that peer group identification is of central importance for the formation of social skills that continue to be a vital part of adult life.

Finally, there is the reputational consequence of joining a particular peer group. As we noted in Chapter 6, there are a variety of peer groupings in every high school, each with its own characteristics and reputation. Once one is associated with the "elites" or the "greasers" or the "jocks" or the "hippies," certain school and community resources may open and others may close. Expectations that peers and adults hold for your behavior as a member of a group will influence their reactions and responses.

One senior who was involved in a small, low-status group whose members were identified by their use of drugs described the consequences for his reputation at school:

"I have a hard time being myself around *people in general,* 'cause like, I play a part, and as time progresses, you get tired of the part you're playing, and you try to change, and people act as if they expect you to be your old self . . . the drug-crazed hippy, which I play pretty good." (Gottlieb, 1975, p. 216)

Over time, participation in the social status system of the peer culture sensitizes adolescents to the costs and the benefits of certain kinds of reputations. In some smaller communities, one's reputation during high school can follow well into adult life, providing a positive "halo" effect on adult activities for some and isolating others (Jones, 1958). To some extent, once the status hierarchy

of the peer culture is established, it continues to have self-perpetu-
ating reputational features. Perhaps the early-maturing boys and
the good-looking girls did show some social maturity as they entered the high school scene. By the senior year, however, physical
maturation and social competence are well distributed among the
student population. Yet this early "elite" group continues to benefit
during its high school career from the status that it achieved during
the first months of high school. In this sense, adolescents learn
about the power of reputation and they begin to evaluate reputational claims in a more critical light.

## Political Socialization

The formulation of a political ideology is influenced both directly
and indirectly through the high school experience. Courses in American history and civics provide a structured exposure to the principles of political decision making and the democratic form of government. High school activities, especially student government and
student-faculty committees, offer students the opportunity to participate in decisions that will directly influence school life. Indirectly,
through conflicts with teachers, administrators, or peers, students
begin to recognize the effective strategies for conflict resolution.
They develop a sense of the patterns of power and influence in
the high school organization. In this regard, powerlessness is a
major source of the dissatisfaction that students express about
high school (Thornburg, 1975). Powerlessness is reflected in students' feelings that decisions are made arbitrarily, that many adults
are unwilling to make changes to meet student needs, and that
students have minimal responsibility for the decisions that directly
concern them (Fisher, 1976; Morgan and Wicas, 1972).

In an attempt to understand how students perceive conflicts in
their own school environment, Richards and DeCecco (1975) asked
junior and senior high school students to describe specific events
that involved conflicts over problems of democracy within the
school. In general, the students saw most conflicts as problems
in decision making. They tended to see only one strategy for conflict
resolution. These problems were most often resolved by the decision of an authority. In only 17 percent of the incidents did the
students mention negotiation as a strategy for resolution. The
younger students did not tend to differentiate their own position
from the point of view of the antagonist. The older students showed
an increasing ability to appreciate the different perspectives represented in the conflict. In general, students' direct experience with
civil liberties and the political process involves conflict over matters of self-governance and over individual rights that appear to

be violated by the authoritarian decision-making structure of the school. Students do not appear to have a varied repertoire of strategies for conflict resolution, nor do they report much variation in the models that adults provide for them.

Another view of the political socialization of high school students is provided by a comparison of students from the same high school graduation class four years after graduation (Montero, 1975). Each subject was asked to complete a ten-item Libertarian Index, each item of which was designed to test the subject's support of a provision of the Bill of Rights. The scores were divided at the median, giving two groups described as not highly libertarian and highly libertarian. For every item, more college students than high school graduates with no college gave libertarian responses. Seventy-five percent of the high school graduates, but only 27 percent of the college seniors, were characterized as not high on libertarianism. In this comparison, other factors come into play. Sex, social class, and religious affiliation are also related to libertarian values. Students who do not attend college may be expressing lower libertarian values due to the influences of these background characteristics as well as the influences of high school experience. Nonetheless, the two studies combined suggest that the high school environment does not generally provide a climate in which students learn that their rights will be protected or that they have some form of legitimate power to counteract the existing authority structure. This delay in political socialization has become particularly serious because of the lowered voting age. At 18, adolescents are still likely to be functioning within the framework of the political reality of their high school environment, even if they are recent graduates. They may not be certain enough of their own rights or clear enough about the strategies available to defend those rights if they continue to see political decisions in terms of their high school's authoritarian power structure.

## ADAPTATION TO THE HIGH SCHOOL ENVIRONMENT

Throughout this chapter we have described a number of ways in which high schools differ. When one looks more closely at the organization, the curricular emphasis, and the atmosphere, one notices important differences among institutions that are called high schools. Differences in physical design, in school size, in curricular emphasis, in control or surveillance, and in the quality and quantity of interactions among students and faculty all contribute to the quality of the environment to which a high school student must adapt.

Students, for their part, bring differences in competences, in expectations, and in aspirations that will guide their orientation to school. In earlier chapters we have described a variety of differences in physical, intellectual, and social development that will influence peer group membership, academic achievement, and the willingness to interact with adults. Adolescents differ in their physical size, in their level of intellectual development, in their predisposition to creative responses, in their needs for independence or dependence, in their orientations toward peers, and in their needs for affiliation. These and other differences make students more eager for some experiences than for others, more responsive to some opportunities than to others.

The question of adaptation, then, is the question of how students with diverse abilities and motives respond to the expectations, the demands, and the opportunities of the school environment. We anticipate a process of interaction in which students change in response to environmental realities and in which the schools change in response to the diverse needs of students. Neither the person nor the organization is static. Each has a history and a future. Although the students may despair over their powerlessness, the school must continue to meet student, parent, and community needs in order to survive.

What are some of the adaptations that students make to their schools? The examples that follow suggest a few of the very many ways in which students make unique responses to special school characteristics. The physical design of the school stimulates unique student uses. In the older school buildings, there were locker rooms in which students would congregate. In more modern school buildings, lockers line the hallways, limiting opportunities for student privacy. Thus, students create their own territories or regions in which friendship groups or classmates congregate. In one school, each class met at a particular window ledge or a particular area of the corridor. Sophomores did not sit on the junior ledge (Newman, 1971). Some school settings may be dominated by a deviant peer group. The students who want to smoke marijuana or drink alcohol may be found at a particular athletic field, in a certain bathroom, or in a particular part of the basement.

Adaptation also takes place in response to the size of the school. In the smaller schools, the greater need for students to run activities and to populate school events leads to greater student involvement and stronger commitment. Even students who are not heavily involved in school activities feel a strong sense of obligation to the smaller school. This kind of psychological investment seems to contradict expert views that we should move in the direction of eliminating small high schools in favor of larger, centralized schools that can offer a greater variety of resources and greater academic expertise. The fact of positive student adaptation to the smaller schools has contributed to the school-within-a-school model, in which an effort is made to preserve the characteristics of the small school.

Schools also differ in the quantity of student-teacher interaction that takes place across settings. Where the quantity of interaction is relatively high, students adapt by having more personal, informal interactions with teachers. Teachers are more likely to become objects of identification, so that students and teachers show more agreement about perceived norms and values. Where the quantity of interaction between students and teachers is low, students have a greater involvement with peers. In such schools, the peer culture is the more active socialization agent (P. Newman, 1979; Iacovetta, 1975).

Even within the same school, different subcultures adapt differently to the available resources. Gottlieb (1975) described two such subcultures as the "elites" and the "deviants." The elites are a high-status group whose members are visible participants in school activities and athletics. They are very competitive academically and tend to be concerned about their plans after graduation, particularly their admission to college. The deviants are a low-status group whose members are not highly involved in either academic or extracurricular activities. They are identified primarily by their excessive use of drugs.

The elites make particularly high use of school personnel for help in problem solving. Because of their high involvement in athletics, the coach is a particularly important school adult for elites. In contrast, peers are rarely mentioned as sources of help. Elites see peers as troubled by the same problems and hindered by a lack of experience and expertise.

Deviants look for help from people who are open, sincere, and accepting. Their criteria guide them to people who will accept them for who they are, without forcing them to put on a front. Thus, deviants are much more likely to find helpers among peers, siblings, or parents rather than school personnel. They identify only one or two school adults as approachable. In this group, any person who can help a deviant gain insight into his or her own problems is a valued helper. Experience, status, or authority in the school does not make school adults particularly useful resources if those adults hold a negative evaluation of this group of students.

A final example of adaptation to school is dropping out. If one thinks of involvement with school on a continuum from highly involved to highly alienated, dropping out might be viewed as an extreme expression of alienation. Studies of dropouts suggest that the socioeconomic class of the student's family is a very strong predictor of dropping out as well as a strong predictor of school success (Elliott, Voss, and Wendling, 1966; Bachman, Green, and Wirtanen, 1971; Alexander and Eckland, 1975). Students from lower socioeconomic levels are less likely to aspire to college; less likely to have high test scores in vocabulary, reading, or general intelligence; and more likely to experience early school failure. Although lower-class students may hold high aspirations for their future occupation, they are confronted by the daily reality of low status in the school because of their academic failure, their inability to conform to the expectations of their teachers, or their feeling that school simply does not teach useful or meaningful information.

The following responses from students who had dropped out of school suggest some of the ways that the school itself is seen as the primary alienating factor.

"I was mostly discouraged because I wasn't passing."

"I was failing, so I quit school. I was working and didn't have time to study. I wasn't interested in it either."

"School in general. It didn't teach me true things. It didn't teach me how to cope with society once I got out of school doors."

"They wanted me to do too much of what they wanted and none of what I wanted."

"They said I could drop out or they'd drop me out. They said I was a rebel. I wore my hair long." (Bachman et al., 1971, pp. 155 and 157)

These examples suggest that students can reach a point at which the effort to stay in school no longer seems worthwhile. What is more, the immediate rewards of having a full-time job may seem quite a bit more appealing than the continuation of a role that involves failure, submissiveness to authority, or learning "meaningless" material.

In earlier sections we have described some of the general effects that attending high school has on intellectual and social development. Participation in the high school environment fosters greater information, a more differentiated understanding of complex social institutions, and an ability to read the characteristics of the local peer group structure. In addition to these and other effects that we would expect from all high school settings, we have argued that there are specific adaptations that occur in certain kinds of schools.

The student in the small school is likely to be more involved in school activities. The student in the school with a high frequency of interactions with adults will develop more personal, less role-bound relationships with school adults. The student who is perceived as a deviant within the school is less likely to find help or problem-solving resources among school adults.

How enduring are these and other adaptations to specific characteristics of the school environment? The sparse evidence on this
question suggests that this depends on the degree of similarity
between the high school environment and subsequent environments. Students at small high schools, for example, are more likely
to remain high participants if they attend small colleges than if
they attend large colleges (Baird, 1969). Students who receive high
grades in high school are likely to achieve greater occupational
success than students with low high school grades (Hess, 1963).
Social involvement and high visibility in school activities are more
likely to endure if the student goes on to college or joins the military
service, where structured activities are also made available. They
are less likely to endure if the person moves from the student role
to participation in the worker, spouse, and parent roles (Jones,
1958; Hess, 1963).

On the other hand, some specific adaptations, such as dropping
out of school, are not necessarily predictive of future responses.
Although dropouts without a diploma have more trouble finding
work than do high school graduates, those who obtained employment did not show any disadvantage in salary and were as well
satisfied with their jobs as those with diplomas. In other words,
they did not respond to the work setting with the feelings of discouragement or alienation that characterized their response to school.
In fact, close to 75 percent of the dropouts expected to eventually
return to school to get their diploma (Bachman et al., 1971). This
suggests that the postschool environment can influence the reversal
of an adaptive response by offering new opportunities and new
responses to an individual's talents or competences.

## CHAPTER SUMMARY

The high school is a major educational institution which is encountered by over 90 percent of American adolescents. In this chapter we have described some characteristics of this institution, its
impact on intellectual and social development, and some of the
adaptive responses that students make to it.

The early 1900s marked a period of building high schools as
an expression of civic pride. This resulted in huge, impersonal buildings. More recent high schools have followed the campus design,
which uses more outdoor space and provides more flexibility of
function. The physical characteristics of the school can influence
patterns of interaction, the amount of student involvement in school
activities, and concerns about security.

The programmatic emphasis of the school has always been a
disputed issue. The early *Cardinal Principles* emphasized health,

citizenship, vocation, the worthy use of leisure, worthy home membership, ethical character, and the command of fundamental processes. These goals continue to deserve attention in the high school curriculum. Three basic questions about the high school program are how the high schools should handle the three objectives of general education, vocational training, and college preparation.

The effect of high school attendance on intellectual growth can be described as having more information about school-related topics. This gain is highly influenced by initial abilities, since those who gain the most begin with higher aptitudes in the ninth grade. The cognitive effects of high school attendance continue well into adulthood. Both peers and teachers can influence cognitive growth, depending on the extent to which they encourage achievement and educational aspirations.

High school attendance influences social development in both planned and unplanned ways. Students learn about participation in a complex social institution. They become involved with school adults. They observe and participate in the social status system of the peer culture. Their experience with the decision-making and conflict resolution strategies of the school contributes to their political socialization.

Adaptation to school can best be understood as the response of individual students with unique talents and needs to unique environmental characteristics. Examples of adaptation include the use of the school building, involvement in school activities, the pattern of interactions with teachers, the different uses of adult resources by different student subcultures, and dropping out of school. In general, we expect the patterns of specific adaptation that are learned in high school to endure insofar as students encounter similar subsequent environments.

# REFERENCES

Alexander, K. L., and Eckland, B. K.   School experience and status attainment. In S. E. Dragastin and G. H. Elder, Jr. (Eds.), *Adolescence in the life cycle: Psychological change and social context.* New York: Wiley, 1975. Pp. 25–47.

Alexander, L., Epson, B., Means, R., and Means, G.   Achievement as a function of teacher-initiated student-teacher personal interactions. *Psychological Reports,* 1971, *28,* 431–434.

American Association of School Administrators.   *The high school in a changing world: Thirty-sixth yearbook.* Washington, D.C.: National Education Association of the United States, 1958.

Architectural Research Laboratory.   *The effect of windowless classrooms on ele-*

*mentary school children.* Ann Arbor: University of Michigan Department of Architecture, 1965.

Bachman, J. G., Green, S., and Wirtanen, I. D. *Youth in transition,* vol. 3: *Dropping out—Problem or symptom?* Ann Arbor, Mich.: Institute for Social Research, 1971.

Baird, L. L. Big school, small school: A critical examination of the hypothesis. *Journal of Educational Psychology,* 1969, *60,* 253–260.

Barker, R. G., and Gump, P. V. *Big school, small school: High school size and student behavior.* Stanford, Calif.: Stanford University Press, 1964.

Brown, B. F. *The reform of secondary education: A report to the public and the profession.* National Commission on the Reform of Secondary Education. New York: McGraw-Hill, 1973.

Bureau of Education. *Cardinal principles of secondary education.* Bulletin no. 35, 1918.

Coleman, J. S. The adolescent subculture and academic achievement. *American Journal of Sociology,* 1960, *65,* 337–347.

Coleman, J. S. *The adolescent society.* New York: Free Press, 1961.

Coleman, J. S., Campbell, E. Q., Hobson, C. J., McPartland, J., Mood, A. M., Weinfeld, F. D., and York, R. L. *Equality of educational opportunity.* Washington, D.C.: U.S. Government Printing Office, 1966.

Conant, J. B. *The American high school today.* New York: McGraw-Hill, 1959.

Damico, S. B. The effects of clique membership upon academic achievement. *Adolescence,* 1975, *10,* 95–100.

Deal, T. E., and Roper, D. A dilemma of diversity: The American high school. In J. G. Kelly (Ed.), *The high school: Students and social contexts in two Midwestern communities.* Hillsdale, N.J.: Lawrence Earlbaum, 1978.

Eitzen, D. S Athletics in the status system of male adolescents: A replication of Coleman's *The adolescent society. Adolescence,* 1975, *10,* 267–276.

Elliott, D. S., Voss, H. L., and Wendling, A. Capable dropouts and the social milieu of the high school. *Journal of Educational Research,* 1966, *60,* 180–186.

Findley, O., and O'Reilly, H. M. Secondary school discipline. *American Secondary Education,* 1971, *2,* 26–31.

Fisher, R. J. A discussion project on high school adolescents' perceptions of the relationship between students and teachers. *Adolescence,* 1976, *11,* 87–95.

Fitzsimmons, S. J., Cheever, J., Leonard, E., and Macunowich, D. School failures: Now and tomorrow. *Developmental Psychology,* 1969, *1,* 134–146.

Friesen, D. Academic-athletic-popularity syndrome in the Canadian high school society. *Adolescence,* 1968, *3,* 39–52.

Getzels, J. W. A social psychology of education. In G. Lindzey and E. Aronson (Eds.), *The handbook of social psychology* (2d ed.), vol. 5. Reading, Mass.: Addison-Wesley, 1969.

Gottlieb, B. H. The contribution of natural support systems to primary prevention among four social subgroups of adolescent males. *Adolescence,* 1975, *10,* 207–220.

Havighurst, R. J.   Unrealized potentials of adolescents. *National Association of Secondary School Principals Bulletin*, 1966, *50*, 75–96.

Hess, R. D.   High school antecedents of young adult achievement. In R. E. Grinder (Ed.), *Studies in adolescence*. New York: Macmillan, 1963. Pp. 401–416.

Hyman, H. H., Wright, C. R., and Read, J. S.   *The enduring effects of education*. Chicago: University of Chicago Press, 1975.

Iacovetta, R. G.   Adolescent-adult interaction and peer-group involvement. *Adolescence*, 1975, *10*, 327–336.

Jenks, C., et al.   *Inequality: A reassessment of the effect of family and schooling in America*. New York: Basic Books, 1972.

Jones, M. C.   A study of socialization patterns at the high school level. *Journal of Genetic Psychology*, 1958, *93*, 87–111.

Jones, S. S.   High school social status as a historical process. *Adolescence*, 1976, *11*, 327–333.

Karmel, L. J.   Effects of windowless classroom environment on high school students. *Perceptual and Motor Skills*, 1965, *20*, 277–278.

Katz, D., and Kahn, R. L.   *The social psychology of organizations* (2d ed.). New York: Wiley, 1978.

Krug, E. A.   *The shaping of the American high school, vol. 2: 1920–1941*. Madison: University of Wisconsin Press, 1972.

Martin, E. C.   Reflections on the early adolescent in school. In J. Kagan and R. Coles (Eds.), *12–16: Early adolescence*. New York: Norton, 1972.

McCandless, B. R., Roberts, A., and Starnes, T.   Teachers' marks, achievement test scores, and aptitude relations with respect to social class, race, and sex. *Journal of Educational Psychology*, 1972, *63*, 153–159.

McClintock, E.   Adolescent socialization and the high school: A selective review of literature. In J. G. Kelly (Ed.), *Adolescent boys in high school: A psychological study of coping and adaptation*. Hillsdale, N.J.: Lawrence Erlbaum, 1979.

McDill, E. L., Meyers, E. D., and Rigsby, L. C.   Institutional effects on the academic behavior of high school students. *Sociology of Education*, 1967, *40*, 181–199.

Montero, D.   Support for civil liberties among a cohort of high school graduates and college students. *Journal of Social Issues*, 1975, *31*, 123–136.

Morgan, L. B., and Wicas, E. A.   The short, unhappy life of student dissent. *Personnel and Guidance Journal*, 1972, *51*, 33–38.

Myrick, R., and Marx, B. S.   An exploratory study of the relationship between high school building design and student learning. Washington, D.C.: U.S. Department of Health, Education, and Welfare, Office of Education, Bureau of Research, 1968.

Newman, P. R.   Persons and settings: A comparative analysis of the quality and range of social interaction in two suburban high schools. Unpublished doctoral dissertation, University of Michigan, 1971.

Newman, P. R.   Persons and settings: A comparative analysis of the quality and range of social interaction in two high schools. In J. G. Kelly (Ed.), *Adolescent boys in high school: A psychological study of coping and adaptation*. Hillsdale, N.J.: Lawrence Erlbaum, 1979.

Poole, R. L.   A teacher-pupil dilemma: Student evaluation and victimization. *Adolescence*, 1976, *11*, 341–347.

Porter, J. W.   *The adolescent, other citizens, and their high schools: A report to the public and the profession.* Task Force '74; A National Task Force for High School Reform. New York: McGraw-Hill, 1975.

Ravitch, D.   The born-again school. *New York*, May 15, 1978, pp. 41–44.

Richards, A. K., and DeCecco, J. P.   A study of student perceptions of civic education. *Journal of Social Issues*, 1975, *31* (2), 111–121.

Ringness, T. A.   Identification patterns, motivation, and school achievement of bright junior high school boys. *Journal of Educational Psychology*, 1967, *58*, 93–102.

Sarason, S. B.   *The culture of the school and the problem of change.* Boston; Allyn and Bacon, 1971.

Shaycoft, M. F.   Cognitive growth during high school. *Project Talent*, bulletin no. 6, 1967.

Snyder, E. E.   High school athletes and their coaches: Educational plans and advice. *Sociology of Education*, 1972, *45*, 313–325.

Snyder, E. E.   Athletic team involvement, educational plans, and the coach-player relationship. *Adolescence*, 1975, *10*, 191–200.

Stern, G. G.   Measuring noncognitive variables in research on teaching. In N. L. Gage (Ed.), *Handbook of research on teaching.* Chicago: Rand McNally, 1963.

Thornburg, H.   The adolescent and school. In H. Thornburg (Ed.), *Contemporary adolescence: Readings* (2d ed.). Monterey, Calif.: Brooks/Cole, 1975. Pp. 188–195.

Trickett, E. J., Kelly, J. G., and Todd, D. M.   The social environment of the high school: Guidelines for individual change and organizational redevelopment. In S. Golann and C. Eisdorfer (Eds.), *Handbook of community psychology.* New York: Appleton-Century-Crofts, 1972.

Trump, J. L., and Miller, D. F.   *Secondary school curriculum improvement: Challenges, humanism, accountability* (2d ed.). Boston: Allyn and Bacon, 1973.

Wicker, A. W.   Undermanning, performances, and students' subjective experiences in behavior settings of large and small high schools. *Journal of Personality and Social Psychology*, 1968, *10*, 255–261.

Wicker, A.   Cognitive complexity, school size, and participation in school behavior settings: A test of the frequency of interaction hypothesis. *Journal of Educational Psychology*, 1969, *60*, 200–203.

Willems, E. P.   Sense of obligation to high school activities as related to school size and marginality of student. *Child Development*, 1967, *38*, 1247–1260.

Williamson, R. C.   Variables in adjustment and life goals among high school students. *Adolescence*, 1977, *12*, 213–225.

*Delinquent acts are common behavior problems in early adolescence.*

# 8

# Deviance in Early Adolescence

Early adolescence is a period of rapid growth and change in physical, cognitive, social, and emotional development. Chapters 4, 5, and 6 have presented the nature of these changes in depth. Chapter 7 has helped to make us aware that individuals during this stage of life spend a good part of their time in a highly organized and evaluative social institution—the high school. In addition to participating in the high school environment, adolescents are usually deeply involved with their families, friendship groups, and neighborhoods. During early adolescence, people are becoming sexually mature and potent. They are dealing with the internal impulses, wishes, fantasies, and fears that accompany this development. They are also dealing with the social implications and conflicts of maturing sexuality in their interpersonal relationships. They are facing rapid changes in height, weight, and strength that tend to leave almost every person somewhat awkward and peculiar looking for some part of early adolescence. All people must reexamine their body image during this time of their lives.

Formal operations provide new possibilities for thinking and reality testing. New intellectual skills are available to the person, but these possibilities must be developed and properly utilized in order to provide increased cognitive capacity. The developing sense of the future, for example, can lead to more effective anticipation and coping, or it can lead to a greater preoccupation with fantasies of the future that are less threatening than facing the anxieties of the present. In the former instance, the new cognitive capacity leads to adaptive, personally enhancing behavior. In the latter instance, it leads to maladaptive, defensive behavior that may result in the development of serious problems. Individual differences in intellectual functioning become more visible during early adolescence. The high school presents greater intellectual challenges than do the elementary, junior high, and middle schools. For the first time, students from various parts of a community are brought together in a single educational setting. Many people who did very well in elementary school now find that their work is only average in comparison with that of the larger more competitive group. They must face this challenge to self-concept, self-esteem, and intellectual potential. For most people this realization is a challenge to be coped with, but for some it is a realization that leads to serious psychological problems.

All of these changes and challenges give rise to strong feelings of excitement and anxiety. Usually these feelings help to motivate behavior that leads to the development of new skills and increased feelings of competence. Most people remember some periods of intense anxiety during early adolescence. Some people have great difficulty in overcoming these feelings and become preoccupied with efforts to deal with them.

The relationship with one's parents is usually reexamined during early adolescence. Adolescents' increased physical and cognitive skills make it necessary for adolescents and their parents to redefine their relationship. In many cases, this redefinition is accomplished with respect, confidence, and mutual compromise. In other cases, rebellion and hostility reach incredible levels. Peer relations change in both complexity and importance. Dealings with members of the opposite sex introduce an interrelationship between physical and social development. The need to be part of a group and to develop skills that are appropriate to group experiences are particularly sensitive to development in early adolescence. The problem of alienation may face an adolescent who, for some reason, is not easily accepted by others or who has not developed the interpersonal skills necessary to make oneself known to others.

The highly structured nature of the high school environment, the new challenges of the academic curriculum, the greater number of students, and the idiosyncratic expectations of particular adults must be faced by adolescents. For some individuals, the challenges and demands are too much to handle and problems in functioning in the complex setting begin to become visible.

These examples are intended to alert the reader to some of the problems that may occur during early adolescence. The developmental issues of this period lead to specific kinds of problems that may be called deviant or psychopathological. Werkman (1974) makes a very clear differentiation between the psychological disorders of early and later adolescence. He states that because the developmental issues of the two stages are quite different, the observed forms of psychological disorders will also be quite different. We would expect, for example, to find that disorders related to difficulties in adjusting to sexual changes and physical maturation are fairly frequent among early adolescents. By later adolescence, however, this type of problem will be less frequent, because no new physical changes are occurring. In later adolescence, problems and disorders related to career choice are likely to become more visible as social pressures mount to resolve uncertainties regarding career choice. We may ask early adolescents what they want to be, and we try to stimulate their thinking about career. For the most part, however, it is the later adolescent whom we expect to be actively making the career decisions.

In the discussion above as well as in the previous chapters, we have documented that adolescence is a period of sweeping change and maturation in many aspects of personal development.

Hall (1904) believed that early adolescence was a period of Storm and Stress for all people. Current research (Douvan and Adelson, 1966; Offer, 1969; Offer and Offer, 1975; Donovan, 1975) tends to dispel this notion. Many people experience this stage of life in a well-integrated development of new skills and competences that are made possible by physical, intellectual, social, and emotional maturation. New behaviors are made possible because of growth, and these behaviors enhance personal functioning. In a longitudinal study of well-adjusted, middle-class adolescent males, Offer and Offer (1975) found that four out of five youths demonstrated patterns of uniform personal development and accomplishment from the time they entered high school until they were 22 years old. The fifth youth experienced the period of Storm and Stress that was once thought to be characteristic of all.

As a result of all the changes that are occurring, the opportunities for problem behavior are plentiful. Our estimate is that 20 percent of early adolescents will experience serious psychological conflicts. Anna Freud (1969) pointed out that most of these problems should be thought of as developmental disturbances. They occur because the individual experiences difficulties in coping with new internal states or new external demands, or both. They may also occur because maturation alters the established balance within the personality and forces the individual to seek new levels of personal integration and stability. For many, this condition represents opportunity; for some, it represents the need to reestablish the integration of physical, intellectual, social, and emotional characteristics in an extremely difficult process.

Developmental disturbances may produce many lapses from normal functioning and sweeping upheavals in a person's behavior (A. Freud, 1969; Werkman, 1974). "Storm in stress" might be the appropriate phrase. The clinicians point out that personality upheavals and deviations from normal behavior may be very sweeping in the person who has problems in adjusting to the developmental issues of early adolescence. These problems, however, may be only transitory. For some people, disorganization is necessary before reorganization can occur. The process may begin spontaneously, look extremely patholological, and end in a spontaneous cure (A. Freud, 1969). Although clinical treatment may be necessary and beneficial for early adolescents with psychological problems, the prognosis for a positive personal outcome is high. Treatment may be necessary because of the severity of the problems, but in most cases the probability of successful recovery and normal later adjustment is very good. The clinician must be extremely skillful in differentiating problems that are developmental disturbances from problems that represent deeper distortions of adjustment that are rooted much earlier in the person's life. The successful treatment of problems of either type will require the correct diagnosis of the developmental disturbances and of the longer term characterological disturbances. Whereas 20 percent of the population may experience the former, a much smaller percentage are likely to experience the latter.

In the preceding discussion, we have made the following points:

1. The developmental issues of early adolescence will determine the kinds of psychological problems that are observed in people during this stage.
2. Early adolescence is not a period of Storm and Stress for everyone. One estimate suggests that it is a period of upheaval for 20 percent of the population.
3. Developmental disturbances may lead to numerous lapses from normal functioning and to very sweeping upheavals in a person's character.
4. Developmental disturbances may end with a spontaneous cure, or they may be cured through skillful psychotherapy which helps the individual to cope with new drives and expectations and to attain a new level of personal integration and stability.
5. Developmental disturbances must be carefully distinguished from more basic, more pervasive psychopathology.

In the rest of this chapter we will discuss the various kinds of psychological problems that are experienced during early adolescence. We will also discuss the implications of these problems for the later life of the individuals who experience them. Finally, we will present the kinds of services and community resources that are available to treat the problems discussed.

## NEUROSES OF EARLY ADOLESCENCE

The psychoanalytic theory of neuroses (Fenichel, 1945; S. Freud, 1959, 1963; A. Freud, 1946, 1965; Blos, 1962) posits that restrictions against the expression of a person's impulses place the person in psychological conflict. This situation is thought to confront the person as a result of developmental issues that are related to the experience of sexuality and/or aggression. The conflict produces tension or anxiety in the person, and in order to ward off this unpleasant feeling the person may develop behaviors called symptoms. Symptomatic behaviors may be effective in providing short-term relief of anxiety, but the person continues to need them because they do not really address the causes of the problem or provide effective resolution of the developmental disturbance.

Often repression is used as a primary mechanism to shield the person from conflict, impulse, and anxiety. Repression distorts the disturbance that is causing the problem by blocking the impulses, the conflict, and the restrictions from the person's conscious awareness. The conflict continues to exist, however, and the impulses continue to seek expression.

Actually, if repression were truly effective the conflict would be retained totally in the unconscious. The fact that repression is not effective is what causes neurosis. Some distortion of the conflict becomes conscious or threatens to become conscious. This condition produces anxiety. Anxiety is experienced as unpleasant, and usually the person is driven to reduce it. Symptoms develop that provide temporary relief but do not resolve the conflict. Symptoms are thought to express the conflict, but only at a very distorted level. The expression of impulses through symptomatic behavior is never enough to resolve the conflict because it is so indirect and distorted.

Let's look at an example. Person X has strong sexual impulses and strong, internalized restrictions against the expression of sexuality. As X begins to experience sexual fantasies, strong guilt is also experienced. This combination upsets X. In order to protect itself, X's ego drives the sexual impulses and the restrictions on sexual expression out of consciousness. Now X begins to worry about cleanliness. Dirt and germs become preoccupations. In order to stay clean, X initiates handwashing. This gives X relief from the worry of contamination. The relief is short-lived, however. Thoughts of contamination occur again, and further handwashing is necessary. X washes three or four times an hour at first. After a while, 10–12 washings an hour are necessary and it becomes increasingly difficult for X to do much else.

After repression occurs, X's thoughts of dirt and disease represent both the impulse and the restriction. Sexuality is "dirty." By thinking of dirt and contamination, X gains an extremely distorted expression for his or her impulses. It is like thinking about sex. The thoughts of contamination also cast sexual impulses in a negative light. The preoccupation, or *obsession,* is one symptom. The anxiety becomes too strong for X to endure, and the behavior symptom occurs.

Handwashing provides X with both the pleasure of physical stroking and the restriction of physical pleasure by cleansing. The behavioral symptom represents the impulse, the restriction, and some resolution of the conflict.

Learning theorists (Davison and Neale, 1978; Ullman and Krasner, 1975) take a somewhat different view of neuroses. They believe that neurotic behavior is learned over time through the experience of reinforcement. A person who experiences a stressful situation may become extremely anxious in that situation. Fear persists even when the stressful stimuli are removed, and the person is motivated to reduce the fear. Behaviors are developed to accomplish the reduction of fear. Over time these fear-reducing behaviors become firmly established in the person's behavioral repertoire. When these behaviors are ineffective and peculiar, they are called neurotic.

There probably is validity to the psychoanalytic view that some psychological neuroses are the result of ineffective attempts to deal with internal conflicts. There is also validity to the learning theorists' notion that neurotic behavior is a current behavioral structure that was built in response to a traumatic event of the remote past. We would offer the additional concept that neurotic behavior is an attempt to reduce anxiety induced by environmental experiences that cannot be dealt with directly or effectively. An adolescent who cannot get along with an important teacher develops a strong fear of attending school that leads to strong strain in the family and great tension for the adolescent. Dealing with the teacher directly would be more appropriate, but this strategy is not even identified because of differences in status. The child and the parent may consider it legitimate for the teacher to be arbitrary and demeaning, because of the status and expertise that they attribute to the teacher. Because of role discrepancies, they do not view direct confrontation and conflict resolution as possible ways of resolving the problem. The adolescent is fearful of confronting the teacher and unable to escape the relationship. As the adolescent's fear and anxiety grow, school itself becomes a frightening experience.

We may, then, discuss impulse neuroses, learned neuroses, and environmentally induced neuroses. Anxiety and the development of symptoms to reduce anxiety are common to all three forms. The fact that the first form is caused by difficulties in managing internal impulses, the second by the development of ineffective and peculiar habits, and the third by difficulties in relating to the external environment does not mean that the behavioral symptoms will be different. The inability to admit and gain expression for sexual conflicts, a fearful past association to a setting, or a poor relationship with an important teacher may all lead to a strong fear of going to school—a school phobia. Although the causes may be very different, the outcomes in behaviors and thoughts may be very much the same. This is likely in part because the person is unable to face or recognize the cause of the problem. The neurotic adaptation is an effort to provide relief for a problem that the individual is unable to face directly. The real problem will not be solved, and the individual is free to select from among a wide range of neurotic symptoms a symptom or symptoms that will serve as an acceptable distortion.

Common experiences also tend to provide some of the possible content for neurotic symptoms. Children from birth to the age five and adults beyond college rarely develop school phobias. People who attend school develop school phobias. Although some of these people may have problems that are caused by their school experience, not all of them do. The school is a setting in which all people of this age group are involved, and it serves as a target for phobias that may be caused by any of the three etiological factors. In treating neuroses, the clinician must try to understand the cause of the problem as well as the symptoms. Proper understanding of the cause is necessary in order to help guide the individual toward self-undertanding, to dissolve the symptom patterns, and to establish new, more effective coping efforts.

The final general statement that we would like to make about neuroses is that although they may be extremely unpleasant and upsetting, they do not usually make a person unable to test the difference between fantasy and reality. Neurotics may have some extremely unpleasant and upsetting fantasies, and they may not be able to rid their minds of those fantasies. However, they know that these mental experiences are fantasies. Reality testing is maintained. There are two primary exceptions to this which may have serious consequences. The first is anorexia nervosa, a condition that results in severe restrictions on food intake (Bruch, 1978). After prolonged starvation, a person may be unable to think logically. Too great a restriction of food intake for too long a time can result in death (Sours, 1969). The second condition is neurotic depression. Here the person is filled with anxiety and feelings of worthlessness. Early adolescents may never have experienced depression of this intensity before. Neurotic depression may involve thoughts of self-destruction. Although most aspects of reality testing remain intact, the anxiety, the feelings of worthlessness, and the lack of prior experience may lead depressed adolescents to conclude that they must try to take their own life (Yasin, 1973; Gallagher and Harris, 1976). We would argue that an attempt at suicide caused by thinking that is generated by depressive anxiety is a failure of the reality-testing mechanism. We would conclude, then, that although neurotics for the most part are able to test the difference between reality and fantasy, there may be occasional lapses of reality testing. In the remainder of this section, we will describe some of the common neuroses of early adolescence.

## Anxiety Reactions

Anxiety plays an important role in every neurosis. In anxiety reactions, emotional tension and high levels of anxiety are the dominant symptoms. The person feels continually apprehensive and has no clear sense of what the threat is or where the anxiety comes from. The major symptoms include anxiety states that produce increased levels of anxiety and heightened activity in an already tension-filled person. The person attempts to get rid of the anxiety by discharging it directly (Cameron, 1963).

Most people experience emotional tension as part of life. The person who is neurotically anxious simply feels more anxious more often. Such a person's capacities for relaxation and enjoyment are seriously diminished. Usually, anxious individuals accept their high levels of anxiety and adapt their lives to accommodate their tension (Cameron, 1963). The anxiety itself is a mechanism for relieving anxiety by direct discharge. This adaptation often exacts heavy costs. Common symptoms of the chronically anxious and worried person include a vigilant, unrelaxed attitude; high levels of driven activity; aches, pains, and hypochondria; stomach or intestinal upset; shallow, irregular breathing; heart palpitation; sleep disturbances; depressed appetite, diarrhea, and constipation; and sexual dysfunctions, including excessive masturbation, impotence, frigidity, and menstrual irregularities (Cameron, 1963; Gallagher and Harris, 1976; Coleman, 1976; Davison and Neale, 1978). The neurotically anxious person constantly worries about danger (Beck, Lande, and Bohnert, 1974). Acute episodes of diffuse tension sometimes occur. These are called anxiety attacks. An extremely serious anxiety attack is called a panic reaction. It is usually the end result of unbearable tension that has built up over a long period of time. Panic reactions may result in serious disorganization of the personality.

In early adolescence, there are many potential causes of anxiety reactions. Among the common experiences that cause some early adolescents to develop serious anxiety reactions are conflict with parents and insecurity in the home; new demands for independent behavior; heightened sexual and aggressive drives and increased demands for sexual activity; school change from elementary, middle, or junior high school to high school; increased academic demands; poor progress in school; peer expectations; and peer rejection (Weiner, 1970; Werkman, 1974; Reynolds, 1976; Gallagher and Harris, 1976). Generally, people with anxiety reactions make use of the wide range of symptoms described above. The symptomatology is diffuse rather than specific.

## Anorexia Nervosa

Anorexia nervosa has been called "nervous malnutrition" (Bliss and Branch, 1960). Table 8–1 presents the primary and secondary

**Table 8–1: Phenomenology of the Anorexia Nervosa Syndrome**

A. *Primary signs and symptoms*
   1. Elective restriction of food.
   2. Pursuit of thinness as pleasure in itself.
   3. Frantic efforts to establish control over the body and its functions.
   4. Food avoidance and preoccupation.
   5. Hyperactivity and increased energy output. } Can be prodromal
   6. Amenorrhea.

B. *Secondary signs and symptoms*
   1. Manipulation of environment around food and diet.
   2. Distrustful attitude to significant objects.
   3. Sadness and guilt, but no clinical depression.
   4. Occasional bulimia.

Source: J. A. Sours, "Anorexia Nervosa: Nosology, Diagnosis, Developmental Patterns, and Power-Control Dynamics," in G. Caplan and S. Lebovici (Eds.), *Adolescence: Psychosocial Perspectives* (New York: Basic Books, 1969), Table 15–2, p. 189. © 1969 by Basic Books, Inc.

signs and symptoms of anorexia nervosa. Bruch (1962, 1966, 1973, 1974, 1978) has pointed out that anorexia nervosa is a set of symptoms that is utilized by people with a variety of psychopathological diagnoses ranging from anxiety neuroses to schizophrenia. Her latest book, *The Golden Cage* (Bruch, 1978), presents a sensitive portrayal of the more common neurotic problem. For the clinician, the problem is to differentiate between the less serious neurotic problem and the more serious psychotic problem. Bruch discusses three main sources of disturbance in anorexia nervosa: (1) disturbances in body image; (2) disturbances in accuracy of perception or cognitive interpretation of body needs and messages; (3) disturbances in one's sense of effectiveness. Many early adolescents, particularly girls, respond to changes in bodily functions and size, and feelings of lack of control over body changes, by denying information concerning good nutrition and messages from their bodies. They go on very strict, restrictive diets whether they are overweight, of normal weight, or underweight (Dwyer and Mayer, 1968–69). For some of these adolescents, this dieting becomes too strict and the signs and symptoms of Table 8–1 begin to show up. In most cases, an early adolescent anxiety reaction with anorexia nervosa symptomatology would be the diagnosis.

One reason why anorexia nervosa deserves specific attention here is that the condition is often observed in early adolescence. The second reason is that the physiological effects can be very serious in advanced stages of the condition. Persons with anorexia nervosa are often characterized by high activity levels. The denial of body messages and a reluctance to take it easy can lead to physical problems that appear to come on rather suddenly. Sours (1969) has described many of the pathophysiologic effects that have been discovered in anorexia nervosa patients. These are presented in Table 8–2. Extremely serious cases can result in death (Lesser et al., 1960; Sours, 1969). Beck and Brockner-Mortensen (1954) estimated that 7 percent of anorexia nervosa patients die. For most

**Table 8–2: Pathophysiological Disturbances in the Anorexia Nervosa Syndrome**

| | |
|---|---|
| 1. Emaciation. | 11. Anemia—decreased RBC Volume. |
| 2. Lanugo hair. | 12. Leukopenia—decreased polys. |
| 3. Hypothermia. | 13. Relative lymphocytosis. |
| 4. Hypotension. | 14. Endocrine studies in normal range or after refeeding. ?Insulin response. ?Gonadotrophins. |
| 5. Bradycardia. | |
| 6. Amenorrhea or delayed menarche. | |
| 7. Decreased libido. | 15. High turnover of $N_{15}$ glycine during refeeding. |
| 8. Dehydration. | |
| 9. Carotenemia. Vitamin A deficiency. | 16. Possible circulatory collapse and death. |
| 10. Hypoproteinemia. | 17. ?Dystrophic cerebral damage. |

Source: J. A. Sours, "Anorexia Nervosa: Nosology, Diagnosis, Developmental Patterns, and Power-Control Dynamics," in G. Caplan and S. Lebovici (Eds.), *Adolescence: Psychosocial Perspectives* (New York: Basic Books, 1969), Table 15–3, p. 189. © 1969 by Basic Books, Inc.

patients the prognosis is favorable, but there is no doubt that the condition must be properly diagnosed and carefully treated.

## Phobias

Phobias are strong fears which are focused upon specific objects or situations. These objects and situations are then avoided as much as possible. Unlike people who have anxiety reactions, persons with phobias believe that they know what causes their strong, unpleasant anxiety attacks even though they may not know why the causative factor affects them in this way (Ferber, 1959; Grinker and Spiegel, 1945; Greenson, 1959; Cameron, 1963; Coleman, 1976; Sarason, 1976). Whereas people with anxiety reactions usually have a wide variety of symptoms, phobic persons usually use strong fear and target avoidance as their major symptom pattern. Many phobics have only a single strong fear, whereas others have multiple phobias. A phobia usually plays an adaptive function for the phobic person. As long as the target of the phobia can be avoided, the phobic person can remain free from anxiety. The symptoms of the phobic person fall, therefore, into two categories: (1) techniques for avoiding the object of anxiety and (2) anxiety attacks whenever avoidance attempts fail (Cameron, 1963). Table 8–3 lists

**Table 8–3: Some Common Phobias**

| | |
|---|---|
| Accident phobia ................. | Accidents, collisions, crashes, injury |
| Acrophobia ..................... | High places—cliffs, roofs, high windows, airplanes, stairwells, ladders |
| Agoraphobia .................... | Open places—halls, wide streets, fields, parks, beaches (sometimes in recent years, a few of all places outside one's house) |
| Algophobia ..................... | Pain |
| Anthropophobia ................. | People |
| Astraphobia .................... | Natural dangers—storms, thunder, lightning |
| Bacteriophobia ................. | Bacteria |
| Claustrophobia ................. | Enclosed places—small rooms, closets, elevators, alleys, subways |
| Cynophobia ..................... | Dogs |
| Demonophobia ................... | Demons, monsters |
| Equinophobia ................... | Horses |
| Hematophobia ................... | Blood |
| Herpetophobia .................. | Lizards or reptiles |
| Mysophobia ..................... | Contaminants—dirt, germs, poisons, certain foods |
| Monophobia ..................... | Being alone |
| Nyctophobia .................... | Darkness |
| Ochlophobia .................... | Public gatherings—crowds, meetings, lectures, theaters, stadiums, concerts, churches |
| Ophidiophobia .................. | Snakes |
| Pathophobia .................... | Disease |
| Pyrophobia ..................... | Fire |
| School phobia .................. | School |
| Strangophobia .................. | Strangers, unfamiliar places, unidentified sounds and movements, the unknown |
| Vehicle phobia ................. | Cars, trains, planes, ships, buses, subways, escalators |
| Weapons phobia ................. | Guns, knives, scissors, bombs, clubs, axes |
| Zoophobia ...................... | Animals |

some of the common phobias. As you can see, there are numerous targets of fear.

Phobias are common at every stage of life. Cameron (1963) calls the phobia "the normal neurosis of childhood." Most of us can remember strong fears that we had as children. Darkness, monsters, certain animals, and school are some common targets of childhood phobias.

We would consider extending Cameron's comment to call the phobia "the normal neurosis of life." Almost every person has one or two strong fears which are managed by avoiding the targets of the fear. If a person is made anxious, it is quite logical for the person to identify the cause of the anxiety. As was noted earlier, a causative target is easy to select. Why the target causes the anxiety is less easily understood. If a person is experiencing the conflict and anxiety of unconscious impulse and restriction, then the phobic target may be selected through the mechanisms of displacement and projection (Cameron, 1963). The target will have symbolic meaning, and it will be something involved in the person's daily experience. For an early adolescent who is experiencing heightened sexual impulses and their corresponding restrictions, a strong fear of high places may develop. This target is selected because high places may have symbolic meaning for the adolescent. "Sexual activity in the dominant position is desired," or "high places generate a sensory experience that is similar to aspects of sexual activity." The fear represents punishment for unconscious impulses, and the avoidance of high places represents the appropriate restrictions on the impulses. The phobic symptom pattern is rather far removed from the actual topic of sexuality, but it protects the person from having to deal with sexuality directly. The pattern also allows the person to avoid anxiety successfully. If the sexual impulses diminish in their intensity or find mature methods of expression, then the phobia will retreat. If the phobia remains the primary vehicle for dealing with sexual impulses and sexual impulses remain intense or increase, then the phobia will remain strong or will increase in intensity. The person might be unable to attend classes on upper floors of the school building or be unable to tolerate the upper floor of the home. If the phobic behavior begins to interfere with the person's ability to function, then therapeutic intervention is necessary.

If, as a child, a person is on the upper floor of a building or the sight-seeing platform of a monument when a thunderclap, a sonic boom, or some other loud noise occurs, fear of high places may result. Over the years the person may elaborate this fear as a simple kind of avoidance learning. The selection of a fear of high places is not symbolic. The learned habit of avoiding high places can be changed through a process of desensitization in which the person is taught to remain relaxed while thinking of experiences in high places. Eventually the person will be able to relax and to overcome this early fear and the resulting habit pattern. For most people, early childhood fears never cause much restriction of behavior and are simply retained as habitual fears through adolescence and into adult life.

Finally, the cause of a phobic reaction may lie in the individual's environment. As we discussed earlier, the fear of the upper floors of the school building may result from a negative relationship between a student and a teacher. The student may be unable to express hostility, anger, rage, or a sense of unfairness directly, but may develop a strong fear of the place where the dreaded teacher is powerful. Eventually the fear of the upper floor of the building may spread to a generalized fear of school and an extreme unwillingness to attend. In this situation, the alteration of environmental conditions may diminish the need for the phobic symptom pattern.

Phobic reactions are common in early adolescence, as they are in other periods of life. Table 8–3 lists some common fears that one might expect to find among adolescents. Most phobic problems will not come to the attention of anyone other than the immediate family and close friends of the phobic person. For most people, phobias will disappear in time or remain very mild. If a phobic fear escalates in intensity and begins to produce extreme restrictions on behavior, then psychological treatment is necessary. One of the psychodiagnostician's main tasks would be to differentiate between impulse phobias, learned phobias, and environmentally induced phobias. The technique for treatment depends upon the cause.

Irving Weiner (1970) presents a detailed account of school phobia in adolescence, including several case examples, in his book *Psychological Disturbances in Adolescence*. LeUnes and Siemsglusz (1977) describe the successful treatment of a school phobia.

### Neurotic Depression

Neurotic depressive reactions are defined as mood disturbances in which worry and anxiety are expressed in the form of dejection and self-deprecation; physical disturbances; and complaints of feeling inferior, worthless, and without hope. Feelings of guilt play an important part in the mental life of the neurotic depressive. Constant complaining corresponds to the person's feeling state, but it often plays the adaptive function of calling forth caring and reassurance from significant people (Cameron, 1963).

Although depression is observed in early adolescence, it is not as common then as it is at other stages of life (Weiner, 1970). Certainly early adolescents have some reasons for becoming depressed. Physical ugliness or awkwardness, increased demands for independence, intensive questioning about one's worth as a

Matthew Klein/Magnum

*Neurotic depression involves feelings of worry, anxiety, and worthlessness.*

group member, and difficulties and failure in school are all circumstances that might be expected to produce depressive mood states in early adolescents. We believe that two reasons account for the above observation: (1) The psychosocial crisis of group identity versus alienation produces a biogenetic push for social relationships during the early adolescent years that makes pervasive feelings of worthlessness difficult to maintain. (2) Early adolescents demonstrate behavioral substitutes which mask the traditional depressive symptom pattern. There is something about the genetic

makeup of early adolescents which pushes them toward relationships and makes it difficult for them to be extremely self-critical,
gloomy, hopeless, and self-deprecating about themselves.

Weiner (1970) discusses in detail the kinds of symptoms that
adolescents develop to mask depressive symptoms. He feels that
part of the reason for the use of substitute symptoms is that early
adolescents are not inclined to express their feelings openly. In
addition, Gould (1965) points out, the relative impulsivity of early
adolescents leads them to express depressive states somewhat
more behaviorally than adults might. Five equivalents for depression are observed regularly in early adolescents: (1) boredom and
restlessness, (2) fatigue and bodily preoccupation, (3) difficulty in
concentration, (4) acting out, and (5) flight to or from people (Toolan,
1962; Glaser, 1967; Weiner, 1970). It is believed that the behaviors
associated with each of these depressive equivalents cover up an
underlying depressive state.

Some adolescents alternate between boredom and the sudden
development of preoccupations in which interest is quickly lost.
They constantly crave excitement and activity to overcome boredom. They cannot tolerate being by themselves. According to Weiner's analysis, these adolescents are fighting against feelings of
worthlessness and isolation. He argues that the early adolescent
who is constantly tired (even after plenty of sleep) and occasionally
buoyant is demonstrating a behavioral equivalent of a depressive
state. One feels empty when one is depressed; thus one has no
energy. Very fatigued adolescents are often preoccupied with physical concerns and may develop a variety of aches and pains.

According to Weiner, difficulties in concentration are extremely
significant indicators of underlying depression in early adolescents.
Declining school performance usually brings this problem to the
attention of parents, teachers, and psychologists. Building on the
prior work of Bonnard (1961) and Burks and Harrison (1962), Weiner
holds that

acting out behavior—including temper tantrums, running away, and a
variety of defiant, rebellious, antisocial, and delinquent acts—serves to
defend early adolescents against coming to grips with underlying concepts
of themselves as unloved, inadequate and unworthy people. Not only
does acting preclude thinking—as the common adage prescribes, "Try
to keep busy and not think about it"—but the actions themselves, to
the extent that they are hazardous or exploitative may be designed to
inflate the youngster's self-image as a tough, brave, and clever person.
(Weiner, 1970, pp. 164–165)

The final behavioral equivalent for depression in early adolescents involves a rather exaggerated approach to or avoidance of

people. As Weiner points out, an underlying feeling of unworthiness may motivate heightened interpersonal involvement and even sexual promiscuity in an attempt to confirm one's worth. Or this underlying feeling may motivate withdrawal and isolation because of a fear of being proved unworthy. The above behavioral equivalents of depression are observed more often in early adolescents than are the traditional symptoms of depression. The traditional symptoms will be discussed in Chapter 12.

## Hysterical Reactions

Two main forms of hysterical neuroses have been identified: conversion reactions and dissociative reactions (American Psychiatric Association, 1968). Since the symptomatologies associated with these forms are quite different, we will discuss each form separately.

**Conversion Reactions.** In a conversion reaction, the individual's unconscious conflict is transformed (converted) into a physical symptom. There is a physical reaction, but there is no physiological cause. As Cameron (1963) points out, the function of a part of the body is literally dedicated and sacrificed to the expression of a forbidden impulse, or to defense against such an impulse, or to a denial of the impulse, or as a self-punishment for having the impulse. All of these meanings can be combined in a single symptom. Persons may develop a partial paralysis and then enjoy the care and support that this causes others to give. The symptom may persist because the person learns to use it for positive outcomes. Finally, a conversion reaction may develop as a way of avoiding some environmental situation that is too threatening to face. The reasons for a conversion reaction are not known to the person. The person is not malingering or practicing any form of conscious deception. In the conversion reaction, the person's tension and anxiety are unconsciously transformed into physical disability. The meaning of the symptom is repressed, and often the person appears to be relatively anxiety free and unconflicted. The disability is the price that the person pays for relative freedom from anxiety (Sperling, 1973).

There are many kinds of major conversion reactions. We will list some in order to give you an idea of the wide variety of bodily symptoms that people use in order to resolve psychological conflict. Cameron (1963) presents an expanded discussion of each of these.

1. Loss of speech. As a conversion symptom, this may be quite complete and may last for several days. Stammering, stuttering,

and the inability to speak above a whisper are less serious conversion reactions.

2. Muscular paralysis. As a conversion symptom, this will involve relatively serious and long-lasting loss of motor functions, including paralysis of the arms or legs.
3. Skin anesthesia—a relatively serious and long-lasting loss of feeling in some part or parts of the body, with no neurological impairment. Often, but not always, this accompanies conversion paralysis.
4. Visual disturbances—blindness, usually selective or in a single eye, which indicates that the person is blotting out the image of something threatening and anxiety provoking.
5. Deafness—sometimes complete, but usually partial. As with blindness it is used to shut out threat.
6. Tremor—usually begins as a part of emotional excitement but persists because it expresses unconscious impulses symbolically. Trembling in the leg may keep an early adolescent from participating in sports where failure may be threatening.
7. Spasms or cramps. These are sudden or painful muscle contractions that actively interfere with the performance of a skilled act. Writer's cramp may make it impossible for an adolescent to do homework.
8. Tics. These are exaggerated gestures that recur intermittently.
9. Postural peculiarities—unusual posture, such as a stoop, which, as a conversion reaction, is greatly exaggerated.

Conversion symptoms involve some physical expression of a psychological conflict in the absence of physiological causes. The symptoms tend to express certain aspects of the conflict symbolically. Thus, the selection of a limb paralysis or a particular tremor is seen as no accident by the clinician. The symptom is seen as providing clues to the causes of the problem. Almost any part of the body can serve as the site for a conversion symptom.

**Dissociative Reactions.**   These are the kinds of hysterical reactions that most people are familiar with, because they have been popularized in literature and the mass media. Stevenson's *Dr. Jekyll and Mr. Hyde* is a fictional example, and the case of Eve, popularized as *The Three Faces of Eve,* is a rather dramatic real-life example (Lancaster and Poling, 1958; Thigpen and Cleckley, 1954, 1957). A recent case of multiple personality describes the three faces of Evelyn both clinically and experimentally (Jeans, 1976; Osgood, Luria, and Smith, 1976). Dissociative reactions separate one or more components of the personality system from the rest (Cameron, 1963). They represent ways of avoiding stress by escaping from conflicts, even though the separation that occurs may lead to unusual, dramatic, or peculiar outcomes. Abnormal dissociative reactions are rather rare, constituting less than 2 percent of all neuroses (Abse, 1966; Coleman, 1976; Davison and Neale, 1978).

People often make use of dissociation in a normal way during extreme stress, as when they learn of the death of a loved one or view a terrible accident. The temporary distancing from emotion that often occurs at such times enables the individual to mobilize resources for coping successfully with a massive threat.

The various types of pathological dissociation include (Cameron, 1963):

1.  Object estrangement—an attempt to relieve anxiety by making the object world seem unfamiliar. Examples include an inability to listen to and understand what someone says and alterations in one's perception of objects.
2.  Somatic estrangement. The body, some part of the body, or the body image seems to be unfamiliar or unreal.
3.  Depersonalization. The person feels that some change in the self has occurred. The person feels that the self is unfamiliar, detached, or unreal. The early adolescent often experiences a sense of depersonalization because of actual bodily changes.
4.  Sleepwalking. This is relatively common in childhood and adolescence. Certain objects or experiences are sought without wakeful cognitions or inhibitions. This symptom can lead one into dangerous situations, such as walking on a roof or a ledge.
5.  Hysterical convulsions—a nonphysiologically-caused convulsive state in which the person becomes suddenly unaware of the surroundings while acting out some fantasy that has been repressed. The convulsive state allows anxiety to be obliterated while the person expresses the problem.
6.  Trances. People become immersed in regressive preoccupations which they cannot express in words. People are not easily aroused from trances.
7.  Psychogenic stupor. The person sits almost motionless and appears to be in a coma, but is preoccupied with internal, previously unconscious fantasies.
8.  Massive amnesia without fugue. The person wanders around near home but doesn't remember his or her identity or home environment.
9.  Massive amnesia with fugue. The person doesn't remember his or her identity or home environment and runs away from the home situation.
10. Dissociated personality—includes alternating personality, in which two or more alternating personalities become almost completely dissociated from one another, and double or multi-

ple personality, in which one personality dominates while one or more other personalities occasionally take over in relatively childlike ways.

Dissociative reactions represent attempts to avoid experiencing anxiety by separating aspects of personality and experience (Briss, 1966). Although such reactions are relatively rare, they tend to be noticeable and dramatic. Early adolescents often sleepwalk, which may be dangerous. Trancelike states and similar conditions have often been valued preoccupations of adolescents in recent times. We would argue that such preoccupations attempt to ritualize escape from anxiety and tension. Amnesia, multiple personality, and stupor are much rarer, but they do occur in early adolescence. Adolescents experience some depersonalization as the body and mental capacities change. They feel that "this is not exactly me." Most adolescents manage to integrate the changes into their personalities, but some require therapeutic intervention in order to learn to accept the "new self."

## Obsessive-Compulsive Reactions

In obsessive-compulsive reactions, emotional tension and anxiety are expressed openly in what appear to be senseless repetitious thoughts, words, actions, rituals, ceremonies, doubts, or ruminations (Alchter et al., 1975). The major conflicts of obsessive-compulsive neurotics are love and hate, right and wrong, cleanliness and dirt, orderliness and disorder. Sadism and masochism are often expressed freely, and strong feelings of guilt are common. Magical thinking and superstitious behavior are often observed. Obsessive-compulsive individuals are usually aware that they are in conflict, although they usually don't understand what the conflict is about (Cameron, 1963).

The pattern of obsessive thoughts and compulsive behavior is illustrated in the following example: "A boy of twelve suffered from repetitious thoughts of calling his parents obscene names. He would control these impulses by saying 'Stop it! Stop it!' to himself out loud. Then he would repetitively swear at himself for having the obsessive thoughts" (Cameron, 1963, p. 373). In this example the boy is obviously in conflict about love and hate feelings toward his parents. The boy's method for controlling anxiety and tension about this conflict involves the development of obsessive thoughts that provide an expression of his forbidden impulses to aggress against the parents and the compulsive use of words to deny such expression and to punish himself for having had the impulses in the first place. As this pattern occurs over and over again, it becomes a predictable ritual that provides relief from tension through indulgence, restraint, and punishment.

Obsessive-compulsive behaviors are very observable in normal people and in society. Freud (1955) believed that such ritualistic manners of behaving were very important in maintaining social order. Rules, orders, procedures, traditions, and customs characterize most well-run social organizations. Society places a high value on orderly, well-mannered people who are concerned with obeying rules and organizing their personal behavior so as to be effective. When children and adolescents develop an interest in work and a corresponding interest in good work habits, we feel that new levels of social commitment and responsibility are being demonstrated. People may engage in ritualistic patterns of behavior before they undertake stressful work. Some students have certain rituals of behavior and dress that they use before taking exams. Some baseball pitchers perform repetitive gestural behaviors before each pitch. We carry good luck charms, feel nervous on Friday the thirteenth, and celebrate a holiday of superstition—Halloween. Human society makes great use of behaviors that resemble those of the obsessive-compulsive neurotic.

The difference is that the neurotic is usually preoccupied with a particular conflict or a set of conflicts which usually produces symptoms that are highly related to the conflict and are usually great exaggerations of normal obsessions, compulsions, rituals, and doubts. The handwashing compulsion discussed above is an example of an obsessive-compulsive neurotic symptom pattern. Trivial preoccupations; intensely driven, elaborate mental constructions; and bizarre, repetitive behavioral rituals are the characteristic kinds of exaggerated behaviors that we observe in obsessive-compulsive reactions (Alchter et al., 1975).

Early adolescents often demonstrate obsessive-compulsive symptoms. Obsessive preoccupation with sexuality and aggression is common. New size and new physical and intellectual capabilities occur before appropriate mastery skills have been learned. The adolescent often develops obsessions over how to present oneself to a member of the opposite sex. Preoccupations with fantasies of war or with athletic expressions of violence are common. Prior to acquiring experience and skills, many early adolescents utilize obsessive-compulsive techniques to gain expression for their conflicts and to master anxiety. For most such adolescents, these behaviors recede as more effective behaviors are developed. For others, they do not. The latter have more serious problems or less effective coping mechanisms.

## Summary

We have discussed the neurotic process as one in which emotional tensions and anxieties are relieved in a variety of ways. In anxiety reactions, tension is discharged directly. A wide variety of symptoms are observed, but general anxiety, anxiety attacks, and panic reactions are the primary symptoms. The source of the anxiety is usually unknown to the person. In phobic reactions, a strong irrational fear or set of fears is used to free the person from generalized anxiety. The person can identify the cause of fear even though there is no awareness of why it is the cause. In considering the neurotic depression of early adolescence, we have discussed depressive equivalents that appear to mask a more basic condition of feelings of worthlessness. Feelings of boredom and restlessness sometimes alternate with each other. Fatigue and preoccupation with the body may be observed. Serious difficulties in concentrating are often indicative of an underlying problem of depression. Acting-out behavior is often an attempt to assert one's worth and self-definition and to gain attention because one has an underlying sense of lacking value. Hysterical reactions are of two types: conversion reactions and dissociative reactions. In conversion reactions, bodily symptoms develop in the absence of physiological causation in order to express psychological conflicts. Although body functioning becomes limited, the person generally remains free from tension and anxiety. In dissociative reactions, aspects of the personality are separated from one another in order to reduce tension. Trances, sleepwalking, amnesia states, and multiple personality are examples of types of dissociative reactions. Finally, in obsessive-compulsive reactions we find the rather direct expression of impulse, restrictions on the expression of impulse, and punishment for the expression of impulse. This occurs through the development of patterns of repetitious thoughts, words, acts, rituals, ceremonies, and doubts that have a great deal of personal meaning but little shared meaning. These types of neurotic reactions are not typical of all early adolescents, but they are all observed in some. For some early adolescents, the symptoms are temporary and will disappear spontaneously as more effective mastery skills are learned and as more effective coping mechanisms for impulse expression are developed. For others, the neurotic symptomatology of early adolescence represents a step in a maladaptive direction that will eventuate in a more debilitating set of problems in adulthood. The neurotic symptomatology of early adolescence may be so debilitating that treatment is obtained during this period. On the other hand, many people may pass through early adolescence with relatively serious problems and symptoms that go unnoticed.

## THE PSYCHOSES OF EARLY ADOLESCENCE

Psychoses are more serious forms of psychopathology than neurotic reactions. These are the conditions that people are usually referring to when they speak of mental illness or "craziness." Very pronounced emotional disturbances ranging from extreme agitation to extreme emotional flatness may be observed. Uncontrolled and inappropriate fits of giddy laughter are common in some types of psychoses; extreme uncontrollable and inappropriate sadness may be observed in other types. Thought disorders are common in psychotic reactions, but are just about nonexistent in neurotic reactions. Delusions, hallucinations, and psychotic logic are common in psychotic reactions. They are usually indicative of the person's loss of the ability to differentiate between reality and fantasy. Delusions are false cognitions or sets of cognitions that continue to be believed even in the face of evidence that the cognitions are wrong. Delusional people may truly believe that they are religious prophets, that they are from other planets, or that they play an important part in government. Such people may act on the basis of their delusions, which often makes their behavior bizarre and unpredictable. Hallucinations are sensory and perceptual experiences that occur in the absence of external stimuli. Hallucinating individuals may hear voices or other sounds, feel things touching them, or see things that are not there. Hallucinations often persist over time and are also evidence of the failure of reality-testing mechanisms.

Psychotic logic is characterized by massive violations of the rules of mature human logical thinking. The psychotic may reason as follows: "A person is president of the United States. I am a person. Therefore I am president of the United States." The psychotic may respond to the sound of a word in a question rather than to the meaning of the question. "How are you feeling?" "Quite congealing." This is called a clang association. There are numerous other examples of logical mechanisms which demonstrate the flawed and distorted reasoning of the psychotic. Once again, we observe the way in which thought processes interfere with the ability to test reality.

Often, psychotic people have experienced deep disturbances in interpersonal relations. Psychotics often demonstrate extreme withdrawal from relations with others. The withdrawal of the catatonic is so extreme that the catatonic may sit in a rigid physical position and not say a word to anyone for months or years. It is not usually the case that the psychotic can have good relations but doesn't want to. Rather, the psychotic's ability to make appropriate social responses is often seriously impaired. In other instances, such as in the manic-phase of the manic-depressive psychosis, psychotics may hurl themselves upon others. Once again, we note the extreme disturbance of normal interpersonal relations.

Extreme disturbances of emotion, thought, and interpersonal relations work to produce an element that often characterizes psychotic reactions—bizarre behavior. Other people easily note—and may be frightened by—a response of giddy laughter when a person is told that someone has died; the statement that a small rocket ship is hovering alongside one's head; or a rigid, withdrawn noncommunicative posture. Each of these kinds of symptoms is severe and is often indicative of a serious inability to function in the world and take care of oneself.

The various kinds of psychoses include schizophrenia, paranoia, manic-depressive psychosis, psychotic depression, and involutional psychoses. Most clinicians agree that the onset of paranoia does not usually occur until adulthood (Cameron, 1963; Swanson, Bohnert, and Smith, 1970; Coleman, 1976). This is also true for involutional psychoses, which tend to occur during the climacteric toward the end of middle adulthood (Cameron, 1963; Rosenthal, 1968; Coleman, 1976; Davison and Neale, 1978, Sarason, 1976). The more serious forms of depression do not usually become manifest until later adolescence (Weiner, 1970). Schizophrenia is observed in early adolescence (Bellak, 1958; Weiner, 1970; Lidz, 1974; Coleman, 1976). In the following section we will discuss schizophrenia as the primary psychosis of early adolescence. Manic-depressive psychosis and psychotic depression will be discussed in Chapter 12. Paranoia and involutional psychoses will not be discussed in this book.

## Schizophrenia

Schizophrenia is one of the most debilitating psychological disorders. The degree of disturbance of emotion, thought, interpersonal relations, and behavior is extensive. Sometimes a schizophrenic episode occurs very suddenly in someone who has never demonstrated schizophrenic behavior before. The episode may be extremely disabling and filled with many pathological symptoms. At other times, schizophrenic behavior may represent a pattern of symptoms of personality disorganization that has gradually developed over many years. One of the main differences between these patterns of onset is with the prognosis for recovery. When the onset of schizophrenic symptomatology is acute, there is a much better chance for recovery than when the condition has developed over a long period of time (Cameron, 1963; Vaillant, 1962, 1964). Studies which focus specifically on adolescent schizophrenia support this conclusion (Carter, 1942; Masterson, 1956; Brown, 1966; Weiner, 1970; van Krevelen, 1971). Acute schizophrenic reactions sometimes disappear after a relatively short period of time in a process called spontaneous remission. At other times, after an intensive therapeutic effort the individual makes a recovery and never experiences another episode. For some persons, however, the first episode is only the beginning of recurring episodes that lead to the development of chronic schizophrenia.

The American Psychiatric Association (1968) lists ten subtypes of schizophrenia. These are summarized in Table 8–4. Adolescent schizophrenia has been compared to adult schizophrenia, and the results have confirmed similarities in disturbances of emotion, thought, interpersonal relations, and behavior (Edelston, 1949; Burns, 1952; Neubauer and Steinart, 1952; Sands, 1956; Masterson, Tucker, and Berk, 1963; Kates and Kates, 1964; Spivack, Haimes, and Spotts, 1967; Weiner, 1966, 1970; van Krevelen, 1971; Lidz, 1974). Table 8–5 compares schizophrenic adolescents with schizophrenia adults as to subtype. All subtypes appear in adolescence. The main differences are a greater incidence of paranoid schizophrenia in adulthood and a greater incidence of the acute, undifferentiated type of schizophrenia in adolescence. One characteristic of adolescent schizophrenia that presents a special diagnostic problem is that often the more serious underlying condition may be masked by what initially appears to be a less serious psychopathological condition. Eating disorders (Bruch, 1958, 1962b, 1969, 1971, 1974; Sours, 1969), psychopathy and delinquency (Binder, 1959), and school phobias (van Krevelin, 1971) may on occasion be hiding a much more serious schizophrenic disturbance. The clinician must be very careful to differentiate between a less serious neurotic or behavior problem and the more devastating schizophrenic reaction.

Many questions are currently being evaluated in order to shed more light on the causes of schizophrenic reactions. Is schizophrenia hereditary? Are there biochemical causes? Do schizophrenics have aberrant neurophysiological development? Is schizophrenia related to a particular form of family interaction or to socioeconomic status? Is schizophrenia the product of excessive stress and overwhelming trauma? An abundant literature has developed around each of these questions as researchers try to better understand schizophrenia. For the moment, it is safe to say that although we are concerned with the condition, we do not fully understand

**Table 8–4: Summary of Types of Schizophrenia**

| | |
|---|---|
| Acute type | Characterized by a sudden onset of undifferentiated schizophrenic symptoms, often involving perplexity, confusion, emotional turmoil, delusions of reference, excitement, dreamlike dissociation, depression, and fear. The individual seems to undergo a massive breakdown of filtering processes, with the result that experience becomes fragmented and disorganized, taking on the qualities of a nightmare. |
| Paranoid type | A symptom picture dominated by absurd, illogical, and changeable delusions, frequently accompanied by vivid hallucinations, with a resulting impairment of critical judgment and erratic, unpredictable, and occasionally dangerous behavior. In chronic cases, there is usually less disorganization of behavior than in other types of schizophrenia, and less extreme withdrawal from social interaction. |
| Catatonic type | Often characterized by alternating periods of extreme withdrawal and extreme excitement, although in some cases one or the other reaction predominates. In the withdrawal reaction there is a sudden loss of all animation and a tendency to remain motionless for hours or even days, in a stereotyped position. The clinical picture may undergo an abrupt change, with excitement coming on suddenly, wherein the individual may talk or shout incoherently, pace rapidly, and engage in uninhibited, impulsive, and frenzied behavior. In this state, the individual may be dangerous. |
| Hebephrenic type | Usually occurs at an earlier age than most other types of schizophrenia, and represents a more severe disintegration of the personality. Emotional distortion and blunting typically are manifested in inappropriate laughter and silliness, peculiar mannerisms, and bizarre, often obscene, behavior. |
| Simple type | An insidious depletion of thought, affect, and behavior, beginning early in life and gradually progressing until the individual impresses others as being curiously inaccessible, isolated, colorless, and uninteresting. Because psychological disorganization is typically less severe than in other types of schizophrenia and some superficial contact with reality is usually maintained, hospitalization is less frequent. |
| Schizo-affective type | Characterized by a mixture of general schizophrenic symptoms, in conjunction with more pronounced obvious depression or elation—not typical of the usual surface pattern of "flattened affect." |
| Latent type | Characterized by various symptoms of schizophrenia but lacking a history of a full-blown schizophrenic episode. |
| Chronic undifferentiated type | Although manifesting definite schizophrenic symptoms in thought, affect, and behavior, not readily classifiable under one of the other types. |
| Residual type | Mild indications of schizophrenia shown by individuals in remission following a schizophrenic episode. |
| Childhood type | Preoccupation with fantasy, and markedly atypical and withdrawn behavior prior to puberty. |

Source: J. C. Coleman, *Abnormal Psychology and Modern Life,* 5th ed. (Glenview, Ill.: Scott, Foresman, 1976), p. 308. © 1976 by Scott, Foresman and Company. Reprinted by permission.

**Table 8–5: Subcategories of Schizophrenia in Adolescent and Adult Patients Terminated from Psychiatric Clinics***

| Subcategory | Adolescents† | | Adults‡ | |
|---|---|---|---|---|
| | Males | Females | Males | Females |
| Paranoid...................... | 18.6 | 14.5 | 39.2 | 34.4 |
| Acute undifferentiated .......... | 11.6 | 16.4 | 5.3 | 6.7 |
| Chronic undifferentiated ........ | 27.9 | 25.5 | 32.2 | 31.3 |
| Childhood .................... | 20.9 | 12.7 | § | § |
| Other ........................ | 21.0 | 30.9 | 23.3 | 27.6 |

*Expressed as percentage of total.

† From Rosen et al. (1965, p. 1566), based on approximately 2,550 schizophrenic adolescents.

‡ From *Outpatient Psychiatric Clinics* (1963, pp. 150–151), based on approximately 17,000 schizophrenic adults.

§ Category not listed.

Source: I. B. Weiner, *Psychological Disturbances in Adolescence* (New York: Wiley-Interscience, 1970), p. 105. Reprinted by permission.

it. It appears that hereditary, biological, psychological, and social factors may interact with one another to produce schizophrenic reactions. Currently, the prognosis for schizophrenics is not too good. Acute onset usually indicates a greater chance of recovery than does chronic development. There is no doubt about the extremely serious and disabling nature of a schizophrenic disturbance. In order to give you a feeling for the seriousness of adolescent schizophrenia, the case of Joan R. is presented. This case originally appeared in Cameron (1963).

## A Schizophrenic Reaction in an Adolescent Girl

Joan R., a Kansas City high school girl, was admitted to a psychiatric clinic after she had attempted suicide by drinking iodine. We shall begin with her childhood. She had suffered the loss through death of two important mother figures, one when she was two years old, the other when she was fourteen. These are critical ages in personality development, ages when a mother figure plays her most significant roles. Joan's mother had been ill for some time before her death, so that the little girl lacked the ego support which should have been available to her for the structuring of her early personality. At fourteen, when an adolescent normally lives through an altered form the oedipal conflicts of early childhood, Joan's foster mother died, and Joan was again left with no one to help her build her adolescent personality. To further complicate matters for Joan, her foster mother was her father's sister, a domineering widow with a daughter of her own. It will be simplest if we present briefly the patient's life history.

As we have said, Joan was two years old when her mother died. Her father's sister moved at once into the home, taking Joan's mother's place, and bringing with her Peggy, an eight-year-old daughter. We shall see how Joan tried to repeat what her foster mother had done as soon as death left her place vacant. Peggy's mother was an anxious, probably superstitious woman who encouraged Joan to be overdependent. The two girls apparently hated each other. When Peggy's mother died, Joan was fourteen and Peggy was a grown woman of twenty. The household now consisted of Joan, Peggy and Joan's father, a scholar with little psychological understanding.

To her father's surprise Joan showed no sorrow over the death of her foster mother. Instead, she tried at once to take her place in the home, just as her foster mother had immediately taken her own mother's place. She became self-assertive, arrogant and demanding. The home, she said, was now hers, and Peggy could henceforth obey her orders. Joan's father spent the next two years trying unsuccessfully to keep the peace between these two girls, rivals for control of the home.

Without a mother figure and without a stable personality of her own, Joan soon got out of control. She continued for the time being to be affectionate to her father, but she also behaved toward him as a nagging wife rather than as a young adolescent daughter. She openly criticized his appearance and his ways, even in front of guests. She demanded that he give her more attention and more money. She reminded her father that her foster mother, her father's sister, had been afraid of the house, often saying that there was a curse upon it. She protested violently against his going out in the evening and leaving the latchkey under the mat, where strangers might find it. As we shall see Joan was already beginning to develop delusional fears in relation to this evening situation. Toward Peggy, her grownup cousin, she remained relentlessly hostile. Once during a quarrel over the radio she hit Peggy severely, giving her a wound that took two weeks to heal. From other evidence it is clear that Joan's emotional problems, with which no one helped her, were precipitating a general personality disorganization.

When Joan was sixteen, her cousin married. This removed her rival from the home; but it also left Joan, in a state of emotional turmoil, alone in the house with her father. Her attitude toward him abruptly changed. She no longer gave or accepted tokens of affection. The hate that she had visited upon her cousin she now directed toward her father. She behaved insolently toward him, accusing him even before visitors of mistreating her. These accusations, which completely mystified her father, were actually the product of delusional experiences that she was having, experiences in which weird primary process fears and wishes had escaped repression and were mingling with preconscious and conscious organization. What these were we shall soon see. Whenever Joan had frightening dreams she would make her father join her in bed, as her aunt had always done, but later she would rail against him for having done this and accuse him of mistreatment. He was greatly disconcerted by all this contradiction and confusion; but he did not know what to do about it. He thought she would outgrow it. One night he came home late to find his daughter thrashing about the room with a cane—killing snakes, she said. She used to keep her light on all night long because she was having "frightening dreams," which were probably delusional and hallucinatory experiences rather than dreams.

As might be expected, after the aunt's death, when Joan was fourteen, her school work grew poorer and poorer. She seemed bored, inattentive and irritable. By the time she was fifteen and a half she needed a tutor to keep her from being dropped from school. Eventually even this help was not enough. When she was sixteen, Joan was dropped from school, and her father was told to consult a psychiatrist. The psychiatrist recommended immediate treatment, but his recommendation was not followed. Joan simply stayed at home.

Joan showed a corresponding decline in her social relationships. Undoubtedly because of her personality defects, and because she was over-dependent upon her foster mother, Joan had never reached an adequate level of social skill. She frightened and repelled the neighborhood children with her temper tantrums and uncompromising demands. As an adolescent she was far too much involved in the rivalry with her cousin for domination of the home, in her own revived oedipal conflicts and her preoccupations with frightening experiences to be able to interact normally with her peers, the boys and girls around her.

The climax came when Joan was sixteen, a year before she came to the hospital. She bought a new dress for a high school dance, but when her escort arrived she refused at first to see him. After considerable persuasion she finally consented to go with him; half an hour later she returned home without her escort. Perhaps she knew that her father had arranged to have her escorted when he found that nobody had invited her to the dance. At any rate this was her last social engagement. Following Joan's withdrawal from school, her father arranged little parties for her, "to help her get well," but she would shut herself in her room until the guests left the house. The best he could do about the situation was to engage a housekeeper.

During the months between leaving school and entering the hospital Joan was living in a nightmare. She was afraid to sleep at night because of all that seemed to be going on. During the day she lay around the house, preoccupied, worn out and doing next to nothing. Her behavior became obviously strange, reflecting the hopeless confusion of her thinking. For example, her father gave her forty dollars to buy some clothes, and she spent it all on history books which she never read. On another occasion she went out and spent twelve dollars on cosmetics, but a few days later she destroyed the lot. She got up early one morning, collected all the playing cards in the house and burned them, saying that they were sinful. She began talking about religion, the church, sin, charity and the hereafter. She gave the housekeeper five dollars because she had to be charitable "to get to heaven."

Joan said that all her troubles came from masturbation. At fifteen she concluded without telling anyone that this was driving her crazy. Her conclusion increased her already intolerable guilt, anxiety and confusion, and contributed to her belief that she would burn in hell for her sins, and that her hands were diseased. "I have leprosy!" she said at the hospital, "look at my hands. But that's not punishment enough for all my evil. Faust, yes, he gave himself to the devil. That's what I've done. Don't touch me! You'll be sorry, you'll get leprosy too!"

The girl's unconscious material, which ultimately emerged and over-whelmed her, seems to have appeared first as anxiety dreams and frightening nighttime fantasies—of snakes, assault, strangers in the house and murder. "I used to read stories and things," she said, "and then I'd go to bed and lie awake and think about them. I'd be scared silly to be in the room by myself. That house is so spooky." The last statement repeats what her foster mother had always said. When Joan closed her eyes and tried to sleep, she would have horrible visions, and see faces that seemed to grow enormous. She thought men were walking on the roofs, which were flat and connected with one another, and that they were climbing in the window. Eventually a man across the street seemed to control the house; and she began hearing voices. Finally a man's voice dominated, telling her to do whatever she was told.

Joan now used weird delusions to reconstruct the reality that she had lost in her steady regression and disorganization, delusions which would help explain her previously unconscious fantasies, now fully conscious. Her home, she told herself, was now the headquarters of a dope ring. Her father had been murdered and an impostor put in his place. "My father wouldn't treat me the way this man has treated me," she said. "My father and I were friends. This man will get into bed with me. I've been love-starved and forsaken; and I thought someone was bringing in opium." The similarity of this tale to the common dope ring mystery story is obvious, and its appeal is probably to the same unconscious needs.

In her fantasies, which Joan considered real, people seemed to beat her and tie her up. They seemed able to read her mind, to control her by reading her thoughts. She tried to keep back her thoughts; but the effort hurt the back of her head.

Joan began having horrible dreams and fantasies of killing her father and other people, of cutting them up and chewing their flesh, of being God, and of being murdered as a sacrifice. She felt at times that she was someone else, that her body was changing, that she might be going to have a baby, that she had a brain tumor and was going crazy.

In the hospital, where people listened to her when she spoke, some of her sadomasochistic fantasies became obvious. Joan said that her suicidal attempt was an act of self-punishment. She was going to hell for her sins, she thought, and the quicker she got there the better. "I thought it would make me suffer. If I hadn't become so hardened, it would have hurt terribly." At times she was sure she would be executed for her crimes, which seemed real to her, or that she would get life imprisonment. She wished that she would "get black smallpox or something." She said, "I got hipped on the subject of Christianity. I thought I should torture myself. . . . I try to figure out ways of torturing people. It seems I have been in so much pain; and I want other people to have the same thing."

Joan had many outbursts of rage. One night a nurse found her trembling and wringing her hands. "I think I'm pushing people's eyes in. I'm dreadfully wicked. . . . It's those awful thoughts that go through my head." Once in the daytime she cried to a group of patients, "If I had the strength of Christ I would kill every one of you! Yes, I would kill you all because a more horrid doom awaits you than death." There is a sign of confusion between herself and the others in this histrionic statement. Another day Joan became angry and struck an inoffensive depressed patient. "That's nothing in comparison with what I'm going to do," she cried, "I'm going to chop off your heads, every one of you. You'd better go home and chop off your families' heads. . . . You're not going to keep me here and make me bear children!" In the more permissive atmosphere of the hospital, Joan was giving vent to the violent aggression that she had felt for years at home. After expressing it, she excused herself on the grounds that she would be saving the patients from something worse by killing them.

There were grandiose delusions also. Joan said that she felt she had a powerful influence over people and was responsible for everything that happened. She thought that she might get superhuman ideas, "such as how Christ turned water into wine—I had to find out how it was done." As God, she thought, she must suffer to help others; and because of her sins she ought to kill herself. But the attempt failed. "So," she said, "I came to the conclusion that I would have to forget. As time goes on, I'll forget all my troubles, my experiences and so forth." This was just what Joan seemed to be achieving. She expressed, in well-organized secondary process speech, the disintegration which she was experiencing, and to which she was resigned.

Years before, when her foster mother died, Joan had begun a struggle at home with a tangled personal situation involving real persons, her father, her cousin and herself. For such a struggle, with no one around to understand her, Joan's personality organization was unprepared. As time went on, this shared social community was gradually replaced by the even greater complexities of Joan's delusional pseudocommunity, with its mixture of real and imagined persons, of fact and reconstructed delusion. Now she seemed to be making a final retreat. She was withdrawing into an autistic community which consisted mainly of fantasied persons and action with the background of her own private fantasies.

There were two definite catatonic episodes. One day, while telling her therapist that she liked dreamy states, Joan slipped into a stupor. Her eyes closed, her eyeballs rolled upward, and her limbs went limp. Her eyelids resisted opening, however, and her jaws and limbs grew stiffer as they were manipulated. When she was left alone she soon recovered. Another day Joan was lying on her side on her bed, just before lunch, when there was a sudden loud clap of thunder close by. Joan instantly became so rigid that the nurses could pick her up and place her in a sitting position with no more change in her posture than if she had been a statue. Then the lunch trays arrived, and an experienced nurse began coaxing her gently and spoon-feeding her. After about ten minutes of this, the girl suddenly got up, rubbed her eyes as though she had just awakened, and ate her lunch with the others as if nothing had happened.

Therapy was unsuccessful with Joan. She slept well at night without medication, in spite of occasional disturbing dreams. In the daytime she spent most of her time daydreaming. She became less and less communicative, her talk developed more and more disorganization. She was frequently observed talking excitedly to herself. Sometimes she smiled and laughed as though she were hallucinating. Often she stood straight against the wall with her hands high above her head; but she would give no explanation of this posturing. Her father decided to place Joan in a state hospital near her home. Her prognosis for social recovery was poor.

**Discussion.** In this case we see the progressive disorganization of an adolescent girl during a period of over three years. Joan suffered two severely traumatic losses. Her mother fell ill and died when Joan was only two, before she had had time to establish her own childhood personality. Her foster mother confused the child by immediately taking the dead mother's place, and by introducing a rival girl into the home. The fact that the woman who took the place of Joan's mother in the house was the sister of Joan's father must have added to the confusion, although we have no information about this. What we do know, however, is that neither girl seems to have been adequately protected from the hostility of the other, at least after the foster mother died. The death of her domineering foster mother when Joan was only fourteen was the second severe trauma. It was compounded by the father's ineptness in handling emotional situations.

The affectional situation was suddenly complicated when the foster mother died. If Joan had been four years older or younger, she might have weathered it, in spite of having always been overdependent and overprotected. We have seen how unskillfully Joan tried to identify with her dead foster mother and take over the household immediately, as her foster mother had done. Her growing confusion can in part be attributed to the conflicts and contradictions, the tumult of early adolescent love and hate, which Joan's ineffectual attempts must have stimulated. A fourteen-year-old girl with such a background could hardly take the role of a domineering mother toward her twenty-year-old cousin; neither could she transform her dependent daughter role into that of the woman of the house in relation to her father. She had been reared an anxious, socially immature child without adequate opportunity to develop a mature ego-superego organization. As such, she was left alone to work out her multiple conflicts, including her clearly expressed guilt over sex and hostility, in a household with a man who did not understand her and a woman whom she hated.

Another important factor in promoting Joan's disorganization was the progressive intrusion of primary process fantasy into her nighttime and daytime thinking, once she had been abandoned to the complex home situation by the death of her aunt. Long before her aunt's death, probably throughout her life, Joan had found difficulty in distinguishing between dream and daydream. She had utilized fantasy freely in satisfying need, and she had also experienced terrifying dreams and hypnagogic visions which drove her to seek the protection of her aunt's bed. We have seen how she carried her conflicts, her wishes, fears and furies, over into her waking and sleeping fantasy life after her aunt was dead.

This procedure settled nothing. On the contrary, the confusion of fantasy and fact only increased Joan's anxiety and complicated her problems. There was now no adult to whom she could flee for comforting in the night, no adult who could act as substitute ego in support of her own inadequate one. The childhood fantasies came tumbling out of repression, through the defective defensive boundaries, and into Joan's daytime thinking. She was able to halt her regression by constructing fantastic delusions, which sounded like murder mystery stories, but this halt did not last. Even before she was admitted to the hospital Joan had already regressed into the jungles of primary process thinking. Therapy did not succeed in rescuing her. She continued regressing into an autistic world of fantasy where she ignored all of her surroundings that she could.[1]

## BEHAVIOR DISORDERS OF EARLY ADOLESCENCE

We will categorize certain problems that are relatively common in early adolescence as behavior problems. These problems include juvenile delinquency, drug usage, and running away from home. There are counterparts to each of these forms of deviant behavior in adulthood. As we will see, each of these three problems is very complex. There are many causes for each and many types of each. What the problems have in common is that each demonstrates behaviors that are not acceptable to the society at large. The problem comes to someone's attention because the main behaviors that are expressed are antisocial or asocial and because these behaviors are simply not tolerated by the person's society. Often there is particular concern when these problems become manifest in early adolescence because there is the sense that a young person going "bad" is a tragic loss for the community. There is also the hope that proper treatment may restore the person to the "right" path.

### Juvenile Delinquency

The word *delinquency* is defined by the dictionary as "conduct that is out of accord with accepted behavior or the law" (Webster, 1977, p. 300). "Juvenile delinquency" is defined as "a status in a juvenile characterized by antisocial behavior that is beyond parental control and therefore subject to legal action" (Webster, 1977, p. 629). These definitions tell us that we are discussing someone who does something that is unacceptable to society. Society takes this behavior as an indication that the person is out of parental control and must therefore be controlled by society as a whole through its legal system. States differ quite a bit in their classifications of juvenile delinquency. What is usually defined by the law as juvenile delinquency is behavior that would be criminal in an adult, who would be held fully responsible for it, and behavior

---

[1] Source: N. Cameron, *Personality Development and Psychopathology.* Copyright © 1963 by Norman Cameron. Reprinted by permission of Houghton Mifflin Co.

*The school is a common target for antisocial behavior.*

for which a child (usually under eight) would not be considered intellectually mature enough to be responsible. The juvenile delinquent is thought to be *(a)* mature enough to be somewhat responsible for the deviant behavior; *(b)* out of parental control; and *(c)* in need of control, guidance, and rehabilitation from the society. What most authors point out is that many, many adolescents commit acts that would be considered delinquent if these acts were observed and if those who committed them were brought to the attention of juvenile court authorities (Porterfield, 1943; Murphy, Shirley, and Witmer, 1946; Offer, Sabshin, and Marcus, 1965; Marwell, 1966; Weiner, 1970; Schimel, 1974; Coleman, 1976; Sarason, 1976). The data from court records and other such sources would seem to underestimate the actual amount of delinquent behavior that exists during the early adolescent years. Yet Schimel (1974) and Sarason (1976) estimate that one out of every nine children will be brought to the attention of the juvenile authorities before their 18th birthday. Coleman (1976) and the *Uniform Crime Reports* (Federal Bureau of Investigation, 1975) provide estimates that 1 out of every 15 adolescents in the nation was arrested in 1974. The problem of juvenile delinquency is quite prevalent, and the problem of delinquent behavior among adolescents is even more widespread.

For most adolescents who commit delinquent acts, the antisocial behavior is a brief, episodic experience. The breakthrough of aggressive impulses, peer group coaxing, crowd behavior, rebellion, a state of deprivation, thrill-seeking, a reaction against depression, and feelings of low self-esteem are among the reasons for episodes of delinquent behavior. Many "one-timers" are not caught by the police committing delinquent acts. Often, however, the effect of such unobserved indiscretions is to bring the issue of the failure of socialization and personal control to the attention of the adolescent and sometimes to the attention of parents. The delinquent behavior and the fear of one's own potential immorality serve to straighten out the offender. The unobserved delinquent behavior serves to warn the offender that there is a potential problem in behavioral control, and the offender is able to use this information adaptively to prevent the recurrence of such episodes.

The involvement of early adolescents in the total crime statistics in the United States is significant. In 1966, the FBI estimated that juveniles comprised 22.9 percent of all arrests in 1965 (Federal Bureau of Investigation, 1966). This figure has been rising faster than the rise in the proportion of adolescents in the population (Federal Bureau of Investigation, 1975). Between 1968 and 1975, arrests of persons under 18 years of age for serious crimes increased 100 percent. This was four times as fast as the rise in the population of this age group. (Federal Bureau of Investigation, 1975; Coleman, 1976). In 1974, adolescents accounted for one out of three arrests for robbery, one out of five arrests for rape, and one out of ten arrests for murder (Federal Bureau of Investigation, 1975; Coleman, 1976).

More males become delinquents than females. Estimates indicate that 80 percent of delinquents are males (Lunden, 1964; Wolfgang, Johnston, and Savitz, 1970; Schimel, 1974). The rate of delinquency for females has been on the rise recently (Coleman, 1976), particularly in the categories of running away and drug abuse. We will discuss these two problems separately in later sections. The main crime areas for boys are larceny, burglary, disorderly conduct, curfew violation, vandalism, auto theft, running away, and violation of liquor and drug laws. To a lesser degree, boys are also arrested for crimes against people, such as armed robbery and aggravated assault. The main crimes for girls are drug usage, sexual offenses, running away from home, incorrigibility or disorderly conduct, and larceny (Lunden, 1964; Schimel, 1974; Coleman, 1976).

There appears to be a developmental pattern to delinquent behavior. The age during which delinquency is most frequently observed is between 14 and 15. This is true for both boys and girls. The incidence of delinquent behavior at different ages may vary according to the kind of offense. At 14 the main kind of observed delinquent behavior is stealing. At 16 and 17 peak incidences are observed for malicious mischief, vandalism, auto theft, carrying an offensive weapon, and assaults (West, 1967). Thus we find a pattern in which delinquency may be observed early (because of state laws, the age of 8 may be the earliest period of observation), increase to a peak at 15, and then decline. Less serious delinquent behavior is observed at earlier ages, whereas more serious crime tends to be observed as children grow older. The evidence also appears to suggest that those who begin to commit delinquent acts at an early age are more likely to continue criminal behavior into adulthood (West, 1967; Sarason, 1976).

The patterns of delinquency tend to suggest the following analysis. For the vast majority of adolescents who commit delinquent acts, the experience goes unobserved by agents of the society, and the episode itself serves as a warning to the culprit to institute measures to gain greater personal control. The next largest number of adolescents committing delinquent acts come to the attention of the police and courts, and this experience serves to warn such adolescents and their families to institute greater mechanisms for behavioral control. The smallest group begin to commit relatively minor delinquent acts at an early age. They continue to perform delinquent acts which become increasingly serious, and during the adolescent years they develop into criminal personalities. Many more boys than girls are involved in this type of behavior problem, indicating a greater ability by girls to institute mechanisms of behavioral control over aggressive and antisocial impulses.

Researchers and clinicians have described many types of delinquents (Weiner, 1970; Coleman, 1976; Sarason, 1976). We will describe five types in order to give you some idea of the complexity of delinquency and of the varied psychopathological problems that find an outlet in antisocial behavior.

1. The psychopathic delinquent—a personality structure which is characterized by impulsivity, defiance, an absence of guilt feelings, inability to learn from experience, and inability to maintain close social relationships. This kind of delinquent behavior is found in females as well as males (Konopka, 1964, 1967; Fine and Fishman, 1968; Cloninger and Guze, 1970; Coleman, 1976). Multiple arrest records and difficulties in altering personality structure are characteristic of this type (Ganzer and Sarason, 1973; Sarason, 1976; Coleman, 1976).

2. The neurotic delinquent. Delinquent behavior is thought to be a product of psychological conflict and anxiety. The behavior of this type may involve the symptomatic expression of (a) needs that cannot be expressed otherwise, including needs for punishment, recognition, admiration, status, and help; (b) the effects of inadvertent parental fostering of antisocial behavior through covert stimulation and inadvertent reinforcement; and (c) the effects of "scapegoating"—the selection, usually unconscious, of a particular youngster to receive the family's implicit encouragement to delinquency (Weiner, 1970).

3. The psychotic delinquent. The delinquent behavior of this type, often violence, is one symptomatic indication of the person's inability to test reality, control personal impulses, and utilize good judgment (Weiner, 1970; Coleman, 1976).

4. The organic delinquent. The two main classes of organic delinquency are (a) mental retardation, in which low intelligence impedes adequate judgment and may make the person a willing instrument for a brighter delinquent; and (b) brain damage, which interferes with behavioral control and may induce periodic displays of violence (Weiner, 1970; Coleman, 1976).

5. The gang delinquent. Once thought to be the typical delinquency pattern, current research reveals gang delinquency to be less common than it had been thought to be. Gang delinquency serves a social purpose, often involving the protection of territory and other resources. Just as social cliques such as those of the frats or preppies fill the social needs of their members for status, resources, and relationship, so juvenile gangs fill the needs of their

members for status, resources, and relationship. Erikson (1959) has pointed out that the type of person who joins a gang often develops a "negative identity." This is an integrated personal identity which stands opposed to the values and goals of the traditional society. Earlier we discussed the importance of the development of a sense of group identity during early adolescence. We believe that gang delinquency is a method by which adolescents who have been rejected by other social groups attain a sense of group identity.

There are many causes of delinquency. At this point we should be able to speculate about some. For the adolescent who engages in a single delinquent act or a small number of delinquent acts, the cause has to do with increased aggressive impulses that accompany physical and psychological maturation. The breakthrough of aggressive behavior signals the need for the further development of judgment, for anticipating the consequences of one's actions, and for a future orientation. Most adolescents are able to heed this behavioral warning and to develop new coping skills as a result of it. For the organic delinquent, the causes are genetic and physical. For the neurotic and psychotic delinquent, the causes of delinquency are rooted in emotional turmoil and personality disorganization. The delinquent behavior is a symptom of these problems. The etiology of the neuroses and psychoses of early adolescence have been discussed above.

The psychopathic delinquent is an integrated character structure. Research indicates that this personality structure appears to be the product of the following factors (Bowlby, 1944; Berman, 1959; Bender, 1961; McCord and McCord, 1964; Glueck and Glueck, 1962, 1970; Weiner, 1970; Bandura, 1973, Sarason, 1976):

1.  Rejection in childhood.
2.  The experience and expectation of hostility and aggression from others as a part of this rejection.
3.  Aggressive behavior as a reaction to rejection and to observing aggressive models.
4.  Lack of support for social achievement in school.
5.  Peer group rejection.

Although this combination of factors does not always lead to the development of a psychopathic personality, it is commonly found in delinquents who have developed this type of personality structure.

The causes of gang delinquency seem to involve *(a)* the rejection of the person by socially favored groups, *(b)* knowledge of and association with others who have been similarly rejected, *(c)* the development of a socially meaningful group that meets needs for group identity, and *(d)* the rejection by the group of traditional societal methods for attaining resources.

## Runaways

Whereas delinquency as discussed above usually involves an aggressive striking out against society, running away involves leaving one's situation, usually for a short period and sometimes for good. This "dropping out" of one's existing settings and relationships is not sanctioned by society either, and many runaways come to the attention of police or juvenile authorities. "Running away," like "striking out," represents a behavioral mode for dealing with internal conflict and/or environmental stress. It has been argued that runaways, like delinquents, are sometimes involved in stealing (Shellow et al., 1967) and drug abuse (Pittell, 1968; Stierlin, 1973), but the data tend to show that these behaviors occur after the person runs away rather than before (Robins and O'Neal, 1959; Pittell, 1968; Stierlin, 1973; Justice and Duncan, 1976). We take the position that running away is an attempt to cope with one's life by leaving the immediate field of one's existence for a time.

Many definitions of running away are used. The National Center for Health Statistics (1975) uses "leaving or staying away on purpose, knowing you would be missed, intending to stay away from home, at least for some time." Walker (1975) summarizes some of the key factors included in definitions of "runaway" that she encountered in her review of the literature. These include (1) age, (2) the parents' permission or consent, (3) psychological characteristics, (4) inclusion in missing person records, (5) identification by a juvenile court, (6) child knowledge about the consequences of the action, (7) time gone, (8) where ran from, (9) where ran to, and (10) previous runaway behavior. The most commonly used definitions are similar to that of the National Center for Health Statistics. Some studies focus in detail on adolescents who run away from institutions (Baer, 1970; Clarke, 1968; Coleman, 1968; Farrington, Shelton, and MacKay, 1963; Levine, 1962; Bartollas, 1973). These occurrences are in the nature of escapes from prisons by adolescents who have been confined for other forms of delinquency. In this section we will focus on the situation of running away from home.

As with delinquency, the prevalence of this kind of behavior is difficult to estimate. The *Uniform Crime Reports* indicate that there were 163,863 runaway arrests (based on 3,601 agency reports) in 1972 and 121,600 runaway arrests (based on 3,256 agency reports) in 1973 (Walker, 1975). Justice and Duncan (1976), using National Center for Health Statistics data, estimated that 2,139,000 youths in the United States had run away from home at least once. The National Center for Health Statistics (1975) calculates that 300,000 ran away in 1974. Arrest records would seem to identify less than half of the adolescents who run away in any particular year. The center also indicates that 10.1 percent of all boys and 8.7 percent of all girls between the ages of 12 and 17 run away from home at least once. Other researchers tend to confirm this finding. Bachman (1970) reports that 11 percent of a sample of 2,213 tenth-grade boys had run away from home. Akers (1964) found that 12.7 percent of a sample of youths between the ages of 13–17 had run away. Short and Nye (1958) found comparable percentages in Western and Midwestern locations. Although many runaways come to the attention of authorities, at least as many receive only the notice of family and friends. Some authorities estimate that there may be as many as 500,000 runaways per year, with most going undetected (Ambrosino, 1971; Gold and Reimer, 1974; Walker, 1975).

Most runaway youths seem to stay close to their hometown, and many actually go to the homes of relatives or friends (Beyer et al., 1974; Brennan et al., 1975). As age increases, so does the length of time away from home. Every study that reports the frequency of runaway episodes indicates that most (probably 70–80 percent) of runaways are on their first and only run (Walker, 1975). Most of the episodes are poorly planned and reflect impulsive behavior (Wein, 1970; Beyer et al., 1974; Brennan et al., 1975). Adolescents run away for many reasons (Walker, 1975). Some of these are:

1. Impulse.
2. To seek good times.
3. To seek a better life.
4. To get away from stressful families.
5. To get away from school stress.
6. To escape after a crime.
7. To get away from a bad reputation.
8. To get attention.
9. To show independence.
10. To show aggression.
11. To travel.
12. To accompany friends.
13. To escape a crisis.
14. To withdraw from the peer group.
15. Restlessness.
16. To escape anxiety.
17. To be free.
18. To join a girlfriend or a boyfriend.
19. Psychotic disorganization.
20. To become a hobo.
21. Loneliness.

One of the common reasons given for running away is conflict and rejection in the family (Shellow et al., 1967; Walker, 1975; Justice and Duncan, 1976). For many, such conflict leads to a single, impulsive, temporary flight. This behavior may serve notice to the

parents and the child that a problem exists, and the family resources may then be mobilized for more effective coping. For others,
rejection and punishment may lead to running away (Wolk and
Brandon, 1977). When rejection is serious, the first run may not
be the last. Females appear to utilize running away more than
other form of delinquency in reaction to rejection and punishment.
as the list above demonstrates, running away also occurs for many
other reasons. Just as Dick Whittington went to London to seek
his fortune, so do some young men and women today go off to
seek their fortune. As Huckleberry Finn ran away to seek adventure, so do some youths today run away to seek adventure. For
some, the "wanderlust" of youth motivates running away. Neuroses, psychoses, psychopathy, and criminal tendencies force some
adolescents to run. Crises produce temporary flights. A wide variety
of motivations lead to the utilization of a single behavioral mode
of adaptation.

## Drug Use

We have discussed delinquency as a form of deviance in which
the person strikes out against property or other people. Sometimes
the aggressive behavior is symbolic of underlying conflicts. Running
away from home is a form of behavior in which people try to
change their environment in order to adapt to internal or external
conditions. Drug use is a form of behavior in which people try to
change their internal state for one reason or another. Drugs may
be used for a wide variety of reasons, but in general terms the
intent is always the same—to alter the physical or psychological
state of the person. (We will not be at all concerned here with
drugs that are used to combat infection and disease, such as antibi-
otics). Sometimes individuals will wish to become more aroused,
and they will then use drugs that act as stimulants to the central
nervous system. Such drugs are called "uppers." Sometimes they
will wish to become more relaxed. In this case they will elect
drugs that act as depressants to the central nervous system. Sometimes people will wish to "expand their consciousness" or alter
their perceptions. In these cases they will seek drugs that produce
these effects on the central nervous system. Such drugs are called
hallucinogens or psychodelics. Each of these types of drug effects
can be induced in a mild, moderate, or severe form, depending
upon the type of drug used and to some extent upon the dosage
that is ingested. Thus, alcohol, which is categorized as a mild depressant, can cause death if a person's blood contains more than
.55 percent alcohol (Coleman, 1976; Kleinhesselink, St. Dennis, and
Cross, 1976; *New York Times,* 1978).

State-altering drugs may be used in five different ways:

1. Proper use—when a drug is prescribed by a physician for a medical purpose.
2. Addictive use—when a person develops a physiological or psychological dependence upon the drug.
3. Misuse—when a drug is used by mistake, as when a child accidentally ingests medication or an adult takes a tranquilizer thinking that it is a Bufferin. This would also include the situation in which someone unknowingly ingests a hallucinogen that someone has put in a drink.
4. Abuse—excessive use of a drug which a person is well aware is excessive, whether or not there is dependence. Excessive use often leads to dependence.
5. Illegal use—when it is against the law for (1) a person to use a drug, (2) a drug to be used, or (3) a particular behavior to be performed while the person is under the influence of the drug.

A drug may be used in more than one of these ways. What the above listing points out to us is that except for a morning cup of coffee (which contains caffeine) almost all drug use in early adolescence is illegal use. Table 8–6 lists common drugs which are addictive and are abused, misused, or illegally used by adolescents. The table categorizes central nervous system depressants, stimulants, and hallucinogens of mild, moderate, and severe toxicity.

Data about the use of drugs informs us that early adolescents are involved in the use of every kind of drug (Boyd, 1971; Milman and Su, 1973; Jessor, Jessor, and Finney, 1973; Johnson, 1973; Galli, 1974; Chafetz, 1974; Lerner, Linder, and Burke, 1974; Kleinhesselink et al., 1976; O'Donnell et al., 1976). As it is illegal for early adolescents to use all of these drugs, including alcohol, drug usage itself would have to be classified as a form of deviant behavior. Milman and Su (1973) substantiate this in a study of drug use in which they find that patterns of drug use are most pronounced in youth who deviate from "currently accepted norms of behavior and adjustment."

Why do early adolescents use drugs? As with the types of behavior problems discussed earlier, there seem to be a multitude of reasons. Often the reasons are directly related to the type of drug used and to the intensity of use.

Early adolescents are often introduced to drugs by friends who have already become involved in drug use (Becker, 1953; Goode, 1970; Boyd, 1971; Johnson, 1973; Chafetz, 1974). Another reason that probably accounts for a great deal of initial and, for most,

**Table 8–6: Common Drugs of Abuse and Addiction (CNS Intoxicants) Employed by Adolescents**

| Usual Toxic Effects | Physical and Psychological Addiction: | Mainly Psychological Addiction | |
|---|---|---|---|
| | CNS depressants | CNS stimulants | CNS Hallucinogens* |
| Mild | 1. Organic solvents (e.g. toluene, acetone, benzene, carbon tetrachloride, ether)<br>2. Alcohol (e.g., ethyl alcohol) | 1. Xanthines ( e.g., caffeine)<br>2. Sympathomimetics (e.g., ephedrine, isoprenaline) | 1. Nutmeg (Myristica fragrans)<br>2. Morning glory seeds (Convolvulacea)<br>3. Cannabis (Cannabis sativa) |
| Moderate | Hypnotics-sedatives<br>1. Barbiturates (e.g., pentobarbitone [s-a], amylobarbitone [1-a], phenobarbitone [1-a])<br>2. Miscellaneous (e.g., Mandrax = methaqualone and diphenhydramine; Doriden = glutethimide; Librium = chlordiazepoxide; Valium = diazepam; Equanil = meprobamate) | Anorectics<br>1. Amphetamines (e.g., Benzedrine = amphetamine; Dexedrine = dexamphetamine; Methedrine = methylamphetamine)<br>2. Miscellaneous (e.g., Preludin = phenmetrazine; Ritalin = methylphenidate; Tenuate = diethylpropion) | 1. Mescaline (peyote)<br>2. Psilocybin (psylocybe)<br>3. DMT = dimethyltryptamine |
| Severe | Opiates<br>1. Natural or semisynthetic (e.g., opium [Papaver somniferum]; morphine; heroin = diacetylmorphine)<br>2. Synthetic (e.g., methadone, pethidine) | Cocaine (Erythroxylum coca or truxillense) | 1. LSD = Lysergic acid diethylamide (lysergide)<br>2. STP = 4-methyl-2,5-dimethoxy-alpha-methyl phenethylamine |

* This word is chosen in preference to others, as it describes the most common manifestation. Other names given to these drugs include: psychotomimetics = producing psychotic manifestations, psychodysleptics = producing delusional manifestations, psychodelics—producing expansion and distortion of mental perceptions.

Source: P. R. Boyd, "Drug Abuse and Addiction in Adolescents," in J. G. Howells (Ed.), *Modern Perspectives in Adolescent Psychiatry* (New York: Brunner/Mazel, 1971), p. 294. Reprinted by permission.

limited use has to do with the excitement of experimentation (Pros-kauer and Rolland, 1973; Newman and Newman, 1975; Kleinhes-selink et al., 1976; Sarason, 1976). Widespread knowledge about the effects of different drugs coupled with the desire to heighten the experiences associated with the physical, cognitive, social, and emotional changes of early adolescence is a strong inducement for many. The National Institute on Alcohol Abuse and Alcoholism (Chafetz, 1974) estimates that 60 percent of seventh graders and 71–93 percent of high school students are experimental users of alcohol. Marijuana is another drug that a large number of early adolescents experiment with (Proskauer and Rolland, 1973; Victor, Grossman, and Eisenman, 1973). Estimates of the extent of mari-juana use vary considerably, but most estimates indicate a wide-spread use on an experimental (sometimes only one time) basis. In terms of widespread use for experimentation, marijuana's popu-larity increased considerably during the 60s and the early 70s (Na-tional Commission on Marijuana and Drug Abuse, 1972), and the use of alcohol surged forward in the 70s (Chafetz, 1974; Kleinhes-selink et al., 1976). Some early adolescents, depending on their degree of daring and the preferences of their companions, will try other drug experiences for experimentation and excitement. "Glue sniffing" and intoxication from other organic solvents are most prevalent among 10–15-year-olds (Press and Done, 1967; Boyd, 1971). Organic solvents produce a quick, short state of intoxication along with a wide variety of unpleasant side effects, including head-ache, nausea, and vomiting. For this reason, most early adolescents abandon this habit rather quickly. LSD, cocaine, or heroin are used experimentally for the thrilling effects by some adolescents, but, we would argue, only by the most daring under circumstances of availability and heavy peer pressure. Amphetamines and barbitu-rates may also be used by thrill seekers when they are available, and they can become truly dangerous when used in conjunction with each other (Boyd, 1971; Kleinhesselink et al., 1976; Coleman, 1976).

Using drugs for experimentation will be a single experience for most of the adolescents who try them. For the next largest group, moderate drug use will continue as a social experience in much the same way as it does for many adults. Drinking groups and marijuana smoking groups can be found in most high school cul-tures. The use of one drug or the other reflects availability, historic trends, and political orientations and attitudes. The next largest group of users would be the people who are seeking thrills, highs, and intoxication. They may be trying to escape from boredom (Sara-son, 1976), a stressful situation (Kleinhesselink et al., 1976), or feel-ings of depression (Proskauer and Rolland, 1973). Some early adolescents use drugs as a method for adapting to and expressing neurotic or psychotic conflicts and problems (Boyd, 1971; Sarason, 1976; Coleman, 1976; Gallagher and Harris, 1976; Kleinhesselink et al., 1976). Just as delinquent behavior or running away may be used as a behavioral expression of a neurotic or psychotic problem, so may taking drugs serve this purpose.

A final reason why some adolescents use drugs is because it is an aspect of the life-style of people like themselves. Jessor and Jessor and their co-workers (Jessor et al., 1968; Jessor et al., 1970; Jessor and Jessor, 1977) have described a group of psychosocial variables which are associated with adolescent drug use as well as other forms of deviant behavior. Psychologically the person feels helpless, hopeless, and socially isolated. This is called *alienation.* the person also feels that social norms and laws can be disregarded because there are no restrictions from parents or peers. This is called *anomie.* There must also be a tolerance for deviance and an access to opportunities to learn deviant behaviors. These factors combine to produce problem behavior as part of a deviant life-style in which the so-called deviant behavior is really an integral part of the individual's subcultural experiences; coming from a lower-class home, having high exposure to opportunities for and models of deviant drug use, high personal dissatisfaction, and a sense that it is acceptable to engage in deviant drug use combine to account for drug use in a particular segment of the population (Kleinhesselink et al., 1976; Jessor and Jessor, 1977). The absence of social controls seems to be the single most powerful predictive variable (Jessor et al., 1968; Jessor et al., 1970; Glueck and Glueck, 1968; Kleinhesselink et al., 1976). This life-style is related to delinquency and running away as well as to drug use. Jessor and Jessor (1977) have been able to demonstrate the ways in which these underlying factors lead to a wide variety of problem behaviors in a subgroup of adolescents. Where there is deprivation, alienation, anomie, tolerance for deviance, and lack of control, there is a strong likelihood of drug use and delinquency and running away from home.

There are many risks of drug use at every age and some particular risks for the early adolescent. Physiological or psychological dependence are serious consequences which often lead to heavy and continuous drug use. The need to support an illegal and often expensive habit sometimes leads to drug-related stealing. The heavy use of certain drugs may lead the person to neglect hygiene and nutrition, which can lead to a wide variety of health problems. The dangers of overdoses of many drugs, including alcohol, are particularly noticeable in early adolescents (Boyd, 1971; Kleinhesselink et al., 1976; Coleman, 1976). Overdoses often lead to death, so that this risk is extremely serious. The impulsive use of drugs, including the combining of drugs to increase their potency, is common in early adolescents and can also be extremely dangerous, sometimes leading to death. The dangers of using solvents, including urinary tract infections, damage to the nasal and oral membranes, and brain damage, are almost exclusively dangers of the early adolescent period, as most other drug-using groups do not use solvents. Impulsive behaviors related to the drug experience, including reckless automobile driving and attempts to fly out of upper-story windows, are common. Such behaviors point to the risks of drug use for even very occasional users, who because of their unfamiliarity with a drug may make a decision that leads to death or serious injury.

In this section we have examined the behavioral problem of drug use during early adolescence. We have discussed five types of use: proper use, addictive use, misuse, abuse, and illegal use. We have discussed the various common central nervous system depressants, stimulants, and hallucinogens that are used by early adolescents. We have discussed a variety of reasons for early adolescent drug use, including social participation, experimentation, thrill seeking, intoxication, escape from boredom, stress or depression, neurotic or psychotic conditions, and life-style. Finally, we have described the serious risks of adolescent drug use, which include addiction, physical or psychological injury, and death.

## CHAPTER SUMMARY

In discussing deviance during early adolescence, we have pointed out that although there are many physical, cognitive, social, and emotional changes as the individual enters puberty and moves through this stage, turmoil, conflict, and serious deviance seem to be characteristic of about 20 percent of early adolescents. Most adolescents seem to accommodate change in a gradual, learning-oriented manner that leads to healthy personality development. Some adolescents experience turmoil and conflict that may lead to temporary periods of upheaval and disorganization. A small group of early adolescents may experience extremely serious deviance in their efforts to cope with and adapt to life. Table 8–7 summarizes the various kinds of psychological problems that are observed during this period of life. The schizophrenic psychoses often reflect a very serious set of disturbances that may lead to institutionalization and ineffective functioning for one's entire life. A single acute episode has the best prognosis for recovery, but an increasing number of episodes and chronic development often lead to a lifetime of debilitation. Psychopathic delinquency is a forerunner of adult

**Table 8–7: Psychological Problems of Early Adolescence**

| | |
|---|---|
| Neuroses | Anxiety reactions |
| | Anorexia nervosa |
| | Phobias |
| | Depression |
| | Hysterical reactions |
| |     Conversion reactions |
| |     Dissociative reactions |
| | Obsessive-compulsive reactions |
| Psychoses | Schizophrenia |
| |     Acute type |
| |     Paranoid type |
| |     Catatonic type |
| |     Hebephrenic type |
| |     Simple type |
| |     Schizo-affective type |
| |     Latent type |
| |     Chronic undifferentiated type |
| |     Residual type |
| Behavior Disorders | Juvenile delinquency |
| | Running away |
| | Drug use |

criminal life patterns which often find the person alternating between periods of lawbreaking and periods of institutionalization. Most delinquent behavior, however, appears to disappear as the person grows into adulthood and assumes work and family responsibilities. A few drug users die in early adolescence as a result of overdoses or of fatal behaviors that are related to drug use. Some drug users begin a pattern of long-term dependence and problem behavior in adolescence that continues into adulthood. This may become more serious, particularly as cumulative physical and psychological effects evolve. Many adolescent drug users continue a mild use of drugs into adult life. For some people, learning to drink socially occurs in early adolescence and continues into adulthood. Some people who use drugs in adolescence become abstainers as they grow older. Running away from home is a single impulsive act for most of the people who try it. They return home and incorporate the experience into their family constellations in a variety of ways. Running away changes the lives of others completely, leading to an entirely different existence than they would have had if they had remained at home. The behavior of multiple runaways is often tied to a pattern of delinquency and drug abuse. It reflects serious hostility, rebellion, and usually a character problem which continues into adulthood. Neurotic disturbances are in many ways the least serious psychological disturbances, particularly because they are rarely characterized by disturbances of reality testing. Anorexia nervosa, conversion symptoms, school phobia, and amnesia are among the most serious problems of adolescent neurotics. Suicide is relatively rare in early adolescence. The effective diagnosis and treatment of neurotic problems in early adolescence is thought to produce improved coping skills, personal insight, and personal problem solving. Some neurotic symptoms are the products of developmental disturbances and will disappear as the causal factor subsides or is integrated into the personality in a more mature way. Other neurotic problems do not go away by themselves. One of the important implications of neuroses for later functioning is that if ineffectual symptomatic behavior goes on for many years and is untreated, the maladaptive but repetitive behavior may preclude mature development in the area of conflict and symptom. This may lead to more serious neurotic problems in adulthood.

## REFERENCES

Abse, D. W.   Hysteria and related mental disorders. Baltimore: Williams and Wilkins, 1966.

Alchter, S., Wig, N. N., Varma, V. K., Pershad, D., and Varna, S. K.   A phenomenological analysis of symptoms in obsessive-compulsive neurosis. *British Journal of Psychiatry*, 1975, *127*, 342–348.

Ambrosino, L.   Runaways. *Today's Education*, 1971, *60*, 26–28.

American Psychiatric Association.   *Diagnostic and statistical manual of mental disorders* (2d ed.). Washington, D.C.: American Psychiatric Association, 1968.

Bachman, J. G.   *Youth in transition*, Ann Arbor, Mich.: Institute for Social Research, 1970.

Baer, D. J.   Taxonomic classification of male delinquents from autobiographical data and subsequent recidivism. *Journal of Psychology*, 1970, *76* (1), 27–31.

Bandura, A.   *Aggression: A social learning analysis*. Englewood Cliffs, N.J.: Prentice-Hall, 1973.

Bartollas, C. L.   Runaways at the training institution, Central, Ohio. *Dissertation Abstracts International*, 1973, *34*, 2789A (University Microfilms No. 73-26, 769).

Beck, A. T., Lande, R., and Bohnert, M.   Ideational components of anxiety neurosis. *Archives of General Psychiatry*, 1974, *31*, 319–325.

Beck, J. C., and Brockner-Mortensen, K.   Observations on the prognosis in anorexia nervosa. *Acta medica Scandinavia*, 1954, *149*, 409.

Becker, H. S.   Becoming a marijuana smoker. *American Journal of Sociology*, 1953, *59*, 235–243.

Bellak, L.   *Schizophrenia: A review of the syndrome*. New York: Logos, 1958.

Bender, L.   The concept of pseudopsychopathic schizophrenia in adolescents. *American Journal of Orthopsychiatry*, 1959, *29*, 491–512.

Bender, L.  Psychopathic personality disorders in childhood and adolescence. *Archives of Criminal Psychodynamics*, 1961, *4*, 412–415.

Berman, S.  Antisocial character disorder: Its etiology and relationship to delinquency. *American Journal of Orthopsychiatry*, 1959, *29*, 612–621.

Beyer, M., Holt, S. A., Reid, T. A., and Quinlan, D. M.  *Runaway youths: Families in conflict.* Paper presented at meeting of Eastern Psychological Association, Washington, D.C., May 1973.

Bliss, E. L., and Branch, C.  *Anorexia nervosa.* New York: Hoeber, 1960.

Blos, P.  *On adolescence: A psychoanalytic interpretation.* New York: Free Press, 1962.

Bonnard, A.  Truancy and pilfering associated with bereavement. In S. Lorand and H. I. Schneer (Eds.), *Adolescents: Psychoanalytic approach to problems and therapy.* New York: Hoeber, 1961. Pp. 152–179.

Bowlby, J.  Forty-four juvenile thieves: Their characters and homelife. *International Journal of Psychoanalysis*, 1944, *25*, 19–53, 107–128.

Boyd, P. R.  Drug abuse and addiction in adolescents. In J. G. Howells (Ed.), *Modern perspectives in adolescent psychiatry.* New York: Brunner/Mazel, 1971. Pp. 290–328.

Brennan, T., Blanchard, F., Huizinga, D., and Elliot, D.  *Final report: The incidence and nature of runaway behavior.* Report prepared for the Office of Assistant Secretary for Planning and Evaluation, DHEW. Boulder, Colo.: Behavioral Research and Evaluation Corporations, 1975.

Brown, G. W.  Working with "unrecovered" patients. *International Journal of Psychiatry*, 1966, *2*, 627–629.

Bruch, H.  Developmental obesity and schizophrenia. *Psychiatry*, 1958, *65*, 21.

Bruch, H.  Perceptual and conceptual disturbances in anorexia nervosa. *Psychosomatic Medicine*, 1962, *24*, 187. (a)

Bruch, H.  Falsification of bodily needs and body concept in schizophrenia. *Archives of General Psychiatry*, 1962, *6*, 18. (b)

Bruch, H.  Anorexia nervosa and its differential diagnosis. *Journal of Nervous and Mental Disease*, 1966, *141*, 555.

Bruch, H.  Obesity in adolescence. In G. Caplan and S. Lebovici (Eds.), *Adolescence: Psychosocial perspectives.* New York: Basic Books, 1969. Pp. 213–225.

Bruch, H.  Obesity in adolescence. In J. G. Howells (Ed.), *Modern perspectives in adolescent psychiatry.* New York: Brunner/Mazel, 1971. Pp. 270–273.

Bruch, H.  *Eating disorders.* New York: Basic Books, 1973.

Bruch, H.  Eating disturbances in adolescence. In G. Caplan (Ed.), *American handbook of psychiatry,* vol. 2: *Child and adolescent psychiatry, Socio-cultural and community psychology.* New York: Basic Books, 1974.

Bruch, H.  The golden cage: The enigma of anorexia nervosa. Cambridge, Mass.: Harvard University Press, 1978.

Burks, H. L., and Harrison, S. I.  Aggressive behavior as a means of avoiding depression. *American Journal of Orthopsychiatry*, 1962, *32*, 416–422.

Burns, C.  Pre-schizophrenic symptoms in pre-adolescents' withdrawal and sensitivity. *Nervous Child*, 1952, *10*, 120–128.

Buss, A. H. *Psychopathology.* New York: Wiley, 1966.

Cameron, N. *Personality development and psychopathology: A dynamic approach.* Boston: Houghton Mifflin, 1963.

Carter, A. B. Prognostic factors of adolescent psychoses. *Journal of Mental Science,* 1942, *88,* 31–81.

Chafetz, M. *Alcohol and health: New knowledge.* Second special report to the U.S. Congress from the secretary of health, education, and welfare. Washington, D.C.: U.S. Government Printing Office, 1974.

Clarke, R. V. G. Absconding and adjustment to the training school. *British Journal of Criminology,* 1968, *8,* 285–295.

Cloninger, C. R., and Guze, S. Psychiatric illness and female criminality: The role of sociopathy and hysteria in the anti-social woman. *American Journal of Psychiatry,* 1970, *127,* 303–311.

Coleman, J. C. *Abnormal psychology and modern life* (5th ed.). Glenview, Ill.: Scott, Foresman, 1976.

Coleman, R. Racial differences in runaways. *Psychological Reports,* 1968, *22,* 321–322.

Davison, G. C., and Neale, J. M. *Abnormal psychology: An experimental clinical approach* (2d ed.). New York: Wiley, 1978.

Donovan, J. M. Ego identity status and interpersonal style. *Journal of Youth and Adolescence,* 1975, *4,* 37–55.

Douvan, E., and Adelson, J. *The adolescent experience.* New York: Wiley, 1966.

Dwyer, J., and Mayer, J. Psychological effects of variations in physical appearance during adolescence. *Adolescence,* 1968–69, *3,* 353–380.

Edelston, H. Differential diagnosis of some emotional disorders of adolescence. *Journal of Mental Science,* 1949, *95,* 961–967.

Erikson, E. H. The problem of ego identity. *Psychological issues,* 1959, *1* (1), 101–164.

Farrington, D. S., Shelton, W., and MacKay, J. R. Observations on runaway children from a residential setting. *Child Welfare,* 1963, *42,* 286–291.

Federal Bureau of Investigation, U.S. Department of Justice. *Uniform crime reports for the United States.* Washington, D.C.: U.S. Government Printing Office, 1966.

Federal Bureau of Investigation, U.S. Department of Justice. *Uniform crime reports.* Washington, D.C.: U.S. Government Printing Office, 1975.

Fenichel, O. *The psychoanalytic theory of neurosis.* New York: Norton, 1945.

Ferber, L. Phobias and their vicissitudes. *Journal of the American Psychoanalytic Association,* 1959, *7,* 182–192.

Fine, R. H., and Fishman, J. J. Institutionalized girl delinquents. *Diseases of the Nervous System,* 1968, *29* (1), 17–27.

Freud, A. *The ego and the mechanisms of defense.* New York: International Universities Press, 1946.

Freud, A. *Normality and pathology in childhood: Assessments of development.* New York: International Universities Press, 1965.

Freud, A. Adolescence as a developmental disturbance. In G. Caplan and S.

Lebovici (Eds.), *Adolescence: Psychosocial perspectives.* New York: Basic Books, 1969. Pp. 5–10.

Freud, S.   Inhibitions, symptoms, and anxiety. In J. Strachey (Ed.), *The standard edition of the complete psychological works of Sigmund Freud,* vol. 20. London: Hogarth Press, 1959. (Originally published in German in 1926.) Pp. 75–176.

Freud, S.   General theory of the neuroses. In *Introductory Lectures on Psychoanalysis* (lectures 16–28). In J. Strachey (Ed.), *The standard edition of the complete psychological works of Sigmund Freud,* vol. 16. London: Hogarth Press, 1963. (Originally published in German in 1916–17.) Pp. 241–477.

Gallagher, J. R., and Harris, H. J.   *Emotional problems of adolescents* (3d ed.). New York: Oxford University Press, 1976.

Galli, N.   Patterns of student drug use. *Journal of Drug Education,* 1974, *4,* 237–247.

Ganzer, V. J., and Sarason, J. G.   Variables associated with recidivism among juvenile delinquents. *Journal of Consulting and Clinical Psychology,* 1973, *40,* 1–5.

Glaser, K.   Masked depression in children and adolescents. *American Journal of Psychotherapy,* 1967, *21,* 565–574.

Glueck, S., and Glueck, E.   *Family environment and delinquency.* Boston: Houghton Mifflin, 1962.

Glueck, S., and Glueck, E.   *Delinquents and non-delinquents in perspective.* Cambridge, Mass.: Harvard University Press, 1968.

Glueck, S., and Glueck, E.   Toward a typology of juvenile offenders: Implications for therapy and prevention. New York: Grune and Stratton, 1970.

Gold, M., and Reimer, D. J.   Testimony presented on the "Runaway Youth Act" to the Subcommittee on Equal Opportunity of the United States House Committee on Education and Labor, May 2, 1974.

Goode, E.   *The marijuana smokers.* New York: Basic Books, 1970.

Gould, R. E.   Suicide problems in children and adolescents. *American Journal of Psychotherapy,* 1965, *19,* 228–246.

Greenson, R. R.   Phobia, anxiety, and depression. *Journal of the American Psychoanalytic Association,* 1959, *7,* 663–674.

Grinker, R. R., and Spiegel, J.   *Men under stress.* Philadelphia: Blakiston, 1945.

Hall, G. S.   *Adolescence: Its psychology and its relations to physiology, sociology, anthropology, sex, crime, religion, and education,* vol. 1 and 2. New York: D. Appleton, 1904.

Jeans, R. F.   An independently validated case of multiple personality. *Journal of Abnormal Psychology,* 1976, *85,* 249–255.

Jessor, R., Graves, T. D., Hanson, R. C., and Jessor, S.   *Society, personality, and deviant behavior.* New York: Holt, Rinehart and Winston, 1968.

Jessor, R., and Jessor, S. L.   *Problem behavior and psychosocial development.* New York: Academic Press, 1977.

Jessor, R., Jessor, S. L., and Finney, J.   A social psychology of marijuana use: logitudinal studies of high school and college youth. *Journal of Personality and Social Psychology,* 1973, *26,* 1–15.

Jessor, R., Young, H. B., Young, E., and Tesi, G.   Perceived opportunity, alienation, and drinking behavior among Italian and American youth. *Journal of Personality and Social Psychology,* 1970, *15,* 215–222.

Johnson, B. D.   *Marijuana users and drug subcultures.* New York: Wiley-Interscience, 1973.

Justice, B., and Duncan, D. F.   Running away: An epidemic problem of adolescence. *Adolescence,* 1976, *11,* 365–372.

Kates, W. W., and Kates, S. L.   Conceptual behavior in psychotic and normal adolescents. *Journal of Abnormal and Social Psychology,* 1964, *69,* 659–663.

Kleinhesselink, R. R., St. Dennis, R., and Cross, H.   Contemporary drug issues involving youth. In J. F. Adams (Ed.), *Understanding adolescence: Current developments in adolescent psychology* (3d ed.). Boston: Allyn and Bacon, 1976. Pp. 369–411.

Konopka, G.   Adolescent delinquent girls. *Children,* 1964, *11* (1), 21–26.

Konopka, G.   Rehabilitation of the delinquent girl. *Adolescence,* 1967, *2,* 69–82.

Lancaster, E., and Poling, J.   *The final face of Eve.* New York: McGraw-Hill, 1958.

Lerner, S. E., Linder, R. L., and Burke, E. M.   Drugs in the junior high school, part 2. *Journal of Psychedelic Drugs,* 1974, *6,* 51–56.

Lesser, L. I., et al.   Anorexia nervosa in children. *American Journal of Orthopsychiatry,* 1960, *30,* 572.

LeUnes, A., and Siemsglusz, S.   Paraprofessional treatment of school phobia in a young adolescent. *Adolescence,* 1977, *12,* 115–122.

Levine, S.   Runaways and research in the training school. *Crime and Delinquency,* 1962, *8,* 40–45.

Lidz, T.   Schizophrenic thinking. *Journal of Youth and Adolescence,* 1974, *3,* 95–98.

Lunden, W. A.   *Statistics on delinquents and delinquency.* Springfield, Ill.: Charles C Thomas, 1964.

Marwell, G.   Adolescent powerlessness and delinquent behavior. *Social Problems,* 1966, *14,* 35–47.

Masterson, J. F.   Prognosis in adolescent disorders—Schizophrenia. *Journal of Nervous and Mental Disease,* 1956, *124,* 219–232.

Masterson, J. F., Tucker, K., and Berk, G.   Psychopathology in adolescence: IV. Clinical and dynamic characteristics. *American Journal of Psychiatry,* 1963, *120,* 357–366.

McCord, W., and McCord, J.   *The psychopath: An essay on the criminal mind.* New York: Van Nostrand Reinhold, 1964.

Milman, D. H., and Su, W.   Patterns of illicit drug and alcohol use among secondary-school students. *Journal of Pediatrics,* 1973, 314–320.

Murphy, F. J., Shirley, M. M., and Witmer, H. L.   The incidence of hidden delinquency. *American Journal of Orthopsychiatry,* 1946, *16,* 686–696.

National Center for Health Statistics.   *Self-reported health behavior and attitudes of youths 12–17 years, United States vital and health statistics.* PHS Publication no. 1000, series 11, no. 147. Washington, D.C.: U.S. Government Printing Office, 1975.

National Commission on Marijuana and Drug Abuse. *Marijuana: A signal of misunderstanding.* Washington, D.C.: U.S. Government Printing Office, 1972.

Neubauer, P. B., and Steinart, J.   Schizophrenia in adolescence. *Nervous Child,* 1952, *10,* 128–134.

Newman, B. M., and Newman, P. R.   Development through life: A psychosocial approach. Homewood, Ill.: Dorsey Press, 1975.

*New York Times.* L. I. youth dead, 2 others hospitalized after party for fraternity's pledges. February 26, 1978, section 1, p. 27.

O'Donnell, J. A., Voss, H. L., Clayton, R. R., Slatin, G. T., and Room, R. G. W. *Young men and drugs—A nationwide survey.* Rockville, Md.: National Institute on Drug Abuse, 1976.

Offer, D.   The psychological world of the teenager: A study of normal adolescent boys. New York: Basic Books, 1969.

Offer, D., and Offer, J.   *From teenage to young manhood.* New York: Basic Books, 1975.

Offer, D., Sabshin, M., and Marcus, D.   Clinical evaluation of normal adolescents. *American Journal of Psychiatry,* 1965, *121,* 864–872.

Osgood, C. E., Luria, Z., and Smith, S. W.   A blind analysis of another case of multiple personality using the semantic personality technique. *Journal of Abnormal Psychology,* 1976, *85,* 256–270.

*Outpatient psychiatric clinics: Special statistical report, 1961.*   Bethesda, Md.: National Institute of Mental Health, 1963.

Pittell, S. M.   The current status of the Haight-Ashbury hippie community. San Francisco: Haight-Ashbury Research Project, 1968. Mimeographed.

Porterfield, A. L.   Delinquency and its outcome in court and college. *American Journal of Sociology,* 1943, *49,* 199–208.

Press, E., and Done, A. K.   Solvent-sniffing: I and II. *Pediatrics,* 1967, *39,* 451, 611.

Proskauer, S., and Rolland, R. S.   Youth who use drugs. *Journal of the American Academy of Child Psychiatry,* 1973, *12,* 32–47.

Reynolds, D. J.   Adjustment and maladjustment. In J. F. Adams (Ed.), *Understanding adolescence: Current developments in adolescent psychology* (3d ed.). Boston: Allyn and Bacon, 1976. Pp. 334–368.

Robins, L. N., and O'Neal, P.   The adult prognosis for runaway children. *American Journal of Orthopsychiatry,* 1959, *29,* 752–761.

Rosen, B. M., Bahn, A. K., Shellow, R., and Bower, E. M.   Adolescent patients served in outpatient psychiatric clinics. *American Journal of Public Health,* 1965, *55,* 1563–1577.

Rosenthal, S. H.   The involutional depressive syndrome. *American Journal of Psychiatry,* 1968, *124,* 21–34.

Sands, D. E.   The psychoses of adolescence. *Journal of Mental Science,* 1956, *102,* 308–316.

Sarason, J. G.   *Abnormal psychology: The problem of maladaptive behavior* (2d ed.). Englewood Cliffs, N.J.: Prentice-Hall, 1976.

Schimel, J. L.   Problems of delinquency and their treatment. In G. Caplan (Ed.),

*American handbook of psychiatry* (2d ed.), vol. 2: *Child and adolescent psychiatry, socio-cultural and community psychiatry.* New York: Basic Books, 1974. Pp. 264–274.

Shellow, R., Schamp, J. P., Liebow, E., and Unger, E. Suburban runaways of the 1960's. *Monographs of the Society for Research in Child Development,* 1967, *32* (3, Serial No. 111).

Short, J. F., and Nye, F. I. Extent of unrecorded juvenile delinquency: Tentative conclusions. *Journal of Criminal Law and Criminology,* 1958, *49,* 296–302.

Sours, J. A. Anorexia nervosa: Nosology, diagnosis, developmental patterns, and power control dynamics. In G. Caplan and S. Lebovici (Eds.), *Adolescence: Psychosocial perspectives.* New York: Basic Books, 1969. Pp. 185–212.

Sperling, M. Conversion hysteria and conversion symptoms: A revision of classification and concepts. *Journal of the American Psychoanalytic Association,* 1973, *21,* 745–771.

Spivack, G., Haines, P. E., and Spotts, J. Adolescent symptomatology and its measurement. *American Journal of Mental Deficiency,* 1967, *72,* 74–95.

Stierlin, H. Characteristics of suburban adolescent runaways. In *Runaway youth: Hearing before the Subcommittee to Investigate Juvenile Delinquency, Committee on the Judiciary, United States Senate.* Washington, D.C.: U.S. Government Printing Office, 1973.

Swanson, D. W., Bohnert, P. J., and Smith, P. J. *The paranoid.* Boston: Little, Brown, 1970.

Thigpen, C. H., and Cleckley, H. M. A case of multiple personality. *Journal of Abnormal and Social Psychology,* 1954, *49,* 135–151.

Thigpen, C. H., and Cleckley, H. M. *The three faces of Eve.* New York: McGraw-Hill, 1957.

Toolan, J. M. Depression in children and adolescents. *American Journal of Orthopsychiatry,* 1962, *32,* 404–415.

Ullman, L., and Krasner, L. A. *Psychological approach to abnormal behavior* (2d ed.). Englewood Cliffs, N.J.: Prentice-Hall, 1975.

Vailliant, G. E. The prediction of recovery in schizophrenia. *Journal of Nervous and Mental Disease,* 1962, *135,* 534–543.

Vailliant, G. E. Positive prediction of schizophrenic remissions. *Archives of General Psychiatry,* 1964, *11,* 509–518.

van Krevelen, D. A. Psychoses in adolescence. In J. G. Howells (Eds.), *Modern perspectives in adolescent psychiatry.* New York: Brunner/Mazel. 1971. Pp. 381–403.

Victor, H. R., Grossman, J. C., and Eisenman, R. Openness to experience and marijuana use in high school students. *Journal of Consulting and Clinical Psychology,* 1973, *41,* 78–85.

Walker, D. K. *Runaway youth: An annotated bibliography and literature overview.* Office of Social Service and Human Development, DHEW, SS-HD Technical Analysis Paper, no. 1.

*Webster's New Collegiate Dictionary.* Springfield, Mass.: G. and C. Merriam, 1977.

Wein, B. *The runaway generation.* New York: David McKay, 1970.

Weiner, I. B.   *Psychodynamics in schizophrenia.* New York: Wiley, 1966.

Weiner, I. B.   *Psychological disturbances in adolescence.* New York: Wiley-Interscience, 1970.

Werkman, S. L.   Psychiatric disorders of adolescence. In G. Caplan (Ed.),
*American handbook of psychiatry* (2d ed.), vol. 2: *Child and adolescent psychiatry, sociocultural and community psychiatry.* New York: Basic Books,
1974. Pp. 223–233.

West, D. J.   *The young offender.* New York: International Universities Press, 1967.

Wolfgang, M. E., Johnston, M., and Savitz, L. (Eds.).   *The sociology of crime
and delinquency* (2d ed.). New York: Wiley, 1970.

Wolk, S., and Brandon, J.   Runaway adolescents' perceptions of parents and
self. *Adolescence,* 1977, *12,* 175–188.

Yasin, A. S.   Attempted suicide in an adolescent—The resolution of an anxiety
state. *Adolescence,* 1973, *8,* 17–28.

# Part III

*Without the skills of formal operational thought, work on identity cannot be completed.*

**9**

# Cognitive Development
# in Later Adolescence

The integrating theme of later adolescence is the formation of a personal identity. Identity reflects a convergence of one's past identifications, an appreciation of one's competences and talents, and a commitment to a vision of oneself persisting into the future. Many different roles contribute to the content of one's identity, including the roles of child, student, worker, lover, and citizen. Along with these roles, there is a growing commitment to values, to certain kinds of relationships, and to aspirations that are viewed as meaningful, as worthy of one's energy and investment. As might be expected, a major part of the formation of identity involves the maturing of social and emotional competences. For this reason, our detailed discussion of identity formation is reserved for Chapter 10. However, it is also evident that certain kinds of cognitive competences are essential for work on identity to take place. In Chapter 5 we focused on the emergence of formal operational thought during early adolescence. It must be clear that without the skills of hypothesis raising, conceptualization of the future, logical problem solving, and the ability to anticipate the consequences of an action, work on identity formation could not really begin.

When we speak of identity, we are speaking of a set of hypothetical formulations about the self. We are playing with the convergence of abstract ideas of commitment, meaning, historical continuity, and life goals. Without the capacities of formal thought, identity would be tied to the observable, the readily measurable or manipulatable dimensions of experience. But with the door of abstract reasoning opened, identity becomes a vision of what might be possible as well as of what has already been experienced. Because of formal thought there is a chance to conceive of an identity that is a unique integration, a new combination of past, present, and future that takes a person along a new course.

In this chapter we focus on three areas of conceptualization that contribute to the formation of identity: morality, political ideology, and career choice. Each of these themes involves values, roles, and aspirations that will be integrated into the content of the person's own identity formation. Of course, each theme has its origins early in childhood. We do not arrive at later adolescence with a blank slate on which a set of moral values is inscribed. Rather, we experience a continuous reformulation of the content of our morality that begins in childhood and persists through later adulthood. So too with political ideology and career choice, there is a developmental process of conceptualization and revision.

Our goal in this chapter is to look closely at these three important components of adult thought in order to understand what new conceptual development occurs during the later adolescent years. One's morality, one's political ideology, and one's career choice have consequences for the course of young adulthood and beyond. Each of these commitments will direct the later adolescent toward relationships, settings, and activities that will encourage the expression of the values inherent in them. Some opportunities will be rejected because they do not reflect a person's moral, political, or work commitments. In this sense, we cannot underestimate the contributions of conceptual growth during later adolescence insofar as it fosters a new formulation of ideas and commitments in the areas of morality, political ideology, and career.

# MORALITY

In this section, two rather different perspectives on morality are presented. First, we consider the quality of moral thought and moral reasoning as it develops during later adolescence. This discussion focuses on the criteria that people use to evaluate whether behaviors are right or wrong and whether persons have been treated justly or unjustly. Second, we consider the implications of one's religious commitment for moral thought. To what extent does involvement in a formal religion or the practice of religious rituals influence moral thought or moral action? How are later adolescents involved in religious movements or religious organizations? Our assumption is that during later adolescence there is an opportunity to make a more independent commitment to a particular religious orientation, a commitment that does not necessarily reflect the beliefs of one's parents or relatives. Religion becomes more a matter of choice and less a matter of obligation or habit. In this sense, religious commitments suggest a particular value orientation that will contribute to one's moral code.

## The Quality of Moral Thought

Moral thought begins in early childhood when a three-year-old child pulls a dog's tail and sternly says out loud, "No! No! Don't hurt the doggy." Throughout childhood and adolescence there is a gradual reformulation of moral principles that reflects a growing understanding of the other person's point of view, of the consequences of one's actions for others, and of the principle of reciprocity ("Do unto others"). Building on Piaget's early analysis of moral thought, Kohlberg (1968, 1969) has developed a technique for assessing the quality of logic or reasoning that underlies a moral judgment. Using situational dilemmas in which a person is usually confronted with a choice between obeying a law and meeting a personal obligation or commitment, he asks subjects to explain what they think would be the right way to behave and why. From the responses,

Kohlberg has evolved a stage theory of moral thought. This theory supposes that there is a stepwise progression in thinking about moral dilemmas that is associated with increasingly abstract and logical principles of thought. At each new stage, the person redefines right and wrong in line with a new appreciation for motives, consequences, and cultural contracts or commitments that might explain the behavior. Table 9–1 defines the three general levels of moral thought—preconventional, conventional, and postconventional morality—and the two stages for evaluating right and wrong at each level. There is an assumption that these six stages are achieved in the same order, regardless of social class, educational background, or culture. However, not all individuals reach the last two stages.

Stages 1 and 2 are characteristic of childhood, when the person is involved in relationships in which adults control most of the resources and make most of the decisions. At this level, what is good is what is rewarded and what meets one's own needs. Stages 3–6 can be found among adolescents and adults. In stages 3 and 4 the person expresses a loyalty to the existing social order either through an affiliation to the members of the immediate social group or to the laws and rules of the social group. The moral judgments of people at stages 5 and 6 reflect an independence from the specific people or authorities who have created the laws or who enforce them. At these levels, morality is based on a recognition of the logical implications of certain kinds of agreements or commitments that people make to one another. At the highest stage, there is a formulation of a personal moral philosophy that guides moral judgments regardless of their similarities to or differences from the existing cultural laws and norms. Few subjects respond consistently at a stage 6 level (Kohlberg, 1970; Kohlberg and Kramer, 1969). In several studies, only about 5 percent of the subjects responded at the stage 6 level (Kohlberg and Kramer, 1969; Haan, Block, and Smith, 1968; Holstein, 1969). In a longitudinal study that followed subjects from high school age into young adulthood, Kohlberg (1973) suggested that true postconventional thought was not fully formulated until the adult years. The model, then, offers a picture of the kinds of moral judgments that are possible and the path toward mature moral thought. It does not predict the level of thought that will be attained by a particular age or for a particular person.

Several factors seem to contribute to the maturation of moral thought. Chronological age and, more importantly, mental age or intelligence are associated with higher levels of moral thought (Froming and McColgan, 1977). However, the development of formal operational thought does not guarantee postconventional

**Table 9–1: Definition of Moral Stages**

*I. Preconventional Level*

At this level the child is responsive to cultural rules and labels of good and bad, right or wrong, but interprets these labels in terms of either the physical or the hedonistic consequences of action (punishment, reward, exchange of favors) or in terms of the physical power of those who enunciate the rules and labels. The level is divided into the following two stages:

Stage 1: *The punishment and obedience orientation.* The physical consequences of action determine its goodness or badness, regardless of the human meaning or value of these consequences. Avoidance of punishment and unquestioning deference to power are valued in their own right, not in terms of respect for an underlying moral order supported by punishment and authority (the latter being stage 4).

Stage 2: *The instrumental relativist orientation.* Right action consists of that which instrumentally satisfies one's own needs and occasionally the needs of others. Human relations are viewed in terms like those of the marketplace. Elements of fairness, of reciprocity and equal sharing, are present, but they are always interpreted in a physical pragmatic way. Reciprocity is a matter of "you scratch my back, and I'll scratch yours," not of loyalty, gratitude, or justice.

*II. Conventional Level*

At this level, maintaining the expectations of the individual's family, group, or nation is perceived as valuable in its own right, regardless of immediate and obvious consequences. The attitude is not only one of *conformity* to personal expectations and social order, but of loyalty to it, of actively *maintaining,* supporting, and justifying the order and of identifying with the persons or group involved in it. At this level, there are the following two stages:

Stage 3: *The interpersonal concordance or "good boy–nice girl" orientation.* Good behavior is that which pleases or helps others and is approved by them. There is much conformity to stereotypical images of what is majority or "natural" behavior. Behavior is frequently judged by intention—"he means well" becomes important for the first time. One earns approval by being "nice."

Stage 4: *The "law and order" orientation.* There is orientation toward authority, fixed rules, and the maintenance of the social order. Right behavior consists of doing one's duty, showing respect for authority, and maintaining the given social order for its own sake.

*III. Postconventional, Autonomous, or Principled Level*

At this level, there is a clear effort to define moral values and principles which have validity and application apart from the authority of the groups or persons holding these principles and apart from the individual's own identification with these groups. This level again has two stages:

Stage 5: *The social-contract legalistic orientation,* generally with utilitarian overtones. Right action tends to be defined in terms of general individual rights and in terms of standards which have been critically examined and agreed upon by the whole society. There is a clear awareness of the relativism of personal values and opinions and a corresponding emphasis upon procedural rules for reaching consensus. Aside from what is constitutionally and democratically agreed upon, the right is a matter of personal "values" and "opinion." The result is an emphasis upon the "legal point of view," but with an emphasis upon the possibility of changing law in terms of rational considerations of social utility (rather than freezing it in terms of stage 4 "law and order"). Outside the legal realm, free agreement and contract is the binding element of obligation. This is the "official" morality of the American government and Constitution.

Stage 6: *The universal ethical principle orientation.* Right is defined by the decision of conscience in accord with self-chosen *ethical principles* appealing to logical comprehensiveness, universality, and consistency. These principles are abstract and ethical (the golden rule, the categorical imperative); they are not concrete moral rules like the Ten Commandments. At heart, these are universal principles of *justice,* of the *reciprocity* and *equality* of human *rights,* and of respect for the dignity of human beings as *individual persons.*

Source: L. Kohlberg and R. Kramer. Continuities and discontinuities in childhood and adult moral development. *Human Development,* 1969, *12,* p. 100–101. Reprinted by permission.

thought. For example, although 60 percent of a sample of 16-year-olds had achieved formal operational thought, only 10 percent were responding to the moral dilemmas at a postconventional level (Muuss, 1976; Kuhn et al., 1977).

Social interaction and discussions with peers are likely to foster the development of moral thought. This is especially true if these force adolescents to confront ideas that are slightly ahead of their own level of thinking. Role-taking skills, involvement in peer interaction, and exposure to training in which higher levels of moral ideology are presented all contribute to a reorganization of moral thought to a higher level (Keasey, 1971; Turiel, 1966; Kohlberg and Blatt, 1972).

Moral growth is also stimulated by a temporary withdrawal from the conventional moral code that permits some reformulation of the logic underlying one's moral judgments. This process is especially important during later adolescence, as the person moves from the conventional to the postconventional level of morality. The period of reformulation tends to occur between the end of high school and the second or third year of college. In early studies, it was described as a temporary "regression," involving a drop from a mixture of stage 4 and some stage 5 judgments to a stage 2 level (Kohlberg and Kramer, 1969). This "regression" involved responses that suggested defying existing laws, rejecting any laws or principles as meaningful ("It's all a game"), or testing out the possibility of a guilt-free existence. Feelings of disappointment were expressed as adolescents discovered that the world does not play by the rules of conventional morality or that being "good" does not seem to have very clear competitive advantages. These realizations stimulate a need to break from the intensity of moral obligations that are bound to the child role. They promote a need to see what moral principles would really emerge if one abandoned all earlier conceptions of morality. As a result of their ability to reconceptualize earlier moral teachings, later adolescents are likely to experience a transitional phase of "hedonistic rebellion" against conventional ways. What is most important is that this transition does appear to facilitate moral growth. Recent reanalyses of these so-called regressive responses have shown them to reflect a step forward toward a higher, more stabilized stage 5 or stage 6 moral orientation (Kohlberg, 1973; Turiel, 1974). In order for adolescents' moral thought to catch up to their commitments to occupational goals and political, religious, and interpersonal values, it may be necessary to take a hard, critical look at the morality of one's childhood. In the process of loosening the bonds to a morality that had its origin in the family group, one begins to form a commitment to a personally meaningful moral code that will have increasing applicability throughout adult life.

Kohlberg's approach to the development of moral thought relies heavily on the cognitive capacity to detect the logical principles that underlie a moral conflict. His system emphasizes the value of principled moral reasoning apart from involvement in the actual circumstances or relationships of the moral dilemma. In general, this has led to a rather weak relationship between the level of moral thought as it is assessed in a moral dilemmas interview and moral action in real or even simulated moral situations (Hogan, 1976b). For example, Haan (1975) evaluated the moral reasoning of students with regard to civil disobedience. She reported that in evaluating an actual example of civil disobedience that they had witnessed or participated in, most of the students used a stage of moral reasoning that was different from the stage that they used in response to Kohlberg's hypothetical situations. She argues that the demands of the situation as well as commitments to the other participants are authentic and important components of a moral judgment. Moral decisions have a strong interpersonal component. They reflect the person's experiences of being threatened or of being in control. The morality of a particular situation depends on the sensitivity of the participants to the needs of others as well as on a desire to protect the self. In this sense, morality can be viewed as a negotiated definition of right or wrong behavior rather than an a priori definition of the logically right or wrong behavior.

In order to illustrate the difference between logical morality and interpersonal morality, Haan (1978) involved adolescent subjects who were already members of friendship groups in five games that presented different kinds of moral dilemmas. Both kinds of moral reasoning were coded during pretest and posttest interviews and during the games themselves. The relationships between the moral reasoning expressed in the interviews and that evidenced during the games were much weaker than the relationships among the stages of moral reasoning in the interviews themselves. When moral reasoning took place in an interpersonal context, especially one that involved stress, logical morality fluctuated quite dramatically. In contrast, interpersonal morality remained more consistent, reflecting the person's ability to control emotions, to empathize with others, and to understand the social demands of the situation.

Speaking in support of the need to incorporate an understanding of the interpersonal component into our view of moral thought, Haan described an important difference between the two systems:

Interpersonal reasoning is basically an inductive process, whereas formal reasoning is primarily a deductive process . . . ; consequently, new or emergent moral solutions can be more readily achieved with interpersonal than with formal reasoning. Because all situations are new in some degree, the person using interpersonal reasoning has a better chance of finding an apt, actionable solution. Moreover, persons using formal reasoning may find that their principles are not germane or suggest impossibly "pure" actions. Consequently, they cannot act and may need to attenuate their commitments. What to do, when all that can be done is to corrupt one's self by choosing between the lesser of two evils? What to do, when one cannot be an agent of justice all over the world all the time? (Haan, 1978, p. 303)

## Religion and Morality

One way to express a commitment to a moral life is through involvement in the personal and congregational activities that are associated with religious affiliation. A number of theorists have anticipated that adolescence would involve a period of doubt and even rebelliousness toward traditional religious practices (A. Freud, 1946; Allport, 1950; Savin-Williams, 1977). Because of adolescents' increased capacity for logical thought and growing desire for emotional autonomy, adolescence has been viewed as a period when cultural myths of all kinds are targets for evaluation and, perhaps, for hostility. In particular, the adolescent's sensitivity to hypocrisy makes religion a vulnerable institution, because throughout history religion has provided a cloak of self-righteousness for people who have acted cruelly and inhumanely to others.

Given both theoretical and commonsense expectations that adolescence is a period for doubting, rejecting, and even scorning religion, what evidence do we have to confirm or reject these expectations? What is the nature of adolescents' involvement in religion?

Savin-Williams (1977) described the responses of younger adolescents aged 10–16 to the task of describing Jesus. The general reaction to the image of Jesus was quite favorable. More than 80 percent of the sample saw Jesus as a "supernatural figure or a good human being." Among the older subjects, aged 15–16, there were increasing expressions of doubt about the special or divine qualities of Jesus. Yet only 34 percent of the males and 29 percent of the females in this group expressed such doubts.

In a study of a large sample of adolescents from three Midwestern communities, the subjects were asked about their agreement with a number of statements that reflected a traditional or orthodox religious orientation (Vener, Zaenglein, and Stewart, 1977). Although the religious orthodoxy index declined with age, the decline varied, depending on the statement. The statement about belief in an afterlife showed an increase in agreement from the group under 13 to the group 17 and over. On the other hand, the belief in a God who watches over us and protects us dropped from 81 percent in the youngest group to 66 percent in the oldest group.

Still, these data suggest that two thirds of older adolescents continue to hold this personalized view of God. According to these two assessments of adolescent orientation toward religion, traditional components of religious belief continue to be a part of many adolescents' belief system.

Johnson et al. (1974) sampled a cross-sectional national sample of Lutheran church members ranging in age from 15 to 65. Although religious participation increases with age, the greatest decline in involvement appears for the age group 19–23, or later adolescents. During this period, fewer respondents attend weekly worship or Holy Communion, or participate in congregational activities. The subjects in the age group 19–23 showed the greatest variability in beliefs. In contrast, the subjects in the age group 50–65 showed the greatest similarity of beliefs.

An important element in the assessment of religious involvement is the extent to which adolescents reflect or deviate from their parents' religious orientation. In the Johnson et al. (1974) sample, adolescents in the age ranges 15–18 and 19–23 were more likely than older groups to say that they were less religious than their parents. They also perceived their own parents as more involved

*Bill Stanton/Magnum*

*Today's youth are expressing a new religious orientation.*

in church activities than did the older age groups. It may be that adolescents perceive themselves to be less religious because they have more doubts and questions about religion than do their parents. It may also be that this particular group of adolescents really does have exceptionally involved parents who offer a model of commitment that is difficult to imitate. In any case, we still find that over 60 percent of adolescents aged 19–23 are involved with religion as much as or more than their mothers and that 75 percent are involved with religion as much as or more than their fathers. We must remind ourselves, however, that many adolescents who are not affiliated with any church or who have abandoned a religious commitment would not be caught in this or any other sampling of church members. Nevertheless, on the basis of these data, we can conclude that adult religious values and orientations are being transmitted to later adolescents quite successfully despite any increase in doubt or any involvement in competing cultural systems on the part of such adolescents. The evidence suggests that religion is alive and well during later adolescence.

In fact, there are those who argue that today's youth are creating a new religious orientation that will influence the course of religion for future generations. Interest in the Jesus Movement emphasizes the blending of an antitechnological hippie life-style with a fundamentalist religious orientation (Graham, 1973; Balswick, 1974). Jesus people use the Bible as a guide for living. They seek to let Jesus enter their lives, providing a sense of meaning, love, and connectedness. As a religious sect, they oppose the formality of church worship and the professionalism of the clergy. They also reject certain current cultural values, including materialism, impersonalism, and the high priority given to reason over intuition. As a new religious movement, they blend informality and spontaneity with very traditional religious concepts, including prayer, fellowship, and the desire to let the Holy Spirit guide their daily lives.

## POLITICAL IDEOLOGY

The growth of political thought among children raised in the United States begins with an image of the president as an important and powerful person and culminates in an appreciation of the purposes and functions of the complex group of institutions that we call government (Greenstein, 1965). In this section we consider some of the ways in which political thought changes from childhood through adolescence. We also evaluate the contribution of family socialization and parental views to the emergence of the adolescent's political thought.

In an attempt to understand what concepts children and adolescents bring to an analysis of the political system, Adelson and

O'Neil (1966) posed the following hypothetical situation: "Imagine that a thousand men and women, dissatisfied with the way things are going in their country, decide to purchase and move to an island in the Pacific: once there, they must devise laws and modes of government." Within the context of this situation, specific problems were posed and the subjects were asked to explain how they should be handled. The sense of government and community changed markedly from the youngest subjects, who were 11 years old, to the oldest, who were 18. An example of the responses to

Table 9-2: Should Men over 45 Be Required to Have a Yearly Medical Checkup?

|  | Age | | | |
|---|---|---|---|---|
|  | 11 | 13 | 15 | 18 |
| Yes, otherwise they would not do it ............ | .50 | .07 | .00 | .03*** |
| Yes, good for person and/or community ........ | .50 | .80 | .70 | .60 |
| No, infringement on liberties ................... | .00 | .13 | .27 | .37** |

Note: The $p$ level refers to the row designated by the asterisk.
  ** $x^2(3) = 11.95$; $p > .01$.
  *** $x^2(3) = 33.10$; $p > .001$.
  Source: J. Adelson and R. P. O'Neil, "Growth of Political Ideas in Adolescence: The Sense of Community," *Journal of Personality and Social Psychology*, 1966, *4*, p. 303. Copyright (1966) by the American Psychological Association. Reprinted by permission.

one question will illustrate some of the differences that emerged with age. One question suggested that a law be passed to require men over 45 to have a yearly medical checkup. This question was designed to put a personal good in conflict with a political value. Table 9-2 shows the proportion of the subjects at each age who gave one of three answers. The youngest children were unanimously in favor of the requirement. Although many of the oldest subjects continued to see the requirement as a good for both the person and the community, over one third of them saw the requirement as an infringement of individual freedom.

In general, younger subjects were more authoritarian and more likely to see the need for a coercive, powerful authority. They were less suspicious that government could function in an irrational or manipulative way. With age, adolescents became more aware of the interrelatedness and multiple functions of governmental institutions. Older subjects were able to use their formal operational skills to think about the chain of a sequence of actions and to anticipate the future consequences of governmental decisions. Many of the older adolescents still did not have a well-integrated political ideology. This may not be achieved until the mid-20s, and not at all by some. Nevertheless, the oldest subjects understood the principles they held and were able to give reasoned, consistent arguments for the positions they took. In a cross-cultural assessment of political ideology, the same hypothetical situation generated a similar developmental pattern of responses from American, British, and German adolescents (Gallatin and Adelson, 1971). Despite some national differences in emphasis, there were clear increases in sensitivity to governmental intrusion in individual privacy, more commitment to the principle of liberty and the need to safeguard individual rights, and greater awareness of the complexity and diversity of governmental functions.

Another aspect of political ideology is an understanding of laws and legal justice. In order to understand how governments work, it is necessary to conceptualize the purpose and nature of laws. Tapp and Kohlberg (1971) have applied a cognitive orientation to describe some of the steps in the development of a sense of legal justice. Using Kohlberg's category system of moral thought as a guide, they explored three levels of responses about the value, function, and modifiability of laws. In the U.S. sample, they drew children from three age groupings; K–2, 4–8, and college age. Their findings were similar to Adelson's findings on conceptions of government. The younger children saw rules and laws as prohibitions designed to prevent violence and crime. The older subjects could not imagine a world without laws. These subjects viewed laws as a protection against anarchy and chaos and as providing predictability and order. Only a few of the oldest subjects argued that humans are rational, and capable of regulating their own behavior by inner principles without the use of rules and laws.

Most of the older subjects moved past the preconventional to the conventional view of laws and the legal system. They saw the purpose of laws as maintaining a social order, as preventing chaos and the exploitation of others while encouraging conformity. Few of even the oldest subjects offered responses that suggested a postconventional orientation. That is, few college students (less than 30 percent) saw the rational or beneficial purpose behind laws as a strategy for achieving personal or social welfare. Only 11 percent of the oldest group suggested that one should conform only to laws and rules that are in line with personal values. On the other hand, 94 percent of the college-age subjects thought that it would be right to break a rule. Of this group, the largest segment (54 percent) argued that morally wrong rules, that is, rules violating essential human rights, should not be followed. There is a picture of the emergence during the later adolescent years of an ethic or ideology that guides political judgments. Although this ideology is not as carefully articulated or as rational as some social scientists might expect, it is clear that the process of conceptualization is under way.

An understanding of political ideology requires an appreciation of the antecedent socialization experiences that contribute to a particular orientation toward government and law. Hogan (1976a) has suggested that there are three levels of socialization in the development of a political ideology. At the first level, one internalizes rules by accommodating oneself to loving but controlling parents. At the second level, one internalizes principles by accommodating oneself to a peer community in which certain standards (for example, fairness, cooperation) are maintained by virtue of judicious adult supervision. At the third level, one organizes these rules and principles under an ideology, usually by accommodating oneself to one's cultural and ethnic history (Hogan, 1976a).

The final stage is not fully achieved until later adolescence or young adulthood. The similarity between this conception of political ideology and personal identity is strong. In order to develop an integrated ideology, one must organize past experiences, cognitive understanding, and rules or principles into a personally meaningful orientation. This orientation is resistant to pressure from parents or peers to hold a more popular view. In this sense, political ideology requires the achievement of socioemotional autonomy as well as cognitive maturation.

Given the assumption that a basic element in the formation of political ideology is parental identification, what do we know of the family background of students who take radical political positions? Two rather different explanations of student radicalism have been offered. One view argues that adolescent activism is a form of rebellion or rejection of parental values (Feuer, 1969; Bettelheim, 1969). This analysis, which builds on the Freudian concept of the unresolved Oedipal conflict, emphasizes the symbolic equation between parents and governmental authorities. It interprets the rejection of political values as a displacement of hostility toward parents.

The other view sees political radicalism or activism as an extension of parental values (Flacks, 1967; Keniston, 1968; Smith, Haan, and Block, 1970). According to this position, politically involved adolescents who hold a radical orientation have parents who also hold liberal values. Such adolescents come to their radicalism as an extension of an independent, questioning orientation that was encouraged at home. Rather than rebelling against parents, activists are continuing the action orientation and critical evaluation that was encouraged by their parents (Block, 1972).

Among college-age adolescents who are described as radical or liberal-radical, it appears that both hypotheses hold true. In other words, some radical students are in conflict with their parents, whereas others are in harmony with parental views. We can understand this diversity among radical adolescents in the following way. Several studies of college students suggest that there are many more left-wing students than left-wing parents (Berns, Bugentol, and Berns, 1972; Silvern and Nakamura, 1973). College students are likely to be more liberal than their parents, regardless of whether the parents rate their own political preferences or the students rate their parents' views. Thus most parents are somewhat to the "right" of, or more conservative than, their adolescent children. Therefore, some radical students will have liberal parents and others will have conservative parents. The former group would be seen as evidence for the continuous socialization hypothesis, whereas the latter group would be seen as evidence for the discontinuous, rebellious hypothesis.

Block (1972) described some of the differences between these two groups. The parents of the adolescents who were in conflict with parental values were concerned with conventional values and with the need to make a good impression. Thus child-rearing practices were more authoritarian and restrictive than the child-rearing practices of parents who shared their adolescent children's values. They made more use of physical punishment and gave their children less opportunity to question decisions and less freedom to play unsupervised. These parents appeared somewhat unsure of their role and were more likely to use anxiety and guilt-inducing messages to control their children.

The parents who shared their adolescent children's political views emphasized their children's individuality and the importance of respect. They practiced a combination of high expectations for responsibility and greater permissiveness. They also tended to be in more agreement with one another about child rearing than did the parents of children whose values conflicted with their own.

We see, then, that radicalism or political activism can be an expression of at least two different socialization patterns. It can reflect the reaction of adolescents to restrictive, conflictual parental relations. For such adolescents, radicalism is a displacement of anger toward parents to rejection of societal laws. Political activism can also be a thoughtful evaluation of governmental decisions in the light of a well-developed political ideology that reflects continuity with parental values and the expression of an active, questioning orientation encouraged by family child-rearing practices.

## CAREER DECISION MAKING

A career can be thought of as any composite of work experiences that permits a person to make use of talents and skills in a productive manner. The career of an artist, for example, could involve work in many media, including oil painting, sculpture, ceramics, sketching, collages, watercolor, and pen and ink. It is not the medium, the project, or the theme of the work that defines the career, but the artist's personal definition of all these activities as the expression of a unique set of talents and goals. In the same way, one might think of an entrepreneur's career as a series of involvements in a variety of small businesses or of a salesperson's career as the providing of many different products. The concept of career change needs to be reevaluated in this light.

If a person continues to pursue some kind of work, we understand that he or she continues to have an occupational career in the broadest sense of the word. The specific changes in work activities reflect changes in the life structure that can no longer be adequately expressed in one particular form of work. The lifelong occupational career is a continuously changing set of activities that express changing competences, emerging goals, and a revised appreciation of the meaning of certain types of work and certain types of reward. From this perspective, it does not make sense to expect that a career decision made during later adolescence will endure throughout life. Even if that decision is made in a most rational, planned way, using a broad range of information about personal competences and the content of a variety of work roles, a sound decision may not be a permanent one. As adults grow and change, their awareness of possibilities and their appreciation of their own skills change. When we describe the phases of decision making and the factors that may contribute to career choice during later adolescence, we do so with an eye toward the likelihood of change. In fact, we anticipate that a person's occupational career will undergo repeated evaluation and revision throughout adulthood (Levinson, 1977; Moreland, 1977; Riegal, 1976).

## The Decision-Making Process

As you will recall from the discussion of career choice in Chapter 5, we can think about the process of career choice from a developmental perspective. In Ginzberg's model, realistic thinking about career choice is foremost during later adolescence. At this time, the cognitive competences necessary for effective career choice are of primary importance.

When we think of career choice from a cognitive perspective, we are thinking about the purposeful choices and decisions that individuals make at various points in the selection of a career. Career-related tasks may include a decision to attend college, a decision about a particular major, or a decision about a particular occupation. From a cognitive perspective we are interested in the process of logical thought about the consequences of particular career choices, the ability to evaluate the suitability of particular work activities, and the planning that contributes to career choice.

Tiedeman has proposed a model of career decision making that reflects a view of the person as responsible and purposeful. The overall goal of career definition involves confronting a number of separate tasks during adolescence and early adulthood. With the effective problem solving of each task, the person gains increased control over life events and is prepared to confront subsequent decisions. Tiedeman's theory offers seven stages in the career decision-making process. These stages include four that emphasize planning or clarification of the choices and three that involve implementation or action. For each of the career-related decisions, including the decisions about college, major, occupation, job change, and career redirection, effective decision making would involve all seven phases (Tiedeman, 1961; Tiedeman and O'Hara, 1963; Miller and Tiedeman, 1972; Tiedeman and Miller-Tiedeman, 1975).

### Seven Phases of Career Decision Making

*1. Exploration.* This stage is marked by unrestricted exploratory considerations. It is characterized by generalized, vague concerns with little or no progress toward choice. Knowledge of self and the occupational world is a felt need, but the individual has developed no strategy or plan of action for satisfying this need. There is an absence or a near absence of negative choices (exclusions of alternatives from the range of possibilities). This stage is accompanied by vague anxieties about the future.

*2. Crystallization.* This stage represents progress toward choice but not its attainment. The individual recognizes alternative choices and at least some of their consequences. Conflicts are recognized; advantages and disdvantages are weighed; and the bases for a decision are being developed, at least implicitly. The range of possibilities is being narrowed down through negative choices. False steps and inappropriate earlier decisions are recognized and are used as bases for further decisions.

*3. Choice.* This stage represents a definite commitment to a particular goal. That commitment is accompanied by expressions of satisfaction and relief for having made it. The individual may focus on aspects of self which are evidence that the decision was appropriate. This stage further represents a swing from the pessimism characteristic of the exploratory stage to a kind of naive optimism about the future. The individual usually expresses a singleness of purpose and an unswerving attitude of goal direction, as well as eagerness and impatience to reach the goal. A focus upon the consequences of the decision and further planning are not yet in evidence.

*4. Clarification.* This stage represents a process of closure in which the individual is involved in clarification and elaboration of the consequences of commitment, as well as in planning the details and next steps to be taken to follow through on the commitment. The individual is usually engaged in a process of elaboration and perfection of the self-image and the image of the future. Although planning and overt action to carry out the commitment are characteristic of this stage, the overt action may be delayed until the environmental conditions are appropriate for action.

5. *Induction.* This stage marks the beginning of the implementation of a decision, the point at which the individual comes into actual contact with a new environment. One begins the process of accommodating to a new group of people and a new situation in the living out of one's career decision. The primary mode of interaction is passive. The individual is hesitant and is looking for cues from others in the group to determine what the group's values and goals are and what the group's expectations of one are. Although there is a general defense of self and a giving up of aspects of self to group purpose, the individual needs to feel some level of acceptance of one's uniqueness by the group. Gradually, one identifies with the group through the assimilation of one's individual values and goals into the group's values, goals, and purposes. This stage ends when a person becomes aware of being accepted by the group.

6. *Reformation.* In this stage, the individual's primary mode of interaction is assertive. One is highly involved in the group, enjoins the group to do better, and acts upon the group in order to bring its values, goals, and purposes into greater conformity with one's own values and goals (which have become somewhat modified during induction). One also acts upon the out-group to bring its view of one's identification with the in-group into greater consistency with one's own view. There is a strong sense of self, which is somewhat lacking in objectivity. At the same time, self is abandoned to solutions and group purposes. The result of this stage is a modification of the group's values, goals, and purposes.

7. *Integration.* In this stage, older group members react against the new member's force for change, which causes the individual to compromise or modify intentions. This results in a greater objectivity toward self and toward the group's purposes. A synthesis is achieved which both the individual and the group strive to maintain through collaborative activity. The individual is satisfied, at least temporarily, has an image of self as successful, and is considered successful by the group. (Harren and Kass, 1977, pp. 2–3. Reprinted by permission)

## Cognitive Styles in Decision Making

Although the phases of the decision-making process are likely to be encountered by every person in the process of choosing a career, there are different decision-making styles that determine the ways in which people make use of information and how much responsibility they take for the decisions they reach (Dinklage, 1969; Harren, 1976; Lunneborg, 1977).

Harren (1976) has described these differences in decision-making styles in three categories. The *Planning* style is the most rational. It involves assuming personal responsibility for a decision and seeking out information to evaluate both personal competences and the characteristics of the situation. The *Intuitive* style emphasizes the use of fantasy and emotions. A decision is reached without much information seeking. Rather, it is based on what feels right or best at the time. The *Dependent* style is influenced by the expectations and evaluations of others. The decision maker takes little responsibility for the decision and tends to see circumstances as forcing the decision or limiting the availability of options.

Harren and Kass (1977) evaluated the progress of 578 college undergraduates in decision making and decision-making style. The decision-making progress was determined in reference to three tasks; the decision to come to college, the decision about a major, and the decision about a future occupation. Both academic class standing and having made a satisfying decision about one's major or one's future occupation were significantly related to the career decision-making score. However, academic class standing was not as strongly related to the career decision-making score as was satisfaction with the decision that had been reached.

When the correlation between progress in decision making and cognitive style was examined, the Planning style was positively associated with decision making about occupation (r = .16). The Intuitive and Dependent styles were negatively associated with decision making (r = −.22, r = −.19, respectively). In a similar assessment, Lunneborg (1977) reported that the Planning style was positively related, and the Dependent style negatively related, to vocational maturity. In that analysis, however, the Intuitive style was independent of vocational maturity. Interestingly, Lunneborg reported that the Intuitive style had the highest mean score for both male and female subjects. In other words, students tended to respond favorably to items that reflected an instinctive sense of what would be a good career decision. They preferred this strategy to the more tedious activities associated with the Planning style. Nevertheless, the Intuitive style was not related to decisiveness, to the crystallization of a vocational self-concept, or to work values. The orientation that emphasizes fantasy, awareness of feelings, and a sense of one's inner states may be highly valued as a path toward personal adjustment, but it does not appear to be the most effective coping strategy for career decision making.

## Sex Differences in Career Decision Making

In recent years, more and more women have entered the labor force and more and more women have attempted to combine the roles of wife, mother, and worker. Despite the many difficulties that confront women in integrating their adult roles, there is no indication that this trend toward increased employment of women is going to decline in the near future. In fact, the census data suggest that women are delaying marriage and childbearing longer and that increasing numbers of women are voluntarily childless (Glick, 1977). These data are evidence of a growing involvement in work,

*The photography of H. Armstrong Roberts*

*Increasingly, more young women are committed to preparation for a lifelong occupational career.*

combined with a decision to limit the demands of competing roles.

Despite the increased participation of women in the labor force, there continues to be concern about the unequal participation of males and females in various areas of employment (Bernard, 1971; Parsons, 1977). Even though women do as well as men in college, fewer women aspire to graduate training (Astin, 1977; Baird, 1976). Women continue to cluster in a few traditional careers, and many women are "underemployed," considering their level of ability and education (Tangri, 1972; Severance and Gottsegen, 1977).

Several kinds of explanations have been offered to account for these differences in participation. We will present four explanations and some of the evidence for supporting or rejecting them.

1. Men and women use different cognitive styles to make career choices. Women use the Intuitive style, and men use the Planning style. As we discussed above, the Intuitive style is a less effective coping strategy and would therefore lead to less carefully planned or less mature career decisions. Comparisons of male and female college students do not find differences in decision-making styles (Barrett and Tinsley, 1977; Lunneborg, 1977; Harren and Kass, 1977).

2. Men and women have different perceptions of specific careers. Their career choices are influenced by the attributes they assign to particular fields. Baird (1977) asked a national sample of college seniors to evaluate five careers: medicine, law, college teaching and research, elementary and senior school teaching, and business. For each career, the subjects told whether each of 18 statements was true or not true. Except for business, men and women had different perceptions of these careers. For example, more women than men thought that law provided challenge and interest, that it required a high level of intelligence, and that it offered opportunities to contribute to the advancement of knowledge. More women than men saw success in law as affected by one's political views. Women saw law as a high-pressure profession requiring hard work, long hours, and a lot of time away from one's family. In this sense, women may see law as a less desirable career, particularly if they have already made a strong commitment to marriage and family. Other studies confirm that males and females differ in their evaluation of particular careers and work settings (Cartwright, 1972; Arvey, Passino, and Lounsbury, 1977).

3. The absence of female models in particular industries or in highly visible leadership positions contributes to the imbalance in the career aspirations of men and women (Shafer, 1975; Severance and Gottsegen, 1977). Following this hypothesis, Tidball (1973) found a correlation of +.95 between the number of women faculty at an undergraduate institution and the number of women graduates who pursued successful careers. In the Soviet Union, where there

is an attempt to make full use of women in the labor force, 36 percent of engineers and 45 percent of scientific workers are women (Chaband, 1970). Russian girls are more likely than American girls to have mothers who are in professional roles and to hear about professional women who are in positions of responsibility.

4. The level of career aspirations is determined by attitudes, personality factors, and socialization experiences. Women who are most committed to a traditional view of their participation in the roles of wife and mother will hold relatively less innovative career aspirations. Tangri (1972) reported that female students who choose occupations in which there are fewer than 30 percent women are likely to have educated, working mothers. Such women are characterized as autonomous, individualistic, and internally motivated. They have a strong career commitment, but they are also likely to have support for their career goals from faculty, female friends, and a boyfriend. In a more recent study of female college students, a number of attitudes were important contributors to high career aspirations (Parsons, Frieze, and Ruble, 1975). These attitudes included a belief that women's demands for equality are justified, a sense that men perceive women's demands for equality as justified, and a belief that career and family roles are not incompatible. A female with high aspirations was likely to have a mother who had a career or a mother who was dissatisfied with her work. In this analysis, the strength of the female's commitment to her own career appeared to be strengthened by her understanding of the ways in which discrimination has influenced the pattern of women's participation in careers.

In summary, males and females appear to bring the same cognitive competences to the process of career decision making. Women do not use a less effective cognitive style than men. On the other hand, women do tend to have different perceptions than men about the desirability of certain careers. This is most likely due to past discrepancies in the participation of males and females in various professions. The absence of female models appears to reduce the likelihood that females will aspire to particular careers. However, the more females understand about how these patterns of participation have come about and the more support they have from parents, faculty, and peers, the more likely they are to select more innovative career aspirations.

## Opportunities for Work Experiences

Some changes in the economic and social conditions of the last 15 years have serious implications for the opportunities for early experimentation in employment. Between 1968 and 1972, the proportion of high school students going on to college dropped from 55 percent to 49 percent (Young, 1973). The drop was especially great among white males. Several factors may be contributing to the decrease in college enrollments, including the end of college enrollment as a means of delaying military service, the rising costs of college tuition, and increasing difficulties in finding work after college (Perrella, 1973).

At the same time that the pool of high school graduates who do not go on to college has been increasing, the availability of jobs for high school graduates has been decreasing. Businesses that are required to pay an increasingly.high minimum wage are becoming less willing to hire young employees who come with limited skills and have a high chance of leaving for another position (Coleman, 1972). Work settings are requiring more educational credentials and providing fewer opportunities for part-time work experiences. Thus, of the class of 1972 high school graduates in the labor force who were not enrolled in college, 14.7 percent were unemployed. In addition, of the class of 1972 high school dropouts who were in the labor force, 26.5 percent were unemployed.

For those adolescents who do go on to college, the first two years are a particularly unstable period, marked by changes in program and indecision about the desired level of education (Borow and Hendrix, 1977; Angrist and Almquist, 1975). Interactions with peers, experiences with new subject areas, and socialization toward changing values and aspirations all provide input for a reevaluation of career goals. On the other hand, the student role tends to be a relatively passive one. There are few chances to evaluate the effectiveness of new competences or to assume the responsibilities of a particular work role. Progress toward career choice is achieved at an abstract, intellective level, with limited opportunities for translating learning into action. Except for those who are enrolled in career programs that include field placements or internships, college students have limited opportunities to feel productive or to test their work-related problem-solving abilities.

## CHAPTER SUMMARY

Work in the areas of morality, political ideology, and career decision making provides evidence of the growing cognitive competences that contribute to the formulation of personal identity during later adolescence. Moral thought is seen as a developmental process. Kohlberg's formulation of three levels of moral thought emphasizes the ability to identify the logical principles that underlie moral decisions. The highest level, postconventional morality, begins to emerge during the high school years. However, evidence suggest that few people function consistently at this level. Experiences that foster the development of moral thought include role taking, peer interactions, and training or planned exposure to higher levels of reasoning. A period of regression in moral reasoning appears to occur after high school, as later adolescents experiment with a hedonistic orientation that frees them from traditional views of morality.

In contrast to Kohlberg's orientation, others emphasize the interpersonal nature of moral decisions. With age, adolescents become more sensitive to the feelings of others, understand the social demands of situations better, and become more skillful at controlling their emotions. In the midst of ongoing moral dilemmas, these interpersonal competences provide a stable orientation toward moral decision making.

Religion continues to provide a value structure to which many later adolescents adhere. Although doubts increase and orthodoxy declines during later adolescence, the general orientation toward religion appears to remain rather positive. The Jesus Movement has been described as an important generational contribution to American religion. It offers a blend of commitment to fundamental religious beliefs and the interpersonal informality and authenticity that are highly valued in the counterculture.

Changes in political ideology reflect increases in cognitive competence similar to those described by students of moral thought. Older adolescents are more aware of the complexity and the multiple functions of government. They are capable of anticipating the consequences of governmental decisions. Although they may not have an integrated political ideology, they are sensitive to the importance of individual rights and to the need to safeguard those rights from governmental intrusion.

Several hypotheses have been raised to explain adolescent radicalism. One view sees it as an expression of rebellion against parental authority, whereas another view sees it as a continuous enactment of liberal parental beliefs. Evidence supports both views, suggesting that political radicals encompass a rather diverse group of adolescents with varied socialization experiences.

We think of occupational career as a lifelong pattern of work experiences. Shifts in focus or emphasis reflect changes in competences, knowledge, and perspective. During later adolescence, individuals are involved in a number of career decision-making tasks. Tiedeman's model suggests that there are seven phases of planning and implementation for career decision making: exploration, crystallization, choice, clarification, induction, reformation, and integration. Each career task would involve working through these phases. Career decision making can also be carried out through a variety of cognitive styles. Although the Planning style appears to be the most effective in reaching a vocational decision, later adolescents tend to prefer the Intuitive style.

A major concern of students of adolescent development is the unequal participation of males and females in the labor force. This inequality results in a "waste" of the talents of many highly competent females. Differences in career aspirations do not appear to result from differences in decision-making styles or competences. Rather, they are due to differences in perceptions of various careers, differences in the visibility of male and female models, the influence of working mothers, lack of understanding about how sex discrimination has influenced existing patterns, and doubts about the feasibility of integrating family and career roles.

One of the most problematic issues in thinking about career development is the limited opportunity for early work experiences. Although adolescents are eager to try out their emerging competences and to assume work-related responsibilities, few work settings are designed to incorporate adolescents before they have completed their educational training or made a career commitment.

## REFERENCES

Adelson, J., and O'Neil, R. P.   Growth of political ideas in adolescence: The sense of community. *Journal of Personality and Social Psychology,* 1966, *4,* 295–306.

Allport, G. W.   *The individual and his religion.* New York: Macmillan, 1950.

Angrist, S. S., and Almquist, E. M   *Careers and contingencies.* New York: Dunellen, 1975.

Arvey, R. D., Passino, E. M., and Lounsbury, J. W.   Job analysis results as influenced by sex of incumbent and sex of analyst. *Journal of Applied Psychology,* 1977, *62,* 411–416.

Astin, A. W.   *Four critical years.* San Francisco: Jossey-Bass, 1977.

Baird, L. L.   Entrance of women to graduate and professional education. Paper presented at American Psychological Association meetings, Washington, D.C., 1976.

Baird, L. L.   Men and women college seniors' images of five careers. Paper presented at American Psychological Association meetings, San Francisco, 1977.

Balswick, J.   The Jesus people movement: A generational interpretation. *Journal of Social Issues,* 1974, *30* (2), 23–42.

Barrett, T. C., and Tinsley, H. E. A.   Vocational self-concept crystallization and vocational indecision. *Journal of Counseling Psychology,* 1977, *24,* 301–307.

Bernard, J.   *Women and the public interest.* Chicago: Aldine-Atherton, 1971.

Berns, R. S., Bugental, D. E., and Berns, G. P.   Research on student activism. *American Journal of Psychiatry,* 1972, *128,* 1499–1504.

Bettelheim, B.   Obsolete youth. *Encounter,* 1969, *23,* 29–42.

Block, J. H.   Generational continuity and discontinuity in the understanding of social rejection. *Journal of Personality and Social Psychology*, 1972, *22*, 333–345.

Borow, H., and Hendrix, V. L.   Educational career patterns of community college students: A national study. Paper presented at American Psychological Association meetings, San Francisco, 1977.

Cartwright, L. K.   Conscious factors entering into decisions of women to study medicine. *Journal of Social Issues*, 1972, *28* (2), 201–215.

Chaband, J.   *The education and advancement of women.* Paris: UNESCO, 1970.

Coleman, J. S.   How do the young become adults? *Review of Educational Research*, 1972, *42*, 431–439.

Dinklage, L. B.   *Student decision-making studies: Studies of adolescents in the secondary schools.* Report no. 6. Cambridge, Mass.: Harvard Graduate School of Education, 1969.

Feuer, L.   *The conflict of generations: The character and significance of student movements.* New York: Basic Books, 1969.

Flacks, R.   The liberated generation: An exploration of the roots of student protest. *Journal of Social Issues*, 1967, *23* (3), 52–75.

Freud, A.   *The ego and the mechanisms of defense.* New York: International Universities Press, 1946.

Froming, W. J., and McColgan, E. B.   Comparing the defining issues test and the moral dilemma interview. Paper presented at American Psychological Association meetings, San Francisco, 1977.

Gallatin, J., and Adelson, J.   Legal guarantees of individual freedom: A cross-national study of the development of political thought. *Journal of Social Issues*, 1971, *27* (2), 93–108.

Glick, P.   Updating the life cycle of the family. *Journal of Marriage and the Family*, 1977, *39*, 5–14.

Graham, W. F.   Technology, technique, and the Jesus movement. *Christian Century*, 1973, *90*, 507–510.

Greenstein, F.   *Children and politics.* New Haven: Yale University Press, 1965.

Haan, N.   Hypothetical and actual moral reasoning in a situation of civil disobedience. *Journal of Personality and Social Psychology*, 1975, *32*, 255–270.

Haan, N.   Two moralities in action contexts: Relationships to thought, ego regulation, and development. *Journal of Personality and Social Psychology*, 1978, *36*, 286–305.

Haan, N., Block, J., and Smith, M. B.   Moral reasoning of young adults: Political-social behavior, family background, and personality correlates. *Journal of Personality and Social Psychology*, 1968, *10*, 184–201.

Harren, V. A.   An overview of Tiedeman's theory of career decision making and summary of related research. Unpublished manuscript, Southern Illinois University—Carbondale, 1976.

Harren, V. A., and Kass, R. A.   The measurement and correlates of career decision making. Paper presented at American Psychological Association meetings, San Francisco, 1977.

Hogan, R.   Legal socialization in *Psychology and the law* by Battelle Memorial Institute. Lexington, Mass.: D. C. Heath, Lexington Books, 1976. (a)

Hogan, R.   Moral development and the structure of personality. In D. DePalma and J. Foley (Eds.), *Moral development: Current theory and research*. Hillsdale, N.J.: Lawrence Erlbaum, 1976. Pp. 153–167. (b)

Holstein, C.   The relation of children's moral judgment to that of their parents and to communication patterns in the family. Unpublished doctoral dissertation, University of California, Berkeley, 1969.

Keasey, C. B.   Social participation as a factor in the moral development of preadolescents. *Developmental Psychology*, 1971, *5*, 216–220.

Keniston, K.   *Young radicals: Notes on committed youth*. New York: Harcourt, Brace and World, 1968.

Kohlberg, L.   Moral education in the schools: A developmental view. *School Review*, 1966, *74*, 1–29.

Kohlberg, L.   Stage and sequence: The cognitive developmental approach to socialization. In D. Goslin (Ed.), *Handbook of socialization theory*. Chicago: Rand McNally, 1968.

Kohlberg, L.   *Stages in the development of moral thought and action*. New York: Holt, Rinehart and Winston, 1969.

Kohlberg, L.   Moral development and the education of adolescents. In R. F. Purnell (Ed.), *Adolescents and the American high school*. New York: Holt, Rinehart and Winston, 1970.

Kohlberg, L.   Continuities in childhood and adult moral development revisited. In P. B. Baltes and K. W. Schaie (Eds.), *Life-span developmental psychology: Personality and socialization*. New York: Academic Press, 1973. Pp. 180–204.

Kohlberg, L., and Blatt, M.   The effects of classroom discussion on level of moral development. In L. Kohlberg and E. Turiel (Eds.), *Recent research in moral development*. New York: Holt, Rinehart and Winston, 1972.

Kohlber, L., and Kramer, R.   Continuities and discontinuities in childhood and adult moral development. *Human Development*, 1969, *12*, 93–118.

Kramer, R.   Moral development in young adulthood. Unpublished doctoral dissertation, University of Chicago, 1968.

Kuhn, D., Langer, J., Kohlberg, L., and Haan, N.   Logical operational foundation of moral judgment. *Genetic Psychology Monographs*, 1977, *95*, 97–188.

Levinson, D.   The mid-life: A period of adult psychosocial development. *Psychiatry*, 1977.

Lunneborg, P. W.   Sex and career decision making styles. Paper presented at American Psychological Association meetings, San Francisco, 1977.

Miller, A. L., and Tiedeman, D. V.   Decision making for the 70's: The cubing of the Tiedeman paradigm and its application in career education. *Focus on Guidance*, 1972, *5* (1).

Mincer, J.   Youth, education, and work. *Teachers College Record*, 1973, *74*, 309–316.

Moreland, J. R.   Career decision making within life-span human development. Paper presented at American Psychological Association meetings, San Francisco, 1977.

Muuss, R. E.   Kohlberg's cognitive-develomental approach to adolescent morality. *Adolescence*, 1976, *11*, 39–59.

Parsons, J. E.   Attributional factors mediating female underachievement and low career aspirations. Paper presented at American Psychological Association meetings, San Francisco, 1977.

Parsons, J. E., Frieze, I. H., and Ruble, D. N.   Intrapsychic factors influencing career aspirations in college women. Mimeographed, 1975.

Perrella, V. C.   Employment of recent college graduates. *Monthly Labor Review*, February 1973, pp. 41–50.

Riegal, K.   The dialectics of human development. *American Psychologist*, 1976, *31*, 689–700.

Savin-Williams, R. C.   Age and sex differences in the adolescent image of Jesus. *Adolescence*, 1977, *12*, 353–366.

Severance, L. J., and Gottsegen, A. J.   Modeling influences on the achievement of college men and women. Paper presented at American Psychological Association meetings, San Francisco, 1977.

Shafer, S. M.   Adolescent girls and future career mobility. In R. E. Grinder (Ed.), *Studies in adolescence* (3d ed.). New York: Macmillan, 1975. Pp. 114–125.

Silvern, L. E., and Nakamura, C. Y.   An analysis of the relationship between students' political position and the extent to which they deviate from parents' position. *Journal of Social Issues*, 1973, *29* (4), 111–132.

Smith, M. B., Haan, N., and Block, J. H.   Social-psychological aspects of student activism. *Youth and Society*, 1970, *1*, 261–288.

Tangri, S. S.   Determinants of occupational role innovation among college women. *Journal of Social Issues*, 1972, *28* (2), 177–199.

Tapp, J. L., and Kohlberg, L.   Developing senses of law and legal justice. *Journal of Social Issues*, 1971, *27* (2), 65–91.

Tidball, M. F.   Perspective on academic women and affirmative action. *Educational Record*, 1973, *54*, 130–135.

Tiedeman, D. V.   Decision and vocational development: A paradigm and its implication. *Personnel and Guidance Journal*, 1961, *40*, 15–21.

Tiedeman, D. V., and Miller-Tiedeman, A.   Choice and decision processes and careers. Paper presented at Conference on Career Decision Making, American Institute of Research, March 1975.

Tiedeman, D. V., and O'Hara, R. P.   *Career development: Choice and adjustment.* New York: College Entrance Examination Board, 1963.

Turiel, E.   An experimental test of the sequentiality of developmental stages in the child's moral judgments. *Journal of Personality and Social Psychology*, 1966, *3*, 611–618.

Turiel, E.   Conflict and transition in adolescent moral development. *Child Development*, 1974, *45* (1), 14–29.

Vener, A. M., Zaenglein, M. M., and Stewart, C.   Traditional religious orthodoxy, respect for authority, and non-conformity in adolescence. *Adolescence*, 1977, *12*, 43–56.

Young, A. M.   The high school class of 1972: More at work, fewer in college. *Monthly Labor Review*, 1973, *96*, 26–32.

The photography of H. Armstrong Roberts

*Social relationships in later adolescence blend greater personal autonomy with increased social skills.*

# 10

# Social Development in Later Adolescence

In later adolescence, social relationships have an emotional buoyancy. Young people have come through the period of strong peer pressure during early adolescence with a sense of confidence about their own social competences. They have experienced the first struggles for autonomy from parents and the first pangs of falling in love. The high school environment provided a relatively complex arena for playing out social roles and for reading the social expectations of others. By later adolescence, we are all more accomplished players. Although there are still new moves to learn and new strategies to develop, one enters the social relationships of later adolescence with a greater sense of certainty and effectiveness.

For most of us, the challenges of social development in later adolescence are met eagerly. We anticipate a more collaborative relationship with parents, the formation of close and enduring friendships, and the experience of loving with excitement and pleasure. The more clearly our personal identity is articulated, the more pleasure we can derive from using that sense of meaning and purpose to guide decisions and to evaluate experiences. After many years of doubting, wondering, and waiting, the first comfortable solution to the question "Who am I?" is finally at hand. With the achievement of identity, we tie together the shreds of evidence about ourselves and finally grasp the whole picture of a unique being with a history, a present, and a future.

Four areas of social development are treated in this chapter: parent relations, sex role development, peer group relations, and the formation of loving relationships. At the end of the chapter, the theory and research on identity formation will be used as a vehicle for integrating the themes that have been presented in this and the preceding chapter. There can be no doubt that the gains that older adolescents make in social relationships are built in part on the cognitive competences discussed in Chapter 9. The widening base of information, the ability to conceptualize complex and multifunction organizations, and the emergence of an integrated ideology all contribute to a broadening of perspective that makes for more empathic, effective social interactions. On the other hand, certain areas of emotional growth also feed into the later adolescent's social competences. The ability to control impulses and to find alternative routes for expressing feelings gives later adolescents a degree of interpersonal composure that is often missing in younger people. Older adolescents have a greater capacity to understand the concerns and feelings of adults, although they may begin to lose touch with younger children, especially infants, toddlers, and children of elementary school age. Finally, older adolescents tend to be more confident about their competences, and therefore less defensive and less in need of reassurance than adolescents of high school age.

This is not to say that the height of maturity is reached in later adolescence. The later adolescent has yet to confront the complex realities of the marriage relationship, parenting, or intense involvement with occupational settings. What is more, the later adolescent has not yet had to negotiate the tensions and contradictions among roles that demand creative social problem solving. In the years to come, there will be a growing appreciation for the merging of the ideals and aspirations of later adolescence and the realities of adult commitment. There will be new demands for a psychological orientation toward others and a new ability to tolerate the contradictions of adult life. Nevertheless, in later adolescence there is a convergence of new skills that makes the young person especially well suited to take on the challenges that lay ahead.

## PARENT-CHILD RELATIONS IN LATER ADOLESCENCE

The goal of parent-child relations during later adolescence is the establishment of mutual respect and emotional autonomy. This goal must be understood within the framework of a lifelong career as a child in a family context. As long as you live, you are someone's child. Although the content of that role may evolve, it always carries with it the memories and emotions of an early period of dependency and vulnerability. It carries with it as well your experiences of realizing your parents' weaknesses and limitations and your efforts to win their respect or approval. It would be difficult to imagine a parent-child relationship that evolved to a fully autonomous level at which ideas, criticisms, and aspirations could be shared comfortably without feelings of guilt, embarrassment, or anger. Parents hide aspects of their personality from their children, and children hide aspects of their personality from their parents. In order to maintain the role expectations of the relationship, adults and children play out parts that disguise certain needs or fears. From the early years when parents tell children "Stop that, it's not nice," children learn to do some things in private, away from their parents. They also come to believe that their parents would never do those "not nice" things. After years of trying to appear well socialized to each other, parents and children find it difficult to achieve mutual respect and emotional autonomy.

The picture of parent-child relationships in later adolescence appears to be a blend of three dimensions that are considered in detail below. First, parental behaviors continue to provide models for adolescents' ideals and aspirations. Second, family socialization practices contribute to the self-concept and the social behaviors of adolescents. Third, there is a gradual differentiation of values and beliefs that reflects the adaptation of a new generation to a changing social and historical era.

## Parents as Models

The notion of a model is most fully elaborated in social learning theory (Bandura, 1978). By observing the model's behavior, we can learn new skills, imitate expressions, or learn a set of appropriate behaviors. The more important the model is to us, the more likely we are to want to copy his or her behaviors. Over time, we even emulate the emotional states that we identify as part of the model's experience. If swimming makes the model feel relaxed, swimming makes us feel relaxed. If talking about politics makes the model excited and energetic, then talking about politics makes us excited and energetic. Eventually, the learning that occurred in the presence of the model becomes internalized. We are no longer deliberately imitating the admired person. Rather, through imitation we have acquired a set of behaviors that belong to us.

In psychoanalytic terms (Freud, 1964), modeling a loved object eventually results in identification. We not only behave as the model behaves, but we derive satisfaction in experiencing a similarity of values and beliefs. Throughout childhood, identification provides children with a comforting means of achieving independence from parents while still remaining close to them. Due to identification, children know how their parents would want them to behave even in their parents' absence. They can direct their own actions, using internalized parental values as a guide.

Parents continue to serve as models during later adolescence. Several examples will help to illustrate this function. Working mothers make an important contribution to the attitudes and aspirations of their college-age children. Both the sons and daughters of employed mothers have less stereotyped views of the masculine and feminine roles than do the children of mothers who are homemakers. The sons of employed mothers see men as warmer than do the sons of homemakers. The daughters of employed mothers see women as more competent than do the daughters of homemakers (Vogel et al., 1970). College-age women whose mothers were not employed were more likely to devalue female competence and to perceive career-related achievements as masculine (Baruch, 1972).

The experiences of an employed mother also contribute to the occupational aspirations of her adolescent daughter. When mothers successfully combine the work and family roles, their daughters are much likelier to see that dual role pattern as desirable; when mothers experience a lot of conflict in their dual role, either because they are dissatisfied with their work or because their husbands do not accept their career involvement, daughters tend to be less supportive of the dual role and more conservative in their occupational aspirations (Baruch, 1972; Tangri, 1972). On the other hand, daughters whose mothers are dissatisfied with their role as homemaker tend to have relatively high career aspirations (Parsons, Frieze, and Ruble, 1975).

Fathers, too, are important role models for career aspirations. In a longitudinal study, Bell (1969) reported that there was a strong, positive relationship between a young adult's attainment of occupational goals and job satisfaction at age 25 and his father's involvement as a role model when the young adult was 15. A change in the importance of the father's role was also described in this study.

Burt Glinn/Magnum

*Parents continue to serve as important models for value decisions.*

Although involvement with a parental role model at age 15 was strongly associated with occupational attainment and effective career problem solving at age 25, this relationship between fathers and sons did not hold true when the sons were 25. At that point, high career satisfaction was associated with moderate or minimal involvement with the father as a role model. By early adulthood, fathers declined in importance for most sons and nonparents increased in significance as role models. This shift reflects the son's growing involvement in a broader sphere of personal, educational, and work settings. It also reflects the father's willingness to withdraw gradually from the son's decision-making activities.

Parents serve as models for a whole range of behaviors in addition to career orientation. In Chapter 9 we discussed the possibility of continuity between parental values and adolescent values, especially in the areas of religion and political ideology. There is considerable evidence that for some students political activism is an expression of the dedication and involvement with political issues that these students have observed in their parents. This activist orientation reflects a continuation of the autonomy, respect, and involvement in decision making that parents have encouraged in their child rearing and have demonstrated through their own political involvements (Flacks, 1967; Thomas, 1971; Lewis and Kraut, 1972).

Parents also provide a model for interpersonal behavior and expressiveness (Balswick and Avertt, 1977). Through their interactions with each other, their ability or willingness to express a wide range of feelings, and their involvement with friends, parents provide their adolescent children with a view of how adults handle feelings and how they establish meaningful personal relationships. High parental expressiveness may give adolescents some insight into the array of feelings that are aroused by the challenges and achievements of adult life. Low parental expressiveness may convey the expectation that adults have things under control, that they remain invulnerable in the face of conflict or crisis. Low parental expressiveness may also be associated with a feeling that parents do not really understand. The inability to share emotional reactions may suggest to adolescents that their feelings of gentleness, anxiety, concern, or anger are simply not shared by their parents.

## Parents as Socialization Agents

During later adolescence, we anticipate a loosening of parental controls. Adolescents come to depend more on their own judgments than on the judgments of parents or friends. They have the physical

strength and endurance to handle the minimal physical tasks of
adult life, such as carrying groceries, climbing a ladder, painting
a room, and shoveling snow. They have the conceptual skills to
handle the minimal daily intellectual tasks of adult life, such as
making change, filling out forms, reading the newspaper, and paying
bills. There is a marked decrease in the areas of dependence. Finally, most parents believe that by later adolescence their children
have learned the basic expectations and norms of the culture, that
they have internalized a set of values and beliefs that reflect parental attitudes, education, and peer group values.

Within a context of increasing freedom and the loosening of
parental controls, there are still considerable differences among
families in the pattern of child-rearing practices that have an impact
on later adolescents. In an eight-year longitudinal study of adolescent character development, Peck (1958) described four clusters
of family variables that were related to adolescent development.
The four clusters and the characteristics that are included in each
cluster are as follows:

F1  Consistency in family life
    *a.* Regularity of home life.
    *b.* Consistency of parental control.
    *c.* Common family participation in activities.
F2  Democracy—autocracy
    *a.* The child's degree of sharing in family decisions.
F3  Mutual trust and approval
    Good father-mother relations.
    Parental trust and faith in the child.
    The child's willingness to share confidences with parents.
    Parental approval of the child.
    Parental approval of the child's peer activities.
F4  Severity—leniency
    The severity of parental control.

Peck reported that trust and consistency were closely related
to three very important aspects of adolescent personality development: emotional and intellectual maturity, willing social conformity,
and mature moral behavior. Adolescent spontaneity and friendliness were associated with trust and democracy. A final personality
characteristic, described as hostility and guilt, was associated with
severity, lack of trust, and lack of democracy in the family. This
pattern of associations between family characteristics and adolescent development was based on data collected during the 1940s.
More recent studies of adolescents and their families bear out the
importance of these dimensions for contemporary adolescents and
their families.

Roll and Millen (1978) described the responses of 20 college males who had very positive feelings of being understood by their fathers and 20 college males who felt seriously misunderstood by their fathers. The responses of these young men illustrate the relevance of Peck's earlier description of family variables. For those young men who felt understood, the following themes emerged from in-depth interviews:

1.  A feeling of security and safety in knowing that their fathers would always be there in times of crisis.
2.  A feeling of acceptance by and interest from their fathers.
3.  The sharing of common interests with their fathers.
4.  The father's discipline was fair and reasonable.
5.  The fathers encouraged the independence of their sons.
6.  The sons wanted to be like their fathers because they loved and respected them.
7.  The sons recognized a change from an earlier period of respect and idolization to a period of greater equality with their fathers.

In contrast, sons who felt misunderstood described their relationships with their fathers along the following dimensions:

1.  A feeling of loneliness and isolation, a lack of connectedness with the father.
2.  A feeling of being unimportant to the father.
3.  The use of irrational, harsh punishment by the father.
4.  Being pressured into activities by the fathers; feeling coerced or dominated by the father's insistence.
5.  Conflict between the mother and the father and a sense that the father might be jealous of the mother's relationship with the son.
6.  A commitment never to act or treat others in the way that the father did.
7.  A lack of hope that the relationship would ever change.

Here we see clear evidence that the amount of interest that parents show, their communication of trust, and their ability to include the children in a rational, democratic decision-making process all contribute to feelings of closeness and support that are important to the development of a positive self-concept in the children.

Another approach to the question of family patterns of socialization is an analysis of the stimuli or antecedents of adolescent rebellion. As we pointed out in Chapter 6, the evidence suggests that adolescent rebellion is not a very frequent or predominant characteristic of adolescents' recollections.

In one sample of 417 college students, 21 percent of the males and 23 percent of the females reported a very rebellious or an extremely rebellious adolescence (Balswick and Macrides, 1975). In another small sample, 25 percent described deliberate, overt rebellious actions and 55 percent showed no rebelliousness at all (Frankel and Dullaert, 1977).

What are the family experiences of students who describe themselves as rebellious or who openly reject parental values? Although there is agreement about some of the antecedents of rebellion, there is disagreement about others. First, rebellion appears to be associated with marital unhappiness and a relatively large amount of parental conflict (Block, 1972; Balswick and Macrides, 1975). The parents of rebellious children are in less agreement with each other about child-rearing practices, less satisfied with their marriage, and more involved in overt expressions of aggression than are other parents.

Second, rebellion is associated with restrictive, controlling child-rearing techniques (Block, 1972; Balswick and Macrides, 1975; Frankel and Dullaert, 1977). There are, however, important exceptions to this pattern. First, not all children of controlling parents become involved in rebellious behaviors. Second, adolescents who describe their parents as very permissive are also likely to be rebellious. Balswick and Macrides (1975) argue that both extremes of child-rearing provide sources of frustration that stimulate rebellion.

Third, the parents of rebellious children are more preoccupied with making a good impression and conforming to social conventions than with the child's own individuality (Block, 1972). This orientation tends to increase the use of guilt-oriented disciplinary techniques and to lead parents to sacrifice the child's needs for the approval of others.

From these studies, we can infer that rebellion is really a rather extreme form of coping that occurs when the environment poses restrictions or barriers to growth. In families where there is a more gradual evolution of autonomy and a clear expression of parental interest in the child's emerging individuality, rebellion is not necessary. In fact, even in restrictive families it would appear that overt, hostile acts of rejection are not the child's preferred course of action. Rather, rebelliousness occurs when the child has no other avenues to express his or her legitimate needs and authenticity in an adult-dominated world.

## The Differentiation of Values

Although adolescent rebellion may be unusual, the process of individuation is not. Most adolescents are confronted by the realization that they are indeed different from their parents in some important ways and that they face a different future. As one college-age student describes it:

I'm beginning to start a life of my own "with a little help from my friends." And it hurts drawing away from my mother. At times, I'm almost overcome, yearning for that time of perfect knowledge between the two of us. . . . I don't want to try to "get even" with her, and I hope this distance between us isn't permanent. As soon as I feel like a unique person, unique and separate from her, then those boundaries will be enough and I can relax the artificial ones. (Goethals and Klos, 1976, pp. 40–41)

Evidence about the emerging of new attitudes and values during later adolescence suggests that there are clear areas of disagreement or difference. For example, membership in an organized religion was viewed as unimportant by three times more college-age respondents than older respondents (Yankelovich, 1970). A marked decline in trust of the government was reported for subjects aged 21–24, who evidenced much greater mistrust than older groups (Miller, Brown, and Raine, 1973). However, on many attitude or opinion surveys, the differences between later adolescents and adults are not dramatic (Thomas, 1974). For example, in one attitude survey college-age adolescents and their parents showed statistically significant differences on 28 of 36 issues. However, on only 10 of the scales did the differences exceed two scale points, and on 20 of the scales the differences were differences of intensity, not direction. In other words, the adults may have said "Strongly agree" and the adolescents may have said "Agree" (Lerner, 1975).

There do seem to be some underlying value issues that reflect a changing view of the meaning of life and of the place of human beings in the natural order (Yankelovich, 1972; Baldwin, 1971). Adolescents are increasingly oriented toward the present rather than the future. They see the goal of human beings as harmony with nature, living off the land and preserving its resources, rather than domination or control of nature. Adolescents appear to be more inclined toward a view of human beings as good and resources as abundant than to a view of human beings as neutral and resources as scarce. These kinds of philosophic differences are not necessarily reflected in opinion surveys, but they will be reflected in the life-style patterns that adolescents view as attractive or satisfying (Thomas, 1974).

Another important difference between the generations is the perception of differences. Lerner (1975) asked adolescents and their parents how much the attitudes of the other group differed from their own. In reality, there were ten scales that showed a difference of two points or more. The adolescents expected that there would be two-point differences on 19 scales. The parents expected that there would be two-point differences on only two scales. The over-estimation of differences by the adolescents and the underestimation of differences by the parents suggest a very important area of discontinuity. At this particular phase of development, adolescents may have a need to distance themselves from their parents and parents may have a need to emphasize the continuity and linkage from their generation to the next. Both sets of needs may blind parents and children to their real areas of agreement or disagreement.

It is important to realize that the process of individuation and the reevaluation of values takes place in a spirit of adaptation and growth. It is not easy to set off in a new direction. The comfort and support of parental approval are given up for the intellectual conviction that another way makes more sense. In the absence of adequate life experiences, in the absence of opportunities for participation in decision making, and often in the absence of an appreciation of the life experiences of earlier generations, each new adolescent generation arrives at its formulation of the "good life." Without this exertion of intellectual reason and emotional commitment to a new version of adult life, cultural evolution would not occur.

## SEX ROLE DEVELOPMENT

The notion of sex role refers to the attitudes and behaviors that the family and the larger culture see as appropriate to each gender (Dreyer, 1977). In this view, each society develops a set of sex role expectations or standards that are based on what the culture requires of males and females during their adulthood. Sex role expectations are based on the differential participation of men and women in the economy, the government, the religion, and the family structure of the culture. These expectations will reflect the power and status that men and women hold in a particular society as well as the particular competences that are valued for each gender. The more continuous the participation of the child in adult activities or relationships, the more similar are the sex role expectations for young children, adolescents, and adults. The more discontinuous the roles of child and adult, the more discrepancy one might expect in the content of sex role expectations for children, adolescents, and adults. In Chapter 2, we described the Aranda as an extreme example of cultural discontinuity. In childhood, Aranda boys and girls stay closely tied to the mother. The mothers and children are all kept in relative ignorance of the secrets of the religion. They are forbidden to enter certain settings, and they have minimal contact with adult males. In order to bring young males into harmony with the sex role expectations for adult males, it is necessary for adolescent males to participate in severe and prolonged initiation ceremonies (Murdock, 1934; Benedict, 1938; Muuss, 1970).

Most theories of the development of sex role identity emphasize the relative importance of early childhood for learning the gender label, for learning the cultural expectations for males and females, and for experiencing strong identifications with male and female models (Stein, 1976). By the age of two, children can appropriately apply gender labels such as Mommy and Daddy or boy and girl (Thompson, 1975). At the preschool level, children show clear understanding that certain toys, clothes, and activities are sex-typed. Their play activities reflect a preference for games and materials that are associated with their own sex or are viewed as neutral (Flerx, Fidler, and Rogers, 1976; Diepold, 1977). As part of sex role identity, children are drawn toward certain behaviors and away from others. This does not necessarily mean that they would not be good at the negatively valued activities or that they excel at the positively valued activities. Rather, it reflects their understanding of the rewards or punishments that might be encountered for engaging in sex-inappropriate and sex-appropriate (Fagot, 1977) behaviors. It also reflects their pressing need to establish a sense of equilibrium about just how they fit into the larger scheme of boys and girls, men and women.

Although sex role identity may be formulated during childhood, there can be no question that events of adolescence foster a broadening of this early conceptualization. The physical changes of puberty bring the adolescent closer to an image of himself or herself as an adult. Sexual maturation and sexual experimentation during adolescence contribute a sexual dimension to the sex role identity that cannot be appreciated before puberty. The impending life choices about career, marriage, and parenting force adolescents to clarify just how their own sex role identity will be expressed in these adult roles. An expanded conceptual understanding of the ties between sex role expectations and earlier forms of traditional society gives adolescents a sense of choice about how they will interpret sex-related norms for their own behavior. A young man may come to understand that although the male's aggressiveness may have fostered survival in an earlier historical period, contemporary marriages require men to be nurturant and expressive. A young woman may come to understand that although every society depends on women to bear and nurture children for the survival of the culture, modern society does not depend on every woman to serve this function. Adolescents redefine the early formulations of sex role identity that are expressed in the traditional game of "house," in which mother hands father the briefcase and sends him off to work so that she can give baby a bath. Young people begin to express their sex role identity in line with what they perceive to be contemporary opportunities for men and women to participate in each component of cultural life.

What, then, are the contemporary views of appropriate sex role behavior? How do these views influence the life choices of adolescents? The evidence suggests that sex role stereotypes continue to operate in the perceptions of male and female adolescents. Male and female adolescents generally agree that women are sensitive, warm, and expressive and that men lack these qualities. They also agree that men are competent, independent, objective, and logical and that women lack these qualities. What is more, stereotypically masculine qualities are viewed by both sexes as more desirable than stereotypically feminine qualities (Broverman et al., 1972).

When college-age adolescents were asked to describe the ideal sex role for children, 40 percent of them felt that there should be no differences. The remaining 60 percent identified a pattern of preferred qualities for males and females. They thought that it would be more desirable for males to be dominant, aggressive, autonomous, exhibitionistic, heterosexual, and achievement oriented. They thought that females were best characterized by order, succorance, deference, nurturance, and abasement (Hamilton, 1977). There appears to be a rather large group of adolescents who maintain what might be described as a traditional view of sex role attributes.

One of the factors that may serve to impede movement toward a more egalitarian view of male and female roles is the conflict of interests between men and women in our society. Stated very simply, if occupational success is a zero-sum game, then adding players can only result in increasing the chances of being a loser. The more competent women there are who participate in careers that are currently dominated by men, the more intense the competition will be and the greater will be the chances that some men will fail. Since the gains that men can make by participating more actively in household chores and child care are less clear at present, self-interest encourages men to maintain a more traditional stance toward sex role definitions. Several studies of sex role attitudes confirm this "gender gap" in contemporary adolescent populations. Roper and Labeff (1977) surveyed undergraduates and their parents. They used the same questionnaire that had been used 40 years earlier by Kirkpatrick (1936a and 1936b) to assess attitudes in four areas of cultural life: political, economic, domestic, and social conduct. In both 1934 and 1974 the same pattern of responses was observed:

1. Students were more egalitarian or liberal in their views of women than parents.

2. Female students were considerably more liberal than male students.
3. Female parents were more liberal than male parents.
4. The two greatest gaps in scores were between female students and their fathers (mean difference for 1974 sample = 10.3 points) and between female students and male students (mean difference for 1974 sample = 8.2 points).
5. In both 1974 and 1934 there was a bigger difference between male and female students than between male and female parents.

In other words, in both generations college-age males retained a relatively conservative view about the changing roles of females. What is more, both men and women, both parents and adolescent children, hold considerably more conservative views about the domestic role and the social conduct of women than about women's participation in the economic and political areas. What these respondents are saying is that it is all right for women to work or to be active in government as long as they still assume major responsibility for child care, the home, and family social life.

Other assessments of parent and adolescent sex role values have found the same general pattern (Zey-Ferrell, Tolone, and Walsh, 1978; Mason, Arber, and Czajka, 1976). The younger generation is more liberal than the older, females are more liberal than males, and adolescent females are by far the most progressive of all four subgroups. This means that although it may be in the best interest of the young female to open up the traditional limitations on female achievement and occupation aspiration, she will have to be prepared to experience criticism and competition from both her parents and her male contemporaries. Since not all women are equally committed to a more egalitarian view, the women who hold liberal values will also have to confront the implications from their traditionalist female contemporaries that they are "unfeminine" or that they are striving after unimportant goals.

The definition of sex role identity that one arrives at in later adolescence has important implications for later life choices. In our discussion of career choice in Chapter 9, we noted the connection between a traditional view of the female role and the limits that such a view places on career aspirations. Women who hold marriage and motherhood as central values are likely to be less innovative in their career choices and less willing to pursue advanced training in order to achieve career goals (Tittle, Chitayot, and Denker, 1977). Think back to the common orientation of adolescent women in the 40s and 50s. Many of them did not even realize that they had a choice about marriage or parenthood. These were "givens," essential expressions of the female role. With these two roles as givens, the desire to increase one's intellectual competences or to develop the skills necessary for a responsible career role was minimal. Today many of those women have discovered that they are in fact involved in a work role, and they are dissatisfied with the work they do (Tangri, 1972). Lacking a college degree or professional training, they are unable to find work that provides them with stimulation and responsibility.

Today's young women see the error in their mothers' sex role definition. They are more likely than their mothers to see career as an important component of adult life that can be interwoven with marriage and parenting if they desire. Still, the kind of work they choose will depend on how firmly they believe in the egalitarian view of the female role and how confident they are about their own competence and autonomy (Parsons et al., 1975; Tangri, 1972).

There appears to be less divergence about the male sex role. Most men and women agree that "masculine" characteristics are valued and are positively associated with mental health. Yet there is a growing appreciation of the strain of role conflicts that are embedded in a total endorsement of the traditional male sex role (Pleck, 1976). Individual males may find it increasingly difficult to base their sense of worth so heavily on work and career achievements. They may feel interpersonally isolated, having less elaborated expressive skills and fewer opportunities for the formation of close personal relationships. As wives move more fully into the world of work, husbands may feel the desire to have more satisfying relationships with their children. The developmental literature is already beginning to document the important contributions that fathers make to the socialization and intellectual growth of their children. Now we may begin to see the emergence of a generation of men who look forward to a close, nurturant relationship with their children. How will the traditional male sex role definition accommodate this important personal and social interest? Finally, as women enter more male-dominated work settings, we can expect them to introduce some of their own interpersonal competences into the work ethic. Men who have been socialized to value assertiveness and competition may find that these traditional male sex role attributes are of less value in an atmosphere of greater collaboration, interpersonal responsiveness, and social empathy. In all of these ways, the particular formulation of sex role identity that a male achieves will determine his involvement and satisfaction in marriage, parenting, and career. The need for a more flexible definition of one's sex role seems adaptive for both men and women. Such flexibility does not involve a rejection of competences that have been associated with the male and female roles, but rather an extension of competences to include the strengths of what had previously been the domain of the opposite sex (Rebecca Hefner, and Oleshansky, 1976; Bem, 1975; Sherman, 1976).

## PEER GROUP RELATIONS

There can be no question that friendships made during the college years have the potential for providing deep and lasting relationships. As adolescents free themselves from the intense peer pressures of the high school peer group, friendships begin to reflect a growing sense of personal identity. A desire and an expectation for intimacy and understanding brings later adolescents together. Of course, this need to be understood may result in disappointments if friendships fail to provide the sense of closeness that is hoped for.

### Developmental Changes in Adolescent Friendships

The more work adolescents do on the resolution of their own identity, the more important it is for them to find friends who share their values and understand their questions. During later adolescence, young people become less conforming and more independent

*Friendships offer a context of mutual support and understanding.*

in their judgments (Lehman, 1963; Costanzo and Shaw, 1966; Boyd, 1975). They are less likely to seek peer friendships in order to be accepted by a clique or crowd and are more interested in honesty and commitment in a friendship. In a survey of Soviet adolescents, two characteristics were predominant in the definition of friendship: "(1) the requirement of mutual aid and loyalty; and (2) the expectation of empathetic understanding" (Kon and Losenkov, 1978, p. 196). The former became less important with age, and the latter became more important. At every age, loyalty was more important to males and understanding was more important to females.

Increased emphasis on friendships that facilitate work on identity can be inferred from several studies of college-age adolescents. Newcomb (1962) described the process of peer group friendship formation in a student rooming house. At first, friendships were based on proximity. Men who lived on the same floor or who shared a room became friends. After four months, it was a commonality of values that drew friends together. Newcomb's subjects felt closest to others who were struggling with the same problems and who were committed to similar values.

Tangri (1972) asked women whom she had typed as Role Innovators to discuss their friendship relations. The Role Innovators were college women who had selected male-dominated careers. They tended to have more males among their ten closest friends than did traditional women (women who had chosen occupations with 50 percent or more women). These males were likely to support the idea of having a wife pursue a career and to encourage this career orientation for the benefits or satisfactions that it would give her. Role Innovators were also likely to find female friends who supported their career aspirations. Thus, the female students who have made what might be described as a high-risk or a potentially conflict-laden career choice have managed to find encouragement and support from both male and female friends who share their values.

A student at a small New England liberal arts college describes the quality of her closest college friendship. In this description we begin to understand how opening oneself up to the vulnerability of intimacy can help foster real progress in self-awareness and personal growth.

Junior year I formed the closest relationship to anyone I've ever had, not only at Berkshire but anywhere. Lisa and I became extremely close. She cared about what I thought, and many times, even though she had reservations about what I was feeling, she never attacked but asked questions, her questions making me question in turn and generally causing me to at least reevaluate those feelings. We talked hours on end about Berkshire and what was happening to us and everyone else here. I didn't like Berkshire because it placed me in a state of, I guess, being nowhere. The academics of Berkshire seemed so unreal, the people seemed unreal, and increasingly it became harder to identify with other black students since it seemed the college was doing some grand experiment in coming up with the perfect black Berkshire student. I didn't identify with any black student who felt comfortable here because it implied being comfortable in other places also. I can't be comfortable because I know where I came from and am going back to, and the black people in the world out there, the real world, are terribly uncomfortable. (Goethals and Klos, 1976, p. 234)

## Friendships between Males and Females

Individuals differ in the patterns of friendships they desire. Some adolescents have both male and female friends, some have friends of only the same sex, some have friends of only the opposite sex, and some have only one intimate friendship that combines sexuality and understanding. In the sample of Soviet adolescents discussed above, 75 percent agreed that it would be possible to have a friendship with someone of the opposite sex without being in love. However, among the oldest males (age 20), more than half doubted that this would be possible. In general, among all age groups in the Soviet sample more males preferred same-sex friendships and more females preferred opposite-sex friendships. If this pattern was reflected in real friendship choices, one could expect that more females would feel disappointed in not being able to have the close friendships they desired. This was in fact the case. At every age, the Soviet girls were less optimistic about the possibility of finding a "genuine friendship."

Opposite-sex friendships are viewed as both desirable and problematic. In a study of black college students, friendships across sex were more intimate than friendships between members of the same sex (Peretti, 1976). Opposite-sex friendships were characterized by more sharing of information about the self, more participation in shared activities, and greater feelings of reciprocity than same-sex friendships. We know from Tangri's (1972) study of Role Innovators that male friends can be very important in supporting women's untraditional aspirations. We also expect adolescent males to benefit from close friendships with females. In these friendships it is possible for males to share some of their doubts and weaknesses, that is, to disclose more of their personal thoughts without being viewed as overly dependent or incompetent. Usually, women are more comfortable than men about sharing intimate aspects of themselves. Since this makes them more vulnerable to exploitation or rejection, they are likely to encourage their male friends to do the same. If a male friend is able to collaborate with a female friend in the process, it is possible that the male will benefit by increasing his feelings of being understood (Derlega and Chaiken, 1977; Cozby, 1973).

Although friendships between males and females may have some beneficial and satisfying consequences, there are some serious barriers to opposite-sex friendships. If we think of one of the goals of friendship as the facilitation of identity formation and value clarification, then relationships that interfere with a developing sense of competence and personal values would be counterproductive. It is from this standpoint that male-female friendships are most likely to run into difficulties.

We have already discussed studies of attitudes toward the female sex role that suggest a gap between males and females in their acceptance of feminism. Male and female adolescent peers do not share the same commitment to the equal participation of women in all spheres of cultural life (Roper and Labeff, 1977; Zey-Ferrell et al., 1978). Furthermore, males and females tend to agree with a stereotyped image of women as less competent, more submissive, and less independent than men (Broverman et al., 1972). Women who reject the traditional female sex role and strive for academic competence or innovative careers will find it difficult to find male friends who really share those values.

Both males and females bring stereotypes about the opposite sex that may interfere with the development of a friendship. Females tend to expect that males will have much fewer "feminine" characteristics that they actually have (Nicol and Bryson, 1977). Thus, females will expect males to be less supportive, empathic, dependent, or nurturant than the males feel they are. In this sense, females may not be ready to accept or support the interpersonal or emotional qualities that are part of a male friend's personality. In contrast, males have trouble accepting the intellectual challenge of a bright female friend. Despite the growing value in finding a life partner who will provide intellectual companionship, many males have difficulty with heterosexual relationships in which they do not feel superior (Komarovsky, 1973). Such males either avoid heterosexual relationships that might threaten their feelings of intellectual competence or try to turn their female companions into "good listeners." For their part, some women play into the male superiority stereotype by pretending to be less competent or by disguising their abilities. Although this kind of charade is becoming less acceptable among college women, it continues to be an expectation that females identify in the college environment. Obviously a productive friendship would not be easy to achieve in a relationship in which one partner had to disguise her intellectual abilities.

As adolescents work toward their own solutions to the challenges of political, occupational, family, and moral ideologies, they can ill afford friendships with either males or females that do not support the expression of their fullest potential. If understanding, support, and empathy are the goals of friendship, then self-doubt, competition, and shame are its pitfalls. It is important that a friendship begin on a foundation of respect and acceptance. Otherwise, the price of companionship is likely to be the abandonment of personal growth.

## LOVING RELATIONSHIPS

By the age of 25, the majority of Americans have experienced their first marriage. For women born in the 1950s, the median age at marriage was 21.2 years (Glick, 1977). Although young people in the working class marry somewhat earlier than do young people in the middle class, there can be no doubt that for most adolescents the period of later adolescence is a time for experimenting with intimacy. The process of achieving a loving relationship usually involves three phases, acquaintance with members of the opposite sex, emotional commitment, and sexual intimacy, though not necessarily in that order (Gagnon and Greenblat, 1978). The heterosexual activities of older adolescents, then, have as their foci meeting new people, falling in love, and providing and receiving physical pleasure. Many adolescents do not see these activities as a prelude to marriage or as a part of courtship per se. Nevertheless, the experiences that are gained in each of these areas help young people to identify members of the opposite sex whom they find attractive and to clarify their own capacity to participate in a close, emotionally involving relationship.

### Mixing

Our society seems to encourage frequent social interaction among males and females. There are few experiences that are designed to keep males and females apart, and increasing opportunities for males and females to collaborate or interact. In the college environment, probably the biggest change in opportunities for meeting members of the opposite sex is the coeducational dormitory. An estimated 70 percent of colleges offer coed dormitories as an option for residential living (Pierson and D'Antonio, 1974). Such dormitories validate the important need of college students to have casual, spontaneous interactions with members of the opposite sex. They also provide more opportunities for males and females to interact in private settings and to develop cross-sex friendships.

The pattern of opportunities for heterosexual interaction is quite different for those later adolescents who do not go on to college and those who do. For adolescents who do not go to college, high school is the last context in which there are frequent opportunities for males and females to meet and mix. After high school, contacts between males and females may be limited to the work setting and the neighborhood. For this age group, the "singles" bar is becoming an alternative setting for mixing. For the most part, however, adolescents who do not go on to college are likely to move more quickly toward sexual intimacy and emotional commitment during high school, so that soon after graduation they are ready to make a decision about a marriage partner. The period for finding a marriage partner among working-class adolescents who do not attend college is fairly short. If a suitable partner is not found among high school, work, or neighborhood contacts, the young person may feel the need to move to another town or to take an apartment in a building in which other "singles" are likely to live (Starr and Carns, 1972).

In contrast to those adolescents who do not go to college, college students have to begin the process of mixing, emotional involvement, and sexual intimacy all over again in the college setting. College-bound students tend to resist a final marriage commitment during high school. College-bound females are also less likely to experience sexual intercourse during high school than are females who are not going to college (Simon, Berger, and Gagnon, 1972). The expectation of meeting a whole new pool of partners and the commitment to a higher level of educational and career aspirations act to delay the desire for a serious commitment during high school. This does not mean that college-bound adolescents do not go steady or fall in love. They simply tend to impose limits on high school relationships in recognition of the potential for future growth that is symbolized by the desire for a college education.

At the college level, adolescents who resisted serious commitments during high school may be more open to the possibility of a long-term commitment. They may even experiment with sharing the same living quarters. Loving relationships formed during college are very likely to include sexual intimacy. Once again, however, their openness to marriage depends on future career aspirations and the decision to pursue an advanced degree. The more involved students are with their academic goals and the more selective the institution is about admitting students, the less likely students are to marry during college (Bayer, 1972).

During the college years, then, adolescents continue to seek close, loving relationships, usually with the understanding that these relationships are not permanent. Thus, we must understand adolescent loving relationships as a contemporary need for understanding and as an increasing desire for sexual expression. In these relationships, important work on identity and value clarification continues. Away from the supervision of parents and neighbors, college adolescents have the opportunity to develop intimate bonds with a person who may come from a very different home background, have quite different political or religious views, or have a very different outlook on future aspirations. Through the intellectual sharing that occurs in an intimate relationship within a context of mutual support, there is important growth in perspective and outlook.

## Emotional Commitment

Falling in love is about as common a college experience as forgetting about an exam; it happens to almost everyone at least once. Experiences in a loving relationship tend to increase somewhat during the four years at college, but very few males or females report having been in love more than twice during their college years (Simon and Gagnon, 1967). Within the context of movement toward a more egalitarian view of women and increased openness about sexuality, what is the quality of love during later adolescence? Is love still "a many-splendored thing"? Do adolescent lovers get lovesick, do they pine for each other, are they starry-eyed innocents standing at the ocean's edge? Or is it freeze-dried insta-love—fast and easy? We have very little data about the quality of loving relationships during later adolescence. Most studies of couples have focused on the sexual dimension. Far fewer studies have tried to evaluate the perceptions couples hold about their relationship or the kinds of needs that the relationship most often satisfies. We do have a sense, however, that changes are taking place in what young men and women look for in a loving relationship and in how they define and enact intimacy.

Vreeland (1972) described the responses of two groups of Harvard males, a sample of students who were enrolled in 1964 and 1965 and a sample of students who were enrolled in 1970. They were asked to tell their reasons for dating, to describe their dating activities, and to give the characteristics of a good or bad date. Vreeland found that some important aspects of dating had changed from the older to the more recent sample. The primary reason for dating had shifted from recreation to companionship. Dating activities seemed to have shifted from a public to a private focus. There were many more young men in the 1970 sample who most enjoyed sitting and talking as a dating activity. There seemed to have been a decline in such dating activities as going to dances, football games, or parties. Only a small percentage of the freshman in both cohorts reported sex as a primary dating actvity (11 percent in the 1960s and 8.9 percent in 1970). By their senior year, however, 21 percent of the Harvard males saw sex as an important dating activity. The primary orientation toward dating was a search for an opposite-sex friend who could participate in a relationship that combined sexuality and understanding.

Among contemporary adolescents there continues to be a degree of variability about the kinds of expectations that couples hold for a loving relationship—the more traditional males or females are about their sex role definition, the more they tend to base their relationship on infatuation and on a romantic dependence on the other partner to complete their personality. In other words, the traditional view of sex roles sees men and women as having rather opposite characteristics. The love relationship offers a completion of the missing parts through the blending of contrasting qualities. Males and females who hold a more egalitarian view of sex roles tend to emphasize trust and understanding as the basis for love. These adolescents do not see such extreme differences between males and females. In a love relationship, they look for a friend who will offer support and compassion.

Peplan, Rubin, and Hill (1977) described the expectations of dating couples who attended four colleges in the Boston area. They were especially interested in the way sexuality fitted into the couple's orientation toward intimacy and love. Three patterns were discussed. Sexually traditional couples felt that marriage was a necessary condition for sexual intimacy. Within this framework, abstaining from intercourse was viewed as an indication of a couple's love and respect for each other. Among sexually moderate couples, sexual intercourse was viewed as an appropriate expression of love, even without the more permanent commitment of marriage. For these couples, the feelings of love and caring that develop in a love relationship are eventually expressed in the act of intercourse. The third group were sexually liberal. They did not view love as a necessary condition for sexual intercourse. Among these couples, "recreational sex" was a part of the erotic fun of dating. Thus, sex may be seen as a way of getting to know another person that does not necessarily have to be connected to love.

We see, then, that for contemporary adolescents love, sex, and marriage are three separate experiences that may or may not be combined in the same relationship (Dreyer, 1975). Not all adolescents see marriage as a prerequisite for sex or sex as an expression of love. There is much more flexibility in the definition of loving relationships and a greater sense of choice about the outcome of a loving relationship than there was in the past. This does not mean that adolescents are not interested in intimacy. Quite the contrary seems to be true. Caring for others; being able to have open, honest communication, and being understood are highly valued interpersonal goals. In fact, we have a sense of much less patience with the game playing and status seeking that were an important part of dating in the past.

## Sexual Intimacy

The pattern of increasing sexual permissiveness that was described in Chapter 4 continues during the college years. When attitudes and behaviors are studied over the four years of college, males and females become increasingly "single standard." That is, they do not differentiate between the sexual behaviors that are appropriate for males and those that are appropriate for females. What is more, this single standard becomes increasingly permissive over the college years. Students move from a standard that emphasizes restraint or abstinence to a standard that endorses sexual expression for both sexes (Ferrell, Tolone, and Welsh, 1977).

King, Balswick, and Robinson (1977) compared the responses of university students in 1965, 1970, and 1975 to questions about sexual behavior and attitudes about sex. Table 10–1 compares the percentage of students who had experienced intercourse and the percentage who had experienced heavy petting at the three time periods. These data suggest that there has been increasing participation in intense sexual activity by both males and females, but markedly more involvement by females. As sexual experience has increased, there has been an accompanying increase in the permissiveness of attitudes toward sex. Over the ten-year period, fewer students viewed premarital sex as immoral and fewer students felt that having sexual intercourse with a number of different people was sinful or immoral.

The double standard, though fading, continues to make its contribution to the formation of intimate relationships. Although the gap between males and females has been closing, fewer females

Table 10–1: Percentage of Students Experiencing Sexual Intercourse and Heavy Petting at Three Time Periods: 1965, 1970, and 1975.

|  | Sexual Intercourse | | Heavy Petting* | |
| --- | --- | --- | --- | --- |
|  | Male | Female | Male | Female |
| 1965 .......... | 65.1% | 28.7% | 71.3% | 34.3% |
| 1970 .......... | 65.0 | 37.3 | 79.3 | 59.7 |
| 1975 .......... | 73.9 | 57.1 | 80.2 | 72.7 |

* Manual and oral manipulation of genitals.

Source: Karl King, Jack O. Balswick, Ira E. Robinson, The continuing premarital sexual revolution among college females. *Journal of Marriage and the Family*, 1977, *39*, pp. 455–459. Copyrighted 1977 by the National Council on Family Relations. Reprinted by permission.

than males report being sexually active. Also, both males and females are slightly more critical of women who have many sexual encounters than they are of men who have many sexual encounters (King et al., 1977).

In seeking sexual intimacy, males and females have somewhat different orientations and expect each other to act differently. Among the dating couples interviewed by Peplan et al. (1977), the males and females advocated identical standards for sexual conduct in a loving relationship. However, more males than females mentioned sex as the best thing in the relationship or as an important goal in dating. When the couple had not yet had intercourse (which was the case for 42 of the 231 couples), it was usually the female who exerted the restraining influence. Among couples who had had intercourse, the less sexually experienced the female, the longer the couple dated before intercourse occurred.

McCormick (1977) provided students with examples of strategies that might be used to have or to avoid having sexual intercourse. The students were asked to guess whether a male or a female would be more likely to use each strategy. Both the males and the females judged the strategies as masculine when they were designed to have intercourse and as feminine when they were designed to avoid intercourse. When the students described the strategies that they would actually use, both sexes tended to try indirect strategies such as body language, or seduction as a means of moving toward sexual intercourse and direct strategies such as coercion, moralizing, or the use of rational arguments to avoid having intercourse. Although males and females described their behavior in quite similar ways, they perceived the two sexes as employing very different strategies—males active and females passive.

A final view of the double standard is provided by the ways in which males and females act when they have already experienced intercourse. Carns (1973) interviewed college students at 12 colleges and universities in the United States. His focus was on the persons to whom adolescents talked about their sexual experiences and how these listeners reacted to the information. Carns' assumption was that sexual behavior had a different meaning for males and females, and that this difference would be reflected in the extent to which they shared their sexual experiences with others. He found that males were quite a bit more likely than females to share their experiences with many friends. Over half of the males (53.4 percent) had told five or more friends about their first sexual experience. Of the females, 26 percent had told no one and another 29.3 percent had told only one or two friends. Over half of the females (57.1 percent) had never told a parent about their sexual experience, whereas two thirds of the males had shared this experience with parents. Finally, 61.6 percent of the males had talked about their first sexual experience immediately or within one month. Only 39.1 percent of the females had told anyone about their sexual experience immediately or within one month. These data suggest that for males, the experience of sexual intercourse is something that is expected and approved of by peers and parents. Adolescent males, for the most part, are proud to have had a sexual encounter and receive relatively strong support for their behavior. For females, however, sex is something that continues to be shrouded in ambivalence. Females may anticipate less approval for their behavior. They may also feel that the intimacy of a sexual encounter is too personal to disclose. What is clear is that the sexual script for male and females continues to differ. Males tend to begin their sexual activity within a context of peer support, conquest, and validation of their masculinity. Females tend to begin their sexual activity as an expression of intimacy and loving feelings, with greater ambivalence about the reactions that such behavior will generate.

## PERSONAL IDENTITY

Erik Erikson has provided a comprehensive treatment of the meaning and functions of personal identity. From his inclusion of this concept in the theory of psychosocial development (1950) to his recent analysis of American identity (1974), Erikson has evolved a notion of identity that involves the merging of past identifications, future aspirations, and contemporary cultural issues. The major works in which he discusses identity are "The Problem of Ego Identity" (1959) and *Identity: Youth and Crisis* (1968). Our presentation of the concept is based upon these works.

Later adolescents are preoccupied with questions about their essential character in much the same way that the early-school-age children are preoccupied with questions about their origin. In their efforts to define themselves, later adolescents must take into account the bonds that have been built between themselves and others in the past, as well as the direction that they hope to be able to take in the future. Identity serves as an anchor that allows the person an essential experience of continuity in social relationships. Erikson (1959) states:

The young individual must learn to be most himself where he means the most to others—those others, to be sure, to have come to mean most to him. The term identity expresses such a mutual relation in that it connotes both a persistent sameness within oneself (self-sameness) and a persistent sharing of some kind of essential character with others. (p. 102)

The photography of H. Armstrong Roberts

*Personal identity—the merging of past identifications, current competences, and future aspirations.*

In addition to the emerging integration of self which is part of identity formation, Erikson posits a cultural component to identity. The personal definition reflects the roles and accompanying expectations that individuals are involved in, as well as the roles and expectations that they expect to become involved in. Personal identity must reflect some of the value orientation of the individual's reference groups. It must also reflect the value orientation of the nation. Americans feel that certain values (which are, in fact, American values) are part of their psychological makeup. The resolution of the search for identity is, therefore, the final step in the internalization of cultural values.

As young people move through the stage of later adolescence, they find that the family, the neighborhood, teachers, friends, the ethnic group, and the nation hold certain expectations for the behavior of a person at this stage. One may be expected to work, marry, serve the country, attend church, and vote. These expectations are different from cultural values, but they must also be accommodated in the formation of the individual's identity. The persistent demands of meaningful others produce certain decisions that might have been made differently or might not have been made at all if the individual were the sole agent involved in identity formation. There is, in fact, a threat to identity formation that results from external demands. People may slip easily into the roles which are expected of them, without ever identifying themselves and their personal goals with those social expectations. In making this point, Erikson (1959) quotes from the autobiography of George Bernard Shaw:

I made good in spite of myself, and found, to my dismay, that Business, instead of expelling me as the worthless imposter I was, was fastening upon me with no intention of letting me go. Behold me, therefore, in my twentieth year, with a business training in an occupation which I detested as cordially as any sane person lets himself detest anything he can not escape from. In March, 1876 I broke loose. (p. 103)

For those who do not "break loose," the situation described by Shaw is called identity foreclosure (Marcia, 1966). This is a resolution of the identity crisis which involves a series of premature decisions about one's identity, often in response to the demands of others. Young people may decide early in their adolescence that they will become what parents or grandparents wish them to become, and may never question this decision in relation to their developing personality. Individuals may be firm in their commitment to these decisions without having identified the particular ways in which the decisions strengthen their own ego.

Sometimes cultural expectations and demands provide the young person with a clearly defined self-image that is completely contrary to the cultural values of the community. This is called a negative identity (Erikson, 1959). Epithets such as "failure," "good-for-nothing," "juvenile delinquent," "hood," and "greaser" are labels that the adult society commonly applies to certain adolescents. In the absence of any indication of the possibilities of success or of contribution to the society, the young person accepts these negative labels as a self-definition and proceeds to validate this identity by continuing to behave in ways that will strengthen it.

The negative identity can also emerge as a result of a strong identification with someone who is devalued in the family or the community. A loving uncle who is an alcoholic or a clever, creative parent who commits suicide can stimulate a crystallization of oneself as a person who might share these undesired characteristics.

The foreclosed identity and the negative identity are both resolutions of the identity crisis which fall short of the goal of a positive personal identity and yet provide the person with a concrete identity. A more psychologically acute resolution of the crisis is role diffusion. In this state, young people are unable to make a commitment to any single view of themselves. They are unable to integrate the various roles they play. They may be confronted by opposing value systems or by a lack of confidence in their ability to make meaningful decisions. In either case, the condition of diffusion arouses anxiety, apathy, and hostility toward the existing roles, none of which can be successfully adopted.

Dolores, an unemployed college dropout, describes the feeling of aimless, meaningless drifting that is associated with role diffusion.

I have two sisters, and my father always told me I was the smartest of all, that I was smarter than he was, and that I could do anything I wanted to do . . . but somehow, I don't really know why, everything I turned to came to nothing. After six years of analysis I still don't know why. (She looked off into space for a moment and her eyes seemed to lose the train of her thought. Then she shook herself and went on.) I've always drifted . . . just drifted. My parents never forced me to work. I needn't work even now. I had every opportunity to find out what I really wanted to do. But . . . nothing I did satisfied me, and I would just stop . . . Or turn away . . . Or go on a trip. I worked for a big company for a while. . . . Then my parents went to Paris and I just went with them. . . . I came back . . . went to school . . . was a researcher at Time-Life . . . drifted . . . got married . . . divorced . . . drifted. (Her voice grew more halting.) I feel my life is such a waste. I'd like to write, I really would; but I don't know. I just can't get going . . . (Gornick, 1971, pp. 77–84, 209–210)

In the process of evolving a personal identity, one undoubtedly experiences temporary periods of confusion and depression. The task of bringing together the many elements of one's experience into a coordinated, clear self-definition is difficult and time-consuming. The adolescent is likely to experience moments of self-preoccupation, isolation, and discouragement as the diverse pieces of the puzzle are shifted and reordered into the total picture. Thus, even the eventual positive identity formation will be the result of some degree of role confusion. The negative outcome of role diffusion, however, suggests that the person is never able to formulate a satisfying identity which provides for the convergence of multiple identifications, aspirations, and roles. In this case, individuals have the persistent fear that they are losing hold on themselves and on their future.

**Role Experimentation.**   During later adolescence, young people experiment with roles that represent the many possibilities for their future identity. In the area of occupational role, later adolescents may think of themselves in a variety of career roles in order to anticipate what it would be like for them to be a member of a specific occupational role group. This experimentation may include taking a number of different summer jobs, changing the college area of specialization, doing extensive reading, and daydreaming.

In the area of sex role, the later adolescent may consider whether or not to marry, the marriage format, and types of personal relationships with members of the opposite sex. Dating is a form of role experimentation that permits different self-presentations with each new date. In the area of value orientation, later adolescents may evaluate their commitment to their religion, consider religious conversion, and experiment with different rationales for moral behavior. In the area of political ideology, they may examine a variety of political theories, join groups that pursue political causes, and campaign for political candidates.

Particularly for the college student, the environment encourages experimentation. Later adolescence is a period when people have few social obligations that require long-term role commitments. They are free to start and stop, to join and quit, without serious repercussions to reputation. As long as adolescents do not break any laws in the process of experimenting with different roles, they can play as many roles as they wish, in order to prepare themselves for the resolution of the identity crisis, without risking serious social censure.

Parents sometimes become concerned because an adolescent son or daughter appears to be abandoning the traditional family value orientation or life-style. The adolescent talks of changing religions, remaining single, or selecting a "low-status" career. The more vehemently the family responds to these propositions, the more likely it is that the young person will become locked into a position in order to demonstrate autonomy, instead of being allowed to continue the experimentation until a more suitable personal alternative is discovered. Parents may be well advised not to take the role experimentation of the later adolescent too seriously. If anything, it might be beneficial for a loved and trusted parent to "play along" with the young person as he or she evaluates the characteristics of various roles.

**The Psychosocial Moratorium.** Role experimentation takes many forms. Erikson uses the term *psychosocial moratorium* (1959) to describe a period of free experimentation before a final identity is achieved. Under ideal conditions, the moratorium would allow individuals freedom from the daily expectations for role performance. Their experimentation with new roles, values, and belief systems would result in a personal conception of how they could fit into society so as to maximize their personal strengths and gain positive recognition from the community.

The concept of the psychosocial moratorium has been partially incorporated into those college programs that provide two years of pass/fail courses before the student is required to select a major. The philosophy is to eliminate the student's concern with external evaluation during the decision-making process. Perhaps an even more effective translation of this concept would be to encourage high school students to take a year for work, travel, or volunteer service before deciding about college or a career. In any case, the notion of the psychosocial moratorium suggests the need for some temporary relief from external demands in order to establish one's identity most effectively.

The intensity of later adolescence is both agonizing and heroic. Adolescents seek to discover those essential characteristics that will satisfy their longing for self-definition and yet will not alienate them drastically from their social environment. The crisis of identity versus role diffusion suggests a fusion of earlier identifications, present values, and future goals into a consistent self-concept. This unity of self is achieved only after a period of questioning, reevaluation, and experimentation. Efforts to resolve questions of identity may take the adolescent down paths of overzealous commitment, emotional involvement, alienation, or playful wandering.

## Research on Identity Resolution

In the discussion of the psychosocial crisis of identity versus role diffusion, a number of potential resolutions of the crisis were suggested. At the positive pole is identity achievement; at the negative pole is role diffusion. We have also discussed the premature resolution (identity foreclosure), the postponement of resolution (the psychosocial moratorium), and the negative identity.

James Marcia (1966) has devised a questionnaire to evaluate the status of identity resolution. Using Erikson's conceptualization (1950, 1959), he assesses identity status on the basis of two criteria: crisis and commitment. Crisis is conceived of as implying a period of role experimentation and active decision making among alternative choices. Commitment includes the demonstration of personal involvement in the areas of occupational choice, religion, and political ideology. On the basis of subjects' completion of Marcia's questionnaire, the status of their identity development is assessed. People who are classified as identity achieved have already experienced a crisis and have made occupational and ideological commitments. People who are classified as identity foreclosed have not experienced a crisis, but demonstrate strong occupational and ideological commitments. Their occupational and ideological beliefs appear to be very close to the beliefs of their parents. People who are classified as being in a state of psychosocial moratorium are involved in an ongoing crisis. Their commitments are diffuse. People who are classified as role diffused may or may not have experienced a crisis and demonstrate a complete lack of commitment. Marcia mentions that the identity-diffused group has a rather cavalier, playboy quality that allows its members to cope with the college environment. He suggests that more seriously diffused persons (such as those described by Erikson, 1959) may not appear in his sample because they are unable to cope with college.

Marcia gave the identity status questionnaire and a group of other test instruments to 86 male college students. He found that the identity-achieved group demonstrated somewhat greater ego strength than any of the other three groups. He also found that the identity-foreclosed group had a strong commitment to obedience, strong leadership, and respect for authority. Of the four groups, this group demonstrated the most vulnerable self-esteem and the least ego strength.

It must be noted here that the group that Marcia has identified as identity diffused is probably made up of immature adolescents who have not yet begun the work on identity that is represented in the other groups. It is unlikely that out of a sample of 86 subjects one would find a group of 21 subjects characterized by role diffusion, as Marcia has. His instrument does not measure a condition of anxiety about identity which is characteristic of truly identity-diffused subjects. What Marcia has demonstrated is that, for males, identity achievement produces the strongest personality, identity foreclosure is a somewhat brittle and vulnerable resolution, and the psychosocial moratorium is a period of transition and flux between childhood and adulthood.

Marcia and Friedman (1970) repeated Marcia's identity status research with women. They found that the identity-achieved women and the identity-foreclosed women were most similar on dependent measures of ego strength. This was in contrast to the findings for males, in which identity-achieved and moratorium subjects were most similar. Marcia and Friedman proposed that while the status groupings for males were based on approximation to mature achievement, the status groupings for females reflected an underlying dimension of stability versus instability.

A later study by Schenkel and Marcia (1972) found that identity formation among females was more related to issues of sexuality and religion, as compared to the concern of males with occupation and politics. The similarity between identity-achieved and identity-foreclosed women was validated in a study relating identity status to conformity in an Asch-type situation (Toder and Marcia, 1973). Women who had been identified as having either an achieved or a foreclosed status conformed to peer pressure significantly less than did women who had been identified as either moratorium or diffuse status. The identity-achieved and identity-foreclosed groups were also similar in indicating less negative affect than the other two groups. These studies suggest that although identity achievement is clearly the most mature resolution of the identity crisis for both men and women, identity foreclosures (or perhaps it could be seen as temporary foreclosure) is also a positive adaptation to reality for women (Marcia and Friedman, 1970; Donovan, 1975).

The process of identity formation appears to be a dynamic, changing integration of competences and aspirations rather than

Table 10–2: Changes in Identity Status from 1967–1968 to 1974

| Current Identity Status: 1974 | Previous Identity Status: 1967–1968 | | | |
|---|---|---|---|---|
| | Identity Achievement (N = 7) | Moratorium (N = 7) | Foreclosure (N = 9) | Identity Diffusion (N = 7) |
| Identity Achievement | 3 | 3 | 0 | 1 |
| Moratorium | 0 | 0 | 2 | 0 |
| Foreclosure | 3 | 2 | 3 | 0 |
| Foreclosure/ Diffusion* | 1 | 0 | 4 | 2 |
| Identity Diffusion | 0 | 2 | 0 | 4 |

* This is a new status composed of two types of individuals: Foreclosures, whose commitment to parental values has weakened, and Identity Diffusions, who are reaching toward some parental values.
Source: J. E. Marcia, "Identity Six Years After: A Follow-up Study," mimeographed, 1975, p. 14. Reproduced by permission.

a fixed typology or a clear stagewise progression. Studies of changes in identity status across age ranges have confirmed several of Erikson's notions about identity. In a cross-sectional comparison of 13- and 14-year-olds with 19–24-year-olds, the older subjects scored higher on all aspects of ego identity (Protinsky, 1975). Longitudinal studies of college students have found increases in identity achievement from the freshman to the senior year (Constantinople, 1969; Waterman, Geary, and Waterman, 1974). In the Waterman et al. study, which was done at an Eastern engineering school, there was a general shift away from moratorium status and toward achievement. Surprisingly, about 30 percent of the seniors remained in a diffused state with regard to either occupation or ideology.

Marcia (1975) has provided an even longer time perspective in a six-year follow-up of males who were first interviewed during college. Table 10–2 shows the relationship between identity status during college and in young adulthood. As can be seen, all of the moratorium-status subjects had changed their status. What is more surprising, four subjects who had been described earlier as identity achieved and two who had been described as in moratorium were described as foreclosed during young adulthood. These six subjects seemed to have abandoned the search and experimentation that had been part of their college orientation for a more conservative, restricted life-style. One of the subjects who changed from achievement to foreclosure was described as follows:

The first, interviewed at his insurance office after hours, was pin-neat in a gray sharkskin suit. He, like several other Foreclosures, had also married his high school sweetheart. About the "revolution", he said, "It's safe to say that I didn't get too involved." He questioned the value of his college education; he would rather have been in a work-study program "where you get hooked into a company right from the beginning." Of his future, he said, "I believe that family and professional life are the basis for personal happiness. We're satisfied, although we feel that we should be making more money."

In this follow-up study, Marcia also looked at the relationship between identity and intimacy. Both previous and current identity status were associated with the successful achievement of an intimate relationship. The subjects who had achieved identity also experienced intimacy. Those who had changed to a foreclosed or diffuse status had stereotyped relationships or were experiencing isolation. In other words, work on identity continued to play a part in the young adults' ability to participate in a mutually satisfying personal relationship.

We can understand identity, then, as a complex formulation about one's personal meaning that requires both cognitive and socioemotional competences. The person who experiences some degree of questioning and role experimentation is seeking to discover the logic of his or her own reality. How do the values that are held, the competences and talents that exist, and the aspirations that are emerging combine to orient one toward a plan for future decision making? A search for identity is a cognitive problem-solving task with a sense of personal fulfillment as the goal. What is more, identity achievement requires self-awareness, an ability to tolerate temporary uncertainty, and an emotional willingness to make the kinds of commitments to values, to work, and to other people that will allow others to know and understand you. In these ways, identity formation is a socioemotional challenge, drawing on the person's resilience, flexibility, and capacity to cope with challenge. For every person who experiences crisis and questioning and is eventually able to make personally authentic commitments about values, ideology, work, and social relationships, the process of identity achievement can be understood as the most profound, creative work of the first 25 years of life.

## CHAPTER SUMMARY

Four areas of social development have been discussed: parent relations, sex role development, peer relations, and the formation of loving relationships. The goal of parent-child relations in later adolescence is the achievement of personal differentiation while still maintaining a bond of affection and respect. Parents continue to serve as important models for career choice, political and religious involvement, and interpersonal behavior. Their socialization practices continue to influence adolescent development. The dimensions of parental behavior that seem to be repeatedly identified as relevant during later adolescence are consistency, support and trust, the involvement of children in decision making, and the leniency or restrictiveness of controls. The point is made that while rebellion is not a usual outcome, it may be an important response to an overly restrictive or controlling home setting. In this generation, the differentiation from parental values tends to emphasize a more trusting view of human beings and a more mistrustful view of large organizations, especially government and religion. Although adolescents and their parents agree on many issues, adolescents tend to be moving away from their parents' view of the place of human beings in nature and of the relative importance of the present and the future.

Sex role development begins in early childhood. In later adolescence, one's sex role is redefined, incorporating sexual experiences, more adult role expectations, and participation in close opposite-sex friendships. There is evidence that sex role stereotypes continue to be held by males and females. Males tend to be more traditional, resisting the full, egalitarian participation of men and women in all aspects of cultural life. However, changing attitudes about involvement in work, changing work norms, and a growing interest in the active integration of work, marriage, and parenting may foster a more flexible definition of the male and female roles.

Friends become increasingly important as a source of support and understanding during later adolescence. As work on identity continues, adolescents seek others who share their values and will participate with them in a process of questioning. It is especially important during later adolescence to have friends who believe in one's ability to achieve aspirations and who do not place unnecessary limits on those aspirations.

Later adolescence can be seen as the prelude to marriage. During these years, experiences in mixing, emotional involvement, and sexual intimacy provide information about the desirability of a marriage partner and about one's capacity for loving.

In general, loving relationships have more variability today than they had in the past. Love, sex, and marriage are separate aspects of a loving relationship. The primary goal of an intimate relationship appears to be understanding and friendship. If that relationship involves sex, so much the better. Not all adolescents view sex as an expression of love, and some continue to believe that love means refraining from sex until marriage.

Although most adolescents endorse a single standard of sexual behavior for males and females, some remnants of the double standard remain. These include less sexual activity among females than males, more restrictive attitudes toward female "promiscuity," and a greater likelihood that the female rather than the male will exert the restraining influence about having sexual intercourse.

The concept of personal identity refers to a synthesis of values, roles, and aspirations that blends past identifications with a vision about oneself moving through the future. Identity is an achievement that requires both cognitive and social competences. As an accomplishment of later adolescence, it marks the person's ability to make sense out of the events of childhood and to plan out a course for adult life. Identity is achieved through a process of crisis, questioning, reevaluation, and eventual commitment to a set of values and beliefs that can guide action. It is generally achieved through role experimentation. Adolescents must try out various images of themselves, becoming temporarily committed to a number of life possibilities in order to discover which roles make a comfortable blend with personal competences and values. Although work on identity can be seen in a developmental perspective, that work can be ended in ways that fall short of the achievement of identity. A person's identity status can be described as achieved, foreclosed, or diffuse. Adolescents can delay commitment through a period of moratorium, or they can claim as their identity values that are in opposition to cultural ideals (negative identity). The capacity to resolve one's work on identity in a creative and fulfilling manner depends on one's personal resources and on the support of the family, college, and peer group cultures.

## REFERENCES

Baldwin, D. C., Jr. The generation gaps: A question of changing values. *Forum,* Fall/Winter 1971, pp. 10–11.

Balswick, J. O., and Avertt, C. P. Differences in expressiveness: Gender, interpersonal orientation, and perceived parental expressiveness as contributing factors. *Journal of Marriage and the Family,* 1977, *39,* 121–127.

Balswick, J. O., and Macrides, C. Parental stimulus for adolescent rebellion. *Adolescence,* 1975, *10,* 253–266.

Bandura, A. *Social learning theory.* Englewood Cliffs, N.J.: Prentice-Hall, 1978.

Baruch, G. K.   Material influences upon college women's attitudes toward women and work. *Developmental Psychology,* 1972, *6,* 32–37.

Bayer, A. E.   College impact on marriage. *Journal of Marriage and the Family,* 1972, *34,* 600–609.

Bell, A. P.   Role modeling of fathers in adolescence and young adulthood. *Journal of Counseling Psychology,* 1969, *16,* 30–35.

Bem, S.   Sex-role adaptability: One consequence of psychological androgyny. *Journal of Personality and Social Psychology,* 1975, *31,* 634–643.

Benedict, R.   Continuities and discontinuities in cultural conditioning. *Psychiatry,* 1938, *1,* 161–167.

Block, J. H.   Generational continuity and discontinuity in the understanding of societal rejection. *Journal of Personality and Social Psychology,* 1972, *22,* 333–345.

Boyd, R. E.   Conformity reduction in adolescence. *Adolescence,* 1975, *10,* 297–300.

Broverman, I. K., Vogel, S. R., Broverman, D. M., Clarkson, F. E., and Rosenkrantz, P. S.   Sex-role stereotypes: A current appraisal. *Journal of Social Issues,* 1972, *28* (2), 59–78.

Carns, D. E.   Talking about sex: Notes on first coitus and the double sexual standard. *Journal of Marriage and the Family,* 1973, *35,* 677–688.

Constantinople, A.   An Eriksonian measure of personality development in college students. *Developmental Psychology,* 1969, *1,* 357–372.

Costanzo, P. R., and Shaw, M. E.   Conformity as a function of age. *Child Development,* 1966, *37,* 967–975.

Cozby, P. C.   Self-disclosure: A literature review. *Psychological Bulletin,* 1973, *79,* 73–91.

Derlega, V. J., and Chaiken, A. L.   Privacy and self-disclosure in social relationships. Paper presented at American Psychological Association meetings, San Francisco, 1977.

Diepold, J. H.   Parental expectations for children's sex-typed play behavior. Paper presented at 85th Annual Convention of American Psychological Association, San Francisco, 1977.

Donovan, J. M.   Identity status: Its relationship to Rorschach performance and to daily life pattern. *Adolescence,* 1975, *10,* 29–44.

Dreyer, P. H.   Changes in the meaning of marriage among youth: The impact of the "revolution" in sex and sex role behavior. In R. E. Grinder (Ed.) *Studies in adolescence* (3d ed.). New York: Macmillan, 1975. Pp. 352–374.

Erikson, E. H.   *Childhood and society,* New York: Norton, 1950.

Erikson, E. H.   The problem of ego identity. *Psychological Issues,* 1959, *1* (1), 101–164.

Erikson, E. H.   *Identity: Youth and crisis.* New York: Norton, 1968.

Erikson, E. H.   *Dimensions of a new identity,* New York: Norton, 1974.

Fagot, B. I.   Consequences of moderate cross-gender behavior in preschool children. *Child Development,* 1977, 902–907.

Ferrell, M. Z., Tolone, W. L., and Walsh, R. H.   Maturational and societal changes in the sexual double-standard: A panel analysis (1967–1971, 1970–1974). *Journal of Marriage and the Family,* 1977, *39,* 255–271.

Flacks, R.   The liberated generation: An exploration of the roots of student protest. *Journal of Social Issues,* 1967, *23* (3), 52–75.

Flerx, V. C., Fidler, D. S., and Rogers, R. W.   Sex-role stereotypes: Developmental aspects and early intervention. *Child Development,* 1976, *47,* 998–1008.

Frankel, J., and Dullaert, J.   Is adolescent rebellion universal? *Adolescence,* 1977, *12,* 227–236.

Freud, S.   New introductory lectures on psychoanalysis. In J. Strachey (Ed.), *The standard edition of the complete psychological works of Sigmund Freud,* vol. 22. London: Hogarth Press, 1964. (Originally published in German in 1933.)

Gagnon, J. H., and Greenblat, C. S.   *Life designs: Individuals, marriages, and families.* Glenview, Ill.: Scott, Foresman, 1978.

Glick, P. C.   Updating the life cycle of the family. *Journal of Marriage and the Family,* 1977, *39,* 5–13.

Goethals, G. W., and Klos, D. S.   *Experiencing youth: First person accounts* (2d ed.). Boston: Little, Brown, 1976.

Gornick, V.   Consciousness. *New York Times Magazine,* January 10, 1971.

Hamilton, M. L.   Ideal sex roles for children and acceptance of variation from stereotypic sex roles. *Adolescence,* 1977, *12,* 89–96.

King, K., Balswick, J. O., and Robinson, I. E.   The continuing premarital sexual revolution among college females. *Journal of Marriage and the Family,* 1977, *39,* 455–459.

Kirkpatrick, C.   Content of a scale for measuring attitudes toward feminism. *Sociology and Social Relations,* 1936, *20,* 512–526. (a)

Kirkpatrick, C.   The construction of a belief-pattern scale for measuring attitudes toward feminism. *Journal of Social Psychology,* 1936, *7,* 421–437. (b)

Komarovsky, M.   Cultural contradictions and sex role: The masculine case. *American Journal of Sociology,* 1973, *78,* 873–884.

Kon, I. S., and Losenkov, V. A.   Friendship in adolescence: Values and behavior. *Journal of Marriage and the Family,* 40, 143–155.

Lehmann, I. J.   Conformity in critical thinking, attitudes, and values from freshman to senior years. *Journal of Educational Psychology,* 1963, *54,* 305–315.

Lerner, R. M.   Showdown at generation gap: Attitudes of adolescents and their parents toward contemporary issues. In H. D. Thornburg (Ed.), *Contemporary adolescence: Readings* (2d ed.). Monterey, Calif.: Brooks/Cole, 1975. Pp. 114–126.

Lewis, S. H., and Kraut, R. E.   Correlates of student political activism and ideology. *Journal of Social Issues,* 1972, *28* (4), 131–149.

Marcia, J. E.   Development and validation of ego identity status. *Journal of Personality and Social Psychology,* 1966, *3,* 551–558.

Marcia, J. E.   Identity six years after: A follow-up study. Mimeographed, 1975.

Marcia, J. E., and Friedman, M. L.   Ego identity status in college women. *Journal of Personality,* 1970, *2,* 249–263.

Mason, K. O., Arber, S., and Czajka, J. C.   Change in U.S. women's sex-role attitudes, 1964–1974. *American Sociological Review,* 1976, *41,* 573–596.

McCormick, N. B.   Power strategies in sexual encounters. Paper presented at American Psychological Association meetings, San Francisco, 1977.

Miller, A., Brown, T., and Raine, A.   Social conflict and political estrangement, 1958–1972. Cited in *Institute of Survey Research Newsletter,* Spring–Summer 1973.

Murdock, G. P.   *Our primitive contemporaries.* New York: Macmillan, 1934.

Muuss, R. E.   Puberty rites in primitive and modern societies. *Adolescence,* 1970, *5,* 109–128.

Newcomb, T. M.   Student peer group influence. In N. Sanford (Ed.), *The American college.* New York: Wiley, 1962. Pp. 469–488.

Nicol, T. L., and Bryson, J. B.   Intersex and intrasex stereotyping on the Bem Sex Role Inventory. Paper presented at American Psychological Association meetings, San Francisco, 1977.

Parsons, J. E., Frieze, I. H., and Ruble, D. N.   Intrapsychic factors influencing career aspirations in college women. Mimeographed, 1975.

Peck, R. F.   Family patterns correlated with adolescent personality structure. *Journal of Abnormal and Social Psychology,* 1958, *57,* 347–350.

Peplau, L. A., Rubin, Z., and Hill, C. T.   Sexual intimacy in dating relationships. *Journal of Social Issues,* 1977, *33* (2), 86–109.

Peretti, P. O.   Closest friendships of black college students: Social intimacy. *Adolescence,* 1976, *11,* 395–403.

Pierson, E. C., and D'Antonio, W. V.   *Female and male: Dimensions of human sexuality.* Philadelphia: Lippincott, 1974.

Pleck, J. H.   The male sex role: Definitions, problems, and sources of change. *Journal of Social Issues,* 1976, *32* (3), 155–164.

Protinsky, H. O.   Eriksonian ego identity in adolescents. *Adolescence,* 1975, *10,* 428–432.

Rebecca, M., Hefner, R., and Oleshansky, B.   A model of sex-role transcendence. *Journal of Social Issues,* 1976, *32* (3), 197–206.

Roll, S., and Millen, L.   Adolescent males' feeling of being understood by their fathers as revealed through clinical interviews. *Adolescence,* 1978, *13,* 83–94.

Roper, B. S., and Labeff, E.   Sex roles and feminism revisited: An intergenerational attitude comparison. *Journal of Marriage and the Family,* 1977, *39,* 113–119.

Schenkel, S., and Marcia, J. E.   Attitudes toward premarital intercourse in determining ego identity status in college women. *Journal of Personality,* 1972, *3,* 472–482.

Sherman, J. A.   Social values, femininity, and the development of female competence. *Journal of Social Issues,* 1976, *32* (3), 181–196.

Simon, W., Berger, A. S., and Gagnon, J. H.   Beyond anxiety and fantasy: The coital experiences of college youth. *Journal of Youth and Adolescence,* 1972, *1* (3), 203–221.

Simon, W., and Gagnon, J. H.   Selected aspects of adult socialization. Unpublished paper, 1967.

Starr, J. R., and Carns, D. E.   Singles in the city. *Society*, 1972, *9*, 43–48.

Stein, A. H.   Sex role development. In J. F. Adams (Ed.), *Understanding adolescence: Current developments in adolescent psychology* (3d ed.). Boston: Allyn and Bacon, 1976. Pp. 233–257.

Tangri, S. S.   Determinants of occupational role innovation among college women. *Journal of Social Issues*, 1972, *28* (2), 177–199.

Thomas, L. E.   Family correlates of student political activism. *Developmental Psychology*, 1971, *4*, 206–214.

Thomas, L. E.   Generational discontinuity in beliefs: An exploration of the generation gap. *Journal of Social Issues*, 1974, *30* (3), 1–22.

Thompson, S. K.   Gender labels and early sex role development. *Child Development*, 1975, *46*, 339–347.

Tittle, C. K., Chitayot, D., and Denker, E. R.   Sex role values: A neglected factor in career decision making theory. Paper presented at American Psychological Association meetings, San Francisco, 1977.

Toder, N. L., and Marcia, J. E.   Ego identity status and response to conformity pressure in college women. *Journal of Personality and Social Psychology*, 1973, *26*, 287–294.

Vogel, S. R., Broverman, I. K., Broverman, D. M., Clarkson, F. E., and Rosenkrantz, P. S.   Maternal employment and perception of sex roles among college students. *Developmental Psychology*, 1970, *3*, 384–391.

Vreeland, R. S.   Is it true what they say about Harvard boys? *Psychology Today*, 1972, *5* (8), 65–68.

Waterman, A. S., Geary, P. S., and Waterman, C. K.   A longitudinal study of changes in ego identity status from the freshman to the senior year at college. *Developmental Psychology*, 1974, *10*, 387–392.

Yankelovich, D.   The generation gap: A misleading half truth. Paper presented at Eastern Sociological Association meeting, 1970.

Yankelovich, D.   *The changing values on campus.* New York: Simon and Schuster, 1972.

Zey-Ferrell, M., Tolone, W. L., and Walsh, R. H.   The intergenerational socialization of sex-role attitudes: A gender or generation gap? *Adolescence*, 1978, *13*, 95–108.

Jean-Claude Lejeune

*Parental expectations play a major role in the decision to attend college.*

**11**

# The College Environment

If you are reading this book, you are more than likely doing so as part of your participation in a program of higher education. Colleges have become a major educational and socialization setting for American adolescents. For the most part, later adolescents do not arrive at college by chance. They are drawn toward postsecondary institutions because of parental expectations, peer pressure, career aspirations, the lack of job opportunities for high school graduates, or because they are in search of new ideas and new information. Whatever their rationale or their goals, they have chosen to participate in yet another complex educational institution.

As a result of their participation in the college environment, adolescents hope to reach their own educational or occupational goals. At the same time, they will be touched by the mission, the value orientation, and the expectations of this new environment. In the role of college students, later adolescents experience presses toward logical thought, scholarship, community participation, and camaraderie that can retain their influence on intellectual and social activity throughout adulthood. During college, adolescents are introduced to new standards of excellence, new levels of competition, and new opportunities for intellectual growth that stand out as models, inspiring later achievements. During college, students also gripe and groan, fall asleep over books, and waste incredible amounts of time deciding about or avoiding work. Students try to protect themselves from the overwhelming flood of information that sensitizes them to their own ignorance. They step cautiously from course to course, from friend to friend, trying to keep hold of the threads of purpose and self-definition that instigated the effort in the first place. As they move along, however, the voyage itself transforms their intentions, so that by the end they seek new goals and expect new things of themselves.

The purpose of this chapter is to consider college environments as contexts for growth during later adolescence. Three themes are discussed. First, we ask, Who goes on to college, and how is the process of selection negotiated? Second, we describe a variety of college settings in order to provide a sense of the diversity of postsecondary experiences. Third, we discuss the process of adaptation and change. In this last section, we examine the consequences of coping with some specific characteristics of the college environment.

## THE DECISION TO ATTEND COLLEGE

In 1974, 33.5 percent of all people aged 18–24 were enrolled in a degree-credit program at an institution of higher education. That figure represents over 9 million Americans aged 18–24 who were involved in some type of college program. It does not include an-other million students in that age range who were enrolled in non-degree-credit programs (Grant and Lind, 1976).

American college freshmen can be described as follows: Over 90 percent are either 18 or 19. Over 90 percent have graduated from high school. Almost half of the women and one third of the men have a high school grade average of B+ or better. They tend to come from relatively affluent families. Less than one fourth of them say that their parents' annual income is less than $10,000 (Grant and Lind, 1976). In 1978–79, the estimated charges for room, board, and tuition were $1,794 a year at public undergraduate insti-tutions and $3,855 at private undergraduate institutions (Simon and Frankel, 1976). Because of steadily rising costs, a major concern of college freshmen and their families tends to be financing a college education.

The transition from high school to college involves a process of negotiation and decision making for the college and the student. Some public universities and community colleges have an open admissions policy. These schools will admit any day high school graduate who has a minimum grade point average of C and is a resident of the state. Among the private, "prestige" universities and colleges, however, there continues to be an active selection procedure that will ensure a balanced class of freshmen that is designed to meet the diverse needs of the institution. Moll (1978) described five admission categories that guide the decisions of those schools that continue to have many more applicants than they can accommodate. The *intellects* are students who have high Scholastic Aptitude Test (SAT) scores and have earned excellent grades in difficult high school courses. These are the students who are sought by the faculty in order to provide the creativity and intellectual stimulation that make college teaching exciting. The *special talent* group are students who have a skill that is particu-larly valued by the college. This may be musical, dramatic, or artis-tic talent, but it is usually a sports skill. Colleges try to select the outstanding athletic talent for the particular sports they empha-size. The *family* group are the children of alumni. These students ensure continued alumni support. The fourth group are the *"All American Kids."* These are the students who will help run the school organizations, the student government, clubs, and activities. They will be the glue that keeps the class together, and they will carry the reputation of the college to the community. This is the most "crowded" category, since most applicants fall into this group and are therefore competing against the largest number of other applicants. The last group are described by Moll as the *social conscience* group. These students are admitted as part of the college's commitment to enroll minority students in proportion to their numbers in the population. The important point is that in most admissions procedures students do not compete for space against all other applicants. Rather, they compete with the other students who have been placed in a similar admissions category. In this way, each college tries to pick the best mix of students it can.

High school students who are deciding about college make their decisions on the basis of their high school achievements, their career aspirations, the reputation of the school, the geographic location of the school, and financial considerations. Because of rising costs, public education is becoming increasingly attractive. Students also have high expectations for a career "payoff" from their college degree. College continues to be an avenue of social mobility. In 1973, the median income for males 25 years or older who had finished college was $14,704. The comparable income for males who had only finished high school was $10,832. Only 3.4 percent of males with high school degrees were earning over $25,000 a year, as compared to 13.6 percent of males with bachelor's degrees. The monetary benefits of a college education for women are less dramatic. The median income of female high school graduates in 1973 was $3,970, and the median income of female college graduates was $6,214. Less than 1 percent of females who graduated from college earned over $25,000 a year (Grant and Lind, 1976). Nonetheless, students continue to view a college education as a prerequisite to a good job and as the training ground for certain specialized careers.

In addition to career expectations, high school students expect the college environment to provide some kind of social and intellectual atmosphere. This is where the school's reputation in a community and the public relations efforts of the school's admissions staff can seriously influence student applications. In order to evaluate adolescents' expectations about college, Goodman and Feldman (1975) asked high school seniors who had been accepted at a specific college to rate their ideal college and the actual college that they would be attending. The many attributes of a college environment were combined into seven scales that seemed to summarize the relevant dimensions of an "ideal college." These seven variables are as follows:

1. Permissive ambience (four items): "Permissive attitudes toward drugs," "permissive attitudes toward sexual activities," "opportunity to do just about what you want," "strict drug regulations" (reverse scoring).
2. Primary-group emphasis (four items): "Mostly small classes,"

"close contact with faculty," "friendly student body," "many cultural activities."

3. Liberal arts emphasis (four items): "Emphasis on liberal arts," "emphasis on arts," "emphasis on science" (reverse scoring), "can meet academic pressure without strain."

4. Specialized and useful training reputation (five items): "Has the special curriculum I want," "good reputation for helping to get into graduate school," "good reputation for getting a job," "a lot of hard work but worth it," "meet different kinds of people."

5. An inexpensive and convenient college (four items): "Close to home," "away from home" (reverse scoring), "relatively mild winter," "low cost."

6. A high-quality institution (four items): "High scholastic standards," "faculty of high academic quality," "intellectual stimulation," "small city."

7. Opportunities for student involvement (three items): "An opportunity to become politically active," "student voice in administration," "good athletic program." (Goodman and Feldman, 1975, p. 152)

In the semester before attending college, these seniors perceived their ideal college as somewhat better on all the scales except permissive ambience than the school that they planned to attend. Two years later, while the students were college sophomores, they were asked to rate their own college and the ideal college again. In four areas, the initial evaluation of the actual college was higher than the evaluation of that college after the student had been there for two years. The students reported that there was less primary-group emphasis, less of a specialized and useful training reputation, less emphasis on high-quality instruction, and less opportunity for student involvement than they had expected. In all of these ways, the students demonstrated that they had had higher expectations of the college they chose before they entered the college than they had after they had been enrolled in it for some time. What is more, over time the students de-emphasized the importance of a high-quality institution in their definition of an ideal college. Perhaps they became more sensitive to the actualities and more suspicious about the reputation of an institution after having participated in one for a while.

For the most part, we are impressed by how poorly informed adolescents are as they approach a decision about college. Decisions tend to be guided by such variables as the prestige or reputation of a school, convenience, cost, and the availability of a particular professional program. Adolescents know very little about the quality of instruction, the teacher-student relationship, the availability of laboratory or library resources, or the quality of dormitory life. These and other critical aspects of college life are left to be discovered as part of the "college experience."

One might argue that part of this lack of information is the fault of students and parents who do not actively search out relevant information. At least among competent high school seniors, however, it has been observed that considerable effort is expended in trying to obtain information about college (Silber et al., 1961). These students wrote to colleges, talked with college-age friends, visited campuses, and talked with teachers or counselors to try to get a sense of what the new role of college student might entail.

Colleges, for their part, do not tend to provide the most useful information to prospective students. For example, Speegle (1969) analyzed the kinds of information that appeared in college catalogs. He found no description of the informal social atmosphere of the schools. He also found that most catalog descriptions did not correspond very accurately to students' perceptions of colleges. In order to make information about the college environment more accurate for incoming students, Baird (1974) offered colleges free tests and scoring services for a questionnaire on student and college characteristics. This questionnaire would provide prospective applicants with information about the rules, the amount of faculty-student interaction, student activism, the emphasis on intellectual rigor, the nonacademic activities, and the flexibility of the curriculum. Only 25 percent of the 200 colleges involved in Biard's project made use of the questionnaire results. Students are left to learn by experience whether their choice of a college was based on accurate information, whether the college they chose will meet their personal needs, and whether it will make the kinds of contributions to personal growth that the students anticipated at the outset.

## KINDS OF COLLEGE EXPERIENCES AND THEIR IMPACT

In Chapter 7 we tried to convey the diversity of high school experiences that might be available for American adolescents. Here, we must take into account an even broader range of settings under the general heading of post-secondary education. In 1974–75 there were 2,747 institutions of higher education, including universities, other four-year institutions, and two-year colleges. In addition, 8,846 postsecondary schools offered occupational programs that did not lead to an associate or bachelor's degree (Grant and Lind, 1976). At all levels of postsecondary education, a number of variables influence the kinds of experiences that students will have at a particular institution. The size of the institution and whether it is public or private, coeducational or single-sex, and a residential or a commuter school will all contribute to the impact of the school and to the satisfaction that students feel in their participation.

In an assessment of over 200,000 students at 300 postsecondary institutions, Astin (1977) has presented some facinating findings about the impact of college environments on students. In the academic year 1969–70, seniors were asked to rate the same institution that they had rated as freshmen in 1966. On a 5-point scale, in which 5 was "very satisfied" and 1 was "very dissatisfied," the mean rating was 3.7 (between "on the fence" and "satisfied"). Students were most pleased about the friendships they had made and least pleased about the variety of courses that they were able to take and about the administration of the college.

Several institutional characteristics were closely related to student satisfaction. Institutions that were highly selective and prestigious had students who were quite positive in their overall rating as well as their rating of classroom instruction, the curriculum, and the academic reputation of the school. Students at large institutions were very satisfied with the social life, the varied curricula, and the academic reputation, but dissatisfied about faculty-student contacts. Students at teacher's colleges were satisfied about their

Susan Meiselas/Magnum

*The residential climate contributes to satisfaction with college.*

peer friendships, but dissatisfied about student-faculty relations, classroom instruction, and the intellectual climate. Satisfaction was lowest at technological schools. Males attending all-male colleges and females attending all-female colleges were considerably more positive about many aspects of their college experience than were students at coeducational settings. The only exception was in the area of social life, with which males at men's colleges expressed strong dissatisfaction. Finally, students who were commuters or who lived at home were less satisfied than students in residence.

These patterns of student satisfaction are especially important in light of changing trends in higher education. Degree-credit enrollment was 9 million in 1974. It is expected to increase to about 10.2 million in 1981 and then to decrease to 9.8 million by 1984. In addition, non-degree-credit enrollment is expected to increase to 1.8 million by 1984. In the face of these projections, the costs of postsecondary education continue to rise. In order to control costs and, at the same time, to offer postsecondary education to an expanding population, several changes have been instituted in higher education over the past 30 years. There has been an expansion of state-supported universities and public community colleges. As these institutions grew, many smaller private institutions closed because they could not compete financially for the pool of students. Because of the increased competition for students, and the growing emphasis in federal laws against sex discrimination in federal spending, many single-sex institutions have become coeducational. In the mid-1960s there were 236 colleges for men and 281 colleges for women. Currently there are 127 and 142, respectively (Grant and Lind 1976). Finally, the press toward publicly funded universities and two-year colleges and the need to cut costs have resulted in an increased number of commuter students and a decreased commitment to the residential component of the college experience.

In other words, institutions of higher education are becoming larger, less selective, less invested in a residential component, and more fully coeducational. Astin's analysis of student satisfaction suggests that these features of the college environment are not the ones that have, in the past, been closely associated with a highly positive college experience. In describing the process of education at Earlham College, Cottle (1977) provides a feeling for some of the special advantages of the small private institution.

There is no Earlham type, just as there is no Quaker type, but there is a barely detectable packet of qualities and predispositions that makes a man or woman an appropriate choice for this school. For despite their sophistication and the punctuations of urbanity that make so many of the Earlham family uncomfortable using words like community and openness, many have become rather taken, if not enthralled, by the gentle spiritualism that sits rather nicely alongside their educational policies and determined life-styles. Earlham has no desire to scour graduate school departments for the "most promising scholars." With a budget that prevents them from offering salaries anywhere near what some of their own faculty members are offered every day by other schools, they listen for the sounds of teachers who have temporarily or, even better, permanently disavowed their connections with high-pressure educational institutions where prestige is king and intellectual honesty and care for a student's welfare are remnants of an antiquated currency. For more than a few of its faculty members, one visit to Berkeley, Cambridge, or Ann Arbor, or to the turmoil of large cities, was enough to convince them that those places were not for them. Compared with the schools where they have previously taught, "Earlham is heavenly." So, if their unseen colleagues in New York, Boston, and San Francisco wonder seriously how human beings can survive in the vacuous wastelands, in the sticks, in the Midwest, well, let them wonder, for Earlham loses only a few of its faculty, and anyway, the air is clean here, the chance for freedom, albeit an insular freedom, rather great, and airplanes can always transport one to the big towns or to the ocean for the summer months. There are many forms of renewal, not all of them urban.[1]

Given that colleges provide different kinds of opportunities and satisfactions, it is extremely important that students try to be more adequately informed before they choose a college. It is, of course, difficult to weigh any particular set of costs and benefits. In making a decision about college, it is important to consider one's needs and competences. What is more, it is important to have a glimpse of the kind of person that one hopes to become. This kind of projection is difficult to achieve at the end of early adolescence, because most of the work on identity formation is yet to be completed. In its place, one must hope for an effective coping strategy in which new information, the ability to understand and control one's emotions, and the capacity to maintain freedom of movement help students to see the implications of the available options and to make a personally enhancing choice.

## THE ADAPTATION OF COLLEGE STUDENTS TO THEIR SCHOOLS

Adaptation is the result of the interaction between individuals with specific competences and needs and environments with unique characteristics and presses. In thinking about adaptation during the college years, we are especially interested in the ways college students respond to institutions and in the ways institutions make

---

[1] T. J. Cottle, *College: Reward and betrayal.* Chicago: University of Chicago Press (1977), pp. 68–69. © 1977 by the University of Chicago. All rights reserved. Reprinted by permission.

their enduring contributions to the development of college students. We are trying to sort out the changes in attitudes, values, or skills that might occur because of maturation or a broader context of ongoing socialization from those that are the direct result of interaction with the educational institution. In other words, we are asking two kinds of questions: (1) Does going to college make a difference? (2) Does going to a particular kind of college make a difference?

There are four areas in which the question of adaptation to college has been considered in some detail. First, living in a college dormitory, fraternity, or residence hall has been identified as an important element of the college experience. The impact of the college is transmitted in part through experiences in the college residence. Second, college environments have been differentiated according to the expectations and resources they provide. Adaptation to college includes adjustment to the basic climate of the institution. Third, adaptation to college can be understood as a process of value change in response to the college experience. Fourth, adaptation to college can be viewed in terms of the academic competences or the intellectual growth that results from a college education. Each of these four themes provides part of the total picture of the means by which colleges make an impact on their students and of the ways in which students are changed by their participation in a college environment.

## Adaptation to College Residences

Think for a moment about some of the experiences that are encountered in a college dormitory. Students from different family groups, different neighborhoods, and different parts of the country are brought together to share bedrooms, bathrooms, hallways, laundry rooms, dining areas, and study space. There is a convergence of diverse individuals into a relatively high-density space. Students may have to ask one another to hold down the noise, take shorter showers, or make shorter phone calls. Students may depend on one another to take phone messages, to find another room for a night or two if a "guest" is visiting, or to share toothpaste or shaving cream in an emergency. Amid the stresses of course work, exams, papers, conflicts with parents, faltering love relationships, and feelings of confusion about future aspirations, dormitory residents come to share one another's crises and triumphs. The tomblike silences during exam week, the nervous laughter about a broken date, the screams and shouts of triumph over an A paper, and the crash of wastebaskets and beer cans during a weekend celebration are part of the dormitory's climate. The sounds of college life are shared within its walls.

*Roommates share the triumphs, the uncertainties, the gripes, and the failures of college life.*

Two rather different aspects of college residences, the architectural design and the social climate, contribute to their impact. The earliest contacts and the first phase of friendship making are likely to occur among residents who live near one another. The increased interaction among roommates or suitemates contributes to the formation of friendships that have a good chance of remaining important throughout the college career (Newcomb, 1962; Dressel and Lehman, 1965). Thus, physical proximity and opportunities for interaction are consequences of the design of a dormitory that contribute to its impact on interpersonal growth.

Interactions are not always viewed as desirable or pleasant. Baum and Valins (1977) compared the patterns of social behavior in two different kinds of dormitories, one modeled on the corridor design and one on the suite design. Corridor residences had rectangular wings and floors. Each wing consisted of 16–17 double-occupancy rooms off a long central hallway. There was a central bathroom and a lounge at the end of the hall. The suite design consisted of four–six-person suites, each with two or three bedrooms, a small lounge, and a bathroom. Each floor consisted of five or six suites along a central hallway. Thus both the corridor design and the suite design were intended to accommodate about 34 students along a wing, but the differences in their arrangement of living space led to considerably different patterns of interaction and perceptions of the environment.

Corridor residents had more contacts with a larger number of students, but these contacts were less predictable and less controlled than those of suite residents. Corridor residents were more likely than suite residents to perceive the dormitory as "crowded." The feeling of being crowded was especially strong for students who lived on the end of the hall near the lounge or right near the bathroom.

The frequent, uncontrolled interactions seemed to generate a social distance among corridor residents. These students had fewer friends on the floor than did suite residents. They were also less likely than suite residents to know their neighbors.

Baum and Valins offer the following statement about the impact of dormitory design on social development:

The clustering of residents in smaller groups around semiprivate or controlled-access public space allows for more positive interactions and more rapidly developing group control over common space. As a result, interaction may be frequent but is generally more predictable and more easily regulated. The distribution of neighbors and the spatial relationships between semiprivate, group-controlled spaces and the individual bedroom unit can encourage group formation and enhance positive and sufficiently controllable interaction. The large group sizes promoted by the corridor and long-corridor designs result in social interference (unwanted interaction, goal-blocking) and inhibit processes of group development. Because residents do not generally exert control over adjacent hallway space, the corridor design does not provide a counterpart to the suite lounge, and the regulation of social interaction becomes more difficult. The architectural clustering of residents in varying group sizes appears to be central to the quality of life in dormitory environments.[2]

The impact of the college residence results from social factors as well as architectural design. The daily life of dormitory residents is influenced by the diversity of residents; the attitudes that residents hold toward social activities, academic achievement, and occupational goals; and the pattern of dormitory regulations. Brown (1968) intervened in the living arrangements of about 400 college freshmen in order to demonstrate the potential impact of the dormitory experience on academic and vocational goals. Brown placed 44 science students and 11 humanities students on two floors of a residence hall and 44 humanities students and 11 science stu-

---

[2] Reprinted with the permission of the authors and publisher from A. Baum and S. Valins, *Architecture and social behavior: Psychological studies of social density.* Pp. 104–105. Hillsdale, N.J.: Lawrence Erlbaum Associates, Publishers, 1977.

dents on the other two floors. One science-dominated floor and one humanities-dominated floor also had an enrichment program, including talks and discussions that provided a chance for informal interaction with faculty members.

The impact of the majority-minority living arrangement was striking. Minority students were more likely to change their major or to become less certain about their major over the year. They were also less likely to have three best friends with the same occupational goals and more likely to be dissatisfied with their residence hall and with the total college experience. These findings suggest that the lack of homogeneity of aspirations and interests created a pervasive feeling of conflict and uncertainty among the minority students. If we think about the chance placement of students in dormitory housing, without regard to their majors or their occupational goals, it seems quite possible that some students would experience this lack of consensus or peer support as part of their early college life.

The enrichment program also had an impact on the students. It stimulated students to become more involved in other school activities. Participants in the program showed more interest in abstract thought and science and placed more emphasis on reason and scientific problem solving than did nonparticipants. These results suggest the desirability of planting the seeds of inquiry and analysis in the context of the living unit instead of making the classroom and the dormitory two distinct settings in which only very different kinds of learning can take place.

The social climate of the college residence can be described by the perceptions of the residents as well as by their characteristics. These perceptions are determined by asking the residents of a particular housing unit what they experience as the dominant patterns of behavior and orientations of the other people who live in it. The University Residence Environmental Scale (URES) was developed to differentiate the social climate among college residences (Gerst and Moos, 1972; Moos, 1976). The scale, described in Table 11-1, consists of ten subscales that measure perceptions about interpersonal relations, personal growth, intellectual growth, and system change and maintenance. Using this scale, a profile can be constructed for a particular residence hall and a number of different questions can be asked. First, do coed residences differ from all-male or all-female residences? Coed dormitories were seen as more innovative and higher in intellectuality than either all-male or all-female dorms. They were also viewed as lower in competition than all male dorms and lower in traditional social orientation than all-female dorms. All three types of housing were perceived to be quite similar in involvement, academic achievement, and student influence.

**Table 11–1: University Residence Environmental Scale: Subscale Definitions**

**Interpersonal Relationships:** The emphasis on interpersonal relationships in the house.

1. *Involvement* (10)*—the degree of commitment to the house and the residents; the amount of social interaction and feeling of friendship in the house.
2. *Emotional Support* (10)—the extent of manifest concern for others in the house; efforts to aid one another with academic and personal problems; emphasis on open and honest communication; etc.

**Personal Growth:** Social pressure dimensions related to the psychosocial development of residents.

3. *Independence* (10)—the diversity of residents' behaviors that are allowed without social sanctions, versus socially proper and conformist behavior.
4. *Traditional Social Orientation* (9)—the stress on dating, going to parties, and others "traditional" heterosexual interactions.
5. *Competition* (9)—the degree to which a wide variety of activities, such as dating and grades, are cast into a competitive framework. (This subscale is a bridge between the Personal Growth and Intellectual Growth areas.)

**Intellectual Growth:** The emphasis that is placed on academic and intellectual activities related to the cognitive development of residents.

5. *Competition*—as above.
6. *Academic Achievement* (9)—the extent to which strictly classroom accomplishments and concerns are prominent in the house.
7. *Intellectuality* (9)—the emphasis that is placed on cultural, artistic, and other intellectual activities, as distinguished from strictly classroom achievement.

**System Change and Maintenance:** The degree of stability versus the possibility for change of the house environment from a system perspective.

8. *Order and Organization* (10)—the amount of formal structure or organization (e.g., rules, schedules, and following established procedures); neatness.
9. *Innovation* (10)—organizational and individual spontaneity of behaviors and ideas; the number and variety of activities; new activities.
10. *Student Influence* (10)—the extent to which student residents (not staff or administration) perceive that they control the running of the house; formulate and enforce the rules; control the use of the money; select staff, food, and roommates; make policies; etc.

---

* Number of items in each subscale.
Source: M. S. Gerst and R. H. Moos, "The Social Ecology of University Student Residences," *Journal of Educational Psychology*, 1972, *63*, 513–525. Copyright 1972 by the American Psychological Association. Reprinted by permission.

Another question that has been raised focuses on the differences between dormitories and fraternities. Using the URES, three men's dormitories and eight fraternities were compared (Gerst and Moos, 1972). Figure 11–1 shows the areas of contrast and similarity across the ten subscales. Dormitories are most divergent from fraternities in the areas of involvement, traditional social orientation, innova-

Figure 11–1: URES Profile Comparisons of Fraternities and Men's
Dormitories from the Same University

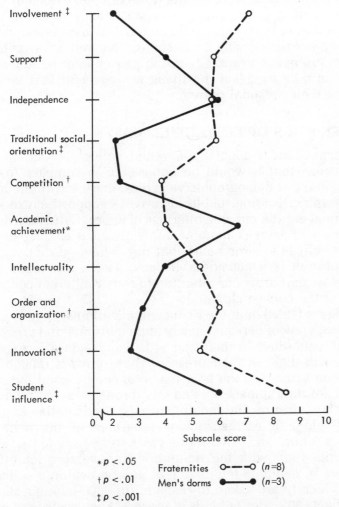

Subscale score

*$p < .05$        Fraternities   O— — O  ($n=8$)
†$p < .01$        Men's dorms   ●———●  ($n=3$)
‡$p < .001$

Source: M. S. Gerst and R. H. Moos, "The Social Ecology of University
Student Residences," *Journal of Educational Psychology,* 1972, *63,* p. 22. Copyright 1972 by the American Psychological Association. Reprinted by permission.

tion, and student influence. Clearly the smaller size of the fraternity,
the emphasis on loyalty and involvement, and the effort to create
a homier environment all result in the creation of a special atmosphere that is readily perceived by fraternity residents.

The URES can be used to differentiate the perceptions of different
groups of residents, to trace the impact of a change in dormitory

regulations or a programmatic intervention, and to compare dormitories with different kinds of residents (for example, freshmen versus upperclassmen, graduate students versus undergraduates). The fact that dormitories have unique characteristics has implications for dormitory placement during the freshmen year and for dormitory selection in subsequent years. Given the proper information, students might be able to select the living arrangement that would most enhance their personal growth.

## THE CHARACTERISTICS OF COLLEGE CLIMATES

At first inspection, it might appear that colleges differ on so many dimensions that it would be impossible to compare them. If one simply looks at demographic variables, there are differences in size, geographic location, public or private support, single-sex or coeducational enrollment, and offerings of undergraduate, graduate, or professional degrees, to name a few. Summarizing the characteristics of college environments that might have an impact on student adaptation is a considerable task. Two approaches are described below that draw our attention to rather different conceptualizations of the college climate.

Pace and Stern (1958) built their conceptualization around Henry Murray's (1938) view of personal needs and environmental presses. If college students differ in their needs, it makes sense to expect that colleges will differ in their presses. These presses reflect the practices, the policies, and the programmatic emphases of the college. They make their impact on students through student interactions with administrators and faculty, through participation in particular academic and extracurricular programs at the college, through observation and interaction with other students, and through identification with the reputation and value orientation of the college. To evaluate the dominant presses within a college, students and faculty are asked to respond to a 300-item questionnaire that reflects 30 scales or kinds of presses. Each scale is scored from 0 to 10. Pace (1967) defined a noticeable press as any scale with a mean score of 6.6 or higher and a lack of press as any scale with a mean score of 4.4 or lower.

Using the College Characteristics Index (CCI), Pace (1967) compared the atmospheres of 32 colleges. He found that differences among colleges tended to cluster around five orientations: humanistic, scientific, practical, welfare, and rebellious. These differences in college atmosphere had predictable consequences for student adaptation. The following description of the presses at College A suggests the ways in which perceived institutional characteristics are translated into patterns of activity, policies, and interaction.

The major press in College A are toward orderliness and friendly helpfulness, with overtones of spirited social activity. This is suggested by high scores on the scales for Order, Objectivity, Conjunctivity, Nurturance, Play, Ego Achievement, Exhibitionism, and by low scores on the scales for Abasement, Impulsion, and Aggression.

The stress on Order, Deliberation (opposite of Impulsion), and Conjunctivity is indicated by such highly shared observations as the following: students have assigned seats in some classes, professors often take attendance, papers and reports must be neat, buildings are clearly marked, students plan their programs with an advisor and select their courses before registration, courses proceed systematically, it is easy to take clear notes, student activities are organized and planned ahead.

Within this orderliness, student life is spirited and a center of interest. For example, big college events draw lots of enthusiasm, parties are colorful and lively, there is lots to do besides going to classes and studying, students spend a lot of time in snack bars and in one another's rooms, and when students run a project everyone knows about it.

At the same time, amid this student-centered culture, there is a stress on idealism and service. Students are expected to develop an awareness of their role in social and political life, be effective citizens, understand the problems of less privileged people, be interested in charities, etc.

The total picture of the environment, then, is one of high social activity, esprit de corps, and enthusiasm combined with an emphasis on helping others and idealistic social action and all within a fairly well understood set of rules and expectations which are deliberative and orderly. One would expect some of the explicit objectives of such an institution to stress personal and social development, idealism and social action, and civic responsibility. (Pace and Stern, 1958, p. 273)

The second approach to the college climate emphasizes the objectively quantifiable characteristics of the college and the student body rather than the subjective assessment of the environmental climate. The Environmental Assessment Technique (EAT) of Astin and Holland (1961) is based on the idea that the climate of an institution can be best understood by knowing about the characteristics of the people who "inhabit" it. The scale includes eight variables: (1) the size of the student body; (2) the intelligence level of the student body; and (3–8) the proportion of students in each of six occupational groupings: Realistic, Intellectual, Social, Conventional, Enterprising, and Artistic. These groupings were based on the major fields elected by the students. Table 11–2 describes the personality characteristics and the major fields associated with each occupational orientation.

The EAT provides an analysis of the pattern of vocational orientations that dominates an institution. This pattern affects students in several ways. First, the students whose major is congruent with the dominant orientation of the college are likely to attain higher

Table 11-2: College Major Fields Corresponding to Each of Six Personal Orientations

| Orientation | Description (from Holland, 1961) | Relevant Major Fields |
|---|---|---|
| Realistic | "Masculine, physically strong, unsociable, aggressive . . . prefers concrete to abstract" | Agriculture, agricultural education, physical education, recreation, industrial arts, engineering, forestry, trade, and industry |
| Intellectual | "Task-oriented, intraceptive, asocial, prefers to think through rather than act out; needs to understand" | Architecture, biological sciences, geography, medical technology, pharmacy, mathematics, philosophy, physical sciences, anthropology |
| Social | "Sociable, responsible, feminine . . . needs attention . . . avoids intellectual problem-solving, orally dependent" | Health education, education of exceptional children and mentally retarded, speech correction, education (unclassified), nursing, occupational therapy, physical therapy, scholastic philosophy, social science (general), American civilization, sociology, social work |
| Conventional | "Prefers structured numerical and verbal activities and subordinate roles . . . conforming . . . identifies with power, externals, and status" | Accounting, secretarial, business and commercial (general and unclassified), business education, library science, economics |
| Enterprising | "Verbal skills for dominating, selling, leading others . . . orally aggressive" | Hotel and restaurant administration, hospital administration, history, international relations, political science, foreign service, industrial relations, public administration |
| Artistic | "Asocial; avoids problems which are highly structured or require gross physical skills . . . intraceptive . . . need for individualistic expression" | Art education, music education, English and journalism, fine and applied arts (all fields), foreign language and literature (all fields) |

Source: A. W. Astin and J. L. Holland "The Environmental Assessment Technique: A Way to Measure College Environments," *Journal of Educational Psychology*, 1961, *52*, p. 310. Copyright 1961 by the American Psychological Association. Reprinted by permission.

levels of academic achievement and to show greater stability in their career goals (Holland, 1963, 1968). Second, when students were tested at the beginning and end of their college years, the career choices of the graduating seniors were more likely to reflect the dominant vocational orientation of the college than the career choices of the entering freshmen (Astin, 1965). In other words, the climate of the school generated a press for occupational conformity. Third, colleges can be homogeneous or heterogeneous with respect to the dominant occupational orientations of the students (Moos, 1976). In the homogeneous colleges, most of the students are of one or two compatible orientations, say Realistic and Intellectual, and few are of conflicting orientations. In heterogeneous colleges, there is a fairly equal representation of all orientations. In heterogeneous colleges, any student is much likelier to find companions who share his or her interests. In homgeneous colleges, some significant minority of students are likely to find that they are really outcasts or misfits in the college culture. Thus, although homogeneity may produce focused academic goals and encouragement for achievement, it is also likely to foster social alienation among students whose goals differ from the goals of the majority (Astin and Panos, 1969).

As might be expected, the EAT and the CCI are not unrelated (Astin and Holland, 1961; Astin, 1963). The CCI scales that correlated most closely with the size of the student body were Aggression (.64), Achievement (−.59), Counteraction-Infavoidance (−.58), Understanding (−.58), Passivity (.55), Fantasied Achievement (−.55), Deference (.54), Sex (.54), Exhibition (.53), and Pragmatism (.52). Students at large schools perceive others in their environment as aggressive, heterosexual in orientation, exhibitionistic, and deferent toward authorities. In comparison, students at small schools perceive others as more achievement oriented, more understanding, and more actively involved in campus activities.

Each of the six occupational orientations was also significantly correlated with particular CCI subscales. The Realistic orientation is associated with pragmatism and is negatively correlated with humanistic or abstract thought. The Intellectual orientation is associated with a need to understand and analyze, independence, and a preoccupation with achievement. The Social orientation is linked to a desire for attention, hetersexual interaction, and a rejection of intellectual problem solving. The characteristics of the Conventional orientation include passivity, a desire for attention, and the rejection of an emphasis on achievement. Both the Enterprising and the Artistic orientations show associations with humanism, reflectiveness, the need to avoid blame or harm, and a rejection of pragmatism. These patterns of association suggest that the six personal orientations do, in fact, reflect different patterns of personal needs. If persons with those orientations were present on a particular college campus, they would most certainly contribute to the social climate through their participation in campus activities, their demands for certain kinds of activities or resources, and their reactions to school events.

## VALUE CHANGE DURING THE COLLEGE YEARS

Many studies of the impact of college have emphasized the question of value change. In their analysis of research over a 40-year period, Feldman and Newcomb (1969) concluded that attending college had a liberalizing effect on many value areas. They found that college attendance was associated with decreases in dogmatism, authoritarianism, religious orthodoxy, and rigidity and with an increasing openness to aesthetic experiences. Two questions have been raised about this pattern of changes. First, is the liberalizing trend equally characteristic of students with all kinds of occupational orientations and at all kinds of colleges, or does it only hold true for special groups of students at particular colleges? Second, is there a liberalizing trend among noncollege students who are of the same age as college students? In other words, is there a maturational factor at work, or is the change really attributable to the college environment? We draw heavily on Astin's (1977) 1966–70 longitudinal analysis for answers to these questions. The areas of value change that are discussed here are liberalism versus conservatism; altruism; artistic, athletic, business, and musical interests; status needs; and religious beliefs.

**Liberalism versus Conservatism.** Both the student and college factors were associated with changes on a self-evaluation of liberal or conservative ideology. Freshman characteristics associated with increased liberalism during the college years included having Jewish parents, being black, having high academic ability, and scoring high on artistic interest, altruism, hedonism, and drinking. The students who were more likely to show an increasingly conservative orientation were female, older than the average freshman, and high in religiousness and had strong business interests. Greater increases in liberalism appeared among social science majors than among majors in engineering, mathematics, or the physical sciences. There is some evidence that social science majors begin their college years with a more liberal orientation. This predisposition is enhanced by contact with liberal faculty and by campus confrontations over social issues (Rich, 1977).

Characteristics of the college experience are also influential in promoting a liberal orientation. Increases in liberalism are largest at prestigious, selective four-year colleges. They are smaller at nonselective public universities, men's colleges, Protestant colleges, and Southern colleges. Certain aspects of college involvement also contribute to an increasingly liberal orientation. Students who live in a dormitory and participate in student government show greater than average increases in liberalism. On the other hand, students who are heavily involved in academic or athletic activities become somewhat more conservative over the college years. In other words, not all kinds of participation in the college experience foster the exposure to diversity or to social issues that would generate a more liberal political outlook.

**Six Value Areas (altruism; artistic, athletic, business, and musical interests; status needs).**   Astin reports that over the four years of college the importance of each of the six value areas decreases. The only exception is artistic interest, which begins as one of the less essential values for freshmen and increases in importance for the sample as a whole. Interest in business and status needs (becoming an authority on a special subject, obtaining recognition from colleagues) decline considerably over the four college years.

College factors do influence the patterns of decline or increase in certain value areas. Altruism decreases among university students and increases among students at Catholic and Protestant colleges. Artistic interest is especially fostered by attendance at private rather than public institutions. Interest in business declines more at selective private institutions and remains more stable at large institutions and men's colleges.

There is some evidence that the patterns of value change during the college years are different for males and females. Among these six value areas, women showed greater declines in athletic interests, business interests, and status needs than did men. Women also showed greater increases in artistic interest. These findings suggest that for most women the college experience is not serving to generate the kinds of participation in the world of work that it generates among men. The additional fact that involvement in academic and honors programs slows down the decline in status needs suggests that women are not experiencing the same kinds of satisfaction in intellectual participation that men experience during their college years.

**Religious Beliefs.**   Astin found a clear pattern of decreasing commitment to a specific denomination and increasing preference for no religious affiliation during the four years of college. Only 9 percent of freshman students had no religious affiliation. This group increased by 14.9 percent by the end of college. In contrast, there were 11 percent fewer students who claimed a Protestant affiliation, 5.7 percent fewer Roman Catholics, and 1 percent fewer students with a Jewish preference. Students whose parents share their religious preference are less likely to drop that preference than are students whose religious preference differs from that of their parents. Students who live at home are also more likely to retain their original religious preference. Students whose parents have no religious preference and students who attend selective, prestigious nonsectarian colleges are most likely not to have a religious preference at the end of four years of college.

We can conclude, then, that some of the general patterns of

value change that occur during later adolescence appear to be retarded or enhanced by participation in particular college environments. Increased liberalism is fostered at the more prestigious and selective schools. It is greater among residents than among commuters, among social science majors, and among participants in student government. The increase in liberalism is less strong among athletes and among "scholars," who may be relatively isolated from some of the more liberalizing experiences of college life.

With the exception of artistic interests, there is a general decline in the emphasis on specific values or on religious commitment as essential life goals. College adolescents become more selective about which values are really important and which are unimportant to their happiness. The college experience has the general effect of raising students' awareness of artistic experiences and of decreasing their investment in business, academic status, and religion as meaningful life commitments. It is hard to assess the meaning of these changes. One view would suggest that the college experience fosters a cynical depreciation of traditional values. Another view would suggest that freshmen come to college with an unrealistic and uncritical perspective that matures over four years toward a more carefully differentiated personal ideology.

## ACADEMIC COMPETENCES AND INTELLECTUAL GROWTH

If my college days ended two decades ago (in the late 1950s), my dreams of it have not. Several times a year I awake from a fitful sleep, perspiring, anxious. It is always the same dream: an examination is coming up and I am wholly unprepared for it. As I attempt to discipline myself and get down to serious study, I remember my other courses and their examinations and suddenly, with terror, I realize that I cannot pass, that I cannot graduate, that the degree I genuinely thought I had earned was illusory. I remain years away from the successful completion of my studies, while everyone else is progressing normally and successfully. In my dream I tell myself, this is only a dream; you know you have finished your work, you have earned your diploma. No, I tell myself, in the past it was a dream, but this is real; this time it is actually happening. I am still in college, well on my way to abysmal failure, humiliation, and quite possibly dismissal. And it is the most portentous moment in my life. (Cottle, 1977, p. 3)

In order to understand the process of intellectual growth during the college years, it is necessary to look in two rather different directions. First, as Cottle emphasizes, there is the subjective experience of being a student. We must try to get a glimpse of the ways in which students function in the classroom; of their emotional involvements with teachers, exams, and grades; and of the extent to which they experience intellectual stimulation. Second, we can evaluate the more objective indices of academic performance, including grades, honors, graduate study, and evidence of new intellectual competences. Although the objective indices may be the things that scholarships, graduate admissions, and hiring practices are based on, they do not tell the whole story of intellectual adaptation to college.

Students bring different needs and concerns as well as different levels of ability to their college experience. We can begin to understand the process of intellectual adaptation to college by examining some of the student styles that have been observed. In an observational study of introductory psychology courses, Mann et al. (1970) describe eight clusters of students. These student groups show different patterns of involvement with the work of the course, react differently to the teacher, and express different emotions during the course. For some of the clusters, the work of the course did not seem to be the primary focus of involvement. Table 11–3 lists the eight clusters, the number of males and females in each, and the primary characteristics of each. The largest group, the anxious-

Table 11–3: Student Styles

| Cluster | Males | Females | Description |
|---|---|---|---|
| The compliant students | 5 | 7 | Consistently task oriented |
| The anxious-dependent students | 12 | 15 | Angry on the inside but frightened on the outside; anxious about being evaluated |
| The discouraged workers | 3 | 1 | Involved in class but discouraged about themselves |
| The independents | 8 | 2 | Older students self-confident and somewhat detached from classroom issues |
| The heroes | 10 | | Involvement in the class includes both productivity and hostile resentment |
| The snipers | 7 | 3 | Low investment and frequent attacks on the teacher |
| The attention seekers | 5 | 6 | Social orientation; trying to please by showing off, bragging, or joking |
| The silent students | 8 | 12 | Fewer than 20 scorable acts for the whole semester |

Source: Adapted from R. D. Mann et al. *The college classroom: Conflict, change and learning.* New York: Wiley, 1970.

dependent students, evidence a chronic anxiety about grades, exams, and evaluation. For them, the focus of the class is to try to "please the teacher," while at the same time they suspect that they will be unfairly evaluated. This orientation is similar to that described by Becker, Geer, and Hughes (1968) in their study of the academic orientation of students at the University of Kansas. Such students depend on their grade point average for staying in school, for scholarships, for membership in fraternities or sororities, and through these organizations for participation in a certain kind of college social life. Thus, although grades may not be accepted as a true reflection of what has been learned, they remain an important "currency" and a continuing source of frustration for many students.

The next largest cluster of students in Table 11–3 are the silent students. This group alerts us to a strategy of adaptation that is pervasive in both high school and college settings. Many students do not take advantage of the opportunities for interaction or involvement that college provides. The students in this group are either afraid of the teacher's authority or of their own possible failure. They take a passive stance in order to avoid conflict or failure. Meanwhile, they may have a variety of private reactions to the class, including feelings of distance, feelings of being overlooked, and efforts to be admired for their silence and passivity.

Finally, there are two groups, the heroes and the snipers, who are openly hostile toward the teacher. Thus, the hidden anger of the anxious-dependent students and the silent students is articulated by these two more verbally aggressive groups. The heroes and snipers suggest that a well of feelings exists about the legitimacy of the teacher's authority, attack the teacher's competence, or attempt to assert their individuality by resisting the role of compliant student. From the teacher's perspective, the difference between the heroes and the snipers is important. Although the latter will never really become involved in the work of the class, the former can be "won over" and may provide the element of creative tension that makes class discussion exciting.

Students seem to resent the mechanical orientation of teachers toward teaching and grading. Mass testing procedures, large classes, and teachers who read their lectures or appear bored with class are a disappointment to most students. As one college junior puts it:

"Yes, I have been turned off by a few professors. They didn't have a positive attitude about what they were doing. To them it was just another class to teach. This was most common in introductory classes, which are primarily designed as distribution fillers. The attitude was that most of the students wouldn't be continuing in that particular area, so why bother spending a lot of time with them?" (*Michigan Alumnus,* 1978, p. 7)

Put another way, the dimensions of high student-faculty interaction and orientation toward personal growth are important factors in the academic achievement of college students. Cohesiveness, flexibility, and a strong emphasis on relationships tend to be related to student persistence (a low dropout rate), high productivity, and the pursuit of further educational or professional aspirations (Thistlethwaite, 1959; 1960, Centra and Rock, 1971).

When one turns to the objective data about the effects of a college education on knowledge or competence, there can be no doubt that college attendance makes a lasting contribution. Hyman, Wright, and Reed (1975) looked at survey data that were collected in the early 1950s, the late 1950s, the early 1960s, and the late 1960s. For each period, they evaluated the responses of subjects in the age ranges 25–36, 37–48, 49–60, and 61–72. At each period, the less well educated subjects had less knowledge than the more highly educated subjects in the areas of civics, domestic policy, foreign affairs, science, geography, history, and the humanities. Comparing subjects who had completed college with subjects who had completed high school and subjects who had completed elementary school showed that each successive level of education was associated with a broader range of knowledge and with greater involvement in seeking new information.

Another way of assessing the impact of college on intellectual growth is to evaluate changes in educational attainment or aspirations. Overall, only about 50 percent of entering freshmen actually earn their B.A. or B.S. in four years. Another 12 percent complete a degree in five years, and of course some students return to school years later to finish their undergraduate degree (Astin, 1977; El-Khawas and Bisconti, 1974). A number of environmental factors influence whether or not one remains in college. These include living in a dormitory, attending a four-year rather than a two-year college, and involvement in a variety of academic or social activities at college (Astin, 1977). Although some studies suggest that students who attend large universities are more apt to drop out of college than are students at smaller colleges, the strength of this variable remains in question (Astin, 1975; Kamens, 1971).

Aspirations for graduate or professional training are also influenced by college attendance. About half of freshmen students have plans to take a postgraduate degree. This percentage increases to 65 percent four years later (Astin, 1977). The pattern of changes depends on the student's initial plans. About 40 percent of the freshmen expect to stop at the bachelor's degree. By the senior year, 53 percent of these students have plans to go on for a graduate degree. In contrast, about 30 percent of the freshmen plan to go on for a master's degree, but only 77 percent of those freshmen actually retain that plan by their senior year. Students who enter college with plans to be a lawyer, doctor, dentist, or veterinarian are the most stable groups in retaining their initial aspirations. The college environment appears to provide differential reinforcement for males and females with regard to further educational attainment. "Although women earn higher grades than men, they are less likely to persist in college and to enroll in graduate or professional school. Moreover, women's aspirations for higher degrees decline, while men's aspirations increase during the undergraduate years" (Astin, 1977, p. 129).

The importance attached to the impact of the college environment on academic attainment must be tempered by the realization that high school grades are a very strong predictor of college grades, of failure in a college course, and of participation in college honors programs. Students who begin college with greater ability are likely to continue to perform at a high level, to make greater gains in the development of academic competences, and to graduate with honors (Astin, 1977). This pattern of success appears to continue during the early work experiences of young adults. College grades are positively associated with the successful attainment of postgraduate education and with higher starting salaries in most careers (Astin, 1977). Thus, although college clearly makes a general contribution to intellectual growth, that contribution is severely modified by the competences and academic skills that students bring to the college experience.

## IDENTITY FORMATION AND THE COLLEGE EXPERIENCE

In preceding sections we have discussed some of the many ways in which college environments differ. We have also described some of the consequences that these differences have for value change and intellectual growth during the college years. Here we offer our own speculations about the interrelationships between identity formation and the college experience. We propose that the amount of influence that the college has on personal growth and identity formation depends on three factors; (1) the amount of student-faculty interaction; (2) the identity status of the student; and (3) the degree of fit between the value orientation of the college and the value orientation of the entering freshman (Newman and Newman, 1978).

First, the college's influence on the identity formation and value consolidation of its students depends on the identity status of the individual student. The notion of identity status suggests that students differ in their degree of commitment to particular values (Marcia, 1966). Identity-foreclosed and identity-achieved students have well-defined values. Moratorium and role-diffuse students are confused about their values. Their values are susceptible to change. In the formation of identity, moratorium is a period of experimentation that precedes identity achievement. Some college students may be in a state of foreclosure, having determined their social, occupational, religious, and political views prior to entering college. Other college students may be in a state of psychosocial moratorium during which they seek to clarify their value positions. Toward the end of their college years, such students may feel strong presses to consolidate their values, and these presses may lead to identity achievement. Or the students may persist in their inability to integrate or clarify their value system and may enter a state of role diffusion. It is unlikely that many students enter college with an achieved identity. Older students who are returning from military service, who are married and are returning to complete a degree, or who have deliberately postponed college attendance in order to gain work experience may be exceptions. It is also unlikely that many role-diffused students would enter college. The degree of ego strength necessary to attend and succeed in college is incompatible with role diffusion. Moreover, role diffusion is more likely to occur at the end of a long period of search and confusion about value commitment rather than at the beginning of the college years. Upon entering college, most students are either foreclosed in their value commitments or they are experiencing the sense of uncertainty and freedom for experimentation which characterizes the moratorium.

We would predict that the foreclosed students would be less likely to change their values due to the influence of the college culture than would the moratorium students. For the foreclosed student, the choice of college, the selection of a major, and participation in college activities would all be directed by a value system which has already been articulated. The college culture would either serve to maintain that value system or to disrupt, it depending on the degree of fit between the content of the student's values and the content of the college's programmatic input. If foreclosed students select a college which mirrors their own value system, no matter how little or how great the amount of interaction between such students and the faculty, that value system will remain intact. If foreclosed students select a college that is at odds with their value system, and if there is minimal student-faculty interaction, the foreclosed students will remain that value system in the knowledge that it differs from the value system of others in the college setting. If there is a great amount of student-faculty interaction and disparity between the values of the college and the values of the foreclosed student values, the foreclosed student will feel very uncomfortable. He or she may need to leave the college—feeling very alienated from the college community. Such a student may, in fact, develop some adaptive behaviors in order to defend against the stress of this discrepancy between personal values and the values of the college culture. Because of the fragile balance between ego strength and value commitments that characterizes foreclosure, we would hypothesize that it would be difficult for the foreclosed student to permit value change.

The moratorium student who is part of a low-interaction environment will experience value change as a product of role experimentation, logical thought about value issues, the values of peers, and the gradual integration of cultural, historical, and family values. The college itself will make no predictable contribution to the student's value system. In a high-interaction environment, the moratorium student will be engaged in an evaluation of values and goals that are important to the college community. Because the college student is developmentally sensitive to issues of value clarification, interactions which convey a particular value orientation will have a strong influence on the adolescent's thoughts. We do not suggest that other influences on value change will have no impact. Rather, we would emphasize that a highly interactive college culture becomes a primary setting for socialization in the adolescent's life space. It will therefore play a comparatively powerful role in the development of the student's value system. One implication of this analysis is that in a highly interactive college, moratorium students of a particular cohort will, toward the end of moratorium, share certain values that are a product of having attended the same college at the same time.

This analysis of the interaction between identity status and the college environment leads us to an interpretation of the concept of identity crisis. Identity crisis may be the result of two different phenomena which share the same demands for rapid, intense work on value issues. It may occur for students in a state of identity foreclosure if they attend a high-interaction college environment that is discrepant from their value system. In this case, the foreclosed students realize that values which differ from their own are held by people with whom they wish to identify. These students feel at a sudden loss as the fabric of their value system is challenged by significant others who share a discrepant perspective. Identity crisis for the foreclosed person results in strong anxiety about this new state of uncertainty. They may desperately try to replace their old value structure with a new system. What is more important to the foreclosed person than the content of the values adopted is the sense of control and order that adopting a value system provides.

Identity crisis may also occur for moratorium students if external demands force them to make a value commitment while they are still in a state of uncertainty and confusion. The need to make a decision may demonstrate to such young persons just how well developed their values are. If that happens, the identity crisis fosters identity achievement. On the other hand, the demand for commitment may throw adolescents into deeper confusion. Because of a lack of certainty about which values best reflect the inner self, a press for commitment is experienced as a threat to the self-concept. Under these conditions, adolescents fear that they will be wedded to a decision that is inauthentic.

A second determinant of the impact of the college environment on the consolidation of student values is the fit between the programmatic input of the college culture and the student's value system. Stern's (1962) research on student needs and college presses found that the greatest discrepancy between needs and presses existed at the liberal arts colleges. We take this finding to mean that the liberal arts colleges have the greatest opportunity to provide institutional input that leads to new values.

A college's influence on the identity formation and value consolidation of its students depends on the degree of similarity between the students' precollege values and the value orientation of the college. The greater the similarity between the values of students and the values of the college culture, the less opportunity there is for value change; the greater the discrepancy between the two, the more opportunity there is for value change.

Greater student-faculty interaction will result in new value positions only if there is some degree of discrepancy between the content of the students' value system and the content of the college value system. If the students and the college share the same values, then student-faculty will serve to maintain or solidify existing values. In fact, a high degree of interaction under these circumstances may even serve to inhibit the achievement of identity by making role experimentation difficult. Because the input of the institution is the same as that of the students' value system, the students will not have the opportunity to observe alternative value structures and their implications for behavior.

Where the discrepancy between student and college values is very great, the person in a state of moratorium will find abundant food for thought. Although the process of value clarification may be extremely difficult, the opportunity to experiment with many value systems and to identify with adults who hold different points of view from one's own promises a more fully internalized value system once it is crystallized. However, for the person who has a foreclosed identity, as we have suggested earlier, a great discrepancy between an already crystallized value system and the value system of the college culture will generate stress. Although a possible response to such stress is to change one's values, that response is unlikely. It is more probable that these alienated students will find a peer group that will support their values and help them to wall off the impact of the college or that they will leave the college setting.

In other words, the amount of difference between the values of the college culture and the values of the student does not, in itself, result in value change. One must know the identity status of the student in order to predict whether the student is susceptible to new views on value issues. One must know how much interaction there is between students and faculty in order to predict whether students are actually exposed to the novel content of the college culture.

## CHAPTER SUMMARY

About one third of all American 18–24-year-olds go on to post-secondary, degree-granting institutions. Another million enroll in noncredit professional programs. The questions raised in this chapter focus on the impact of these college environments on development during adolescence. The process of selecting a college is a two-way street. Among the criteria that colleges use in selecting students are intellectual ability, special talent, connection with alumnae, high school participation in extracurricular activities, and the commitment to include minority students in each freshman class. Although colleges have quite a bit of information about prospective students, students choose their colleges on the basis of comparative ignorance. A criterion often used by students is that they expect some career payoff from their college degree. Students' choice of college may also be based on expectations about the social life and the intellectual stimulation that the school will provide. The evidence suggests that students are usually disappointed in regard to these early expectations.

The variety of colleges is impressive. Among the ways in which schools differ are size; prestige and selectivity; public or private support; single-sex or coeducational; religious affiliation; and two-year, four-year, or graduate enrollment. In general, students seem moderately satisfied with their college experience across all kinds of schools. They tend to be most satisfied about the friendships they have formed and less satisfied about the courses or the administration. Selective and prestigious colleges, single-sex colleges, and colleges with live-in residence are associated with greater than expected satisfaction.

Student adaptation to college was considered in relation to four areas: student residences, the college climate, value change, and academic competences. Student residences make their impact through their physical design and their social climate. Proximity is the first factor that influences interaction and the formation of early friendships. In a comparison of dormitory designs, however, it was found that the large number of uncontrolled interactions in the corridor design had unfavorable consequences for the formation of friendships and led to feelings of being crowded. A dormitory's social climate can be influenced by the predominance of students with a particular academic major, as well as by the quality of interpersonal relations, the rules, and the academic or social emphasis of the residence. Using the University Residence Environment Scale, it is possible to differentiate the social climate of dormitories of different populations and different designs.

Two measures of college climate were described, the College Characteristics Inventory (CCI) and the Environmental Assessment Technique (EAT). The former emphasizes perceived presses, whereas the latter is based on indices of school size and indices of the intellectual ability and the personal orientation of the students. Several themes emerge in studies of the college climate. First, the greater the conformity between the student's orientation and the college climate, the greater is the stability of the student's goals and the higher is the student's academic achievement. Second, there is a trend toward conformity to the prevailing orientation of the college. Third, the degree of homogeneity of the college population influences the extent to which some students are likely to experience alienation during their college years.

Studies of value change during the college years find a general pattern of increased liberalism and decreased commitment to a range of other values, including business interests, status needs, and religious orientation. The greatest gains in liberalism are made at the prestigious, selective four-year schools, especially among social science majors.

Academic competence and intellectual adaptation are discussed as a subjective experience of participation in the academic activities of the college and as an objective assessment of student competences and aspirations. Students bring different styles to the classroom. These styles reflect differences in participation, differences in anxiety about evaluation, and differences in needs for relating to authorities. Students are generally sensitive to grades as a cur-

rency that has broad implications for college life and later entry
into the world of work. Although the meaning and value of grades
have been questioned, both students and faculty seem to want
to retain this strategy of evaluation. Currently there is concern
about "grade inflation" and the need to establish objective performance criteria for grading. Students experience depersonalization,
faculty with low involvement in teaching, and unclear course expectations, all of which interfere with motivation and academic
achievement. High student-faculty interaction and an emphasis on
personal growth are two factors that are positively related to student achievement.

Looking at more objective assessments of intellectual attainment,
college attendance appears to result in more knowledge and more
openness to new information. Especially for students who begin
with minimal expectations for advanced degrees, college attendance increases educational aspirations. The impact of college on
intellectual growth is tempered by the student's initial level of ability and especially by high school performance. High school grades
are a strong predictor of college grades. Students with a record
of high precollege achievement are most likely to be high achievers
at college and afterward.

The contribution of the college experience to identity formation
is just beginning to be evaluated. Based on our view of identity
and our knowledge of the diverse factors that are part of the impact
of college, we offer a view of the mechanisms by which going to
college can influence identity. Three factors play a part in this
analysis: the amount of student-faculty interaction, the identity status of the student, and the degree of fit between the values of
the college and the values of the student. Maximal influence on
identity formation will occur where the student is still in a state
of moratorium or experimentation, where there is a moderate discrepancy between student and college values, and where there
is a high amount of student-faculty interaction.

## REFERENCES

Astin, A. W.  Further validation of the Environmental Assessment Technique.
    *Journal of Educational Psychology*, 1963, *54*, 217–226.

Astin, A. W.  Effect of different college environments on the choices of high
    aptitude students. *Journal of Counseling Psychology*, 1965, *12*, 28–34.

Astin, A. W.  *Preventing students from dropping out.* San Francisco: Jossey-Bass,
    1975.

Astin, A. W.  *Four critical years.* San Francisco: Jossey-Bass, 1977.

Astin, A. W., and Holland, J. L.  The environmental assessment technique: A way to measure college environments. *Journal of Educational Psychology,* 1961, *52,* 308–316.

Astin, A. W., and Panos, R. J.   *The educational and vocational development of college students.* Washington, D.C.: American Council on Education, 1969.

Baird, L. L.   Big school, small school: A critical examination of the hypothesis. *Journal of Educational Psychology,* 1969, *60,* 253–260.

Baum, A., and Valins, S.   *Architecture and social behavior: Psychological studies of social density.* Hillsdale, N.J.: Lawrence Erlbaum, 1977.

Becker, H. S., Geer, B., and Hughes, E. C.   *Making the grade: The academic side of college life.* New York: Wiley, 1968.

Brown, R. D.   Manipulation of the environmental press in a college residence hall. *Personnel and Guidance Journal,* 1968, *46,* 555–560.

Centra, J., and Rock, D.   College environments and student academic achievement. *American Educational Research Journal,* 1971, *8,* 623–634.

Cottle, T. J.   *College: Reward and betrayal.* Chicago: University of Chicago Press, 1977.

Dressel, P. L., and Lehman, I. J.   The impact of higher education on student attitudes, values, and critical thinking abilities. *Educational Record, 46,* 248–257.

El-Khawas, E., and Bisconti, A.   *Five and ten years after college entry.* Washington, D.C.: American Council on Education, 1974.

Feldman, K. H., and Newcomb, T. M.   *The impact of college on students,* vol. 1: *An analysis of four decades of research.* San Francisco: Jossey-Bass, 1969.

Gerst, M. S., and Moos, R. H.   The social ecology of university student residences. *Journal of Educational Psychology,* 1972, *63,* 513–525.

Goodman, N., and Feldman, K. H.   Expectations, ideals, and reality: Youth enters college. In S. E. Dragastin and G. H. Elder, Jr. (Eds.), *Adolescence in the life cycle: Psychological change and social context.* New York: Wiley, 1975. Pp. 147–169.

Grant, W. V., and Lind, C. G.   *Digest of educational statistics.* Washington, D.C.: U.S. Government Printing Office, 1976.

Holland, J.   Explorations of a theory of vocational choice and achievement: II. A four-year predictive study. *Psychological Reports,* 1963, *12,* 547–594.

Holland, J.   Explorations of a theory of vocational choice and achievement: VI. A longitudinal study using a sample of typical college students. *Journal of Applied Psychology,* 1968, *52* (monograph supplement), 1–37.

Hyman, H. H., Wright, C. R., and Reed, J. S.   *The enduring effects of education.* Chicago: University of Chicago Press, 1975.

Kamens, D. H.   The college "charter" and college size: Effects on occupational choice and college attrition. *Sociology of Education,* 1971, *44,* 270–296.

Mann, R. D., Arnold, S. M., Binder, J., Cytrynbaum, S., Newman, B. M., Ringwald, B., Ringwald, J., and Rosenwein, R.   *The college classroom: Conflict, change, and learning,* New York: Wiley, 1970.

*Michigan Alumnus.*   What are you getting out of college? February 1978, pp. 5–8.

Moll, R. W.   The college admissions game. *Harper's*. March 1978, pp. 24–30.

Moos, R. H.   *The human context: Environmental determinant of behavior*. New York: Wiley, 1976.

Murray, H. A.   *Explorations in personality*. New York: Oxford University Press, 1938.

Newcomb, T. M.   Student peer-group influence and intellectual outcomes of college experience. In R. Sutherland, W. Holtzman, E. Koile, and B. Smith (Eds.), *Personality factors on the college campus*. Austin, Tex.: Hogg Foundation, 1962. Pp. 69–92.

Newman, P. R., and Newman, B. M.   Identity formation and the college experience. *Adolescence*, 1978, *13*, 312–326.

Pace, C. R.   *College and university environment scales: Technical manual* (2d ed.). Princeton, N.J.: Educational Testing Service, 1967.

Pace, C. R., and Stern, G. G.   An approach to the measurement of psychological characteristics of college environments. *Journal of Educational Psychology*, 1958, *49*, 269–277.

Rich, H. E.   The liberalizing influence of college: Some new evidence. *Adolescence*, 1977, *12*, 200–211.

Silber, E., Hamburg, D., Coelho, G., Murphey, E., Rosenberg, M., and Pearlin, L.   Adaptive behavior in competent adolescents: Coping with the anticipation of college. *Archives of General Psychiatry*, 1961, *5*, 354–365.

Simon, K. A., and Frankel, N. M.   *Projections of education statistics to 1984–85*. Washington, D.C.: U.S. Government Printing Office, 1976.

Speegle, J.   College catalogs: An investigation of the congruence of catalog descriptions of college environments with student perceptions of the same environments as revealed by the College Characteristics Index. Unpublished doctoral dissertation, Syracuse University, 1969.

Stern, G. E.   Environments for learning. In N. Sanford (Ed.), *The American college*. New York: Wiley, 1962. Pp. 690–730.

Thistlethwaite, D. L.   College press and student achievement, *Journal of Educational Psychology*, 1959, *50*, 183–191.

Thistlethwaite, D. L.   College press and changes in study plans of talented students. *Journal of Educational Psychology*, 1960, *51*, 222–239.

*Deviance in later adolescence is often characterized by turning inward or self-destruction.*

# 12

# Deviance in Later Adolescence

In Chapter 8 we discussed problems of psychopathology during the early adolescent years. We took up three general types of problems: neuroses, psychoses, and behavior disorders. Neuroses are psychological problems that involve emotional disturbances and a variety of relatively ineffective methods for dealing with anxiety. The symptom patterns of neurotics are usually seen as methods that have been developed to express a psychological conflict that includes impulse, the restriction of impulse, and the punishment of impulse. The symptoms provide some expression for psychological conflicts and some relief from the inner tension that the conflicts usually produce. As neurotic symptoms become more elaborate, they often give rise to certain kinds of restrictions on the individual's ability to function successfully. The fact that they are only partially successful in reducing psychological tension means that they must be used repeatedly in order to provide relief. Thus, we observe patterns of somewhat strange behavior that provides some relief from tension but also interferes with effective personal functioning. Neurotic problems may endure for many years; however, they usually do not seriously interfere with the person's ability to test reality.

The psychoses are far more serious disturbances than the neuroses. They usually involve serious disturbances in emotional, cognitive, interpersonal, or behavior functioning. Serious disturbances of thought, including delusions and hallucinations, are common in psychotic behavior, whereas they are virtually nonexistent in neurotic patterns. The psychotic's personality is usually deeply disturbed. Psychotics are often unable to accomplish the routine tasks of life successfully. Extremely bizarre behavior and deep withdrawal from relationships with others are typical of psychotics. The more chronic the psychotic problems are, the worse are the psychotic's chances for recovery.

Behavior disorders involve the selection of some observable, deviant actions which become elaborated by the person and often integrated into the life-style. Often the actions are distinctly antisocial, and as such, they may involve the person in a denigrated and sometimes illegal life-style. The specific behaviors selected by individuals may be a symbolic representation of an inner struggle. Some people elect delinquent behaviors in order to express their aggression or their personal reactions to rejection. The society may be selected as the target of behaviors that might more appropriately be targeted at rejecting parents. Thus the society may serve as a symbolic substitute for personal authority figures. Behavior problems may also reflect a desire to leave a stressful situation or to alter one's internal state in order to cope with stress. The reasons for selecting particular behaviors vary widely. Sometimes deviant behavior is rooted in a neurosis or a psychosis; sometimes a specific constellation of factors leads to the selection of an antisocial life-style. Many other factors may also account for behavior disorders.

In Chapter 8 we discussed certain problems that are observed in early adolescence and also occur in later adolescence. We will review those problems in this chapter. Among the problems taken up in Chapter 8 were problems that are observed primarily in early adolescence, and we will not treat these in detail here. Running away from home and juvenile delinquency, for example, are most common in the years from puberty until the end of high school. There are other psychological problems that are not usually observed in early adolescence and were not treated in Chapter 8. We will discuss those problems in detail in this chapter. Serious problems of depression, for example, including the manic-depressive psychoses and suicide, are not widely observed until the later adolescent period. In general, in discussing problems of psychopathology and the relationship between the two periods of adolescence, we will note: (1) some psychopathological problems occur primarily in one period and are not observed in great numbers either before or after that period; (2) some problems develop in early adolescence and become progressively worse and more noticeable in later adolescence; (3) some problems may occur at any period of life as ways of dealing with stress and conflict; and (4) some psychopathological problems which are not observed until after the adolescent years.

## NEUROSES OF LATER ADOLESCENCE

The neuroses of later adolescence are similar to the neuroses of early adolescence, with the exception that the more classical forms of neurotic depression are observed in later adolescence. In Chapter 8, you will recall, we discussed a variety of depressive equivalents which are commonly observed in early adolescence, but noted that the occurrence of the classical depressive symptoms was relatively rare. In the following discussion we will present the patterns of depressive symptoms that are relatively common during the later adolescent period.

First, let us review the neurotic symptom patterns that are common to early and later adolescence and examine a few cases to help facilitate our understanding of these patterns. Table 12–1 summarizes the types of neuroses and the symptom patterns. Anorexia nervosa is sometimes observed in later adolescence and adulthood, but it is most common during the early adolescent years.

Table 12–1: Common Types of Neuroses and Their Symptoms

| Type | Symptoms |
|---|---|
| Anxiety reactions | 1. Emotional tension.<br>2. High levels of anxiety.<br>3. Anxiety attacks.<br>4. Panic reactions.<br>5. Vigilant attitude.<br>6. Aches, pains, stomach and intestinal upset.<br>7. Respiratory irregularities.<br>8. Hypochondriasis.<br>9. Sleep disturbances.<br>10. Depressed appetite.<br>11. Sexual dysfunction. |
| Anorexia nervosa | 1. Elective restriction of food.<br>2. Pursuit of thinness as pleasure in itself.<br>3. Frantic efforts to establish control over the body and its functions.<br>4. Food avoidance and preoccupation.<br>5. Hyperactivity and increased energy output.<br>6. Amenorrhea.<br>7. Manipulation of the environment around food and diet.<br>8. Distrustful attitude to significant objects.<br>9. Sadness and guilt, but no clinical depression.<br>10. Occasional food cravings. |
| Phobias | 1. Strong, irrational fears that are focused on specific objects or situations. |
| Hysterical conversion reactions | 1. Development of a physical symptom, usually restrictive in nature, in the absence of any physiological cause.<br>2. Relative freedom from anxiety. |
| Hysterical dissociative reactions | 1. Object estrangement.<br>2. Somatic estrangement.<br>3. Depersonalization.<br>4. Sleepwalking.<br>5. Hysterical convulsions.<br>6. Trances.<br>7. Psychogenic stupor.<br>8. Massive amnesia.<br>9. Massive amnesia with fugue.<br>10. Alternating or multiple personality. |
| Obsessive-compulsive reactions | 1. Obsessive thoughts.<br>2. Compulsive behaviors.<br>3. Rituals.<br>4. Ceremonies.<br>5. Superstitions.<br>6. Doubting and rumination.<br>7. Magical thinking. |

# Cases

**Anxiety Reaction.**  In the following selection we see a kind of anxiety problem that is often observed among people who have been sheltered and supported at home and who falter because of their inability to cope with the experience of leaving home for the first time.

*The Case of Jim.*  Jim had always leaned heavily on his mother for protection. She helped him with his homework, she kept him from school when he ate little or no breakfast or when he said his stomach was upset, she shielded him from his father's sporadic attempts to "make a man of him." Nothing was too good for Jim. He had tutoring "because he needed individual attention." At that point he did! He had been helped so much that he couldn't help himself and it took the extra effort of several teachers to get him into college. He had a superficial charm, good manners, good looks, and more than enough intelligence to permit him to do very well in his studies. In college, however, he did miserably.

"They don't seem to take any personal interest in him, doctor. You have to understand Jim. He's lost weight and he doesn't eat well. I think something's worrying him." It was. He was eating little, he had lost weight, and he had all manner of gastrointestinal symptoms. At first he offered one rationalization after another as the cause of his failure, but it was evident that the main trouble was simply that he had started off doing little or no studying and soon was far behind and in the sort of bind where only a more purposeful and independent boy could hope to prevail. Jim wasn't that sort; he just gave up. And then he began to worry about what might happen if he were to flunk out. How would his mother feel; what would his father do; what would his friends think? Casting among these thoughts, he neither faced his fundamental problem nor worked out his present one; and from week to week his anxiety increased. His dilemma was more than he could stand. He became panicky, lost his appetite, and began to have "stomach trouble." "Stomach trouble" had been his means of getting out of school when he was a little boy, and now he could rely on it to get him out of college before he was "fired."

His stomach trouble firmly established as a means of handling his conflict and as an escape from school and from flunking out, it was difficult for him to allow himself to see his symptoms for what they were. It was even more of a task to try to strengthen his personality so that he would have more than symptoms of illness to call upon when a problem faced him. Here was a boy for whom so much had been done that he had had little ability to do for himself, a boy who had little confidence in himself; "after all, no one thinks I can do anything, if they did they'd let me try." Still dependent at an age when he should have been able not only to do for himself but to help others, he had neither the confidence nor the ability to work himself out of his difficulties.[1]

---

[1] Source: J. R. Gallagher and H. I. Harris, *Emotional Problems of Adolescents,* 3d ed. (New York: Oxford University Press, 1976), pp. 74–75. Copyright © 1976 by Oxford University Press, Inc. Reprinted by permission.

It should be noted that Jim's inability to perform is not the result of anxiety. He gives up quickly once his mother is not present to push and coax him to work. Jim's anxiety results from thinking about what his friends will think of him. Rather than respond rationally by trying to rectify his work habits, Jim simply becomes involved in developing a variety of ways of expressing anxiety and tension until he is able to mobilize the attention and pity of his mother.

**Phobias.** In the case of Kenneth E., we see an example of a neurosis that develops because of the inability of the individual to cope effectively with internal impulses which he is afraid and embarrassed to acknowledge even to himself. The phobic solution protects Kenneth from constant anxiety and tension by restricting his access to particular situations.

*A Case of Claustrophobia with Other Phobic Symptoms.* Kenneth E., 22 years of age, could not stay in theaters because they made him feel suffocated and afraid that he would not be able to get out in case of illness or a fire. His fear generalized to elevators, busses and downtown city streets. He sought therapeutic help because his fears were restricting his life without reducing his overall anxiety. In therapy he concentrated at first upon his most recent symptoms and gained his first insight into his phobias.

At the beginning of therapy Kenneth said that whenever he was in downtown streets he felt he might fall ill or be injured in an accident. Since he would be among strangers he might not get the help he needed in time to save his life. There was nothing objective to justify such fears. Later on Kenneth realized that fears of accident and illness were secondary. What he primarily feared was that if he were to "fall in a fit," or be injured, he might lose control of himself and shout something, or talk without realizing what he was saying. Obviously there was something he must hide, something which at the same time he had an impulse to proclaim. This discovery of an impulse to give himself away in public led ultimately to the origin of his phobias.

The onset of his claustrophobic symptoms followed an acute anxiety attack in a theater. The play contained a homosexual theme to which Kenneth was doubly sensitized, by his own trends and by a recent threat to expose them. The anxiety attack was his response to the total stress. When this occurred he became still more frightened that people around him in the theater would notice his agitation and guess its cause. As soon as the curtain fell for the intermission he staggered out, feeling weak, tremulous and nauseated. After this, he could go to the theater only if he sat near an exit, even then he felt so anxious that he lost all pleasure in being there. The phobia generalized to places where he was thrown with strangers under crowded conditions.

Kenneth's experience in the theater had merely dramatized his current conflict and made him for the moment vividly aware of it. His phobias appeared as defensive devices which moved his conflict from the center of the stage and put a group of expanding fears in its place. What he was basically afraid of was not the theater, elevators, busses or downtown city streets. It was not accident or illness in the ordinary sense, or even the danger of not getting medical attention in time. These were all secondary rationalizations used to explain away the otherwise unintelligible anxiety.

What Kenneth *feared basically was the upsurge of his own forbidden impulses, his powerful urge to behave homosexually and give himself away in public.* His phobias shielded him from situations which aroused these impulses, offering him the neurotic compromise of freedom from anxiety in return for restricted activity. The neurotic compromise in his case eventually failed because, as with many severe phobias, the situations continued to generalize and the restrictions became impossible to meet. Therapy was successful to the extent that Kenneth was able to explore the larger background of personality distortion from which he suffered and to cooperate with his therapist in working out a solution.[2]

**Conversion Reaction.** The cases of Deborah W. and "the young man" presented below are examples of later adolescents who develop conversion symptoms to represent conflicts over work. The case of Deborah presents more detailed background information and allows a closer look at this type of problem. At one time it was thought that conversion reactions were almost entirely confined to females. Modern case treatment teaches us that many males also develop hysterical conversion reactions.

*The Case of Deborah W.* Deborah W., a married woman, aged 23, complained that whenever she tried to typewrite her forearms became rigid in a half-raised position and her hands became clenched. She had been obliged to give up a position as secretary a few weeks previously because of this symptom. A general medical and neurological examination revealed no organic pathology to account for the disability, which appeared only in relation to typewriting and not in relation to other activities, even when the same muscles were used. Her only other relevant complaint was that for some years she had been dreaming of little boys lying in the street mangled, apparently having been run over by an automobile or a truck. In the rest of the case abstract we shall limit discussion to just three events forming part of the context of the conversion symptom.

When Deborah was four years of age a brother was born, the first boy in the family. She and an older sister were sent to stay with relatives on a farm just before the brother's birth. She remembered taking a violent dislike to the new baby because of the fuss everyone made over his being a boy. She did not recall any aggressive fantasies about him; but the current dreams of mangled little boys suggest strongly that she had had them as a little girl.

The patient did recall that, after the brother's birth, she and her older sister played in secret at being boys by putting some object between

---

[2] Source: Norman Cameron, *Personality Development and Psychopathology*. Copyright © 1963 by Norman Cameron. Pp. 288–289. Reprinted by permission of Houghton Mifflin Co.

their legs so that it protruded. She remembered that this play was accompanied by much giggling and excitement, and that she and her sister openly ridiculed the brother's genitals which they secretly resented. The patient apparently solved her conflict over the brother's birth by attaching herself passionately to her older sister and ignoring her brother's existence as much as possible. This maneuver was so successful that even after several months of intensive therapy no early memories or fantasies about her brother returned from repression.

This young woman had the misfortune to marry an ineffectual husband. Their low income and her own restlessness and dissatisfaction drove her to prepare for work outside the home. She enrolled in a secretarial school while still feeling that if she were allowed to do what her husand was doing she could certainly do it better. Her frustration over her own awkwardness at the typewriter was heightened by the pressure to work harder from the teacher, her parents and her husband. In spite of her feelings of frustration, and her disillusionment in relation to her home life, she completed the secretarial course creditably and secured a reasonably good position. At work she found that she resented having to do what she was doing and often lived out her working day in a spirit of sullen anger. It was in this setting that her conversion symptom appeared. It repeated in a different mode her resentful, envious childhood play with her sister after the brother's birth, it expressed doubly her masculine protest, and in the form of clenched fists it symbolized both her general aggressive hate and her specific unconscious refusal to do work that she despised.[3]

*The Case of a Young Male College Student.* A college student went numb in his hands and arms after failing in his examinations. This cleared up when he found work, but it returned when he took entrance examinations later in another college, and again just before his graduation. The numbness did not correspond in distribution to that of sensory nerves.[4]

**Dissociative Reactions.** We have selected one case of massive amnesia without fugue and one case of massive amnesia with fugue in order to illustrate the dissociative reactions. In the case of John Doe, we see the way in which a precipitating event, the accident, can mobilize the most basic defenses against facing the situation. In this case the individual changes his own perceptions and realizations in order to escape the burden of remembering. In the case of Samuel O., we see how personal conflicts and fantasies become so threatening that loss of memory and escape to another location are safer than dealing with personal feelings.

*The Case of John Doe.* A young man, dressed in working clothes, appeared at the main entrance of a general hospital one Saturday morning with the complaint that he did not know who he was. He seemed dazed.

---

[3] Source: Norman Cameron, *Personality Development and Psychopathology.* Copyright © 1963 by Norman Cameron. Pp. 331–332. Reprinted by permission of Houghton Mifflin Co.

[4] Source: Norman Cameron, *Personality Development and Psychopathology.* Copyright © 1963 by Norman Cameron. P. 306. Reprinted by permission of Houghton Mifflin Co.

There was nothing on his person by which he could be identified. On the emergency service he was found not to be intoxicated, there was no evidence of bodily injury, and he was not medically ill. He was admitted to the psychiatric in-patient service under the name of John Doe.

There was nothing evasive about this man. He kept asking earnestly, though laconically, for help. He could remember nothing about himself—who he was, where he lived, what work he did, and who his relatives and friends were. Most of the time he sat staring at the floor with his head in his hands, as though deeply preoccupied. Every now and then he raised his head and shook it slowly and sadly, or he looked up at someone and said, "Can't you help me?" Hypnosis was tried with no effect. Narcosis only put the man to sleep. To avoid the publicity which such cases as this arouse no alarm was sent out about him; the staff heard nothing about a missing man over the radio. He spent Saturday and Sunday on a closed ward, going about the usual routines without any noticeable change in his clinical picture.

On Monday morning John Doe awoke in great distress. He demanded to know why he was in a hospital. He told the nurse who he was. He insisted that he must leave at once in order to appear at a coroner's inquest. Here is his story.

At dawn on Saturday morning the patient was driving his produce to the vegetable market. On the outskirts of the city an elderly man stepped from between two parked cars directly in his path. There was no time to put on the brakes. The truck ran over the man and killed him. The police who arrived at the scene seemed convinced that John Doe was not responsible. They released him on condition that he send a report of the accident at once to the Commissioner of Motor Vehicles and appear at the coroner's inquest the following Monday.

Much shaken, John went to the home of friends in town where he filled out a form for reporting accidents which the police had given him. His friends succeeded in alarming him. They appeared to think that he would be found to blame and might go to prison for committing manslaughter. They finally left for work, and John went out alone to send off his report, leaving his wallet in his friends' home. The last thing he remembered was the act of dropping the report into the mail box. It was learned later that a stranger, who probably saw how dazed he was, led him to the door of the hospital and then departed.

The precipitating factors in the case are obvious—the terrible accident at dawn, the police, the shadow of the coroner's inquest, the frightening friends. John Doe had signed a report which amounted to a confession of manslaughter, as his friends had pointed out, and he had mailed it. There was something irrevocable about dropping the letter into the box. The patient reached the limit of his emotional tolerance. Regression and a massive amnesia then shut everything out. He became literally a man who was not responsible. He made no attempt at flight. All that the amnesia gave him—and it was quite a lot—was two days of freedom from a clear recognition that he had killed someone and might be held responsible for it.[5]

---

[5] Source: Norman Cameron, *Personality Development and Psychopathology.* Copyright © 1963 by Norman Cameron. Pp. 355–356. Reprinted by permission of Houghton Mifflin Co.

*The Case of Samuel O.*   Samuel O., a graduate student, impoverished and far from home, was invited to dinner at the home of an instructor whom he had known when they were socio-economic equals in another town. He accepted the invitation because he was lonely and hungry, but he regretted it almost at once because his clothes were shabby. He thought, in retrospect, that the instructor had seemed condescending. That evening he left his rooming house in plenty of time for the dinner, but he failed to show up at the instructor's home. Two days later he was picked up by the police in a neighboring state. He could remember vaguely having ridden a freight train, talking with strangers and sharing their food; but he had no idea who he was, where he had come from or where he was going. The contents of his pockets identified him and he was fetched by relatives.

Later on, this young man was able to remember the events leading up to the fugue and something of what went on during it. He had started for the instructor's house while still in strong conflict over going there. He was ashamed of his appearance, resentful over the condescension, and afraid to express what he felt and call the dinner off. On his way he was held up at a grade crossing by a slowly moving freight train. He had a sudden impulse to board the train and get away. When he acted on this impulse he apparently became amnesic. He retained enough ego integration, however, to be able to carry through complex coordinations, to converse with others and to get food. Nonetheless, he was much less in contact with people than anyone suspected until the police began to question him.

This is almost all that we know for certain about our fleeing graduate student. But from studies of others like him we can assume that throughout his dissociative flight he was deeply preoccupied, caught in a web of conflictual fantasy. Before his encounter with the patronizing instructor an emotional turmoil had probably been seething beneath the surface. The dinner engagement was only a precipitating factor which increased the turmoil and brought its components into sharper focus. This then made flight irresistible once the impulse to flee clearly emerged. Flight under such circumstances, however, is a turning away from realities— from social responsibility, job and future. This kind of turning away, and the regression that makes it effective, can also seriously disturb an already unstable inner equilibrium, and awaken the shades of dormant conflicts to new life.[6]

**Obsessive-Compulsive Reaction.**   In the case of Eliot H., we are able to observe a condition characterized by tremendous amounts of rumination and doubt. Here Eliot's life is not restricted by dramatic symptomatology or behavioral peculiarities. Eliot, because of his personal conflicts and an inability to handle these conflicts effectively, has been reduced to a level of obsessive rumination that inhibits his capacity to make effective decisions. Although less dramatic, this condition is relatively common in late adoles-

---

[6] Source: Norman Cameron, *Personality Development and Psychopathology.* Copyright © 1963 by Norman Cameron. Pp. 357–358. Reprinted by permission of Houghton Mifflin Co.

cence. The guise is one of problems of self-esteem, but the deeper problem is really about serious personal conflicts that the individual cannot deal with effectively.

*The Case of Eliot H.* Eliot H., a college student, went to a telephone booth to call up a wealthy girl whom he had recently met, to ask her for a date. He spent an hour there, anxious and indecisive, unable to put the coin in the slot and unable to give up and go home. Each time his hand approached the telephone he anxiously withdrew it because he felt that telephoning her might ruin his chances with her. Each time he withdrew his hand he seemed to be throwing away a golden opportunity. Every positive argument for telephoning her he matched with a negative argument for not doing so. He went into all the ramifications of his ambivalent motivations. He imagined to himself what the girl and the members of her family—whom he scarcely knew—might think of his attentions to her; and then he had to picture to himself what they would think if he neglected her.

His whole future seemed to Eliot to hang on the outcome of this little act. Had he any right to put his coin in? If he did so would the girl respond favorably? If she did, what would happen next? Eliot fantasied every conceivable consequence as he sat there sweating in the booth, consequences to him and to her, on and on into remote contrasting futures. He was helplessly caught in an obsessive dilemma, as he had been caught before hundreds of times. The more he tried to be sure of what he did, the more things he imagined going wrong, any one of which might ruin everything. In the end he gave up the anxious debate and went home, exasperated and worn out. Later he became convinced that in not making the call at that particular time he had missed the chance of a lifetime for winning security and happiness.

This absurd little episode sounds like the mere exaggeration of a shy suitor's hesitancy, but it was much more than this. It was a condensed symbolic expression of an intensely ambivalent personality, one that was volatile, impulsive and unpredictable. Almost every enterprise upon which Eliot had embarked since early adolescence had involved similar obsessive rumination. Into each decision he funneled all of his ambivalent conflicts—conscious, preconscious and unconscious—and then he found himself unable to follow through to a decision. The same thing unfortunately happened to his search for therapeutic help. He began with despair, switched quickly to great optimism, and then got bogged down in endless doubting and rumination over whether to continue. In the end he withdrew from therapy without ever becoming really involved in it.[7]

**Summary of the Cases.** All of the cases presented above have certain features in common. First, the symptoms persist. Second, the symptoms restrict the individual's ability to function effectively. Third, the symptoms are perceived as unpleasant by the individual. This constellation of features is common in neurotic reactions.

---

[7] Source: Norman Cameron, *Personality Development and Psychopathology.* Copyright © 1963 by Norman Cameron. P. 396. Reprinted by permission of Houghton Mifflin Co.

These patterns usually persevere for an extended period. They may be attempts to deal with internal conflicts or external conditions, or they may be learned behaviors used to avoid fear. The creation of a neurosis requires time and effort, and because the neurosis serves important psychological functions it may endure for a considerable time. The fact that the symptom pattern is, for the most part, maladaptive is evidenced by the increasing behavioral restrictions and emotional involvements that occur. The strength of the underlying personality may be inferred from the fact that although neurotics may not understand the cause of their symptoms, they usually realize that their symptoms are "not typical" and that they are not happy with these symptoms. The above cases illustrate the range of neurotic reactions which are common to both early and later adolescence. Often the initial onset of symptomatology occurs in early adolescence, and the development of structured symptoms in later adolescence. The full-blown neurosis is then carried into later adolescence, when it becomes more noticeable and unacceptable. We will now present the classical symptomatology of neurotic depression, which is often masked in early adolescence but becomes manifest in later adolescence.

## Neurotic Depression

Cameron (1963) states that neurotic depression is primarily a mood disturbance. It is a reaction to loss or threatened loss, to failure, discouragement, and disillusionment. The basic symptoms are self-depreciation, dejection, and appeals for reassurance. The neurotically depressed individual loses interest in people, things, or activities; gives up initiative; repeatedly expresses feelings of inferiority, unworthiness, and hopelessness. The neurotically depressed individual does not totally relinquish relationships. Such a person may derive considerable reassurance from parents and friends who counter the claims of inferiority with arguments extolling the person's worth. Judgment and reality testing may be somewhat distorted, but they are not seriously disturbed.

In discussing depression, Freud (1957) stated: "The distinguishing mental features of melancholia are a profoundly painful dejection, cessation of interest in the outside world, loss of the capacity to love, inhibition of all activity, and a lowering of the self-regarding feelings to a degree that finds utterance in self-reproaches and self-revilings and culminates in a delusional expectation of punishment" (Freud, 1957, p. 244).

Freud points out in his analysis that there are many similarities between normal and neurotic depression. This should make the experience of the neurotic depression relatively easy for most people to understand because most of us have been depressed. Good days and bad days are common experiences which most people come to expect. As the song says, "Rainy days and Mondays always get me down." Normal, everyday mood disturbances may be caused by a bad grade; something someone says to you; the feeling that you didn't live up to personal expectations; the weather; a girlfriend/boyfriend, parent, or best friend taking a trip. Many daily experiences that involve some loss will cause a person to be depressed. A major personal loss such as the death of a loved one will produce an intense depressive reaction in most people that may last for some time. Most people ultimately recover from the depression produced by such a loss, but there is no doubt that the death of a parent, a child, a spouse, or a grandparent will have a lifelong effect on the psychological development of the bereaved individual.

Later adolescents usually experience a loss that they must deal with and that will naturally lead to many depressed days. This is the loss of the childhood home. The process of achieving independence from parents often requires adolescents to distance themselves from parents and home. Although a newer and more mature relationship often results from the attainment of independence, the adolescent rarely returns for long to the physical location which is the subject of many childhood memories, fantasies, and experiences. The loss of the childhood home is quite literally "homesickness," and this loss may produce deep feelings of depression in otherwise normal later adolescents.

The "loss of self" is a second type of loss that is commonly incurred in later adolescence and that may lead to prolonged periods of depression. In searching for a sense of personal identity through a process of turning inward, self-testing, self-evaluation, and role experimentation, the later adolescent will experience periods of negative personal evaluation, failure at certain tasks, and the inability to know and understand the self. Such experiences may produce prolonged and intense periods of depression as the search for personal identity occurs.

Gloomy self-depreciation evolves into a neurotic depressive reaction when persons are chronicially preoccupied with their own worthlessness, failure, and hopelessness. The psychological dejection of such persons will persist despite positive external experiences. These individuals lose their personal initiative and their interest in activities and people. They often repetitively express feelings of despair and futility when their personal situation does not warrant a lack of hope. Physical symptoms similar to those observed in anxiety reactions often occur (Cameron, 1963; Beck, 1967; Weiner, 1970; Coleman, 1976).

## PSYCHOSES OF LATER ADOLESCENCE

We discussed schizophrenia as the major psychotic reaction that occurs in early adolescence. Schizophrenia is also observed in later adolescence. We would suggest that the reader review the section on schizophrenia in Chapter 8 at this time. The types, symptomatology, and patterns of onset remain much the same. In later adolescence some people who experienced initial schizophrenic episodes in early adolescence will continue to experience schizophrenic episodes, and it will become increasingly clear that they are becoming chronic psychotics who will probably have lifelong problems. Other people will have their first encounter with schizophrenia during later adolescence. Among the events that can precipitate a schizophrenic episode in later adolescence are leaving home; the stress of school, work, or military discipline; demands for increasing interpersonal or sexual intimacy; impending marriage plans; the selection of a career; graduation from college; separation from military service; and losing a job. Whether a single acute episode or a chronic pattern will occur, can only be determined by the passage of time. Sometimes sociocultural demands for independence reveal a basically disorganized personality structure in someone who has been sheltered and protected until later adolescence. The demands of living alone and taking care of oneself may reveal a chronic schizophrenic pattern which has been sheltered, protected, and denied by parents, friends, and relatives. In the remainder of this section we will describe the serious psychotic disorders related to mood and affect, which are usually not observed until ages 15 or 16 and beyond (Weiner, 1970). These disorders include psychotic depression and the manic-depressive psychoses. Although these are called affective disorders, it should be remembered that with them, as with all psychoses, there are disturbances of affect, cognition, interpersonal relations, and behavior.

### Psychotic Depressive Reactions

The picture of depression that was begun in the section on neurotic depression becomes intensified in psychotic reactions. An important task is to be able to differentiate between the two. The severity of depression is sometimes determined by diagnostic interview and sometimes by rating scales (Beck, 1972) in which the individual is asked to report degrees of sadness, self-dislike, and crying episodes, among other things.

In psychotic depressive reactions dejection, guilt, and organized delusions of self-depreciation overwhelm the individual's thinking. Hallucinatory experiences are generally not part of the psychotic depressive reaction. The psychotic depressive tends to shut out others much more than the neurotic does. The neurotic depressive often tends to manipulate others into support and praise in order to bolster low self-esteem. The psychotic depressive generally becomes preoccupied with delusions of unworthiness, inadequacy, and failure and with accompanying feelings of guilt, and usually exhibits less personality disorganization than the schizophrenic (Cameron, 1963; Beck, 1967, 1972; Sarason, 1976).

The savage manner in which psychotic depressives turn on themselves and shut out others is striking. Their deep self-hate is often characterized by gradiose delusions concerning the extent of their wickedness. "I am the worst person in the world" and "I am the most sinful person in the world" are common statements. The sense of guilt for this "wickedness" is often accompanied by a strong need for punishment. Plans for how to punish oneself and how to hurt oneself may be a major preoccupation for the psychotic depressive. Suicide (which will be discussed in detail later in this chapter) is a real risk (Cameron, 1963; Sarason, 1976; Becker, 1974). Parents, friends, relatives, children, and others who are close to the psychotically depressed person will usually not have any difficulty in determining the depth and seriousness of this type of depression. The extremely disturbed thoughts about how evil one is and preoccupations with self-injury, cleansing, penitence, and unworthiness are so strong that they replace the psychotic depressive's ability to test reality and make effective judgments.

Psychotically depressed people rebuke others for trying to help them, and they are less disorganized and less unable to perform daily routines than schizophrenics. They may successfully wall themselves off from others. Thus, although they may not go unnoticed, they may go unhelped. This is a particularly serious problem because of the suicide risk. Psychotically depressed later adolescents are especially at risk. These people are often outside the boundaries of former close support structures such as their families and not yet reestablished in their own intimate networks. As they become preoccupied with self-depreciation, guilt, and punishment, there may be no one to notice the loss of reality testing and judgment that is occurring. School or work failure, the death of a parent, or the loss of a lover may initiate a depression that goes unheeded simply because no one notices the clear development of increasingly serious symptoms. Roommates, colleagues, shipmates, or acquaintances may not feel like becoming involved in helping a later adolescent who is obviously seriously disturbed, yet shuns help at every turn. In fact, such individuals may not know how they can be of help. Who to go to? What to do? These questions are hard enough for parents, husbands, wives, and others who feel responsible for the safety and well-being of the psychotically depressed person. The questions may be too difficult, too time-consuming and too unrewarding for a relatively uninvolved person to bother with. Thus the psychotically depressed later adolescent may be left alone to fall deeper and deeper into the depths of the depression—to commit suicide or to become a hermit who walls the self off.

Institutions such as colleges and many communities have developed crisis emergency services and telephone services from which anonymous, relatively isolated persons who are disturbed and desire help may obtain advice, brief therapy, plans for management, or appropriate referral. These services often alert community resources to serious psychotic disturbances which are brewing. The mobilization of support services may help to aid psychotic depressives who won't help themselves. Cameron (1963) points out that there is little adaptive value to psychotic depressive reactions. The condition induces a loss of effective functioning and may drain the resources of the afflicted person's family, friends, and associates. As the condition deepens, it becomes increasingly serious and difficult to cure. Like the prognosis for recovery from chronic schizophrenia, the prognosis for recovery from chronic psychotic depression is poor. Psychotic depressives often pose a real threat to themselves, and sometimes to others.

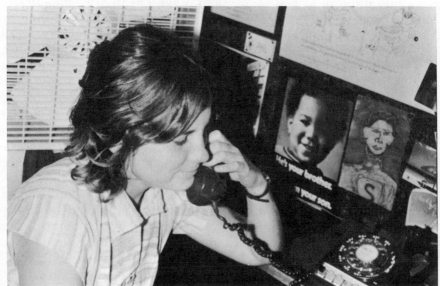

*Courtesy Aunt Martha's Youth Service Center, Inc.*

*Hot lines and emergency services offer help especially to adolescents who are isolated or alienated from their community.*

## Manic-Depressive Psychotic Reactions

This category comprises two somewhat different patterns of symptomatology. One of the patterns is characterized primarily by mania, observed; in the other pattern, the manic-depressive reaction, mania and depression alternate.

**Manic Reactions.** Cameron (1963) points out that although manic-depressive reactions have been described for centuries, manic reactions alone have been more prevalent in his clinical experience. Manic reactions are defined as mood disorders in which extreme euphoria is accompanied by self-assertion and delusions of self-importance. During manic reactions, people are often very talkative, but it soon becomes apparent that their conversation is limited in scope, relatively shallow and rambling (Lorenz and Cobb, 1952; Lorenz, 1953). A great deal of activity often accompanies manic reactions. When one first encounters a person who is having a manic attack, it may appear that the person is very happy and excited. After a while it can be seen that the person having a manic reaction, like a little child, has difficulty in controlling excitement. In fact, manic reactions often last for weeks or months (Cameron, 1963). The person having a manic attack actually loses contact with reality because he or she is so preoccupied with asserting internal states of self-importance and happiness, and often with planning gradiose self-aggrandizing activities that cannot possibly be carried out. The manic state is often a firm barrier to the pleas of friends and relatives for more rational behavior (Lichtenberg, 1959). Sometimes reality-oriented comments from others evoke hostility or increased self-aggrandizement (Cohen et al., 1954).

The manic attack often masks or is used as a defense against a deep underlying sense of depression (Cameron, 1963). Rather than become psychotically depressed, individuals deny the depressive aspects of their lives by self-assertion, self-aggrandizement, and euphoria. Cameron points out that although manic individuals experience very profound disturbances of reality testing and may represent a danger to themselves or others, there may be some value in warding off profound depression with mania.

Manic attacks may be mild or severe. They may occur only once or many times. Sometimes individuals will have a manic episode and then a depressive episode years later. At other times a manic attack is preceded by a mild initial depression (Cohen et al., 1954). The best prognosis for recovery is for people who have a single, mild manic attack. Mania usually indicates underlying difficulties with feelings of self-worth. Often it is an effort to deny a depressive stance. The following case describes a manic attack of a college student.

Barry was a participant in a self-analytic group as part of a course in group dynamics at a large Midwestern university. He was a moderate participant during the first several meetings. When he spoke, his contributions were appropriate to the discussion. When he talked about himself, he mentioned a lack of confidence in dating situations and a career interest in business administration. These disclosures are quite typical for someone his age.

Barry was absent for several sessions, which was clearly a violation of the group's norms. When he returned, other members wanted to know why he had been absent. Barry began to tell a story that lasted for the remainder of the two-hour session and from which he could not be distracted by the other group members.

He said that several weeks before, he had been awakened in the middle of the night by a phone call. The caller was a member of the Beatles, George Harrison. Harrison had told him to take the next available flight to London. He did this and was met upon arrival by the Beatles, who took him to their recording studio. They told him that he was involved in a secret mission of international significance but that they could not disclose the reason to him until the mission had begun.

He said that he spent several days with the Beatles, and then one afternoon they told him that the mission was to get under way. They boarded a plane heading for the United States. It was a U.S. Air Force customized jet. On board, along with several high-ranking Air Force officers and the Beatles, was Lyndon B. Johnson (then president of the United States). Barry was told that the mission was to "look for the hole in the ocean." Although he knew that this was a line from one of the Beatles' songs, he said that he now believed that the Beatles were involved in some type of international intrigue. He realized that secrets were disclosed in their songs. At some point halfway across the Atlantic a huge chasm opened in the water. Everyone on board agreed that this was the hole in the ocean. The significance of the discovery was unclear to Barry. He was then flown to the university town and let off the plane. This had occurred several weeks before. He had been busy telling everyone he knew about his experience.

Barry's case is a good example of the onset of a serious manic episode in a college student. This attack developed after only a mild rejection by a girl whom he had been dating. The euphoria, high-activity level, and grandiosity of mania are well represented. Barry's attack lasted for several weeks. His judgment and reality testing were replaced by a strong belief in his delusional trip. Barry was finally hospitalized after his roommates called his parents to notify them about his condition.

**Manic-Depressive Reactions.** It was once thought that the typical pattern of manic and depressive reactions involved alternations of mania and depression. More recently, it has been recognized that cases of either psychotic depression or mania are much more commonly observed (Cameron, 1963; Coleman, 1976). There are some instances, however, in which a full-fledged manic attack leads directly into a full-fledged depression, and vice versa (Arieti, 1959). Some cases have even been reported in which there is an extremely precise period for the two phases. Jenner et al. (1967) mention a manic-depressive reaction that had lasted for 11 years. A manic phase of exactly 24 hours was followed by a 24-hour depressive phase. Bunney et al. (1972) cite a case in which a woman alternated between manic and depressive periods every 48 hours for two years. Such precision is rare, however. In a more typical manic-depressive reaction, there is a period of one–ten days of relative normality between the end of the depressed period and the start of the manic period. The switch from mania to depression usually occurs more suddenly, with little warning, although in some cases there may be a prolonged period of normality in between (Coleman, 1976).

The patterns of the manic and depressive phases are similar to those that have been discussed above. Persons in the manic phase are extremely elated and very sociable. They are usually overly talkative and move from topic to topic very quickly. They are often hyperactive and rarely tired. They may sleep very little. The self-image is extremely positive, and egocentric grandiose delusions are common. Such persons will often become extremely irritable when criticized about the unreality of their delusions and their other behaviors. During the depressive phase a remarkable change takes place. The opposite conditions prevail. The person is extremely gloomy and self-deprecating. There appears to be a loss of hope in life. The person withdraws markedly from social relationships, often becoming untalkative and preoccupied by obsessional thoughts of guilt, self-depreciation, sin, and punishment. Delusions often develop in these areas of thought. The person's activity level declines markedly: he or she often becomes slow-moving and extremely tired. Insomnia and loss of appetite are common. The self-image is now extremely negative (Arieti, 1959; Cameron, 1963; American Psychiatric Association, 1968; Reich, Clayton, and Winokur, 1969; Becker, 1974; Akiskal and McKinney, 1975).

Studies that have attempted to investigate the personality of manic-depressive individuals often find that such persons are achievement oriented, conventional in their beliefs and values, concerned about how others react to them, ambitious, sociable, and successful. They tend to have rather rigid consciences and often find it difficult to express hostile feelings toward others. Self-depreciation and self-blame when things go wrong are often reported. (Bellak, 1952; Gibson, Cohen, and Cohen, 1959; Arieti, 1959; Becker and Altrocchi, 1968; Grinker, 1969; Beck, 1971, Chodoff, 1972; Ferster, 1973; Libet and Lewinsohn, 1973; Bagley, 1973; Schancke,

1974; Akiskal and McKinney, 1975). There is often a high incidence of depression among the families of people who develop manic-depressive symptom patterns (Poznanski and Zrull, 1970).

The personality pattern which is observed in research is not uncommon. Many people have such characteristics but do not become manic-depressives. The inability to express hostility and a family history of depression may begin to differentiate the manic-depressive from other sociable, achievement-oriented men and women who are concerned with what others think of them. It is obvious from the picture sketched above that there is a strong possibility of observing this type of reaction among college students. Extreme mood swings are not uncommon among students in high-pressure schools. For some, these mood swings are indicators of the first phases of manic-depressive disorders. Cameron (1963) believes that the truly important dynamic for the manic-depressive is a pervasive underlying depression. Mania is seen as a defense against depression. When it does not work, the depression surfaces. When the person regains his defensive position, the mania is used to protect the person from depression.

## BEHAVIOR DISORDERS OF LATER ADOLESCENCE

In examining the behavior disorders of early adolescence, we discovered that delinquency, running away from home, and drug use were common problems. In exploring the behavior disorders of later adolescence, we find that the picture has changed somewhat. Delinquency declines substantially after age 15. It is not considered to be a significant behavior problem of the later adolescent period. This may, in some way, be because the courts regard delinquent acts as juvenile offenses. In later adolescents, the same acts would be regarded as adult crimes. For the greatest number of delinquents, single undetected delinquent episodes cause the person to develop new techniques of personal behavioral control. Delinquency will decline as a risk. For a smaller number, delinquency evolves into a criminal life-style. This is a relatively rare occurrence, and we will not elaborate it further. Running away from home is not considered a common behavior problem of later adolescence. The 18-year-old in American society is often expected to move out of the "family residence" to seek independence. Going to college, joining the military, or taking a job are often accompanied by getting a place of one's own. The later adolescent does not require the same sort of permission to be away from home that the early adolescent does. Leaving the situation is less effective as a coping device and less likely to occur during later adolescence than during early adolescence. There are certainly many later adolescents who wander, but their travels tend to be sanctioned by parents or to be acknowledged as the time when the person "left home" for good.

The primary behavior disorders of later adolescence that we will discuss in this section are drug use and suicide. Drug use begins to be a problem in the early adolescent period, and the problem worsens in later adolescence. In Chapter 8 we discussed definitions of drug usage and the nature of the problem in the early adolescent period. In this section we will document several specific kinds of drug use problems that often become more widespread in later adolescence. We will also discuss suicide as a major behavior disorder of later adolescence. Although there is some self-destructive behavior prior to later adolescence, such behavior rarely becomes a problem before the ages of 16 or 17 (Weiner, 1970). During later adolescence, suicidal behavior is a leading cause of death. The incidence of suicide reaches a peak during the early and middle adulthood years, but it has been rising at the fastest rate during the later adolescent years (Coleman, 1976). The behavior disorders of early adolescence included a problem in which aggression was directed toward society (delinquency), a problem in which people attempted to leave difficult situations (running away from home), and a problem in which people attempted to alter their internal state. The behavior problems of later adolescence involve changing one's internal state and directing aggression toward the self.

## Drug Use

In Chapter 8 we discussed the various kinds of drug use and presented a model of drug categorization based upon the effects of drugs on the central nervous system. In this chapter we will explore many examples of drug use in greater depth. In general, it should be stated that drug problems increase in both incidence and severity during later adolescence. More people take drugs, and more people become involved in serious problems because they use drugs. We will begin our discussion of drug use by discussing the most widely used drug—alcohol.

**Alcohol Use.** Except for a small number of complete abstainers, almost everyone has at least tried alcohol during later adolescence. There is more variability in the legality of alcohol use in later adolescence than there was in early adolescence. In such states as New York, the legal drinking age is 18. In other states, such as Michigan, the legal drinking age is 21. Thus later adolescent drinking is legal in some places and illegal in other places. Whatever the legal status, the most widely used and abused drug in later adolescence is alcohol (Chafetz, 1974a; National Institute on Alcohol Abuse, 1975; Barnes, 1975, 1977). The National Institute on Alcohol Abuse and Alcoholism (Chafetz, 1974b) estimates that problem drinking is characteristic of 10 percent of the adult Americans who drink. Of the 18–20-year-olds who drink, 27 percent are problem drinkers, and of the 20–24-year-olds who drink, 18 percent are problem drinkers. Later adolescents who use alcohol seem to be more prone to develop serious problems than do alcohol users of other ages. This situation becomes even more noteworthy when we realize that during the past 15 years there has been an ever-increasing use of alcohol among later adolescents. The use of marijuana and other hallucinogens increased until the late 60s, but since that time there has been a leveling off (and even some decline) in the use of these drugs. Alcohol use increased continuously throughout the first half of the 1970s (Kleinhesselink, St. Dennis, and Cross, 1976).

Alcohol is a central nervous system depressant. Although most people think that alcohol makes you "high," or intoxicated, at its highest level of concentration in the body it can cause death by depressing breathing (Kleinhesselink et al., 1976). Even though this outcome is extremely rare, it is most often observed during late adolescence after "chugging" large amounts of alcohol. A recent report (*New York Times*, 1978) documents the death of a college student due to forced alcohol consumption during a fraternity initiation.

Although death due to too great a concentration of alcohol in the blood is rare, there are two other extremely serious problems that involve alcohol and often contribute to the death of later adolescents. The first problem is the use of alcohol along with other drugs. Sometimes getting drunk is just a prelude to taking other drugs. Often alcohol is taken along with barbiturates or amphetamines in order to increase the effects of the drug experience. Impaired judgment due to alcoholic intoxication may lead to taking a fatal overdose of the other drug (Kleinhesselink et al., 1976). The other problem is the use of alcohol while driving. It is a well-known and well-documented fact that alcohol use is involved in many automobile accidents. Chafetz (1974b) estimates that approximately half of the 55,000 traffic deaths that occur each year are related to alcohol use. Kleinhesselink et al. (1976) point out something that is less well known. Nearly half of all pedestrians who are killed by automobiles have blood alcohol levels that lead them to be classified as intoxicated. The above examples demonstrate three ways in which the misuse and abuse of alcohol can end in death. The problem is serious. Sometimes the desire for new experiences, impaired judgment, thrill seeking, peer taunting, or personality disorganization can have a fatal outcome in later adolescence. This danger is not necessarily confined to alcoholics. The warning is for all college-age adolescents to be aware that: *(a)* if anyone's blood contains more than .55 percent alcohol, the outcome is lethal; *(b)* taking alcohol and other drugs can be dangerous because the interaction effects of the two substances may be more than the "sum of the two" and because impaired judgment may lead to taking an overdose of a dangerous drug; and *(c)* whether you drink a lot or only occasionally, you should not drive when you've been drinking and you should be careful where you are walking.

Most later adolescents who drink do so with moderation (National Institute on Alcoholism, 1975; Barnes, 1977). Figure 12–1 presents the effects of various amounts of alcohol on most people. The majority of people who drink do so to attain the mild effects described in Figure 12–1, particularly the feelings of warmth and relaxation. This state may also facilitate social relations. One tends to be somewhat less shy and more talkative after having had a couple of drinks. A report of the National Institute on Alcoholism and Alcohol Abuse (Chafetz, 1974b) states that alcohol can be used in a responsible manner if it is used to improve social relationships and if it is not the primary activity. This same report indicates that moderate alcohol consumption may be good for one's physical health. Later adolescents who are away at college, in military service, or in a new area of their hometown will probably engage in some social drinking to help themselves relax and to facilitate social participation.

Unfortunately, certain aspects of the college culture and of the later adolescent's self-concept are likely to encourage more than moderate alcohol consumption. Within the college community, many events are marked by celebrations that include the heavy use of alcohol. The Thank God It's Friday parties that celebrate the end of the week; football, basketball, or hockey victories (and sometimes defeats); the end of classes; the end of exams; graduation; and assorted college weekends (Winter Carnival, homecoming, Spring Fling) are all cultural occasions for letting go. More than likely, part of letting go is getting drunk. What is more, the cultural approval of the use of alcohol for celebration seems to carry over to the approval of alcohol to combat depression or frustration. In the same way that aspirin and lots of juices are seen as a cure-all for colds or the flu, a pitcher of beer or some bottles of wine are seen as a surefire way to handle a failing grade, a disappointment in a love relationship, or a rejection from graduate school.

The other component of this picture of potential alcohol abuse is the later adolescent's self-image. During later adolescence, young

**Figure 12-1: Alcohol Levels in the Blood after Drinks Taken on an Empty Stomach by a 150-Pound Person**

| Effects | Time for all alcohol to leave the body (hours) | Alcohol concentration in blood (percent) | Amount of beverage |
|---|---|---|---|
| Gross intoxication | 10 | 0.15 | 5 highballs ($1\frac{1}{2}$ oz. whiskey each) or 5 cocktails ($1\frac{1}{2}$ oz. whiskey–ea.) or $27\frac{1}{2}$ oz. ordinary wine or $\frac{1}{2}$ pint whiskey |
| Clumsiness – unsteadiness in standing or walking | 8 | 0.12 | 4 highballs or 4 cocktails or 22 oz. ordinary wine or 7 bottles beer (12 oz. ea.) |
| Exaggerated emotion and behavior – talkative, noisy, or morose | 6 | 0.09 | 3 highballs or 3 cocktails or $16\frac{1}{2}$ oz. ordinary wine or 5 bottles beer |
| Feeling of warmth, mental relaxation | 4 | 0.06 | 2 highballs or 2 cocktails or 11 oz. ordinary wine or 3 bottles beer |
| Slight changes in feeling | 2 | 0.03 | 1 highball or 1 cocktails or $5\frac{1}{2}$ oz. ordinary wine or 1 bottle beer |
| | 0 | | |

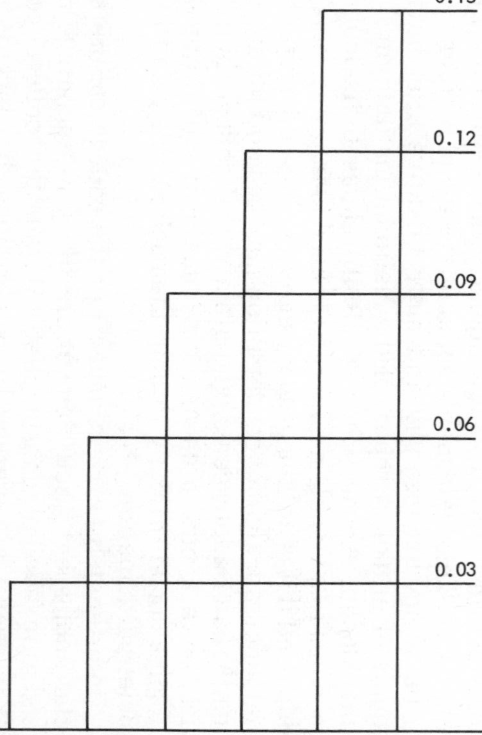

Calories:
5½ ounces of wine—115.
ounces of beer—170.
1½ ounces of whiskey—120.

Bill Ownes/Magnum

*So drink, chugalug.*

people tend to see themselves as vigorous, energetic, and somewhat impervious to harm. They perceive themselves as young and healthy. In fact, they are likely to be in better physical condition and less vulnerable to illness than they were during childhood or than they will be ten years later. This sense of personal vitality encourages later adolescents to scorn moderation. They will stay up late into the night and then engage in a full day of academic, athletic, and work activities. They will go from one party to the next on weekends, giving up sleep for celebration. They will take on responsibilities for a variety of committees, plan to drive a long trip without stopping for rest, or save two or three long papers until the last week of class and then do them all without sleeping. This sense of energy and vitality extends to the later adolescents' orientation toward alcohol. There is no special appreciation of moderation. The fun of drinking is the abandonment of limits. "Guzzling" or "chugalugging" are examples of the heroism attached to consuming great quantities of alcohol. Getting drunk is usually a part of the fun, a sign that caution and restraint were temporarily abandoned. Getting sick or passing out may not be as "cool" as being able to maintain a drunken ambience, but they are more acceptable than staying sober.

**Marijuana Use.** Most evaluations have concluded that marijuana is a relatively harmless drug that has less negative or dangerous effects than alcohol (Brill et al., 1973; Shafer, 1972). A presidential commission on marijuana recommended decriminalization of
the private use of marijuana, but suggested a maintenance of laws
prohibiting the manufacture or sale of the drug (Shafer, 1972; Kleinhesselink et al., 1976). The current status of marijuana in our society
represents a dilemma of values that is bound to generate controversy. Thus, an understanding of the use of marijuana requires
an appreciation of its status as an illegal drug as well as its intoxi-
cating properties.

Marijuana is a widely used drug, especially among college students. There are an estimated 24 million marijuana smokers, of
whom 1.5 million smoke marijuana daily (Rist, 1972). Estimates
of college use range from 49 percent at a large Midwestern university to 87 percent at a college in New England (Levy, 1973; Bonier
and Hymowitz, 1973). In general, marijuana use among these later
adolescents cannot really be considered deviant, even though it
is formally illegal. Most college students who use marijuana believe
it to be a harmless drug that provides a pleasant high, enjoyable
sensory experiences, and feelings of relaxation (Rist, 1972). Heavy
users (three or more times a week) also claim that marijuana increases self-awareness, changes their perceptions about time, and
heightens sexual pleasure (Hochman and Brill, 1973). Marijuana
use is generally not associated with needs to escape reality or to
avoid commitment. Studies of users and nonusers find no significant
differences between the groups in personal adjustment, in the likelihood of dropping out of school, or in feelings of optimism and
self-worth (Hochman, 1972; Knight Sheposh, and Bryson, 1974).
Some studies have reported that the grade point averages of users
are higher than those of nonusers and that marijuana use is most
widespread among some of the more prestigious, competitive colleges (Hochman and Brill, 1973; Gergen, Gergen, and Morse, 1972).
These data clearly discourage any psychopathological interpretation of marijuana use.

On the other hand, there are some differences between marijuana
smokers and nonsmokers that do suggest different patterns of adaptation. Marijuana smokers are usually introduced to the experience
by friends who teach the novice how to smoke, what to look for
as part of a "high," and how to enjoy the sensations of intoxication
(Becker, 1963; Goode, 1970). The more one is involved in the use
of marijuana, the more one is likely to associate with peers who
also use it and who share the perceptual, political, and cognitive
orientations that tend to be associated with heavy marijuana use.
Chronic marijuana users are more likely than nonusers to have

liberal or radical political views, to express pessimism about the future of the U.S. government, and to have experienced harassment, arrest, or questioning by the police (Levy, 1973). Because marijuana users are involved in illegal behavior, they are forced to confront the legal system more directly than are nonusers. They must deal with the reality of being suspected or even arrested for the sale or possession of marijuana. They must also strive to balance the illegality of marijuana use against the pleasure of the marijuana high. In this sense, chronic marijuana users are allied in their rejection of a part of the legal code. Being part of what may begin as inadvertent resistance, chronic users are likely to call into question other aspects of the political system, especially those involving areas of personal freedom and individual rights. In this regard, chronic users tend to be more rebellious, more antiauthoritarian, and more reckless or prone to other deviant behaviors than nonusers (Jessor, Jessor, and Finney, 1973; Hochman and Brill, 1973).

The area of marijuana use that has been least well evaluated is the effect of heavy, long-term use. This level of abuse would amount to being stoned all day long, every day. There is research which suggests that under this condition a variety of physical complications develop, including lung cancer, hormone deficiency, reduced immune responsiveness, and chromosomal damage (Kleinhesselink et al., 1976). On the other hand, research comparing marijuana users and nonusers has not reported any specific health dangers that can be reliably associated with moderate marijuana use.

**Hallucinogenic Drugs.** The psychedelic or mind-expanding drugs include a variety of substances that provide vivid sense experiences, visual and occasionally auditory hallucinations, and a sense of self-detachment. The most commonly used and the most publicized of these drugs is LSD, or "acid" (lysergic acid diethylamide), which can be taken as a colorless liquid or powder. When doses of 100–500 micrograms are taken, the experience of an LSD high will last for as long as 10–12 hours (Boyd, 1971; Kleinhesselink et al., 1976). Thus, LSD has very powerful properties that are readily apparent on the first "trip" and do not have to be learned or socialized, as is the case with marijuana. There is, however, an important contextual component to the way the hallucinogens are used. Davis and Munoz (1968) distinguish between "freaks" and "heads" to clarify this aspect of hallucinogenic drug use. The freak uses the drug for kicks, or for satisfying excessive cravings or emotional needs. Freaks are likely to be highly anxious, aggressive, or paranoid. They are likely to use drugs to the exclusion of other activities or relationships. In contrast, the heads use hallucinogens to heighten their self-awareness or to gain insight into their genetic origins. They use LSD as a means of personal growth in conjunction with other self-expanding experiences. The heads may even give up hallucinogenic drugs in order to achieve this level of consciousness through meditation. One's orientation toward the use of LSD may depend on whether it is taken in the company of freaks or heads.

In general, the hallucinogens are not biologically addictive, although the freak user may become emotionally dependent on this kind of high. If the same dosage is taken several days in a row, the effects are dramatically reduced. Therefore, most users trip only periodically. The use of hallucinogens is very closely associated with the youth culture, especially the college-age population. Studies of college campuses have reported experimentation with these drugs by 2–18 percent of the students (Levy, 1973). In a study of marijuana use, it was found that only 1 percent of nonusers had tried LSD, whereas 29 percent of occasional users and 57 percent of chronic users had tried it (Hochman and Brill, 1973). Although the hallucinogens are not nearly as popular as marijuana or alcohol, many adolescents see them as an intriguing way of experimenting with the totality of conscious experience.

The negative consequences of LSD seem to fall into three categories. First, there is the unwanted trip. In this case, a person ingests LSD at a party or during an outdoor celebration without knowing that the drug was part of the "refreshments." The resulting hallucinations, sensory experiences, and sense of detachment are likely to set off an intense anxiety reaction and a fear of going crazy. Because the effects of the drug last so long and the source of the effects is unknown, the person may become convinced that he or she is psychotic. Even after the effects of the drug have worn off, the memory of the fear of madness and the power of some of the imagery may remain as a source of anxiety. Second, there are "bad trips" during which even experienced users become extremely anxious and paranoid. These trips may result in prolonged periods of psychotic thought, including hallucinations, frightening nightmares, and disorganization that can last for a few days or as long as a few months (Miller, 1974; Cohen, 1967). Third, there are adolescents who appear to experience prolonged or even permanent confusion or affectlessness after heavy use of hallucinogens (Kline, 1971; Miller, 1974). These changes have been attributed to potential brain damage or to the tendency of the hallucinogens to reduce the person's ability to defend against areas of existing pathology. The risks associated with LSD and other hallucinogens are disturbingly unpredictable. Heavy users can continue to trip periodically for several years with no observable negative consequences, and they can stop using the drug without any obvious withdrawal symptoms except for occasional "flashbacks" of a vivid drug-related experience. On the other hand, a novice or an experienced user can encounter acute anxiety, paranoid delusions, terrifying hallucinations, or prolonged confusion as a result of just one dose. The promise that LSD holds of greater self-insight, which is so urgently important for adolescents who are at work on identity, is tied to a threat of identity disruption or dissolution.

**Addictive Narcotics.** This group of drugs, which includes heroin, cocaine, codein, and opium, is considered addictive in the sense that abstinence creates physical discomfort and an intense preoccupation with trying to maintain access to a supply of the drug. "The opiate high provides relief from pain, including hunger, and a gratifying buzz, a feeling that has never been adequately described, of immediate pleasure and transient well-being" (Boyd, 1971, p. 304). The heroin high lasts for about two hours, and withdrawal symptoms begin after about four hours. These symptoms can include anxiety, irritability, sweating, nausea, cramps, vomiting, and diarrhea. A single dose of heroin does not lead to addiction. In fact, adolescents may use heroin every once in a while without suffering unpleasant withdrawal symptoms. This may be because of the small amount of pure heroin that is contained in American heroin or because these drug users are also taking other drugs that mask the effects of heroin withdrawal (Kleinhesselink et al., 1976; Miller, 1974; Boyd, 1971).

Adolescent involvement with heroin and other addictive narcotics is relatively infrequent in comparison to their involvement with alcohol and marijuana. An estimated 1.3 percent of those 18 or over have tried heroin (National Commission on Marijuana and Drug Abuse, 1973). During the Vietnam War there was a significant increase in heroin use because the drug was readily available and inexpensive for American troops in Vietnam. In the United States, heroin is mixed with large quantities of other substances, including lactose. Because of the poor quality and high cost of the domestic supply, soldiers returning from Vietnam have been likely to give up their involvement in this form of drug use. Active methodone maintenance programs have been established to obtain the positive effects of the narcotic high with a clinic-administered substitute drug while providing skill training, recreational opportunities, and psychological counseling that will replace the heroin addict's emotional dependence on the narcotic high.

The controlled use of narcotics does not, in and of itself, create a maladaptive life-style. Rather, it is a convergence of the factors that surround the supply and application of narcotics that usually results in mental and physical distress. Generally, the narcotics purchased on the street are impure. Dirty syringes, unregulated dosages, and malnutrition all contribute to the physical complications associated with heroin use. These complications include tetanus, hepatitis, and local infections. Death may be a direct result of a heroin overdose or a complication of these other conditions (Boyd, 1971). Because heroin use is illegal, the adolescent heroin user is thrown into contact with others who are involved in criminal activity and who perceive themselves as deviants. Often, in order to support the habit, heroin users become involved in illegal and violent activities. There are, however, no generally accepted differences in the personalities or degree of pathology present among users and nonusers. In fact, in one study of suburban, white, middle-class males, the 7 percent who used heroin were no different from nonusers in school grades, number of courses failed, frequency of cheating, or attitudes toward principals or teachers (Rathus, Siegel, and Rathus, 1976). The pathology of heroin addiction consists primarily in what the adolescent is willing to do to avoid withdrawal. There are no characteristics that predict who will become an addict, and there are no common psychological deficits among former addicts that link drug addiction to any of the commonly used categories of psychopathology (Millman and Khuri, 1973).

## Suicide

Suicide is perhaps the most distrubing expressions of the maladaptation of later adolescents. We are frustrated by the premature ending of life, by unrealized potential. We are agonized by our failure to prevent the act. We are haunted by the questioning and doubt that surround suicides. The ambivalence that is implied in most suicides draws upon our own preoccupation with the meaning of life and with the amount of suffering or isolation that we are prepared to absorb into our own existence. The emotions of sadness, guilt, anger, and frustration that we feel in response to another's suicide are the same emotions that are associated with the suicide attempt itself.

Suicide is currently the second most common cause of death in the age group 15–24 (Hendon, 1975). Among this age group, about 4,000 deaths are attributed to suicide each year. Many more suicides are reported as accidents or disguised to protect the reputation of the adolescent or his or her family (Toolan, 1975; Miller, 1975). College students, black youth, and American Indians are more likely to commit suicide than others in their age cohort. The rate of suicide for Indians is almost five times as high as the rate for other 15–24-year-olds (Frederick, 1973; Smith, 1976).

The pattern of suicide attempts is somewhat different from the pattern of suicides that actually result in death. Adolescents have a much higher attempt-to-completed suicide ration than do older adults. Estimates of attempts to completions are as high as 120:1 in adolescent populations, whereas they are closer to 10:1 for older groups (Weiner, 1970; Rosenkrantz, 1978). This disproportion between attempted and completed suicides has been used as evidence that many adolescent suicides are cries for help or efforts to change the pattern of communication that exists between adolescents and significant others.

More females than males are likely to attempt suicide, but more males complete suicide. The primary mode of accomplishing suicide among adolescents is firearms or explosives. The next most frequent method is strangulation for males and poison for females. Among those who attempt but do not complete suicide, poison is by far the most common method (Weiner, 1970). Since the statistical distinction between attempted and completed suicides is based on the outcome, it may not take the intention into account. Some adolescents who plan a violent, immediate death are "saved," and some who do not think they have taken a lethal overdose of some drug actually die. There is clearly no truth to the myth that a person who attempts suicide and fails will not try again.

Coleman (1976) offers four stress factors that are associated with suicide: (1) Interpersonal crises associated with the loss of a loved one or the loss of an important person's love may lead to suicide. (2) Failure and self-devaluation may result in feelings of depression and self-blame that lead to suicide. (3) Inner conflict can lead to suicide if the person simply cannot accept some aspect of his or her own fate. (4) Loss of meaning or hope, especially in the case of a terminal illness or prolonged chronic pain, may lead to suicide. The common theme of depression is found in all of these factors (Leonard, 1974; Weissman, Fox, Klerman, 1973). The suicidal person is preoccupied by feelings of hopelessness and a sense of isolation or an absence of meaningful communication.

Some theorists have suggested that adolescent suicide is an impulsive act that occurs in reaction to a precipitating stress situation (Jacobinizer, 1960; 1965; Gould, 1965). In contrast, Weiner (1970) presents strong evidence for the view that adolescent suicide is a final response to a long series of problems that usually involve feelings of alienation from family or feelings of failure and worthlessness. In many cases, other kinds of symptoms are observed before the suicide attempt. These include sleeplessness, psychosomatic illness, defiant acts, and declining school performance. However painful these symptoms may be, the majority of adolescents who commit suicide do not seek counseling and do not have a history of diagnosed psychopathology (Temby, 1961; Miller, 1975). Nevertheless, their suicide attempt is a last response to a prolonged sequence of personal and interpersonal stress.

The most frequent theme associated with adolescent suicide is some disappointment or loss of intimacy and love. The following was written by a 19-year-old college student:

Dear Jim:
   I've just emptied 40 capsules and put the powder in a glass of water. I'm about to take it. I'm scared and I want to talk to someone but I just don't have anybody to talk to. I feel like I'm completely alone and nobody cares. I know our breakup was my fault but it hurts so bad. Nothing I do seems to turn out right, but nothing. My whole life has fallen apart. Maybe if, but I know.
   I've thought about all of the trite phrases about how it will get brighter tomorrow and how suicide is copping out and really isn't a solution and maybe it isn't but I hurt so bad. I just want it to stop. I feel like my back is up against the wall and there is no other way out.
   It's getting harder to think and my life is about to end. Tears are rolling down my face and I feel so scared and alone. Oh Jim . . . if you could put your arms around me and hold me close . . . just one last time . . . . . . . J . . . . . m. (Coleman, 1976, p. 607)

The dissolution of a love relationship, the death of a parent, and the threat of parental abandonment are all significant kinds of interpersonal loss that can stimulate feelings of depression or worthlessness. If these events occur in conjunction with a history of prolonged stress and articulated plans of suicide or fantasied preoccupations with suicide, the risk that the person will attempt suicide becomes quite high (Griest et al., 1974).

## CHAPTER SUMMARY

During later adolescence we observe the continued expression of some of the forms of deviance described in Chapter 8 as well as the emergence of some new patterns of maladaptation. The neuroses of later adolescence bear a close resemblance to those of early adolescence. Case material on the anxiety reaction, phobia, conversion reaction, dissociative reaction, and obsessive-compulsive reaction illustrates some of the ways in which the structure of these neuroses becomes elaborated during later adolescence. The classic form of neurotic depression is much more likely to be observed during this age period. This loss of initiative and chronic sense of a lack of worth is thought to be a reaction to loss, failure, discouragement, or disillusionment. It is important to differentiate the normal experiences of depression associated with loss of the childhood home or confusion about identity from this more intense, chronic sense of worthlessness.

The psychoses of later adolescence include schizophrenia, the psychotic depressive reaction, and the manic-depressive psychotic reaction. In later adolescence, the full array of expectations for autonomous behavior may reveal the serious limitations of the schizophrenic early adolescent. One or many of the new demands of this period may precipitate a schizophrenic adaptation.

The psychotic depressive reaction involves an overwhelming self-depreciation, deep self-hate, guilt, and a need for punishment. Adolescents may shut off interpersonal contact, believing themselves undeserving of the care or concern of others. This form of psychosis is difficult to treat because the afflicted person usually does not permit close, supportive relationships and may be a participant in a transitional life situation in which he or she has no permanent interpersonal contacts.

The manic-depressive psychosis involves either prolonged mania or alternations of mania and depression. Both forms are viewed as related to intense depression and an inability to express hostility. Both the manic and the depressed phases of this condition involve unrealistic evaluations of the self and the environment.

The primary behavior disorders of later adolescence are drug use and suicide. The most widely used and abused drug is alcohol. Although alcohol can be used to facilitate relaxation and social interaction, its heavy use can have a range of negative consequences. Alcohol has a particular place in the college culture, and it tends to be an expression of the later adolescent's sense of virility and vitality. It is also a common source of relief from discouragement or depression. Patterns of heavy alcohol use that begin during college are likely to continue into adulthood.

Marijuana is another drug that is widely used among later adolescents, but its use, unlike that of alcohol, is illegal. Although there is no evidence that marijuana use leads to reduced achievement or involvement, marijuana users and nonusers do differ on some important dimensions. Users tend to be more liberal, more pessimistic about the government, more rebellious, more reckless, and more antiauthoritarian. It is difficult to know whether the use of marijuana produces these characteristics or whether individuals who possess these characteristics are more likely than individuals who do not possess them to try marijuana and to enjoy its effects.

The hallucinogenic drugs provide a powerful, long-lasting high. They are associated with unpredictable risks, especially the bad trip which precipitates a temporary psychotic episode. In general, the effects of these drugs can be influenced by the orientation of the companions who "guide" the trip.

Addictive narcotics provide a short, intense high with unpleasant withdrawal symptoms. The main maladaptive component of narcotic use comes from the activities involved in maintaining one's supply. Other narcotic-related dangers are associated with impurities in the drug, infections associated with injection, malnutrition, and unregulated dosage. Narcotic users who are able to support their habit and to regulate the conditions of drug administration are able to pursue a productive work life.

Suicide is the second highest cause of death among people aged 15–24. The death rate due to suicide is especially high for college students, blacks, and American Indians. Suicide attempts are viewed as a cry for help, a need for communication. Although the theme of depression is common to many suicides, there is no clear history of psychopathology in the majority of cases. Suicide is usually a final response to chronic stress. Among later adolescents, this stress is primarily a result of a disruption of interpersonal relations or a loss of love.

In all the forms of deviance discussed in this chapter, we cannot help but note the recurrent theme of depression. Both the expression and the denial of depression are central elements in the neurotic depression, psychotic depressive reactions, manic-depressive reactions, alcohol use, and suicide. We might hypothesize the existence of biological changes that stimulate depressive mood states during this phase of adolescence. Certainly the challenges of impending adulthood and the increasing expectations for autonomy and decision making may create feelings of worthlessness and confusion. Finally, the desire for intimacy and the difficulty of achieving emotional and sexual contact produce a sense of isolation that may well generate depression.

## REFERENCES

Akiskal, H. S., and McKinney, W. T., Jr.   Overview of recent research in depression: Integration of ten conceptual models in a comprehensive clinical frame. *Archives of General Psychiatry*, 1975, *32*, 285–305.

American Psychiatric Association.  *Diagnostic and statistical manual of mental disorders* (2d ed.). Washington, D.C.: American Psychiatric Association, 1968.

Arieti, S.   Manic-depressive psychosis. In S. Arieti (Ed.) *American handbook of psychiatry*. New York: Basic Books, 1959. Pp. 419–454.

Bagley, C.   Occupational class and symptoms of depression. *Social Science and Medicine*, 1973, *7*, 327–340.

Barnes, G. M.   A perspective on drinking among teenagers with special reference to New York State studies. *Journal of School Health*, 1975, *45*, 386–389.

Barnes, G. M.   The development of adolescent drinking behavior: An evaluative review of the impact of the socialization process within the family. *Adolescence*, 1977, *12*, 571–591.

Beck, A. T.   *Depression: Clinical, experimental, and theoretical aspects.* Harper and Row, 1967.

Beck, A. T.   Cognition, affect, and psychopathology. *Archives of General Psychiatry*, 1971, *24*, 495–500.

Beck, A. T.   *Depression: Causes and treatment,* Philadelphia: University of Pennsylvania Press, 1972.

Becker, H. S.   Becoming a marijuana smoker. *American Journal of Sociology*, 1953, *59*, 235–243.

Becker, J.   *Depression: Theory and research,* Washington, D.C.: Winston-Wiley, 1974.

Becker, J., and Altrocchi, J.   Peer conformity and achievement in female manic depressives, *Journal of Abnormal Psychiatry*, 1968, *73*, 585–589.

Bellak, L.   *Manic-depressive psychoses and allied conditions.* New York: Grune and Stratton, 1952.

Bonier, R. J., and Hymowitz, P.   Marijuana and college students: Set, setting, and personality. Paper presented at American Psychological Association, Honolulu, September 1972.

Boyd, P. R.   Drug abuse and addiction in adolescents. In J. G. Howell (Ed.), *Modern perspectives in adolescent psychiatry.* New York: Brunner/Mazel, 1971. Pp. 290–328.

Brill, H., Fioramonti, F., Fort, J., Goode, E., and Lang, I. L.   A panel discussion on marijuana. *Contemporary Drug Problems*, 1973, *2*, 267–302.

Bunney, W. E., Jr., Murphy, D. L., Goodwin, F. K., and Borge, G. F.   The "switch-process" in manic-depressive illness: A systematic study of sequential behavioral changes. *Archives of General Psychiatry*, 1972, *27*, 295–302.

Cameron, N.   *Personality development and psychopathology: A dynamic approach.* Boston: Houghton Mifflin, 1963.

Chafetz, M.   Alcoholism: Drug dependency problem number one. *Journal of Drug Issues*, Winter 1974, pp. 64–68. (a)

Chafetz, M.   *Alcohol and health: New knowledge.* Second special report to the U.S. Congress from the secretary of health, education, and welfare. Reprint edition. Washington, D.C.: U.S. Government Printing Office, 1974. (b)

Chodoff, P.   The depressive personality: A critical review. *Archives of General Psychiatry.* 1972, *27*, 666–673.

Cohen, M., et al.   An intensive study of twelve cases of manic-depressive psychosis. *Psychiatry*, 1954, *17*, 103–137.

Cohen, S.   Psychomimetic agents. *Annual Review of Pharmacology*, 1967, *7*, 301.

Coleman, J. C.   *Abnormal psychology and modern life* (5th ed.). Glenview, Ill.: Scott, Foresman, 1976.

Davis, F., and Munoz, L.   Heads and freaks: Patterns and meanings of drug use among hippies. *Journal of Health and Social Behavior*, 1968, *9*, 156–164.

Ferster, C. B.   A functional analysis of depression. *American Psychologist*, 1973, *28*, 857–870.

Frederick, C. J. *Suicide, homicide, and alcoholism among American Indians.* U.S. Department of Health, Education, and Welfare Publication no. ADM 74–42. Washington, D.C.: U.S. Government Printing Office, 1973.

Freud, S. Mourning and melancholia. In J. Strachey (Ed.), *The standard edition of the complete psychological works of Sigmund Freud,* vol. 14. London: Hogarth Press, 1957. (Originally published in 1917.) Pp. 243–258.

Gallagher, J. R., and Harris, H. J. *Emotional problems of adolescents* (3d ed.). New York: Oxford University Press, 1976.

Gergen, M., Gergen, K., and Morse, S. Correlates of marijuana use among college students. *Journal of Applied Social Psychology,* 1972, *2,* 1–16.

Gibson, R. W., Cohen, M. B., and Cohen, R. A. On the dynamics of the manic-depressive personality. *American Journal of Psychiatry,* 1959, *115,* 1101–1107.

Goode, E. *The marijuana smokers.* New York: Basic Books, 1970.

Gould, R. E. Suicide problems in children and adolescents. *American Journal of Psychotherapy,* 1965, *19,* 228–246.

Griest, J. H., Gustafson, D. H., Stauss, F. F., Rowse, G. L., Loughren, T. P., and Chiles, J. A. Suicide risk prediction: A new approach. *Life-Threatening Behavior,* 1974, *4* (4), 212–223.

Grinker, R. An essay on schizophrenia and science. *Archives of General Psychiatry,* 1969, *20,* 1–24.

Hendon, H. Student suicide: Death as a life-style. *Journal of Nervous and Mental Disorders,* 1975, *160,* 204–219.

Hochman, J. S. *Marijuana and social evolution.* Englewood Cliffs, N.J.: Prentice-Hall, 1972.

Jacobinizer, H. Attempted suicides in children. *Journal of Pediatrics,* 1960, *56,* 519–525.

Jenner, F. A., Gjessing, L. R., Cox, J. R., Davies-Jones, A., and Hullen, R. P. A manic-depressive psychotic with a 48 hour cycle. *British Journal of Psychiatry,* 1967, *113,* 859–910.

Jessor, R., Jessor, S., and Finney, J. A social psychology of marijuana use: Longitudinal studies of high school and college youth. *Journal of Personality and Social Psychology,* 1973, *26,* 1–15.

Kleinhesselink, R. R., St. Dennis, R., and Cross, H. Contemporary drug issues involving youth. In J. F. Adams (Ed.), *Understanding adolescence: Current developments in adolescent psychology* (3d ed.). Boston: Allyn and Bacon, 1976. Pp. 369–411.

Kline, N. S. The future of drugs and drugs of the future, *Journal of Social Issues,* 1971, *27* (3), 73–87.

Knight, R. C., Sheposh, J. P., and Bryson, J. B. College student marijuana use and societal alienation, *Journal of Health and Social Behavior,* 1974, *15* (1), 28–35.

Leonard, C. V. Depression and suicidality. *Journal of Consulting and Clinical Psychology,* 1974, *42,* 98–104.

Levy, L. Drug use on campus: Prevalence and social characteristics of collegiate drug users on campuses of the University of Illinois. *Drug Forum,* 1973, *2* (2), 141–171.

Libet, J. M., and Lewinsohn, P. M.   The concept of social skill with special reference to the behavior of depressed persons. *Journal of Consulting and Clinical Psychology,* 1973, *40,* 304–312.

Lichtenberg, J. D.   Theoretical and practical considerations of the management of the manic phase of the manic-depressive psychosis. *Journal of Nervous and Mental Disorders,* 1959, *129,* 243–281.

Lorenz, M.   Language behavior in manic patients: An equalitative study. *Archives of Neurology and Psychology,* 1953, *69,* 14–26.

Lorenz, M., and Cobb, L.   Language behavior in manic patients. *Archives of Neurology and Psychology,* 1952, *67,* 763–770.

Miller, D.   *Adolescence: Psychology, Psychopathology, and psychotherapy.* New York: Jay Aronson, 1974.

Miller, J. P.   Suicide and adolescence. *Adolescence,* 1975, *10,* 11–24.

Millman, R. B., and Khuri, E. T.   Drug abuse and the need for alternatives. In J. C. Schoolar (Ed.), *Current issues in adolescent psychiatry.* New York: Brunner/Mazel, 1973. Pp. 148–158.

National Commission on Marijuana and Drug Abuse.   *Drug use in America: Problem in perspecitve.* Washington, D.C.: U.S. Government Printing Office, 1973.

National Institute on Alcohol Abuse and Alcoholism.   *A national study of adolescent drinking behavior, attitudes, and correlates.* Final report prepared by Research Triangle Institute, Research Triangle Park, North Carolina, 1975.

*New York Times.*   L.I. youth dead, 2 others hospitalized after party for fraternity's pledges. February 26, 1978, section 1, p. 27.

Poznanski, E., and Zrull, J. P.   Childhood depression. *Archives of General Psychiatry,* 1970, *53,* 259–263.

Rathus, S. A., Siegel, L. J., and Rathus, L. A.   Attitudes of middle-class heroin abusers toward representatives of the educational system. *Adolescence,* 1976, *11,* 1–6.

Reich, T., Clayton, P. J., and Winokur, G.   Family history studies: The genetics of mania. *American Journal of Psychiatry,* 1968, *124* (11, supplement), 21–34.

Rist, R. C.   Marijuana and the young: Problem or protest? *Intellect Magazine,* 1972, *101,* 154–156.

Rosenkrantz, A. L.   A note on adolescent suicide: Incidence, dynamics, and some suggestions for treatment. *Adolescence,* 1978, *13,* 211–214.

Sarason, J. G.   *Abnormal psychology: The problem of maladaptive behavior* (2d ed.). Englewood Cliffs, N.J.: Prentice-Hall, 1976.

Schancke, D. A.   If you're way, way down—or up too high. *Today's Health,* 1974, *52* (5), 39–41, 65–67.

Shafer, R.   *Marijuana: A signal of misunderstanding.* National Commission on Marijuana and Drug Abuse. New York: New American Library, 1972.

Smith, D. F.   Adolescent suicide: A problem for teachers? *Phi Delta Kappa,* April 1976, pp. 195–198.

Temby, W. D.   Suicide. In G. R. Blaine and C. C. McArthur (Eds.), *Emotional problems of the student.* New York: Appleton-Century-Crofts, 1961. Pp. 133–152.

Toolan, J. M.   Suicide in children and adolescents. *American Journal of Psycho-therapy,* 1975, *29,* 339–344.

Weiner, I. B.   *Psychological disturbance in adolescence.* New York: Wiley, 1970.

Weissman, M. M., Fox, K., and Klerman, G. L.   Hostility and depression associated with suicide attempts. *American Journal of Psychiatry,* 1973, *130,* 450–455.

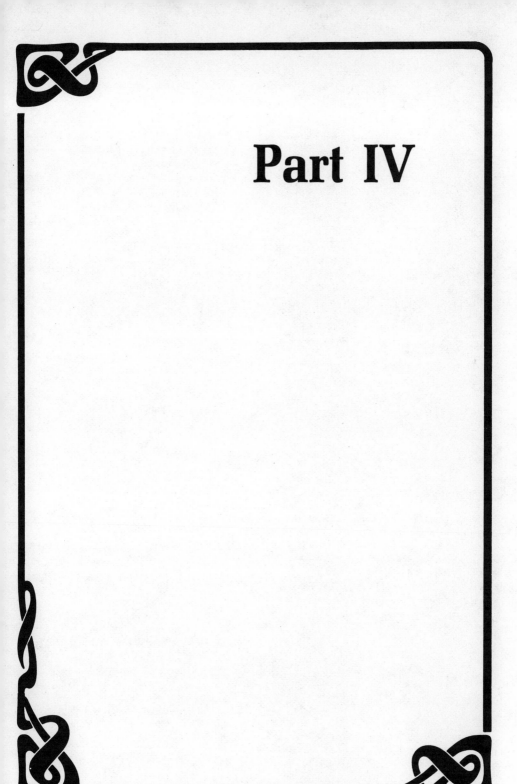

# Part IV

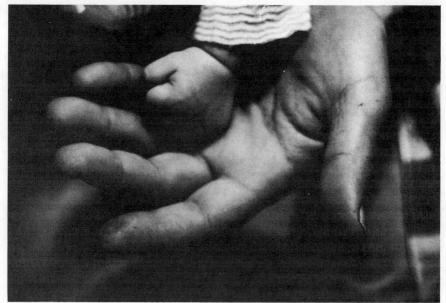

Inge Morath/Magnum

*Continuity and change are central themes in the study of development.*

# 13

# The Place of Adolescence in the Life Span

Throughout the book, we have emphasized a developmental approach to the study of adolescence. The focus has been on the emerging competences of the person in interaction with changing cultural expectations and opportunities. By way of summary and integration, we ask the general question of how to conceptualize adolescence in the context of the life span. In adolescence we see endings and beginnings. We see preparation for future stages and departure from earlier stages. We see experiences similar to those of earlier and later stages of life. We also see unique experiences that belong to this decade of life alone. The first two parts of this chapter examine some of the continuities and changes from childhood to adolescence and from adolescence to adulthood. The third part suggests implications for the development of resources that would enhance the experience of adolescence.

## CONTINUITY AND CHANGE FROM CHILDHOOD TO ADOLESCENCE

"The more things change, the more they stay the same." "Today is the first day of the rest of your life." Continuity and change are two of the puzzling, elusive concepts that confront the student of human development. Our perceptions of continuity are impressive, and they are readily supported by others. From day to day we are the same selves, with the same memories, the same experiences of conscious self-recognition, and, for the most part, the same patterns of motor habits, tastes, and talents. Yet, looking back through the family album to that tiny baby on the fluffy pillow or the chubby toddler sitting proudly on the Shetland pony at the zoo, we cannot help but confront the dramatic changes that have taken place. Changes in our skills, in our body shape, in our information, in our relationships, and in our sense of self-awareness shake our confidence in the perception of continuity and invite us instead to consider the possibility of continuous, far-reaching change. We liken this psychological paradox to the physical motion of the earth. While you sit comfortably in one place reading these words, confident about your stable location in time and space, the earth is moving 18.5 miles per second in its orbit around the sun. In other words, stability and change can both be occurring simultaneously on different dimensions or different planes. Adaptation and growth involve the gradual modification of aspects of the self that are familiar and predictable so that they take into account new information and new competences (Piaget, 1952). The process of adaptation does not cause us to lose contact with our former self but refreshes that self through expansion and innovation.

The threads of continuity from childhood to adolescence are

strong and convincing. Perhaps the most powerful example of continuity is the maintenance of the role of *child.* Well into adolescence, most young people live with their family of origin, dependent on the material and psychological resources of their parents. Although there may be a gradual redefinition of responsibilities and freedoms, adolescents continue to be keenly aware of the areas in which they rely on parental support. Parents too may be slow to modify the relationship they hold with their adolescent children. As compared with children in other cultures, American children tend to live in a context of comparative parental restrictiveness (Kandel and Lesser, 1972). They tend to share many of their parent's values and to see little encouragement for autonomy during early adolescence. Thus the role of son or daughter, with its accompanying expectations for obedience, respect, and duty or obligation, remains an essential element that provides continuity from childhood into adolescence.

The other role that retains a central place in childhood and adolescence is that of student. In both early and later adolescence we have focused on the educational setting as a powerful socialization influence. Beginning with the nursery school experiences of toddlerhood, children learn to play the student role. This role usually includes expectations about the teacher, a sense of oneself as a "learner," norms about how to interact with other students, and some concern about evaluation (Katz and Kohn, 1978). The thread of continuity in the student role means that there is an accumulation of experiences which blend events from elementary school, middle school, high school, and college into a mixture of behaviors and expectations that define the self as a student. When adolescent students raise their hands to ask a question, when they study for an exam, when they sit in confused silence while the teacher is lecturing, or when they discover the connection between two ideas, they relive familiar experiences. Once again, it is not that the student role is identical from year to year. Certainly the competences of students and students' expectations for performance change from one grade to the next. Nevertheless, the background of past evaluations, academic aspirations, and intellectual talents as well as the common organizational features of different educational settings helps to foster a continuity of performance and expectations.

The most marked areas of change from childhood to adolescence include physical and cognitive development. Physical growth and sexual maturation provide an obvious break from the self-image of childhood. Increased height and strength open the way for new levels of endurance and motor skill. Sexual maturation brings a capacity for reproduction as well as an increase in sexual drives and an interest in heterosexual intimacy. The changes of puberty bring the physical status of childhood to an irrefutable close. We do not see childhood as void of sexuality. Sensual pleasure is intimately associated with the experiences of loving, self-discovery, and play that are part of childhood. However, the excitement of sexual arousal and the potential for creating one's own children are experienced in a new and vivid perspective after sexual maturation has occurred.

Cognitive maturation during adolescence provides an increased self-awareness as well as the more abstract, flexible thinking of formal operational logic. Adolescents become aware of their own thoughts and their own existence as objects for reflection. They are freed from the restraints of concrete operational thought and from their commitment to the world as they see and experience it. With formal thought comes a whole range of hypothetical realities that can be vastly different from reality as it is experienced in the here and now. The meaning of this change is difficult to evaluate. We know that for some adolescents the transition to formal thought is slow and that some adolescents make very little use of this potential competence (Dulit, 1972). On the other hand, once formal thought has emerged as a fully expressed mode of thinking, the possibilities for new conceptualizations, new levels of integration, and new insights about the self are enormously expanded.

## CONTINUITY AND CHANGE FROM ADOLESCENCE TO ADULTHOOD

Many theorists emphasize the notion of adolescence as a period of transition from childhood to adulthood (Erikson, 1950; A. Freud, 1965; Blos, 1962). The validity of this orientation comes primarily from the variety of adolescent experiences that can be seen as forms of preparation, introduction, or initiation into adult roles. In our own view, this emphasis on transition tends to mask some of the unique features of adolescence as well as to ignore some of the critical areas of discontinuity from adolescence to adulthood.

First, let us focus on the dimensions of stability or continuity. We see the high school as a powerful training ground for participation in other complex organizations. Adolescents from different communities, with different levels of competence, and with different personal aspirations come together in a relatively closed system. The emphasis on school rules, on community involvement, or on academic excellence sets a pattern of expectations for the next organizational setting, whether it is work, college, or the military. Within the high school, students gain experience in identifying the role structure of the institution and in recognizing the network of peer associations. They begin to identify the costs and benefits of various reputational associations. Being known as an athletic star, an honor student, or a school leader has implications for how one is treated and what resources are made available. Those lessons in the working of reputation and status are powerful guidelines for anticipating the social organization of adult settings.

Another area of continuity involves the growing focus on work and career. Beginning with the tracking system in junior high or high school, students are asked to make decisions about vocation (Shafer and Olexa, 1971). Although these decisions may not close the door on other alternatives permanently, they make some career directions much less accessible than others. The choice about whether to follow a college preparatory, vocational, or general education curriculum has obvious implications for one's adult work life. At the same time, adolescents are beginning to identify specific areas of work that they wish to pursue. For students who go on to college, the specific focus may guide the choice of a college, the choice of a major, and the array of courses that are elected. Career decisions may also influence the kinds of summer employment or part-time work that the adolescent seeks. Many students are involved in work experiences during their high school years. These experiences prepare adolescents for the demands and benefits of employment. Some adolescents have their first taste of joblessness (Havighurst and Gottlieb, 1975). The bitter experiences of being turned away, trained and never hired, or fired because of a lack of seniority are common for adolescent workers. For some adolescents, these early job failures or disappointments simply enforce the importance of obtaining a high school diploma. For others, these initial experiences of frustration set a pattern of hostility about work and expectations of subsequent failure.

We have emphasized peer group identification as a central experience of early adolescence (Newman and Newman, 1976). Positive affiliation with peers provides a source of satisfaction that continues to be important throughout life. Friends offer support and understanding. They share exposure to the contemporary culture and values that provide a basis for rapport. All through adulthood, we treasure the bonds we share with others who have gone through similar crises or similar role changes. Because of shared experiences, there are certain assumptions that do not need explanation or clarification. Friends who have raised their families during the same period, who have lived through a war or a disaster, or who have gone through the same phases of job training can provide a unique form of reassurance or comfort that members of other age cohorts may not be able to offer.

Peer associations also open the way to the more complex peer network of the high school (Dunphy, 1963). In the company of friends, adolescents are likely to participate more actively in the social and political activities of the school. This same pattern of peer involvement extends to participation in the adult community. Friends encourage one another's membership in political, charitable, or social organizations that expand the social network and create a sense of involvement or belonging.

We have also talked about adolescence as a time for the formation of loving relationships. Loving begins in infancy and is continuously redefined throughout life. In adolescence, some very special aspects of loving are added to the picture. We experience the awkward anxiety of early dating. We fantasize about intimate encounters with members of the opposite sex. We hold secret affections, waiting to be noticed. We turn each other on with magazines and movies, with lotions and colognes, with tight jeans and bikinis. We have our first kiss, our first love, our first opportunity for physical intimacy. The many doors of romance, dating, and sexual pleasure are open. Adolescent loving is a form of experimentation all its own, with its own moments of exhilaration and despair. Adolescent loving is also one part of the process of achieving adult intimacy. Through adolescent experiences in love we begin to learn about our own needs in a love relationship as well as about how to satisfy the needs of others. We become more skilled at blending sexuality and interpersonal intimacy. If these loving relationships are successful, we grow increasingly optimistic about the possibility of making a lifelong commitment to another person. If they are unsuccessful, we may begin to develop other strategies for satisfying the need to experience intimacy in adulthood.

Perhaps the most widely discussed link between adolescence and adulthood is the achievement of personal identity. As we have discussed it, identity provides a bridge from past identifications and historical origins to future aspirations (Erikson, 1959). It is a conceptual system of values, commitments, and goals that will serve as a guide for significant life choices. In that sense, the formation of a personal identity provides a stable framework from which to build the life-style of adulthood. Commitments to work, to a marriage partner, to a religious or political ideology all reflect the sense of oneself that is formulated toward the end of later adolescence. Perhaps no other single concept more adequately reflects the creative achievement that is possible during this period of life.

Given the importance of the areas of continuity, one might well ask what more is to come in adulthood. In fact, many theories of development have ended their story of growth with adolescence viewing adult life as "more of the same" or as a reworking of

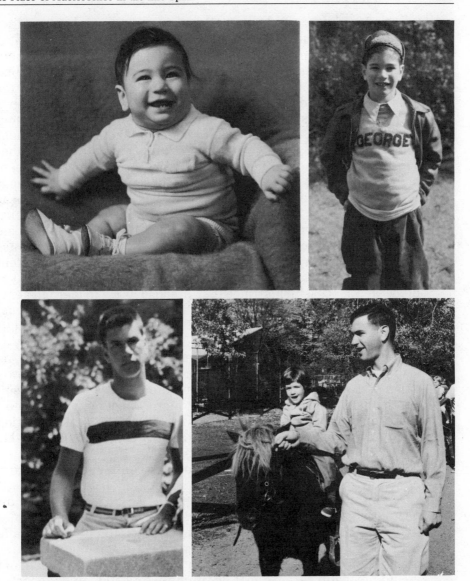

*Looking through the family album from the smiling infant . . . to the eager schoolboy . . . to the preoccupied adolescent . . . to the responsive parent.*

earlier conflicts. Here we would like to offer some ideas about the potential for new growth during adulthood that is not ordinarily accomplished during the two stages of adolescence.

After some years of experimentation, training, or apprenticeship, adults tend to define a particular set of work activities as their career. In adulthood, the meaning of work changes, especially as other family members come to count on the steady income of the worker. Issues of promotion, salary increases, employment benefits, retirement policies, and the risks of being transferred or fired begin to tie workers more closely into the socialization network of their jobs. The demands, the rewards, and the hazards of the job set many of the limits of the adult's life-style (Newman and Newman, 1979). Eventually, the older adult begins to take on more responsibility in the work setting, training, guiding, hiring, or firing others. Through experience in the world of work, adults develop a sense of how businesses operate, about the kinds of skills that are needed for success in work, and about strategies of administration and management that facilitate productivity. In this sense, experiences in the world of work contribute to the adult's education and alter his or her perspective on the meaningful rewards of employment.

Participation in a marriage relationship provides another avenue for change. Marriage partners are apt to become more like each other. In a successful marriage they are also likely to learn to negotiate conflicts and to discover each other's areas of strength (Rausch et al., 1975). Over the years, through periods of varying satisfaction and intimacy, marriage provides a background of mutuality between peers that is often not experienced during adolescence. Adolescents may rely on their peers for understanding or loyalty, but when it comes to certain important life choices they feel some doubt that their peers will be any more adequately prepared to guide them than they are themselves (Curtis, 1975). In marriage, the partners learn to respect each other's judgment and to share the consequences of their joint decisions.

Parenting is another role that provides continuous potential for new growth. As parents, adults are called upon to anticipate the needs of children who may not be able to articulate their own needs very well. Parents learn to create a responsive environment, to differentiate the needs and talents of different children at different ages, and to plan ahead for the stages that are to come. Parenting brings with it a new commitment to a whole range of concerns, including health care, education, traffic safety, nutrition, opportunities for physical activity, play space, toys and games, holiday celebrations, and grandparents, to name a few. At each stage of the child's growth, parents are confronted with new opportunities for their own growth. The child's needs and interests have the potential for bringing to light elements in the parent's childhood that were missing or frustrating or defined too narrowly. With the help of the child as a stimulus, the parent has the opportunity to reexperience or redefine his or her own childhood in a more enjoyable and more enhancing way (Newman and Newman, 1978).

As a final example of change in adulthood, let us consider the single notion of an expected future. If the life span is about 75 years, the early adolescent has a projected future life of about 60 years and the later adolescent has a projected future life of about 55 years. By the age of 40, adults recognize that they have lived about half their life already and that there is half left to live. At 65, there is the realization that there may be only a few years of life ahead. At 80, there is joy at having survived and some bewilderment about just how long this can go on. In adolescence, most young people do not really confront the reality of their own mortality. The game is just beginning, the wheel is just starting to spin, and the possibilities are as far reaching as the imagination. The passage of time carries us toward an uncertain but predictable end point. With age, our perspective on the meaning of life goals, the priorities we have given to certain relationships, and the urgency with which we face life's tasks changes. "The youth gets together his materials to build a bridge to the moon, or, perchance, a palace or temple on the earth, and, at length, the middle-aged man concludes to build a woodshed with them" (Henry David Thoreau, *Journal*, July 14, 1852).

## THE REALLOCATION OF RESOURCES FOR THE ENHANCEMENT OF ADOLESCENT DEVELOPMENT

In this final section, we take a look at some of the "rough spots" of early and later adolescence. Our goal here is to begin to consider ways in which material, social, and informational resources could be redistributed or redefined in order to enhance the experience of development during the adolescent years. The society is already structured so that certain rights and responsibilities are made available for the first time during adolescence. Driving a car, purchasing cigarettes and alcohol, voting, and enlisting in the military are among the privileges that are extended to adolescent citizens. As we look across the previous chapters, what are some of the areas in which the need for change is evident?

### Adolescent Pregnancy

Our assessment of adolescent pregnancies is that they currently have far greater probability of leading to misfortune and unhappiness than to a successful parent-child relationship. Adolescent mothers are likely to disrupt their education, to cut short their opportunities for career training or job experimentation, and to experience isolation from age-mates. They are more likely to give birth to underweight babies that have postnatal complications.

They are also likely to experience conflict with their parents and with the baby's father during the pregnancy and shortly after childbirth (Furstenberg, 1977).

There are two approaches to intervention that should alleviate some of the stress of this kind of experience. First, there is a need for early and ongoing education about sexuality, reproduction, and contraception. This kind of information should be presented on television, in comic book form, in school curricula, and in books that parents read to their young children. There is simply no reason why adolescents should conceive babies because "they didn't know you could get pregnant doing that." We take great precautions to teach our children about how to cross a street carefully, about how to take care of their teeth, and about the nutritional value of different foods. Certainly the topic of sexuality with its implications for the production of new life is worth as much of our energy as learning how to prevent dental cavities.

The second approach to change with regard to adolescent pregnancy is the creation of resources for the young mother. Resources have to be made available so that she can maintain continuity in education, in job training, and in peer group contact. Support systems are required to work with the parents of young mothers, with adolescent fathers, and with the young mothers themselves. There is no reason why the adolescent mother and her baby should be isolated from the important people in their lives. In some cultures, a marriage is not fully accepted until the wife becomes pregnant. Why, in our society, should adolescent pregnancy lead to so many forms of alienation? We need to add resources, not take them away, in order to give the adolescent mother and her baby the time they need to develop their own competences.

## Work

Thoughts about work are a major preoccupation of adolescents. As we pointed out, participation in a work setting during adolescence has the potential for stimulating intellectual growth as well as for providing a sense of responsibility and autonomy (Piaget, 1972). The desire to work is clearly a positive link between the adolescent's aspirations and his or her image of adult life. Yet we are struck by the inadequacy of the opportunities to work and learn about work that are available to either early or later adolescents.

Once again, there is a need for two directions of change. First, at the elementary, high school, and college levels there should be more direct education about work, work roles, and the process of finding work. This kind of career education can include an identification of the variety of work activities that exist, the strategies for selecting a work role, and the kinds of preparation or training that are needed. At a very concrete level, students in high school should have training in completing a job application and in being interviewed. College students should have some instruction in preparing a résumé and in finding appropriate job descriptions. The "nuts and bolts" of finding and keeping a job do not need to be left entirely to trial and error.

The second intervention requires opening up the world of work to the observation and participation of adolescents. The kinds of work that adolescents of high school age usually do is often of no help to them in identifying their career direction. Making french fries or bagging groceries does not offer much experience in the kinds of job-related challenges that are part of adult work. Adolescents have far too few opportunities for career-related experimentation. A commitment is needed from all kinds of work settings to create more ways in which adolescents can experience work firsthand. Apprenticeships, internships, summer fellowships, orientation programs, and part-time employment are some of the ways in which businesses, professions, and the skilled trades could provide meaningful learning opportunities for early and later adolescents.

## Parent-Child Relations

Adolescent-parent relations are a peculiar area of stress. It could be argued that there is a need for stress in this area, that such stress enhances growth. Indeed, to the extent that loosening parental bonds and evaluating earlier identifications foster work on personal identity, we would agree. Yet the theme of misunderstanding and lack of communication suggests that something more than the desired developmental stress is occurring. Young adolescents have relatively infrequent interactions with adults, including their parents, and yet they claim to value their parents' opinions on many matters (Newman, 1971; Czikszentmihalyi, Larson, and Prescott, 1977). College-age students complain that they do not receive encouragement for autonomy from their parents, and yet they closely reflect their parents' values (Lerner, 1975). Conflict with parents and familial disruption continue to be associated with a number of forms of deviant adolescent behavior, including juvenile delinquency, running away, drug abuse, and suicide. In other words, the pattern suggests that the quality of adolescent-parent relations and the background context of the parent's relationship with each other continue to be relevant dimensions that can support or disrupt adolescent growth (Peck, 1958). Our sense is that both parents and adolescent children are unaware of the ways in which they contribute to each other's development. The parents of adolescents are uncertain about the ways in which their parenting behaviors are needed or about how to modify those behaviors as their children more through adolescence. Adolescents are unaware that their parents are actively responding to their growth. The fact that parents may envy their child's freedom, delight in their child's educational accomplishments, or suffer feelings of shame because of their own lack of achievement is usually not noticed by the child. The parents, on the other hand, may not appreciate the child's continuing need for support, the child's desire to learn about love from the parents, or the child's need for the parents' information and past experiences in the process of finding work or planning a career.

The directions for intervention in this area are less obvious than they are in the areas of pregnancy and work. Here, we really begin to see the need for a variety of efforts to increase parent-child communication, to educate parents about their role as their children move through adolescence, and to educate both parents and adolescents about the developmental needs of adolescence and young, middle, and later adulthood. There are some ways for fostering interaction that have an interesting potential. Communities or high schools might create parent-exchange nights in which groups of adolescents talk with the parents of other students about values, intimacy, work, or the community. High schools could try to incorporate parents more actively into the school curriculum, using their expertise to offer minicourses in special work or skill areas or to present lectures or demonstrations to larger audiences. Colleges might establish a foster parent program in which families from the community would volunteer to "adopt" a college student, inviting the student for occasional meals or encouraging the student to spend afternoons or evenings at their home. The effectiveness of such efforts would depend on the context of support for intergenerational interaction. There is a need to emphasize the interdependence of adolescents and adults, encouraging the validity of their different perspectives and the possibility of their mutual enhancement.

## Isolation

We have discussed the theme of group identity versus alienation in early adolescence (Newman and Newman, 1976). The implication of this crisis is that alienation, or the feeling of being set apart from meaningful peer group associations, is a negative experience that has far-reaching consequences for subsequent development. Alienation can result from peer rejection or from the person's inability to make a commitment to any of the existing peer groups. In either case, alienation suggests that the young adolescent lacks the support or the sense of personal enhancement that results from peer group affiliation.

We have also discussed the self-conscious egocentrism of early adolescence as a form of alienation (Elkind, 1967; Looft, 1971). To some extent, all adolescents experience the feelings of isolation and separateness that result from being overly invested in the way others perceive them.

In later adolescence, isolation may be an inevitable part of the introspection that is required for work on identity. As adolescents leave home and loosen parental ties, they are at least temporarily likely to be more isolated than they have been during their childhood years.

Again, some experiences of isolation can be seen as positive and growth producing. Such experiences suggest a process of self-differentiation. The boundaries of the self become more clearly articulated, separating each of us from others. Loneliness, in this sense, is a positive outcome of a more mature selfhood. The fantasies of blending with another, of incorporating the other person into ourselves or of being taken in and totally surrounded by the other person, are fantasies of the past. As our own boundaries become more well defined, we inevitably confront feelings of separateness or isolation.

Yet there is a sense in which isolation can be a trap for adolescents. Adolescents may be caught with their social bridges down, especially if they are trying to demonstrate the strength of their newly emerging autonomy. We have described young adolescents who drift through high school, failing to make meaningful contacts with teachers or peers. (Newman and Newman, 1974). We have described college students who lose hope of any meaningful communication and end their lives (Coleman, 1976). We have described young males' strong desires to be understood by their fathers and their feelings of frustration at not being understood (Roll and Miller, 1978). We have described the resentment of students at being treated as numbers, as the target for one more bored professor. All of these examples reflect the continued need for connection, for a sense of belonging.

The issue of isolation is particularly relevant as adolescents begin to cope with growing feelings of depression. Such feelings are relatively new to adolescents (Weiner, 1970). Young people may not have developed the coping strategies for modifying these feelings. Strong feelings of worthlessness or hopelessness may make the adolescent an unattractive object for interaction. Adults and other students may be loath to approach the sad-eyed youth who is preoccupied with his or her own miseries. Having set off to demonstrate autonomy, adolescents may find themselves confronting shame and doubt.

Several strategies can be adopted to prevent the unproductive consequences of isolation. First, we must examine our institutions in order to ascertain the degree of heterogeneity of their populations. We recall that isolation is considerably more likely in homogeneous environments. When environments are identified as homogeneous, there must be an active effort to support and validate the contributions of the divergent minorities.

Second, in both the high school and the college we can create settings that encourage informal faculty-student interaction. We can also do more to make the advisement systems in these settings work. Instead of being limited to signing a paper or filling out a form, faculty advisement could become a more interpersonally meaningful contact point. Third, we need to consider the noncollege high school graduates in the community. These young people are especially likely to experience isolation as they leave the social structure of the high school and the intimacy of the family group. Probably the most predictable points of contact are the work settings in which these young people are employed. We would encourage businesses to create social occasions at which young employees can interact, as well as interagency social occasions at which the workers from several department stores, or banks, or computer centers, can come together. Here is a need that churches, synagogues, or community centers could readily meet by developing a "young adults" series of athletic, craft, or social events.

All of these suggestions are intended to reflect the legitimate need of adolescents to make contact with adults and peers. The suggestions cast doubt on our current "laissez-faire" attitude toward adolescents, our tendency to let them "make it" on their own. This attitude is too often interpreted as a lack of caring, even as an expression of the older generation's hostility to the younger generation. There is a strong need to have messages of generativity reach the adolescent population.

## REFERENCES

Blos, P. *On adolescence: A psychoanalytic interpretation.* New York: Free Press, 1962.

Coleman, J. C. *Abnormal psychology and modern life* (5th ed.). Glenview, Ill.: Scott, Foresman, 1976.

Curtis, R. L. Adolescent orientations toward parents and peers: Variations by sex, age, and socioeconomic status. *Adolescence,* 1975, *10,* 483–494.

Czikszentmihalyi, M., Larson, R., and Prescott, S.   The ecology of adolescent activity and experience. *Journal of Youth and Adolescence,* 1977, *6,* 281–294.

Dulit, E.   Adolescent thinking à la Piaget: The formal stage. *Journal of Youth and Adolescence,* 1972, *1,* 281–301.

Dunphy, D. C.   The social structure of urban adolescent peer groups. *Sociometry,* 1963, *26,* 230–246.

Elkind, D.   Egocentrism in adolescence. *Child Development,* 1967, *38,* 1025–1034.

Erikson, E. H.   *Childhood and society.* New York: Norton, 1950.

Erikson, E. H.   Identity and the life cycle. *Psychological Issues,* 1959, *1* (1), Monograph 1.

Freud, A.   *Normality and pathology in childhood: Assessments of development.* New York: International Universities Press, 1965.

Furstenberg, F. F.   *Unplanned parenthood: The social consequences of teenage childbearing.* Riverside, N.J.: Free Press, 1977.

Havighurst, R. J., and Gottlieb, D.   Youth and the meaning of work. In R. J. Havighurst and P. H. Dreyer (Eds.), *Youth: The seventy-fourth yearbook of the National Society for the Study of Education.* Chicago: University of Chicago Press, 1975. Pp. 145–160.

Kandel, D. B., and Lesser, G. S.   *Youth in two worlds.* San Francisco: Jossey-Bass, 1972.

Katz, D., and Kahn, R. L.   *The social psychology of organizations* (2d ed.). New York: Wiley, 1978.

Lerner, R. M.   Showdown at generation gap: Attitudes of adolescents and their parents toward contemporary issues. In H. D. Thornburg (Ed.), *Contemporary adolescence: Readings* (2d ed.). Monterey: Brooks/Cole, 1975. Pp. 114–126.

Looft, W. R.   Egocentrism and social interaction in adolescence. *Adolescence,* 1971, *6,* 485–494.

Newman, B. M., and Newman, P. R.   *Infancy and childhood: Development and its contexts.* New York: Wiley, 1978.

Newman, B. M., and Newman, P. R.   *Development through life: A psychosocial approach* (2d ed.). Homewood, Ill.: Dorsey Press, 1979.

Newman, P.   Persons and setting interactions: A comparative analysis of the quality and range of social interaction in two suburban high schools. Unpublished doctoral dissertation, University of Michigan, 1971.

Newman, P. and Newman, B.   Naturalistic observation of student interactions with adults and peers in the high school. Paper presented at Eastern Psychological Association Convention, Philadelphia, 1974.

Newman, P. R., and Newman, B. M.   Early adolescence and its conflict: Group identity versus alienation. *Adolescence,* 1976, *11,* 261–274.

Peck, R. F.   Family patterns correlated with adolescent personality structure. *Journal of Abnormal and Social Psychology,* 1958, *57,* 347–350.

Piaget, J.   *The origins of intelligence in children.* New York: International Universities Press, 1952.

Piaget, J.   Intellectual evolution from adolescence to adulthood. *Human Development,* 1972, *15,* 1–12.

Rausch, H. L., Barry, W. A., Hertel, R. K., and Swain, M. A. *Communication, conflict, and marriage.* San Francisco: Jossey-Bass, 1975.

Roll, S., and Miller, L. Adolescent males' feeling of being understood by their fathers as revealed through clinical interviews. *Adolescence,* 1978, *13,* 83–94.

Schafer, W. E., and Olexa, C. *Tracking and opportunity: The locking-out process and beyond.* Scranton, Pa.: Chandler, 1971.

Weiner, I. B. *Psychological disturbance in adolescence.* New York: Wiley, 1970.

# Index of Names

# Index of Subjects

*This book has been set VideoComp, in 11 and 10 point Vermilion, leaded 1 point. Part numbers are 40 point Vermilion Bold. Chapter numbers are 48 point Vermilion Bold and chapter titles are 24 point Vermilion Bold. The size of the text area is 28 by 47 picas.*